Big Data Analytics for Healthcare

Big Data Analytics for Healthcare

Datasets, Techniques, Life Cycles, Management, and Applications

Edited by

Pantea Keikhosrokiani

Senior Lecturer, School of Computer Sciences. Universiti Sains Malaysia, Minden, Penang, Malaysia

ELSEVIER

ACADEMIC PRESS

An imprint of Elsevier

Academic Press is an imprint of Elsevier
125 London Wall, London EC2Y 5AS, United Kingdom
525 B Street, Suite 1650, San Diego, CA 92101, United States
50 Hampshire Street, 5th Floor, Cambridge, MA 02139, United States
The Boulevard, Langford Lane, Kidlington, Oxford OX5 1GB, United Kingdom

ISBN: 978-0-323-91907-4

For information on all Academic Press publications visit our website at https://www.elsevier.com/books-and-journals

Publisher: Stacy Masucci
Acquisitions Editor: Rafael E. Teixeira
Editorial Project Manager: Kristi L. Anderson
Production Project Manager: Omer Mukthar
Cover Designer: Miles Hitchen

Typeset by TNQ Technologies

Contents

16. Skin cancer prediction using big data analytics and AI techniques

Piyush Kumar, Rishi Chauhan, Radhika Goyal, Nishi Bhati, Shubham Garg and Shuchi Mala

Section V
Big medical fake news analytics for preventing medical misinformation and myths

17. COVID-19 fake news analytics from social media using topic modeling and clustering

Sherrylin Anak John and Pantea Keikhosrokiani

18. Big medical data mining system (BigMed) for the detection and classification of COVID-19 misinformation

Nurul Husna Binti Rosli and Pantea Keikhosrokiani

Section VI
Challenges and future of big data in healthcare

19. Privacy security risks of big data processing in healthcare

Zhihan Lv and Liang Qiao

Contributors

S. Abirami, Department of Information Science and Technology, College of Engineering Guindy, Anna University, Chennai, Tamil Nadu, India

Nur Hidayah Ilham Ahmad Azri, Universiti Sultan Azlan Shah (USAS), Kuala Kangsar, Perak, Malaysia

Faiza Ahmed, Department of Biomedical Engineering, Military Institute of Science and Technology (MIST), Dhaka, Bangladesh

Md Habib Al Mamun, School of Computer Sciences, Universiti Sains Malaysia, Minden, Penang, Malaysia

Anika Anjum, Department of Biomedical Engineering, Jashore University of Science and Technology (JUST), Jashore, Bangladesh

Katpadi Varadarajan Arulalan, A.A. Child Care Centre, Vellore, Tamilnadu, India

Md. Ashrafuzzaman, Department of Biomedical Engineering, Military Institute of Science and Technology (MIST), Dhaka, Bangladesh

Paul Barach, Interdisciplinary Research Institute for Health Law and Science, Sigmund Freud University Vienna, Vienna, Austria; Jefferson College of Population Health, Philadelphia, PA, United States

Gopi Battineni, University of Camerino, School of Medicinal and Health Products Sciences, Camerino, Italy

Ebru Aydindag Bayrak, Istanbul University-Cerrahpasa, Istanbul, Turkey

Nishi Bhati, Zuora, Chennai, Tamil Nadu, India

Nurul Husna Binti Rosli, School of Computer Sciences, Universiti Sains Malaysia, Minden, Penang, Malaysia

Saurabh Biswas, Delhi Technological University, Department of Biotechnology, New Delhi, India

Carlo Biz, University of Padova, Orthopedics and Orthopedic Oncology, Department of Surgery, Oncology and Gastroenterology DISCOG, Padova, Italy

Nicola Luigi Bragazzi, Laboratory for Industrial and Applied Mathematics (LIAM), Department of Mathematics and Statistics, York University, Toronto, ON, Canada

Zehra Nur Canbolat, Istanbul Medipol University, Department of Management Information Systems, Istanbul, Turkey

Pritha Chakraborty, Integrative Biochemistry and Immunology Laboratory, Department of Animal Science, Kazi Nazrul University, Asansol, West Bengal, India

Nabarun Chandra Das, Integrative Biochemistry and Immunology Laboratory, Department of Animal Science, Kazi Nazrul University, Asansol, West Bengal, India

Rishi Chauhan, Amity University, Department of Computer Science and Engineering, Noida, Uttar Pradesh, India

G. Deepalakshmi, Kongu Engineering College, Anna University, Chennai, Tamil Nadu, India

Kushan De Silva, Monash Centre for Health Research and Implementation, Monash University, Melbourne, Australia

Shankar Dey, Department of Obstetrics and Gynaecology, ESI Hospital, Asansol, West Bengal, India

Ozge Doguc, Istanbul Medipol University, Department of Management Information Systems, Istanbul, Turkey

Joanne Enticott, Monash Centre for Health Research and Implementation, Monash University, Melbourne, Australia

Shubham Garg, Amity University, Department of Computer Science and Engineering, Noida, Uttar Pradesh, India

K. Gokul, Department of Computer Science and Engineering, College of Engineering Guindy, Anna University, Chennai, Tamil Nadu, India

Radhika Goyal, Amity University, Department of Computer Science and Engineering, Noida, Uttar Pradesh, India

Cameron Graydon, Monash Centre for Health Research and Implementation, Monash University, Melbourne, Australia; Centre for Health Services Research, University of Queensland, Brisbane, Australia

Pratiyush Guleria, National Institute of Electronics and Information Technology (NIELIT) Shimla, Shimla, Himachal Pradesh, India

Yasha Hasija, Delhi Technological University, Department of Biotechnology, New Delhi, India

Norbik Bashah Idris, Department of Information System, Department of Computer Sciences, Department of History, Health Research Institute, International Islamic University Malaysia (IIUM), Kuala Lumpur, Malaysia

Sherrylin Anak John, School of Computer Sciences, Universiti Sains Malaysia, Minden, Penang, Malaysia

Suna Kang, Korea Environment Institute, Sicheong-daero, Sejong-si, Republic of Korea

Mustafa Asim Kazancigil, Department of Management Information Systems, Yeditepe University, Istanbul, Turkey; Department of Information Systems and Technologies, Yeditepe University, Istanbul, Turkey; Department of Information Security Technology, Yeditepe University, Istanbul, Turkey

Pantea Keikhosrokiani, School of Computer Sciences, Universiti Sains Malaysia, Minden, Penang, Malaysia

Farzana Khanam, Department of Biomedical Engineering, Jashore University of Science and Technology (JUST), Jashore, Bangladesh

Pinar Kirci, Bursa Uludag University, Bursa, Turkey

Piyush Kumar, Amity University, Department of Computer Science and Engineering, Noida, Uttar Pradesh, India

Donghyun Lee, Department of Business Administration, Tech University of Korea, Gyeonggi-do, Republic of Korea

Zhihan Lv, Faculty of Arts, Uppsala University, Uppsala, Sweden

Kevin Sheng-Kai Ma, Center for Global Health, Perelman School of Medicine, University of Pennsylvania, Philadelphia, PA, United States; Graduate Institute of Biomedical Electronics and Bioinformatics, College of Electrical Engineering and Computer Science, National Taiwan University, Taipei, Taiwan

Shuchi Mala, Amity University, Department of Computer Science and Engineering, Noida, Uttar Pradesh, India

G. Manikandan, Department of Computer Science and Engineering, College of Engineering Guindy, Anna University, Chennai, Tamil Nadu, India

Md. Mahmudul Haque Milu, Department of Biomedical Engineering, Jashore University of Science and Technology (JUST), Jashore, Bangladesh

Dimitrios V. Moysidis, Hippokration General Hospital of Thessaloniki, Aristotle University of Thessaloniki, Thessaloniki, Macedonia, Greece

Najhan Muhamad Ibrahim, Department of Information System, Department of Computer Sciences, Department of History, Health Research Institute, International Islamic University Malaysia (IIUM), Kuala Lumpur, Malaysia; University of Limerick, Limerick, Ireland

Suprabhat Mukherjee, Integrative Biochemistry and Immunology Laboratory, Department of Animal Science, Kazi Nazrul University, Asansol, West Bengal, India

Ajaypradeep Natarajsivam, School of Computer Science and Engineering, Vellore Institute of Technology, Vellore, Tamilnadu, India

Andreas S. Papazoglou, Athens Naval Hospital, Athens, Attiki, Greece

Ritwik Patra, Integrative Biochemistry and Immunology Laboratory, Department of Animal Science, Kazi Nazrul University, Asansol, West Bengal, India

António Pesqueira, Bavarian Nordic A/S, Zürich, Switzerland

Md. Asadur Rahman, Department of Biomedical Engineering, Military Institute of Science and Technology (MIST), Dhaka, Bangladesh

Omanin Siddiqua Prova, Department of Biomedical Engineering, Military Institute of Science and Technology (MIST), Dhaka, Bangladesh

Liang Qiao, College of Computer Science & Technology, Qingdao University, Qingdao, Shandong, China

Rehab A. Rayan, Department of Epidemiology, High Institute of Public Health, Alexandria University, Alexandria, Egypt

R. Sasikala, School of Computer Science and Engineering, Vellore Institute of Technology, Vellore, Tamilnadu, India

Parth Sarthi Sen Gupta, Department of Chemical Science, Indian Institute of Science Education and Research (IISER) Berhampur, Chemical Sciences, Berhampur, Odisha, India

Gokhan Silahtaroglu, Istanbul Medipol University, Department of Management Information Systems, Istanbul, Turkey

Maria José Sousa, Instituto Universitário de Lisboa, Business Research Unit, Lisboa, Portugal

Clair Sullivan, Centre for Health Services Research, University of Queensland, Brisbane, Australia

Jafrin Sultana, Department of Biomedical Engineering, Military Institute of Science and Technology (MIST), Dhaka, Bangladesh

Helena Teede, Monash Centre for Health Research and Implementation, Monash University, Melbourne, Australia

Christos Tsagkaris, Novel Global Community Educational Foundation, Hebersham, New South Wales, Australia

Liew Set Yee, School of Computer Sciences, Universiti Sains Malaysia, Minden, Penang, Malaysia

Imran Zafar, Department of Bioinformatics and Computational Biology, Virtual University of Pakistan, Punjab, Pakistan

Preface

1. Overview of big medical data and analytical infrastructure for decision-making in healthcare: healthcare intelligence

Traditional decision-making process in healthcare and medical era relies on decision-makers points of view, their perception of a task, their experience, intuition, and rule of thumbs. Particularly, traditional decision making was based on the preconceived guidelines rather than the facts. Therefore, decision-making was time consuming which led to reduced competitive advantages, upsurge healthcare provider burden, and endanger patients' health and well-being. Furthermore, human intervention was necessary in different parts of the decision-making process and therefore, systematic linkage between strategic planning, execution, and reporting was missing. Traditional decision-making hinders healthcare organization's ability to make fully informed decisions. Hence, this book introduces Healthcare Intelligence (HI) which refers to the use of various tools, techniques, and methods to analyze Big Medical Data (BMD) and transform it into the valuable information which can be utilized for efficient decision-making in healthcare organizations.

Advancement of new technologies in healthcare and medical field such as wearable sensors, information systems, computing, networking, mobility, etc., increases the volume, variety, veracity, and velocity of data (Keikhosrokiani, 2019). Evolution of big data technologies opens new horizons in medical fields such as Healthcare Intelligence (HI). Big data analytics offers a comprehensive view of the overall picture as a consequence of processing data from multiple sources. Furthermore, big data analytical solutions assist healthcare organizations to make streamlined, and fast decision, gain competitive advantages, save time, and energy.

In order to provide a data management guideline for Healthcare Intelligence (HI), a Big Medical DataPath (BMDP) with different tiers is designed as shown in Fig. 1. BMD can be generated from various sources such as medical wearables, Electronic Health Record (EHR), patient behavior and satisfaction in social media, decision support systems, health survey, remote healthcare information systems, administrative data, etc. These medical related data are extremely large data sets that may be computationally analyzed to show patterns, trends, and associations, particularly in the context of human behavior and interactions. These data are very voluminous that cannot be stored in traditional databases, cannot be processed with traditional software, and cannot reveal proper patterns for decision making. The BMD needs to be ingested which means prioritized and categorized to make data flow smooth for further processing. Then, the data will be collected and transported to data storages. Selecting a proper data storage, which can store and manage BMD efficiently, is very challenging and requires careful consideration. In order to solve the issue of BMD storage, the idea of Polyglot Persistence is proposed (Deka, 2018; Roy-Hubara et al., 2022), which focuses on using multiple databases in parallel to power a single application. Different types of data storage tools such as Hadoop Distributed File System (HDFS), Dependable Distributed File System (GlusterFS), and Amazon S3 Storage Service can be used to handle BMD.

After successful storage of BMD, data need to be decoupled and routed to different destinations to start data analytics process. Thus, BMD processing tier focuses on processing the collected data using batch processing, real-time processing, or hybrid processing. Batch processing refers to offline data analytics which utilizes some tools such as Apache Sqoop, whereas real-time processing provides pure online processing using some tools like Apache Storm, Apache Spark, and Apache Flink.

The next tier in BMDP is data query processing where the active analytical processing takes place and data value will be gathered. Various tools such as Apache Hive, Apache Spark SQL, Amazon Redshift, and Presto are used in this layer to provide interactive queries. Data visualization or presentation tier is the most prestigious tier in BMDP which measures the success of the project, drags people attention, and ensures the findings are well understood by decision-makers. Various data visualization tools such as Tableau, PowerBI, etc., can be utilized to visualize the data or creates analytical dashboards. Finally, based on the proper visualizations, report can be generated for the healthcare decision-makers to make the proper decision and solved the organizations problems which could not be tackled before.

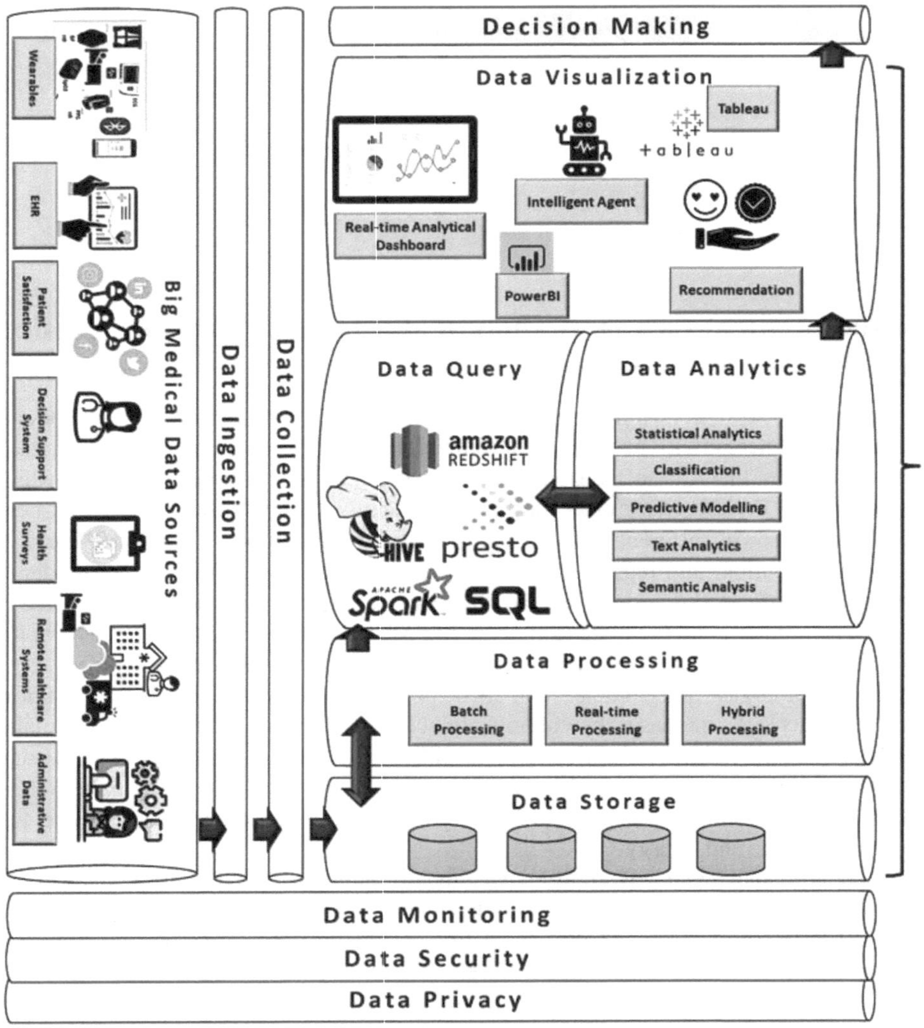

FIGURE 1 Big medical DataPath (BMDP) for healthcare intelligence (HI).

Healthcare data privacy refers to a collection of rules and regulations to ensure that only authorized persons and organizations have access to patient data and medical records. It may also apply to healthcare organization's procedures for safeguarding patient health information and keeping it out of the hands of criminal actors (Keikhosrokiani, 2019). Therefore, data privacy is considered as a crucial part of BMDP which needs careful attention in all tiers. Furthermore, data security is essential for all tiers where data are involved starting from data ingestion, storage, analytics, and discovery. Various techniques such as BMD authentication, access control, encryption and data masking, auditing data access by users, etc., can be utilized to secure the healthcare information system. Finally, data monitoring tier is responsible for monitoring, cleaning, auditing, testing, managing, and controlling the BMD for the overall analytical process. Data profiling and lineage, data quality assurance, data cleansing, and data loss and prevention are considered as some of the tasks of data monitoring layer.

2. Purpose of the book

Healthcare industry plays an important role in people health and well-being. It requires proper strategies, technologies, and decision-making process to deliver effective healthcare services to people. Therefore, this book aims to introduce Healthcare Intelligence (HI) which includes tactics and technologies utilized by healthcare organizations for data analysis, information management, and prediction. Due to the emergence of Big Medical Data (BMD), this book presents the use of artificial intelligence and big data analytics in healthcare and medical sciences. It focusses on theories, methods, and approaches in which data analytic techniques can be used to analyze medical data to provide a meaningful pattern for classification, diagnosis, treatment, and prediction of disease. In addition, it covers social, behavioral, and medical fake news analytics to prevent medical misinformation and myths. The present book contains information that can benefit healthcare organizations in achieving sustainable development goals such as SDG3 (good health and well-being) and SDG9 (industry, innovation, and infrastructure).

This book is a valuable resource for graduate students, researchers, members and decision-makers of biomedical field, and healthcare providers who are interested in learning more about analytical tools, applications, and big data management to support their work.

The outstanding features of this book are as follows:

- Provides a guideline for Healthcare Intelligence (HI) to manage Big Medical Data (BMD)
- Presents theories, methods, and approaches in which data analytic techniques are used for medical data
- Brings practical information on how to use big data for classification, diagnosis, treatment, and prediction of diseases
- Discusses social, behavioral, and medical fake news analytics for medical information systems

3. Organization of the book

This book consists of seven main sections which includes twenty four chapters as follows:

3.1 Section I: Theories and concepts of big data analytics in healthcare

1. Big data analytics in healthcare: theory, tools, techniques and its applications
2. Driving impact through big data utilization and analytics in the context of a Learning Health System
3. Classification of medical big data: a review of systematic analysis of medical big data in real-time setup
4. Towards big data framework in government public open data (GPOD) for health

3.2 Section II: Big medical data: Techniques, managements, and applications

5. Big data analytics techniques for healthcare
6. Big data analytics in precision medicine
7. Recent advances in processing, interpreting, and managing biological data for therapeutic intervention of human infectious disease
8. Big data analytics for health: a comprehensive review of techniques and applications

3.3 Section III: Diagnosis and treatment: Big data analytical techniques, datasets, life cycles, managements, and applications for diagnosis and treatment

9. Recent applications of data mining in medical diagnosis and prediction
10. Big medical data analytics for diagnosis
11. Big data analytics and radiomics to discover diagnostics on different cancer types
12. Big medical data, cloud computing, and artificial intelligence for improving diagnosis in healthcare

3.4 Section IV: Prediction: Big data analytical techniques, datasets, life cycles, managements, and applications for prediction

13. Use of artificial intelligence for predicting infectious disease
14. Hospital data analytics system for tracking and predicting obesepatients' lifestyle habits
15. Predictions on diabetic patient datasets using big data analytics and machine learning techniques
16. Skin cancer prediction using big data analytics and AI techniques

3.5 Section V: Big medical fake news analytics for preventing medical misinformation and myths

17. COVID-19 fake news analytics from social media using topic modeling and clustering
18. Big medical data mining system (BigMed) for the detection and classification of COVID-19 misinformation

3.6 Section VI: Challenges and future of big data in healthcare

19. Privacy security risks of big data processing in healthcare
20. Opportunities and challenges in healthcare with the management of big biomedical data
21. Future direction for healthcare based on big data analytics

3.7 Section VII: Case studies of big data in healthcare arena

22. Big data in orthopedics: between hypes and hopes
23. Predicting onset (type-2) of diabetes from medical records using binary class classification
24. Screening programs incorporating big data analytics

Finally, I would like to thank the contributors and reviewers for their high-quality intellectual work. My special appreciation and thanks to Mr Rafael Teixeira, Ms Kristi Anderson, Mr Moosa Omer Mukthar, Swapna Praveen, and all the Elsevier staff for their unlimited support to publish this book.

References

Deka, G. C. (2018). Chapter nine - NoSQL polyglot persistence. In P. Raj, & G. C. Deka (Eds.), *Advances in computers* (Vol. 109, pp. 357–390). Elsevier. https://doi.org/10.1016/bs.adcom.2017.08.003

Keikhosrokiani, P. (2019). *Perspectives in the development of mobile medical information systems: life cycle, management, methodological approach and application*. Academic Press. https://doi.org/10.1016/C2018-0-02485-8

Roy-Hubara, N., Shoval, P., & Sturm, A. (2022). Selecting databases for polyglot persistence applications. *Data and Knowledge Engineering, 137*, 101950. https://doi.org/10.1016/j.datak.2021.101950

Section I

Theories and concepts of big data analytics in healthcare

Chapter 1

Big data analytics in healthcare: theory, tools, techniques and its applications

G. Manikandan[1], S. Abirami[2], K. Gokul[1] and G. Deepalakshmi[3]

[1]*Department of Computer Science and Engineering, College of Engineering Guindy, Anna University, Chennai, Tamil Nadu, India;* [2]*Department of Information Science and Technology, College of Engineering Guindy, Anna University, Chennai, Tamil Nadu, India;* [3]*Kongu Engineering College, Anna University, Chennai, Tamil Nadu, India*

1. Introduction

Over the last 2 decades, data science has become one of the most important fields of study in various domains, such as bioinformatics, machine learning, pattern recognition, etc. The term "data" is the lowest raw format of knowledge or information. The rapid growth of consumer technology, along with the increased digitization of many essential processes, has made this drastic increase in data. With analytics as the driving force behind some of the most powerful algorithms currently in use, every industry, be it finance, healthcare, or security, has a vested stake in the development of related technologies (Bajaber, Sakr, Batarfi, Altalhi, & Barnawi, 2020). It is important that there is proper understanding of what the phrase big data refers to. It mostly deals with any and all bulk information either collected from various independent sources or assimilated over a period of time. This can also include the constant influx of new information uploaded to the internet or generated through various online interactions each and every second. Leveraging the vast amount of data available to gain valuable insight in an efficient and effective manner requires consideration of the various related factors. This may include the identification of data, its collection, cleaning, storage, and curation, as well as an overall understanding of the current data analytics tools. This chapter covers the analytics lifecycle in depth along with the different types of analytics and their related tools. This survey also summarizes some of the most current applications of the various types of analytics.

Applying data analytics in a real-world scenario requires an understanding of the opportunities and limitations of the tools at hand. Similar algorithms and approaches are applied in vastly different industries, such as healthcare (Pramanik et al., 2020), banking, etc. With the increase in automation of customer interactions as well as a rising need to fully understand the data at hand, there are numerous new technologies made available for every layer of the data analytics process. Several factors influence how one chooses how to proceed with the task at hand. One of the most prevalent approaches to understanding the data considers three main factors. These are Volume, Velocity, and Variety (Hwang & Chen, 2017; Kambatla, Kollias, Kumar, & Grama, 2014).

1.1 Volume

Volume refers to the amount of data being generated or collected from various sources. Nowadays, the data used can be in the magnitude of many Zettabyte (ZB) and Yottabyte (YB). Social media is one of the main sources that generate large amounts of data and the most important source for big data as it can provide valuable insights regarding current trends and preferences of consumers. Over 500 h of videos are uploaded every minute on YouTube. It is found that in the past 2 years, 90% of the world's data has been created and around 1.7 MB of data is created every second by every person in 2020 (Bajaber et al., 2020).

Big Data Analytics for Healthcare. https://doi.org/10.1016/B978-0-323-91907-4.00008-X

1.1.1 Impact of increasing volume in healthcare data

With the advent of telehealth and an exponentially growing population, the last few years have seen an unparalleled growth in healthcare data. According to RBC Capital Markets, about 30% all data generated on a day-to-day basis is by the healthcare sector. This number is only projected to grow, surpassing many other major industries and allowing researchers and analysts access to a tremendous amount of material. With the advent of more complex diagnostic tools, even results of a single patient can take up many megabytes of space. This increase in the volume of data has facilitated new research and allowed more accurate study of diseases and cures. It allows for a more evidence-based approach in solving problems. Collection of data across several stages in the healthcare providing process has allowed more efficient hospital management and customer service (Furht & Villanustre, 2016).

1.2 Velocity

Velocity refers to the speed with which new data is generated. Every organization obtains different types of data from a variety of sources. Some data may be real time, collected as and when the end-users interact with the system. Others may be collected in bulk and sent in bursts. An organization's back end must be capable of processing and storing this data efficiently (Kune, Konugurthi, Agarwal, Rao Chillarige, & Buyya, 2016).

1.2.1 Impact of increasing velocity in healthcare data

Not only has the volume of healthcare adjacent data increased but the rate at which this data is produced has also sky rocketed. With more and more research being done on collecting and leveraging data, the speed with which this information is generated has increased. Data generating tasks such as Internet of Things (IoT)-based healthcare solutions have become common in many parts of the world resulting even higher velocities of data generation. In 2020 alone there has been a huge surge in the velocity of data owing to better collection methods and an increased interest in studying data (Kune et al., 2016). This increase in velocity has forced the industry to consider newer and better methods to store and use this data, keeping patient privacy standards in mind.

1.3 Variety

With evolving technologies, the data can be stored and transmitted in a variety of formats. Previously, only a limited number of file types were in use such as excel or CSV. However, now data can be in the form of images, videos, XML, JSON, or several other types (Kankanhalli, Hahn, Tan, & Gao, 2016). While this variety is useful in accurately representing data, care needs to be taken in consolidating information from different sources and ensuring that systems have the capability of understanding newer formats.

1.3.1 Impact of increasing variety in healthcare data

The healthcare industry generates a large variety of data including but not limited to X-rays, lab tests, patient information, CT scans, patient vitals, etc (Kankanhalli et al., 2016). Different healthcare processes from administration, testing, diagnosis, operation, observation, and long-term care generate different types of data. One problem many institutions faced, when attempting to utilize a large variety of data, is the lack of uniformity when it comes to the different sources. Different countries may have different standards when it comes to handling data, storing information in different formats, and inconsistent structure.

1.4 Other factors influencing in big data

Apart from this, there are other factors to consider such as veracity, variability, volatility, validity, and vulnerability when collecting data especially from external sources that may need verification. The rise in cybercrimes has necessitated a closer look into how vulnerable and compromised our data is. However, increased digitization has far more pros than cons with a plethora of applications being discovered every year. Every aspect of our lives leads to the generation of data that can be stored and analyzed to provide meaningful insights. The widespread use of handheld electronics and the use of internet-based services have made the collection of customer data streamlined. With storage and processing technologies making leaps and bounds in the past decade and cloud technology becoming more mainstream, this process has become easier than ever before. With this rise in data, it is no surprise that many industries have taken advantage of the available information (Chen, Hao, Hwang, Wang, & Wang, 2017; Hwang & Chen, 2017).

Perhaps the biggest impact of the widespread use of data analytics can be seen in the healthcare industry. It is used in various capacities at every stage, from identification to treatment. Analytics has sped up disease prediction and tracking, allowing professionals to handle spread better. Hospital data and demographic details can allow outbreaks to be identified and neutralized quickly. Predictive algorithms facilitate more accurate diagnosis in tough cases. During the Covid-19 pandemic, various institutions and corporates used real-time data to track the spread of the disease. It has been used to identify high-risk patients (Pham, Nguyen, Huynh-The, Hwang, & Pathirana, 2021). It is also used in clinical monitoring, keeping track of a patient's vitals by use of sensors used in combination with IoT technology. This technology is even more widely deployed in the wearables market, with smart watches allowing remote monitoring and alerting physicians or emergency responders in case of irregularities (Zhang, Qiu, Tsai, Hassan, & Alamri, 2015).

The growth in cloud-based computing and IoT technology has allowed for smarter homes in addition to being efficient and user friendly. Technologies such as automatic lights and sensor-based temperature controllers have proven to be more energy efficient. Data analytics has allowed the adoption of greener technologies at a wider scale (Wu, Guo, Li, & Zeng, 2016). Another application is in the cybersecurity field. This branch of analytics called cyber analytics includes the use of ML concepts for intrusion detection and network security. It also allows for the identification of bogus links and malicious URLs (Buczak & Guven, 2015). Apart from this, analytics has many applications from advertising online to social media recommendations, analytics in healthcare applications, etc. The applications for data analytics are only set to grow with the wide-scale adoption of 5G technology. Apart from enabling companies to leverage available information to streamline their operations and gleaning current customer requirements, a major application of analytics is to help visualize data. Be it the results of the latest census, the progress of a global pandemic, or current market trends, data analytics through visualization gives form to abstract concepts and large numbers. Everyone from regular people to management representatives can see for themselves the figure and results manipulated into a more tangible form. Data science tools such as tableau allow for a better understanding of the data at hand in an easy way.

2. Challenges in big data analytics

While data analytics can be very lucrative to implement, almost every stage of the process has the potential to pose some challenge due to financial, temporal, or physical constraints. There may also be concerns regarding the security and reliability in large-scale decentralized computing environments. Apart from this, handling and storing exponentially increasing data is a resource-intensive process which can place a variety of demands on an organization (Acampora, Cook, Rashidi, and Vasilakos, 2013; Buczak & Guven, 2015).

2.1 Management of big data

One of the major issues faced is the need to integrate and store this vast amount of data. While this number continues to skyrocket every day, the current capacity of even some large tech companies is only in the range of zettabytes. Managing this data also becomes a difficult yet crucial task, with data derived from various distributed sources. Cleansing, validation, and aggregation of big data need to be done in a reliable and efficient manner. With the advent of cloud computing, access storage and updating this data has become vital role in the field of big data (Chen, Mao, & Liu, 2014). Access to such databases needs to be closely monitored to ensure security and integrity of the information stored.

2.2 Security and privacy concerns

With more and more financial, healthcare, and government institutions incorporating data analytics to better their operations, security and privacy becomes a major concern. In many countries, personal information of citizens such as social identification numbers, clinical databases, healthcare data phone numbers, bank details, and biometric information is stored in outdated or otherwise vulnerable databases. Apart from security concerns in such institutions, social media and tech companies also store vast amounts of user data including but not limited to passwords, email addresses, photos, and private messages. In April 2021, Facebook revealed that 533 million user accounts had been hacked, affecting consumers across the globe (Acampora et al., 2013).

2.3 Scalability

While data analytics technologies have seen several major leaps in the last 2 decades, changing digital landscapes guarantee that even more innovations are yet to come. It is important that any systems designed right now must be able to operate using future datasets (Hu, Wen, Chua, & Li, 2014). Shifting preference in storage formats must be accommodated with potential support.

3. Data analytics life cycle

This section describes various stages of data analytics and its phases in detail. From the initial proposal of the project to the final deployment, each phase of data analytics is important. This life cycle starts with a basic understanding of what problems the stakeholders expect to be solved and then the required data is identified and gathered. In this phase the previously discussed factors come into play, determining how storage and other logistics are utilized. After any necessary data cleaning is completed, the modeling begins. This stage involves the actual application of analytics principles. Finally, the results are evaluated and deployed. This can range from the visualization of the data to creating new strategies. This process will be later expanded upon in detail and the diagrammatic representation is shown in Fig. 1.1.

3.1 Data generation

Data generation can be addressed by considering the different types of data that is collected as well as the possible methods of collection. Every aspect of modern human life results in the generation of piece of data that can be collected and stored if needed. All of the transactions, interactions, and browsing carried out on digital platforms such as internet browsers, social media sites, and service websites are recorded for a variety of reasons. Even phone records and in store transactions are linked to phone numbers and stored for market analysis.

Big data is classified in numerous ways based on a variety of factors. As previously discussed, the three important characteristics are Volume, Velocity, and Variety. Further classifications are made based on data type and the use cases. With the vast number of instances where data can be stored in day-to-day life, it is crucial to understand the different ways this data is identified and mined for analytics. Firstly, we address the levels of structure applied to stored data. These are structured, unstructured, semistructured, and quasi structured (Bajaber et al., 2020).

3.1.1 Structured data

Structured data is data that is already stored in an ordered manner. Such databases can be in the form of tables with well-defined rows and columns also called relational databases. It is usually text data that can be neatly arranged in a two-dimensional form. In such datasets, all published information can be approached one row at a time, with each row describing one particular entity. While all the objects described by the dataset may belong to a same class, each row is a unique instance. Its main benefit is that it is easy to search and manipulate. This type of arrangement does pose some challenges when it comes to expanding to include new information. Some applications for such a system of arranging data are in storing student details, passenger details, inventory management, clinical data, and such. All these systems would deal with one type of item in a row with supporting details for describing the characteristics of the data (Pramanik et al., 2020).

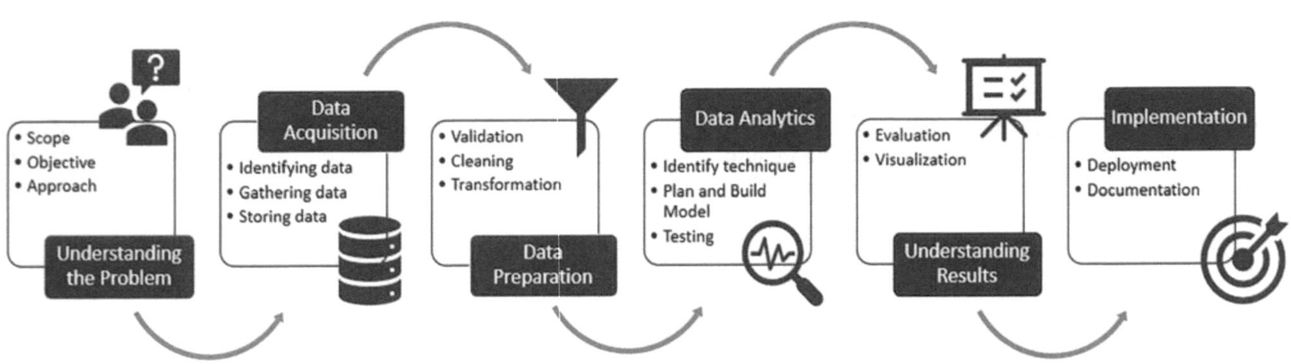

FIGURE 1.1 The data analytics life cycle.

3.1.2 Unstructured data

Unstructured data is data that has no clear manner of storage. Unlike the more traditional structured data, this can include a variety of data types such as images, MP4 files, video clips, images, text, and more. Most data generated these days fall into this category, as various modes of information sharing online cannot always have a fixed format. This accounts for up to 80% of all existing data (Kambatla et al., 2014). It is not as easy to search through seeing as it has no clear format of storage. Until recently, this type of data had very few applications. However, with the advent of newer technologies, unstructured data has found numerous new uses such as predictive analysis, etc.

3.1.3 Semistructured data

Semistructured data can be difficult to define as it can often be confused with unstructured data. However, this type of information contains some form of organization, with partially well-defined data. No-SQL documents can be considered semistructured data as they do not adhere to traditional relational database principles. Semistructured data cannot be stored in traditional tabular structure. It contains the data that is separated according to its individual elements by means of tags that accurately describe the data enclosed within. Unlike structured data, semistructured data can have entities with varying or nonuniform attributes. Some of the most common formats for storing semistructured data are XML and JSON, with the data in such files defined within tags (Bajaber et al., 2020; Pramanik et al., 2020). This type of data can be represented by graphs or trees with root nodes ascribed to the outermost parent tag. While the order and number of attributes may vary in such datasets, they are structured enough to make processing significantly easier than completely unstructured data.

3.1.4 Quasi structured data

Quasistructured data is similar to unstructured data in the sense that it has no fixed format, file type, or structure. It however consists mostly of textual content unlike unstructured data. The variation in formats can be handled by concentrated effort and specialized tools that allow better usage of the data. One example of quasistructured data is in click streams. Click streams are the series of web sites, links, and resources visited by a browser one after the other. Such click streams contain the list of content visited in text form, but the resources themselves may be of different formats. Analysis on click streams is valuable in determining user interests and browsing habits (Dehghantanha & Choo, 2019). It can allow companies to understand what users find useful or interesting among related web content.

3.2 Big data acquisition in healthcare

Data related to healthcare can be amassed from a variety of sources and can include government records, research databases, patient details from hospitals, information from IoT devices, smart phones, etc. Many of these records are often is the form of electronic health records (EHRs), images, genome sequences, and other similar formats. Many smart healthcare devices can collect information on a patient's vitals by use of sensors. Internal hospital records are more robust than ever, owing to the digitization of many internal processes (Saranya & Asha, 2019). Depending on the organization and purpose for collecting the data, there are some limitations to accessing this data. Patient confidentiality laws are often in place to protect the interest of individual patients. However as stated above, there are many sources delivering different types of information. This is true especially during the Covid-19 pandemic in end of 2019, when many research organizations and government bodies collected, curated, and released massive amounts of healthcare information in an effort to better study and understand the progression of the disease.

4. Data analytics during the Covid-19 pandemic

The Covid-19 pandemic which gained momentum in the end of 2019 posed one the most serious challenges to modern healthcare infrastructure. With an alarming number of new cases reported every day and newer variants surfacing, also proper tracking of peoples and tracing the disease became invaluable. One of the most important applications was visualization, which gave the public regular information on various factors. Covid dashboards used access to publicly available numbers to constantly update their database and provide better visual understanding of the severity of the disease. Such dashboards were used in analytics in order to identify hotspots and danger zones for breaking the spread chain. Similar analytics also aided government bodies in implementing various lockdown policies and precaution measures for arranging the hospitals, doctors, and other necessary requirements. Similarly, studying this data influenced when and how businesses could open back up (Al-Fuqaha, Guizani, Mohammadi, Alechari, & Ayyash, 2015).

Another application is in the diagnosis of the disease itself. The current standard is the reverse transcription polymerase chain reaction (RT - PCR) test which is time consuming and requires access to physical kits. One proposed solution was medical image analysis of the lung X-rays and CT scans to identify if the disease has spread to the respiratory tract. This was accomplished by implementing a deep CNN model on an open-source image dataset and was able to achieve a good accuracy (Al-Fuqaha et al., 2015). Such diagnosis would be quicker and allow prioritization of patients who are in a more critical condition in order to reduce the death rate.

Apart from this, there have been a number of studies (Guraya, 2020) to identify drugs that can help in treating the symptoms of Covid-19 where a number of drugs are selected, and their effect studied. There have also been efforts to study the spread of the virus in order to flag potential outbreaks. Contact tracing efforts by many governments have also been backed by analysis of Covid Data resources. In order to show the importance of the big data analytics in healthcare, an application of Covid-19 data is considered as an example; with this, X-rays, CT scans, patient details, regional outbreak details, etc., are the inputs to the big data system for predicting the outbreaks effects, contact tracing, diagnosis, vaccination suggestions, etc., are the useful insights of the analytics which are shown in Fig. 1.2. Some of these efforts are summarized in Table 1.1 and Covid data sources and analytics are shown in Fig. 1.2.

TABLE 1.1 Data analytics during Covid-19 pandemic.

Topic of concern	Reference	Summary of work
Visualization of Covid data	Rahmanti, Ningrum, Lazuardi, Yang, and Li (2021)	Visualization of epidemiological Covid-19 data by making use of data mining and data analytics. An innovative tool is proposed that is more flexible and provides a clear understanding of patterns and trend.,
Unsupervised learning for classification of chest X-rays	Wang et al. (2020)	Use of a self-organizing feature map (SOFM) to classify unlabeled chest X-rays. This network found a distinct difference between the X-ray of sick and healthy patients. The SOFM network was able to successfully cluster the X-rays and extract features without requiring a labeled dataset for training.
Face mask detection	Çallı, Sogancioglu, van Ginneken, van Leeuwen and Murphy (2021)	Method for detecting face masks through implementing image classification. It uses the MobileNetV2 architecture to differentiate between people who are wearing a mask and those who are not wearing a mask with a reported of accuracy of 96.85%.

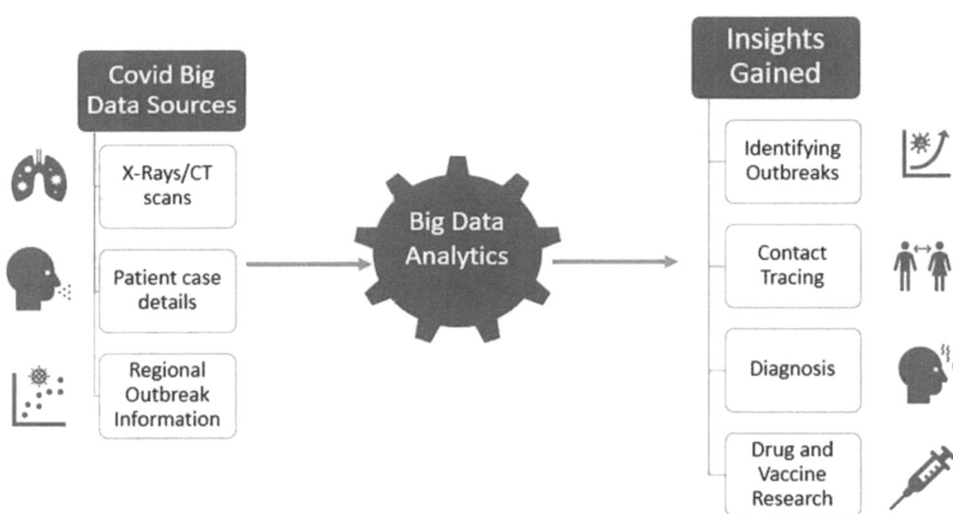

FIGURE 1.2 Covid big data sources and big data analytics.

5. Big data tools in healthcare

The rapid advancements in wireless sensors and mobile communication technologies and stream processing systems monitor the people's health status in real time and generate large amounts of structured and unstructured streamed data. Medical tests, photographs, and descriptions from professionals all result in clinical information about patients, which is collected through records which comes in a variety of shapes and sizes. Personal Health Records (PHRs), unlike EHRs and Electronic Medical Records (EMRs), are often administered by patients and are easily understandable, lifetime instruments for managing important health information, promoting health maintenance, and assisting with chronic disease management.

EMRs , EHRs, and PHRs are the most popular big data management application areas in the perspective of storage and analytics. EMRs are real-time patient health records, which may be used to assist clinicians in decision-making. EHRs are used to report episodes of care across multiple care delivery organizations.

By supplying vast amounts of data, EHRs can enable advanced analytics and aid clinical decision-making. However, a significant percentage of this information is now unorganized since the presence of unstructured data that does not follow a predetermined model or organizational system. It's possible that we choose this format since we can record it in a variety of forms. Another reason to choose an unstructured format is because structured input methods typically fall short when it comes to gathering complex data. It cannot be capture the nonstandard data about a patient's clinical suspicions, socioeconomic data, patient preferences, key lifestyle characteristics, and other associated information in any format other than an unstructured format. It could manifest in terms of better management, care, and low-cost therapies in the healthcare sector. At present it is still a long way from fully grasping the benefits of big data and utilizing the insights it provides since must handling and analyzing large data in a systematic manner in order to attain these objectives.

The data must be saved in a file format that is easily accessible and understandable for efficient analysis before it can be made available to the scientific community. Another key problem in the context of healthcare data is the application of high-end computing tools, protocols, and high-end hardware in clinical settings. The main big data open source tools that are used in healthcare analytics are Apache Hadoop, Kaggle, Hive, R, MongoDB, Lumify, Tableau, Oozie, Knime, Datawrapper, etc. Based on the importance among these tools we have explained few tools based on the importance and role in the big data system (Prasad & Agarwal, 2016).

Hadoop has the ability to be employed in the development of a healthcare analytics system. However, as previously stated, it is a batch-only system. As a result, it is unable to fully use the potential of real-time crises such as ECG reading, in which a patient's heart rate is measured in milliseconds (Prasad & Agarwal, 2016). **Apache Spark** has in-memory data processing that is provided by implementing resilient distributed datasets, which can make Spark 100 times quicker than Hadoop in multipass analytics. Spark is a platform for large data analytics in healthcare. It takes advantage of its stream computing capacity to perform better analysis without the requirement for additional frameworks (Salloum, Dautov, Chen, Peng, & Huang, 2016). For event-driven applications. **Apache Flink** is an ideal platform. Furthermore, health analytics must transition from a typical reactive to a proactive strategy. As a result, a streaming platform is an excellent solution for real-time health monitoring applications (Bergamaschi, Gagliardelli, Simonini, & Zhu, 2017).

Many aspects influence your decision to use a big data platform for your health solution, including real-time requirements, data quantity, speed, scalability, and throughput. Some healthcare applications, such as EMR records, may not require real-time processing; therefore, a nonstreaming platform like Hadoop MapReduce can suffice. Others, like ECG analysis, may require real-time action; thus, streaming will be critical, but scalability will not be an issue to consider. Some recommendation applications, such as diagnosis suggestion support, will necessitate a platform that can scale and accommodate massive amounts of data; in this case, vertical scaling platforms such as CUDA or High-Performance Computing will be useless, but horizontal scaling systems such as Spark will be extremely useful. Another thing to think about is fault tolerance. This refers to the platform's ability to keep running in the event of a failure. In this regard, horizontal scaling systems such as Hadoop and Spark, though not equally, win since they disperse work across multiple clusters, whereas vertical scaling platforms have a single point of failure. Various firms have utilized AI to assess published findings, textual data, and image data to obtain meaningful conclusions in order to manage big data difficulties and perform smoother analytics. IBM Corporation is a commercial provider of healthcare analytics services. Watson Health is an AI platform that allows hospitals, providers, and researchers to share and analyze health data.

5.1 Big data management and analysis

Tools and applications for big data management and analysis are constantly being developed, especially for real-time data streaming and visualization tools that can assist integrate EMRs with healthcare better. One of the main issues faced is storing massive amounts of data. After acquisition, the data must be cleansed or scrubbed to ensure accuracy, correctness, consistency, relevancy, and purity. To achieve high levels of correctness and integrity, this cleaning process can be done manually or automatically using logic rules. Machine learning algorithms are used in more complex and precise technologies to save time and money while also preventing bad data from derailing big data projects.

Every issue listed above must be overcome in order to establish a healthcare system based on big data that can exchange large data and offer us with reliable, timely, and useful information. Overcoming these obstacles would necessitate a significant investment of time, money, and commitment. The accomplishment of these ambitious measures, like other technology improvements, would appear to reduce the current demands on healthcare, particularly in terms of price (Alsubaiee et al., 2012). By lowering the hospital readmission rate, big data analytics can help save money by allowing for better diagnosis and disease prediction. Healthcare organizations do not have a thorough understanding of the factors that cause readmissions. By determining these links thoroughly, healthcare organizations would be able to enhance their practices for dealing with patients and reduce readmission. Big data analytics can also be used to bolster the pharmaceutical supply chain by optimizing workforce, anticipating operating room demand, and accelerating patient care.

6. Summary

In this chapter, we have discussed detailed introduction of the big data and its Vs such as volume, variety, and velocity in detail and also it extended with its impact of increasing volume, velocity, and variety in healthcare data. Further, this chapter provides the challenges and issues present in the big data with respect to the healthcare domain. In order to project the actual requirement of big data technologies, we also provided the big data life cycle in the perspective of data sources, acquisition, storage management, and analytics in detail. With the application perspective, we explained various open-source tools that are required for dealing with these kinds of voluminous data. Finally, the role and importance of the big data analytics in healthcare is discussed in detail with the consideration of the use case as Covid-19 and its impact on the big data.

References

Acampora, Giovanni, Cook, Diane J., Rashidi, Parisa, & Vasilakos, Athanasios V. (2013). A survey on ambient intelligence in healthcare. *Proceedings of the IEEE, 101*(12), 2470–2494. https://doi.org/10.1109/JPROC.2013.2262913

Al-Fuqaha, Ala, Guizani, Mohsen, Mohammadi, Mehdi, Aledhari, Mohammed, & Ayyash, Moussa (2015). Internet of things: A survey on enabling technologies, protocols, and applications. *IEEE communications surveys & tutorials, 17*(4), 2347–2376. https://doi.org/10.1109/COMST.2015.2444095

Alsubaiee, Sattam, Altowim, Yasser, Altwaijry, Hotham, Behm, Alexander, Borkar, Vinayak, Bu, Yingyi, et al. (2012). ASTERIX: an open source system for" Big Data" management and analysis. *Proceedings of the VLDB Endowment, 5*(12), 1898–1901. https://doi.org/10.14778/2367502.2367532

Bajaber, Fuad, Sakr, Sherif, Batarfi, Omar, Altalhi, Abdulrahman, & Barnawi, Ahmed (2020). Benchmarking big data systems: A survey. *Computer Communications, 149*, 241–251. https://doi.org/10.1016/j.comcom.2019.10.002

Bergamaschi, Sonia, Gagliardelli, Luca, Simonini, Giovanni, & Zhu, Song (2017). BigBench workload executed by using Apache Flink. *Procedia Manufacturing, 11*, 695–702. https://doi.org/10.1016/j.promfg.2017.07.169

Buczak, Anna L., & Guven., Erhan (2015). A survey of data mining and machine learning methods for cyber security intrusion detection. *IEEE Communications surveys & tutorials, 18*(2), 1153–1176. https://doi.org/10.1109/COMST.2015.2494502

Çallõ, Erdi, Sogancioglu, Ecem, van Ginneken, Bram, van Leeuwen, Kicky G., & Murphy, Keelin (2021). Deep Learning for Chest X-ray Analysis: A Survey. *Medical Image Analysis*, 102125. https://doi.org/10.1016/j.media.2021.102125

Chen, Min, Mao, Shiwen, & Liu, Yunhao (2014). Big data: A survey. *Mobile Networks and Applications, 19*(2), 171–209. https://doi.org/10.1007/s11036-013-0489-0

Chen, Min, Hao, Yixue, Hwang, Kai, Wang, Lu, & Wang, Lin (2017). Disease prediction by machine learning over big data from healthcare communities. *Ieee Access, 5*, 8869–8879. https://doi.org/10.1109/ACCESS.2017.2694446

Dehghantanha, Ali, & Choo, Kim-Kwang Raymond (Eds.). (2019). *Handbook of big data and IoT security*. Springer. https://doi.org/10.1007/978-3-030-10543-3

Furht, Borko, & Villanustre, Flavio (2016). Introduction to big data. In *Big data technologies and applications* (pp. 3–11). Cham: Springer. https://doi.org/10.1007/978-3-319-44550-2_1

Guraya, Salman Y. (2020). Transforming laparoendoscopic surgical protocols during the COVID-19 pandemic; big data analytics, resource allocation and operational considerations. *International Journal of Surgery, 80*, 21–25. https://doi.org/10.1016/j.ijsu.2020.06.027

Hu, Han, Wen, Yonggang, Chua, Tat-Seng, & Li, Xuelong (2014). Toward scalable systems for big data analytics: A technology tutorial. *IEEE access, 2*, 652–687. https://doi.org/10.1109/ACCESS.2014.2332453

Hwang, Kai, & Chen, Min (2017). *Big-data analytics for cloud, IoT and cognitive computing*. John Wiley & Sons.

Kambatla, Karthik, Kollias, Giorgos, Kumar, Vipin, & Grama, Ananth (2014). Trends in big data analytics. *Journal of parallel and distributed computing, 74*(7), 2561–2573. https://doi.org/10.1016/j.jpdc.2014.01.003

Kankanhalli, Atreyi, Hahn, Jungpil, Tan, Sharon, & Gao, Gordon (2016). Big data and analytics in healthcare: introduction to the special section. *Information Systems Frontiers, 18*(2), 233–235. https://doi.org/10.1007/s10796-016-9641-2

Kune, Raghavendra, Konugurthi, Pramod Kumar, Agarwal, Arun, Rao Chillarige, Raghavendra, & Buyya, Rajkumar (2016). The anatomy of big data computing. *Software: Practice and Experience, 46*(1), 79–105. https://doi.org/10.1002/spe.2374

Pham, Quoc-Viet, Nguyen, Dinh C., Huynh-The, Thien, Hwang, Won-Joo, & Pathirana, Pubudu N. (2021). Artificial intelligence (AI) and big data for coronavirus (COVID-19) pandemic: A survey on the state-of-the-arts. *arXiv*. https://doi.org/10.1109/ACCESS.2020.3009328. preprint arXiv:2107.14040.

Pramanik, Md Ileas, Lau, Raymond YK., Azad, Md Abul Kalam, Hossain, Md Sakir, Chowdhury, Md Kamal Hossain, & Karmaker, B. K. (2020). Healthcare informatics and analytics in big data. *Expert Systems with Applications, 152*, 113388. https://doi.org/10.1016/j.eswa.2020.113388

Prasad, Bakshi Rohit, & Agarwal, Sonali (2016). Comparative study of big data computing and storage tools: a review. *International Journal of Database Theory and Application, 9*(1), 45–66. https://doi.org/10.14257/ijdta.2016.9.1.05

Rahmanti, Annisa Ristya, Ningrum, Dina Nur Anggraini, Lazuardi, Lutfan, Yang, Hsuan-Chia, & Li, Yu-Chuan Jack (2021). Social media data analytics for outbreak risk communication: public attention on the "new normal" during the Covid-19 pandemic in Indonesia. *Computer Methods and Programs in Biomedicine, 205*, 106083. https://doi.org/10.1016/j.cmpb.2021.106083

Salloum, Salman, Dautov, Ruslan, Chen, Xiaojun, Peng, Patrick Xiaogang, & Huang, Joshua Zhexue (2016). Big data analytics on Apache Spark. *International Journal of Data Science and Analytics, 1*(3), 145–164. https://doi.org/10.1007/s41060-016-0027-9

Saranya, P., & Asha, P. (2019). Survey on Big Data analytics in health care. In *2019 International Conference on Smart Systems and Inventive Technology (ICSSIT)* (pp. 46–51). IEEE. https://doi.org/10.1109/ICSSIT46314.2019.8987882

Wang, Yiting, Wang, Ting, Cui, Ying, Mei, Honghui, Wen, Xiao, Lu, Jinzhi, et al. (2020). COVID-19 data visualization public welfare activity. *Visual Informatics, 4*(3), 51–54. https://doi.org/10.1016/j.visinf.2020.09.003

Wu, Jinsong, Guo, Song, Li, Jie, & Zeng, Deze (2016). Big data meet green challenges: Big data toward green applications. *IEEE Systems Journal, 10*(3), 888–900. https://doi.org/10.1109/JSYST.2016.2550530

Zhang, Yin, Qiu, Meikang, Tsai, Chun-Wei, Hassan, Mohammad Mehedi, & Alamri, Atif (2015). Health-CPS: Healthcare cyber-physical system assisted by cloud and big data. *IEEE Systems Journal, 11*(1), 88–95. https://doi.org/10.1109/JSYST.2015.2460747

Further reading

Chew, Alvin Wei Ze, Pan, Yue, Wang, Ying, & Zhang, Limao (2021). Hybrid deep learning of social media big data for predicting the evolution of COVID-19 transmission. *Knowledge-Based Systems*, 107417. https://doi.org/10.1016/j.knosys.2021.107417

Hu, Songhua, Xiong, Chenfeng, Yang, Mofeng, Younes, Hannah, Luo, Weiyu, & Zhang, Lei (2021). A big-data driven approach to analyzing and modeling human mobility trend under non-pharmaceutical interventions during COVID-19 pandemic. *Transportation Research Part C: Emerging Technologies, 124*, 102955.

Hyman, Meleik, Mark, Calvin, Imteaj, Ahmed, Ghiaie, Hamed, Rezapour, Shabnam, Sadri, Arif M., et al. (2021). Data analytics to evaluate the impact of infectious disease on economy: Case study of COVID-19 pandemic. *Patterns*, 100315. https://doi.org/10.1016/j.patter.2021.100315

Sethi, Shilpa, Kathuria, Mamta, & Kaushik, Trilok (2021). Face mask detection using deep learning: An approach to reduce risk of Coronavirus spread. *Journal of Biomedical Informatics, 120*, 103848. https://doi.org/10.1016/j.jbi.2021.103848

Chapter 2

Driving impact through big data utilization and analytics in the context of a Learning Health System

Cameron Graydon[1,2], Helena Teede[1], Clair Sullivan[2], Kushan De Silva[1] and Joanne Enticott[1]
[1]*Monash Centre for Health Research and Implementation, Monash University, Melbourne, Australia;* [2]*Centre for Health Services Research, University of Queensland, Brisbane, Australia*

1. Introduction

Fundamentally, all countries, independent of their national resources or health system maturity, face similar health system drivers—socioeconomic demands for value and expectations from citizens for better experience and quality health care. Macroeconomic trends are similar as well, increasing life expectancy, an "aging population" with increasing comorbidities, increasing medical care costs with economies, and health impacted negatively by global events such as pandemics and climate stress (Patrick et al., 2021). The reality is that maintaining these fundamental aims with the projected increase in demand and finite resources will challenge the aspirational human right of Universal Health Coverage (Nomura et al., 2020).

With the realization that the current models of healthcare are unsustainable, and not "fit for purpose" for rapidly changing demands (Bircher, 2020; Rifkin, 2020), we must accept that system level change is required. The World Health Organization (WHO), Organization for Economic Co-operation and Development (OECD), World Bank Group, the Lancet Commission, and governments have a clear mandate and moral obligation to enable systems level change to achieve affordable, sustainable, and universal high-quality healthcare. The optimal approaches to deliver such change are not yet established. However, in this chapter we explore the concept of the Learning Health System (LHS) and how it can utilize data and be iteratively applied to address the significant future challenges ahead for health care. Here we provide an overview of the goals and priorities for healthcare, the concepts of the LHS, big data, and how they might be applied to deliver on these goals.

2. What matters for healthcare?

Healthcare does not follow a simple linear process and is indeed a complex adaptive system (Miller & Page, 2007). It is a dynamic process where the interactions and relationships of different components simultaneously affect and are shaped by the system (The Health Foundation, 2010), often via nonlinear processes where context has critical influence (Melder et al., 2020). The consequence of this is that positive impacts in one area may mask or contribute to negative impacts in other areas and that impacts vary according to settings, requiring tailoring of interventions to context.

An initial exploration of what is meant by impact and the leverage points to optimize impact is required. An impact is a positive or negative, direct or indirect, and intended or unintended change produced by an intervention (Clarke et al., 2019). Impact as it pertains to the health system can be upon an individual, group, or population and can refer to the health economics, clinical practice, health outcomes, or the healthcare system as a whole. Impact generally refers to the immediate effects of a health intervention, process, or policy, while the term outcome is used to refer to the distant or ultimate effect (Frankish et al., 2001). Because of the nature of complex adaptive systems, the ultimate measure of impact necessarily

Big Data Analytics for Healthcare. https://doi.org/10.1016/B978-0-323-91907-4.00019-4

needs to be against a goal or set of values—for healthcare, the ultimate measure should be the health outcomes of individuals at a population level, while also considering sustainability and resources.

The Institute of Healthcare Improvement (IHI) describes three dimensions to consider for optimizing health system performance in the Triple Aim (Berwick et al., 2008) framework: (1) *Population Health*, (2) *Experience of Care*, and (3) *Value*. A fourth component, *Provider Experience*, has been added to become the "Quadruple Aim" (Sikka et al., 2015) of health and care in recognition of the fundamental role employees have in achieving optimum performance of organizations and customer satisfaction. These four aims are fundamental to optimizing healthcare and are all vital dimensions to consider in any transformative initiatives in health systems. The aims in themselves reflect the complexity of the health care system, often with competing drivers, and only through approaches that recognize the healthcare system as a complex adaptive system will meaningful change be achieved.

Alongside safe, high-quality healthcare, improved health outcomes, and value or sustainability, end user and consumer experience is important; to date, this has not been a key focus of health system reform (Vinn, 2000) and moving forward must be incorporated front and center, acknowledging that the community are ultimately the funders and beneficiaries of healthcare and deserve a system that serves them well.

3. Global strategies for impact on health

While the healthcare system itself is complex, social determinants of health add an additional layer of complexity. The WHO has described in the European Program of Work 2020–25 three overarching core priorities to respond to their citizens' future health needs: moving toward universal access to quality care without financial hardship; to protect against health emergencies, and to ensure better health and well-being at all ages (Regional Committee for Europe European Program of Work, 2020). WHO (2008) and other organizations (Cosgrove et al., 2020; Fichtenberg et al., 2019) are focusing on the "determinants of health" as a mechanism of understanding how to influence population health outcomes. It is estimated that healthcare is only responsible for 15%–40% of population health outcomes (Alderwick et al., 2016). Hence, these factors also need consideration when aiming to optimize health outcomes.

Indeed, in attempting to understand variations in health outcomes WHO described five conditions required to live a healthy life (Barr, 2020). To provide targets for increasing equity and to understand their relative contributions to health outcomes in certain socioeconomic contexts, data on each of the five conditions is required, with only one being the healthcare system: (1) Health services, (2) Income security and social protection, (3) Living conditions, (4) Social and human capital and (5) Employment and working conditions. In recognizing these further layers of complexity, WHO further describe the need to develop strategic intelligence on levels and inequalities of health and well-being, improving patient safety and the need for improved efficiency through innovation in terms of digitalization, technology, and organization (Regional Committee for Europe European Program of Work, 2020).

WHO go on to say "There is a need for a quantum leap in the ability to generate timely, disaggregated, and comprehensive data that provide credible, reliable, and actionable information. Classic data collection will need to be complemented by robust use of big data, online surveys, consensus panels, and expert opinion. This will ensure that decisions are data driven and facilitate public health monitoring and forecasting."

A range of aggregated and nonaggregated data will be needed to understand the health of the population, the needs of different groups, and where best to allocate resources for maximum impact. The data should focus on the determinants of health, not just healthcare (Alderwick et al., 2016), enabling data-driven allocation and the means to evaluate interventions.

The WHO has also highlighted in its various drafts and reports the importance of digital technologies, including big data to help increase universal access to affordable person- and community-centered care and services (WHO Big Data, 2017; WHO Draft Global, 2020). The global internet coverage is extending rapidly with almost two-thirds of the population having some access, and a half are online with nearly all of them using personal devices (WorldBank, 2021); this will become both a means to collect information and impart information—it could be a key enabler of the quantum leap forward.

4. What is big data?

Big data can be characterized by the "5 Vs"; it is an information asset characterized by the high *volume*, *velocity* of creation, and transmission, the *variety* of structured, semistructured and unstructured formats, *veracity*, and that because of its complexity requires specific technology and analytical methods for its transformation into *value* (De Mauro et al., 2016).

In the preceding decade, there have been several enablers that have matured to make the collection and analysis of large datasets feasible. Computing power, cloud-based storage, and sophisticated analytic tools that can cope with large datasets have developed. Even when the "noise" in the data is high, and there are complicated relationships between the inputs, we can now use artificial intelligence and machine learning (ML) analysis to identify relationships.

The opportunity to integrate social determinants to influence public health is significant. Within health care itself, it is estimated 30% of healthcare is waste, duplication, or of low value (Braithwaite et al., 2020; Couffinhal & Socha-Dietrich, 2017; Hackbarth, 2012), and another 10% leads to harm, of which nearly 50% is considered preventable (Panagioti et al., 2019) if even a fraction of this could be identified and avoided, then significant savings could be achieved (Slawomirski et al., 2017). The application of big data to optimize healthcare is a significant priority internationally and can be further enhanced by integrating precision or personalized medicine.

5. Applying big data—precision medicine

The overarching goal of "precision medicine" is to use data to facilitate clinical decision-making that is personalized, predictive, preventive, participatory, psychosocial, and public (6P Medicine) (Overby & Tarczy-Hornoch, 2013; Pravettoni & Triberti, 2020). It is the patient-centric model which fundamentally relies on big data (both from the individual and aggregated data). Precision medicine can be used to avoid empiric treatments that "on average" show an effect, but benefit a few, are wasted on many and harm some, and for patient engagement and empowerment for self-care (Parikh et al., 2017; Schüssler-Fiorenza Rose et al., 2019).

Through the analysis of a patient's personal health record—encompassing integrative Personalized Omics Profiling (iPOP) (Chen et al., 2012), Real World Data from the electronic medical record, patient-reported indicators, personal monitors and the internet of things, combined with an individual's psychological disposition, and other determinants of health data—an intervention or specific targeting of resources could be used at leverage points that have proven impact. It can benchmark an individual's potential risks or outcomes, comparing the individual to aggregated outcomes from a similar cohort—this can help with shared decision-making between the patient and their clinician. In the future, it may also be possible to develop specific novel treatments designed for that individual patient—truly personalized medicine.

A good illustration of how big data can advance precision medicine is in the field of "omics"—the study of the biological molecules that translate in the structure, function and dynamics of an organism, and can contribute to the understanding of disease and risk. Initially referring to the field of genomics; there are now epigenomics, proteomics, lipidomics, immunomics, metabolomics, metagenomics, transcriptomics, microbiomics, glycomics, fluxomics, and connectomics—the latter encompassing the totality of the neural connections in the brain. A single human genome has 3 billion base pairs and is a somewhat manageable dataset using conventional analytic techniques, while the connectome is estimated to have 10^{15} synaptic connections and 100 billion neurons, each one having a three-dimensional relation, and is beyond current technological capabilities. A concrete example is that mapping 1 millimeter of mouse brain required 2000 terabytes (10^{12}) of data and five electron microscopes (Deweerdt, 2019). Further examples lie outside of biology in the medical, environmental, financial, geographic, and social media datasets that are being created through the routine collection of data—it is estimated that by 2025 there will be more than 200 zettabytes (10^{21}) or 2^{70} bytes of data in cloud storage and more than 40 billion devices connected to the internet. This proliferation of data sources can be aggregated with financial, employment, environmental, healthcare, and social services data to provide insights into the most impactful interventions.

Advances in data utilization, both recent and unforeseen, will usher in a new approach to understanding the determinants of disease from social determinants, personal factors and health system support, and will inform vital transformations of the health system around, and with these determinants, to optimize outcomes.

6. Learning Health System—a paradigm for the future?

Braithwaite et al. (2014) has highlighted that application of simple frameworks to multifaceted and constantly changing systems is flawed. In complex adaptive systems, an over reliance on theories and linear frameworks essentially "blinds" clinicians, and more agile, simpler, high-level approaches that recognize complexity and support and incentivize change, alongside a focus on what makes clinical practice work well and what motivates and engages clinicians, are more constructive (Melder et al., 2020). The system of the future that will operationalize the potential of big data and artificial intelligence will need to be flexible and responsive to health challenges and the inherent risks of digital systems. It will make use of multiple sources of evidence and will utilize research for evaluation and implementation to maximize impact (Enticott et al., 2020, 2021b).

With ever-increasing data, there is a clear need to effectively harness this to deliver on the four IHI aims and deliver impact (Melder et al., 2020). Systems are needed to ensure the most relevant information and evidence can guide healthcare decision-making (Budrionis & Bellika, 2016; Flynn, 2019). LHSs have been variously described (Enticott et al., 2020; Foley & Vale, 2017; Safaeinili et al., 2020; Enticott et al., 2021b) and implemented into health and healthcare at local, regional, or national levels (Enticott et al., 2021a). Interest and investment is increasing in LHSs as an approach that considers elements of complex adaptive systems, is responsive to new and emerging evidence (Pomare et al., 2021), and where multiple effective exemplars are now demonstrated across North America, Europe, and Oceania (Enticott et al., 2021a).

An LHS was originally defined by the Institute of Medicine as a broader system in which "science, informatics, incentives, and culture are aligned for continuous improvement and innovation, with best practices seamlessly embedded in the delivery process and new knowledge captured as an integral by-product of the delivery experience" (Institute of Medicine, 2007, p. 374). It combines the socio-technical components of healthcare, the scientific method for iterative testing of hypotheses—to get less and less wrong—and embeds knowledge generation processes and decision support into daily clinical practice. It is dependent on data, and on application or use of that data in rapid virtuous learning cycles, taking practice to data, data to knowledge, and knowledge to practice. It is proposed to bring value and impact to health compared to the traditional linear translational research model. An essential component of an LHS is "measurement for action," which is recommended for all healthcare systems (Kruk et al., 2018). A fundamental recommendation from the Lancet Commission was the need for healthcare delivery systems to contribute, measure, and report on what matters and is effective, meeting patients', not just providers' needs, and supplying high-quality care to the maximum achievable level. It also highlighted the need for better use of existing resources, for providers to take a systems perspective and adopt practices known to deliver better care, e.g., adherence to evidence-based guidelines, use of IT known to improve decision-making and treatment, and scaling up of good practices nationally.

While there are multiple different frameworks in use, most are derived from singular perspectives, be that a single health condition, an isolated research or healthcare perspective, and few consider the consumer and stakeholders as key to the system. Given that current healthcare improvement strategies and conventional project-based approaches to transform care have been inadequate (Braithwaite et al., 2020; Langendam et al., 2020; Melder et al., 2018, 2020; Robinson et al., 2020), a systems level approach is required for sustainability and scalability. However, it is important that the LHS is broad and considers all dimensions of the complex adaptive system to succeed.

Arguably, the most potential will come when national level data ecosystems enable a patient—or community—centric, "cradle to the grave" approach. Coproduced, efficiently collected information on the determinants of health and evidence from stakeholders (especially patients), research, data, and implementation can be analyzed to guide value-based interventions to achieve the greatest impact. To enable this, incentives, resourcing, structure, and governance must align (Zurynski et al., 2020) to enable the people, culture, and infrastructure for transformational change. Such an approach can be developed in a "learning organization" (Senge, 2006), with smart data providing insights (Barnett et al., 2019), design science and implementation science combining with healthcare improvement to maximize the capacity for change, and where stakeholder engagement, codesign, coproduction, and partnerships ensure that efforts are relevant to population health outcomes. It should be acknowledged that the "raison d'être" behind research is for achieving the core obligation of continuous improvement in health.

Frameworks for LHSs have been described (Friedman et al., 2010; Institute of Medicine, 2013; Palakshappa et al., 2020; Zurynski et al., 2020); each follows a similar cycle of assembling, analyzing, and interpreting data, followed by feeding the learnings back into practice and creating change (Foley & Fairmichael, 2015). An evidence-based process has been used in Australia to develop an LHS framework (Enticott et al., 2021b) (Fig. 2.1).

Through stakeholder engagement, systematic review of LHSs has delivered impact (Enticott et al., 2021a,b), qualitative interviews, and workshops (Enticott et al., 2020; Monash Partners, n.d.). The key components that emerged were evidence sources coming from stakeholders, data, implementation, evaluation, and research (Fig. 2.2).

Evidence from the community and stakeholders is essential for problem identification, priority setting, and solution codesign, as well as implementation evaluation and iterative improvement. Evidence from research can come from economic and policy data, guidelines, synthesis reviews, and traditional sources. Despite enormous resources, good will, and effort, research can take over a decade from initial data collection before it begins to be translated into practice. The evidence to translation gap in translational research is well accepted (Bero et al., 1998; Rudd et al., 2020) and requires a model that responds to this problem. Data evidence is knowledge generated from real-time health-related data, patient reported indicators, benchmarking, and analysis. The data needs to be meaningful and actionable, as well as being able to be accessed in a timely manner. Contextual evidence from implementation can be understood using theory driven and

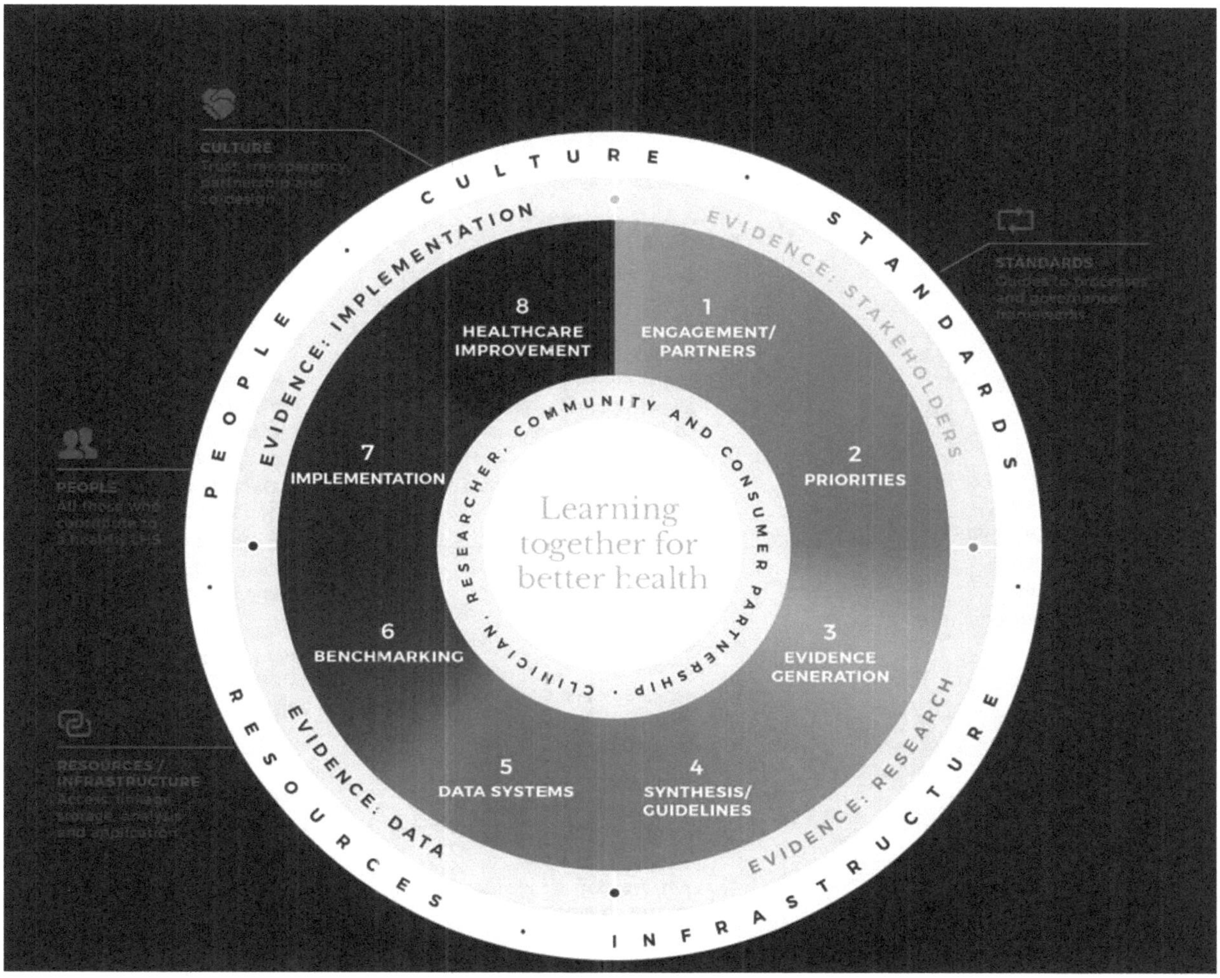

FIGURE 2.1 Monash Partners Learning Health System Framework. The framework with stakeholders and patients at the center with the principles underpinning the LHS (Enticott et al., 2021b). *Reproduced with permission from Monash University.*

formative evaluations such as using Realist Methods (Stoto et al., 2017), "What works, for whom, and under what circumstances?" and can broaden the appreciation of what is impactful, sustainable, and can aid in refining interventions.

The framework also describes the enabling principles pertaining to the *People*, *Culture*, *Governance*, and *Resources* (Enticott et al., 2021b). People contribute through a broad range of capabilities from community, frontline clinical/nonclinical staff, IT and information experts, technologists, analysts, data, and implementation researchers and policy makers. A continuous improvement culture of trust, transparency, partnership, and codesign underpin the LHS with commitment, of clinicians and management, and support for integration of new approaches into standard care to achieve sustainable, scalable change. Governance: Transparent, agreed processes, and governance, including compliance with legal and legislative standards for data sharing and linkage, consent processes for data use, robust data governance systems, and security. Resources and infrastructure need to enable linkage and analysis of data, interoperability between the electronic medical record platforms, external data sources and software, then effective presentation and visualization of data at point of care, with real-time data access, meaningful end-user targeted feedback, and benchmarking.

7. Driving big data utilization in an LHS

To realize the full potential of data within an LHS, core requirements include collecting the right data—accurate, broad, relevant, and equitable—using the right aggregation and analytic techniques for knowledge formation, and then benchmarking with audit and feedback to iteratively optimize outcomes.

COMPONENTS

STAKEHOLDER DERIVED EVIDENCE

1 ENGAGEMENT OF PEOPLE

- Consult
- Engage
- Involve
- Collaborate
- Empower
- Inform

2 IDENTIFYING PRIORITIES

- Formal engagement
- Agreed priorities
- Ranked priorities
- Prioritised outcome measures

RESEARCH DERIVED EVIDENCE

3 EVIDENCE BASED INFORMATION

- Cohort trials
- Randomised and pragmatic clinical trials
- Epidemiology based research
- Economic analysis
- Qualitative and Quantitative research

4 EVIDENCE SYNTHESIS AND GUIDELINES

- Systematic reviews
- Meta- analysis: aggregate and individual data
- Secondary research
- Consideration of stakeholder and evidence based priorities
- Guidelines, standards and policies

DATA DERIVED EVIDENCE

5 DATA AND INFORMATION SYSTEMS

- Quality, timely, harmonised, meaningful and actionable data
- Data from health care and other sources
- Patient reported experience and outcome measures
- Compliance with 5 safes*, FAIR data principles** and legislative and privacy requirements
- Governance, data sharing, linkage, analysis and interpretation
- Big data analytics, machine learning
- Technology and infrastructure

6 BENCHMARKING

- Transparency and equity
- Adjustments for service variation
- Real time visual representation at individual, service and organisational levels
- Measurement to iteratively and continuously drive improvement
- Evaluation
- Learning feedback

IMPLEMENTATION EVIDENCE

7 IMPLEMENTATION

- Leadership
- Theory driven
- Economically sound
- Methodologically rigorous
- Addressing barriers and enablers
- Capability in change management
- Consideration of the Burden of data collection
- Sustainable and scalable
- Demonstrating healthcare improvement

8 HEALTHCARE IMPROVEMENT

- Leadership
- Pragmatism
- Contextual/ local
- Outcome improvement
- Quality improvement
- Change management
- Evaluation

*Five Safes: Safe Projects, People, Settings, Data and Outputs
** FAIR data principles: Findable, Accessible, Interoperable and Reusable

FIGURE 2.2 Components of the Monash Partners Learning Health System Framework. Four components that contribute to the evidence embedded into the LHS (Enticott et al., 2021b). *With permission from Monash University.*

Modern computing capabilities have enabled artificial intelligence tools like ML to find generalizable predictive patterns within big data, as opposed to the hypothesis/probability model of classical statistical methods. Artificial intelligence uses different learning algorithms that can analyze large data sets and outcomes at all levels of granularity and can improve over time. As the data and information available exponentially increases, and the number of variables exceeds a human's capacity to process them, the various tools in artificial intelligence will become essential to help us with predictive analysis and data-driven intelligence. Design and implementation science will play a pivotal role in making this data impactful. Currently, artificial intelligence is being used to assess risk of disease onset and estimating treatment success; in an attempt to manage or alleviate complications; to assist with patient care during the active treatment or procedure phase; and in research aimed at elucidating the pathology or mechanism and/or the ideal treatment for a disease (Becker, 2019).

8. Challenges

Arguably the barriers to leveraging big data lie in the lack of integrated systems, the lack of system approaches, the lack of agreed harmonized processes, and human barriers unrelated to technology, such as data governance, sharing, linkage, access, etc. Often cited concerns for the use of big data pertain to security, veracity, privacy, ethics, ownership, and secondary use. Likewise, artificial intelligence brings its own set of concerns related to regulation, ethics, law, bias, interpretability, and equity.

Personal data regarding physical, physiological, genetic, mental, economic, cultural, online, or social identity can be related to an identified or identifiable person needs secure management. This demand for confidentiality together with maintenance of integrity, authenticity, and availability is stimulating technological solutions using Isolated and Trusted Execution Environments (Asclepios Project, 2021), Blockchain (Chang, 2020), Multiparty Homomorphic Encryption (Scheibner et al., 2021), Polymorphic Encryption, and Pseudonymization (Verheul et al., 2016). Additional infrastructure, authentication tools, and data access controls will be required to bring these technologies to fruition, and engender the trust required for individuals to relinquish control of their data or "gifting" it for research and improvement purposes. Through standards and data governance, ethical review, demonstrating that the data will be equitably used for social value and not be misused, a social contract and culture of consumer trust will enable the benefits of big data, with the acknowledgment that no data is irrefutably secure.

Selection, accuracy, and analysis of big data can lead to biases that may lead to bad data, incorrect conclusions, and misapplication of knowledge. However, this can equally apply to traditionally formulated knowledge. The analysis of big data is strongly limited by the quality and the breadth of the aggregated data, like in the analogy of a chain—where it is only as strong as its weakest link—the act of collecting more data will not necessarily bring validity and a better analysis. big data is observational in nature and analyses are essentially "data mining" and should be considered as hypothesis generating initially—they are liable to many biases such as selection, confounding variables, and lack of generalizability (Khoury & Ioannidis, 2014). It should also be emphasized that "association is not prediction" in the same way as "correlation is not causation"—the Bradford Hill criteria for causation can be applied to the basic sciences as well as to big data analysis (Fedak et al., 2015). Even after robust associations are established, predictive tools will need to be regulated, validated, and evidence of clinical significance and utility (i.e., assessing balance of benefits vs. harms) is still needed (Ioannidis & Khoury, 2013).

The incursion of Big Tech (Apple, Amazon, Alphabet, Microsoft, Facebook and in China, Alibaba, Baidu, Tencent) into the health space is inevitable, and while it may bring benefits for interoperability, data aggregation, and data use, it will also bring commercial conflicts of interests that do not prioritize the Quadruple Aim. The historian and popular author Yuval Harari (Harari, 2020) alludes to a future where enough biological knowledge, computing power, and data will allow the manipulation of human behavior—the "ability to hack humans." This may sound like a far-fetched futuristic concern; however, it is not; it is the fundamentals of the LHS—using data to change human behavior and culture. "Culture," the result of collective behavior and behavioral traits, is the response to specific environmental stimuli, so the change of human behavior and culture, intended for the greater good, could cause unintended consequences or be misused for profit or nefarious means.

9. Conclusion

Health has multiple determinants, including health services, income security, social protection, living conditions, social and human capital, employment, and working conditions. Within the healthcare system, four key aims have been identified: Population health outcomes, (2) Experience of care, (3) Value, and (4) Provider Experience. With rapidly changing demands, there is a need for rapid transformation of a complex adaptive system to deliver impact upon these aims. The LHS framework is an evidence-based, systems level approach to rapid transformation, and leverages off the plethora of data on determinants of health, on the healthcare system itself and on individual or personal factors. A rigorous process has identified the key components of an LHS as evidence from stakeholders and consumers; evidence from research and best practice; evidence from data, including big data; and evidence from implementation. Within this, big data and new digital technologies, including AI cognitive architectures, neural networks, and quantum computing, will be integral to progress deep learning, and will alter the fundamental relationships between data, information, knowledge, and wisdom.

We can only see a short distance ahead, but we can see plenty that needs to be done

Alan Turing, British mathematician.

Funding statement

CG: Australian Government Research Training Program Scholarship.
HT: is funded by an NHMRC MRFF fellowship.
JE, KDS, CS have no funding to declare.

References

Alderwick, H., et al. (2016). *Healthy populations: Designing strategies to improve population health.*

Asclepios Project. (2021). *Advanced secure cloud encrypted platform for internationally orchestrated solutions in healthcare.* Available from: https://www.asclepios-project.eu/blog-post/isolated-and-trusted-execution-environments-in-healthcare/.

Barnett, A., et al. (2019). Digital transformation of hospital quality and safety: Real-time data for real-time action. *Australian Health Review, 43*(6), 656.

Barr, B. (2020). HESR innovation in analysis that supports decision making and action. *The European Journal of Public Health, 30*(Suppl. 5).

Becker, A. (2019). Artificial intelligence in medicine: What is it doing for us today? *Health Policy and Technology, 8*(2), 198–205.

Bero, L. A., et al. (1998). Closing the gap between research and practice: An overview of systematic reviews of interventions to promote the implementation of research findings. *BMJ, 317*(7156), 465–468.

Berwick, D. M., Nolan, T. W., & Whittington, J. (2008). The triple aim: Care, health, and cost. *Health Affairs, 27*(3), 759–769.

Bircher, J. (2020). Meikirch model: New definition of health as hypothesis to fundamentally improve healthcare delivery. *Integrated Healthcare Journal, 2*(1), e000046.

Braithwaite, J., et al. (2020). Transformational improvement in quality care and health systems: The next decade. *BMC Medicine, 18*(1).

Braithwaite, J., Glasziou, P., & Westbrook, J. (2020). The three numbers you need to know about healthcare: The 60-30-10 challenge. *BMC Medicine, 18*(1).

Braithwaite, J., Marks, D., & Taylor, N. (2014). Harnessing implementation science to improve care quality and patient safety: A systematic review of targeted literature. *International Journal for Quality in Health Care, 26*(3), 321–329.

Budrionis, A., & Bellika, J. G. (2016). The learning healthcare system: Where are we now? A systematic review. *Journal of Biomedical Informatics, 64*, 87–92.

Chang, A. C. (2020). Chapter 10 - key concepts of the future of artificial intelligence. In A. C. Chang (Ed.), *Intelligence-based medicine* (pp. 415–430). Academic Press.

Chen, R., et al. (2012). Personal omics profiling reveals dynamic molecular and medical phenotypes. *Cell, 148*(6), 1293–1307.

Clarke, G. M., et al. (2019). Evaluating the impact of healthcare interventions using routine data. *BMJ*, l2239.

Cosgrove, L., et al. (2020). A critical review of the Lancet Commission on global mental health and sustainable development: Time for a paradigm change. *Critical Public Health, 30*(5), 624–631.

Couffinhal, A., & Socha-Dietrich, K. (2017). *Ineffective spending and waste in health care systems: Framework and findings.*

De Mauro, A., Greco, M., & Grimaldi, M. (2016). A formal definition of Big Data based on its essential features. *Library Review, 65*(3), 122–135.

Deweerdt, S. (2019). How to map the brain. *Nature, 571*(7766), S6–S8.

Enticott, J., Braaf, S., Johnson, A., Jones, A., & Teede, H. (2020). Leaders' perspectives on Learning Health Systems: A qualitative study. *BMC Health Services Research, 20*(1).

Enticott, J., Johnson, A., & Teede, H. (2021a). Learning Health Systems using data to drive healthcare improvement and impact: A systematic review. *BMC Health Services Research, 21*(1).

Enticott, J., Melder, A., Johnson, A., Jones, A., Shaw, T., Keech, W., Buttery, J., & Teede, H. (2021b). A learning health system framework to operationalize health data to improve quality care: an Australian perspective. *Frontiers in Medicine*. https://doi.org/10.3389/fmed.2021.730021

Fedak, K. M., et al. (2015). Applying the Bradford Hill criteria in the 21st century: How data integration has changed causal inference in molecular epidemiology. *Emerging Themes in Epidemiology, 12*(1).

Fichtenberg, C. M., Alley, D. E., & Mistry, K. B. (2019). Improving social needs intervention research: Key questions for advancing the field. *American Journal of Preventive Medicine, 57*(6), S47–S54.

Flynn, A. (2019). Informatics and technology enable us to learn from every patient: Pharmacists' many roles in Learning Health Systems. *American Journal of Health-System Pharmacy, 76*(15), 1095–1096.

Foley, T., & Fairmichael, F. (2015). *The potential of learning healthcare systems.* The Learning Healthcare Project.

Foley, T. J., & Vale, L. (2017). What role for Learning Health Systems in quality improvement within healthcare providers? *Learn Health Syst, 1*(4), e10025.

Frankish, C. J., et al. (2001). Health impact assessment as a tool for health promotion and population health. *WHO Regional Publications European Series*, (92), 405–437.

Friedman, C. P., Wong, A. K., & Blumenthal, D. (2010). Achieving a nationwide Learning Health Systems. *Science Translational Medicine, 2*(57), 57cm29.

Hackbarth, A. D. (2012). Eliminating waste in US health care. *Journal of the American Medical Association, 307*(14), 1513.

Harari, Y. (2020) *How to survive the 21st century* [Aug 2021]; Available from: https://www.weforum.org/agenda/2020/01/yuval-hararis-warning-davos-speech-future-predications/.

Institute of Medicine. (2007). *The learning healthcare system: Workshop summary*. Washington, DC: The National Academies Press.

Institute of Medicine. (2013). A Learning Health System activity roundtable on value science-driven health care. In *Observational studies in a Learning Health System: Workshop summary*. Washington (DC): National Academies Press (US). Copyright 2013 by the National Academy of Sciences. All rights reserved.

Ioannidis, J. P., & Khoury, M. J. (2013). Are randomized trials obsolete or more important than ever in the genomic era? *Genome Medicine, 5*(4), 32.

Khoury, M. J., & Ioannidis, J. P. A. (2014). Big Data meets public health. *Science, 346*(6213), 1054–1055.

Kruk, M. E., et al. (2018). High-quality health systems in the sustainable development goals era: Time for a revolution. *The Lancet Global Health, 6*(11), e1196–e1252.

Langendam, M. W., et al. (2020). Approaches of integrating the development of guidelines and quality indicators: A systematic review. *BMC Health Services Research, 20*(1), 875.

Melder, A., Burns, P., Mcloughlin, I., & Teede, H. (2018). Examining 'institutional entrepreneurship' in healthcare redesign and improvement through comparative case study research: A study protocol. *BMJ Open, 8*(8), e020807.

Melder, A., Robinson, T., McLoughlin, I., Iedema, R., & Teede, H. (2020). An overview of healthcare improvement: Unpacking the complexity for clinicians and managers in a Learning Health System. *Internal Medicine Journal, 50*(10), 1174–1184. https://doi.org/10.1111/imj.14876

Miller, J. H., & Page, S. E. (2007). *Complex adaptive systems: An introduction to computational models of social life*. STU - student edition. Princeton University Press.

Monash Partners. (n.d.). *Learning health systems*. [cited Aug 2021]; Available from: https://monashpartners.org.au/initiatives/learning-health-system/.

Nomura, S., et al. (2020). Contributions of information and communications technology to future health systems and Universal Health Coverage: Application of Japan's experiences. *Health Research Policy and Systems, 18*(1).

Overby, C. L., & Tarczy-Hornoch, P. (2013). Personalized medicine: Challenges and opportunities for translational bioinformatics. *Personalized Medicine, 10*(5), 453–462.

Palakshappa, D., Miller, D. P., Jr., & Rosenthal G. E. (2020). Advancing the Learning Health System by incorporating social determinants. *American Journal of Managed Care, 26*(1), e4–e6.

Panagioti, M., et al. (2019). Prevalence, severity, and nature of preventable patient harm across medical care settings: Systematic review and meta-analysis. *BMJ*, l4185.

Parikh, R. B., Schwartz, J. S., & Navathe, A. S. (2017). Beyond genes and molecules - a precision delivery initiative for precision medicine. *New England Journal of Medicine, 376*(17), 1609–1612.

Patrick, D. R., et al. (2021). Australians report climate change as a bigger concern than COVID-19. *The Journal of Climate Change and Health, 3*, 100032.

Pomare, C., et al. (2021). *Learning Health Systems: A review of key topic areas and bibliometric trends*. Learning Health Systems.

Pravettoni, G., & Triberti, S. (2020). *P5 eHealth: An agenda for the health technologies of the future*. Cham: Springer Open.

Regional Committee for Europe. (2020). European programme of work, 2020–2025. In *United action for better health in Europe*. Denmark: Regional Office for Europe, WHO.

Rifkin, S. B. (2020). Paradigms, policies and people: The future of primary health care. *BMJ Global Health, 5*(2), e002254.

Robinson, T., et al. (2020). Bridging the research-practice gap in healthcare: A rapid review of research translation centres in England and Australia. *Health Research Policy and Systems, 18*(1), 117.

Rudd, B. N., Davis, M., & Beidas, R. S. (2020) Integrating implementation science in clinical research to maximize public health impact: A call for the reporting and alignment of implementation strategy use with implementation outcomes in clinical research. *Implementation Science, 15*(1).

Safaeinili, N., et al. (2020). CFIR simplified: Pragmatic application of and adaptations to the Consolidated Framework for Implementation Research (CFIR) for evaluation of a patient-centered care transformation within a Learning Health System. *Learning Health System, 4*(1), e10201.

Scheibner, J., et al. (2021). Revolutionizing medical data sharing using advanced privacy-enhancing technologies: Technical, legal, and ethical synthesis. *Journal of Medical Internet Research, 23*(2), e25120.

Schüssler-Fiorenza Rose, S. M., et al. (2019). A longitudinal Big Data approach for precision health. *Nature Medicine, 25*(5), 792–804.

Senge, P. M. (2006). *The fifth discipline: The art and practice of the learning organization*. Rev. and updated. New York: Doubleday/Currency.

Sikka, R., Morath, J. M., & Leape, L. (2015). The Quadruple aim: Care, health, cost and meaning in work. *BMJ Quality and Safety, 24*(10), 608–610.

Slawomirski, L., Auraaen, A., & Klazinga, N. (2017). *The Economics of Patient Safety: Strengthening a value-based approach to reducing patient harm at national level.*

Stoto, M., Parry, G., & Savitz, L. (2017). Analytical methods for a Learning Health System: 4. Delivery system science. *EGEMS, 5*(1), 31.

The Health Foundation. (2010). *Evidence scan. Complex adaptive systems*. The Health Foundation.

Verheul, E., et al. (2016). Polymorphic encryption and pseudonymisation for personalised healthcare. *IACR Cryptology ePrint Archive, 2016*, 411.
Vinn, N. E. (2000). The emergence of consumer-driven health care. *Family Practice Management, 7*(1), 46–49.
WHO Big Data. (2017). *And artificial intelligence for achieving universal health coverage: an international consultation on ethics: Meeting report.*
WHO Closing. (2008). *The gap in a generation: health equity through action on the social determinants of health.*
WHO Draft Global. (2020). *Strategy on digital health 2020–2024.*
WorldBank. (2021). *Individuals using the internet* [cited 2021 August]. Available from: https://data.worldbank.org/indicator/IT.NET.USER.ZS?most_recent_value_desc=false.
Zurynski, Y., et al. (2020). *Mapping the Learning Health System: A scoping review of current evidence.* Sydney: Australian Institute of Health Innovation, and the NHRMC Partnership Centre for Health System Sustainability.

Chapter 3

Classification of medical big data: a review of systematic analysis of medical big data in real-time setup

Ajaypradeep Natarajsivam[1], R. Sasikala[1] and Katpadi Varadarajan Arulalan[2]

[1]*School of Computer Science and Engineering, Vellore Institute of Technology, Vellore, Tamilnadu, India;* [2]*A.A.Child Care Centre, Vellore, Tamilnadu, India*

1. Introduction

Information is a vital aspect in all sorts of organizations. The more generic and specific information we have, we can construct and maintain the organization in an efficiently proper way (Dash et al., 2019). Even a single entity of data is information. Hence, gathering of such data is very essential and important for all sorts of organization or enterprise. In the current tremendously developing digital world, wherever we see, we can notice data is collected in various direct and indirect means. For instance, consider an online trading website which sells households and groceries. The website mandatorily needs the user's email id and mobile number as a registration entity if he/she cannot purchase goods through the platform. Similarly, when it comes to social media, we may notice that it is hard to find someone who does not hold an account on social media. Social media sites generate large volumes of data in the form of user accounts, their posts, pictures, messages, etc. Thus, data and information travel with us as an unavoidable element in this digital world. On one hand, we should consider how these large amounts of gathered data are stored, and, on the other hand, how these large amounts of data are processed? Both storing and analyzing the data are complex tasks.

Managing and storing volumes of data in local storage, interpreting the data, and retrieving it when needed is a very hard task for any organization or firm. For this purpose, there has evolved a strategy called "cloud computing." Cloud resources provide online storage access management with enhanced security features. BDA works in an integrated way with cloud strategies, thereby rendering its real-time application to health care and medicine-based analytics. Big data analytics (BDA) tools help corporate and mid-range enterprises to employ advanced computational strategies to manage very large volumes of data. In generic notation, big data is stated as bigger data, bigger data, and bigger data (Aiden & Michel, 2013). For the two questions about how data is stored and how the data is analyzed, cloud storage—based solutions such as IAAS (infrastructure as a service) should be denoted as the best solution. Various cloud service providers, such as Amazon Web Services, Microsoft Azure, and Google Cloud, exist and have services all over the universe. They provide analyzing and storage facilities for all tiers of basic, mid-, and large-scale sectors of organizations. When it comes into the healthcare and medical domains, the application of BDA plays a very important role in manipulating and analyzing the data. Consider a hospital setup where thousands of patients make visits per day. A couple of decades ago, the scenario in developing and under developing countries for managing patient records was the usage of traditional paper-based systems. For patient registration, pharmacy and other patient details etcetera were maintained through such a paper-based system. But the scenario is completely different in the current digital world. It is not possible to maintain thousands of patient data using the paper-based traditional system. Hence, usage of a multidisciplinary platform is indeed a need in health care systems. In such a situation, hospital setups and medical hubs make the application of big data and cloud systems for analyzing and storing data. Though there was the use of computers or modern machines in hospitals and medical centers for local data storage and data entry for a quantity of extremely low entries of patients, the deployment of cloud resources was a notable happening which paved the path for the use of BDA in real-time hospital setups. Thus, the emergence of BDA took place in the real-time hospital and healthcare domains.

Big Data Analytics for Healthcare. https://doi.org/10.1016/B978-0-323-91907-4.00007-8

Analysis of big data can be defined as processing precise, large, and efficient data to gain effective solutions for perusal (Kamble et al., 2019). Medical big data analysis covers a broad umbrella of processing, manipulating, and retrieving data from cloud servers, thereby making the process easier and it tends to be a low-cost practice than the usage of traditional systems. Not only patient records, all radiology "X-ray" images, MRI reports, CT scans, etcetera come under the BDA processing coverage and back tracking of a patient's record who visited the hospital 10 years back too can be performed within seconds.

Fig. 3.1 depicts the pictorial representation of how data centers store, process, and manipulate large volumes of data that are accessed by hospitals. In this chapter, we have extensively discussed various medical big data processing techniques and methods which are applied in order to make health care systems faster and smarter.

This chapter includes six main sections: (1) Introduction, (2) Types of data, (3) Accountancy of BDA in health care domains, (4) Machine learning (ML) based on BDA in real time which focuses on Autism disease diagnosis, (5) Open source tools: cloud resources for health care management, and (6) Conclusion.

2. Types of data

BDA deals with processing the data with advanced analytical strategies. The data for processing is classified broadly into three types, namely "structured data," "unstructured data," and "semistructured data." Table 3.1 lists the data types with their corresponding characteristics, respectively. Data such as address of a person, email id of a person, mobile

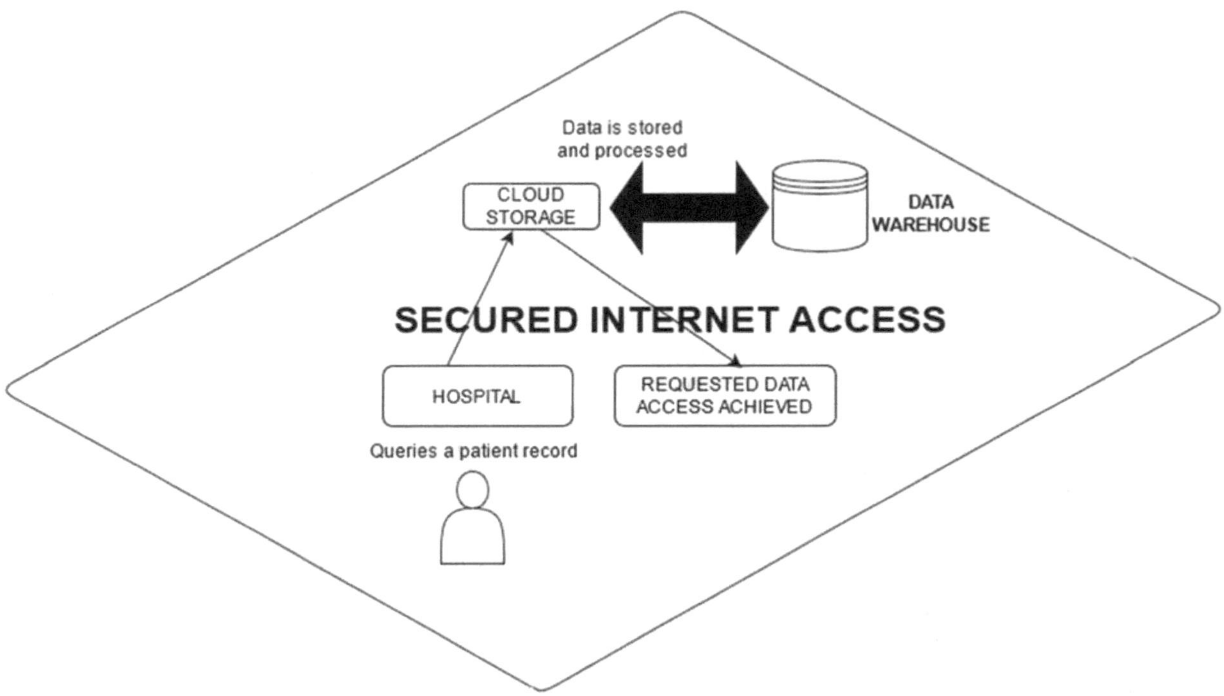

FIGURE 3.1 Data management framework.

TABLE 3.1 Various types of data.

S.No	Types of Data	Characteristics
1	"Structured data"	Has a general format and stored in tables with accurate details.
2	"Unstructured data"	All other forms of data including audios, picture or images, videos come under this classification.
3	"Semistructured data"	Has fused content of both structured and unstructured data.

numbers, ATM/debit/credit wallet details, etcetera are well-structured forms of data and these kinds of data can be said to be examples of "structured data." Under "unstructured data," various formats of files are grouped. For instance, consider a search engine. As a result of the search, the user will be provided with results and suggestions which consist of various file types including images, videos, executable files, etc. All these are grouped under "unstructured data." The final type is the "semistructured data" in which both the above discussed types of data exist. An example of this type of data is a "CSV" file.

2.1 Attributes of big data

Big data has five very important attributes, namely, "Volume," "Velocity," "Variety," "Veracity," and "Value."

Volume: The first attribute is "volume." It refers to the size/proportion of the data. If the existing data is relatively larger in size, then the data in consideration can be said to be big data.

Velocity: The second attribute is "velocity." This term refers to the mean time with which data is accessed and processed. The data in the storage repository should be accessed fast without any time delays or lag.

Variety: The third attribute is "variety." This refers to various different types of data that may exist in a firm. The capability of big data to analyze all types of data which are structured or unstructured is illustrated.

Veracity: The fourth attribute is "veracity." This refers to the efficiency and the precision of the gathered data.

Value: The fifth attribute is the "value." This refers to the perusal of the collected data into a useable end product for a purposeful application (Gills, 2021). Fig. 3.2 illustrates the attributes of big data.

2.2 Core big data analysis strategies

BDA is carried out in all sorts of organizations using some standard procedures. This section covers various core big data analytics strategies using which the data is processed.

2.2.1 A or B testing

This methodology involves mapping of various examination sets against a well-organized set of features. The objective of performing such a test is to identify what change or cause will improve a certain entity. This feature of big data can be applied to any numerously large amount of data and the factors needed for improvising can be found out. In many cases, the examination sets and organization sets are compared to be like a question and answer scenario where the answer set is expected to give the proper solution to the question set (*A Simple Guide to A/B Testing for Data Science*, 2020).

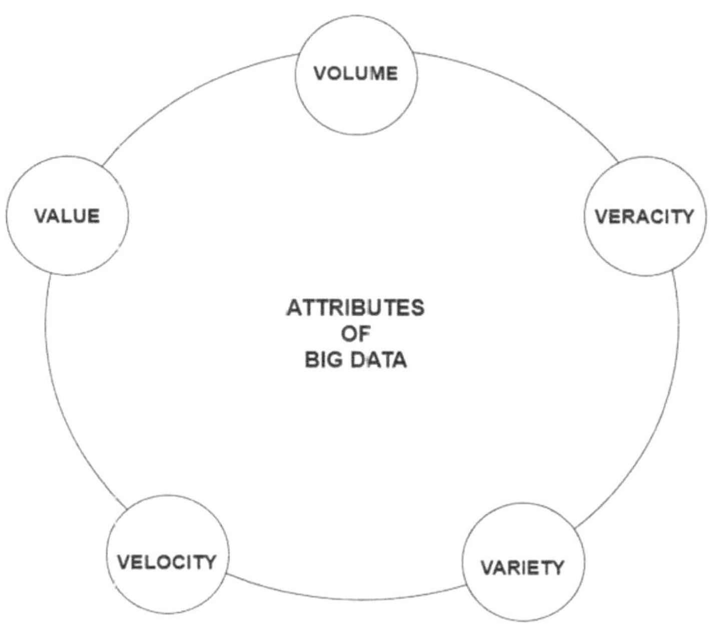

FIGURE 3.2 Various characteristics and attributes of big data analytics.

2.2.2 Unification of data

This methodology recommends combining various forms of data and retrieving effective solutions from them and evolving a new strategy. This tends to demonstrate that when data from a single source is analyzed the end product will not be a perfect model, whereas combing various sources and analyzing them, the corresponding end product will be an effective and precise model. Fig. 3.3 describes the unification of data (Introduction to Oracle Big Data, 2020).

2.2.3 Data feature extraction or mining of data

This is the most common tool used in BDA for extraction of features from data. For this process, advanced computational intelligence techniques like deep learning, ML, and mathematical statistical principles are employed. For instance, consider a hospital dataset. The features which highlight the patient's behavior toward having a disease or illness can be extracted and sorted. These noted features in each occurrence of future datasets may be noted as prone to disease or illness. Likewise, feature extraction plays a vital role in all sorts of BDA (*How to Use Feature Extraction on Tabular Data for Machine Learning*, 2020).

2.2.4 Artificial intelligence and machine learning

In the widely spread domain of artificial intelligence, the branch of ML is applied widely to data analytics. ML-based techniques can be applied to all sorts of data in order to train the machine to predict future outcomes. For instance, if 1000 patient records are used to train the machine with features containing disease, based on attributes (say fever), when a new dataset is given, the machine may be able to predict the existence of disease. This era of disease prediction is a great achievement in the multidisciplinary domains of computation and health care (*Big Data and ML: A Marriage between Giants!*, 2018).

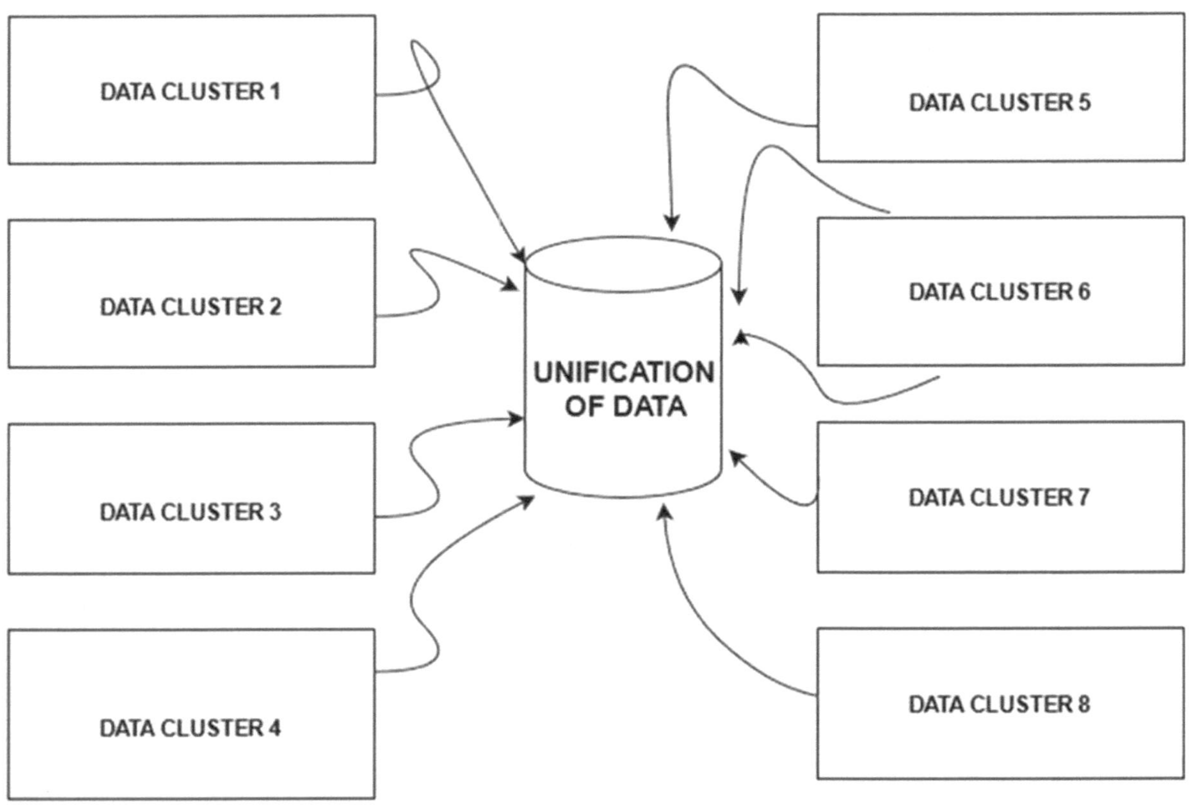

FIGURE 3.3 Unification of data: how data from various sources is made unified and handled.

2.2.5 Math and statistics

Statistical techniques help to gather, process, and manipulate data in an easier way. All sorts of field surveys and opinion polls come under this methodology. This is a common and widely used strategy even in places where computation was not employed decades ago. But statistical analysis in fusion with computation-based techniques forms a more powerful platform to gather, analyze, and process data. ML-based techniques help us to visualize the data and interpret it, while statistical analysis helps us to explore the math-based evaluation of data (Kumar & Singh, 2019; *The Role Of Statistics In The Era Of Big Data?*, 2021).

3. Accountancy of big data analytics in health care domains

The application of BDA plays an important role in the healthcare domain. As briefed, BDA is applied with the help of cloud-based resources. There are vital benefits achieved as an end product. Advanced strategies such as ML coupled with big data processing yield good output. Various disease predictions are also examined. Patient health records, patient charters, appointment rosters, etcetera, can be referred to as primary criteria for BDA applications where patients have direct access or patient involvement and interaction is essential in manipulating data for analytics. Other than this, the data generated by patient's treatment procedures such as X-rays, MRI scan reports, CT scans, etc., involve a doctor or technicians' handling and involvement. This comes under secondary criteria. The discussed criteria are combined together to form the application of real-time data analytics in the medical and health care industries. There are a few applications where BDA is applied directly to medical and healthcare-based systems other than the above discussed criteria, which include disease prediction, diagnosis, and screening. Discussed below are various aspects for which BDA is accountable in healthcare.

3.1 Hospital and health hubs

Various hospitals and health care centers avail cloud storage from service providers and form a common interface for storing, processing, and retrieving the data from the cloud data warehouses. Collecting data through such a common interface has two great benefits. The first benefit is that the ease of storing such large amounts of data is decreased. The second benefit is that the collected data without any personally identifiable information (patient name, address, contact number, etc.) can be gathered and analyzed with advanced ML algorithms. For instance, consider a hospital in Asia and another in Australia that has an agreement to have data stored in a common pool. Consider a scenario for patients with heart disease. Many patients may visit hospitals on these continents, respectively, based on their place of residence. Further, while correlating the data from hospitals of the two continents, the common parameters causing the disease such as age, additional issues such as hypertension, diabetes levels. Table 3.2 illustrates an example of how the parameters causing the disease are split up in a table and a further "*n*" number of data entries like this, without the patient's name or any identifiable details being gathered. The collected data can be processed by employing ML-based algorithms by which the machine can be trained in order to predict disease in the future. For better understanding, if a patient has high levels of diabetes, hypertension, and has a history of heart attack in the past, he is most prone to get affected even in the future. Likewise, by training the machine with various combinations of such features, the machine will be able to diagnose disease with high efficiency if a new dataset is given. This paves the era for multidisciplinary application of computing-based systems and reduces manpower too. The data collected through such an interface is split into storage and analysis.

3.2 Malignancy detection using big data analytics

Another broad field where BDA can be applied is the diagnosis and treatment for malignancy or cancer. BDA helps to organize data efficiently so that retrial is easier. Malignant detection is based on genetics and it will vary from person to

TABLE 3.2 Handling heart disease dataset is handled by big data analytics.

Heart disease	Age of the patient	Diabetes level	Hypertension level	History of cardiac arrest (if any)
	55	Normal	Normal	Yes
	64	Intermediate	Normal	No
	64	High	High	Yes

person (Kumar & Singh, 2019). BDA techniques help to cluster large volumes of human genetic characteristics and this collected data can be mapped into a new patient's gene attributes and the diagnosis of malignancy can be performed. Telemedicine as an automated system in many countries works through this principle.

3.3 Medical intelligence

In the current scenario, people from all tiers of society are applying for medical claims and critical care life support insurance policies. When it comes to insurance providing firms, it is harder for them to segregate fraudsters from the genuine ones. For instance, people may submit false holdings and reports of older claims or may generate false details in order to make use of the insurance service provider's service. By having a well-equipped portal with all data sorted through BDA techniques, the fraudster can be easily identified as every detail is online and computationally validated (Kumar & Singh, 2019; *The Role of Statistics in the Era of Big Data?*, 2021).

3.4 E-health records

The modern era presents you a digital world. Wherever we go, we see the inclusion of digital technology or technological support in any direct or indirect means. E-health records are libraries as discussed in section 3.1, where the data is stored for future perusal. The large volumes of such collected data are stored centrally on cloud servers, which reduce the ease for both concerned hospitals and patients. There are various practical scenarios such as loss of documents, natural calamities, disasters, and pandemics, because of which there may be a situation where a patient's health record could be lost or inaccessible. The E-health record puts an end to this issue as every patient's details, including laboratory test results, radiography results, MRIs, etc., will be kept safe for future use. A patient in 2020 may be treated by a doctor for an orthopedics-based problem, while the same person may consult a doctor in the same hospital after years for any other sort of problem. In such a case, the hospital need not create a new entry for data storage, whereas accessing of older records can be done. Every such patient record holds an editable file through which the doctors can edit the patient's current condition and update them. Hence, there will not be situations where any of the data can merge with other patients' health records (Durcevic, 2020).

3.5 E-medicine

E-medicine or online-based treatments are very popular nowadays. People would like to be in the comfort of their homes and get to all the services through the internet. Initially, this applied only to e-commerce, food orders, and travel reservations. This now further extends to healthcare. The entire world is suffering because of the "COVID 19" pandemic, and the boon for avoiding such tough situations is health care. In many countries, the situation was worse and people suffered a lot to undertake treatment for their diseases and ailments. The application of e-medicine gave a helping hand to making use of "doctor on request" services through online health portals. Treatments and medical prescriptions are generated purely online, by which inclusion of manpower is considerably reduced. Other than this, in certain developed countries, AI-powered robots are employed to assist doctors during surgery and this comes under the umbrella of big data—powered AI, where the automated devices are trained with huge volumes of data and synthesized by ML and deep learning algorithms (Durcevic, 2020).

3.6 Evolution of new medicines and practices in healthcare

The above discussed sections described how big data strategies can be ingeniously applied into health care domains. We also discussed that the advanced strategies of AI and big data can apply to disease predictions too. Likewise, the same can be applied to the evolution and the discovery of new pharmaceutical medicines too. Since big data powered by AI has a vast collection of data processing and visualization methods, the researchers and scientists are boosted with confidence by having efficient resources which assist them to discover new medicine. New combinations and proportions can be framed with the help of AI and which in turn can be tested for its efficiency by using statistical and ML strategies (Durcevic, 2020). Fig. 3.4 depicts the top applications of big data in the healthcare and medical domains.

4. Machine learning based on big data analytics in real time: autism disease diagnosis

As BDA applications are enormously useful in the medical and health care domains, coherent outputs can be attained by supplying medical data to ML algorithms. One such application is the detection and diagnosis of autism. Autism is a

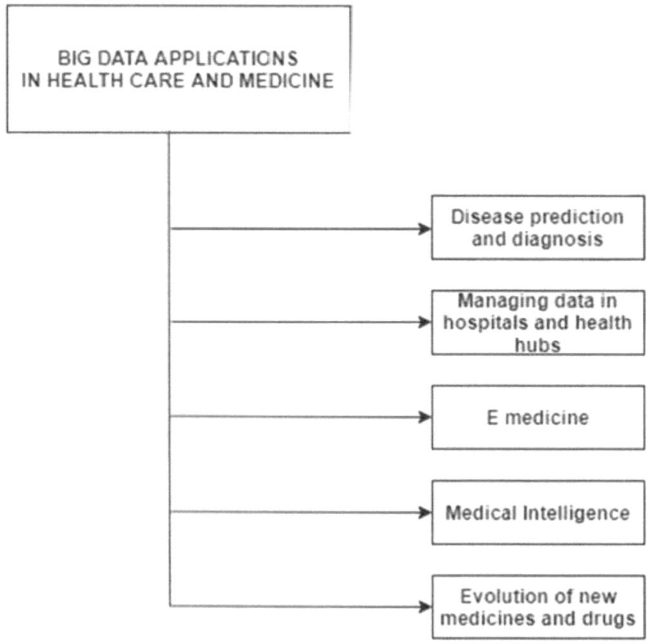

FIGURE 3.4 Top applications of big data in health care.

typical developmental disorder of which indications and early manifestations are found in children below the age of 12 years (Ajaypradeep & Sasikala, 2021). Duda et al. (2016) did a study on applying advanced ML algorithms for diagnosis of autism and thereby differentiating autism with attention deficiency disease (Duda et al., 2016). The authors used data gathered from 2925 participants containing "Social Responsive Scales" (SRS) evaluation. "SRS" is considered to be a standard tool for clinical diagnosis of autism disease and it has around 65 questions related to child behavior. Duda's study found that only "5" crucial parameters out of 65 total parameters were able to distinguish the participants with autism disease from that of attention deficit syndrome. By training the ML model with 2925 features, the author and team were able to achieve high efficiency with "au curve" analysis results like 0.96 (Duda et al., 2016).

Daniel Bone performed a study to enhance autism diagnosis and detection using ML-based algorithms. The authors recruited 1726 participants with 1264 participants who are prone to be affected by autism and 462 participants with various other disorders. The authors performed analysis with various advanced ML algorithms to differentiate the persons as an autism affected category and others as nonautism affected. The authors derived high efficiency outputs with sensitivity of 89.2% (Bone et al., 2016). The discussed studies suggest how efficient the performance of ML algorithms delivers in analysis of large scale datasets. For better interpretation, we discuss benchmark datasets collected and devised by Thabtah for autism diagnosis and screening (Thabtah et al., 2018). The autism datasets compiled by the authors can be stated as a perfect application of medical data analytics in real-time systems. In the concerned study, the authors designed a mobile application to gather data from various sorts of people. The app was designed in a way that all age groups of people can be evaluated. The app was segregated into four major segments of age groups: below 3 years, 4–11 years, 12–16 years, and above 17 (Thabtah et al., 2018). The app consisted of a questionnaire from a gold standard autism detection methodology called, "Q chart," which is accepted universally.

The authors claim that the data given as input by various individuals is gathered and the same can be used to train the ML model in order to deliver an efficient output. The app comprises of 10 questions and based on the response given by the user for those questions, a threshold value is set which differentiates whether the patient is prone to be affected by autism or not (Thabtah et al., 2018) For instance, while applying the above strategy, consider we have a data instance of 3000 features, and we attain efficiency of 80%. While gathering more and more data and adding it to our repository and retraining the machine, the end product will be more efficient output. Likewise, any ML or deep learning model will require very large volumes of data, so that the analysis will be more stringent and precise delivery of results can be guaranteed. Thus, the real-time application of BDA applies to the prediction of autism. There are various such diseases and disorders which can be diagnosed by the application of BDA.

5. Open source tools: cloud resources for health care management

Previous sections discussed how BDA is applied in healthcare and this section narrates the tools and cloud service providers for processing and storing the collected data. There are wide sources of various tools which are either open source or proprietary tools available. In generic terms, managing "structured data" is somewhat easier, such that the user may consolidate the data into tables, graphs, or charts and thus manipulation and storage is easier. When it comes to "unstructured data," the interpretation is very hard as it contains various file formats and all together cannot be clustered into a single entity, such as "structured data." Serving as a solution for this purpose, "Hadoop" from Apache provides various free-to-use technologies by which data analytics can be performed. Various "Hadoop"-based tools which are available as part of apache distribution can be used effectively for data analysis. Briefed below are a few distributions which are used extensively by health care organizations and hubs for data analytics.

5.1 Apache "Hadoop"

The term Apache "Hadoop' refers to the most common distribution consisting of tools bundled to analyze and process large amounts of datasets (The Apache software foundation, 2021). Not only are the healthcare-based datasets, but the data generated and obtained from social media and other bulk volumes can be processed and storage platforms for equipping data's centralized storage for easy access are provided. The data under apache "Hadoop" is structured into the following modules, which act as the core functioning fragments of the entire system. The "Hadoop" system integrates the following components, which are collectively described as the Apache "Hadoop." Fig. 3.5 represents the collective distribution of "Hadoop" components.

"Hadoop" common: This library consists of common files required for the functioning of "Hadoop" systems.

"Hadoop" YARN: This repository holds the responsibility of setting up the process of allocating resources and their management.

"Hadoop" Map reduce: This works on the basis of "Hadoop" YARN, by which huge data sets are processed simultaneously without any hindrances or interruptions.

"Hadoop" Ozone: The new implementation of ozone will be held during 2020. This serves as a repository for the storage of objects for "Hadoop" (Kumar & Singh, 2019, 2021).

5.1.1 HDFS or "Hadoop" distributed file system

HDFS is the heart of the "Hadoop" environment where storing of large volumes of data takes place. HDFS has the capability of storing large sums of structured and unstructured data and it has the tendency to make note of directory names

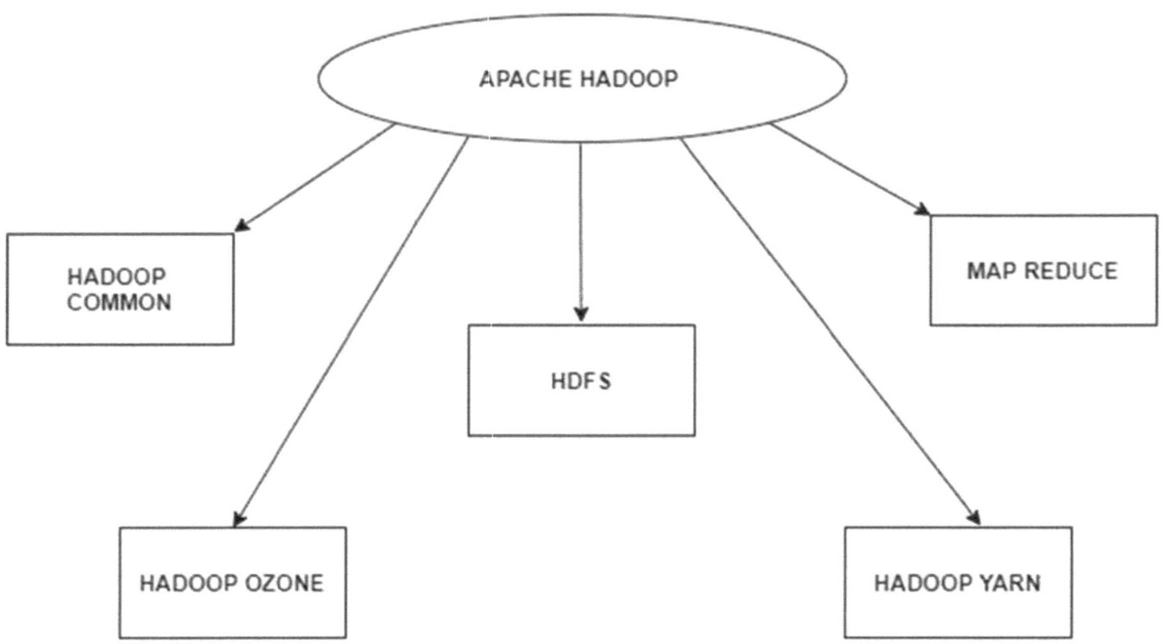

FIGURE 3.5 Hadoop system components.

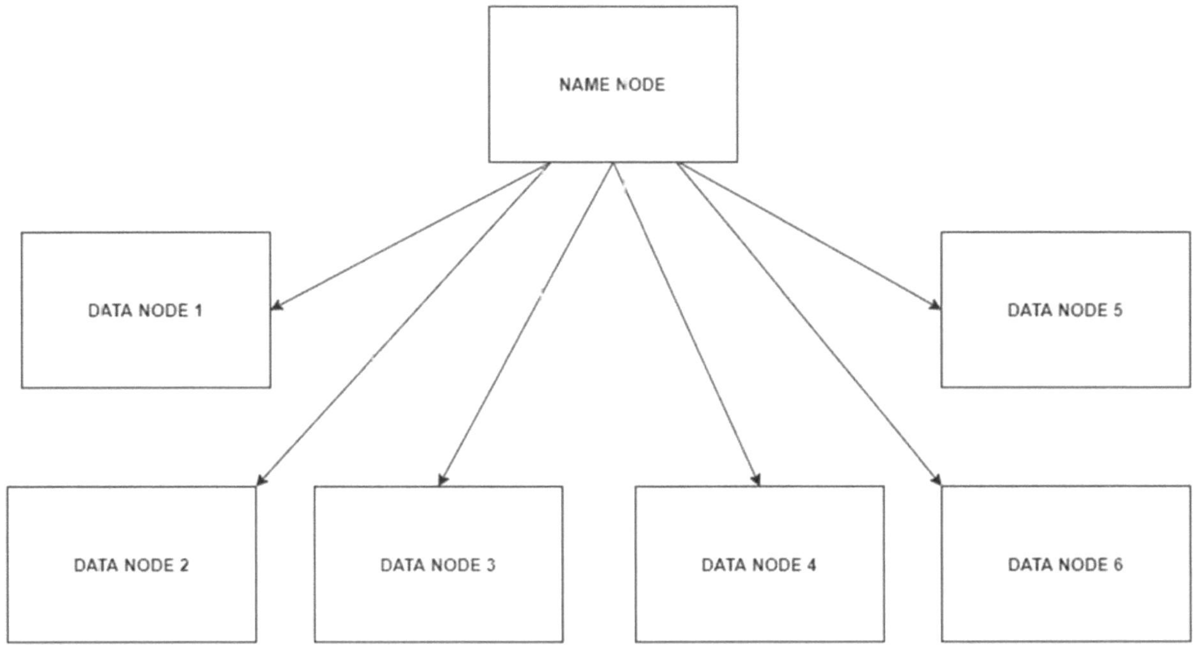

FIGURE 3.6 Nodes in HDFS system.

as labels. Labels act as the id to access data files stored in the repository. The HDFS acts as the core functionality of the "Hadoop" and it performs the function of storing and retrieving files. HDFS's functionality is structured into two fragments, namely, the "name node" and the "data node." Fig. 3.6 narrates the functionality of HDFS. As discussed earlier, the "name node" consists of labels of files stored in the repository. "Data nodes" are the real place where the data is stored (Kumar & Singh, 2019, 2021).

6. Conclusion

This chapter briefed on the strategy of BDA, its application in the medical and health care domains, real-time disease diagnosis, and various resources available for employing BDA in health care. As part of advancements in technology, day to day newer and newer concepts and strategies are discovered. In those, employing ML-based systems and artificial intelligence–powered machines for disease prediction and diagnosis which are in existence can be boosted with additional features. This will rule the future medical industry and health care domains. The section accountability of BDA under health care discussed how various hospitals and health care hubs gather, organize, and process patient data. This extends to how, without human intervention, world-class health solutions can be provided. In real time, this is being in practice now universally as part of the existence of "COVID 19." E-health record maintenance and e-medicine sections discuss how patient records are maintained on the cloud and how that data is accessed remotely by doctors and technicians. Malignancy detection and autism diagnosis in real-time sections discuss how effective ML models help in detecting ailments among all age groups. Relatively, BDA techniques work ethically and under all devised gold standard operating procedures. Hence, applying these methods on a large scale will help society to apply the same methodology in detecting various other diseases and disorders in real time. This may save valuable human lives too. Likewise, bringing more advancement in cloud-based online health care systems can improve the services provided to the targeted public. In this chapter, we discussed applications of open source cloud solutions, whereas there are service providers who may provide these cloud-based services on subscription too. Based on user requirements and the amount of data being in consideration, the user may opt for any of these services and make use of BDA. In developed countries, there is already a full-scale deployment of data analytics using various cloud resources, whereas in many developing and underdeveloped countries, the reach is not as much as that of the developed countries. Many factors such as devices, a high-speed internet, nonavailability of experts with intact knowledge, etcetera, may be reasons for the same. This can be overcomed by creating awareness about technologies and funding countries which require resources. Thus, the applicability of BDA and usage of cloud-centric resources will increase, thereby reducing human ease and improving efficiency universally.

References

A Simple Guide to A/B Testing for Data Science.(2020). https://towardsdatascience.com/a-simple-guide-to-a-b-testing-for-data-science-73d08bdd0076.

Aiden, E., & Michel, J. B. (2013). *Uncharted: Big data as a lens on human culture* (Vol. 11). Riverhead Books.

Ajaypradeep, N., & Sasikala, R. (2021). 2021. "Statistical perspectives and machine learning algorithms: Research analysis of technological support for autism diagnosis. In *Education and technology support for children and young adults with ASD and learning disabilities*. IGI Global.

Big Data and ML: A Marriage between Giants!.(2018). https://towardsdatascience.com/big-data-and-ml-a-marriage-between-giants-1d6dc52d54de.

Bone, D., Bishop, S. L., Black, M. P., Goodwin, M. S., Lord, C., & Narayanan, S. S. (2016). Use of machine learning to improve autism screening and diagnostic instruments: Effectiveness, efficiency, and multi-instrument fusion. *Journal of Child Psychology and Psychiatry, 57*(8), 927–937. https://doi.org/10.1111/jcpp.12559

Dash, S., Shakyawar, S. K., Sharma, M., & Kaushik, S. (2019). Big data in healthcare: management, analysis and future prospects. *Journal of Big Data, 6*(1), 1–25. https://doi.org/10.1186/s40537-019-0217-0

Duda, M., Ma, R., Haber, N., & Wall, D. P. (2016). Use of machine learning for behavioral distinction of autism and ADHD. *Translational Psychiatry, 6*(2). https://doi.org/10.1038/tp.2015.221

Durcevic, S. (Retrieved October 21, 2020). 18 Examples Of Big Data Analytics In Healthcare That Can Save People. *Business Intelligence*. from https://www.datapine.com/blog/big-data-examples-in-healthcare/.

How to Use Feature Extraction on Tabular Data for Machine Learning.(2020). https://machinelearningmastery.com/feature-extraction-on-tabular-data/.

Kamble, S. S., Gunasekaran, A., Goswami, M., & Manda, J. (2019). A systematic perspective on the applications of big data analytics in healthcare management. *International Journal of Healthcare Management, 12*(3), 226–240. https://doi.org/10.1080/20479700.2018.1531606

Kumar, S., & Singh, M. (2019). Big data analytics for healthcare industry: Impact, applications, and tools. *Big Data Mining and Analytics, 2*(1), 48–57. https://doi.org/10.26599/bdma.2018.9020031

Thabtah, F., Kamalov, F., & Rajab, K. (2018). A new computational intelligence approach to detect autistic features for autism screening. *International Journal of Medical Informatics, 117*, 112–124. https://doi.org/10.1016/j.ijmedinf.2018.06.009

The Apache software foundation. (2021). *Apache Hadoop*. https://hadoop.apache.org/.

The Role of Statistics in the Era of Big Data?.(2021). https://analyticsindiamag.com/the-role-of-statistics-in-the-era-of-big-data/.

Chapter 4

Towards big data framework in government public open data (GPOD) for health

Najhan Muhamad Ibrahim[1,3], Nur Hidayah Ilham Ahmad Azri[2] and Norbik Bashah Idris[1]

[1]*Department of Information System, Department of Computer Sciences, Department of History, Health Research Institute, International Islamic University Malaysia (IIUM), Kuala Lumpur, Malaysia;* [2]*Universiti Sultan Azlan Shah (USAS), Kuala Kangsar, Perak, Malaysia;* [3]*University of Limerick, Limerick, Ireland*

1. Introduction

Nowadays, data has become one of the world's most valuable resources. Data can be used for various types of solution such as to generate a set of useful of information for the future, all of which are driven by creativity and innovation. In order to obtain information and provide services, data is also a critical component. In recent years, in the global economy, big data (BD) has become a contentious issue. Big data is a piece of new evidence and comprehension managing phenomena where enormous data amounts are composed and managed to be adopted in different of domains such as research, enterprise, industry, marketing, e-learning, health, and media social. John Mashey invented the term "big data" in 1998 to describe the amount of data generated by information technology and the storage capacity required to keep it. Big data also can be defined as an ever-increasing number of resources in a digital format with various forms, comprising social media, public open data and network sensors, image, spreadsheet, video, and email (Hamzah et al., 2020).

According to Gartner (2019), big data can be referred to as the huge amount of volume, increasing the velocity, and various types of data source that need to reduce the cost to manage, innovation way to execute for wiser view and better decision-making. Big data can also be described as collections of basic information, with the features of BD in terms of 3V concept, which are volume, velocity, and variety necessitating the use of complex application system to record, capture, and evaluate the information. BD has been formerly exclusively well known in a few domains, currently extended to every sector in the globe. Despite the fact that the business sector dominates DB adoption, the government or public agency is starting to see the power of open Data and DB, which is capable to generate data pattern for making decision (Ali et al., 2016). As the government is under increasing pressure to provide better service while working within tighter financial constraints, big data may be one of the options to consider. Furthermore, the public sector has been identified as one of the industries with the most data acquired and stored.

Academics and nonprofit organizations with a close relationship to the open data movement have impacted the definition and popular understanding of the phrase open data in the recent years. Open data is information that is available for free online which can then be used, reused, and disseminated by someone for whatever purpose and with no technical restrictions or prohibitions. The term Government public open data (GPOD) or government open public sector data (GOPD) focuses on data that has been made publicly available in an open platform and has been released on the Internet without restriction for sharing, reuse, and dissemination (Haini et al., 2020). GPOD innovation can promote government accountability and transparency, empower citizen engagement in government service, and boost economic growth through the reuse of data. Openness and transparency are, of course, important objectives. Governments are more inclined to launch open data projects if they feel it would also drive economic growth, increase the efficiency of public service delivery, and lead to innovation, according to years of research and practice. It is also critical to keep emphasizing these value propositions, emphasizing the full range of benefits that open data might potentially be important to hold governments accountable (Mustapa et al., 2019).

Big Data Analytics for Healthcare. https://doi.org/10.1016/B978-0-323-91907-4.00024-8

Currently, most of the country invests in technology that reflects the government's revolutionary to make digital technology an essential pillar of the country's development strategy, which will enable the collection of more useful data in the future. For example, The Government of Malaysia has already shown willingness to adopt big data by listing as being among the goals in the Country Blueprint from 2016 to 2020 that further intends to use data to enhance achievements and also save costs in government organizations. The state government has developed public data that is readily accessible throughout ministries, supported cross-agency information exchange, and implemented big data technologies (BDTs). Malaysia's government has made efforts to make data more accessible from 2014. MAMPU (Malaysia Administrative Modernization and Management Planning Unit) is a prominent organization within the Prime Minister's Department in Malaysia, is in charge of campaign management in Malaysia, and directs strategy in the global context. www.data.gov.my is the website for the Malaysian government's data portal. The remaining chapter will be organized as the following. It starts with a review of the previous study of big data and GPOD as related works section, then follows with the finding, which will be discussed on existing work in detail. Lastly, the study is then concluded with a summary of the research findings as well as recommendations for further research.

2. Related works

Despite the fact that such data has varying degrees of availability, it should be relatively easy to use. According to the broad consensus, open access data should always be freely accessible. Public open data, and from the other perspective of information, generated and maintained by government agencies for public access, therefore fits underneath the open access umbrella (Ijab et al., 2019). Despite the fact that data analytics and open data are related, they are not the same concept, according to Ijab et al. (2019). Large data can become more valuable and democratic if it is made open. Using open data principles, to alleviate some of the problems that have occurred as a result of big data, can be beneficial.

Although open data is a relatively new phenomenon in empirical science, more research is required to fully comprehend this trend and its economic, political, social, and technical implications (Jetzek, 2016). Jetzek (2016) introduced the following common qualities of open data: availability, affordability, shareability, interoperability, primary, high-quality, usability, and accessibility as presented in Fig. 4.1. The below eight traits are divided into five categories: strategic, economic, legal, conceptual, and technical open data. These features, we believe, form the framework for data sharing requirements.

In a concept paper, Bugbee et al. (2020) proposed a virtualized data system architecture that supports evolving cyber infrastructures as presented in Fig. 4.2. The data pool acts as a center to store for many types of datasets. Metadata generation, data input, reconfiguring, description, and regulatory compliances are among the basic requirements for the proposed framework to provide a basic service, as are services that help users search, visualize, and share information. Users can access data in a variety of ways thanks to this architecture. Furthermore, it is stated that data programmes should invest in cloud-native data systems that comply with this conceptual paradigm. It is significant because it shows how investing in collaborative, information sharing stewardship solutions may help open research ideas.

MapReduce is one of the most popular big data frameworks (Inoubli et al., 2018). Two user-written functions, Map and Reduce, are the key aspects of the MapReduce programming methodology. A single key—value pair is passed to the Map function, which returns a list of intermediate key—value pairs. The Reduce function receives a collection of intermediate values associated with the same intermediate key. An intermediate key and a set of values for that key are passed to the Reduce function as input. It combines these values to create a smaller set of numbers. The MapReduce system is depicted in Fig. 4.3 as a whole.

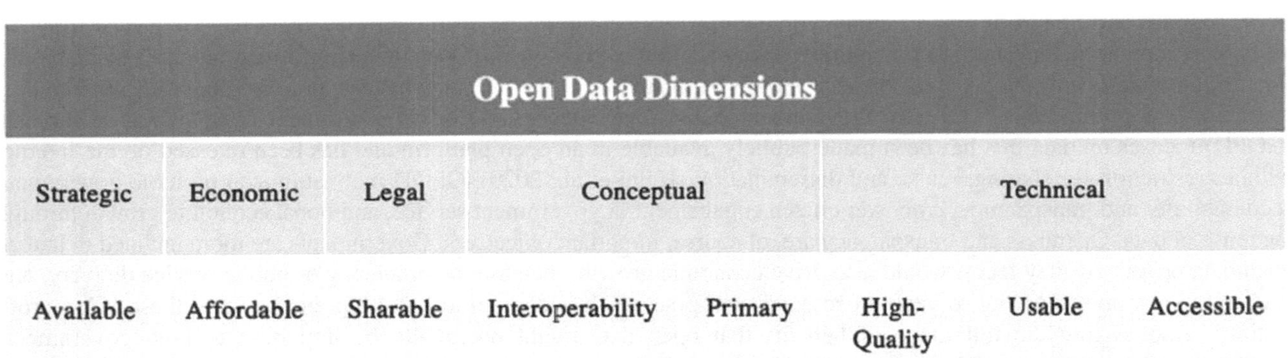

FIGURE 4.1 Open data dimension (Jetzek, 2016).

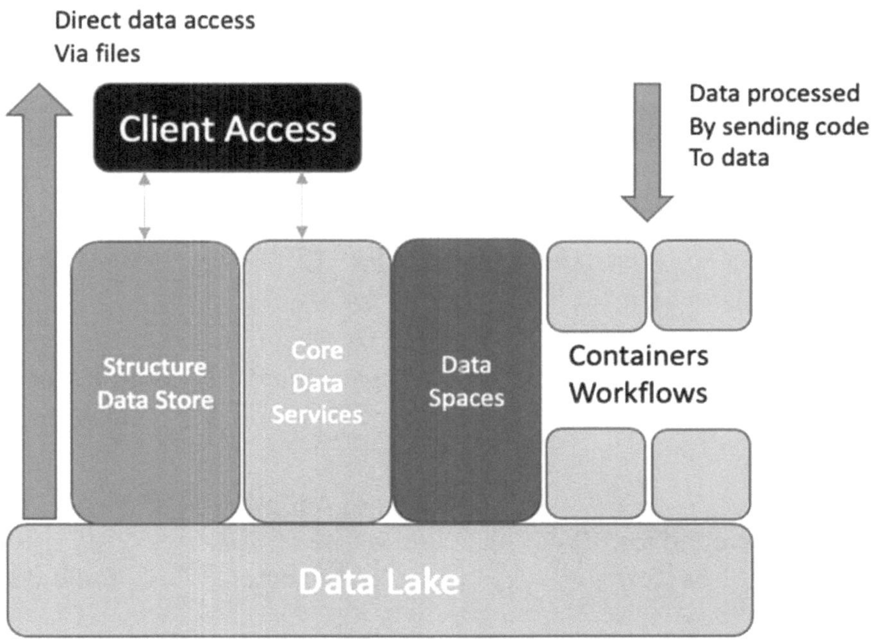

FIGURE 4.2 Conceptual data architecture in the cloud (Bugbee et al., 2020).

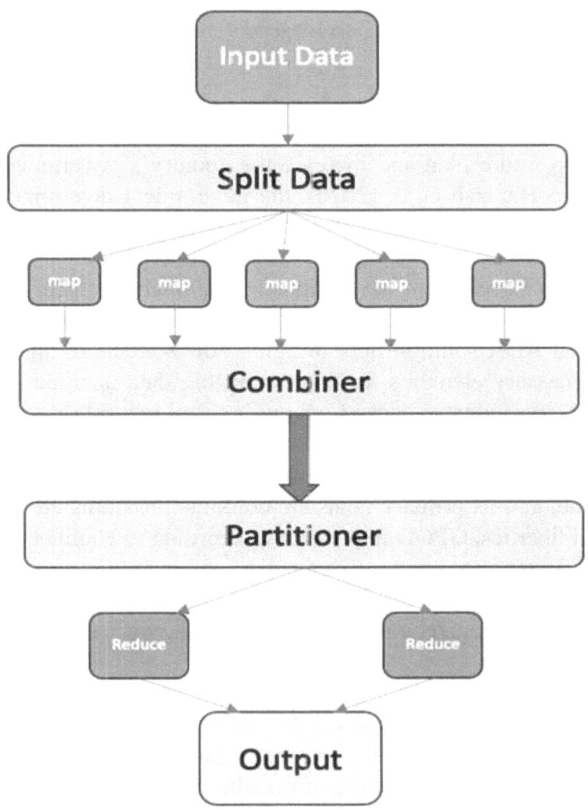

FIGURE 4.3 MapReduce Framework (Wissem et al., 2018).

FIGURE 4.4 Malaysia BD framework (Mampu, 2017).

Since the Multimedia Super Corridor was established in the early 2000s, the Malaysian government has also been implementing an e-government agenda. Similar to other developing nations, Malaysia has begun to adopt BD technology into government strategy to develop future plan and increase the country's government's efficiency in providing public services to its citizens. According to Hamzah et al. (2020), the government determines the regulations that regulate the public sector in Malaysia, making it the most crucial aspect of development for a growing country. Although privatization has been around since the 1980s, the authority still has an influence in what policies are acceptable for government and private firms to adopt. The Malaysian government has designed a national framework for big data implementation at the national level in order to assure its effective and systematic implementation. The fundamental goal of BDA implementation is to position Malaysia as a regional BDA solution hub, bringing new benefits to all industries.

The framework includes all necessary elements for supporting big data analytics (BDA), such as people centricity, government data and policy upholstery, industry-backed operations, and big data processing and support technologies as presented in Fig. 4.4. Big data implementation focuses on both public and commercial sectors to help Malaysia achieve productivity gains, ICT growth, cost savings, and innovation for the benefit of the people. Furthermore, the government service does not operate for revenue, and its primary goals are continue providing services to the public, create economic success, and protect residents' civil liberties. GPOD innovation. According to Haini et al. (2020), reusing data can increase government accountability and transparency, community empowerment in public sector, and economic growth. As a result, given the numerous concerns raised about the public's use of big data, its services are committed to strengthening operational efficiency and engagement for citizens while also addressing current problems (Ali et al., 2016).

3. Methodology

The proposed chapter for big data framework in government open data is conducted adapting SLR (Systematic Literature Reviews) approach. The method is a systematic, explicit, thorough, and repeatable procedure for discovering, evaluating, and summarizing the current body of completed and recorded research, academic, and practitioner work. The advantage of SLR is that it is a well-defined methodology. Using a range of empirical approaches, in a variety of instances, SLR may also give information on the consequences of an occurrence. If studies yield consistent results, systematic reviews confirm that a topic is robust and transferable. If the investigation results are inconclusive, the sources of variation may be investigated.

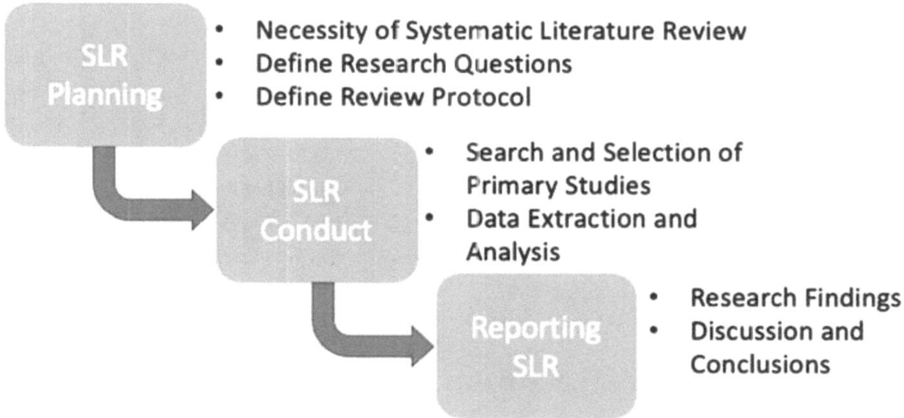

FIGURE 4.5 The steps of systematic literature review (Hussain et al., 2019).

As shown in Fig. 4.5, the research approach relies on Hussain et al. (2019). The SLR's goal is to evaluate and validate current research on the use of BDT in GPOD adoption in government agencies for public service. Planning, conducting, and reporting are the three stages of the SLR procedure. This technique requires a thorough evaluation of a number of primary papers. It allows for data integration by extracting data from studies with similar outcome measures and synthesizing findings from studies using diverse approaches.

A prime example of a public open data architecture is presented in this chapter. Since the accessible data is extensive and has been publicly available for some years with a range of data sources, this study focused on public open data. The literature study, the primary part of the research methodology, for example, is a critical evaluation of current and previous study, which will be focused on published journals, conferences, research papers, and other academic materials. This investigation demands an understanding of current big data framework challenges in public open data. The purpose of this study is to investigate research gaps, requirements, and the best big data framework for public open data. Big data framework has been a popular study issue due to a large amount of data available and the range of data types and sources. This study focuses on the growth of public open data due to a lack of awareness of big data framework for health.

4. THE finding

This section is discussed based on the existing BD framework and architecture for Public Open Data. This part also supports the research by providing a thorough overview of the current research studies. The analysis was carried out by filtering and analyzing papers relating to the issue. We used a few conceptual and theoretical frameworks from previous quality studies to capture relationships between variables. It is significant to undertake a thorough investigation and propose a viable solution for the corresponding big data and GPOD challenges, which have become the primary resources to generate and investigate various types of information. There are currently only a few research studies on the big data framework in GPOD for health.

Table 4.1 summarizes and analyses the existing big data framework based on an adoption of Open Data in Health. The table's row specifies the objectives, focus, and gap of research. There are several types of existing research work: theoretical and practical approaches for big data and open data. The approaches were chosen from a variety of research studies, some of which are theoretical and conceptual frameworks with major highlighted points of view for public open data, while others focus on infrastructure and architecture for the big data framework.

The number of incidents in an inspector acknowledged to have an influence on GPOD user attitude in the public sector was used by Kurshid et al. (2020) to model organizational GPOD implementation attitude determination and validation. This technique can be used to find a wide range of relationships, including significant, nonsignificant, and none. When forming a hypothesis or analyzing the results, this makes it easier to make a group decision. This strategy was also used to construct a conceptual or theoretical model. Moreover, the most often and discussed components approach is suitable to identify the gaps of research study and providing typical research trending, which is explored throughout the investigation.

In order to keep the model relevant, if an analyzer is addressed more than twice, it is said to be modeled. In addition, five distinct layers have been created: (1) technology layer, (2) organization layer, (3) environment layer, (4) benefits, barriers, risks, and losses layer, and (5) business layer. Fig. 4.6 depicts the conceptual/theoretical paradigm of

TABLE 4.1 The literature study comparison table.

Year	References	Objectives	Focus	Research gap
2020	Kurshid et al. (2020)	Development of conceptual model and theoretical model of public open data.	Focus on theoretical concept of pubic open data	Dot not support big data Development for Health
2019	Ijab et al. (2019)	Development of data quality framework for generic view of big data	Focus on big data quality framework	Dot not support big data Development for Health
2016	Ali et al. (2016)	Development of open data theoretical framework	Open data theoretical framework	Dot not support big data Development for Health
2016	Klievink et al. (2016)	Development of big data readiness conceptual model	Focus on intangible factor for big data framework	Dot not support big data Development for Health
2016	Jetzek et al. (2016)	Development of open data value driven framework	Only focus on private sector for open data framework	Dot not support big data Development for Health
2021	Ibrahim et al. (2021)	Development of big data interoperability framework	Focus on integration between multiple types of dataset.	Dot not support big data Development for Health
2017	R. Joaheer and S. D. Nagowah (2017)	Development of big data Architecture for Diabetes	Focus on big data Architecture	The proposed architecture only support for Diabetes
2020	Dinesh et al. (2020)	Development of Open Data Health Heatmap	Focus on Open Data Health Heatmap in general	Dot not support big data Development for Health

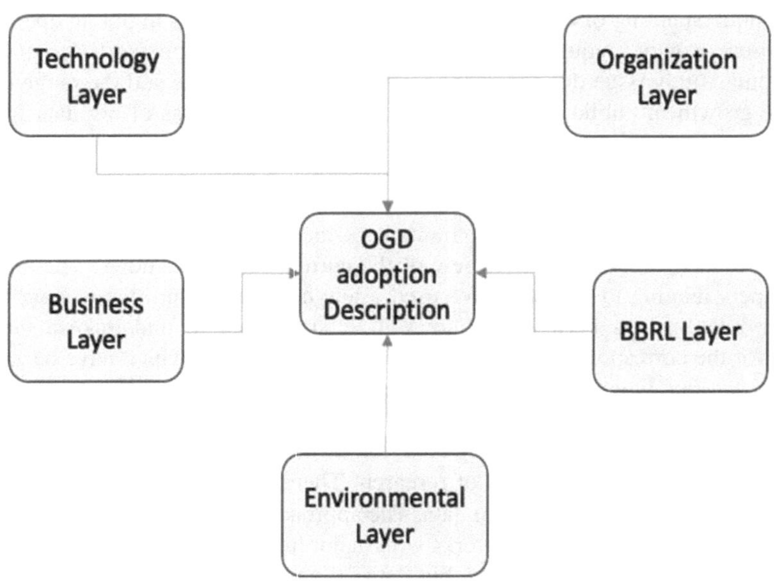

FIGURE 4.6 Conceptual framework for GPOD (Kurshid et al., 2020).

organizational adoption of GPOD proposed by Kurshid et al. (2020). However, this research work was focused more on the development of the conceptual model, which is the overview of Public Open Data. This study also did not support the development of GPOD framework for health.

According to Ijab et al. (2019), MAMPU could theoretically adopt the framework in practice as part of an initiative for Malaysia government Open Data in Public service. Data masters and ownership, for example, will use a measurement tool to examine, evaluate, and analyze information for checking the level of reliability. Once most of the content has collected,

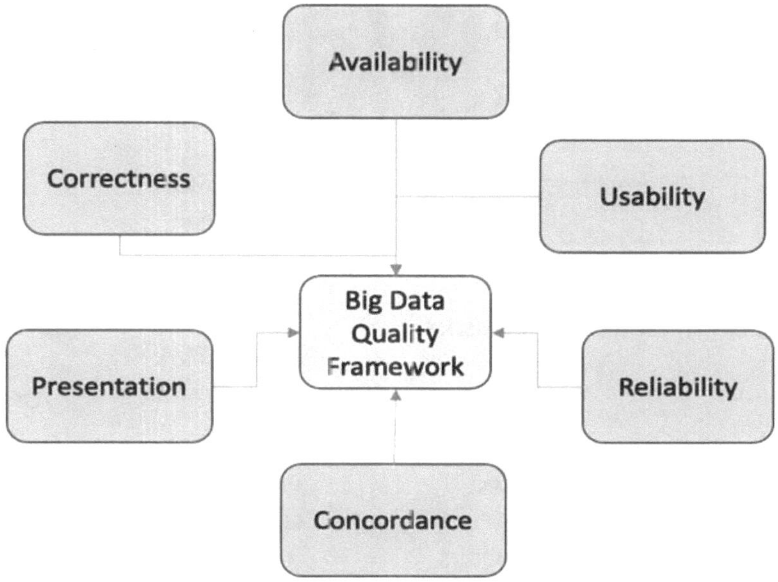

FIGURE 4.7 Big data quality framework (Ijab et al., 2019).

the data masters or system administrators will be allowed to choose preferred db based on the sensor that they have provided, with DQ Level 0 becoming the lowest and DQ Level 6 has always been the highest level of quality control.

The framework shown in Fig. 4.7 illustrates how and why the capability of an enterprise, which is adopted to changes from different source of transition, leads to the development of information technology that can be evaluated from a variety of aspects, recognizing the importance of the organization and its stakeholders (Ali et al., 2016). Infrastructure support, appropriate resource allocation, employee behavior modification, and other external and internal constraints are all factors that must be considered when implementing big data analytics in the public sector. Nevertheless, this research aims to implement BD Quality framework for Public Open Accesses Data. This research work is more conceptual in nature, where it did not provide a depth study for each component of the framework. The proposed study also did not consider any significant viewpoint for big data in Health.

Everyone in the organization should review and prepare BDA using the same amount of requirements, according to the framework. Three basic sections of the framework are precursors, implications, and interpretations, which would bring better adoption. The outcomes will be determined by the organizational and personnel BDA readiness. BDA capabilities, collective performance, BDA supportive behaviors, and organizational attitudes have all been used to explain the outcomes at the organizational level. BDA-assisted behavioral, employee commitment, and employee performance are the outcomes at the employee level.

Infrastructure support, effective budget allocation, staff changing behavior, and other direct and indirect limitations are all necessary conditions for implementing big data within a public institution (Ali et al., 2016). According to the proposed structure, all organizational members should assess preparations that use the same set of guidelines. The framework is divided into three sections: (1) preconditions, which includes elements that contribute to enhanced readiness, (2) perceived BDA preparedness, and (3) projected BDA effects as presented in Fig. 4.8. This research work has provided a valuable discussion on the theoretical framework for Open Data. Nonetheless, this framework did not provide a comprehensive study of the big data component and also there is a lack of Health component in the proposed theoretical framework.

The antecedents also contribute to increased BDA readiness. Organizational BDA implementation is driven by external factors such as industry or technology developments. The three types of antecedents are internal context facilitators, such as changes in the communication process with BDA implementation, and organizational or human qualities. It also implies that organizational members share cognitive beliefs, as well as the institution's or project participants' emotional responses to institutional BDA preparedness, which have an impact on the institution's and members' BDA readiness.

Organizational alignment, organizational maturity, and organizational capabilities are the components of the suggested framework, as shown in Fig. 4.9. The recognized models, according to Klievink et al. (2016), show the interaction between organizations and technology for each component. Organizational alignment is crucial to the success of big data applications. Without it, big data applications cannot offer value to an organization's core functions. Organizational alignment

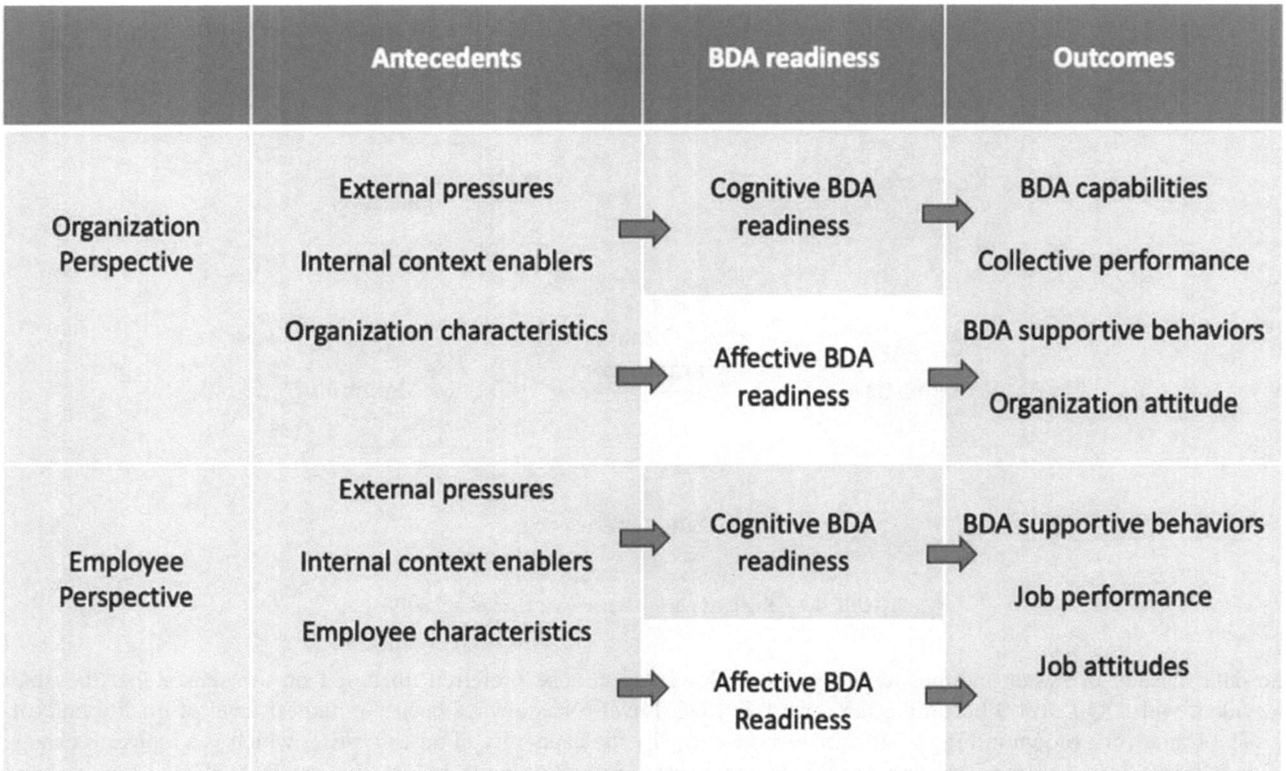

FIGURE 4.8 Open data theoretical framework (Ali et al., 2016).

FIGURE 4.9 Big Data Readiness conceptual model (Klievink et al., 2016).

should not be disregarded, even if organizational competencies are adequately available or developed. Although, this research study has highlighted an important component for Big Data Readiness, yet the view point is still in the conceptual level of study and lacks awareness to include big data for health.

Various efforts in both the private and public sectors have the ability to provide social and economic benefits in this context. When these projects are examined from the perspective of actual implementation, however, substantial differences are emerged. Using the two-by-two matrix to highlight the primary strategic options for government, the value-generating activities in value-driven primarily by the actions of the public sector on the one hand and the private sector, on the other hand, were simplified. The resulting value could be social or economic, but some value propositions are more likely to provide social value than others.

Jetzek et al. (2016) introduced open data-driven value, which was built to describe key events and constructions discovered in the data, as well as to combine previous theoretical frameworks as presented in Fig. 4.10. The model divides the process into four parts, starting with the formulation of an open data infrastructure strategy and ending with implementation, data use, and effect. The transition from an open data infrastructure strategy to impact measurement is a complicated process with many distinct stakeholders and recursive parts. For conceptual clarity, the process is dipicted as a

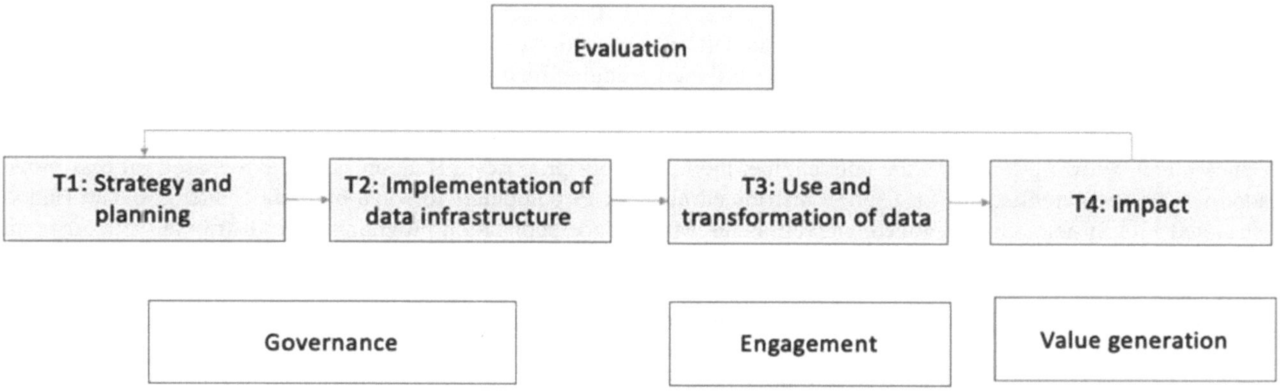

FIGURE 4.10 Open data value-driven infrastructure (Jetzek et al., 2016).

linear process with a cyclical feedback loop and leave stakeholders out of the model. The four value drivers that emerged from the categorization are shown in Fig. 4.6.

The infrastructure reviews two significant aspects. Firstly, the infrastructure that is reflected in the right-hand column by private sector involvement and the proportion of financial advantages determined in the top row has an impact on the value aspect. GPOD has a significant impact on each of these projects, but it also has its own set of integration challenges. Varied financial statement amounts and users, as well as different data sets, licenses, and even business strategies, are all required in operations and infrastructure. The open data infrastructure program is identified through (open) data strategy and (open) data policies, followed by a planning phase for the program itself, according to the process model. The approach also focuses on converting data across multiple aspects of liquid open data, including making data open in a legal and commercial sense, cleaning up data and enhancing data quality and coherence, and ultimately putting in place a technical infrastructure for data distribution. The proposed infrastructure for Open Data has a good review based on the data-driven perspective. However, the proposed work was focused on infrastructure in a conceptual view, which did not provide a study in detail for typical components for the big data framework in Health.

As shown in Fig. 4.11, the authors have introduced big data integration system or framework comprises of four different key data sources: Banci Data sets, Population and Demography Data sets, Department of Statistical Data sets, and Miscellaneous Data sets (Ibrahim et al., 2021). Data from the Banci registration system can be useful. Life-course, Population and demography Data as a life grid, as a particular situation, statistics from the Malaysian Department of

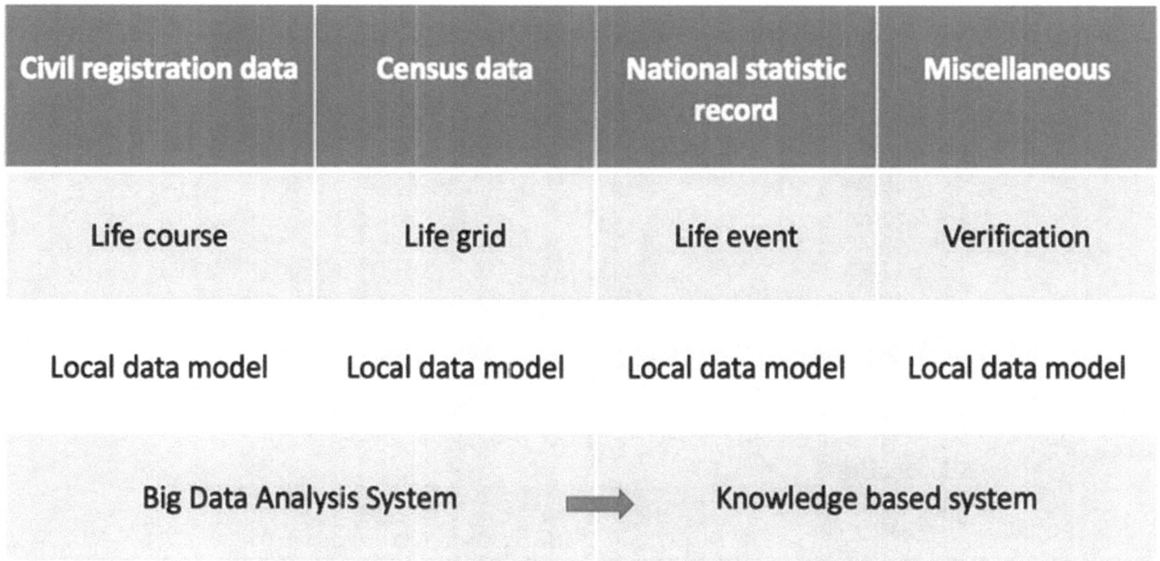

FIGURE 4.11 BD interoperability framework (Ibrahim et al., 2021).

Statistics, and Random as verification data are some of the data kinds that can be classified. In order to develop a Mapreduce Big Data Analysis System, various data will be generated in each local data model (BDAS). Then, to show how the knowledge-based system works, BDAS will be the core engine for the interoperability framework, allowing for the overall integration of a single ontology that reflects each local model from a variety of local data models. Consequently, this would develop an experience and understanding data model to show how the various data sources are related and to produce a new knowing trend. As the core engine, the framework proposes a Hadoop Ecosystem—based process model. Hadoop is an open architecture for using a distributed network of computers to solve big data challenges. The Hadoop Distributed File System was employed, as well as the MapReduce application programmes to distribute the storage and processing of a large dataset. The authors have proposed a significant framework for big data in GPOD in general. Nevertheless, the proposed framework did not include the generation of Health perspective in the framework.

R. Joaheer and S. D. Nagowah (2017) proposed big data framework for diabetes using machine learning for predictions based on biological, demographic, clinical, and environmental factors. Hadoop was used to handle a huge amount of datasets. The framework is built on top of a Hadoop cluster that has been virtualized as presented in Fig. 4.12. They argued that it is critical to examine patterns such as glucose, insulin level, blood pressure, BMI, age, and so on when treating diabetics. The framework will use MapReduce to analyze these parameters. The system will also be able to forecast diabetes problems based on EHR, insurance claims, R&D, and other sources by using machine learning in big data. The framework also highlighted the social media factor, because healthcare experts are not available 24 h a day, 7 days a week to answer endless patient questions, many individuals resort to alternate sources such as Facebook and blogs. Aside from using social media for self-management, this framework will allow users to locate the finest options and healthcare providers based on previous patients' thoughts and sentiments on the network. This information can then be used by hospitals to improve their services. This framework has an important point of view of the big data framework for Diabetes where the framework has cooperation with the big data component in detail. However, the proposed framework was not considered for Public Open Data.

Dinesh et al. (2020) suggested a framework for extracting open data pipeline in various formats such as tables, text, and pdfs from multiple sources as presented in Fig. 4.13. The data pipeline is primarily for the Extract, Transform, and Load service, which allows for the storage of disparately formatted data in a single structure. Source files, files generated from PDFs, curated files, and metadata files are all archived at the end of the extraction process. This provides for a thorough examination of the extraction process as well as the capacity to retrace data back to the origin. For each extracted value, the convert procedure creates a data point, associating it with an indication, a geo object, and other dimensions from the original dataset such as source and time period. The indicators in the source dataset are mapped to the framework indicator schema, allowing data from a variety of sources to be merged and consolidated. The transfer procedure saves the curated and balanced variables, as well as all of their dimensions and information, to an ElasticSearch database system. The proposed framework has developed a comprehensive Health Heatmap for Open Data. Nonetheless, the big data perspective has not been discussed in this framework.

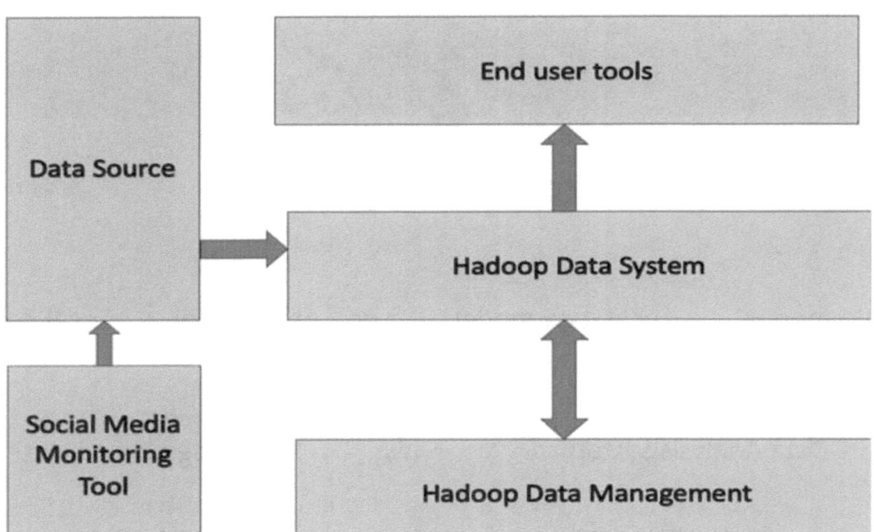

FIGURE 4.12 Big data framework for diabetes (Joaheer & Nagowah, 2017).

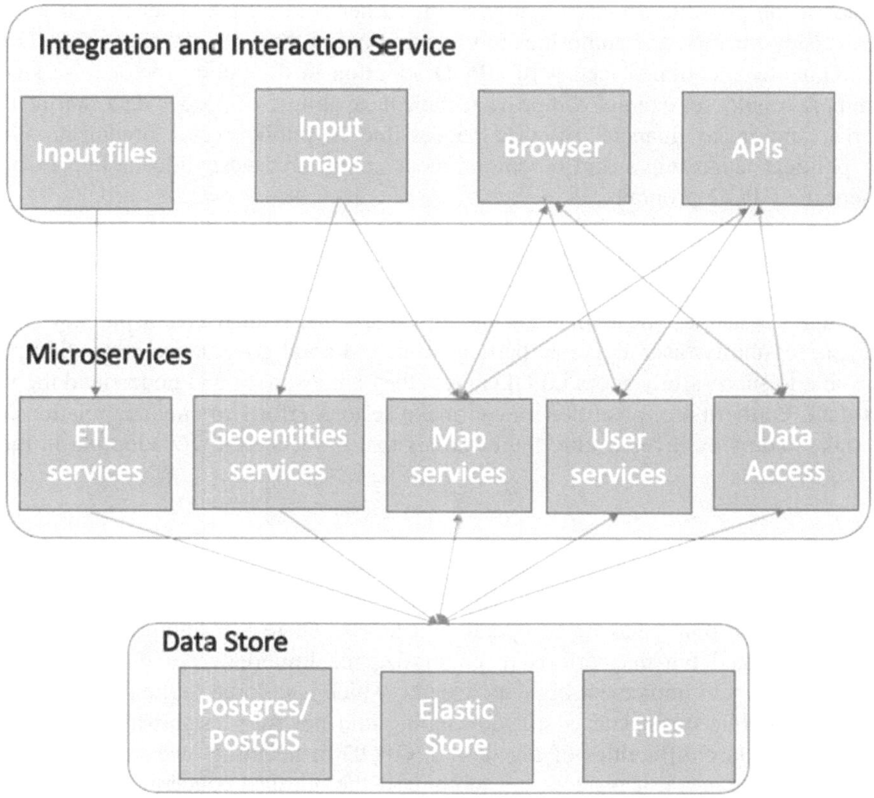

FIGURE 4.13 Open data Health Heatmap framework (Dinesh et al., 2020).

Despite the fact that most existing architecture and infrastructure are capable to handle big data operations and provide a significant solution for processing big data and open data, however, the majority of existing frameworks continue to overlook the requirements of public open data for health to be incorporated. There are two main noteworthy viewpoints that can be drawn from the comparison study. To begin with, less number of previous researches have sophisticated big data framework in GPOD for health. Only one existing research work focuses on big data for diabetes; however, this research was focused more on architecture and still lacks consideration of public open data. Second, while the big data framework is commonly utilized for data management in a larger enterprise, there is still a lack of investment and adoption of big data in the public sector. As a result, the authorities may less utilize the huge amount of valuable datasets available, which may reduce the overall cost for consultancy and system development for the healthcare system in order to generate health patterns for future policy. Collaboration from a variety of disciplines and sources is required for the success of big data in GPOD in health. To achieve the desired outcomes, all aspects of the government agency, including process, technologies adoption, people readiness, and structure innovation, must incorporate at the same time.

5. Contribution, limitation, and discussion

This research presents three main contributions. The study begins with a discussion of the motivations for open data as well as an overview of the present state of open data research. This overview aims to clearly clarify the scope of the public open data research study so that we can take tangible efforts to put public open data principles into practice. Next, we believe that research in big data for GPOD is becoming increasingly necessary to investigate. Therefore, it is significant to study and consolidate the existing framework for GPOD. Finally, the finding presented a list of the best practices that both individual researchers and authorities may employ to make open data relevant for health in the future.

This study approach has the drawback that each case of open data adoption is extremely dependent on a variety of contextual factors. We attempted to report on the backdrop of this particular example in order to make comparisons with different other similar research works. As a result, the different viewpoint has been identified to accommodate contextual elements. Another disadvantage is that the study focuses on typical GPOD in health, which might vary greatly among open data projects based on context as well as the initiative's goals.

By taking into account the possible drivers highlighted in earlier studies, the conceptual and theoretical framework offered practitioners, decision-makers, and authorities to successfully implement and execute GPOD in their practice. The findings of the most frequently mentioned factors of GPOD adoption in the public sector raise significant concerns for policymakers. Governments could, for example, improve technical capabilities, improve data sharing culture, develop legal and policy frameworks, and make financial resources accessible in public sector organizations to facilitate GPOD implementation. The political leadership's aim or commitment could have a significant impact on how organizations embrace and implement the GPOD program.

Apart from that, as representatives of businesses, decision-makers can take initiatives to improve productivity and the use of GPOD and community engagement in decisions. This perspective of undertaking attempts to develop publicly available data in multiple formats influences organizational acceptance of GPOD, in which moral choice should focus on and take necessary initiatives to tackle. The association should address issues such as transparency and confidentiality, data protection and privacy, accessibility, user and civic participation, and good governance generation projects. Furthermore, businesses will not be able to successfully adopt GPOD unless they are aware of and understand the volume, velocity, and value of government data. Furthermore, practitioners can make serious efforts to enhance relationships between organizations and external stakeholders by investigating the elements that influence GPOD adoption in the public sector.

6. Conclusion

Referring to the nature of big data, assembling data in many sectors of an organization necessitates a large size of the structure. Along with its nature of business, the public sector is a suitable sector to focus on big data initiatives because it provides services to people from policymaking to operational levels. There are commonly known that governments in developed countries have adopted big data efforts to emphasize the importance of data inclusion of all government agencies to formalize the policy and implement big data agenda, which is tailored to the country's present condition. The big data study discipline in public open data is still developing and not fully established, and there are few thorough research papers addressing the key difficulties of big data in GPOD in health. However, in order to gain a deeper understanding of the big data phenomena, it is necessary to connect the big data concerns with public open data.

The goal of incorporating big data framework and open data is to enhance the outcomes while lowering costs and better analysis of huge available data. One way to address this is to promote open data among government agencies, encourage data exchange across agencies and take advantage of BDT. The government can use the Public Sector Open Data program to produce innovative data-driven goods with the purpose of increasing public service and availability while taking into account the needs to access quality information. DB technology is a new technology area that a country needs to plan for enormous scientific advances and digitalization. To achieve a beneficial outcome for the boost their performance, the government and government agencies must use technology, particularly when it comes to accurately writing government policy. In perspective of a national initiative and trend, it is expected to continue to change public officials' and agencies' attitudes regarding data transparency. Although the theoretical and conceptual potential of free public data has been established, there are still more works to be done. If public accessible data become a reality, many obstacles as well as significant gaps in our understanding, must be addressed to assist in the resolution of difficult traditional system challenges and the improvement of data analysis for providing relevant knowledge for the future.

Funding Statement: This research is funded by the Kulliyyah (Faculty) of Information and Communication Technology (KICT) Initiative research grant by the International Islamic University Malaysia (IIUM) Award 2021. We are grateful for the full cooperation of the RMC in facilitating this research grant.

References

Ali, R. M., Haslinda, R., Rosli, M., & Sudin, S. (2016). A proposed framework of big data readiness in public sectors. *AIP Conference Proceedings, 1761*, 020089. https://doi.org/10.1063/1.4960929

Bugbee, K., Lynnes, C., Ramachandran, R., Maskey, M., Barciauskas, A., Kaulfus, A., et al. (2020). Advancing open science through inno- vative data system solution: The joint ESA-NASA multi-mission algorithm and analysis platform (MAAP)'S data ecosystem. In *Igarss 2020—2020 IEEE international geoscience and remote sensing symposium*. https://doi.org/10.1109/igarss39084.2020.9323731

Dinesh, A. S., Mathur, V., Ansil, B. R., Chandru, V., Chellam, R., Vanak, A. T., Ramakrishnan, U., Rajagopal, P., et al. (2020). Health Heatmap of India: An open data platform. *Journal of the Indian Institute of Science, 100*, 701—716. https://doi.org/10.1007/s41745-020-00196-z

Gartner. (2019). Retrieved May 15, 2019, from IT Glossary: https://www.gartner.com/itglossary/big-data.

Haini, S. I., Rahim, N. Z., Mohd, N. M., & Ibrahim, R. (2020). Factors influencing the adoption of open government data in the public sector: A systematic literature review. *International Journal of Advanced Science, Engineering and Information Technology, 10*(2), 611—617. https://doi.org/10.18517/ijaseit.10.2.9488 [Online]. Available:.

Hamzah, M. A., Yatin, S. F. M., Yusof, M., Rashid, T. S. L. T. Z., Shuhaimi, H., Suleiman, A. B., Mansor, A. N., & Taib, K. M. (2020). Big data implementation in Malaysian public sector: A review. *International Journal of Academic Research in Business and Social Sciences, 10*(11), 1461–1474.

Hussain, N., Turab Mirza, H., Rasool, G., Hussain, I., & Kaleem, M. (2019). Spam review detection techniques: A systematic literature review. *Applied Sciences, 9*(5), 987. https://doi.org/10.3390/app9050987

Ibrahim, N. M., Hussin, A. A. A., Hassan, K. A., & Breathnach, C. (2021). Big data interoperability framework for Malaysian public open data. In F. Saeed, F. Mohammed, & A. Al-Nahari (Eds.), *Lecture notes on data engineering and communications technologies: Vol. 72. Innovative systems for intelligent health informatics. IRICT 2020*. Cham: Springer. https://doi.org/10.1007/978-3-030-70713-2_39

Ijab, M. T., Mat Surin, E. S., & Mat Nayan, N. (2019). Conceptualizing big data quality framework from a systematic literature review perspective. *Malaysian Journal of Computer Science*, 25–37. https://doi.org/10.22452/mjcs.sp2019no1.2

Inoubli, W., Aridhi, S., Mezni, H., Maddouri, M., & Nguifo, E. M. (2018). An experimental survey on big data frameworks. *Future Generation Computer Systems, 86*, 546–564. https://doi.org/10.1016/j.future.2018.04.032

Jetzek, T. (2016). Managing complexity across multiple dimensions of liquid open data: The case of the Danish Basic Data Program. *Government Information Quarterly, 33*(1), 89–104. https://doi.org/10.1016/j.giq.2015.11.003

Joaheer, R., & Nagowah, S. D. (2017). A big data framework for diabetes in Mauritius. In *International conference on infocom technologies and unmanned systems (trends and future directions) (ICTUS), 2017* (pp. 126–132). https://doi.org/10.1109/ICTUS.2017.8285991

Khurshid, M. M., Zakaria, N. H., Rashid, A., Ahmad, M. N., Arfeen, M. I., & Faisal Shehzad, H. M. (2020). Modeling of open government data for public sector organizations using the potential theories and determinants—a systematic review. *Informatics, 7*(3), 24. https://doi.org/10.3390/informatics7030024

Klievink, B., Romijn, B. J., Cunningham, S., & de Bruijn, H. (2016). Big data in the public sector: Uncertainties and readiness. *Information Systems Frontiers: A Journal of Research and Innovation*, 1–17. https://doi.org/10.1007/s10796-016-9686-2

MAMPU (Malaysian Administrative Modernisation and Management Planning Unit). (2017). *Data terbuka sektor awam (DTSA)*. Retrieved from: https://www.mampu.gov.my/ms/penerbitan-mampu/send/157-tahun-2017/997-.

Further reading

Mustapa, M., Hamid, S., & Nasaruddin, F. (2019). Exploring the issues of open government data implementation in Malaysian public sectors. *International Journal of Advanced Science, Engineering and Information Technology, 9*, 1466. https://doi.org/10.18517/ijaseit.9.4.8850

Section II

Big medical data: Techniques, managements, and applications

Chapter 5

Big data analytics techniques for healthcare

Md. Ashrafuzzaman[1], Md. Mahmudul Haque Milu[2], Anika Anjum[2], Farzana Khanam[2] and Md. Asadur Rahman[1]

[1]*Department of Biomedical Engineering, Military Institute of Science and Technology (MIST), Dhaka, Bangladesh;* [2]*Department of Biomedical Engineering, Jashore University of Science and Technology (JUST), Jashore, Bangladesh*

1. Introduction

In the modern era, information is the power and the key to development. Information conveys the facts about something we would like to know. We can better arrange ourselves to give the greatest results if we have more information (Afzali et al., 2017). Data collection is the procedure of getting information. Data collection is an essential part of any healthcare organization and is also useful to know the trends of the relevant parameters. We can also utilize the information to forecast future occurrences. Different machine learning algorithms and artificial intelligence are extremely used in clinical oncology research (Dlamini et al., 2020). Theories and algorithms of Bioinformatics are hugely implemented in the drug discovery in the pharmaceutical industry (Wooller et al., 2017). Numerous dataset-related machine learning approaches have been used to diagnose and forecast cardiovascular disease (Krittanawong et al., 2017). Data is necessary to predict genetic disorders of humans, digital pathology systems, precision in public health, and the analysis of radiographic images for some famous modalities (Bang et al., 2020; Choi & Kim, 2016; Dolley, 2018; Madabhushi & Lee, 2016).

Today, we are inundated with data in every sphere of our lives, including social activities, the arts, science, employment, health, and so on. In some ways, the current situation may be compared to a data deluge (Sung et al., 2016). This data deluge demands the development of new technologies to contextualize, analyze, and understand such massive amounts of data (Norsigian et al., 2020). Technological advancements have enabled us to generate an increasing amount of data, to a level that it has become impossible to manage with currently available technology (Pastorino et al., 2019). This big database cannot cope with the traditional data management tools and techniques. As a result, the phrase "big data" is used to represent data that is vast and unmanageable.

To fulfill our current and future societal requirements, we must devise innovative techniques for organizing this data and extracting useful information. The healthcare industry is one such social need. Healthcare industries, like any other sector, generate a massive amount of data, which provides both advantages and complications (Mallappallil et al., 2020). In this review, we discuss the basics of big data including its management, analysis, analytical tools and techniques, and prospects, especially in the healthcare sector.

Big data means huge voluminous data that contains greater variety with extensive velocity and overwhelms a database on a day-to-day basis so that traditional data processing software cannot capture, calculate, process, and handle them. The size of big data is always increasing. The size may exceed from a few dozens of terabytes to many zettabytes. A big dataset is nothing but a healthy and complex dataset that cannot be imagined for managing with manual or traditional software. Big data can be very largely structured or nonstructured, dynamic or static, that must be captured, managed, or processed using innovative techniques.

Every day, a large amount of data is generated by different devices from different geographical regions. There are thousands of places where big data is necessary and makes the lifestyle easier. Weather forecasting and prediction, evaluation of disasters, crime investigation, social media homepage, healthcare management, and record-keeping, medical imaging, genomic sequencing, and bioinformatics: these are the different sectors where big data platforms are using to serve the purpose of these fields. Several general sources of big data in healthcare are depicted in Fig. 5.1.

Big Data Analytics for Healthcare. https://doi.org/10.1016/B978-0-323-91907-4.00015-7

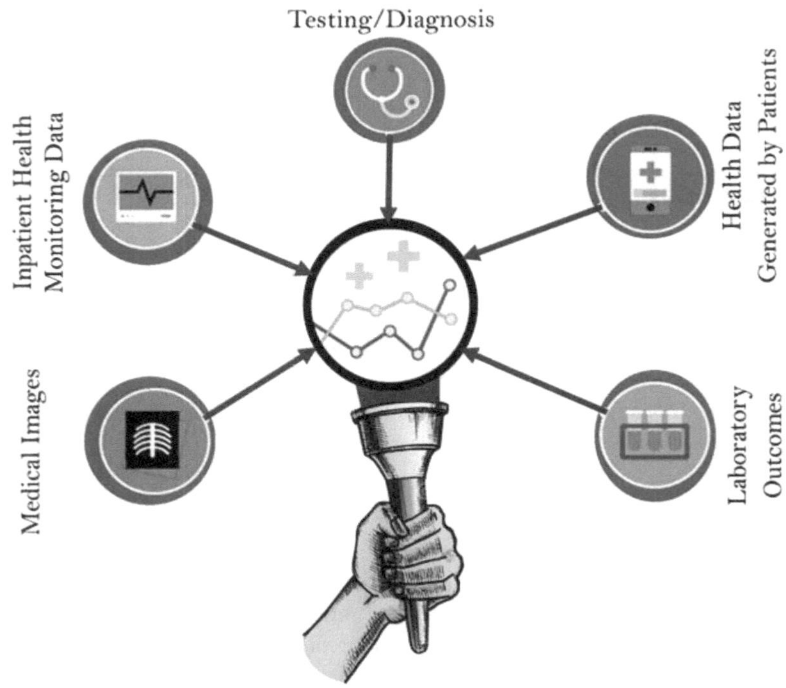

FIGURE 5.1 General sources of big data in healthcare.

The sources and patterns of big data in the healthcare industry are discussed in Section 2 of this chapter. The characteristics of big data with examples are presented in Section 3. In Section 4, the key elements to analyze big data in the healthcare sector are pointed out and demonstrated comprehensively. The available analytical tools to handle big data are discussed with their structures and features in Section 5. The overall concept of big data analytics in healthcare is concluded in Section 6.

2. Big data in healthcare

Massive data is obtained from different healthcare sources. Since this huge data is very diverse in format, type, and context, it is difficult to merge this data into a system. The main motive of a data scientist is to extract the hidden pattern of data accumulated from several sources in a way that can be easily manipulated for the betterment of the patient's life. The possible big data sources which are used in healthcare are shown in a schematic diagram in Fig. 5.2.

2.1 Structured data

Structured data is data that is organized in a tabular scheme and is created using a fixed outline. Structured data is seized and kept in discrete coded values. Such kind of data is stored in a Logical Observation Identifiers Names and Codes (LOINC), which is a medical laboratory observation database (Bora, 2019). A relationship is maintained between the columns of the structured data. Numbers of the elements link the columns that exist in a table. Data stored in a structured way makes the computation and analysis easier for a data handler in a healthcare organization. Structured datasets are getting priority in diagnosis, laboratories, and pharmaceutical industries. For example, some patients have an appointment with doctors in a hospital. The electronic recording systems can be designed like the following table. Table 5.1 is an example of structured data used in a hospital.

2.2 Unstructured data

Unstructured data does not have any predefined format. It has no fixed outlines. It cannot be stored in a relational database like a structured database. It contains 80% of the total data volume in the world. The text is the common type of unstructured data but some nontext data also act like the unstructured type. Some nontext unstructured data are images and video. In the healthcare industry, unstructured data can be found in huge numbers of emails, patient register forms,

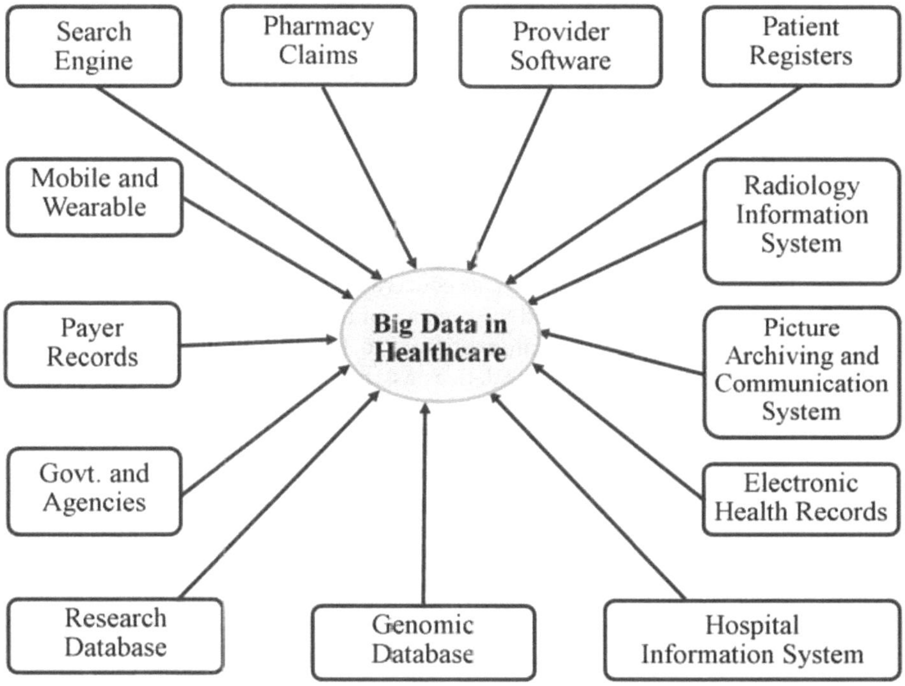

FIGURE 5.2 All possible sources of big data in healthcare.

TABLE 5.1 Example of structured data in a hospital.

Patient ID	Patient name	Doctor name	Department
601	Mr. P	Dr. X	Cardiology
602	Mr. Q	Dr. Y	Ear, nose, throat
603	Mrs. R	Dr. Z	Obstetrics
604	S. Pitt	Dr. M	Pediatrics

survey responses, radiology images, audible sounds, etc. Most of the text-based unstructured data are found in the biomedical sector.

2.3 Semistructured data

When someone would like to experience the pros of both structured and unstructured data, he or she has to deal with a semistructured database. Semistructured data is not a permanent member of the rational database in tabular form, but it has a few organizational properties that create it facile to evaluate. Some examples of semistructured data are electronic data interchange (EDI), NoSQL, etc. A semistructured database does not restrict the information volume that one data handler wants to keep, but it creates some groups of arranged data in the hierarchy and free text.

2.4 Genomic data

Genomic data can be found in the dataset that deals with the genome and DNA data of a living organism. Modern genomic technologies are used in healthcare for genomic data generation, processing, and mining. Genome data mining means computational genome annotation. Various tools and software are used to sequence, sort, and assemble the big genome data. The genomic and DNA data used in healthcare is very big. Heavy bioinformatics software is necessary for processing the structure and functions of genome data. The complete set of DNA of an organism is known as the genome. Each human genome is made up of around three billion bases, approximately 3–4 million, among which vary from different genome arrangements. These differences that occur across the genome are known as genomic variants. There are some essential genome browsers from where a researcher can easily search for a specific region of the genome and can extract the necessary information. Some renowned genome homepages are the University of California, Santa Cruz Genome Browser, EBI's Ensembl, and NCBI's MapViewer.

2.5 Sentiment data

Medical sentiment analysis has been a very emerging and concerning issue in healthcare nowadays. Patients and their relatives want to know about the latest technology and the reviews of the facility of an individual doctor or a hospital or a diagnostic center. The best way of extracting this information is to follow a traditional process of questions–answers (Bansal et al., 2021). In this way, the patients or their relatives ask many questions to the acquaintances that might have used the healthcare facilities of an organization or healthcare providers. This feedback is found on different social media platforms. One of the examples is that one can get these valuable reviews on a blog post. Sentiment analysis is a field that categorizes reviews, comments, or thoughts into two basic and intrinsic emotional indicators, namely positive and negative (Bhatia & Nath, 2020). Sentiment analysis means the understanding of the emotional spirit of any text and the assessment of the nature of opinion of the text (Pang & Lee, 2004). Biomedical literature and Electronic Medical Records (EMRs) are the primary sources of medical sentiment analysis research. Recently, several studies were conducted to capture the social media medical texts in different medical settings. To achieve their goal, the scientists generated domain-specific clinical documents like radiology reports, nurse letters, and discharge forms which were collected from the MIMIC II database. They also collected medication reviews from medical blogs like WebMD and DrugRating.

2.6 Clinical data

Clinical data is the assembly of data associated with patient diagnosis, exposures, demographics, test reports, and family relationships on a cloud platform. Most of the clinical data is collected from the ongoing treatment program of patients. Clinical data can be of several types: electronic health records, patient registers, claims data, health surveys, administrative data, and clinical trials. The administrative and demographic information, patient physiological condition monitoring, prescription of drugs, patient's insurance, etc., can be obtained from an electronic medical record-keeping system. Thus, it can be easily understood that EMR is a perfect source of big data. The registerd patient can be tracked for certain chronic conditions such as Alzheimer's disease, cancer, asthma, heart disease, etc. Some renowned databanks for these types of chronic diseases are as follows: Global Alzheimer's Association Interactive Network (GAAIN), National Cardiovascular Data Registry (NCDR), National Program of Cancer Registries, and National Trauma Data Bank.

3. Characteristics of big data in healthcare

The amount of big data created in healthcare is too large, too complex to understand, and too fast for healthcare practitioners' existing tools to comprehend and interpret. There are six attributes associated with healthcare data which are known as 6 Vs of healthcare big data: Volume, Velocity, Variety, Value, Variability, and Veracity.

3.1 Volume

The volume of big data is huge; specifically, it is uncountable in size. Big data in healthcare has an attribute to ingest, process, and store a very large quantity of data. Healthcare big data does not have any fixed threshold value. US healthcare data has already reached 150 exabytes (10^{18}) 5 years back (Cottle et al., 2013). We are dealing with zettabyte (10^{21}) and yottabyte (10^{23}) for a country with a large population like China and India.

3.2 Velocity

The velocity of data means the speed at which it is increasing and the frequency of delivery. Velocity is the fundamental reason for growing healthcare data exponentially. And the speed of this steeper curve is so fast. The data generation flow is massive, so that high-velocity tools known as streaming analytics are commonly used. The cumulative number of publications respective to years, shown in Fig. 5.3, is a representation of data generation velocity.

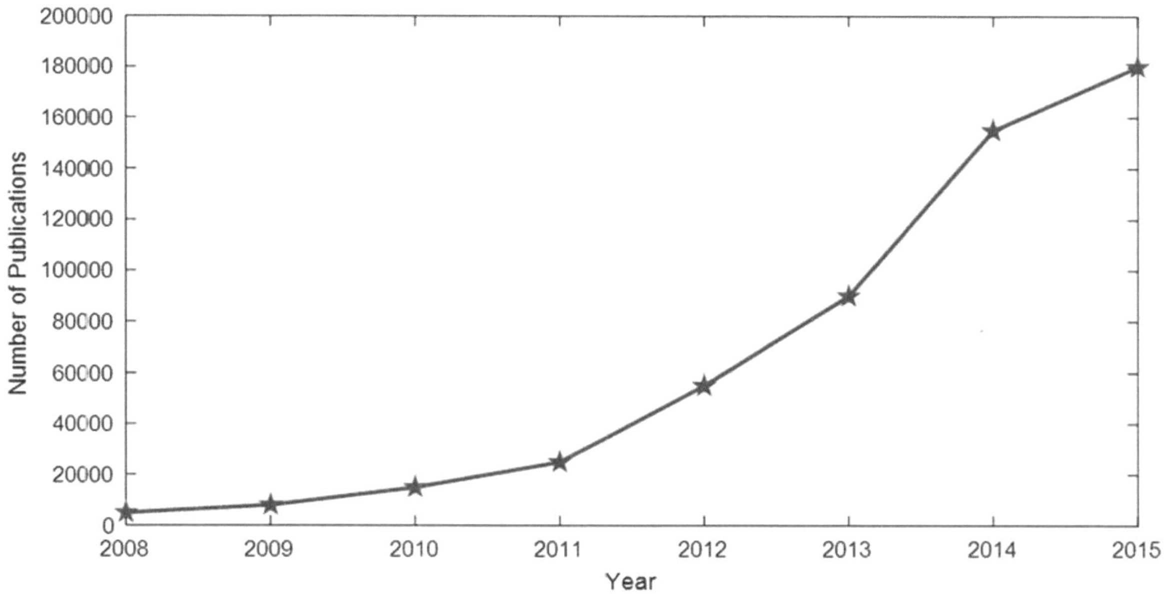

FIGURE 5.3 A proof of data velocity is exponential. This graph shows the cumulative number of publications with respect to years (from 2008 to 2015).

3.3 Variety

A challenge of big data processing is the variety of data. Healthcare big data is generated from various sources. To manipulate these data is not an easy task because these data are mixed of structured and unstructured data. The unstructured data creates problems of data mining and storage. Data heterogeneity and diversity emerge in healthcare as a result of connecting the broad range of accessible biological data sources. Text, audio, videos, images are the various types of data produced in healthcare.

3.4 Value

All data are not valuable. We have to find out the potential data from the massive healthcare dataset. Value refers to turning or making data into significance. Value in data tells a data scientist whether it should be stored or discarded. If one does not find valuable data, it is not necessary to store it for further processing because keeping data reduces the storage and increases the costs.

3.5 Variability

This relates to determining if the data stream's contextualizing structure is regular and reliable, even in a situation of high instability. It outlines the requirement to obtain relevant data while taking into account all conceivable conditions.

3.6 Veracity

Understanding data relevance is the key to value. Veracity refers to the bias, noise, and abnormality of data. A data scientist should know how to utilize the relevant data for acquiring his purpose. It is useless to analyze inaccurate data. The gathering of large amounts of data from diverse sources results in veracity. The target of a data handler should be to increase the signal-to-noise ratio of a dataset. If the cleansing of the dataset does not occur at the preliminary stage, veracity degrades.

4. Key elements of big data analysis

Healthcare organizations have some principal elements for the application of big data analytics. This section describes the key elements of big data analytics in healthcare. Data inputs, functional elements, human elements, and security elements are four key elements of big data in healthcare, which are displayed in Fig. 5.4 with their subsections (Kulkarni et al., 2019).

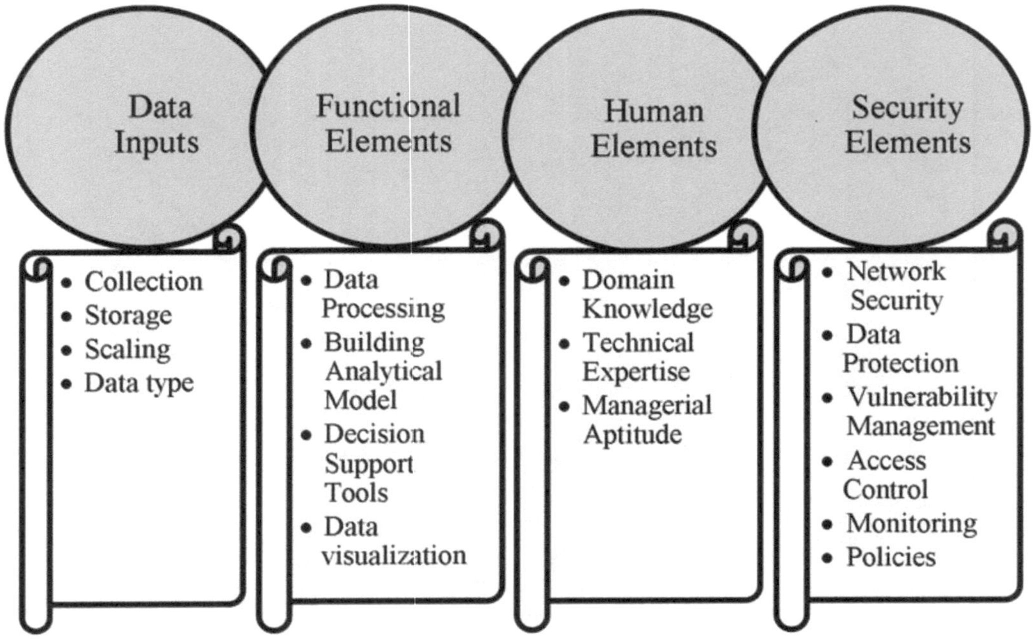

FIGURE 5.4 Key elements of big data analytics in healthcare.

4.1 Data inputs

Input data motivates the application of analytics to gain actionable insights. Hence, extremely rich informative healthcare data are used to improve the quality of service as well as operational efficiency. Identifying and gathering important data sources may necessitate extra infrastructure (Bernard, 2016). The type of data and its structure would dictate the architecture of such information infrastructure for data collection, storage, and scalability. Data may vary from highly structured to unstructured so that doctors can easily use the user data in the shortest possible time.

4.2 Functional elements

When healthcare-related data produces actionable, meaningful insights, organizations need to use seamless, trustworthy data. Some of the functional elements are data preparation and processing, building analytical models, decision support tools, and data visualization.

4.2.1 Data preparation and processing

Since it was mentioned earlier in this chapter that the purpose of big data processing is to ensure high-quality efficient data, the first task of this stage is to clean and format unnecessary data. Tabular format data is needed for analysis which can be extracted from the previously collected structured and unstructured data.

When the data is kept in a relational database or Hadoop Distributed File System (HDFS) or HBase, diverse processing tools are picked depending on the demand, like MapReduce and Spark (batch processing); Storm and Spark Streaming (real-time processing); Mahout and MLib (machine learning); and GraphX (graph processing capabilities) which are illustrated in Fig. 5.5.

4.2.2 Building analytical model

Progressive methodical models are required for data-driven calculation and real-time decision-making in emergency circumstances. Python, NoSQL, R, JavaScript, Prolog, etc., are some widely used programming languages for the progress of analytical models. When the purpose is clear to a data scientist in a healthcare organization, algorithms are designed by descriptive, predictive, or prescriptive analytics methods. For pattern recognition, forecasting, classification, clustering, and prediction, some statistical techniques, and machine learning algorithms can be applied. The necessary steps for building an analytical model are presented in Fig. 5.6. CNN and genetic algorithms, for example, can be used to categorize brain

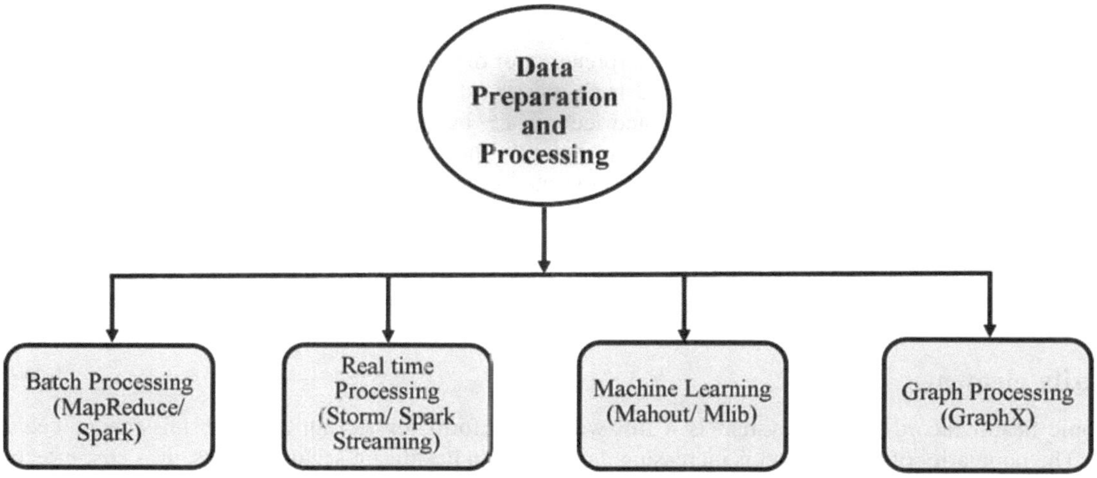

FIGURE 5.5 Data preparation and processing steps.

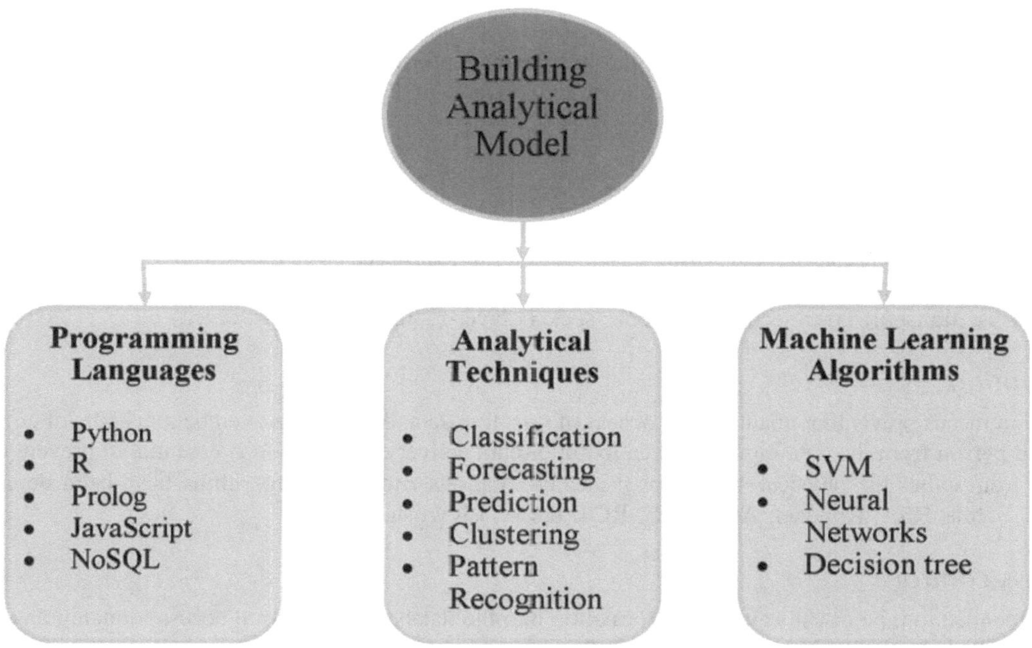

FIGURE 5.6 Steps of building an analytical model.

tumor MRI scans (Anaraki et al., 2019), and health insurance companies can use random trees and SVM to automate the preauthorization acceptance process (Araújo et al., 2016).

4.2.3 Decision support tools and data visualization

Before publishing the results of the analytical model mentioned above, they need to be synchronized with existing data. After making a decision, the results are now ready to be published. We can use Tableau, Jupiter, QlikView, FusionCharts, and Google charts for representing the potential data graphically or in the chart or tabular format.

4.3 Human element

Data analytics is an impressive science. Since the interpretation of big data in healthcare is an art, human involvement is a must thing to find out the insights of the collected data. In the world of big data, many hospitals and healthcare research organizations are focusing too much on the tools and techniques, but they should remember, a plane cannot fly safely without a pilot. Big data analytics is a data-driven science. To manipulate huge data or to predict some results after observing the data, a data scientist, as well as a properly trained human, is necessary. Humans provide great value to the data analysis process by asking the appropriate questions, understanding why data is required, finding available data sources, developing models, and selecting the best tools for the job. Technology is important, but without humans, it cannot work properly. In basic terms, it is said that technology sees the trees, humans see the forest. So to get better insights and interpretation, the involvement of humans in big data analytics is absolutely necessary.

4.4 Security element

An electronic health record-keeping system is a trustworthy platform for storing and transmission of healthcare data nowadays. The popularity of this method is increasing day by day in healthcare sectors because it is cost-effective and not time-consuming. As the number of users of electronic record-keeping systems is increasing day by day, ensuring the security of this system is becoming a concerning issue. The security system should be ensured through health insurance, clinical decision support, disease surveillance, adverse event monitoring, population health management, and treatment optimization for diseases. Every healthcare business must adopt practical, preventative strategies and steps with future security and privacy demands in mind to prevent gaps of sensitive information and other sorts of security events. There are many technologies for giving protection of security and privacy of healthcare data. Some of these technologies are described below.

4.4.1 Authentication

Authentication is the first line of cyber defense. To ensure authentication or the identification of accessible people, many cybersecurity technologies are used from setting a password to fingerprint or face unlock technology. In some applications of HER such as electronic mail, online surfing, voice over IP different cybersecurity protocols are widely used. An organization can use transport layer security or secure sockets layer to authenticate its server.

4.4.2 Encryption

Data encryption means preventing unauthorized access of sensitive data. No data can even be touched without the owner or the authorized person from the data input to the endpoint of data delivery. Encryption is essential to prevent exposure and theft of data from either the physical storage or the cloud. Various encryption algorithms have been deployed to save various data, such as RSA, Rijndael, AES, DES, RC4, IDEA, Blowfish, etc.

4.4.3 Access control

After user authentication, he or she can enter information into the database, but his full access to manipulate the database should be controlled by an algorithm. It ensures that the user can only perform the task for which he or she is authorized. The default access control rule of "denying access when in doubt" is substituted with "granting access when in doubt" for health-related data to be easily available in emergencies. Some popular access control models for EHR are Role-Based Access Control and Attribute-Based Access Control.

5. Big data analytical tools used in healthcare

In this book chapter, the types, characteristics, importance, elements, and architectural framework of big data analytics in healthcare were described broadly. Several tools on different platforms are frequently used in big data analytics, which are explained below.

5.1 Hadoop distribution file system

HDFS is a distributed and open-source data analytics and storage application. Hadoop distributes enormous volumes of data over several processing nodes before combining the findings. HDFS is used to run on low-cost hardware and it is

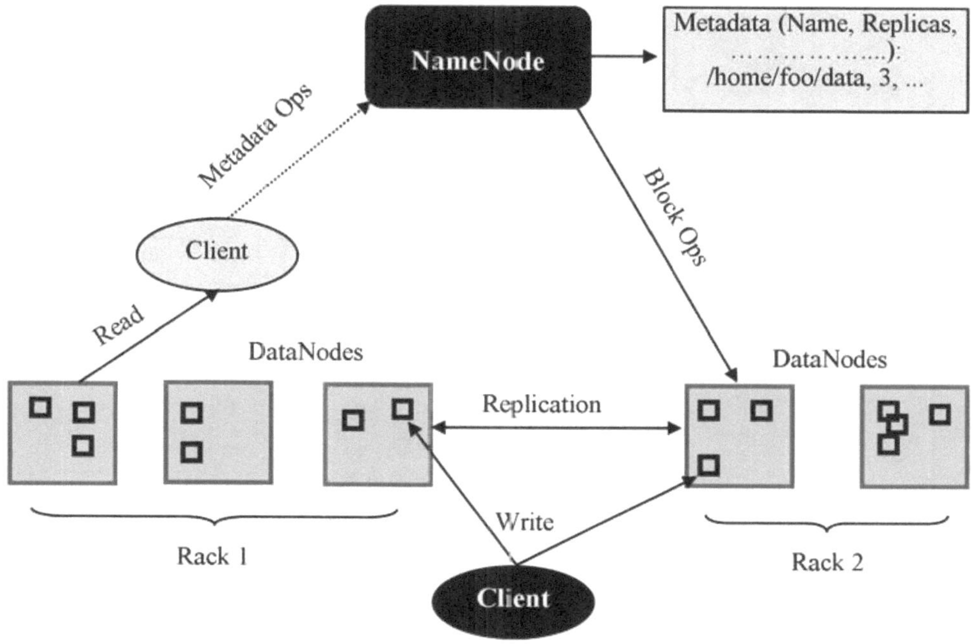

FIGURE 5.7 HDFS architecture.

extremely fault tolerant. HDFS is a distributed file system that uses NameNode and DataNode architecture to offer high-performance data access across highly scalable Hadoop clusters. HDFS organizes and condenses the results into a cohesive answer to a query by filtering and dividing work among the nodes in a cluster. When HDFS receives data, it divides it into distinct blocks and allocates it to altered nodes in a cluster. The NameNode follows the location of storage of file data in the cluster. An HDFS has a master–slave architecture; the master server accomplishes the file system namespace and controls access to files by clients. The DataNode acts as a slave server that manages the nodes that are attached to the storage. DataNodes conduct read–write operations on file systems in response to client requests. They also perform the deletion, block creation, and replication according to the directions of the NameNode. The HDFS architecture and working procedure are sketched as a block diagram in Fig. 5.7. HDFS has some advantages, such as storing massive data, having a simple and robust model, fast scalability, and data accessibility, serving multiple clients by adding more machines to the cluster, reading data multiple times, but the stored data can be written once, and finally, it requires high economy, high efficiency, and high reliability, etc.

5.2 MapReduce

MapReduce is the core component of the Hadoop framework used for writing applications that can process enormous data in big clusters. By dividing petabytes of data into smaller pieces and treating them in analogous on Hadoop commodity, MapReduce makes simultaneous processing easier. MapReduce's job is to save the input and output to the file system. The MapReduce program is executed in three main stages: map stage, shuffle stage, and reduce stage. Sometimes an optional phase helps to execute the desired function named the combiner phase.

The map stage is the first stage of MapReduce whose function is to map and split. The input data is first splited into the smaller chunks and then each smaller chunk is assigned to a mapper for further processing. Hadoop includes a RecordReader that transforms input splits into key–value pairs using TextInputFormat. A coding mechanism is applied to the data blocks during the mapping process. If a file has 100 records to process, for example, 100 mappers can work together to process one record at a time. Alternatively, 50 mappers may work together to process two records at a time. Based on the amount of data to be processed and the memory block available on each mapper server, the Hadoop framework determines how many mappers to employ.

The shuffling phase is combined of two subphases called sorting and merging. The key–value pairs are sorted using the keys in the sorting subphase. This phase makes it easier to get rid of duplicate values. The output of the mapping and shuffling phase is the keys and the values. The output of the shuffling stage is used as input in the reducing phase. A

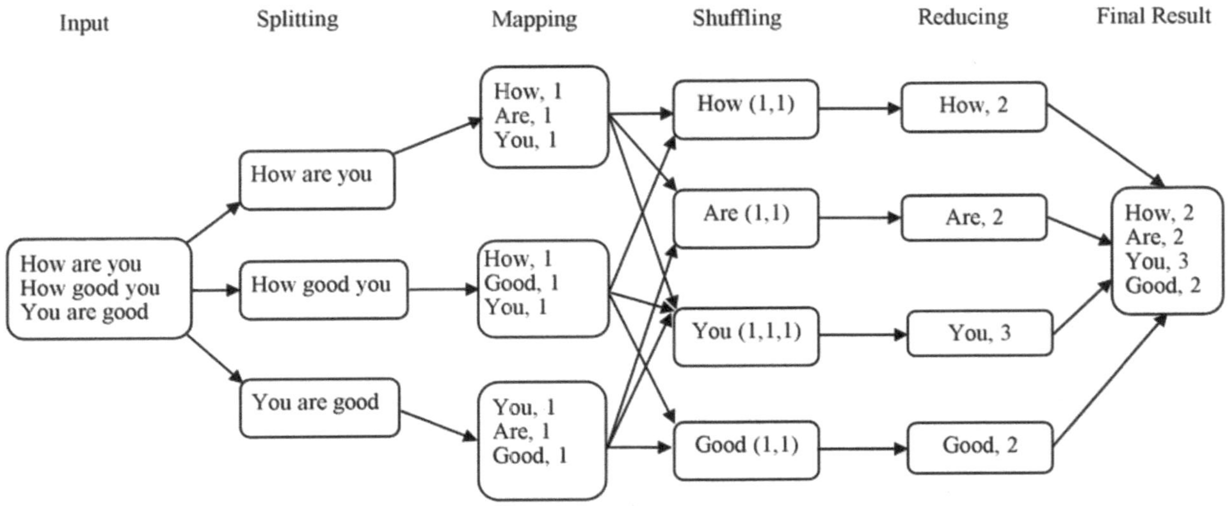

FIGURE 5.8 MapReduce architecture.

reducer cannot be in a working mood, while the map or shuffle stage is functional. After processing, the output of the reducer stage is stored in HDFS. Three simple structured sentences are used to understand the architecture of MapReduce in Fig. 5.8.

5.3 Hive

Hive is a data warehouse platform used to process or analyze a large structured dataset stored in HDFS. It acts to control structured query language (SQL) in the Hadoop system and it is called HiveQL or HQL (Shruti, 2021). Hive is not a relational database and it is not a language for real-time queries. Hive is only designed to manage the structured data stored in tables (Shruti, 2021). The data types of Hive architecture are as follows: numeric type, date/time types, string types, and complex types. Hive architecture is given below in Fig. 5.9.

The first step of Hive data flow is to execute a query that goes into the driver. Then the metadata is obtained from the metastore by the compiler. At this point, the compiler compiles the data and returns the plan to the driver. Now the execution engine receives the execution plan from the driver. To process the query, the execution engine functions as a

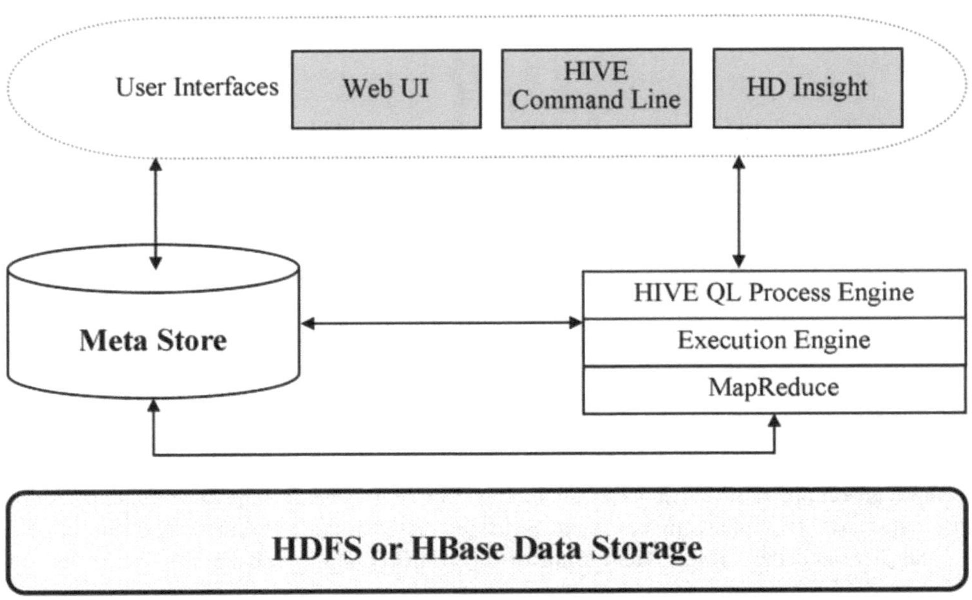

FIGURE 5.9 Architecture of Hive.

bridge between Hive and Hadoop. Furthermore, the execution engine connects bidirectionally with the metastore to execute actions. Finally, we have a bidirectional communication system that allows us to retrieve and provide results to the client.

5.4 Pig and PigLatin

Pig is a high-level tool that uses a high-level programming language to analyze a large dataset. Scientists found the Java language used for MapReduce architecture not so user-friendly. Therefore, a high-level language is used in Pig and it extensively reduces the challenges of maintaining large datasets.

Pig programming is easy to write and to attain parallel execution. In addition, the information flow structures encrypt most of the tasks. There are some optimization opportunities in pig as follows: Pig allows the system to automatically optimize tasks so that the programmer may attain semantic efficiency. Pig comes with a large number of datasets that may be used to execute operations such as join, sort, filter, group, load, and so on. Pig architecture consists of some components such as parser, optimizer, compiler, execution engine, and execution mode.

In the Pig flow system, the programmer or data scientist develops a Pig Latin script that is stored as a function in the local file system. After submitting a pig script, it links to a compiler, which generates a sequence of MapReduce tasks. After MapReduce tasks are completed, the Pig compiler takes raw data from HDFS, performs operations, and saves the results in HDFS. The step-by-step architecture of Pig and PigLatin is drawn in Fig. 5.10.

5.5 ZooKeeper

ZooKeeper is a high-performance centralized service for distributed applications. It maintains configured information, naming, provides group services, and distributed synchronization in a simple interface. ZooKeeper has a straightforward

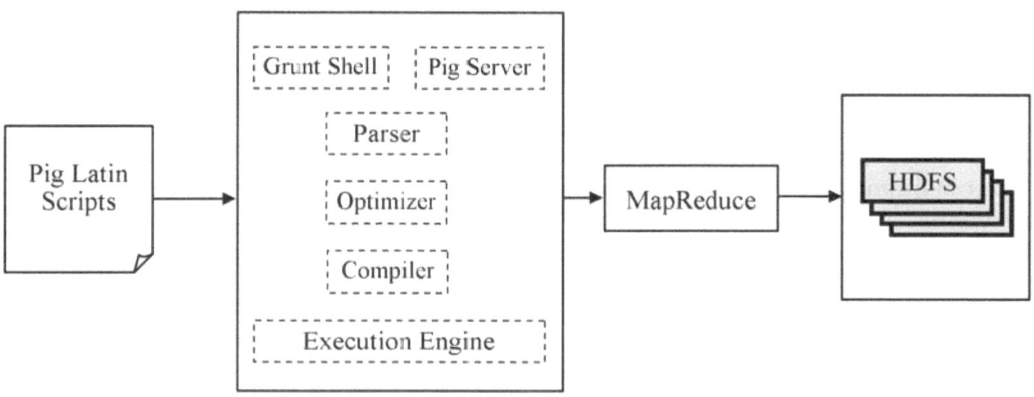

FIGURE 5.10 Pig and PigLatin architecture.

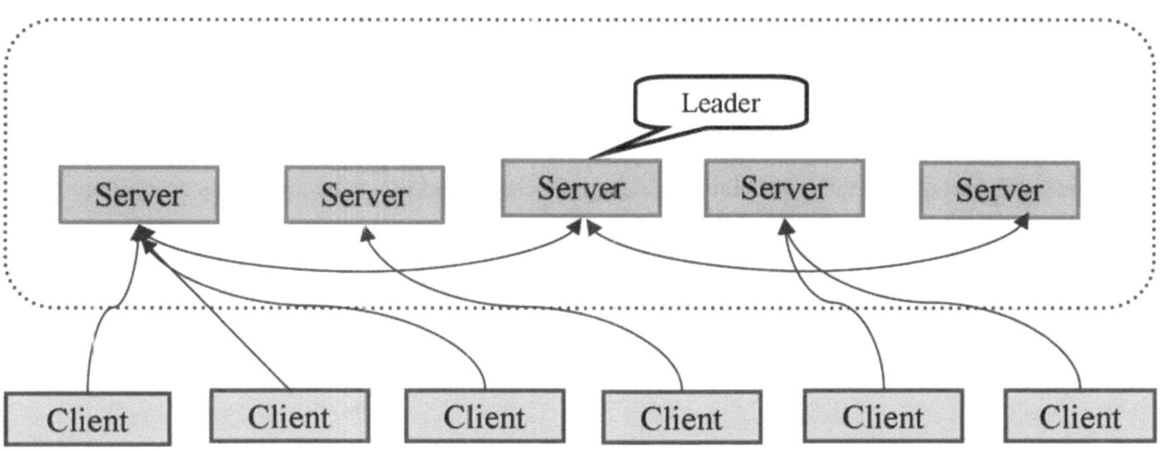

FIGURE 5.11 ZooKeeper architecture.

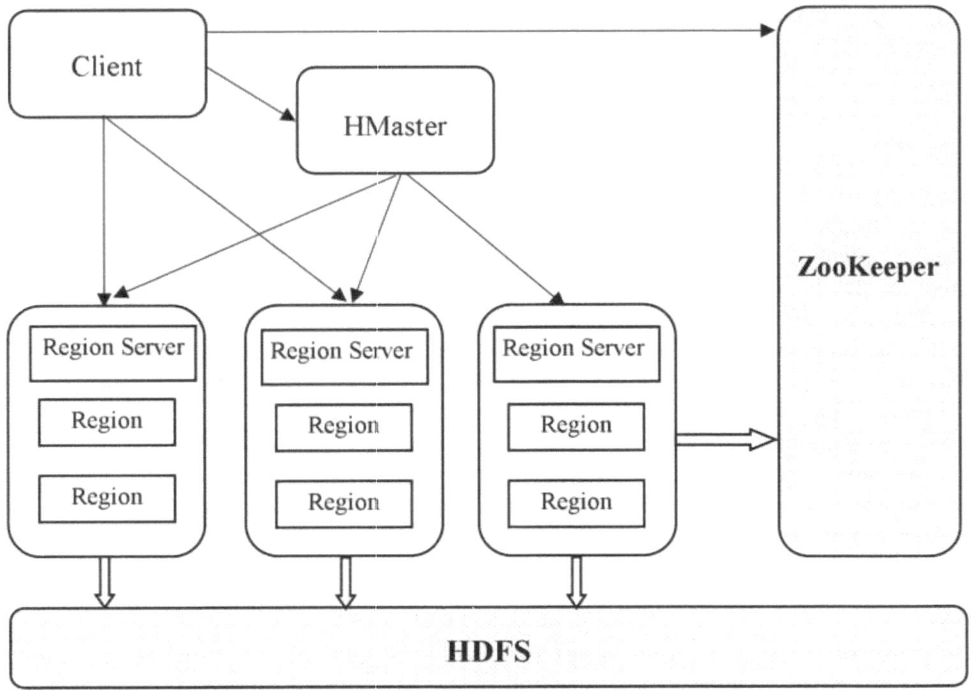

FIGURE 5.12 HBase architecture.

client—server paradigm, in which clients are nodes (i.e., machines) that utilize the service, and servers are nodes that offer the service. It aids in the preservation of a standard categorized namespace, analogous to the files and directories. ZooKeeper follows a client—server architecture. The components of ZooKeeper architecture are client, server, leader, follower, cluster, and ZooKeeper WebUI which are outlined in Fig. 5.11.

When a client connects, the server sends an acknowledgment. If the connected server does not respond, the client immediately transfers the message to another server. The client acts as a node in the distribution cluster which enables to obtain information from the server. The server is allowed to determine whether the client is alive or not by receiving messages from the client at a regular interval. If any connected node fails, the leader which is designated as a server automatically recovers. The follower follows the instructions of the leader (2021). A cluster is a serving ZooKeeper. Finally, to deal with ZooKeeper resource management, an individual must utilize the WebUI. It enables interacting with ZooKeeper using the web user interface rather than the command line.

5.6 HBase

HBase is an open-source, nonrelational, column-oriented, distributed database model. Although HBase is a NoSQL database, it makes data maintenance easier by distributing it evenly across the cluster. Since HBase is a NoSQL database, it consists of the components including HBase table, RowKey, Columns, Column Family, Column Qualifiers, Cell, Time-stamp, etc. The core components of the HBase architecture are illustrated in Fig. 5.12. A short description of these components are described below.

HMaster: The employment of a master server in HBase is called HMaster. It allocates regions to the region server. It handles the management of loading and unloading of servers by unloading the busy servers and connecting them to fewer engaged servers. HMaster takes the responsibility for changing schema and Metadata operations according to the wish of the clients.

Regions: Region servers are the building blocks of HBase architecture which are comprised of column families. The main function of the region server is to handle the customers and data-related actions. HBase region consists of two components: Memstore and Hfile. 256 Mb is the default size of an HBase region.

6. Conclusions

Currently, several biomedical, healthcare tools, and apps are generating huge data which should be analyzed for procedural and technical improvements in specialized healthcare. Combined EHRs, EMRs, and other medical data analysis can establish a better prognostic framework that results in healthcare analytics and clinical transformation service by numerous companies. Cost-reducing, effective Clinical Decision Support systems development, fraud prevention, better treatment, etc., are the common goals of these companies but also face common problems with data confidentiality. Reviewing diagnosis, treatment, and overall healthcare framework in different healthcare and biomedical organizations, most of the medical fraternities comprehended the potentiality of big data analysis. As a result, big data analytics have been implemented, introducing supercomputers to quantum computers in the healthcare sector for meaningful data extraction in seconds. Clinical trials, analysis of pharmacy, and insurance jointly claim that the discovery of biomarkers has revealed a novel way of big data analysis despite infrastructure challenges.

Although there is a gap within structured and unstructured data sources in big data analytics, it may be overcomed through a shifting integrated data environment. Through the exponential growth of the big data market, medical industries get more information, insights, and future predictions in a short period. As a consequence, various domains are investing in computational experts for the design of innovative strategies which can interpret and analyze enormous data in a given timeframe. Integrated signal processing systems have been popular among researchers and medical professionals and might contribute to the innovation of the human body model and the development of unique diagnostic tools. Exploring all healthcare sectors, we can say that rapidly expanded genomic data, including inherent hidden errors, needs further attention, where lots of opportunities can introduce systematic improvements.

In conclusion, a big revolution is suggested to group bioinformatics, health informatics, and personalized treatment analytics in one shed for the betterment of data scientists. New technologies and strategies should be developed to realize data classification, size, and complexity for substantial advancements from medical data management to drug discovery programs. For example, since late 2000s, the healthcare market has perceived advancements in the EHR system in the context of data collection, management, and usability. We can believe and see that the big data market will add on and bolster the existing pipeline of healthcare toward personalized domains instead of replacing skilled experts and intellectuals. It can be projected that big data analytics will hike toward a predictive system from certain geography to the generation of population health information. Introducing prediction of epidemics (concerning population health), providing early warnings of disease conditions, and helping in the discovery of novel biomarkers and intelligent therapeutic intervention strategies for an improved quality of life are the blessings of big data.

References

Afzali, M., Ahmadi, M., & Mahmoudvand, Z. (2017). Data requirements and the basis for designing health information kiosks. *Acta Informatica Medica, 25*(3), 198–202. https://doi.org/10.5455/aim.2017.25.198-202

Anaraki, A. K., Ayati, M., & Kazemi, F. (2019). Magnetic resonance imaging-based brain tumor grades classification and grading via convolutional neural networks and genetic algorithms. *Biocybernetics and Biomedical Engineering, 39*(1), 63–74. https://doi.org/10.1016/j.bbe.2018.10.004

Araújo, F. H. D., Santana, A. M., & de A. Santos Neto, P. (2016). Using machine learning to support healthcare professionals in making preauthorisation decisions. *International Journal of Medical Informatics, 94*, 1–7. https://doi.org/10.1016/j.ijmedinf.2016.06.007

Bang, C. S., Lee, J. J., & Baik, G. H. (2020). Artificial intelligence for the prediction of helicobacter pylori infection in endoscopic images: Systematic review and meta-analysis of diagnostic test accuracy. *Journal of Medical Internet Research, 22*(9). https://doi.org/10.2196/21983

Bansal, A., Maurya, M., Kumar, N., & Tomar, S. (2021). Analysis of hospital reviews through sentiment analysis: An approach to aid patients in the times of covid-19 pandemic. In *CEUR workshop proceedings* (Vol. 2786, pp. 228–236). CEUR-WS. http://ceur-ws.org/.

Bernard, M. (2016). *Building your big data infrastructure: 4 key components every business needs to consider*. https://www.forbes.com/sites/bernardmarr/2016/06/15/building-your-big-data-infrastructure-4-key-components-every-business-needs-to-consider/?sh=2f4ba648577e.

Bhatia, P., & Nath, R. (2020). Using sentiment analysis IN patient satisfaction: A survey. *Advances in Mathematics: Scientific Journal, 9*(6), 3803–3812. https://doi.org/10.37418/amsj.9.6.59

Bora, D. J. (2019). In N. Dey, H. Das, B. Naik, & H. S. Behera (Eds.), *Big data analytics for intelligent healthcare management* (Vol. 3). https://doi.org/10.1016/B978-0-12-818146-1.00003-9

Choi, Y. J., & Kim, N. (2016). Gastric cancer and family history *Korean Journal of Internal Medicine, 31*(6), 1042–1053. https://doi.org/10.3904/kjim.2016.147

Cottle, M., Hoover, W., Kanwal, S., Kohn, M. Strome, T., & Treister, N. W. (2013). Transforming health care through big data. *Institute for Health Technology Transformation*. https://www.healthitoutcomes.com/doc/transforming-healthcare-through-big-data-0001.

Dlamini, Z., Francies, F. Z., Hull, R., & Marima, R. (2020). Artificial intelligence (AI) and big data in cancer and precision oncology. *Computational and Structural Biotechnology Journal, 18*, 2300–2311. https://doi.org/10.1016/j.csbj.2020.08.019

Dolley, S. (2018). Big data's role in precision public health. *Frontiers in Public Health, 6*. https://doi.org/10.3389/fpubh.2018.00068

Krittanawong, C., Zhang, H. J., Wang, Z., Aydar, M., & Kitai, T. (2017). Artificial intelligence in precision cardiovascular medicine. *Journal of the American College of Cardiology, 69*(21), 2657–2664. https://doi.org/10.1016/j.jacc.2017.03.571

Kulkarni, A. J., Siarry, P., Singh, P. K., Abraham, A., Zhang, M., Zomaya, A., & Baki, F. (2019). Elements of healthcare big data analytics. In N. Mehta, A. Pandit, & M. Kulkarni (Eds.), *Big data analytics in healthcare*. Springer. https://doi.org/10.1007/978-3-030-31672-3_2

Madabhushi, A., & Lee, G. (2016). Image analysis and machine learning in digital pathology: Challenges and opportunities. *Medical Image Analysis, 33*, 170–175. https://doi.org/10.1016/j.media.2016.06.037

Mallappallil, M., Sabu, J., Gruessner, A., & Salifu, M. (2020). A review of big data and medical research. *SAGE Open Medicine, 8*, 1–10. https://doi.org/10.1177/2050312120934839, 205031212093483.

Norsigian, C. J., Fang, X., Palsson, B. O., & Monk, J. M. (2020). Pangenome flux balance analysis toward panphenomes. In *The pangenome: Diversity, dynamics and evolution of genomes* (pp. 219–232). Springer International Publishing. https://doi.org/10.1007/978-3-030-38281-0_10

Pang, B., & Lee, L. (2004). A sentimental education: Sentiment analysis using subjectivity summarization based on minimum cuts. In *Proceedings of the 42nd annual meeting on association for computational linguistics*.

Pastorino, R., De Vito, C., Migliara, G., Glocker, K., Binenbaum, I., Ricciardi, W., & Boccia, S. (2019). Benefits and challenges of big data in healthcare: An overview of the European initiatives. *The European Journal of Public Health, 29*, 23–27. https://doi.org/10.1093/eurpub/ckz168

Shruti, M. (2021). *Hive tutorial: Working with data in Hadoop*. https://www.simplilearn.com/tutorials/hadoop-tutorial/hive.

Sung, J., Hale, V., Merkel, A. C., Kim, P. J., & Chia, N. (2016). Metabolic modeling with big data and the gut microbiome. *Applied and Translational Genomics, 10*, 10–15. https://doi.org/10.1016/j.atg.2016.02.001

Wooller, S. K., Benstead-Hume, G., Chen, X., Ali, Y., & Pearl, F. M. G. (2017). Bioinformatics in translational drug discovery. *Bioscience Reports, 37*(4). https://doi.org/10.1042/BSR20160180

Chapter 6

Big data analytics in precision medicine

Saurabh Biswas and Yasha Hasija
Delhi Technological University, Department of Biotechnology, New Delhi, India

1. Introduction

Precision medicine is a medical model that recommends custom-tailored products, techniques, treatments, and decisions for a subgroup of patients having the same biological basis of diseases. Collection, analytics, management imaging, and molecular diagnostics are a few tools used in precision medicine. The US precision medicine initiative states that its aim is "to enable a new era of medicine through research, technology, and policies that empower patients, researchers, and providers to work together toward the development of individualized care" (Prosperi et al., 2018). Due to the huge size and complexity of omics data and dataset of patient features, they cannot be analyzed directly by the doctors. To interpret the different types of data, big data analytics is applied to areas such as sensor informatics, imaging informatics, health informatics, and bioinformatics. For example, the utility of precision medicine can be explained with the use of NNT. The number needed to treat or NNT is a metric used to measure the average quantity of patients that have to be given the treatment to prevent 1 additional bad result, e.g., an NNT of 10 for treatment of hypertension depicts that 1 out of the 10 people receiving the treatment will benefit from it. The remaining 9 people will not gain any assistance from the treatment and could even face adverse effects from the treatment. This demonstrates the requirement of a custom treatment based on factors like lifestyle, ethnicity, and genetics. Precision medicine provides custom-tailored healthcare to patients and decreases the rate of adverse effects due to the treatment. Some other examples of precision medicine include the use of the genetic test to calculate the risk of hypersensitivity to antiretroviral medicine abacavir (Cargnin et al., 2014), determining an individual's genetic susceptibility to quicker metabolism for deciding whether clopidogrel drug should be given (Ph.D., 2010). Therefore, using the patient's information, it is easier to optimize the treatment by predicting the effect of different treatments.

Big data is a term used for complex or large datasets that cannot be accurately processed or stored by traditional management tools. Big data is generally characterized by 5 Vs: Volume (amount of data), Velocity (the speed of data generation and transfer), Variety (diversity of data types), Veracity (accuracy and quality of the data), and Value (worth of the collected data). These characteristics can be applied to medical datasets. The Human Genome Project led to the beginning of the Omics Era. New high-throughput methods can collect genomic, transcriptomic, proteomic, metabolic, and epigenomic data of individuals. Keywords associated with biomedical big data are summarized in Table 6.1. High-throughput methods can also collect environmental, imaging, and histopathological data. Hence, there is an increasing difference in the big medical data generated and our capability for analyzing and understanding it. The National Institutes of Health started the "Big Data to Knowledge" initiative in 2012, to collect a large amount of information present in the big biomedical data (Margolis et al., 2014). In this chapter, we review the methods, challenges, and application of using big data analytics in precision medicine.

2. Biomedical big data

There are two types of biomedical big data, which are Omics data and Electronic Health Record (EHR) data.

Big Data Analytics for Healthcare. https://doi.org/10.1016/B978-0-323-91907-4.00005-4

TABLE 6.1 Glossary of big omics data and big EHR data terms.

Term	Definition
Genome	The complete set of an organism's genetic material (usually DNA).
Transcriptome	The collection of all RNA transcripts existing in the cell of an organism.
Epigenome	A collection of chemical alterations to DNA and proteins associated with DNA, which are heritable, can modify gene expression.
Proteome	The complete collection of proteins present in an organism.
Metabolome	The complete collection of metabolites present in the cell of an organism.
Omics	Study of the -omes (e.g., genome, proteome).
Single nucleotide polymorphism (SNP)	A variation across individuals located at a single spot in the sequence of DNA.
Frameshift mutation (indels)	A mutation in the gene that is produced by an insertion or deletion in the sequence of DNA, which alters the way of reading the sequence.
Copy number variation (CNV)	The difference in the copy number of a gene sequence among people.
Fusion gene	A novel gene is created through the combination of various genes.
Alternative splicing	A procedure that adds or removes exons pre-mRNA to produce a mature mRNA
Histone modification	A posttranslational modification to the histone proteins which can affect the expression of genes.
DNA methylation	The addition of a methyl group to the DNA, which can modify gene functions.

2.1 Omics data

Omics data comprises a collection of molecular profiles (e.g., metabolomic, proteomic, epigenomic, transcriptomic, genomic) in patient samples. The genome is unique, does not change over time, and its information is present in copy number variations (CNVs), frameshift mutations, single nucleotide polymorphisms (SNPs), and other variations; transcriptomic information is present in the form of alternative splicing, gene fusion, transcript expression, and gene expressions; epigenomic information is present as DNA methylation patterns, histone modification patterns, and protein–DNA binding sites; proteomic information is in the form of protein expression, protein–protein interactions, and posttranslational modifications.

2.2 Electronic health record data

EHR data can be present in a structured form (e.g., medications, administrative data, diagnosis codes) or an unstructured form (e.g., clinical notes). Clinical notes define the patient's state and are an effective way for documentation based on human instincts. However, it is difficult to computationally analyze these records due to the presence of domain-specific words, errors and mistakes in grammar and typing, heterogenous, and unstructured data. Structured data can be divided into two classes. The first class is the administrative data, which includes data that is periodically updated (e.g., methods and diagnoses), and those which remain constant throughout the clinical process (e.g., patient demographics). The second class is the ancillary data that is regularly recorded throughout the clinical process, and it can be either continuous (e.g., wearable devices, blood pressure, respiration) or discrete (lab tests, medications).

3. Challenges associated with big data

Challenges in big medical data analytics include heterogeneity, dimensionality, quality, and data frequency.

3.1 Heterogeneous data

Heterogenous multiomics data may be required in the form of molecular fingerprints for classifying disease subtypes. For example, to discover active molecular alterations among healthy and diseased individuals, integrative personal omics profiling combines different expression profiles. However, combining multiomics data is difficult due to factors such as spatiotemporal resolution, identification accuracy, technical and biological noise levels, and differences in the representation of biological processes. For precision medicine to be successful, it is essential to interpret heterogeneous data.

3.2 High dimensionality

Omics data generally have features or dimensions much more than the quantity of the available samples, whereas EHR data can have a big sample size of data with high dimensionality, having thinly populated samples. A challenge in precision medicine is to interpret this data with statistical significance.

3.3 Data quality problems

In omics data, quality problems are produced due to a mixture of environmental, instrumental, and biological factors like low signal-to-noise ratios, and sample contamination. In EHR data, quality problems arise due to errors in data or missing data. For the clarity of waveform data, quality problems can include gaps in the waveform, random noise. The data quality problems may cause an incorrect conclusion to be reached. Therefore, it remains a challenge to correct these problems.

3.4 Frequency of collecting diverse data

Different collection frequencies are present for the diverse data modalities, e.g., the genome in omics data remains constant for a long time and generally requires a single data acquisition. Other omics data differ with time, types of tissues, and environment. The monitoring data in EHR is collected very frequently, whereas lab tests can be taken a small number of times per day. A big challenge is that the rate of data production may depend upon the price (e.g., data generated by different techniques like Next Generation Sequencing [NGS], Mass Spectrometry [MS]). Another challenge is that the rate of data acquisition may be irregular. For example, in EHR, the majority of the variables have unequal sampling rates based on the difficulty of measurement and the criticalness of the patient.

4. Machine learning techniques for big data analytics

As explained previously, big data is complex, diverse, large, and requires effective techniques to obtain the knowledge hidden inside it. Machine learning (ML) techniques are used in big data analytics due to their ability to combine heterogeneous, diverse, and large data. ML techniques can be classified into the following:

Supervised techniques like regression and classification, which take labeled training data as input. A model is developed using a method that gives the maximum performance accuracy on the training set. This model can then utilize the existing labels to map new samples. For example, an input can consist of patient data divided into control and cases. A model is generated that can give the maximum difference between the control and cases. This model will then be used for classifying the new data (illustrated in Fig. 6.1). Some commonly used supervised methods are Logistic regression, kernel-based methods, and Support Vector Machines.

Unsupervised techniques, such as dimensionality reduction and clustering, take unlabeled training data as input. A model is developed by uncovering the hidden patterns and grouping this data into appropriate subsets (illustrated in Fig. 6.2). Unsupervised learning techniques are generally utilized in finding patterns in gene expression data, and molecular subtyping of cancer patients. Some commonly used unsupervised learning techniques are K-means and hierarchical clustering techniques.

Semisupervised techniques take a combination of unlabeled and labeled samples as input. A model is developed which can predict new samples and explain the data structure. For example, to predict drug–disease associations, semisupervised

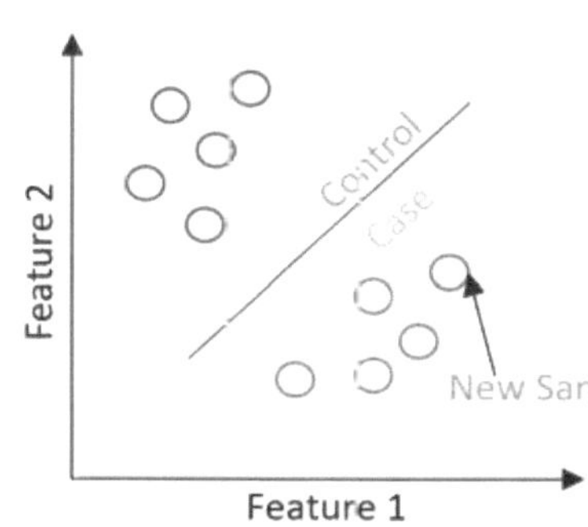

FIGURE 6.1 Classification of a new sample using supervised machine learning techniques. A dataset containing samples labeled as either controls or cases is used for training. A model with the maximum difference between the controls and cases is generated and can be utilized for labeling new samples.

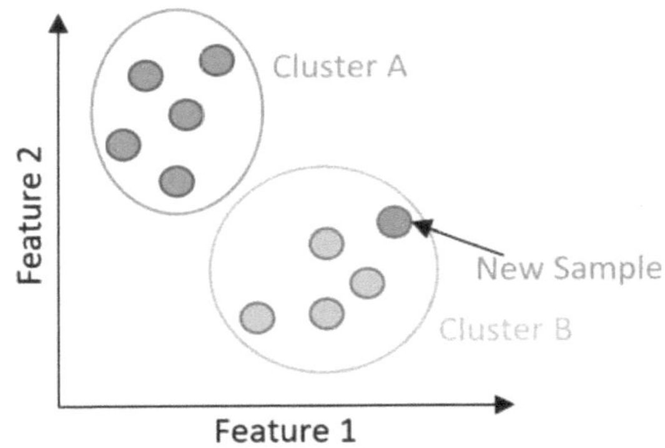

FIGURE 6.2 Classification of a new sample using unsupervised machine learning techniques. Unlabeled samples are used in unsupervised techniques. Samples can be grouped based on the similarities among them.

techniques learn from labeled data for predicting new associations. This technique is useful for integrating data, as different data types can be integrated as prior information. A common example of this technique is the network-regularized matrix factorization.

Depending upon the data needed to be integrated, integration techniques can be classified as either heterogeneous (numerous data types in multiple formats are combined) or homogenous (same data types along different perspectives are combined). The former is more computationally expensive, as it needs a model that can reduce the loss of heterogeneous data during transformation. Most of the currently used models cannot manage this problem and a preprocessing step is required before integration, where the data is transformed into a single form. The techniques used for big data analytics are selected based on the following conditions: (i) The technique should be able to address the challenges in precision medicine, (ii) The technique should be predominantly based on ML techniques, and (iii) The technique must be integrative and applied to big medical data analytics.

5. Methodology

The majority of EHR and omics are data with high dimensionality that affect the accuracy of the analytics and increase the required time. Therefore, dimensionality reduction can be used for finding a subset of factors that conserve the properties of the original data. Two different strategies are used for this purpose: (i) feature extraction that converts the original features into a set of compact dimensions and (ii) feature selection that picks the best subset of the original features.

Feature selection methods include embedded, wrapper, and filtering techniques. Filtering techniques can control the number of features through a score calculated for estimating the importance of all features. Hence, this technique is quicker and does not need the labeling of classes. A filtering technique, mRMR (minimum redundancy maximum relevance), makes a repetitive selection of features that provide the most relevant information with minimum redundancy, whereas the wrapper techniques generate models by selecting a subset of features and utilizing evaluation metrics like cross-validation. Embedded techniques combine the iterative elimination of features with ML methods.

Principle component analysis (PCA) is a basic feature extraction technique that recognizes some orthogonal linear vectors. The performance of this technique depends upon the correct identification of an ideal quantity of components and needs vigilant testing and validation. Nonlinear kernels in PCA and artificial neural networks are other techniques that are used.

5.1 Big data analytics in omics data

5.1.1 Preprocessing of omics data

Different techniques are used for preprocessing MS and NGS assay data. Table 6.2 describes some tools for preprocessing omics data obtained from NGS and MS techniques.

NGS describes DNA sequencing methods that can sequence millions of DNA fragments. Through bioinformatics analysis, these DNA fragments can be joined together by mapping the DNA fragments to the reference human genome. NGS is a commonly used technique for epigenomic, transcriptomic, and genomic research. Sequence mapping in NGS is a common preprocessing step that finds the alignment and origin of every inferred DNA fragment (read). Sequence mapping

TABLE 6.2 Tools for preprocessing of omics data.

Tool	Assay	Function	Description
Genomic mapping and alignment program (GMAP)	NGS	Sequence mapping	A tool used to align and map cDNA sequences to the genome.
Genome analysis toolkit (GATK)	NGS	Discovery of genomic variants	This is a framework to identify genomic variations using multiple samples.
deFuse	NGS	Identification of fusion genes	This is a computational method used for the identification of fusion genes from cancer RNA-seq data.
Model-based analysis of ChIP-seq (MACS)	NGS	ChIP-seq peak calling	This computational technique detects DNA–protein interactions across the genome using CHIP-Seq data.
OpenMS	MS	Peak detection and quantification	This is a framework for quick MS application development.

requires a lot of computing power and supplementary data structures like in-memory computing or multithreading to increase efficiency. Genomic research is aimed at identifying the variants present in a genome. The difference in individual bases between the reference genome and the reads is used to detect small-scale variations like SNP's and indels. Assembly based, split-read-based, read-depth-based, and read pair-based techniques are used to detect large-scale variations like SVs. Transcriptomic research generally aims at the detection of alternative splicing, detection of fusion genes, and expression profiling. Expression profiling is used to associate the genes and isoforms with the mapped reads. Different profiling techniques manage multimapped reads in various ways, like techniques that associate a small number of loci probabilistically to the reads and others that associate all the loci to the reads. Detection of the fusion genes depends upon two features: split read and spanning read pairs. Detection of alternative splicing depends upon either the interpretation of outputs from sequencing mapping or de novo transcriptome assembly. Epigenomic research aims to identify DNA methylation, histone modifications, and DNA–protein interaction locations. Preprocessing of epigenomic data generates a profile that identifies the statistically significant peaks, represents the background noises, and the density of reads through the genome.

MS is an analytical technique to find the molecular weights and identities of the components of a sample. MS is used for metabolomic and proteomic research. Preprocessing steps include peak detection, baseline correction, and alignment. Baseline correction is very useful in MALDI MS, as the background noise produced due to the matrix affects the baseline of the spectrum and should be removed before the analysis. Identification of peaks is done based on thresholds of detection, the shape of the peaks, and the signal-to-noise ratio. During the chromatography-MS, alignment of chromatographic peaks can guarantee the detection of accurate mass and comprehensive retention time, whereas the alignment of the mass to charge ratio can guarantee mass spectra and comparable features throughout the samples.

5.1.1.1 Identification of biomarkers through omics data

Diverse groups of samples are used for different conditions (e.g., healthy vs. diseased) or at different times for collection (e.g., pretreatment vs. posttreatment). A majority of disease biomarkers are detected by identifying the statistically significant variations between the groups. For example, variations in DNA methylations, histone modifications, DNA–protein bindings, alternative splicing, and expression of transcripts or genes. The general principle is to measure and then fit the values of groups into a distribution (e.g., binomial distribution, Poisson distribution). Then, statistical tests (e.g., likelihood ratio test, Fisher's exact test) are used to find the significance of the features. Genome-wide association studies (GWAS) utilize various methods (e.g., logistic regression or chi-squared test) to evaluate the degree of association among the target characteristics and the variants and select the variants with the maximum significance as biomarkers. Generally, GWAS focuses on the SNP association, but sometimes they may focus on SV or CNV association (Kim et al., 2012). A flowchart representing the procedure followed by CNVRuler (a technique for GWAS based on CNV) is illustrated in Fig. 6.3.

5.1.1.2 Utilizing omics data for systems biology models

The modeling and analysis of complicated biological systems is known as systems biology. Biological networks can contain different components interacting with each other, as depicted in Fig. 6.4. To obtain information about complicated molecular systems, systems biology models can be constructed by utilizing "dynamic temporal analysis" or "static network analysis."

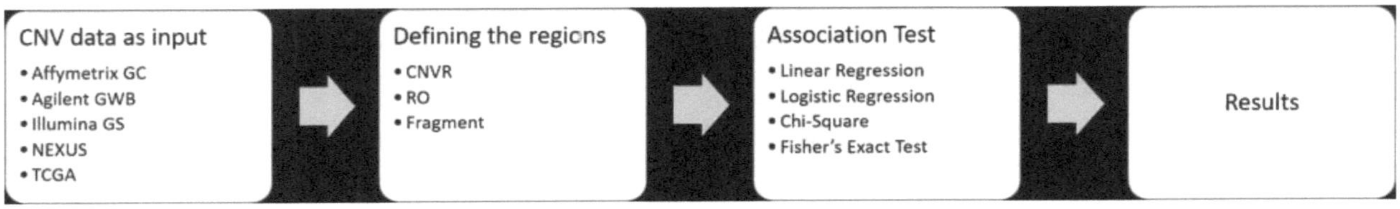

FIGURE 6.3 Flowchart representing the procedure followed by CNVRuler. CNVRuler imports clinical data through various tools. CNV containing regions can be identified as a CNVR, which are composed of CNV's overlapping by at least 1 bp. Regions containing CNV can also be identified by RO (reciprocal overlap), which is the degree of overlap between the two CNVs (CNVRuler has a threshold of 0.5). Another definition of the region involves breaking the overlapping CNV into fragments. CNVRuler can then utilize methods like Linear Regression and the Chi-Square tests for association analysis. Finally, a report containing the results is generated.

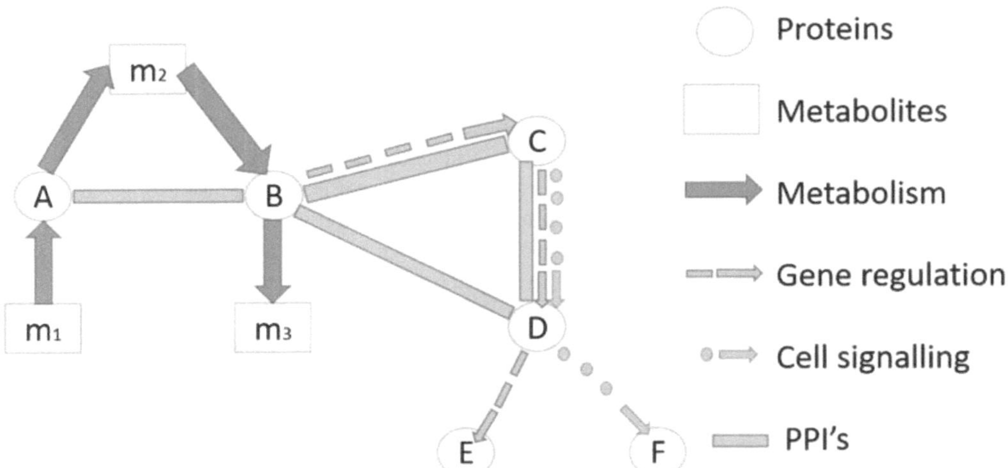

FIGURE 6.4 Representation of different biological processes in a network. Biological networks can represent the interactions among different molecules including genes, proteins, and metabolites.

Dynamic temporal analysis (e.g., Boolean networks, ordinary differential equations) utilizes the temporal measurement of omics data to generate and evaluate models for the prediction of complex systems. For example, research on the plant, *A. thaliana* utilized the Granger causality model to combine two forms of metabolic data collected at different times for understanding the interaction of primary and secondary metabolism (Doerfler et al., 2013). Static network analysis is based on the study of interactomes. It has three steps: finding a network scaffold that explains the interactions among the features, breaking down the network scaffold into modules, and generating a mathematical representation of all network modules for analysis. A majority of networks utilize single omics information like gene regulatory networks and metabolic networks. Some combined multiomics information is used in simple organisms like *C. elegans* and *S. cerevisiae* (Vidal et al., 2011).

5.2 Big data analytics in EHR data

5.2.1 Preprocessing of EHR data

A lot of disorganized information is stored in the EHR. Therefore, systematic preprocessing of EHR data is required. For the missing EHR data, records with missing data are deleted or are filled by the median or mean values. These methods are easy to use, but they generally add extra biases and overlook data structures. Therefore, robust methods such as maximum likelihood, expectation maximization, multiple imputation, and interpolation may be used.

5.2.2 EHR data mining

To obtain important information from complicated EHR data, two different approaches may be used: static endpoint prediction and temporal data mining.

Static endpoint prediction: After dimensionality reduction, relationships among medical features and results can be modeled through three approaches as follows:

1. Associate Rule Learning finds regular and dependable relationships between medical variables and defines if all parts in antecedent take place; all elements in the consequent would take place with particular confidence.
2. Classification is based on creating models which can designate new inputs into defined classes. Different classification methods like SVMs, k-nearest neighbors, and decision trees have been useful in various medical applications.
3. Regression analysis is a statistical method that predicts the relationship among the dependent variables (results) and the independent variables (features). A general linear model for model fitting can be used if distributions like binomial, Poisson, or normal are followed by the dependent variables.

Temporal data mining: EHR stores treatment, diagnosis, and the results along with a clinical encounter. Therefore, it is essential to identify the temporal relationships among the events with the help of temporal data mining methods like Conditional Random Field (CRF) and Hidden Markov Model (HMM). One drawback of these methods is that they need previously defined variables and results, making it difficult to generalize a treatment for a patient. Therefore, to find the connection among the event and the result, temporal association rule mining (TARM) is used. TARM can be used for any event result grouping in different clinical conditions as the selection of the event and result can be varied.

5.3 Enablers for big medical data analytics

Progress in the field of big data has led to the generation of platforms and software for mining, understanding, and defining information from the data for modeling, analytics, and business intelligence. Systems like Apache Hadoop provide a framework to store and process big data. Specialized software is used to resolve more specific problems. For example, real-time streaming data can be managed using Apache Spark Streaming and IBM InfoSphere Streams. Cloud computing services like Amazon Elastic Compute Cloud can give computational power on-demand to help in the generation of big data. Different cloud computing providers are used in bioinformatics like the Galaxy project and Illumina's BaseSpace can be deployed on Amazon Elastic Compute Cloud.

6. Applications

6.1 Disease subtyping and biomarker discovery

Disease subtyping is a method for clustering people into subgroups using medical, epigenomic, transcriptomic, and genomic data. Subtyping aims to achieve higher accuracy in the prediction of decisions that can improve the treatment of diseases like cancer, autoimmune disorders, cardiovascular disorders, and neurological disorders (Saria & Goldenberg, 2015). The most studied disease through subtyping is cancer. In cancer, there is an accumulation of genomic aberrations which finally lead to disturbance in the activity of biological systems. Cancers of similar histology are formed using different molecular subtypes with varying complexity and behaviors at the proteomic, transcriptomic, epigenomic, and genomic stages.

Unsupervised ML methods like K-means and hierarchical clustering are generally used on gene expression data to compare the level of expression of disease genes among the samples to find suitable subgroups. The newest techniques place patients into subgroups through differentially expressed genes comparison (comparing healthy and cancer patient samples). Using the nominated group of differentially expressed genes, the distance between the patients is calculated and followed by hierarchical clustering. The mRNA expression data of lung and breast cancer patients have been used for identifying five lung cancer and four breast cancer subtypes with survival rates having a significant difference. Additionally, as an alternative to identifying individual mutations, mutation modules are identified for every subtype. Specifically, by generating a protein—protein interaction network, followed by locating the most regularly altered genes of every subtype on the network and finally locating an optimal subnetwork containing these genes. These subnetworks are thought to be the driver modules that could be used as novel targets for a combination of recognized drugs. Using omics data and molecular networks, various other techniques have been produced to identify network modules. For example, KeyPathwayMiner created by Alcaraz et al. is a technique to extract unusual network modules in the protein—protein interaction networks by combining DNA methylation and gene expression data (Alcaraz et al., 2014). This is a heuristic-based technique utilizing ant colony optimization for extracting the subnetworks with the most connections and a minimum quantity of differentially expressed genes in the tested patients. KeyPathwayMiner was tested on the cancer genome atlas colorectal cancer patients. The subnetworks obtained were enriched in overexpressed genes in colorectal cancer which could be potentially used as targets for therapy.

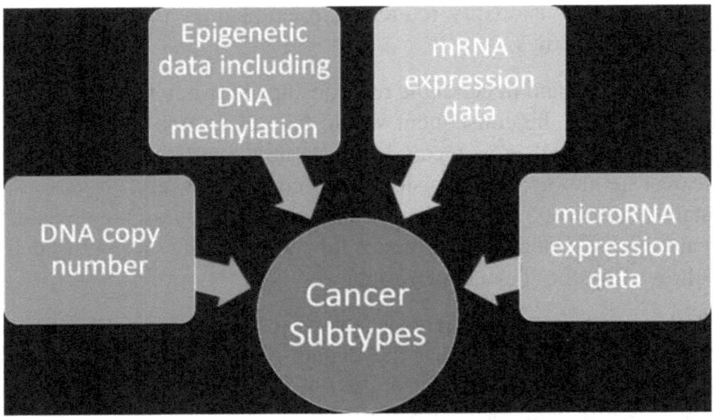

FIGURE 6.5 The iCluster model. Tumor subtypes are predicted from various types of genomic data obtained from the same samples.

Most of the newer techniques combine multiple types of data like protein expression, mRNA expression, DNA methylation, and change in DNA copy number leading to increased accuracy of subtyping. For example, iCluster created by Shen et al. is a model that can perform dimensionality reduction, feature selection, data integration, and clustering (Shen et al., 2010). iCluster utilizes a probabilistic matrix factorization method to continuously break down matrices having various types of data (e.g., mRNA expression, DNA methylation data) across a constant quantity of samples in a 2D matrix. Precisely, they break down the matrices by continuously factorizing all the matrices into a product of 2D matrices with low dimensionality. The dimensionality of these matrices depicts the number of cancer subtypes and their defined parameters. The matrices are known as the coefficient matrix and cluster indicator matrix. The coefficient matrix is different for every data type. The cluster indication matrix collects the dependencies through the data types and designates the cancer samples to the clusters. Fig. 6.5 represents the various types of data utilized by iCluster to predict cancer subtypes. Gene expression and DNA copy number difference data were utilized by iCluster to categorize lung and breast cancer patients. In both cases, subgroups were identified with statistically different results through the combination of data from the two data types. Curtis et al. applied iCluster to the breast cancer patients from the Molecular Taxonomy of Breast Cancer International Consortium (METABRIC) to identify 10 subgroups having significantly different results (Curtis et al., 2012). Additionally, it was stated that there was a significant correlation between the gene expression data and genome variations, which led to the discovery of newly predicted genes for breast cancer.

6.2 Drug repurposing

Dudley et al. classified drug repurposing techniques into disease-based and drug-based techniques (Dudley et al., 2011). Disease-based techniques utilize the similarities among the disease symptoms or other disease similarities such as the similarities in phenotype to cluster diseases into a group and repurpose a new drug by identifying known connections among some diseases in the group and the drug and inferring the remaining diseases in the group. Drug-based techniques utilize the similarities in the side effects of the drugs, similarities among gene expression caused by the action of the drugs, and other drug similarities such as chemical similarities to repurpose a drug in the group to act in the same way as the rest of the drugs in the group. Other techniques utilize the similarities based on the target for inferring new drugs, such as similarity of 3D structures and similarities in protein sequences. All these techniques can also be classified as network-based or ML techniques. Molecular docking methods can predict the location within the 3D structure of proteins where the drug will bind.

A kernel-based technique was used by Napolitano et al. to combine gene expression induced by the drug posttreatment, Protein–Protein Interaction networks, and the chemical similarity of drugs (Napolitano et al., 2013). All information was depicted by a kernel matrix. Specifically, three drug-centered matrices depicting the similarities among the drugs are based upon (i) gene profile correlations induced by the drugs, obtained from the Complement Map Database, (ii) Closeness of the targets in the network, and (iii) chemical structure of the drugs obtained from the DrugBank database. The matrices are then integrated into a single matrix, followed by the application of the SVM technique for classification. The trained SVM classifier achieved an accuracy of 78% and they utilized the highest-scoring misclassified drugs as repurposing candidates.

PreDR is a similar technique developed by Wang et al. where the disease-centered matrix depicts the similarities in the disease phenotypes obtained from the OMIM database (Wang et al., 2013). The drug-centered matrices depict

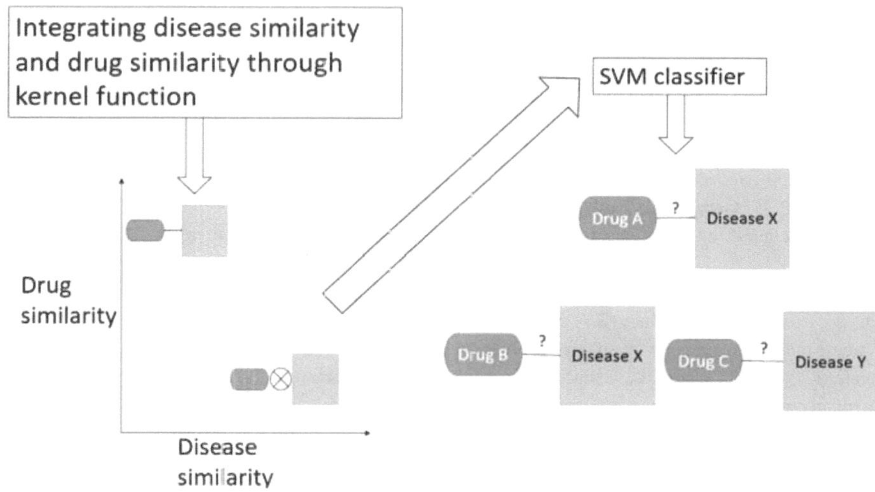

FIGURE 6.6 Representation of the PreDR technique. Application of kernel function for the association of drug and disease similarities, followed by the application of SVM to predict the associations among unknown drugs and diseases.

(i) similarities in adverse drug effects obtained from the SIDER database, (ii) similarities in the sequence of target proteins obtained from the DrugBank and KEGG BRITE databases, and (iii) similarities in the drug chemicals obtained from the PubChem database. The integrated kernel was utilized for training an SVM classifier and identified new drug–disease associations, depicted in Fig. 6.6.

6.3 Integrating omics data into EHR

Electronic medical records or EMR can be used by medical workers for clinical decision support. Therefore, it is essential to combine EMR information with omics data. The eMERGE Network consortium has a goal to find the genomic variants (e.g., SNPs) for EMR-based phenotypes and to combine the known phenotype–genotype connections into the EMR structure (Gottesman et al., 2013). Some proposed ideas for expanding the EMR system are (i) Genomic variants like CNVs and SNPs should be stored in a separate computer format, (ii) Interoperability must be present to ensure easy data transfer and updates in the facilities, (iii) Rule-based decision support systems must be supported, and (iv) A wide range of visualization elements must be present to help in the interpretation of information. EMR is available only in small hospitals and clinics, whereas EHR stores and transfers the records to all the connected hospitals and clinics. Interoperability is essential for utilizing big data in precision medicine. Fast Healthcare Interoperability Resources (FHIR) given by Health Level Seven International aims to solve this issue. For medical genomics, a variety of FHIR definitions and resources can be used for the variant information (Alterovitz et al., 2015). Through a standard data transfer procedure, healthcare workers can use genomic data along with EHR data to find the treatment having maximum efficiency for an individual patient.

7. Conclusion

Omics and EHR data are among the most essential big biomedical data having a strong association with precision medicine. In this chapter, we review the importance of EHR and omics data in precision medicine. Big data plays an essential part in finance, the environment, energy, and other sectors. Big data has progressed due to advances in data retrieval, data mining, data analytics, data visualization, and data storage. Big data has been applied to healthcare in biomarker discovery and disease subtyping, drug repurposing, and integrating omics data into EHR. Further research is required in biomedical areas like patient similarity, waveform and analysis of unevenly spaced time series, and omics data integration to accelerate the growth of precision medicine. As big medical data is in its initial stages, there is a requirement for additional engineers and data scientists to obtain the needed biological knowledge for utilizing a large amount of data due to big biomedical data initiatives. By providing the most appropriate and efficient treatment to every patient on the basis of their subtyping data, the hospitals and clinics can provide more effective and quality care.

References

Alcaraz, N., Pauling, J., Batra, R., Barbosa, E., Junge, A., Christensen, A. G. L., Azevedo, V., Ditzel, H. J., & Baumbach, J. (2014). KeyPathwayMiner 4.0: Condition-specific pathway analysis by combining multiple omics studies and networks with Cytoscape. *BMC Systems Biology, 8*(1). https://doi.org/10.1186/s12918-014-0099-x

Alterovitz, G., Warner, J., Zhang, P., Chen, Y., Ullman-Cullere, M., Kreda, D., & Kohane, I. S. (2015). SMART on FHIR genomics: Facilitating standardized clinico-genomic apps. *Journal of the American Medical Informatics Association*, 1173–1178. https://doi.org/10.1093/jamia/ocv045

Cargnin, S., Jommi, C., Canonico, P. L., Genazzani, A. A., & Terrazzino, S. (2014). Diagnostic accuracy of hla-B*57:01 screening for the prediction of abacavir hypersensitivity and clinical utility of the test: A meta-analytic review. *Pharmacogenomics, 15*(7), 963–976. https://doi.org/10.2217/pgs.14.52

Curtis, C., Shah, S. P., Chin, S. F., Turashvili, G., Rueda, O. M., Dunning, M. J., Speed, D., Lynch, A. G., Samarajiwa, S., Yuan, Y., Gräf, S., Ha, G., Haffari, G., Bashashati, A., Russell, R., McKinney, S., Aparicio, S., Brenton, J. D., Ellis, I., … Caldas, C. (2012). The genomic and transcriptomic architecture of 2,000 breast tumours reveals novel subgroups. *Nature, 486*(7403), 346–352. https://doi.org/10.1038/nature10983

Doerfler, H., Lyon, D., Nägele, T., Sun, X., Fragner, L., Hadacek, F., Egelhofer, V., & Weckwerth, W. (2013). Granger causality in integrated GC-MS and LC-MS metabolomics data reveals the interface of primary and secondary metabolism. *Metabolomics, 9*(3), 564–574. https://doi.org/10.1007/s11306-012-0470-0

Dudley, J. T., Deshpande, T., & Butte, A. J. (2011). Exploiting drug-disease relationships for computational drug repositioning. *Briefings in Bioinformatics, 12*(4), 303–311. https://doi.org/10.1093/bib/bbr013

Gottesman, O., Kuivaniemi, H., Tromp, G., Faucett, W. A., Li, R., Manolio, T. A., Sanderson, S. C., Kannry, J., Zinberg, R., Basford, M. A., Brilliant, M., Carey, D. J., Chisholm, R. L., Chute, C. G., Connolly, J. J., Crosslin, D., Denny, J. C., Gallego, C. J., Haines, J. L., … Williams, M. S. (2013). The electronic medical records and genomics (eMERGE) network: Past, present, and future. *Genetics in Medicine, 15*(10), 761–771. https://doi.org/10.1038/gim.2013.72

Kim, J. H., Hu, H. J., Yim, S. H., Bae, J. S., Kim, S. Y., & Chung, Y. J. (2012). CNVRuler: A copy number variation-based case-control association analysis tool. *Bioinformatics, 28*(13), 1790–1792. https://doi.org/10.1093/bioinformatics/bts239

Margolis, R., Derr, L., Dunn, M., Huerta, M., Larkin, J., Sheehan, J., Guyer, M., & Green, E. D. (2014). The National Institutes of Health's big data to knowledge (BD2K) initiative: Capitalizing on biomedical big data. *Journal of the American Medical Informatics Association, 21*(6), 957–958. https://doi.org/10.1136/amiajnl-2014-002974

Napolitano, F., Zhao, Y., Moreira, V. M., Tagliaferri, R., Kere, J., D'Amato, M., & Greco, D. (2013). Drug repositioning: A machine-learning approach through data integration. *Journal of Cheminformatics, 5*(6). https://doi.org/10.1186/1758-2946-5-30

Ph.D. (2010). Genetic testing for CYP450 polymorphisms to predict response to clopidogrel: Current evidence and test availability. Application: Pharmacogenomics. *PLoS Currents, 2*.

Prosperi, M., Min, J. S., Bian, J., & Modave, F. (2018). Big data hurdles in precision medicine and precision public health. *BMC Medical Informatics and Decision Making, 18*(1). https://doi.org/10.1186/s12911-018-0719-2

Saria, S., & Goldenberg, A. (2015). Subtyping: What it is and its role in precision medicine. *IEEE Intelligent Systems, 30*(4), 70–75. https://doi.org/10.1109/MIS.2015.60

Shen, R., Olshen, A. B., & Ladanyi, M. (2010). Integrative clustering of multiple genomic data types using a joint latent variable model with application to breast and lung cancer subtype analysis. *Bioinformatics, 26*(2), 292–293. https://doi.org/10.1093/bioinformatics/btp659

Vidal, M., Cusick, M. E., & Barabási, A. L. (2011). Interactome networks and human disease. *Cell, 144*(6), 986–998. https://doi.org/10.1016/j.cell.2011.02.016

Wang, Y., Chen, S., Deng, N., Wang, Y., & Chen, L. (2013). Drug repositioning by kernel-based integration of molecular structure, molecular activity, and phenotype data. *PLoS One, 8*(11), e78518. https://doi.org/10.1371/journal.pone.0078518

Chapter 7

Recent advances in processing, interpreting, and managing biological data for therapeutic intervention of human infectious disease

Pritha Chakraborty[1], Parth Sarthi Sen Gupta[2], Shankar Dey[3], Nabarun Chandra Das[1], Ritwik Patra[1] and Suprabhat Mukherjee[1]

[1]*Integrative Biochemistry and Immunology Laboratory, Department of Animal Science, Kazi Nazrul University, Asansol, West Bengal, India;* [2]*Department of Chemical Science, Indian Institute of Science Education and Research (IISER) Berhampur, Chemical Sciences, Berhampur, Odisha, India;* [3]*Department of Obstetrics and Gynaecology, ESI Hospital, Asansol, West Bengal, India*

Abbreviations

BDA Big data analytics
CDC Centers for Diseases Control and Prevention
ChIP Chromatin immunoprecipitation
CLIP Cross-linking immunoprecipitation
CNN Convolutional neural network
COPD Chronic obstructive pulmonary disorder
CTMS Clinical trials management systems
DTx Digital Therapeutics
EDC Electronic data collection
EEG Electroencephalogram
EHRs Electronic health records
FDA Food and Drugs Administration
GLMS Generalized linear models
HDFS The Hadoop Distributed File System
Hi-C High-resolution chromosome conformation capture
HQL Hive Query Language
IBD Inflammatory Bowel Disease
IoT Internet of things
JSON JavaScript Object Notation
LASSO Least Absolute Shrinkage and Selection Operator
NGS Next-generation sequencing
PBM Protein-binding microarrays
PDMS Patient data management system
RNN Recursive neural network
SARS Severe acute respiratory syndrome
SELEX Systematic evolution of ligands by exponential enrichment
SQL Structured Query Language
WHO World Health Organization
XML Extensible Markup Language.

Big Data Analytics for Healthcare. https://doi.org/10.1016/B978-0-323-91907-4.00009-1

1. Introduction

Data has been an omnipresent concept in the modern-day world. It has become a part of different domains including retail, healthcare, education, e-commerce, agriculture, media, entertainment, finance, travel industry, telecom, automobiles, and more on consisting of an enormous amount of information, collectively called "Big Data" (Dash et al., 2019). Characteristics of big data involve the 6 Vs: Value, Volume, Velocity, Variety, Veracity, and Variability (Ristevski & Chen, 2018). Big data and analytics are commonly associated with large datasets formed by collections of large and complex data. The greater amount of data brings more accuracy in outcomes. Management of these data requires computing techniques, including machine learning and deep learning (Garattini et al., 2017). Processing, interpretation, and analysis of large datasets fall under Big Data Analytics (BDA) to discover useful information. BDA has been in use for medicine and healthcare in the areas of bioinformatics, sensor informatics, medical and health informatics, and medical imaging. Developed and developing countries have opted for various healthcare information system models to provide the best healthcare services for patients. They involve personalized, participatory, predictive, and preventive models. All these models are based on biomedical data, also called the "omics data," and Electronic Health Records (EHRs) from public authorities and large hospitals in a structured and/or unstructured format. Analysis of data from thousands of patients has been used to identify correlations and clusters between different datasets using different data mining techniques (Galetsi & Katsaliaki, 2019).

The dawn of big data for surveillance of infectious disease has been a part of healthcare over decades. But traditional surveillance was time consuming and lacked spatial resolution. Thus, analysis of infectious diseases has become a serious need for the treatment of infectious diseases (Kasson, 2020). Traditionally, epidemiological studies of infectious diseases depend on the high quality and accuracy of the data on the diseases. Modern studies on epidemiology are characterized by electronic data produced in large volumes based on existing digital information and repurposing it to identify different patterns related to diseases. BDA helps in disease surveillance, monitoring potential outbreaks, risk of exposure, patient stratification for treatment, and prediction of the treatment outcome (Lee et al., 2016).

Biomedical research driven by data integration and interpretation is a crucial part of the discovery of new therapeutic interventions and disease surveillance. For research advancement in biomedical sciences, data needs to be shareable and traceable, thus integrable. Herein, in which chapter, we will be discussing management of the big biological data as an optimistic view to forecast the trajectory of an outbreak and dispersion of infectious diseases in the public domain of healthcare to anticipate and develop therapeutic interventions for the same. The schematic diagram of big data accumulation, processing, interpretation, and management is depicted in Fig. 7.1. Accumulation of health data from different sources and its storage needs to be done accurately so that we can have a model outline of disease prediction and necessary

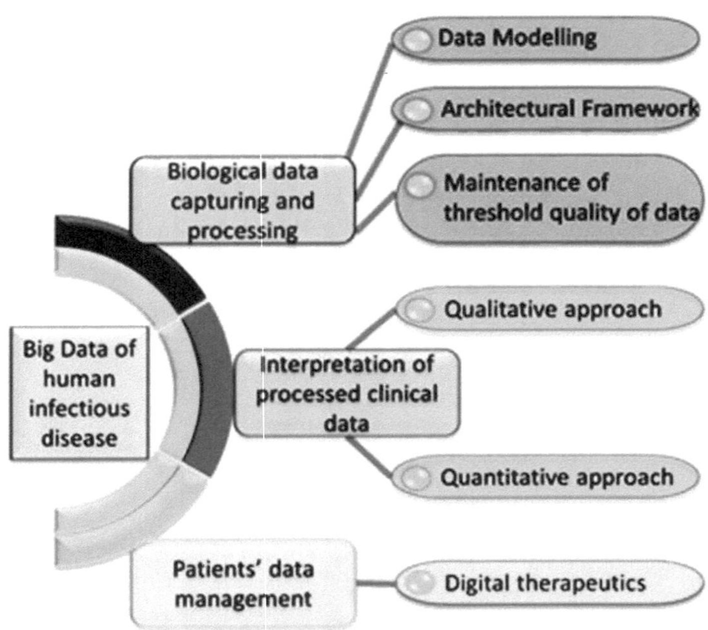

FIGURE 7.1 Schematic diagram depicting big data capturing, processing, interpretation, and management.

management strategies. With the help of EHRs, different databases and storage systems are developed for data modeling that can be used for better understanding of infectious and inflammatory disease processes and management. Maintaining the quality of big data and its interpretation simultaneously is a crucial part that can be achieved using qualitative and quantitative approaches. With the enormous amount of data, there are some limitations that need to be addressed, followed by the development of improved technologies.

1.1 Need of big data in therapeutic intervention

Center for Diseases Control and Prevention (CDC) have noted "Epidemiology" as a method of investigation of infectious diseases using data collection, interpretation, and analysis. Combating infectious diseases relies on the various omics layers ranging from genomics to postgenomics data, tracking of the disease, surveillance systems, and its clinical outcomes (Thacker and Stroup, 1994). Traditionally, data accumulation for the infectious disease was time lagging with lack of spatial resolution; thus, a timely and robust option was the need of the hour. The reemergence of infectious diseases was a serious concern; hence, monitoring of potential infections and reinfections is much needed (Bansal et al., 2016). The World Health Organization (WHO) has reported several outbreaks, pandemics, and epidemics throughout the world over time. Hitherto, infectious diseases like pandemic influenza, Severe Acute Respiratory Syndrome (SARS), tuberculosis, Ebola, Zika, filariasis, and drug-resistant pathogens are of particular interest (Corsi et al., 2020).

BDA has been playing a crucial role in the epidemic and pandemic scenarios. Accessibility to the internet and availability of big data helps in prediagnostic and diagnostic approaches by allowing cloud computing and smart devices. Social media platforms, smartphones, the Internet of Things (IoT) are generating an enormous amount of data which can be used to resolve healthcare challenges (Garattini et al., 2017). Inflammatory diseases like Inflammatory Bowel Disease are heterogeneous diseases with various clinical phenotypes. Using big data approaches like data mining, phenomapping for disease heterogeneity helps in the identification of these phenotypes. Also, predictive models can be prepared to identify high-risk patients to provide better treatment courses. By combing the omics data and clinical data, BDA approaches can repurpose already existed drugs and develop cost-effective new drugs as a therapeutic intervention (Olivera et al., 2019). Currently, the world is facing a pandemic known as Covid-19. According to WHO, 192,284,207 cases of Covid-19 has been reported globally, while 4,134,518 deaths have been reported (Coronavirus, 2021). Along with the WHO, CDC, John Hopkins Platform, GSAID, Oxford University, and Google trends all are providing real-time monitoring of emergence and omics data, statistical data for treatment strategies, and global vaccination programs for Covid-19 worldwide. With the ability to store and explore biological data worldwide, biological research has been transformed to information-driven discovery science (Biological data management, 2021).

2. Biological data capturing and processing

The field of medicine is working on forming the clinical picture to gain a better understanding of their health and diseases. With the help of computational technologies, this picture is transformed measurements to form models like EHR data that depicts accurate clinical pictures and their related comorbidities. Also, data capturing and processing can be done using powerful sensors and wearable devices that store the raw data directly to the cloud-based computing system (Vitabile et al., 2019). Various datasets are prepared based on diagnostic, survey spatial, longitudinal, and time series approaches and analyzed using different methods such as social network analysis, machine learning, regressions, etc (Dash et al., 2019). Individual data in the case of infectious diseases can be collected using questionnaires to estimate the risk of infection, whereas data from a group will provide the risk assessment of infectious diseases within the community (Jarynowski et al., 2018).

2.1 Architectural framework

Traditional healthcare data capturing and processing depends on stand-alone business tools like desktop or laptop. Since big data is itself enormous, the processing is broken down among multiple systems. The working framework of distributed processing has been in use over a long period, but with BDA, healthcare medical professionals and clinical researchers have access to the repository within a single tap of a button to get a deeper insight into the EHRs and have clinical support in decision-making (Raghupathi & Raghupathi, 2014). Algorithms and models for BDA are highly complex with intensive programming as compared to traditional health analytics and require a variety of skills for its application. BDA in healthcare depends on internal and external sources captured from EHRs, clinical decision support systems, government sources, laboratories, etc., in multiple formats from different geographical locations. Different types of data involved in healthcare include web and social media data (Facebook, Twitter healthcare plan websites, etc.), IoTs and smart wearable, billing records, medical insurance, biometric data, and human-generated unstructured and structured data (Mehta et al., 2019). The second component of the framework is the processing of "raw data." Data warehousing is an approach in which data from different sources is retrieved and processed via extraction, transformation, and loading from data sources depending on unstructured and structured data (Raghupathi & Kesh, 2007). The third component is called the conceptual framework, which performs several decisions related to input, distribution, tools, and analysis (Pastorino et al., 2019). The last component of BDA involves the application in healthcare, including data mining, generating reports and queries. These applications are further visualized and used in other fields of healthcare and clinical research. The architectural framework of big data for infectious diseases is shown in Fig. 7.2.

2.2 Data modeling

EHR is documenting all the healthcare activities, but from the perspective of computational technology, EHR data has been accurate and persistent over the years and has been stored in the relational database and accessed by using Structured Query Language (SQL) (Friedman et al., 1990; Schrodt et al., 2020). Further, the NoSQL database management system came into the market which is also based on an EHR system to replace document-orientated database management systems like MongoDB and CouchDB (Klein et al., 2015; Rascovsky, Delgado, Sanz, Radiographics, 2012; Xu et al., 2014). Table 7.1 summarizes the list of platforms and tools currently used in healthcare.

Traditional databases use tables to store the data, but the new data model uses documents written in JavaScript Object Notation and/or Extensible Markup Language (Schrodt et al., 2020). Compared to the document model, another data model is the graph database in which the data is stored based on nodes connected by edges representing the relation between connected nodes. They are much easier than the traditional relational database and documentation in respect of scaling and a higher level of availability (Nayak et al., 2013). Graph databases can store the data directly decreasing the computation time and create queries that can be used in the field of representation of infectious and inflammatory disease networks, integration of biological data, and forming bimolecular pathways (Fabregat et al., 2018; Lysenko et al., 2016; Yoon et al., 2017). This concept of the graphical model has been of great use to healthcare and medicine. Patient EHRs are modeled to determine the diagnosis, therapeutic strategies, as well as the action of the medicine. It will provide a support system to the clinicians or medical professionals related to the clinical decisions of an individual patient and/or for a community.

2.3 Maintenance of threshold quality of data

Integrating big data is a crucial part of the field of healthcare, but maintaining the quality is another challenge. The quality of data is based on the dimensions of data viz., consistency, uniqueness, accuracy, completeness, and timeliness. Consistency is defined as the consistent values among two different datasets without creating any conflict. Uniqueness is achieved within the data accumulated and represented with no entity existing more than once within the dataset. Accuracy

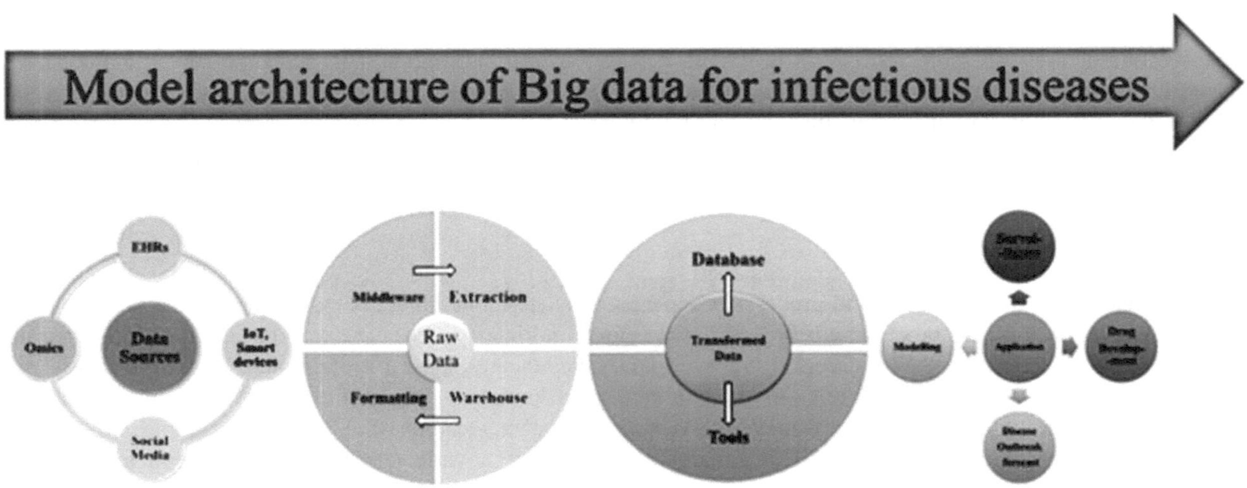

FIGURE 7.2 Architecture of big data for infectious diseases.

TABLE 7.1 The list of platforms and tools currently used in healthcare.

Platforms/tools	Use	References
MongoDB	Cloud-based database using NoSQL language. Generates modular ontologies	Abbes and Gargouri (2016)
CouchDB	Stores IoT information using NoSQL language	Raghavendra Kumar and Lalitha (2018)
The Hadoop distributed file system (HDFS)	Stores the underlying data and distributed across various servers	Saraladevi et al. (2015)
Pig and PigLatin	Assimilation of data	Rathi (2017)
Hive	Used as a Hadoop support architecture to develop Hive query language (HQL) to typical SQL language	Costa et al. (2019)
MapReduce	Processing model with high-level query language in cloud computation	Birjali et al. (2018)
Jaql	Process large sets of data by converting high-level queries into low level with MapReduce tasks	Birjali et al. (2018)
Zookeeper	Synchronizes and coordinates cluster of servers	Anagnostopoulos et al. (2016)
HBase	Column orientated database using non-SQL language	Chrimes and Zamani (2017)
Cassandra	Distributed database system for handling big data using NoSQL system	Stanway et al. (2017); Stanaway et al. (2018)
DynamoDB	Database using NoSQL approach running on Amazon Web Services cloud	Kalid et al. (2017)
Oozie	Open source project to manage the workflow and coordination	Peek et al. (2018)
Lucene	Search application using JAVA application; incorporated in open source project for text analytics	Lydia et al. (2020)

represents the real-life scenario within the predicted model precisely. Completeness refers to mandatory values assigned to the specific data elements expressing optionality and value under specific conditions. Timeliness is the expectation of time required for the access and availability of the information ("Data Quality Dimension - an Overview I ScienceDirect Topics"). Data management also involves improving the quality, which can be achieved by following a particular hierarchy of reliable data sources bearing good quality information. The organization of the accumulated data within the warehouses must be updated, followed by data cleaning mechanisms, while the data management dimensions are careful (Lehmann et al., 2020).

3. Interpretation of processed clinical data

Interpretation of data remains the most vital part of data analysis, which refers to the implementation of the processes and methods to review the data for arriving at an informed conclusion. Data interpretation provides meaning to the analysis, which further determines its importance to the particular field. Once the data is collected, the most important part is to look closely at the findings. While interpreting data, the data analyst has to consider all the involved factors that may lead to the conclusion. One can use various data interpretation methods depending upon the nature of the data. Two broad categories are qualitative and quantitative approaches (What Is Data Interpretation, 2018).

3.1 Qualitative approach

Qualitative data describes qualities or characteristics which cannot be described through numerical values but with descriptive and narrative context such as questionnaires, interviews, or observation. Qualitative data is difficult to measure and analyze but can be examined sometimes through the use of coding. A wide variety of person-to-person techniques used for the interpretation of qualitative data are (I) observational: observation and detailing of various patterns noticed in a group, such as quality, amount of time spent in a specific activity, type of activity, mode of communication, etc. (II) Documentation: types of patterns and resources can be documented and coded based on the type of entity or material it contains. (III) Questionnaires or interviews: questions based on any topic, theme, category, and routines can be asked and recorded. It is one of the best collective methods and allows for highly focused segmentation of data (What Is Data Interpretation, 2018).

3.2 Quantitative approach

Data is either counted or compared on a numeric scale. In a quantitative analysis, one should have to encounter numbers if not then it is not quantitative, for example, the rating of the quality of food in a restaurant on a scale of 1−10. The processes involved in the analysis of these types of numerical data are generally statistical models such as mean, mode, median, standard deviation, and frequency distribution, etc (What Is Data Interpretation, 2018). The software and tools used for the calculation of the statistical parameters are summarized in Table 7.2. Other commonly used processes are regression analysis, cohort analysis, and predictive and prescriptive analysis.

Apart from statistical models, machine learning methods are widely applied in the biomedical field to deliver integrative solutions for multiview data for the prediction of outcomes. The outcomes, in the case of generalized linear models (Agresti, 2006), are linearly related to covariates and factors by a function that permits the estimation of the model parameters by maximum likelihood or Bayesian techniques. Biological data generally possess some form of structure, such as the family of proteins with similar functions, structural regularization methods such as Sparse Group LASSO (Least Absolute Shrinkage and Selection Operator) could be used for supervised multiview feature selection. Ensemble-learning models such as random forest, neural networks, and deep learning are commonly used in recent approaches.

The deep learning method has been used for the analysis of biomedical data, integration, and modeling, such as drug designing, risk of disease and hospitalization prediction, etc. The deep learning method applied in a few biomedical applications is summarized in Table 7.3.

4. Patients' data management for digital therapeutics

Medical decision-making and support require documentation of all the information related to the patient as well as the drug therapy in the form of a computerized medical record (Riou et al., 2018). Detailed statistical analysis of all the components involved in the drug therapy and their interactions with each other and other is integrated for the decision-making of the computerized algorithm in the form of Patient Data Management System (PDMS) database. The basic architecture of the PDMS database has been designed keeping the complexity of medicine and drug therapy in mind. Thus, standardization, modularization, and communication are the key components of the architecture of PDMS.

TABLE 7.2 List of common statistical software/tools used for the clinical data analysis.

Software/tools	Open-source	License	Interface	Language	Common use case
R	Yes	GNU/PL	CLI/GUI	C/Fortan/ C++	Metaanalysis
STATA	No	Proprietary	CLI/GUI	C	Clinical data analysis and healthcare
GraphPad prism	No	Proprietary	GUI	C/C++	Research and clinical data analysis
SAS	No	Proprietary	CLI/GUI	C	Clinical data analysis, life sciences and healthcare
MATLAB	No	Proprietary	CLI	C++/Java	Metaanalysis and clinical data analysis
STATISTICA	No	Proprietary	GUI	C	Clinical data analysis, visualization
IBM SPSS	No	Proprietary	CLI/GUI	Java	Review, survey, and data analysis
JMP	No	Proprietary	CLI/GUI	C++	Clinical data analysis, visualization
Minitab	No	Proprietary	CLI/GUI	Fortan	Clinical data analysis, and healthcare
Excel	Yes	Proprietary	GUI	C/C++	Metaanalysis and clinical data analysis

TABLE 7.3 Few applications of deep learning methods in the area of the biomedical field.

Application	Data type	Method	References
Drug designing	Chemical compounds	RNN	Segler et al. (2018)
Disease risk prediction	Gene variants	CNN	Zhou et al. (2018)
Prediction of hospitalization outcome	EHRs	RNN	Rajkomar et al. (2018)
Prediction of epileptic seizure	EEG	RNN	Tsiouris et al. (2018)
Analysis of medical images	Images of skin lesion	CNN	Esteva et al. (2017)
Binding site prediction of transcription factor	PBM, SELEX, ChIP-seq, and CLIP-seq	CNN	Alipanahi et al. (2015)
Prediction of promoter–enhancer interaction	Hi-C and genomic annotations	CNN	Singh et al. (2018)
Classification of metagenomic	16S rRNA sequences	RNN	Ditzler et al. (2015)
Variant calling	NGS data	CNN	Poplin et al. (2018)

ChIP, chromatin immunoprecipitation; *CLIP*, cross-linking immunoprecipitation; *CNN*, convolutional neural network; *EEG*, electroencephalogram; *Hi-C*, high-resolution chromosome conformation capture; *NGS*, next-generation sequencing; *PBM*, protein-binding microarrays; *RNN*, recursive neural network; *SELEX*, systematic evolution of ligands by exponential enrichment (Cirillo & Valencia, 2019).

The emergence of electronic media such as social media platforms, smartphones, and watches, cloud-based data platforms, etc., witnessed the explosion of digital health in recent times. Thus, now in a digital world, several applications of smartphones are used for the well-being and monitoring of health and are not restricted to hospitals and clinics. As a result, many innovative models are being employed in the digitized health domain, harnessing the potential of open source platforms, and optimizing the potential of professionals from traditional healthcare, and this emergent phenomenon within the digital health space is termed as "Digital Therapeutics" (DTx) (The Rise of Digital Therapeutics, 2021).

Digital Therapeutics (DTx) is a subdivision of digital health representing technologies, products, and services across healthcare industries and formally defined by Sepah et al. (2015) as, "evidence-based behavioral treatments delivered online that can increase accessibility and effectiveness of healthcare" The importance of DTx can be measured by the fact that its value of the global market is estimated at USD 1.8 billion in 2018, and is expected to reach USD 7.1 billion by the year 2025 ("Can Digital Therapeutics Revolutionize Medicine? | Ideo.Com,"). Recent reports suggest the successful implementation of DTx in several diseases in which diabetes, weight loss, chronic obstructive pulmonary disorder, developmental disorders (with the use of computer games), and Posttraumatic Stress Disorder (PTSD) are few notable. Digital Therapeutics is a new class of digital applications that helps in treating diseases using changes in the behavior of patients by monitoring remotely to provide favorable health outcomes. The application brings favorable outcomes from patients by encouraging them to adhere to a particular lifestyle such as diet, exercise routine, and drug regimens. Now, even health authorities are also recognizing its potential and encouraging innovations in the field. Although the application is still in the preliminary stage, growing Research and Development (R&D) investment and its successful implementation will show enormous growth in coming years.

5. Advantages and limitations

Heterogenicity, huge volume, context-dependency, nosiness, and complexity are the biggest issues in managing the biological data. Though clinical data is managed by the Food and Drugs Administration, there is a lack of regulations for industrial standards for data collection, also known as clinical trials management systems and Electronic Data Collection (Mayer, 2009). The existing technology for data management lacks stability and implicit scientific context characterizing the biological data and needs to be evolved with diversifying ability. For an enormous amount of data, there are some challenges as well. High-throughput omics data is accumulated at the cost of expensive experimental measurements such as whole-genome sequencing, etc. Since the omics data is based on various sources, experimental noise, environmental conditions, biological nature, and different protocols followed during the experiment technique make the heterogenicity of the data biased. Due to these contributing factors being biased, the reliability of these data becomes an issue. Also, the omics data and EHR data entries are done manually; thus, there will always be a potential human error, missing values, incorrect data due to misunderstanding, or wrong interpretation (Wu et al., 2017). The intermediating relationship between omics data and EHR is a challenging task due to the high dimensionality of omics data and individual EHR data.

Preprocessing of both the big data is a handful of tasks since it is very noisy and contains missing values, outliers, normalization, and data transformation. Security and privacy of the individual patient is a rising concern with big data since sensitive medical data is being shared digitally. To overcome these challenges, BDA needs to be encrypted using advanced algorithms.

6. Conclusion and future direction

BDA relies on the pillars of more information; deeper will be the insights to predict the future outcomes. A fast-growing world with the generation of an enormous volume of data is growing exponentially; thus, it is mandatory to manage this huge amount of data as it provides insights for improvement in medicine and healthcare. Hitherto, this chapter suggests that BDA has been helping to form a better framework for combating infectious diseases in the form of epidemics and/or pandemics. With the use of BDA from healthcare, biomedical researchers can form better therapeutic interventions against infectious diseases. With digital data and cloud computing, there are always security and privacy issues that need to be addressed and handled carefully to protect sensitive data from fraudsters. Clinical trials, drugs, and biomarker discovery have given new hopes to analyze big data despite the challenges and improve the current status of the healthcare system.

BDA in healthcare can be revolutionized by improving the studies in bioinformatics, immune-informatics, health informatics, and other analytics promoting effective treatments. BDA has overcome the hurdle between structured and unstructured data. These new strategies should be developed for understanding the nature, complexity, and volume of different types of data structures to retrieve useful information and knowledge. In the field of infectious diseases, cancer, and/or neurodegenerative diseases, BDA has been advancing greatly concerning data collection, integration, and management. There will be a possibility that big data will replace skilled manpower with computer-based AI systems, transforming the healthcare system into a completely different level. Inspired by the human brain, AI with deep learning holds the ability to counteract the challenges and issues posed by the current scenario. Also, there will be the possibility for big data to predict futuristic outcomes of an individual patient based on his EHRs and omics data. Upcoming years will provide a prediction of epidemics within the public health domain by providing warnings of disease conditions and developing therapeutic interventions to improve the quality of living.

Acknowledgments

PSSG acknowledges IISER Berhampur for providing him with an Institute Postdoctoral Fellowship to carry out this work. PC acknowledges DST Govt. of India for the award of DST-INSPIRE fellowship. RP acknowledges the Department of Higher Education, Govt. of West Bengal for awarding Swami Vivekananda Merit Cum Means Fellowship.

References

Abbes, H., & Gargouri, F. (2016). Big data integration: A MongoDB database and modular ontologies based approach. In *Procedia computer science* (Vol. 96, pp. 446–455). Elsevier B.V. https://doi.org/10.1016/j.procs.2016.08.099

Agresti, A. (2006). *Generalized linear models. An introduction to categorical data analysis* (2nd ed.). https://doi.org/10.1002/0470114754

Alipanahi, B., Delong, A., Weirauch, M. T., & Frey, B. J. (2015). Predicting the sequence specificities of DNA- and RNA-binding proteins by deep learning. *Nature Biotechnology, 33*(8), 831–838. https://doi.org/10.1038/nbt.3300

Anagnostopoulos, I., Zeadally, S., & Exposito, E. (2016). Handling big data: Research challenges and future directions. *The Journal of Supercomputing, 72*(4), 1494–1516. https://doi.org/10.1007/s11227-016-1677-z

Bansal, S., Chowell, G., Simonsen, L., Vespignani, A., & Viboud, C. (2016). Big data for infectious disease surveillance and modeling. *Journal of Infectious Diseases, 214*, S375–S379. https://doi.org/10.1093/infdis/jiw400

Biological data management. (2021). In *Proceedings of the Thirtieth international conference on Very large data bases* (Vol. 30). Retrieved July 22, 2021, from https://dl.acm.org/doi/10.5555/1316689.1316799.

Birjali, M., Beni-Hssane, A., & Erritali, M. (2018). Evaluation of high-level query languages based on MapReduce in big data. *Journal of Big Data, 5*(1). https://doi.org/10.1186/s40537-018-0146-3

Can Digital Therapeutics Revolutionize Medicine? Retrieved 30 July 2021, from https://www.ideo.com/journal/can-digital-therapeutics-revolutionize-medicine.

Chrimes, D., & Zamani, H. (2017). Using distributed data over HBase in big data analytics platform for clinical services. *Computational and Mathematical Methods in Medicine*. https://doi.org/10.1155/2017/6120820

Cirillo, D., & Valencia, A. (2019). Big data analytics for personalized medicine. *Current Opinion in Biotechnology, 58*, 161–167. https://doi.org/10.1016/j.copbio.2019.03.004

Coronavirus. (2021). *COVID-19) Dashboard | WHO Coronavirus (COVID-19) Dashboard with vaccination data.* Retrieved July 26, 2021, from https://covid19.who.int/.

Corsi, A., de Souza, F. F., Pagani, R. N., & Kovaleski, J. L. (2020). Big data analytics as a tool for fighting pandemics: A systematic review of literature. *Journal of Ambient Intelligence and Humanized Computing*. https://doi.org/10.1007/s12652-020-02617-4

Costa, E., Costa, C., & Santos, M. Y. (2019). Evaluating partitioning and bucketing strategies for hive-based big data warehousing systems. *Journal of Big Data, 6*(1). https://doi.org/10.1186/s40537-019-0196-1

Dash, S., Shakyawar, S. K., Sharma, M., & Kaushik, S. (2019). Big data in healthcare: Management, analysis and future prospects. *Journal of Big Data, 6*(1). https://doi.org/10.1186/s40537-019-0217-0

Data quality dimension - an overview. (2021). ScienceDirect topics. Retrieved July 27, 2021, from https://www.sciencedirect.com/topics/computer-science/data-quality-dimension.

Ditzler, G., Polikar, R., & Rosen, G. (2015). Multi-layer and recursive neural networks for metagenomic classification. *IEEE Transactions on Nano-Bioscience, 14*(6), 608–616. https://doi.org/10.1109/TNB.2015.2461219

Esteva, A., Kuprel, B., Novoa, R. A., Ko, J., Swetter, S. M., Blau, H. M., & Thrun, S. (2017). Dermatologist-level classification of skin cancer with deep neural networks. *Nature*. https://doi.org/10.1038/nature21056

Fabregat, A., Korninger, F., Viteri, G., Sidiropoulos, K., Pablo, M.-G., Ping, P., Wu, G., Stein, L., D'Eustachio, P., & Hermjakob, H. (2018). Reactome graph database: efficient access to complex pathway data. *Plos Computational Biology, 14*. https://doi.org/10.1371/journal.pcbi.1005968

Friedman, C., Hripcsak, G., Johnson, S. B., Cimino, J. J., & Clayton, P. D. (1990). A generalized relational schema for an integrated clinical patient database. In *Proceedings of the annual symposium on computer application in medical care* (p. 335). Retrieved from pmc/articles/PMC2245527/?report=abstract.

Galetsi, P., & Katsaliaki, K. (2019). A review of the literature on big data analytics in healthcare. *Journal of the Operational Research Society, 71*(10), 1511–1529. https://doi.org/10.1080/01605682.2019.1630328

Garattini, C., Raffle, J., Aisyah, D. N., Sartain, F., & Kozlakidis, Z. (2017). Big data analytics, infectious diseases and associated ethical impacts. *Philosophy & Technology, 32*(1), 69–85. https://doi.org/10.1007/S13347-017-0278-Y

Jarynowski, A., Marchewka, D., & Buda, A. (2018). *Internet - assisted risk assessment of infectious diseases in women sexual and reproductive health*. Retrieved from http://arxiv.org/abs/1802.01733.

Kalid, S., Syed, A., Mohammad, A., & Halgamuge, M. N. (2017). Big-data NoSQL databases: A comparison and analysis of "Big-Table", "DynamoDB", and "Cassandra.". In *2017 IEEE 2nd international conference on big data analysis, ICBDA 2017* (pp. 89–93). Institute of Electrical and Electronics Engineers Inc. https://doi.org/10.1109/ICBDA.2017.8078782

Kasson, P. M. (2020). Infectious disease research in the era of big data. *Annual Review of Biomedical Data Science*, 43–59. https://doi.org/10.1146/annurev-biodatasci-121219-025722

Klein, J., Gorton, I., Ernst, N., Donohoe, P., Pham, K., & Matser, C. (2015). Performance evaluation of NoSQL databases: A case study. In *PABS 2015 - Proceedings of the 1st ACM/SPEC international workshop on performance analysis of big data systems* (pp. 5–10). Association for Computing Machinery, Inc. https://doi.org/10.1145/2694730.2694731

Lee, E. C., Asher, J. M., Goldlust, S., Kraemer, J. D., Lawson, A. B., & Bansal, S. (2016). Mind the scales: Harnessing spatial big data for infectious disease surveillance and inference. *Journal of Infectious Diseases, 214*, S409–S413. https://doi.org/10.1093/infdis/jiw344

Lehmann, C., Huber, L. G., Horisberger, T., Scheiba, G., Sima, A. C., & Stockinger, K. (2020). Big data architecture for intelligent maintenance: A focus on query processing and machine learning algorithms. *Journal of Big Data, 7*(1), 1–26. https://doi.org/10.1186/S40537-020-00340-7

Lydia, E. L., Satyanarayan, S., Kumar, K. V., & Ramya, D. (2020). Indexing documents with reliable indexing techniques using Apache Lucene in Hadoop. *International Journal of Intelligent Enterprise, 7*(1–3), 203–214. https://doi.org/10.1504/IJIE.2020.104656

Lysenko, A., Roznovăţ, I. A., Saqi, M., Mazein, A., Rawlings, C. J., & Auffray, C. (2016). *BioData Mining, 9*(23). https://doi.org/10.1186/s13040-016-0102-8

Mayer, G. (2009). *Data management in systems biology I-Overview and bibliography*. Retrieved from https://arxiv.org/abs/0908.0411.

Mehta, N., Pandit, A., & Shukla, S. (2019). Transforming healthcare with big data analytics and artificial intelligence: A systematic mapping study. *Journal of Biomedical Informatics, 100*, 103311. https://doi.org/10.1016/j.jbi.2019.103311

Information, D. P.-I. J. of A., & 2013, undefined Nayak, A., & Poriya, A. (2013). Type of NOSQL databases and its comparison with relational databases. *Citeseer, 5*(4). Retrieved from https://citeseerx.ist.psu.edu/viewdoc/download?doi=10.1.1.402.3372&rep=rep1&type=pdf.

Olivera, P., Danese, S., Jay, N., Natoli, G., & Peyrin-Biroulet, L. (2019). Big data in IBD: A look into the future. *Nature Reviews Gastroenterology & Hepatology, 16*(5), 312–321. https://doi.org/10.1038/s41575-019-0102-5

Pastorino, R., Vito, C. De, Migliara, G., Glocker, K., Binenbaum, I., Ricciardi, W., & Boccia, S. (2019). Benefits and challenges of big data in healthcare: An overview of the European initiatives. *The European Journal of Public Health, 29*, 23–27. https://doi.org/10.1093/EURPUB/CKZ168

Peek, N., Holmes, J. H., & Sun, J. (2018). Technical challenges for big data in biomedicine and health: Data sources, infrastructure, and analytics. *Yearbook of Medical Informatics, 23*(01), 42–47. https://doi.org/10.15265/IY-2014-0018

Poplin, R., Chang, P.-C., Alexander, D., Schwartz, S., Colthrust, T., Ku, A., Newburger, D., Dijamco, J., Nguyen, N., Afshar, P. T., Gross, S. S., Dorfman, L., McLean, C. Y., DePristp, M. A., et al. (2018). A universal SNP and small-indel variant caller using deep neural networks. *Nature Biotechnology, 36*, 983–987. https://doi.org/10.1038/nbt.4235

Raghavendra Kumar, S., & Lalitha, B. (2018). CouchDB: Reliable repository for big data generated by IOT. *International Journal of Research in Advent Technology, 6*(5), 757–761. http://www.ijrat.org/archives/VOLUME-6-ISSUE-5.

Raghupathi, & Kesh. (2007). Interoperable electronic health records design:towards a service-oriented architecture. *e-Service Journal, 5*(3), 39. https://doi.org/10.2979/ESJ.2007.5.3.39

Raghupathi, W., & Raghupathi, V. (2014). Big data analytics in healthcare: Promise and potential. *Health Information Science and Systems, 2*(1). https://doi.org/10.1186/2047-2501-2-3

Rajkomar, A., Oren, E., Chen, K., Dai, A. M., Hajaj, N., Hardt, M., Liu, P. J., Liu, X., Marcus, J., Sun, M., Sundberg, P., Yee, H., Zhang, K., Zhang, Y., Flores, G., Duggan, G. E., Irvine, J., Le, Q., Litsch, K., … Dean, J., et al. (2018). Scalable and accurate deep learning with electronic health records. *NPJ Digital Medicine, 1*(18). https://doi.org/10.1038/S41746-018-0029-1

Rascovsky, S., Delgado, J., Sanz, A., & Radiographics, V. C. (2012). Informatics in radiology: Use of CouchDB for document-based storage of DICOM objects. *Pubs.Rsna.Org, 32*(3), 913–927. https://doi.org/10.1148/rg.323115049

Rathi, M. S. (2017). A brief study of big data analytics using Apache Pig and Hadoop distributed file system. *International Journal of Advanced Research in Computer Engineering & Technology (IJARCET)*. ISSN: 2278-1323, *6*(1).

Riou, C., Pouliquen, B., & Beux, P. Le (2018). A computer-assisted drug prescription system: The model and its implementation in the ATM knowledge base. *Methods of Information in Medicine, 38*(01), 25–30. https://doi.org/10.1055/S-0038-1634147

Ristevski, B., & Chen, M. (2018). Big data analytics in medicine and healthcare. *Journal of Integrative Bioinformatics, 15*(3). https://doi.org/10.1515/JIB-2017-0030

Saraladevi, B., Pazhaniraja, N., Paul, P. V., Basha, M. S. S., & Dhavachelvan, P. (2015). Big data and Hadoop-a study in security perspective. *Procedia Computer Science, 50*, 596–601. https://doi.org/10.1016/J.PROCS.2015.04.091

Schrodt, J., Dudchenko, A., Knaup-Gregori, P., & Ganzinger, M. (2020). Graph-representation of patient data: A systematic literature review. *Journal of Medical Systems, 44*(4), 1–7. https://doi.org/10.1007/S10916-020-1538-4

Segler, M. H. S., Kogej, T., Tyrchan, C., & Waller, M. P. (2018). Generating focused molecule libraries for drug discovery with recurrent neural networks. *ACS Central Science, 4*(1), 120. https://doi.org/10.1021/ACSCENTSCI.7B00512

Sepah, S. C., Jiang, L., & Peters, A. L. (2015). Long-term outcomes of a web-based diabetes prevention program: 2-year results of a single-arm longitudinal study. *Journal of Medical Internet Research, 17*(4), e92. https://doi.org/10.2196/JMIR.4052

Singh, S., Yang, Y., Póczos, B., & Ma, J. (2018). *Predicting enhancer-promoter interaction from genomic sequence with deep neural networks* (p. 085241). BioRxiv. https://doi.org/10.1101/085241

Stanaway, J. D., Afshin, A., Gakidou, E., Lim, S. S., Abate, D., Abate, K. H., … Murray, C. J. L. (2018). Global, regional, and national comparative risk assessment of 84 behavioural, environmental and occupational, and metabolic risks or clusters of risks for 195 countries and territories, 1990–2017: A systematic analysis for the global burden of disease study 2017. *The Lancet*, 1923–1994.

Stanway, J. D., Afshin, A., Gakidou, E., Lim, S. S., Abate, D., Abate, K. H., Abbafati, C., Abbasi, N., Abbastabar, H., Abd-Allah, F., Abdela, J., Abdelalim, A., Abdollahpour, I., Abdulkader, R. S., Abebe, M., Abebe, Z., Abere, S. F., Abil, O. Z., Abraha, H. N., Murray, C. J. L., et al. (2017). Global, regional, and national comparative risk assessment of 84 behavioural, environmental and occupational, and metabolic risks or clusters of risks for 195 countries and territories, 1990-2017: a systematic analysis for the Global Burden of Disease Study 2017. *Lancet, 392*(10159), 1923–1994. https://doi.org/10.1016/S0140-6736(18)32225-6

Thacker, S. B., & Stroup, D. F. (1994). Future directions for comprehensive public health surveillance and health information systems in the United States. *American Journal of Epidemiology, 140*(5), 383–397. https://doi.org/10.1093/OXFORDJOURNALS.AJE.A117261

The Rise of digital therapeutics | navigate the future.(2021). Retrieved July 30, 2021, from https://blogs.3ds.com/northamerica/the-rise-of-digital-therapeutics/.

Tsiouris, K., Pezoulas, V. C., Zervakis, M., Konitsiotis, S., Koutsouris, D. D., & Fotiadis, D. I. (2018). A long short-term memory deep learning network for the prediction of epileptic seizures using EEG signals. *Computers in Biology and Medicine, 99*, 24–37. https://doi.org/10.1016/J.COMPBIOMED.2018.05.019

Vitabile, S., Marks, M., Stojanovic, D., Pllana, S., Molina, J. M , Krzyszton, M., & Salomie, I. (2019). Medical data processing and analysis for remote health and activities monitoring. In *Lecture notes in computer science (including subseries lecture notes in artificial intelligence and lecture notes in bioinformatics)* (pp. 186–220).

What is data interpretation? Definition, methods & examples.(2018). Retrieved July 30, 2021, from https://www.datapine.com/blog/data-interpretation-methods-benefits-problems/.

Wu, P. Y., Cheng, C. W., Kaddi, C. D., Venugopalan, J., Hoffman, R., & Wang, M. D. (2017). Omic and electronic health record big data analytics for precision medicine. *IEEE Transactions on Bio-Medical Engineering, 64*(2), 263–273. https://doi.org/10.1109/TBME.2016.2573285

Xu, W., Zhou, Z., Zhou, H., Zhang, W., & Xie, J. (2014). MongoDB improves big data analysis performance on electric health record system. *Communications in Computer and Information Science, 461*, 350–357. https://doi.org/10.1007/978-3-662-45283-7_36

Yoon, B. H., Kim, S. K., & Kim, S. Y. (2017). Use of graph database for the integration of heterogeneous biological data. *Genomics & informatics, 15*(1), 19–27. https://doi.org/10.5808/GI.2017.15.1.19

Zhou, J., Theesfeld, C. L., Yao, K., Chen, K. M., Wong, A. K., & Troyanskaya, O. G. (2018). Deep learning sequence-based ab initio prediction of variant effects on expression and disease risk. *Nature Genetics, 50*(8), 1171–1179. https:// QCdoi.org/10.1038/s41588-018-0160-6.

Chapter 8

Big data analytics for health: a comprehensive review of techniques and applications

Rehab A. Rayan[1], Christos Tsagkaris[2], Imran Zafar[3], Dimitrios V. Moysidis[4] and Andreas S. Papazoglou[5]

[1]Department of Epidemiology, High Institute of Public Health, Alexandria University, Alexandria, Egypt; [2]Novel Global Community Educational Foundation, Hebersham, New South Wales, Australia; [3]Department of Bioinformatics and Computational Biology, Virtual University of Pakistan, Punjab, Pakistan, [4]Hippokration General Hospital of Thessaloniki, Aristotle University of Thessaloniki, Thessaloniki, Macedonia, Greece; [5]Athens Naval Hospital, Athens, Attiki, Greece

1. Introduction

Electronic healthcare data and electronic health records (EHRs) have contributed to achieving some population healthcare objectives such as healthcare services delivery, clinical research, public health surveillance, and healthcare facilities' logistics (Wang & Alexander, 2020). Telehealth eases conveying health services similarly to urban and rural patients. Managing individual healthcare could be assisted by smartphone apps. Big data fields sustain the prospective to accomplish such objectives and bring prime services (Mendelson & Mendelson, 2017). Individualized prognostic analytics is a growing technique of conveying health services that depend on the sameness of sick persons; when a new patient demands care, alike patients are detected from historical datasets, perceptivities are drawn from the records, and individualized forecasting are done. For instance, such a technique has been practiced in medication-recommending systems, determining hazard elements for alike patients, forecasting cardiac arrest based on telemonitoring data, and providing individualized healthcare (Cano et al., 2017).

Illnesses and healthcare systems frequently rely on many familial factors, ecological statuses, and different elements, like sex, medical data, and workout plans. Individualized healthcare cannot learn everything expressly via clinical experiments. Investigators might employ innovative formulas to examine big clinical data and determine the models or courses of illnesses known as black-box medicine that could greatly propagate individualized healthcare with immense gains (Ii & Nicholson, 2015). Fine-tuned EHR systems could be finer utilized for big data in healthcare contexts. EHR systems in the time to come shall constitute "genetic clinical decision support" for enforcing individualized and timely healthcare. Clinical decision support is needed to translate hereditary fluctuations and their uses in a particular illness or medication for each patient. It eases timely reasoning for a patient's familial chart, like whole-genome sequencing (Mathias et al., 2016). Precision healthcare centers on features of persons which consider ecological, -omics (i.e., genomics, metabolomics, proteomics, etc.), societal, makeup, and mental factors. It is resource driven, patient centered, and data intensive. Its play element is the data derived from whole-genome sequencing and big data analytics that would serve precision healthcare (Rothstein, 2017).

Artificial intelligence (AI) has been employed in investigating pictures in radiology, pathology, and dermatology with rapid diagnosis and ample quality. AI assists lessen healthcare-related faults, suggest precision medical care for complicated illnesses, perfect healthcare processes for prolonged health problems, and improve patient registration into clinical experiments (Miller & Brown, 2018). Unsupervised, supervised, and reinforced learning are types of machine learning (ML) techniques. Unsupervised learning determines concealed constitutions in untagged data. Supervised learning exploits tagged data for training, produces a framework, and sorts fresh observations grounded on that framework. Reinforcement learning employs a response mechanism to increase the additive reward and better outcomes (Ulfarsson et al., 2016). Text mining has been practiced in diverse businesses, like the biomedical business. Three technical arms—AI, ML, and text mining—have been brought to the health sector (Pramanik et al., 2017).

Big Data Analytics for Healthcare. https://doi.org/10.1016/B978-0-323-91907-4.00002-9

Medical data from carers and identities of patients demand confirmation for each entrée. Data cryptography is an efficacious technique for saving delicate data from an unlicensed entrée, defending data possession end-to-end of its lifecycle, and refraining from vulnerability to breach (Abouelmehdi et al., 2017). Defending genetic big data and the internet of things (IoT) has gotten so crucial. Medical sequencing demands to pursue rigorous constructs, chiefly due to the Health Insurance Portability and Accounting Act (HIPAA). Ahead of the current adoption of cloud-driven medical sequencing, information safety in clouds demands to be ascertained. This should be established on a dependable and spirited Internet of Living Things structure with secured privacy, wholeness, and accessibility (Pizzolante et al., 2018). Moral entailments have been referred to when medical subject areas such as the nursing battle over interrogations of informed consent, information possession, and secrecy, among others. Big data analytics is anticipated to let out unexpected links between information parts and forecast succeeding health behavior (Milton, 2017).

There is a growing body of big data applications in healthcare. This growth is reflected in current scientific research (Borges do Nascimento et al., 2021); however, the concept of big data remains vague. At this point, it is useful to summarize the existing findings, provide an overview of relevant literature review and applications, and discuss challenges and paths to advancement in the field.

This chapter aims to present the techniques and technology intelligence, models and tools, improvements and technical advancement, and diverse limitations of big data analytics in healthcare. The following segment presents the sorts, origins, and characteristics of big data in healthcare; Segment 2 entails a tripartite search of the literature containing i) the definition of big data in healthcare ii) an umbrella review of reviews and surveys assessing big data application in various domains of health and healthcare, and iii) an overview of big data applications in healthcare. Segment 3 carries on with the uses and gains of big data and big data analytics in health; Segment 4 shows the improvements and technical advancement of big data analytics in health; Segment 5 deals with the opportunities and limitations or obstacles of big data use in health, and the closing segment is the conclusion and way forward.

2. Literature review

2.1 Methodology

The authors conducted an umbrella review literature search in PubMed/Medline and Cochrane with keywords (Big data, analytics, healthcare, applications, research, digital health, wearables, devices, software). Relevant peer-reviewed reviews of the literature and metaresearch published in English, French, or German between 2015 and 2021 were included. Studies with a significant conflict of interest were excluded. The authors identified the included studies through title and abstract screening and assessed the full text of the studies that fulfilled the inclusion criteria. Papers were deemed appropriate for inclusion by the consensus of at least three authors. 23 review studies were deemed appropriate for inclusion following full-text analysis.

Additionally, gray literature including product licensing reports, policy briefs, and case studies was included in the literature search and discussion subsections related to the definition of big data in healthcare and the applications of big data in biomedicine. Their selection was based on relevance (recent), time of publication, and scientific or technical rigor. The authors declare no financial or other ties guiding to the inclusion of reports and case studies. The study technique applied is descriptive, specifically content analysis, that is meant to comprehensively discuss a message. The structure of this study is not meant to test a specific hypothesis or evaluate the correlation among elements.

2.2 Dimensions of big data in health

Health data involve (Fang et al., 2016; Terry, 2012) genetic data such as genotypic, gene expression, and DNA sequencing; medical data, like temperature, blood pressure, heart rate, and others; man-made data, like doctors' telecommunications, remarks, and report records; electronic data from different clinical sensing elements, domestic monitoring, intelligent devices, and telemedicine (Yang et al., 2014); biometric data such as fingermarks, iris scan, signatures, and others (Erdman et al., 2013); administrative, transaction and business data such as health insurance claims and associated invoicing, fiscal data and listing; Web and social network data; communications such as healthcare acknowledgment Info and medical investigating papers; and different crucial data like diseased person feedback and unfavorable effects.

Biomedical big data has obtained significant care since medical data demand security for their susceptibility and inherent exposure; there is a substantial possibility to amend diagnosis, boost clinical care, and prevent illnesses (Mittelstadt & Floridi, 2016). EHRs consist of big data sources with significant masses of datasets and diversity in arranges such as structured, semistructured, and unstructured data, that pull in obstacles of how to alter unstructured medical data into knowledge and gains for diseased persons (Baro et al., 2015). Medical big data exists in diverse sets of EHR such as mobile devices, CSV, flat files, and others and from either inside origin such as clinical decision support systems, and others or outer origins like labs and insurance organizations (Sabharwal et al., 2016).

The primary roots of medical big data are from remunerators and suppliers and involve EHR, medical imaging, claims, pharmacy registers, and others. Data analytics will continue flourishing from -omics such as epigenomics, genomics, proteomics, and metabolomics data. EHR alone calculates for a limited contribution of healthcare data; genomics brings about twofold the quantity; and patient-produced sources, like Internet activities, detectors, and mobile phones, yield the significant bulk of health big data (Monteith et al., 2016). Additionally, spatial big data, which are vast in mass, speed, and diversity of origins, have been used for epidemiologic investigation (Lee et al., 2016).

Omics are getting big data driven with diverse sorts of natural data involving genomics, proteomics, metabolomics, etc. Systems medicine, a fresh technique of medicine, has been introduced with a general perspective of the living thing and different assemblage factors which interact and organize compound systems. Collective multiomics methodologies exhibit to a greater extent inclusive results since diverse levels of illness-associate data are examined jointly. Several multilayer collective methodologies, such as iCluster and aggregate databases' consolidation, are employed for various sorts of data; however, others such as Camelot and CNAmet are employed for a particular collection of -omics (Castellani et al., 2016). A form of big data in life science is yielded by the advanced output molecular assessment where Microarray is a set of this field which has presented life science to significant data with a broad magnitude, speed, and diversity. It analyzes the expression of messenger RNA of sequences and its uses involve researching the effects of familial alterations or therapies on gene expression, supervising cell development below different states (Karimi et al., 2016).

2.3 Big data—based research in health

Research based on big data can be classified thematically to studies focusing on metabolic diseases, cardiovascular conditions, oncology, mental health, neurological conditions, pulmonology, and public health. A number of these studies focus on specific big data—based methodologies, while other studies provide a comparative assessment of different methodologies and applications such as neural networks, forest plots, etc. The bulk of relevant evidence has been published from 2015 onwards. An overview of these studies is presented in Table 8.1.

2.4 Big data analytics applications for health

The probable estimate of clinically huge information has been shown in Intervention of personal medication; Use of dynamic clinical emotional support networks, such as examination of programmed clinical images and extraction of clinical briefs; Customize the demonstration and treatment options and informational messages to help the patient behave in a desired manner through the use of mobile phones; Population well-being analyzes the dependence on far-reaching information that revealed examples that may have been overlooked (Roski et al., 2014).

The usage of tremendous data for health involves identifying illnesses ahead of time when they could be controlled further expeditiously and with success; controlling the health of a specific group and persons and determining the erroneous rendering of healthcare services further rapidly and suitably and different established profits in the areas of infection control, recognizable evidence of modifiable disease factors, and sexual intercourse plan to change welfare. You can expect and/or evaluate certain events or results depending on a large amount of information recorded, such as residual length; patients choosing an elective medical procedure; patients who are unlikely to earn money from medical treatment; complexities; patients at risk of unexpected problems; patients at risk for sepsis, MRSA, *C. difficile*, or other emergency room disease; patients with disease/disease movement at risk of disease movement; the causative element of the disease/infectious movement; and possible comorbid conditions.

The regions where improved information and research yield the best results are: recognizing patients who are the largest clients of wellness assets or who are more exposed to hostile results; Give people the information they need to make informed decisions and manage their well-being even more profitably, as well as adopt and track more beneficial methods, distinguish drugs, projects, and cycles that do not provide obvious benefits or are too expensive, reduce consumption by recognizing ecological or lifestyle factors that amplify the hazard or trigger outcomes and change treatment design in the same way; Improve results by looking at important family metrics; monitor the welfare of the population by identifying weak intolerant populations during the onset or debacle of the disease; and consolidate clinical, budgeting, and operational information to analyze asset use in a profitable and ongoing manner (Raghupathi & Raghupathi, 2014).

Quantum computing gathers popularity and seems to be a possible solution for big data research. For example, the quantum support vector machine has been used to classify new data for training and classification measures. In several

TABLE 8.1 An overview of the studies discussing big data in health published from 2015 onwards.

The topic of the study	Type of the study	Key findings	Reference
Metabolic diseases/Diabetes mellitus (DM)	Survey	Use of big data analytics (preprocessing methods, feature extraction methods, machine learning–based identification, classification, and diagnosis of DM, artificial intelligence–based intelligent DM assistant and performance measures) to determine the best practices for detection, diagnosis, and self-management of DM.	Chaki et al. (2020)
Metabolic diseases/Diabetes mellitus (DM)	Survey	The application of real-world deep learning–based methodologies in screening patients with DM for diabetic retinopathy leads to a reduction in personnel and screening expenditure but faces ethical limitations related to the accountability of potential medical errors.	Nielsen et al. (2019)
Metabolic diseases/Diabetes mellitus (DM)	Survey	Data-driven prediction and modeling of serum glucose deviation in patients with DM type 1. Several big data–based methodologies (recurrent neural networks, feed-forward neural networks, support vector machines, self-organizing maps, the Gaussian process, genetic algorithm and programs, deep neural networks) can comprehensively predict serum glucose dynamics. Integrating carbohydrates intake in this model remains challenging.	Woldaregay et al. (2019)
Metabolic diseases/Diabetes mellitus (DM)	Survey	Big data–based machine learning can support outcomes' research in DM. Support vector machine and naive Bayesian appear more effective because of their capacity to integrate more variables and targets than other methodologies.	Abhari et al. (2019)
Metabolic diseases/Diabetes mellitus (DM)	Survey	Data mining in enriched datasets that combine clinical and biological information are necessary to advance diabetes care.	Kavakiotis et al. (2017)
Cardiovascular conditions	Survey	Big data–based intelligent systems (neural networks) can be more accurate than established clinical algorithms and scales in the diagnosis of acute coronary syndromes. Such tools will be essential for diagnostic work-up and decision-making in the future.	Sprockel et al. (2018)
Cardiovascular conditions	Survey	Big data–based models predicting QT interval prolongation in the Echocardiogram (ECG) have a major potential to benefit both outpatients and inpatients. However, their cost-effectiveness needs to be further assessed.	Tomaselli Muensterman and Tisdale (2018)
Cardiovascular conditions	Survey	Big data–based machine learning can predict cardiac arrest. The existing evidence needs to be validated in real clinical environments.	Layeghian Javan et al. (2018)
Cardiovascular conditions	Survey	There is sufficient evidence for the efficacy of data mining methodology for the creation of models assessing the presence, the subtype, the severity of heart failure, related adverse events, and mortality. Implementation studies need to be carried out.	Tripoliti et al. (2017)
Neurological conditions	Survey	Big data methodologies including random forests, support vector machines, decision trees, and neural networks have been used for the prediction of cerebrovascular stroke outcomes. Relevant studies need methodological improvement to be assessed in the real-world clinical context.	Wang et al. (2020)

Neurological conditions	Survey	Random forest learning and convolutional neural networks have been used to predict large vessel occlusions—ischemic strokes. Standardized assessment performance tools are necessary to advance relevant research.	Murray et al. (2020)
Mental health	Survey	Big data–based suicide prevention tools yield high levels of risk classification accuracy in the prediction of suicidal behaviors. Ethical limitations remain challenging.	Bernert et al. (2020)
Mental health	Survey	Big data can complement existing models and classifications for the study of suicidal and nonsuicidal self-injurious thoughts and behaviors. Developing common and standardized reporting criteria is essential.	Burke et al. (2019)
Mental health	Survey	Most big data applications in mental health focus on the detection and diagnosis of conditions. Further research is necessary concerning the management and monitoring of these conditions using big data–based digital health.	Shatte et al. (2019)
Mental health	Survey	The application of big data in bipolar disorder (BP) is challenged by the heterogeneity of the clinical presentation of the disease. BP modeling can contribute to screening, personalized diagnosis, and monitoring.	Librenza-Garcia et al. (2017)
Oncology	Survey	Computational decision-making tools can improve process outcomes and adherence to guidelines; however, no improvement in clinical outcomes has been reported.	Klarenbeek et al. (2020)
Oncology	Survey	Support vector machine has yielded a major potential in the prognostic prediction of head and neck cancer utilizing genomic dataset's analysis.	Patil et al. (2019)
Oncology	Survey	Feature-based algorithms are more accurate than deep learning algorithms in the detection of lung cancer across the LIDC-IDRI imaging dataset. Structured reporting systems need to be developed.	Pehrson et al. (2019)
Oncology	Survey	Deep learning algorithms can achieve classification accuracy between 68% and 99.6% and detection accuracy between 80.6% and 94% in images retrieved from databases different from the LIDC-IDRI database.	Li et al. (2019)
COVID-19	Survey	Data mining can optimize response to the dynamic changes occurring in COVID-19's epidemiology. The efficacy of big data research methodologies is subject to the given problem and the available data and infrastructure.	Albahri et al. (2020)
Pulmonology	Survey	The available models for the prediction of asthma exacerbation appear deficient in terms of validation. Concordance statistics (c-statistic) can be used to create an effective model based on existing data	Bridge et al. (2020)
Public health	Survey	Big data research about the pharmacological effects of pregnancy needs to be implemented in (i) obtaining reliable data from clinical records, (ii) optimizing animal experiments and translational studies to validate hypotheses, (iii) improve decision-making support systems.	Davidson and Boland (2020)
Public health	Survey	Logistic regression, support vector machines, naive Bayes, ensemble learning, and deep learning are effective for big data analytics of user-generated content related to mental health and cancer.	Yin et al. (2019)

scientific fields, these quantum methods can be applied. The neural quantum network has been recuperated with an electroencephalogram to improve the separation of the signal. To maximize radiation intensity, quantum annealing has also been used. Likewise, further uses of quantum methods are available in terms of healthcare, for example, quantum and quantum microscopes.

3. Discussion

Big data in biomedicine constitutes a growing field of research. PubMed search reveals more than 1000 original studies assessing various big data-based applications and interventions in healthcare. The exact number varies depending on the search algorithm, while more information is available in tech-oriented databases and gray literature. The above-presented umbrella review describes the major potential of big data-based applications to several domains of health and healthcare including metabolic and cardiovascular health, neurological and mental conditions, oncology, pulmonology, and public health. Big data has served as a pool where AI and machine or big learning techniques were applied to create simple or multivariate models. Studies related to multisystem diseases, such as diabetes mellitus, faced challenges in modeling dynamic processes like carbohydrate intake (Woldaregay et al., 2019). The lack of standardized performance assessments was an additional challenge (Pehrson et al., 2019). Despite the recorded effectiveness of ML, DL, and AI Big data mining applications in a diverse context of disease prediction, diagnosis, monitoring, and management, ethics, and accountability about medical errors or missed diagnoses constitute additional barriers to the integration of big data in healthcare. Standardized reporting and assessment criteria are essential for the integration of big data in clinical practice at a large scale.

In the development of health and science, the rapidly growing field of large-scale data analysis has begun to play a central role. It has provided tools for capturing, managing analyzes, and assimilating large amounts of different, structured, and unstructured data created by existing healthcare systems. To facilitate the method of care delivery and disease research, extensive data collection has recently been used. However, some fundamental problems that exist in the big data paradigm still hamper the pace of research's access and growth in this space. The world goes off the screen and is analyzed every second, either via Google Maps on the phone, Netflix habits, the care system, or what you have booked online in the shopping cart.

The former research confirmed that there are large-scale Big Data technologies that come from different disciplines, such as analytics, computer science, applied mathematics, and economics. Various sources of big data in the healthcare sector include hospital reports, patient records, and results of medical examinations and devices used on the IoT. Much of the big data that applies to public health care also comes from biomedical research. To obtain useful information, this data requires careful handling and analysis. Otherwise, it is easy to find a solution by analyzing Big Data and finding a needle in a haystack. By opening new avenues for modern processing, efficient management, analysis, and understanding of big data, better understanding the real-world will change the game. Therefore, various sectors, such as health, are taking strong action to modify these possible urgent improvements to the facilities and the economic benefits on their own. Modern healthcare organizations can eventually revolutionize medical therapies and personalized medicine by incorporating a vast amount of biomedical knowledge and care. Because these approaches are field based, both large data and other amounts of data, such as the healthcare system, can be added to the different analysis tools and applications.

3.1 Opportunities and challenges

The transformation of several subsectors of healthcare including AI, techniques, infrastructure, cloud computing, data processing, biosensors, wearables, IoT, smart health, privacy and security, health economics, and management by big data analytics has been regarded as a source of both opportunity and controversy (Costa, 2014). The opportunities for such a transformation have been outlined in the United Nations' Sustainable Development Goals (SDGs). The SDGs consist of a global call for action to decrease poverty, protect the planet, and ensure that all people live in peace and prosperity by 2030. This action is oriented to 17 pillars out of which two can be greatly connected with the integration of big data analytics in healthcare.

Goal 3 focuses on health and wellbeing, and Goal 9 focuses on industry innovation and infrastructure that can be promoted with big data analytics. Each goal is analyzed in subtargets. Goal 3 pertains to reducing global maternal mortality, and preventable deaths of newborns and children, combat AIDS, tuberculosis, malaria, hepatitis, and other communicable diseases, reducing premature mortality from noncommunicable diseases, enhance the prevention and treatment of substance abuse, decrease traffic-related mortality, strengthen control over tobacco and other hazardous chemicals, and support the research and development of medicines and vaccines, either directly or by investing in related administration and infrastructure. Meanwhile, Goal 9 pertains to developing reliable, environmentally friendly, and resilient infrastructure, promote sustainable industrialization, making credit and value chains and markets accessible to small-scale enterprises, merging industrial and scientific breakthroughs, supporting the developing countries in terms of industrialization and domestic technology development, and increasing access to internet-based information and communication resources (Nakatani, 2016).

In both cases, the integration of big data to disruptive innovations in healthcare requires the collaboration between science, researchers, and clinicians, on one side and industry on the other side (Dimitrov, 2016). From a scientific point of view, rigorous data analysis can positively impact much of the healthcare crisis brought up by SDG 3 such as the elimination of communicable diseases (AIDS, hepatitis, tuberculosis, etc.) and noncommunicable diseases. At the same time, tackling maternal, neonatal, and child mortality requires enough data to be collected and analyzed, which can be achieved in a big data context. IoT interconnectivity of smart sensors and wearables can be used in the same context (Aceto et al., 2020; Tian et al., 2019). Tobacco control can also be promoted in collecting and analyzing information concerning the addiction traits and patterns to design more efficient interventions (Alemi et al., 2018). The parallel existence of multiple classification systems for tobacco and other substances' addiction has been underlined by Lesch et al. as an obstacle to providing personalized addiction care. Assessing and improving the existing classifications with big data analytics can now shape a deeper understanding of addiction medicine (Schlaff et al., 2011).

On the other hand, developing and testing wearables, sensors, and smart health devices suitable to the needs of national or local communities will encourage small-scale entrepreneurship schemes such as start-ups and spin-offs to engage in positive action upscaling their business plan at the same time. Connecting everyday clinical practice to big data analytics for decision-making or research purposes is also expected to make the internet more accessible. If patients need access to the internet for their smart or wearable sensors, internet access can be provided even "by prescription" to ensure their connectivity (Moro Visconti & Morea, 2019). Apart from big data analytics services, wider access to the internet can subsequently contribute to a higher level of digital and health literacy in our communities (Dicker & Jim, 2018).

However, several challenges arise as well. There are still issues to be resolved concerning the very technology of big data analytics. Particularly, experts are currently facing a dilemma when it comes to checking the validity of the results. This can be done either through statistical tests or through interpretable models. The computational efficacy of statistical tests as well as their capacity to use all the available data and not a part of them is questionable. On the other hand, interpretative models are based on ML, a promising yet developing field, and specialists highlight that several aspects of these models, including their ability to detect rules and patterns, need further improvement (Islam et al., 2015; Zhou et al., 2014).

Additionally, big data usually exists in distributed datasets, with different owners possessing different parts of the dataset. Analyzing the entire data requires that all the owners provide the same level of access to a central user. Technically, experts could overcome this challenge by making the entire data accessible to central users, which is currently not possible for regulatory reasons (Valerio et al., 2017).

At this point, we understand that the establishment of big data analytics in healthcare faces several regulatory challenges as well. There should be harmonized legislation for the use of data at a global level. Although this can be accomplished in specific parts of the world, such as the European Union, this has never been achieved globally. The perception of privacy and data protection differs from country to country, leading policymaking efforts at these ends to a stalemate (Baldini et al., 2018; Cumbley & Church, 2013; Islam et al., 2015).

Besides, actual data protection issues should be considered. Who will be the owners of the dataset's parts, and who will be the central user? Is every hospital, clinic, and healthcare unit provided with the necessary equipment or private or public entities will meditate? The identity of the central user who will be warranted access to the whole datasets—or a great portion of them—is also questionable and may lead to controversy among physicians and patients (Choudhury et al., 2014; Cumbley & Church, 2013). The present study attempts to provide a comprehensive overview, identifying challenges and future directions along the way. It can serve as a source of information for clinicians to increase their big data literacy and support their involvement in relevant research in real world healthcare settings. All in all, big data analytics have great potential in healthcare, if obscure aspects of their technical and regulatory implementation are clarified.

4. Conclusions

Big data analytics has been employed in population, individualized and precision health, timely telemedicine, and e-health, etc. Cloud computing eases big data investigation. Big data analytics in health could be effectuated on open-source platforms and means. Quantum computation is anticipated to highly improve big data analytics in health. Sensing elements have been broadly applied in compiling diseased persons' data. Vital signs, like body temperature, respiratory and cardiac rates, blood pressure, and sugar levels could be systematically compiled via different detectors. Wearable body sensors serve personalized e-health and m-health, where big data analytics and IoT are anticipated to be pivotal assisting techniques. Big data analytics in health depends on a firm basis established on clouds and different advanced innovative techniques, like IoT, holds immense data, allows incorporating well-being assets and healthcare facilities' heritage systems, and sustains secrecy covering and cybersecurity.

Overall barriers of big data in healthcare are associated with great mass, diversity, speed, accuracy, presentation, secrecy, cybersecurity, and others. Additionally, leading disputes of big data and big data analytics in health particularly exist in unifying and managing silo or divided data because of healthcare givers; data mining from broken and disparate origins; cross-border care and EHR governance for various states, languages, and society; and the discrepancy between public big data and subject-centered healthcare, hence, constant interactions between big and small data. Subsequent research issues of big data analytics in healthcare: combining and examining semistructured and unstructured data, scaling, and managing stream data timely, mining fast stream and detector data, accommodating deep learning to stream data, secrecy-conserving data mining, data mining of heterogeneous big data, big data presentation, cloud computing, timely managing of complex data, and adopting big data analytics.

Acknowledgments

We would like to thank all those who contributed to the article.

Funding statement: No sources of funding.

Conflicts of interest: The authors declare that they have no conflicts of interest to report regarding the present study.

References

Abhari, S., Kalhori, S. R. N., Ebrahimi, M., Hasannejadasl, H., & Garavand, A. (2019). Artificial intelligence applications in type 2 diabetes mellitus care: Focus on machine learning methods. *Healthcare Informatics Research, 25*(4), 248–261. https://doi.org/10.4258/hir.2019.25.4.248

Abouelmehdi, K., Beni-Hssane, A., Khaloufi, H., & Saadi, M. (2017). Big data security and privacy in healthcare: A review. *Procedia Computer Science, 113*, 73–80. https://doi.org/10.1016/j.procs.2017.08.292

Aceto, G., Persico, V., & Pescapé, A. (2020). Industry 4.0 and health: Internet of things, big data, and cloud computing for healthcare 4.0. *Journal of Industrial Information Integration, 18*, 100129. https://doi.org/10.1016/j.jii.2020.100129

Albahri, A. S., Hamid, R. A., Alwan, J. K., Al-Qays, Z. T., Zaidan, A. A., Zaidan, B. B., Albahri, A. O. S., AlAmoodi, A. H., Khlaf, J. M., Almahdi, E. M., Thabet, E., Hadi, S. M., Mohammed, K. I., Alsalem, M. A., Al-Obaidi, J. R., & Madhloom, H. T. (2020). Role of biological data mining and machine learning techniques in detecting and diagnosing the novel coronavirus (COVID-19): A systematic review. *Journal of Medical Systems, 44*(7), 122. https://doi.org/10.1007/s10916-020-01582-x

Alemi, F., Avramovic, S., & Schwartz, M. D. (2018). Electronic health record-based screening for substance abuse. *Big Data, 6*(3), 214–224. https://doi.org/10.1089/big.2018.0002

Baldini, G., Botterman, M., Neisse, R., & Tallacchini, M. (2018). Ethical design in the internet of things. *Science and Engineering Ethics, 24*(3), 905–925. https://doi.org/10.1007/s11948-016-9754-5

Baro, E., Degoul, S., Beuscart, R., & Chazard, E. (2015). Toward a literature-driven definition of big data in healthcare. *BioMed Research International, 2015*, e639021. https://doi.org/10.1155/2015/639021

Bernert, R. A., Hilberg, A. M., Melia, R., Kim, J. P., Shah, N. H., & Abnousi, F. (2020). Artificial intelligence and suicide prevention: A systematic review of machine learning investigations. *International Journal of Environmental Research and Public Health, 17*(16), E5929. https://doi.org/10.3390/ijerph17165929

Borges do Nascimento, I. J., Marcolino, M. S., Abdulazeem, H. M., Weerasekara, I., Azzopardi-Muscat, N., Gonçalves, M. A., & Novillo-Ortiz, D. (2021). Impact of big data analytics on people's health: Overview of systematic reviews and recommendations for future studies. *Journal of Medical Internet Research, 23*(4), e27275. https://doi.org/10.2196/27275

Bridge, J., Blakey, J. D., & Bonnett, L. J. (2020). A systematic review of methodology used in the development of prediction models for future asthma exacerbation. *BMC Medical Research Methodology, 20*(1), 22. https://doi.org/10.1186/s12874-020-0913-7

Burke, T. A., Ammerman, B. A., & Jacobucci, R. (2019). The use of machine learning in the study of suicidal and non-suicidal self-injurious thoughts and behaviors: A systematic review. *Journal of Affective Disorders, 245*, 869–884. https://doi.org/10.1016/j.jad.2018.11.073

Cano, I., Tenyi, A., Vela, E., Miralles, F., & Roca, J. (2017). Perspectives on big data applications of health information. *Current Opinion in Systems Biology, 3*, 36–42. https://doi.org/10.1016/j.coisb.2017.04.012

Castellani, G. C., Menichetti, G., Garagnani, P., Giulia Bacalini, M., Pirazzini, C., Franceschi, C., Collino, S., Sala, C., Remondini, D., Giampieri, E., Mosca, E., Bersanelli, M., Vitali, S., Valle, I. F. do, Liò, P., & Milanesi, L. (2016). Systems medicine of inflammaging. *Briefings in Bioinformatics, 17*(3), 527–540. https://doi.org/10.1093/bib/bbv062

Chaki, J., Thillai Ganesh, S., Cidham, S. K., & Ananda Theertan, S. (2020). Machine learning and artificial intelligence based diabetes mellitus detection and self-management: A systematic review. *Journal of King Saud University - Computer and Information Sciences*. https://doi.org/10.1016/j.jksuci.2020.06.013

Choudhury, S., Fishman, J. R., McGowan, M. L., & Juengst, E. T. (2014). Big data, open science and the brain: Lessons learned from genomics. *Frontiers in Human Neuroscience, 8*, 239. https://doi.org/10.3389/fnhum.2014.00239

Costa, F. F. (2014). Big data in biomedicine. *Drug Discovery Today, 19*(4), 433–440. https://doi.org/10.1016/j.drudis.2013.10.012

Cumbley, R., & Church, P. (2013). Is "big data" creepy? *Computer Law & Security Review, 29*(5), 601–609. https://doi.org/10.1016/j.clsr.2013.07.007

Davidson, L., & Boland, M. R. (2020). Enabling pregnant women and their physicians to make informed medication decisions using artificial intelligence. *Journal of Pharmacokinetics and Pharmacodynamics, 47*(4), 305–318. https://doi.org/10.1007/s10928-020-09685-1

Dicker, A. P., & Jim, H. S. L. (2018). Intersection of digital health and oncology. *JCO Clinical Cancer Informatics, 2*, 1–4. https://doi.org/10.1200/CCI.18.00070

Dimitrov, D. V. (2016). Medical internet of things and big data in healthcare. *Healthcare Informatics Research, 22*(3), 156–163. https://doi.org/10.4258/hir.2016.22.3.156

Erdman, A. G., Keefe, D. F., & Schiestl, R. (2013). Grand challenge: Applying regulatory science and big data to improve medical device innovation. *IEEE Transactions on Biomedical Engineering, 60*(3), 700–706 https://doi.org/10.1109/TBME.2013.2244600

Fang, R., Pouyanfar, S., Yang, Y., Chen, S.-C., & Iyengar, S. S. (2016). Computational health informatics in the big data age: A survey. *ACM Computing Surveys, 49*(1), 12:1–12:36. https://doi.org/10.1145/2932707

Ii, P., & Nicholson, W. (2015). Big data, patents, and the future of medicine (SSRN scholarly paper ID 2659797). *Social Science Research Network*. https://papers.ssrn.com/abstract=2659797.

Islam, S. M. R., Kwak, D., Kabir, M. D. H., Hossain, M., & Kwak, K.-S. (2015). The internet of things for health care: A comprehensive survey. *IEEE Access, 3*, 678–708. https://doi.org/10.1109/ACCESS.2015.2437951

Karimi, N., Samavi, S., Soroushmehr, S. M. R., Shirani, S., & Najarian, K. (2016). Toward practical guideline for design of image compression algorithms for biomedical applications. *Expert Systems with Applications, 56*, 360–367. https://doi.org/10.1016/j.eswa.2016.02.047

Kavakiotis, I., Tsave, O., Salifoglou, A., Maglaveras, N., Vlahavas, I., & Chouvarda, I. (2017). Machine learning and data mining methods in diabetes research. *Computational and Structural Biotechnology Journal, 15*, 104–116. https://doi.org/10.1016/j.csbj.2016.12.005

Klarenbeek, S. E., Weekenstroo, H. H. A., Sedelaar, J. P. M., Fütterer, J. J., Prokop, M., & Tummers, M. (2020). The effect of higher level computerized clinical decision support systems on oncology care: A systematic review. *Cancers, 12*(4), E1032. https://doi.org/10.3390/cancers12041032

Layeghian Javan, S., Sepehri, M. M., & Aghajani, H. (2018). Toward analyzing and synthesizing previous research in early prediction of cardiac arrest using machine learning based on a multi-layered integrative framework. *Journal of Biomedical Informatics, 88*, 70–89. https://doi.org/10.1016/j.jbi.2018.10.008

Lee, E. C., Asher, J. M., Goldlust, S., Kraemer, J. D., Lawson, A. B., & Bansal, S. (2016). Mind the scales: Harnessing spatial big data for infectious disease surveillance and inference. *The Journal of Infectious Diseases, 214*(Suppl. 4), S409–S413. https://doi.org/10.1093/infdis/jiw344

Librenza-Garcia, D., Kotzian, B. J., Yang, J., Mwangi, B., Cao, B., Pereira Lima, L. N., Bermudez, M. B., Boeira, M. V., Kapczinski, F., & Passos, I. C. (2017). The impact of machine learning techniques in the study of bipolar disorder: A systematic review. *Neuroscience & Biobehavioral Reviews, 80*, 538–554. https://doi.org/10.1016/j.neubiorev.2017.07.004

Li, D., Mikela Vilmun, B., Frederik Carlsen, J., Albrecht-Beste, E., Ammitzbøl Lauridsen, C., Bachmann Nielsen, M., & Lindskov Hansen, K. (2019). The performance of deep learning algorithms on automatic pulmonary nodule detection and classification tested on different datasets that are not derived from LIDC-IDRI: A systematic review. *Diagnostics, 9*(4), E207. https://doi.org/10.3390/diagnostics9040207

Mathias, B., Lipori, G., Moldawer, L. L., & Efron, P. A. (2016). Integrating "big data" into surgical practice. *Surgery, 159*(2), 371–374. https://doi.org/10.1016/j.surg.2015.08.043

Mendelson, D., & Mendelson, D. (2017). Legal protections for personal health information in the age of big data – a proposal for regulatory framework. Ethics. *Medicine and Public Health, 3*(1), 37–55. https://doi.org/10.1016/j.jemep.2017.02.005

Miller, D. D., & Brown, E. W. (2018). Artificial intelligence in medical practice: The question to the answer? *The American Journal of Medicine, 131*(2), 129–133. https://doi.org/10.1016/j.amjmed.2017.10.035

Milton, C. L. (2017). The ethics of big data and nursing science. *Nursing Science Quarterly, 30*(4), 300–302. https://doi.org/10.1177/0894318417724474

Mittelstadt, B. D., & Floridi, L. (2016). The ethics of big data: Current and foreseeable issues in biomedical contexts. *Science and Engineering Ethics, 22*(2), 303–341. https://doi.org/10.1007/s11948-015-9652-2

Monteith, S., Glenn, T., Geddes, J., Whybrow, P. C., & Bauer, M. (2016). Big data for bipolar disorder. *International Journal of Bipolar Disorders, 4*(1), 10. https://doi.org/10.1186/s40345-016-0051-7

Moro Visconti, R., & Morea, D. (2019). Big data for the sustainability of healthcare project financing. *Sustainability, 11*(13), 3748. https://doi.org/10.3390/su11133748

Murray, N. M., Unberath, M., Hager, G. D., & Hui, F. K. (2020). Artificial intelligence to diagnose ischemic stroke and identify large vessel occlusions: A systematic review. *Journal of Neurointerventional Surgery, 12*(2), 156–164. https://doi.org/10.1136/neurintsurg-2019-015135

Nakatani, H. (2016). Global strategies for the prevention and control of infectious diseases and non-communicable diseases. *Journal of Epidemiology, 26*(4), 171–178. https://doi.org/10.2188/jea.JE20160010

Nielsen, K. B., Lautrup, M. L., Andersen, J. K. H., Savarimuthu, T. R., & Grauslund, J. (2019). Deep learning-based algorithms in screening of diabetic retinopathy: A systematic review of diagnostic performance. *Ophthalmology Retina, 3*(4), 294–304. https://doi.org/10.1016/j.oret.2018.10.014

Patil, S., Habib Awan, K., Arakeri, G., Jayampath Seneviratne, C., Muddur, N., Malik, S., Ferrari, M., Rahimi, S., & Brennan, P. A. (2019). Machine learning and its potential applications to the genomic study of head and neck cancer: A systematic review. *Journal of Oral Pathology & Medicine: Official Publication of the International Association of Oral Pathologists and the American Academy of Oral Pathology, 48*(9), 773–779. https://doi.org/10.1111/jop.12854

Pehrson, L. M., Nielsen, M. B., & Ammitzbøl Lauridsen, C. (2019). Automatic pulmonary nodule detection applying deep learning or machine learning algorithms to the LIDC-IDRI database: A systematic review. *Diagnostics, 9*(1), E29. https://doi.org/10.3390/diagnostics9010029

Pizzolante, R., Castiglione, A., Carpentieri, B., De Santis, A., Palmieri, F., & Castiglione, A. (2018). On the protection of consumer genomic data in the Internet of Living Things. *Computers & Security, 74*, 384–400. https://doi.org/10.1016/j.cose.2017.06.003

Pramanik, M. I., Lau, R. Y. K., Demirkan, H., & Azad, Md, A. K. (2017). Smart health: Big data enabled health paradigm within smart cities. *Expert Systems with Applications, 87*, 370–383. https://doi.org/10.1016/j.eswa.2017.06.027

Raghupathi, W., & Raghupathi, V. (2014). Big data analytics in healthcare: Promise and potential. *Health Information Science and Systems, 2*. https://doi.org/10.1186/2047-2501-2-3

Roski, J., Bo-Linn, G. W., & Andrews, T. A. (2014). Creating value in health care through big data: Opportunities and policy implications. *Health Affairs, 33*(7), 1115–1122. https://doi.org/10.1377/hlthaff.2014.0147

Rothstein, M. A. (2017). Structural challenges of precision medicine: Currents in contemporary bioethics. *Journal of Law Medicine & Ethics, 45*(2), 274–279. https://doi.org/10.1177/1073110517720655

Sabharwal, S., Gupta, S., & Thirunavukkarasu, K. (2016). Insight of big data analytics in healthcare industry. In *2016 International Conference on Computing, Communication and Automation (ICCCA)* (pp. 95–100). https://doi.org/10.1109/CCAA.2016.7813696

Schlaff, G., Walter, H., & Lesch, O. M. (2011). The Lesch alcoholism typology – psychiatric and psychosocial treatment approaches. *Annals of Gastroenterology: Quarterly Publication of the Hellenic Society of Gastroenterology, 24*(2), 89–97.

Shatte, A. B. R., Hutchinson, D. M., & Teague, S. J. (2019). Machine learning in mental health: A scoping review of methods and applications. *Psychological Medicine, 49*(9), 1426–1448. https://doi.org/10.1017/S0033291719000151

Sprockel, J., Tejeda, M., Yate, J., Diaztagle, J., & González, E. (2018). [Intelligent systems tools in the diagnosis of acute coronary syndromes: A systemic review. *Archivos de Cardiología de México, 88*(3), 178–189. https://doi.org/10.1016/j.acmx.2017.03.002

Terry, N. (2012). Protecting patient privacy in the age of big data (SSRN scholarly paper ID 2153269). *Social Science Research Network*. https://doi.org/10.2139/ssrn.2153269

Tian, S., Yang, W., Grange, J. M. L., Wang, P., Huang, W., & Ye, Z. (2019). Smart healthcare: Making medical care more intelligent. *Global Health Journal, 3*(3), 62–65. https://doi.org/10.1016/j.glohj.2019.07.001

Tomaselli Muensterman, E., & Tisdale, J. E. (2018). Predictive analytics for identification of patients at risk for QT interval prolongation: A systematic review. *Pharmacotherapy: The Journal of Human Pharmacology and Drug Therapy, 38*(8), 813–821. https://doi.org/10.1002/phar.2146

Tripoliti, E. E., Papadopoulos, T. G., Karanasiou, G. S., Naka, K. K., & Fotiadis, D. I. (2017). Heart failure: Diagnosis, severity estimation and prediction of adverse events through machine learning techniques. *Computational and Structural Biotechnology Journal, 15*, 26–47. https://doi.org/10.1016/j.csbj.2016.11.001

Ulfarsson, M., Palsson, F., Sigurdsson, J., & Sveinsson, J. (2016). Classification of big data with application to imaging genetics. *Proceedings of the IEEE*. https://doi.org/10.1109/JPROC.2015.2501814

Valerio, L., Passarella, A., & Conti, M. (2017). A communication efficient distributed learning framework for smart environments. *Pervasive and Mobile Computing, 41*, 46–68. https://doi.org/10.1016/j.pmcj.2017.07.014

Wang, L., & Alexander, C. A. (2020). Big data analytics in medical engineering and healthcare: Methods, advances and challenges. *Journal of Medical Engineering & Technology, 44*(6), 267–283. https://doi.org/10.1080/03091902.2020.1769758

Wang, W., Kiik, M., Peek, N., Curcin, V., Marshall, I. J., Rudd, A. G., Wang, Y., Douiri, A., Wolfe, C. D., & Bray, B. (2020). A systematic review of machine learning models for predicting outcomes of stroke with structured data. *PLoS One, 15*(6), e0234722. https://doi.org/10.1371/journal.pone.0234722

Woldaregay, A. Z., Årsand, E., Walderhaug, S., Albers, D., Mamykina, L., Botsis, T., & Hartvigsen, G. (2019). Data-driven modeling and prediction of blood glucose dynamics: Machine learning applications in type 1 diabetes. *Artificial Intelligence in Medicine, 98*, 109–134. https://doi.org/10.1016/j.artmed.2019.07.007

Yang, S., Njoku, M., & Mackenzie, C. F. (2014). "Big data" approaches to trauma outcome prediction and autonomous resuscitation. *British Journal of Hospital Medicine, 75*(11), 637–641. https://doi.org/10.12968/hmed.2014.75.11.637

Yin, Z., Sulieman, L. M., & Malin, B. A. (2019). A systematic literature review of machine learning in online personal health data. *Journal of the American Medical Informatics Association: JAMIA, 26*(6), 561–576. https://doi.org/10.1093/jamia/ocz009

Zhou, Z.-H., Chawla, N. V., Jin, Y., & Williams, G. J. (2014). Big data opportunities and challenges: Discussions from data analytics perspectives (discussion forum). *IEEE Computational Intelligence Magazine, 9*(4), 62–74. https://doi.org/10.1109/MCI.2014.2350953

Section III

Diagnosis and treatment: Big data analytical techniques, datasets, life cycles, managements, and applications for diagnosis and treatment

Chapter 9

Recent applications of data mining in medical diagnosis and prediction

Ozge Doguc, Zehra Nur Canbolat and Gokhan Silahtaroglu
Istanbul Medipol University, Department of Management Information Systems, Istanbul, Turkey

1. Introduction

With the penetration of technology into our daily lives, the amount of data produced by us has started to increase rapidly. In the Data Age 2025 research report made by IDC (International Data Corporation), it was stated that 16 zettabytes of data were produced worldwide in 2016. In this research, it is also predicted that 160 zettabytes of data will be produced worldwide by 2025 (Reinsel et al., 2017). This rapid increase in data size causes the interest in the field of big data which is increasing day by day. Large amounts of data have been analyzed in the fields of minimizing traffic density, reducing crime rates, physics modeling, drug development, and other scientific and medical research (Ohlhorst, 2012).

The first step in exploring the big data universe is finding and understanding what information to be used. E-commerce and social media businesses such as Facebook, Amazon, and Google have used big data tools as part of their marketing plans to serve their customers better. Amazon is a good example where a company makes very good use of the data it collects, as it built an intelligent system to provide purchase recommendations to its customers. Amazon has stored customer's searches, purchases, and personal information and used this data as input for its intelligent systems. Amazon has learned the science of extracting value from the big data universe and has achieved great performance from this situation. For example, suppose a customer who lives in a snowy area buys a jacket. The climatic conditions of the shopping area are determined from the geographical location information of the customer, and product recommendations such as snow boots, snow shovels, and snow chains are offered to the customer for purchase. For a salesperson working in the store, these suggestions may be part of his or her ordinary routine; however, this is only possible for Amazon by using big data analytics to look at which customers bought it where and when, what they have purchased in the past, and to develop an appropriate understanding of this purchasing process. This data—when combined with other public data such as census, meteorology, and even social network data—creates a unique value serving the customer and Amazon (Ohlhorst, 2012).

To understand how big data has been helping us in our daily lives, it is useful to consider its uses in the healthcare industry. In healthcare, big data is used to predict epidemics, improve disease control, improve quality of life, and avoid preventable deaths, beyond increasing profits, and reducing the financial burden of patients. With the increase in the world population and the prolongation of human lifespan, the patterns of delivery of treatment are changing rapidly, and many of the decisions behind these changes are based on data (Marr, 2015). Each patient application made to hospitals and other health institutions, which receive hundreds of patient applications in their daily operations, provides new data for improving the data-driving decision-making process. Different data such as gender, age, complaints, income levels, payment types, and insurance status of the patients who apply are processed into the database of the hospitals. In addition to the data coming from external systems, the distribution of patients within the hospital, the number of daily procedures in the polyclinic and other medical departments, the duration of the procedures, their complete and correct execution, and their follow-up by the hospital management can be considered as the internal dynamics of the hospital. Considering the competition in the health sector, the option to stand out in the sector by managing the information correctly becomes important in hospitals where information flow is intense. For this reason, it is important for the hospital management to review the information stores and make a plan to manage the information. Transformation based on information and

Big Data Analytics for Healthcare. https://doi.org/10.1016/B978-0-323-91907-4.00006-6

communication technologies, when interpreted with the right analysis methods applied to big data, can enable health institutions to better manage their risks, make strategic decisions, and make innovations.

Big data provides the opportunity to provide effective and precise medicine by performing patient classification. This is an important step toward truly personalized healthcare. Better use of medical resources through personalization can lead to well-managed healthcare that can meet the challenges of a rapidly growing and aging population. Thus, advances in big data processing for health informatics, bioinformatics, sensing, and imaging will have a major impact on future clinical research (Andreu-Perez et al., 2015). The next section discusses how big data is being used in the health sector. The rest of this chapter discusses recent applications of data mining in healthcare, and shows how big data can help patients and healthcare providers.

2. Big data and the health sector

In recent years, there have been great developments in using technology to analyze and understand data, as well as collecting data. The intersection of these trends creates what is called "Big Data" and it helps businesses in every industry be more efficient and productive. The use of big data in the health sector is used to improve the quality of life, predict epidemics, cure diseases, and avoid preventable deaths, beyond increasing profits or reducing the burden of excess labor (Marr, 2015; Young, 2014). Huge amounts of data have been collected by healthcare institutions, such as personal health records, genetic data, radiological images, and clinical trial data. All electronic patient records (forms containing all examinations and evaluations performed on patients) can be defined as "big data." In addition, new data types such as genomic and biometric sensor data and three-dimensional images greatly increase this amount. All this data changes according to the conditions and the perspective of health professionals and contains different clues. Both the diversity and production speed of the produced data are quite high. Due to this increase, it is vital that the data quality is high, and the analysis results are error-free, especially in the health sector.

Big data sources in healthcare are the State, Ministry of Health, Health Insurance Companies, health institutions at all levels, health workers, pharmaceutical companies, physicians providing individual health services, researchers, patients and retailers, and telecommunication companies, which we can call new generation players. The nature and importance of big data provided by each source is different. The ways in which the aforementioned sources produce data or reveal the data are also diverse. Fig. 9.1 shows the main data sources and the services they provide. All data from these services will be a part of big data. For example, data such as nutrition and activity reports that patients will provide, PubMed, Bio Bank data obtained from clinical studies, health-related topics discussed on social media, questions and answers, patient complaints and questions asked by healthcare professionals to make them more understandable, and laboratory results. All of them constitute big data as a whole. However, in order to draw meaningful conclusions from this data, all this data must be integrated into each other in a "specific" order.

Today, data sources in the field of healthcare have become quite diversified and accessible to individuals. For example, devices used every day, such as mobile phones, collect data about the daily lives and behaviors of their users and transfer this data for processing. When combined with existing health data, daily (even instantaneous) data from these devices can be used to predict future health conditions of individuals and to identify necessary intervention points. It can also prevent diseases by measuring the heartbeat, rhythm disturbances (e.g., Apple Watch), and thus reduce health care costs. The general framework of data collected and processed for medical and health purposes is summarized in Table 9.1.

In recent years, there has been a massive increase in health data sources such as wearable and implantable devices, smartphones, and real-time sensors. Jalali et al. (2012) revealed in their study that utilizing cloud computing can cause differences in terms of public health. They stated that they have developed an environment where emerging public health threats can be observed in real time and provide instant notification to practitioners through big data analytics, predictive modeling, and cloud computing (Jalali et al., 2012). In one of the first examples of the use of data mining in the health sector, the effects of the pain reliever Vioxx were investigated in the health data of 1.4 million patients by the Canadian-based research company Kaiser Permanente, and it was concluded that the Vioxx drug increased the risk of heart attack and stroke by blocking the COX-2 enzyme. This triggered the process leading up to the removal of the drug from the market. Between 1999 and 2003, 27,000 deaths occurred due to cardiac arrest due to the use of the drug. Working in medicine and bioengineering at Stanford University, Dr. Altman and his team used statistical analysis and data mining techniques applied to the large datasets revealed that Paxil and Pravachol drugs cause serious side effects when used together.

This chapter discusses a number of applications of data mining techniques in the health sector. In the next section, a machine learning powered diagnosis system is discussed based on patient complaints. Section 3 introduces a machine learning model for automated medical diagnosis based on patient complaints. Section 4 explains a method for early prediction and diagnosis of Sepsis based on lab test data. Section 5 summarizes how Creatine Kinase can be detected by

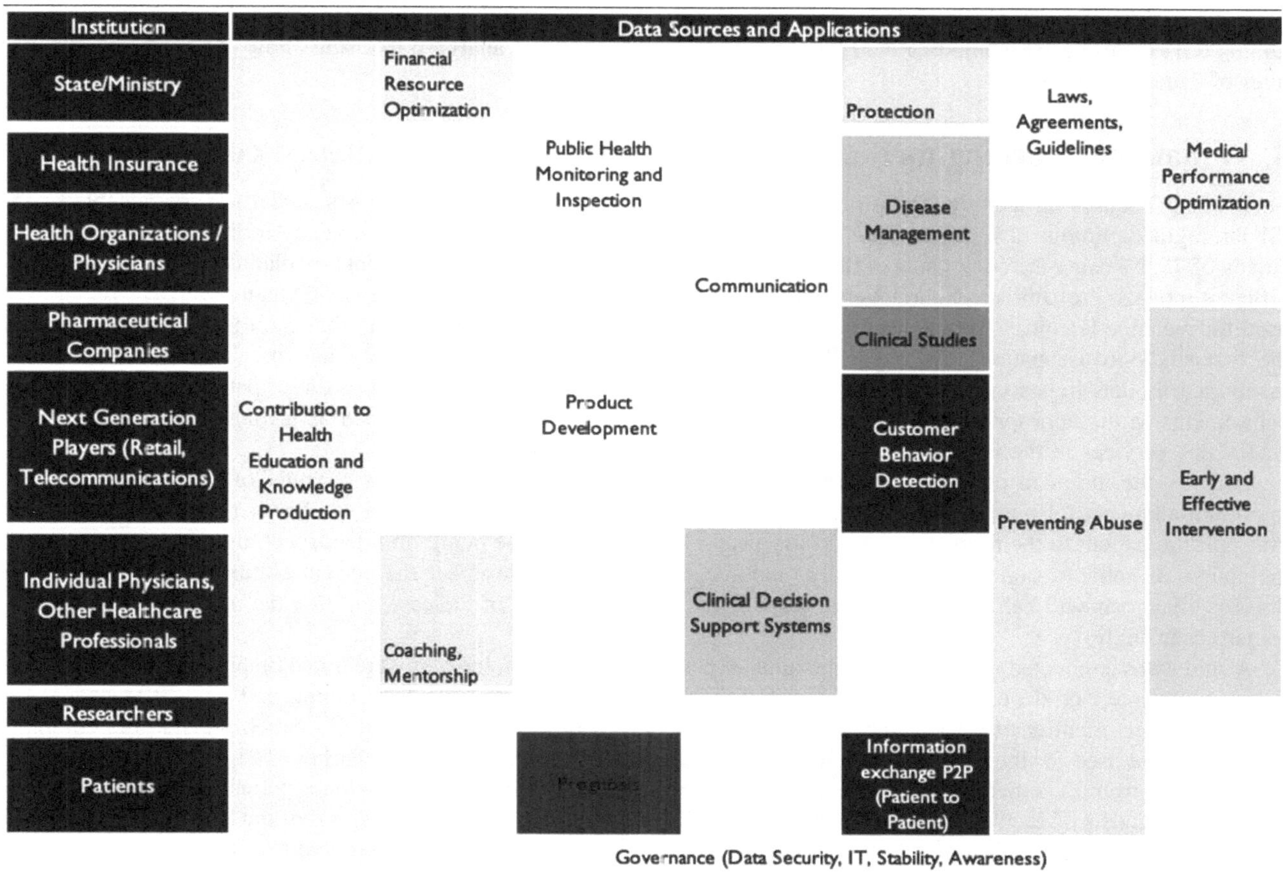

FIGURE 9.1 Health data sources and applications.

TABLE 9.1 Big Data in the Health Sector.
Types of medical data used in data mining applications.

Type of Data	
Medical data	Most traditional medical data available in hospitals, regular follow-up data such as blood pressure assessments, X-rays, or EKGs.
Public health data	Data from municipalities, public health departments, ministries, or international organizations such as the World Health Organization (WHO)—supplemented or associated with data from public institutions.
Insurance data	Data received from Health Insurance Companies regarding patients.
Research data	Data collected during clinical studies or with specific characteristics from medical journal articles.
Data produced by patients	Pain diary, data entered through sensors, is gradually becoming a part of the health system today, causing big data to become more and more massive.
New generation players	Among these, it is stated that social networks (for example, Facebook, Twitter social media posts, status updates, blogs, and web pages), mobile operators, smartwatches, or retailers' data will be used (Langkafel, 2016).

using lab results of patients. Section 7 introduces a study on predicting malignant potential of gastrointestinal stromal tumors (GISTs) using AI methods. Finally, in Section 8, patient data was analyzed to discuss how covid-19 affected daily lives of Turkish citizens.

3. A machine learning medical diagnosis model based on patients' complaints

This section focuses on a study which proposed a machine learning–based prediagnosis model for emergency services (Silahtaroğlu & Yõlmaztürk, 2019). The proposed model can make diagnosis for emergency room patients with an accuracy of 75.5% using the complaints of the patients. In the study, after examining patient complaints with text mining, two different models, Probabilistic Neural Network and Random Forest Decision Tree based on Dynamic Decay Tuning, were used for machine learning. Although there are other studies based on machine learning that can diagnose patients, this is the first study to use patients' verbal and written complaints as input. The accuracy and precision statistics of both mentioned models indicate that this study can be used as a decision support system to direct patients from emergency departments to the appropriate health centers. In addition, this study can be developed as a triage prediction model in emergency services in the future.

Usually, the first step of emergency services begins with ambulance services. As a matter of fact, one of the most important elements for ambulance workers is to evaluate the urgency of incoming cases. Another important factor is to transport the patient to the nearest and least busy health center for the time being. In this respect, it is important to predict the course of patients' conditions as quickly (and accurately) as possible under the current circumstances. A good preliminary diagnosis will help paramedics to accurately assess the urgency of the case and find the most appropriate health center accordingly.

A study was conducted in which the complaints of patients registered in the past were noted by physicians. First, hidden text patterns that can aid diagnosis were extracted from these complaints using text mining and two different machine learning models mentioned earlier were trained to make diagnostic predictions using the patterns inside the complaint notes. The data used for the research was collected from a private hospital in Istanbul, Turkey. The records were collected anonymously from the emergency services and other services. The resulting dataset includes patients' complaints and the definitive diagnosis of each case. The dataset contains 5394 records of 164 different diagnoses and 391 unique complaints after cleaning. During the data preparation phase, the missing values were first removed, and then the data was converted into a format that machine learning algorithms could use. The snowball root separator algorithm (Porter, 2001) was used to find the root of each word in patient complaints. Terms with less than three characters and all punctuation marks were filtered and only terms that could be used for diagnosis were obtained. After finding the terms, the frequencies of each clean word were tagged with the corresponding diagnosis. Fig. 9.2 shows the data preparation framework for customer complaints.

In the study, the decision tree model was used for the training of the machine learning algorithm. Decision trees are known to be weak learners, and therefore, the Random Forest Decision Tree learning model was preferred in the study. Random forests are a combination of tree estimators in which each tree depends on the values of an independently sampled random vector and has the same distribution for all trees in the forest (Breiman, 2001). Rapid and accurate evaluation of cases is of great importance for emergency services due to their natural urgency. Above all, predicting the definitive diagnosis is invaluable.

The complaints and final diagnoses of 5394 patients were used to create a system that could generate prediagnostic results with machine learning. The Random Forest model provided an accuracy of 77.65%, and the PNN's accuracy was 76,367%. The analysis results show that a machine learning diagnostic system can reach 76% accuracy statistics. For further study, the triage of each case can be estimated through machine prediagnosis. For this reason, triage line eligibility can be taken into account when choosing a health center by ambulance paramedics. Tables 9.2 and 9.3 show the results from decision tree and neural network–based training models respectively.

4. An early prediction and diagnosis of sepsis in intensive care units

Sepsis infection is one of the most common causes of death in intensive care units globally. If early diagnosis of sepsis infection cannot be made and treatment does not start immediately after, septic shock may result in multiple organ failures and death becomes almost inevitable. Sepsis affects 27–30 million people each year and kills 7–9 million people Sepsis — Global Sepsis Alliance (n.d.). Sepsis infection is a common cause of high mortality, and the most survivors experience long-term morbidity too. A recent study found that sepsis was the cause of 26% of the mortality in hospitals (Szakmany et al., 2016). Prediction of sepsis and early detection of sepsis provides faster treatment and reveals

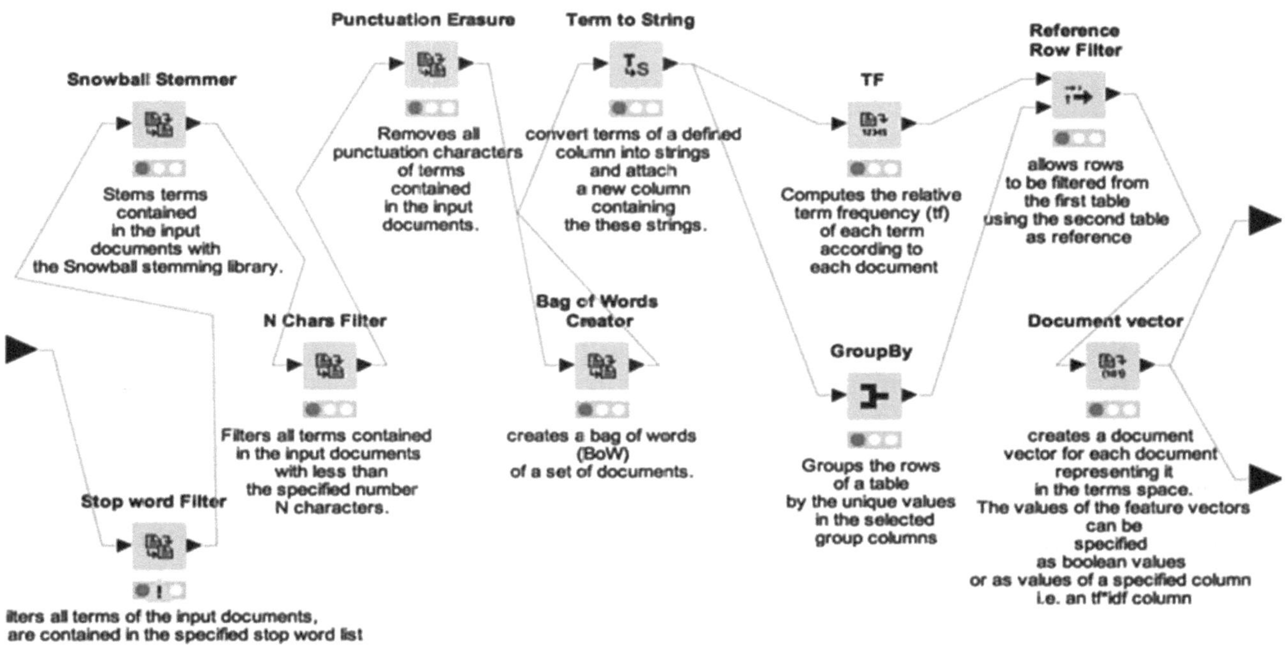

FIGURE 9.2 Data preparation for patient complaints. *From Silahtaroğlu, G., & Yõlmaztürk, N. (2019). Data analysis in health and big data: A machine learning medical diagnosis model based on patients' complaints.* Communications in Statistics - Theory and Methods, 50. *https://doi.org/10.1080/03610926.2019.1622728.*

TABLE 9.2 Statistics of random forest decision tree training.

True positives rate	False positives rate	True negatives rate	False negatives rate
21,128	6,538	4,281,794	6,538
Recall	Precision	Sensitivity	Specificity
0.581	0.915	0.581	0.998
	F-measure	Accuracy	Cohen's kappa
	0.882	0.763	0.756

TABLE 9.3 Statistics of probabilistic neural network training.

True positives rate	False positives rate	True negatives rate	False negatives rate
20,757	6,707	4,277,828	6,707
Recall	Precision	Sensitivity	Specificity
0.557	0.885	0.557	0.998
	F-measure	Accuracy	Cohen's kappa
	0.864	0.755	0.748

better results. However, the diagnosis of sepsis is usually possible only very few hours before the patients are at a high risk of mortality. Therefore, it is crucial to predict the disease before it truly shows itself. In the recent studies, some important parameters that trigger sepsis infection are determined. Lactate and Ph laboratory test parameters are 2 important ones among those 57 determined in the study (Nemati et al., 2018). Permanent increases in lactate for 24 h have been shown to be associated with mortality as high as 89% (Broder & Weil, 1964).

	Lactate_max	Lactate_min	Lactate_ave	Lactate_std	Ph_max	Ph_min	Ph_ave	Pd_std
PozSep_01	6,0	1,2	2,9	1,5	7,5	5,2	6,9	0,6
PozSep_02	1,9	1	1,4	0,3	7,4	5,3	6,8	0,7
PozSep_03	10,3	1,5	4,4	2,6	7,6	5,2	7,1	0,5
PozSep_04	3,6	1,1	2,1	0,8	7,5	5,2	6,8	0,7
PozSep_05	18,1	2	7,6	5,1	7,6	5,3	7,1	0,5
NegSep_01	16,3	4,5	9,2	4,5	7,4	5,7	7	0,4
NegSep_02	1,9	1,1	1,4	0,4	7,3	5,1	6,7	0,8
NegSep_03	8,4	1,9	4,2	2,4	7,5	5,5	7	0,5
NegSep_04	2,0	1,3	1,6	0,5	7,4	6,9	7,2	0,2
NegSep_05	4,2	1,6	2,6	1,1	7,4	5,5	6,9	0,6

FIGURE 9.3 Fuzzy-C learning results. Cluster centers learned by the Fuzz-C algorithm. *From Silahtaroglu, G., & Canbolat, Z. N. (2020). An early prediction and diagnosis of sepsis in intensive care units: An unsupervised machine learning model.* Mugla Journal of Science and Technology. *https://doi.org/10.22531/muglajsci.643554.*

Canbolat and Silahtaroglu provided a study where, in addition to the lactate value of the laboratory tests, which are considered to be of primary importance in the diagnosis of sepsis based on the opinions of the clinicians and the literature studies, the Ph parameter accompanying the lactate was used (Silahtaroglu et al., 2020). Intensive care patient data were used in the study through MIMIC-III international clinical database. Lactate and Ph data were converted into eight separate variables, the lowest, highest, average, and variance (standard deviation) for each patient, regardless of the duration of stay. The machine was trained with nonsepsis 27,321 patients and 1657 sepsis diagnosed patients in the intensive care unit whose lactate and PH values were transformed as mentioned above. This training was conducted separately for each patient group using fuzzy C-means algorithm. Subsequently, dimension reduction was performed using principal component analysis to visualize patients with or without sepsis. There are many parameters associated with sepsis infection and these may vary from patient to patient depending on their living conditions, genetic information, and life history. The study contributes to the literature in that it has conducted a fully unsupervised fuzzy learning model by using two parameters (lactate and Ph) and pioneering multiparameter studies. In addition, the visualization of the model makes it possible to identify the sepsis area and the nonsepsis area in order to see which region the patients tend to head to. Fig. 9.3 shows the learning algorithm results and Fig. 9.4 provides insights into how a new patient is evaluated between sepsis and nonsepsis areas. Fig. 9.4 also displays how a patient moves from the SN (sepsis-negative) region to the SP (sepsis-positive) region based on the lactate and Ph values. After treatment, the patient leaves the SP regions and moves to the ND (no decision) zone.

5. A machine learning approach to predict creatine kinase test results

Laboratory tests are one of the most common methods that doctors use to make an accurate medical diagnosis. Laboratory tests are used not only for diagnostic purposes, but also to guide the treatment procedure and confirm the course (Badrick, 2013). Although laboratory test results are so powerful and important in diagnosis, the use of test results is limited because the results are reported as numerical values at certain intervals and doctors usually focus on values outside a certain reference range (Luo et al., 2016). On the other hand, artificial intelligence–assisted learning algorithms can learn and help diagnosis by evaluating all test results together and each result separately, without focusing only on values outside the range. Canbolat et al. (2020) presents an AI-powered system to accurately predict the results of laboratory tests based on patients' previous tests. In this study, laboratory test results for the years 2017, 2018, and 2019 were collected from a private hospital in Istanbul. All patient data in the collected data set was first anonymized and a test data set containing a total of 449,471 test results was created. This dataset contains a total of 107,646 individual patient data. The study focused on estimating the range of values for Creatine Kinase tests, which generally require more processing time than other tests. At the end of the study, it was shown that using the laboratory test results and the Random Forest Algorithm, the creatine kinase test result could be predicted with 97% accuracy based only on the AST and ALT test values.

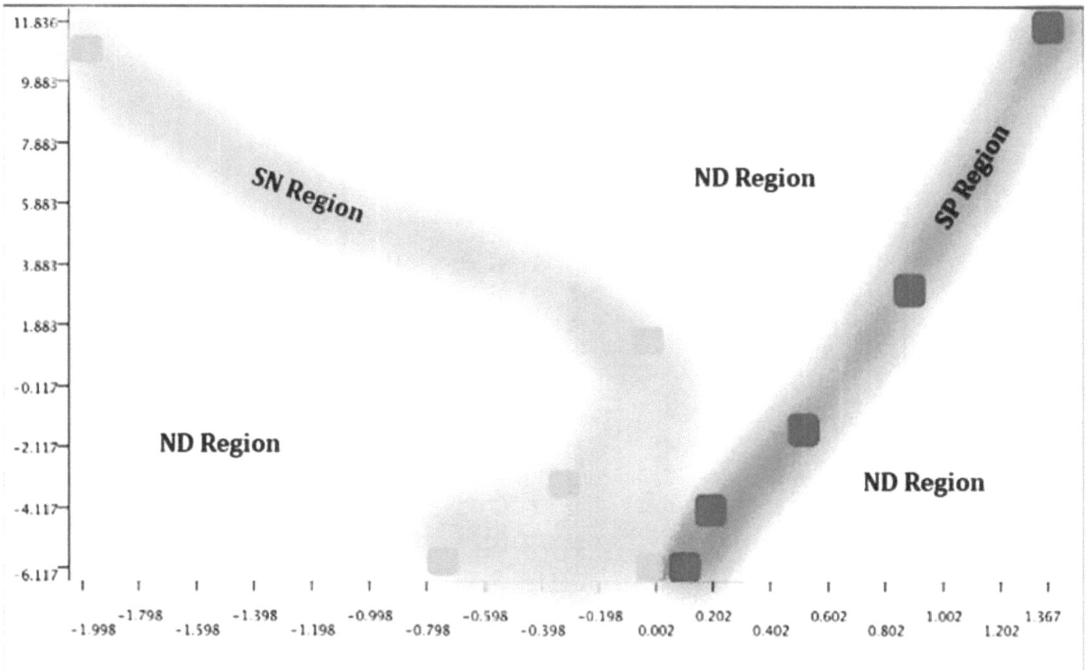

FIGURE 9.4 Traverse of a sepsis positive patient. *From Silahtaroglu, G. & Canbolat, Z. N. (2020). An early prediction and diagnosis of sepsis in intensive care units: an unsupervised machine learning model.* Mugla Journal of Science and Technology. *https://doi.org/10.22531/muglajsci.643554.*

The data set used in the study included seven different laboratory tests, including ALT, AST, and creatine kinase. These records were first removed (cleaned) from the dataset, as the resulting dataset contained many missing patient-related features. Occasionally, multiple results were reported for a patient at the same date and time for the same test, and these values were also excluded from the data set as the correct value to use could not be determined deterministically. In many cases, the dataset was lacking, as all seven tests for patients were unsuitable for various reasons. Missing records had to be removed from the dataset because the dataset had to contain all the tests for each record. In addition, Lactate and Sedimentation test results were retained for very few cases, so these tests were completely excluded from the analysis. Thus, the remaining 221,342 records out of a total of 449,471 records in the data set were used in the study. Deficiencies in the dataset were corrected by adding the age and gender of the patients and correlated with the date/time of the tests. The final dataset included the following variables: Patient's Age, Gender, ALT value, AST value, Urea value, and Creatine Kinase value. Fig. 9.5 shows the summary of data preparation done for this study.

5.1 Model creation

After dividing the dataset into two sections for training and testing, the random forest method emphasized that the AST feature was the most effective in predicting creatine kinase test results after 100 iterations during the training phase. The first rule created by the random forest method is as follows:

Rule #1: If the AST value is greater than 65, the creatine kinase test result will be positive with an accuracy of 97.9%, regardless of gender.

When ALT values are also taken into account, the decision tree provides a more accurate estimation for positive cases, as seen in Rule 2:

Rule #2: If the AST value is greater than 65 and the ALT value is less than 8.64, the creatine kinase test result will be positive with an accuracy of 99.5% regardless of gender.

Also, Rule 3 shows prediction for negative cases can be done with even higher accuracy. Although this estimate also seems to contradict the first rule shown in Fig. 9.4, it provides a highly accurate estimate for the remaining 2% of cases in the first rule. When only the ALT value is considered, it recommends looking at the AST value in the remaining 2% and can diagnose with 100% accuracy according to the AST value.

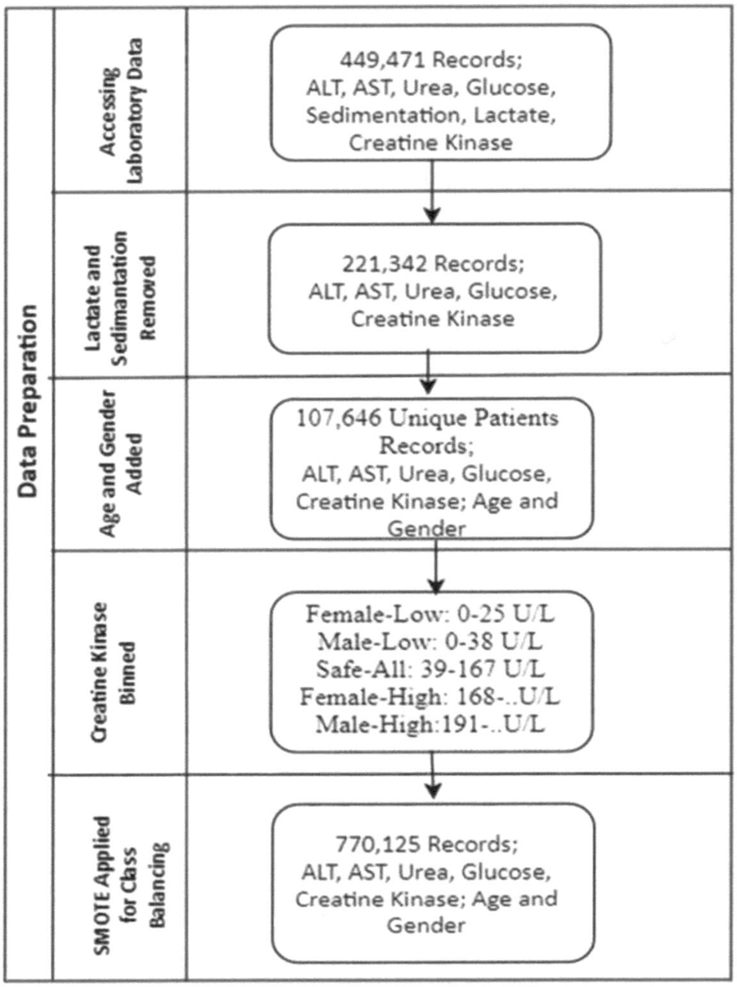

FIGURE 9.5 Summary of data preparation.

Rule #3: If AST value is greater than 65 AND ALT value is greater than 8.64, then the creatine kinase test result will be negative with 100% certainty, regardless of gender.

The three rules shown about creatine kinase test prediction so far highlight a very important conclusion: Test results can be estimated only by using AST and ALT tests without any personal information about the patient (e.g., age or gender). Also, particularly, the rule that is shown in Fig. 9.8 highlights that a negative creatine kinase result (the majority of creatine kinase test results are negative) can be predicted with 100% certainty based on AST and ALT results. This will help reduce waiting times for healthy patients greatly.

In summary, this study showed that by using a relatively simple prediction method (the random forest), creatine kinase test results can be predicted with 97% accuracy, based on data collected from 450,000 laboratory tests. At the same time, the system presented in this study showed that AST and ALT are the two most important tests for deciding creatine kinase results. Therefore, health centers will be able to diagnose creatine kinase with close to 100% accuracy by simply performing AST and ALT tests and using their results.

6. Use of artificial intelligence in the prediction of malignant potential of gastric gastrointestinal stromal tumors

Although GISTs are rare, they are the most common mesenchymal tumors of the gastrointestinal tract. It is most commonly seen in the stomach; on the other hand, it is uncommon in the small intestine and extremely rare in the esophagus (Baysal et al., 2017; Chandrasekhara & Ginsberg, 2011; Miettinen et al., 2005; Søreide et al., 2016). Because GISTs have malignant potential, the risk of progressive disease should be determined according to risk stratification systems when a lesion at resection is confirmed to be GIST (Joensuu, 2008; Miettinen et al., 2006; Miettinen & Lasota, 2006). The risk of recurrence or metastasis of GISTs can be defined mainly by tumor size, mitotic index, and tumor location (Miettinen et al., 2005, 2006). The risk of recurrence varies with the location of the tumor; gastric GISTs, particularly those from the small intestine, are less aggressive than nongastric GISTs (Miettinen et al., 2006). The mitotic index calculated in resected tumors is the main determinant of malignant potential. Promising results in medicine have been demonstrated in previous studies using artificial intelligence—assisted deep learning algorithms (Horie et al., 2019; Kurita et al., 2019; Kuwahara et al., 2019; Le Berre et al., 2020; Maeda et al., 2019; Zhu et al., 2019). However, no studies to date have examined the role of GISTs in predicting their malignant potential.

Seven et al. (2021) proposed a study that uses convolutional neural networks (CNNs) to predict malignant GISTs (Seven et al., 2021). CNN is a deep learning model which is a specialized type of the regular artificial neural network (Goodfellow, 2016). They are distinguished from other artificial neural networks by their superior performance in image, speech, and sound processing. CNNs are widely used in computer vision. In particular, image classification has become the most commonly used technology in visual applications. They are used with very high accuracy to capture lines, patterns, and even eyes and faces in images. These properties make CNNs very powerful for computer vision. Unlike previous computer vision algorithms, CNNs can run directly on a raw image without the need for preprocessing (Fig. 9.6).

In this study, tumor regions were selected from EUS images to create image datasets to be used in the development of the artificial intelligence supported model. For this, all GISTs were manually marked by an experienced endoscopist and transferred to the data set with the outer edges of the tumors drawn. The localization of GISTs was cardia in 10 cases, fundus in 9 cases, trunk in 22 cases, and antrum in 14 cases. 52 tumors originated from the fourth layer of the wall (muscularis propria), while the remaining 3 originated from the second layer (muscularis mucosa). 20 CNN cores were used in the first layer and 50 CNN cores were used in the second layer. Image resolution was halved after each core layer. After these convolutional processes, the extracted image information was introduced into an artificial neural network model to train AI-assisted learning systems. Since the dataset used for training did not have the same size of risk groups or mitotic index, the dataset was expanded with SMOTE; and data from 55 patients were used.

For CNN training, initially 38 of the patients (69%) were categorized as having low malignant potential, and the remaining 17 patients (31%) as having high malignant potential based on the AFIP criteria. It was observed that there was no significant difference between the low and high-risk groups in terms of age and gender ($P > .05$). Also, no statistical significance was noted for shape, lobulation, extra- or intraluminal margins, ulceration, echogenicity, heterogeneity, anechoic spaces, hyperechoic foci, hypoechoic halo, and growth pattern ($P > .05$). However, the study showed fundus location as an important factor in predicting malignancy risk ($P = .019$). Meanwhile, tumor size was not included in the analysis to predict malignancy risk; however, when tumor size was added to the above features, size and fundus location became important factors ($P = .011$ and $P = .013$). The study also showed that "tumor size" in the high mitotic index group was significantly larger than that in the low mitotic index group. An ROC curve was created to more clearly see the distinguishing features of size in estimating the mitotic index. EUS, which was used to estimate the corresponding pathological tumor size, confirmed that the results were successful, with an intraclass correlation coefficient value of 0.864 ($P < .001$).

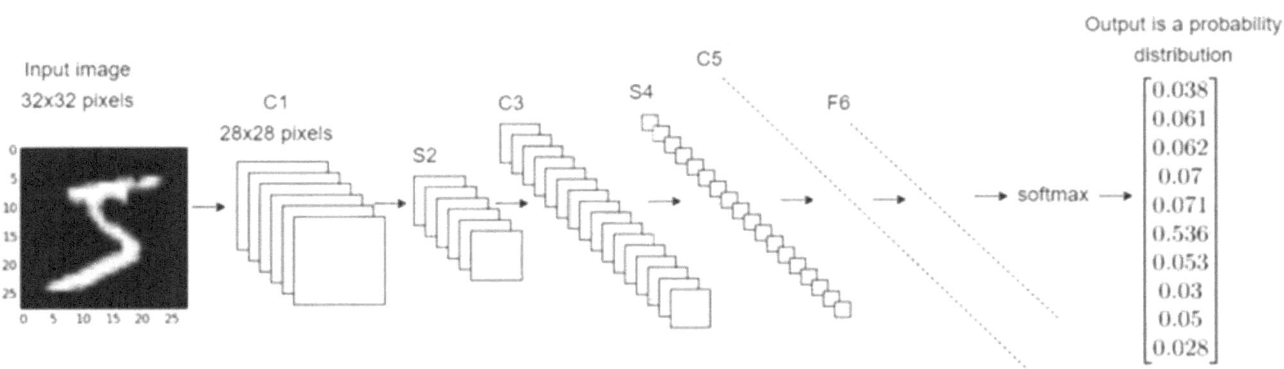

FIGURE 9.6 Convoluted neural networks (CNNs). *From Wood, T. (n.d.).* Convolutional neural network. *Retrieved May 2021, 15 CE., from https://deepai.org/machine-learning-glossary-and-terms/convolutional-neural-network.*

In summary, in this study, it was observed that individual endosonographic morphological features of gastric GISTs were insufficient to predict malignant potential with the help of an artificial intelligence–supported system. On the other hand, the evaluation of EUS images with artificial intelligence gave a very high accuracy rate. The CNN-based AI system described in this study can predict malignant potential and mitotic index in a short time with a high sensitivity and specificity. Briefly, this study shows that CNN-based computer vision systems will find significant application in automatic evaluation of GISTs today and in the future.

7. Weekly emotional changes amidst Covid-19: Turkish experience

The Covid-19 pandemic has affected many people in the world, such as in Turkey, irritating and making them anxious. In the study performed by Silahtaroglu et al. (2020), the reaction of the Turkish society to the epidemic has been examined in the period from March 2020, when the first case has been announced, to June 2020, when the normalization process began (18 March–28 May) (Silahtaroglu et al., 2020). In order to capture these reactions, a total of 567,018 texts using the hashtag #StayHome on the Twitter platform have been collected and analyzed. Sensitivity analysis has been used to see the weekly reactions of individuals that differentiate their positive/negative moods and hope levels. As a result, some differences have been observed in the emotions analyzed in 2-week periods. Analysis of the tweets included text cleaning, frequently used emoji analysis, keyword extraction, 2 and 3 n-grams, and sentiment analysis. Fig. 9.7 shows the framework including the processes and analysis for the tweet content.

In this period, restricting the mobility of people has been one of the most effective measures. For this reason, #StayHome messages have constantly featured in social media tools. Fig. 9.8 shows the number of cases in the process and the line chart containing the Tweets posted with the #Evdekal hashtag. It can be said that the precautions described above and the increase in the number of cases caused an increase in the number of Tweets.

In Fig. 9.9, the most commonly used words and their frequencies in the hashtag #StayHome are included. Accordingly, it was observed that people constantly emphasized staying at home during this period and frequently included words such as quarantine, health, incident, support, curfew, and nationalism in their texts. In Turkey (and also in Italy), frequency of these hashtags also increased during this period of national unity and people's feelings ahead (Italians belt out national anthem during virus lockdown, 2020). In order to support each other and stay strong, the national anthem was sung together on some evenings. This result is also understood by the reflection of the word anthem in the word cloud.

Fig. 9.10 shows the most used 15 emojis in this process. Accordingly, it is seen that the first three most used emojis are home, TR symbol or abbreviation, and book. It can be inferred that people give messages about spending time at home and reading books. Also, it is seen that in this period, people used to draw books and encourage each other to read books, as well as emojis. As with the 2-n-grams, it has been determined that prayer and supplication to God are also present in emoji analysis.

In Fig. 9.11, the general mood for 10 weeks extracted from the texts is expressed. Accordingly, it is seen that positive emotions are in the foreground in general. In this period, people tried to give positive messages to support each other and shared the activities that could be done at home with each other. During this period, the number of live broadcasts increased, concerts, interviews, training, and even TV series continued online. Other emotions seen in the research were determined to be anticipation and trust.

In Fig. 9.12, emotional changes of people are explained by analyzing these 10 weeks, in 2-week intervals. Accordingly, except for the period covering the third and fourth weeks, the general mood of people is positive (30 March–12 April). The prominent feeling in the weeks is negative. The reason for this is thought to be that the first curfews started in those weeks, restrictions were imposed, the depreciation of the TL, the cessation of production, the economic impact of the citizens, and the increased concern. Intense emotional states have experienced between weeks changes as positive, anticipation, trust, and negative.

In our era, Covid-19 created uncertainty wherein people are not sure how to react and struggle. Without a doubt, in some cases, a deadly illness may give way to a "dangerous opportunity" to enrich and develop one's life (Post et al., 2020, p. 6). Actually, in the case of Covid-19, the uncertainty atmosphere and panic created by the illness led to a greater need for optimism and hope. Related research has already shown that optimism and hopeful thinking can have positive effects on both physical and psychological health (Baykal, 2018; Cheavens et al., 2005; Naseem & Khalid, 2010). Actually, an optimal balance between optimism and pessimism is the best strategy for survival. As in the case with most traits, optimism and pessimism are also distributed normally and outliers within the population help to create a balance in group decision-making (Ruch & Zuckerman, 2001).

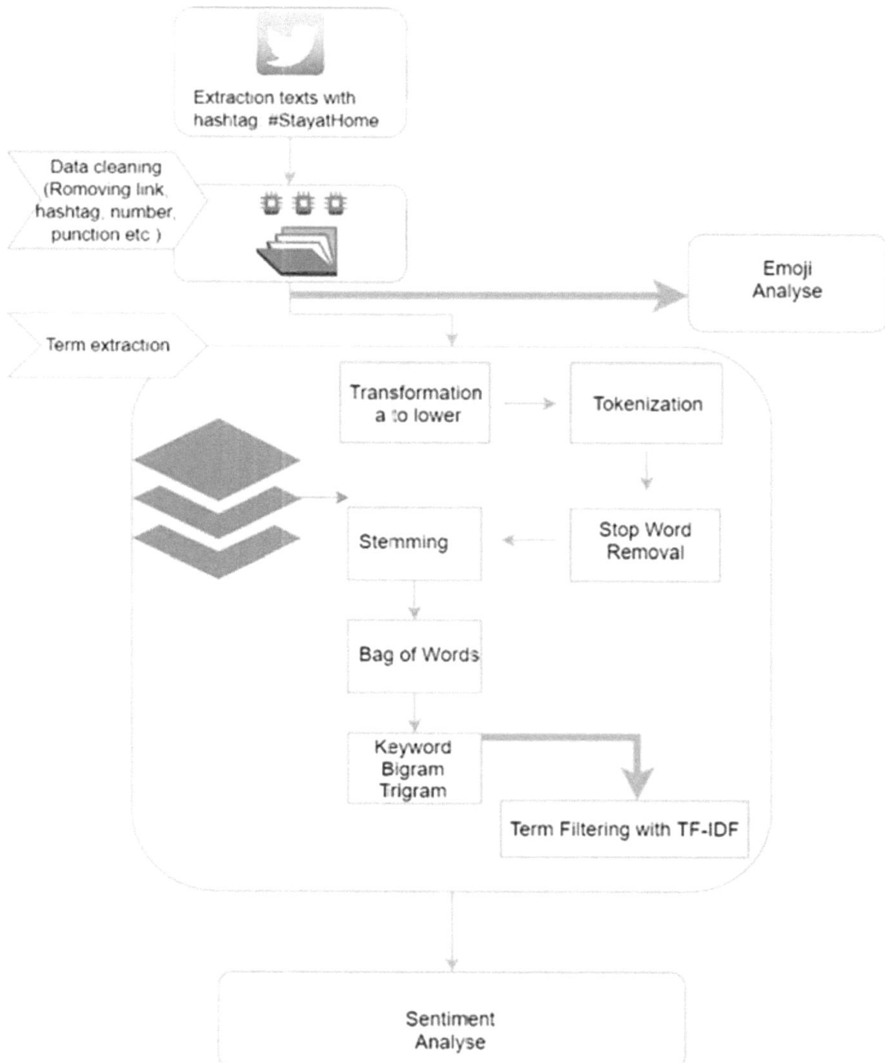

FIGURE 9.7 Framework of data collection and analysis for the study.

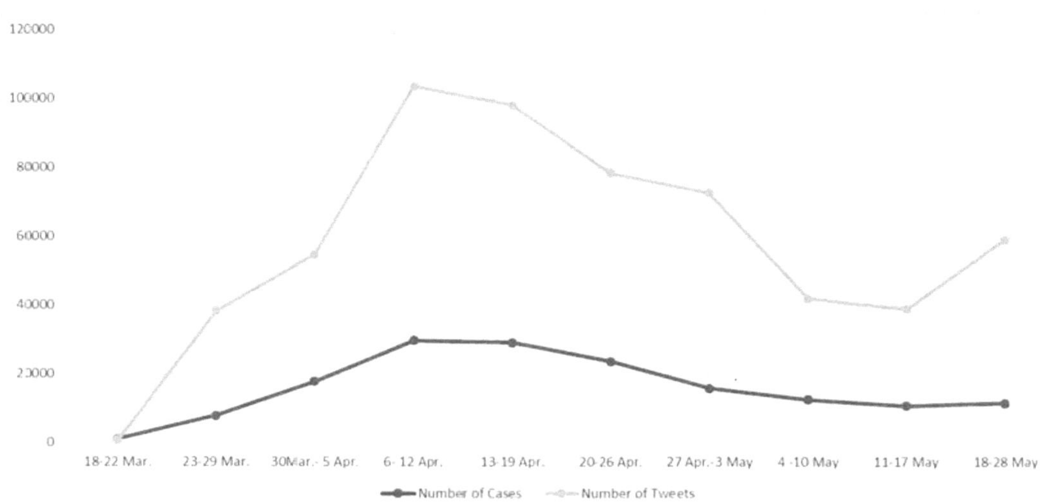

FIGURE 9.8 Weekly number of cases and tweets (for #StayHome hashtag).

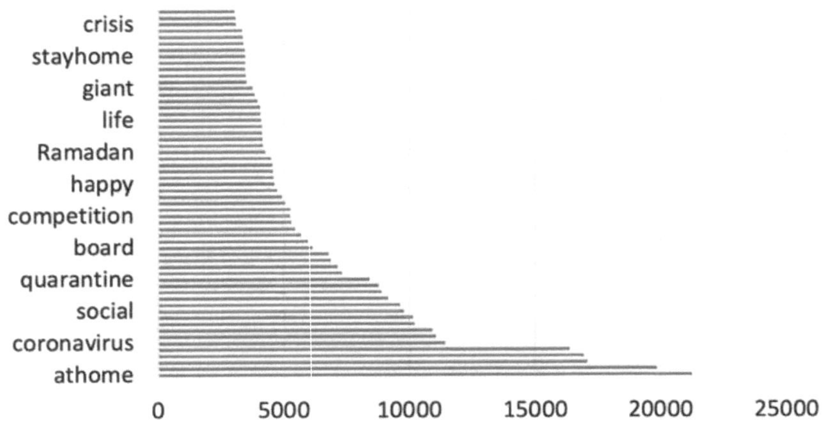

FIGURE 9.9 Most frequently used words and their frequencies.

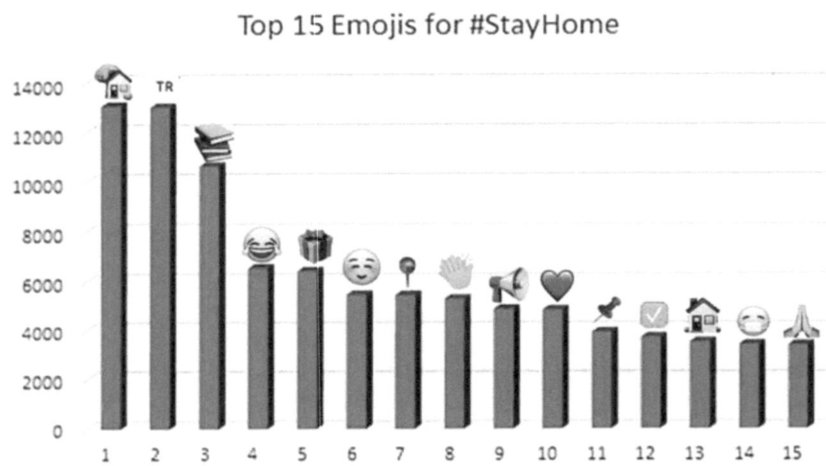

FIGURE 9.10 Top 15 emojis for #StayHome hashtag.

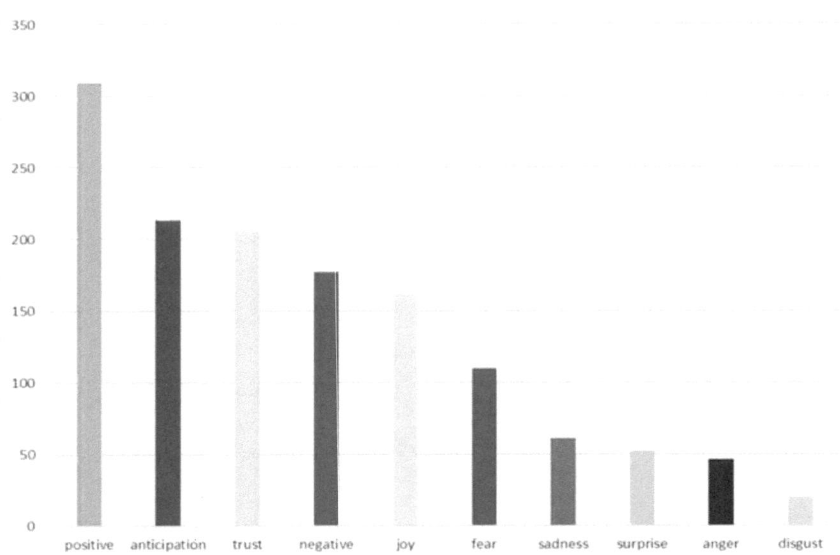

FIGURE 9.11 Sentiment type for hashtag: StayHome.

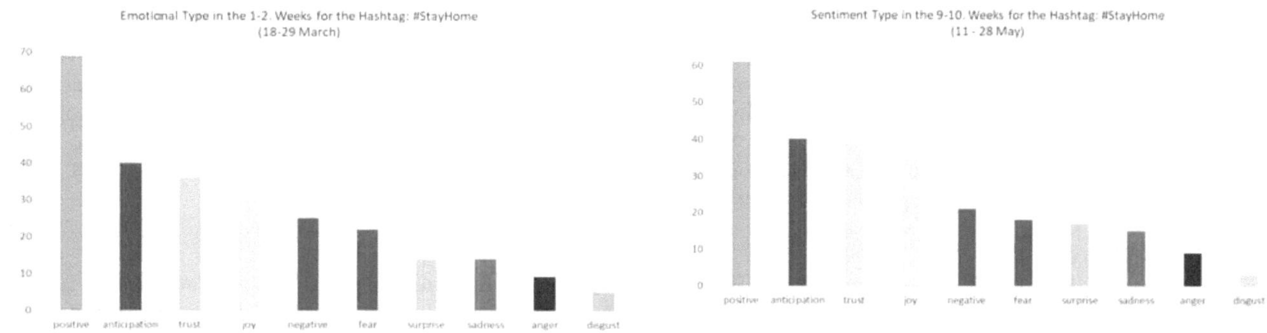

FIGURE 9.12 Emotional changes between weeks.

8. Conclusion

Health data has been steadily increasing in recent years due to sources such as wearable and implantable devices, smartphones, and real-time sensors. Advances in this growing data are causing controversy over the role of big data in clinical practice and research. Appropriate use of big data in the healthcare industry offers great promise. Handling and evaluating the data from the right perspective has the power to prevent misdiagnoses, to develop new treatment options, to develop health tracking systems, and to create a system that will warn you of changes in your body without you being aware of it. For example, population health management, cardiovascular disease risk estimation, precision medicine using genetic information, and clinical decision-making support can be improved using the power of big data. While studies on the opportunities offered by big data in the field of health are rare, these studies are increasing gradually through machine learning algorithms. In the event of a disease, epidemic, or other public health emergency, healthcare professionals often turn to paper reporting. However, online access to the latest report or statistical information about the disease or cases of health professionals can help them to develop an effective response.

In order to use data and information effectively in the health sector, it is necessary to develop the necessary skills to store and share information. People are the most important part of any knowledge management strategy. For effective knowledge management, people should be supported by appropriate technology. Knowledge management should be considered as a business model for improving organizational performance, coordinating, and collaborating efforts by creating, sharing, storing, and applying knowledge. Making the healthcare culture collaborative, transparent and active is a sustainable commitment. Well-practiced knowledge management is expected to transform the health system into a more cost-effective, error-free, and accountable public resource over the next few years.

This chapter discusses a number of recent studies that introduce methods for using big data to create intelligent systems for patient diagnosis, triage, predicting lab results, and even detecting tumors. These studies open ways for researchers in the healthcare sector to improve the quality of services provided to the patients as well as reduce costs for healthcare institutions.

References

Andreu-Perez, J., Poon, C. C. Y., Merrifield, R. D., Wong, S. T. C., & Yang, G. Z. (2015). Big data for health. *IEEE Journal of Biomedical and Health Informatics, 19*(4), 1193–1208. https://doi.org/10.1109/JBHI.2015.2450362

Badrick, T. (2013). Evidence-based laboratory medicine. *Clinical Biochemist Reviews, 34*(2), 43–46. http://www.aacb.asn.au/documents/item/1204.

Baykal, E. (2018). Promoting resilience through positive leadership during turmoils. *International Journal of Management and Administration.* https://doi.org/10.29064/ijma.396199

Baysal, B., Masri, O. A., Eloubeidi, M. A., & Senturk, H. (2017). The role of EUS and EUS-guided FNA in the management of subepithelial lesions of the esophagus: A large, single-center experience. *Endoscopic Ultrasound, 6*(5), 308–316. https://doi.org/10.4103/2303-9027.155772

Breiman, L. (2001). Random forests. *Machine Learning, 45*(1), 5–32. https://doi.org/10.1023/A:1010933404324

Broder, G., & Weil, M. H. (1964). Excess lactate: An index of reversibility of shock in human patients. *Science, 143*(3613), 1457–1459. https://doi.org/10.1126/science.143.3613.1457

Canbolat, Z. N., Silahtaroğlu, G., Doğuç, Ö., & Yõlmaztürk, N. (2020). A machine learning approach to predict creatine kinase test results. *Emerging Science Journal, 4*(4), 283–296. https://doi.org/10.28991/esj-2020-01231

Chandrasekhara, V., & Ginsberg, G. G. (2011). Endoscopic management of gastrointestinal stromal tumors. *Current Gastroenterology Reports, 13*(6), 532–539. https://doi.org/10.1007/s11894-011-0224-6

Cheavens, J. S., Michael, S. T., & Snyder, C. R. (2005). The correlates of hope: Psychological and physiological benefits. In *Interdisciplinary perspectives on hope* (pp. 119–132).

Goodfellow, I. (2016). *Deep learning.*

Horie, Y., Yoshio, T., Aoyama, K., Yoshimizu, S., Horiuchi, Y., Ishiyama, A., Hirasawa, T., Tsuchida, T., Ozawa, T., Ishihara, S., Kumagai, Y., Fujishiro, M., Maetani, I., Fujisaki, J., & Tada, T. (2019). Diagnostic outcomes of esophageal cancer by artificial intelligence using convolutional neural networks. *Gastrointestinal Endoscopy, 89*(1), 25–32. https://doi.org/10.1016/j.gie.2018.07.037

Jalali, A., Olabode, O. A., & Bell, C. M. (2012). Leveraging cloud computing to address public health disparities: An analysis of the SPHPS. *Online Journal of Public Health Informatics.* https://doi.org/10.5210/ojphi.v4i3.4325

Joensuu, H. (2008). Risk stratification of patients diagnosed with gastrointestinal stromal tumor. *Human Pathology, 39*(10), 1411–1419. https://doi.org/10.1016/j.humpath.2008.06.025

Kurita, Y., Kuwahara, T., Hara, K., Mizuno, N., Okuno, N., Matsumoto, S., Obata, M., Koda, H., Tajika, M., Shimizu, Y., Nakajima, A., Kubota, K., & Niwa, Y. (2019). Diagnostic ability of artificial intelligence using deep learning analysis of cyst fluid in differentiating malignant from benign pancreatic cystic lesions. *Scientific Reports, 9*(1). https://doi.org/10.1038/s41598-019-43314-3

Kuwahara, T., Hara, K., Mizuno, N., Okuno, N., Matsumoto, S., Obata, M., Kurita, Y., Koda, H., Toriyama, K., Onishi, S., Ishihara, M., Tanaka, T., Tajika, M., & Niwa, Y. (2019). Usefulness of deep learning analysis for the diagnosis of malignancy in intraductal papillary mucinous neoplasms of the pancreas. *Clinical and Translational Gastroenterology, 10*(5). https://doi.org/10.14309/ctg.0000000000000045

Langkafel, P. (Ed.). (2016). *Big data in medical science and healthcare management: diagnosis, therapy, side effects.* Berlin/Boston: Walter de Gruyter GmbH & Co KG.

Le Berre, C., Sandborn, W. J., Aridhi, S., Devignes, M. D., Fournier, L., Smaïl-Tabbone, M., Danese, S., & Peyrin-Biroulet, L. (2020). Application of artificial intelligence to gastroenterology and hepatology. *Gastroenterology, 158*(1), 76–94. https://doi.org/10.1053/j.gastro.2019.08.058. e2.

Luo, Y., Szolovits, P., Dighe, A. S., & Baron, J. M. (2016). Using machine learning to predict laboratory test results. *American Journal of Clinical Pathology, 145*(6), 778–788. https://doi.org/10.1093/ajcp/aqw064

Maeda, Y., Kudo, S.e., Mori, Y., Misawa, M., Ogata, N., Sasanuma, S., Wakamura, K., Oda, M., Mori, K., & Ohtsuka, K. (2019). Fully automated diagnostic system with artificial intelligence using endocytoscopy to identify the presence of histologic inflammation associated with ulcerative colitis (with video). *Gastrointestinal Endoscopy, 89*(2), 408–415. https://doi.org/10.1016/j.gie.2018.09.024

Marr, B. (2015). *How big data is changing healthcare.* https://www.forbes.com/sites/bernardmarr/2015/04/21/how-big-data-is-changing-healthcare/#3f565b832873.

Miettinen, M., & Lasota, J. (2006). Gastrointestinal stromal tumors: Pathology and prognosis at different sites. *Seminars in Diagnostic Pathology, 23*(2), 70–83. https://doi.org/10.1053/j.semdp.2006.09.001

Miettinen, M., Makhlouf, H., Sobin, L. H., & Lasota, J. (2006). Gastrointestinal stromal tumors of the jejunum and ileum: A clinicopathologic, immunohistochemical, and molecular genetic study of 906 cases before imatinib with long-term follow-up. *The American Journal of Surgical Pathology, 30*(4), 477–489. https://doi.org/10.1097/00000478-200604000-00008

Miettinen, M., Sobin, L. H., & Lasota, J. (2005). Gastrointestinal stromal tumors of the stomach: A clinicopathologic, immunohistochemical, and molecular genetic study of 1765 cases with long-term follow-up. *The American Journal of Surgical Pathology, 29*(1), 52–68. https://doi.org/10.1097/01.pas.0000146010.92933.de

Naseem, Z., & Khalid, R. (2010). Positive thinking in coping with stress and health outcomes: Literature review. *Journal of Research & Reflections in Education, 1.*

Nemati, S., Holder, A., Razmi, F., Stanley, M. D., Clifford, G. D., & Buchman, T. G. (2018). An interpretable machine learning model for accurate prediction of sepsis in the ICU. *Critical Care Medicine, 46*(4), 547–553. https://doi.org/10.1097/CCM.0000000000002936

Ohlhorst, F. J. (2012). *Big data analytics: Turning big data into big money.*

Porter, M. F. (2001). *Snowball: A Language for Stemming Algorithms.* Snowball.

Post, L., Ganzevoort, R. R., & Verdonck-De Leeuw, I. M. (2020). Transcending the suffering in cancer: Impact of a spiritual life review intervention on spiritual re-evaluation, spiritual growth and psycho-spiritual wellbeing. *Religions, 11*(3). https://doi.org/10.3390/rel11030142

Reinsel, D., Gantz, J., & Rydning, J. (2017). *He evolution of data to life-critical don't focus on big data; focus on the data that's big.* https://www.import.io/wp-content/uploads/2017/04/Seagate-WP-DataAge2025-March-2017.pdf.

Ruch, W., & Zuckerman, M. (2001). *Sensation seeking and adolescence* (pp. 97–110). Springer Science and Business Media LLC. https://doi.org/10.1007/978-3-663-11310-2_5

Italians belt out national anthem during virus lockdown. (2020). https://www.wtoc.com/2020/03/13/italians-belt-out-national-anthem-during-virus-lockdown/.

Sepsis — Global Sepsis Alliance. (n.d.). https://www.global-sepsis-alliance.org/sepsis.

Seven, G., Silahtaroglu, G., Kochan, K., Ince, A. T., Arici, D. S., & Senturk, H. (2021). Use of artificial intelligence in the prediction of malignant potential of gastric gastrointestinal stromal tumors. *Digestive Diseases and Sciences.* https://doi.org/10.1007/s10620-021-06830-9

Silahtaroglu, G., Baykal, E., & Canbolat, Z. N. (2020). Covōd-19 Salgōnōnda Yaşanan Haftalōk Duygusal Değişimler: Türkiye Örneği. *Ekonomi İşletme ve Maliye Araştōrmalarō Dergisi*, 280–304. https://doi.org/10.38009/ekimad.825285

Silahtaroğlu, G., & Yōlmaztürk, N. (2019). Data analysis in health and big data: A machine learning medical diagnosis model based on patients' complaints. *Communications in Statistics - Theory and Methods, 50.* https://doi.org/10.1080/03610926.2019.1622728

Søreide, K., Sandvik, O. M., Søreide, J. A., Giljaca, V., Jureckova, A., & Bulusu, V. R. (2016). Global epidemiology of gastrointestinal stromal tumours (GIST): A systematic review of population-based cohort studies. *Cancer Epidemiology, 40*, 39–46. https://doi.org/10.1016/j.canep.2015.10.031

Szakmany, T., Lundin, R. M., Sharif, B., Ellis, G., Morgan, P., Kopczynska, M., Dhadda, A., Mann, C., Donoghue, D., Rollason, S., Brownlow, E., Hill, F., Carr, G., Turley, H., Hassall, J., Lloyd, J., Davies, L., Atkinson, M., & Jones, M. (2016). Sepsis prevalence and outcome on the general wards and emergencydepartments in Wales: Results of a multicentre, observational, point prevalence study. *PLoS One, 11*(12). https://doi.org/10.1371/journal.pone.0167230

Young, S. D. (2014). Behavioral insights on big data: Using social media for predicting biomedical outcomes. *Trends in Microbiology, 22*(11), 601–602. https://doi.org/10.1016/j.tim.2014.08.004

Zhu, Y., Wang, Q. C., Xu, M. D., Zhang, Z., Cheng, J., Zhong, Y. S., Zhang, Y. Q., Chen, W. F., Yao, L. Q., Zhou, P. H., & Li, Q. L. (2019). Application of convolutional neural network in the diagnosis of the invasion depth of gastric cancer based on conventional endoscopy. *Gastrointestinal Endoscopy, 89*(4), 806–815. https://doi.org/10.1016/j.gie.2018.11.011. e1.

Chapter 10

Big medical data analytics for diagnosis

Omanin Siddiqua Prova, Faiza Ahmed, Jafrin Sultana and Md. Ashrafuzzaman
Department of Biomedical Engineering, Military Institute of Science and Technology (MIST), Dhaka, Bangladesh

1. Introduction

1.1 Big medical data

Data is an incredible asset which is found in many structures. The term "big medical data" refers to aggregating and analyzing the myriad amounts of medical/clinical data to bolster early disease detection or provide an early indication of health hazards. Medical data includes a database that is of medical interest and is used in disease diagnosis. Big medical data analytics can reform medical care, support caregivers, medical device/software developers, and policymakers for arranging or executing better treatment policy, quicker disease identification, expanded customized medication, and bringing about cheaper, greater consideration in diagnosis with better results (Sonnati, 2017). Big medical data encompasses characteristics such as volume, variety, velocity (Raghupathi & Raghupathi, 2014; Rumsfeld et al., 2016), with respect specifically to healthcare veracity (Raghupathi & Raghupathi, 2014), and value (Ristevski & Chen, 2018). Fig. 10.1 shows the parameters of big medical data.

Volume: Numerous new data in the healthcare field will be created and stored continuously, which is going to result in a massive volume of potential data. Data of clinical importance is collected from different standard and conventional sources (Raghupathi & Raghupathi, 2014).

Variety: The term "Variety" in big medical data analytics indicates the diverse sources and types of data (Rumsfeld et al., 2016). The data (structured and unstructured data) is coming from numerous sources, the majority of them are collected from real-time data and real human interface (Khan et al., 2014, pp. 1–5).

Velocity: Assimilation of data is done in real-time at a rapid pace, which is termed as "Velocity." It is obvious that new data will continually be created over time and this unstoppable flow of data will generate new challenges. So, velocity is such an important parameter to cope with real-world applications (Dash et al., 2019; Raghupathi & Raghupathi, 2014).

Veracity: Veracity indicates the "trustworthiness" of data, the parameter that is concerned with the authenticity and quality of data (Pastorino et al., 2019). By the scaling of data, proper algorithm of removing errors make the outcome more reliable (Khan et al., 2014, pp. 1–5). Therefore, veracity or "data assurance" makes the data credible (Raghupathi & Raghupathi, 2014).

Value: It indicates the coherent analysis of the given data and the predicted outcome should have importance to clinicians (Ristevski & Chen, 2018). The parameter "Value" mainly infers how much valuable information can be extracted from the data and can create a reliable result (Khan et al., 2014, pp. 1–5).

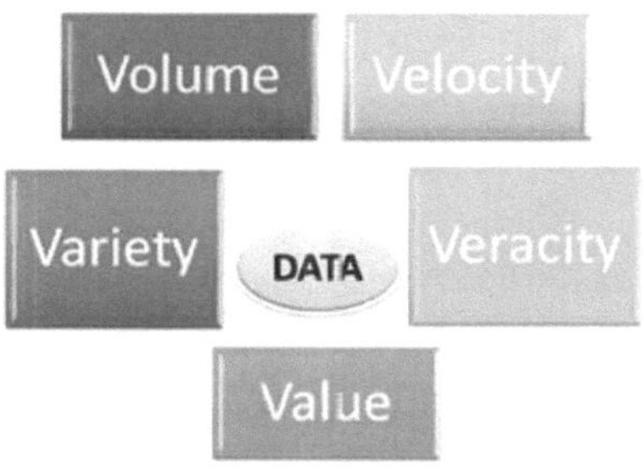

FIGURE 10.1 Parameters of big medical data.

Big Data Analytics for Healthcare. https://doi.org/10.1016/B978-0-323-91907-4.00013-3

1.2 Data lifecycle

Fig. 10.2 shows the data life cycle for big medical data analytics, which includes (1) Data Assortment, (2) Data Pre-preparing, (3) Data Declination and Conversion, (4) Data Analytics, and (5) Data Output. The steps of data life cycle are explained in the following subsections.

1.2.1 Data Assortment

The absolute first phase of the interaction is gathering the data from various archives, sources, and preserving it. Data can be organized, unstructured, and the effect on quality can be estimated through the assortment cycle (Sonnati, 2017).

1.2.2 Data prepreparing

After Data Assortment, this stage assists with purifying the data and sorting data likewise for additional examination. Setting up the data is a significant part of pushing the interaction forward (Sonnati, 2017).

1.2.3 Data declination and conversion

This stage assists in handling the data from the pipeline by lessening the least noticeable data segments. Data changes mean to change the data by applying different numerical and pressure calculations, but the system will not lose any data (Sonnati, 2017).

1.2.4 Data analytics

Data Analytics plays a significant part in breaking down the data by making determinations. Utilizing these results, plans of action can be improved; lucid connections can be made (Sonnati, 2017).

1.2.5 Data output

The factual, scientific data is introduced dependent on the information sources given. The produced reports are deciphered properly in different configurations for the client to view. The yield data is the significant data that assists in accomplishing the objective (Sonnati, 2017).

1.3 Impact of big medical data on the healthcare system

The capability of big medical data is that it could alter the results in regards to the most reasonable or precise patient determination and the exactness of data utilized in the wellbeing informatics framework. All things considered, the examination of immense measures of data will powerfully affect restorative administration structure in five regards, or "pathways" as shown in Fig. 10.3 (Kumar & Singh, 2019).

1.4 Digitized big medical data analytical applications for the health industry

Medical data are generally heterogeneous complex data, thus, it is difficult to extricate significant information regarding patient's condition, clinical activities, and examination. The assortment of programming utilities known as the Hadoop

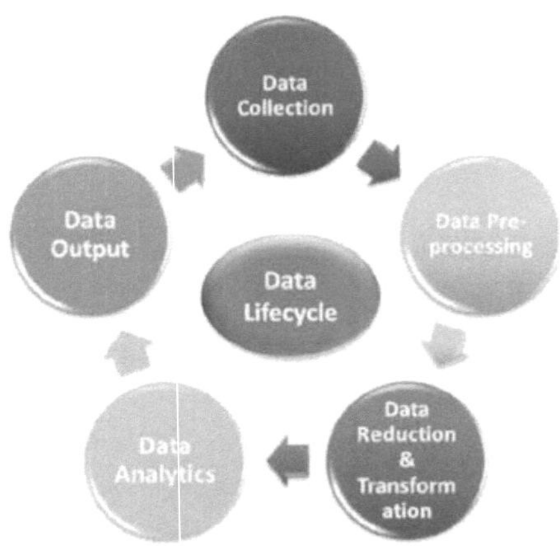

FIGURE 10.2 Data lifecycle.

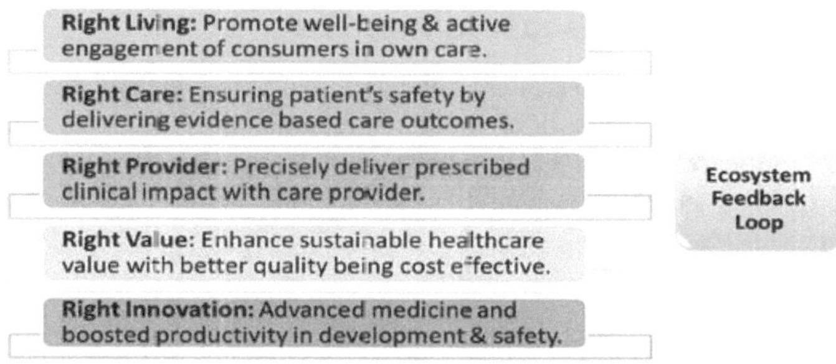

FIGURE 10.3 Revolutionary pathways impact on big medical data.

biological system can help the medical area to deal with profuse diverse data (Kumar & Singh, 2019). Different aspects of the Hadoop environment in the medical area are the following:

1.4.1 Cancer and genomics treatment

Human DNA contains three billion base sets. Data coordination in an equitable way is pivotal to learn about diseases and to plan treatments for fighting against the disease. MapReduce (Hadoop innovation) efficiently deals with these billion data sets of DNA base and provides a pertinent treatment plan in accordance to the specificity of the disease, which gives premise to treatment through a big medical data examination to save patients' lives (Kumar & Singh, 2019).

1.4.2 Monitoring of patient vitals

Hospital staff associate their work with big data innovation and use Hadoop-based segments in Hadoop Distributed File System (HDFS). Hospitals are furnished with equipment that tracks the heartbeat, pulse, and other imperative signs of patients. An alarm system keeps the staff knowing any issue to ensure the wellbeing of patients (Kumar & Singh, 2019).

1.4.3 Healthcare intelligence

Hospitals, clinics, and healthcare agencies utilize the Hadoop innovation with big medical data analytics that assist in yielding the best outcome. Hadoop biological system's Pig, Hive, and MapReduce measure datasets to extricate significant data (e.g., wanted age) for insurance agencies (Kumar & Singh, 2019).

1.4.4 Prevention and detection of frauds

With Hadoop, organizations use applications dependent on a forecast model to recognize extortion through data in regards to their past wellbeing claims, voice accounts, wages, and socioeconomics (Kumar & Singh, 2019). Fig. 10.4 shows interconnected Hadoop applications in healthcare with big medical data analytics.

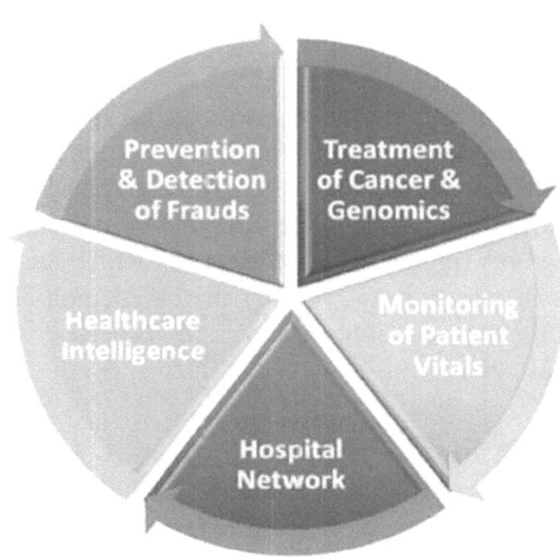

FIGURE 10.4 Hadoop applications in healthcare with big medical data analytics.

2. Big medical data analytics in disease diagnosis

In big medical data analytics, huge complex databases are collected, evaluated, and the result is delivered (Rumsfeld et al., 2016). Medical data analytics is collected via patient reports, wearable devices, telemedicine services, genomic data, pharmaceutical data, electronic healthcare records (EHRs), clinical trials, etc (Pastorino et al., 2019; Rumsfeld et al., 2016). In this section, the importance of big medical data analytics in diagnosis of diseases are highlighted.

2.1 Cardiology

Availability of huge amounts of data and proper use of these data analytics can assist in risk stratification (Sladojević et al., 2015). In the case of cardiology, big medical data analytics can play a prominent role in detecting cardiovascular diseases and can ameliorate the treatment procedure to a greater extent. However, there is some gap regarding the evidence-based treatment in the case of cardiovascular diseases. In this section, we are going to cover the potential of big data analytics in the case of decision-making and further treatment steps in the cardiovascular field (Xiao et al., 2021).

Cardiovascular medication has been a forerunner in the clinical utilization of models created utilizing these strategies. Models incorporate the rules for preoperative heart hazard appraisal, the thrombolysis in myocardial localized necrosis hazard score for visualization in intense coronary syndrome (Antman et al., 2000), and the CHA2DS2-VASc score for stroke forecast in atrial fibrillation (Lip et al., 2010). Conversely, big medical data examination can conceivably utilize a huge number of factors, to deliver dynamic prescient models that are consistently educated by recently gathered data, rather than the static models produced by standard multivariable relapse techniques.

2.1.1 Big medical data analytics in heart attack prediction

Among different cardiovascular diseases, heart attack (acute myocardial infarction-AMI) is one of the most dangerous diseases which occurs due to insufficient flood circulation within the heart. Plaque (a substance that is built up by cholesterol/fat cells) is the most common cause of heart attack (Alexander & Wang, 2017). In many research studies, it is mentioned that big medical data analytics tools can benefit in determining possibilities of heart attack early. Data mining is such a tool (Alexander & Wang, 2017; Ghadge et al., 2015). The data mining process can bolster clinicians with efficient methodology and technology to extract useful, pertinent information from the database (Koh & Tan, 2005). Data mining and machine learning algorithms can be utilized to develop software that can identify possibilities of heart attack at an early stage (Alexander & Wang, 2017; Ghadge et al., 2015; Wanaskar et al., 2016).

2.1.2 Troponin and implanted sensors for heart attack prediction

Detection of the risk factors can be assessed by an implanted sensor that senses abnormalities of heart activity. One such sensor is the troponin detector. Troponin is a chemical substance produced by the heart muscles when ischemia occurs. Troponin levels increase the blood within the heart just before a heart attack takes place. Various research institutes have developed some sensors that can detect troponin T/I and can immediately send the data to the care givers via smart phones. Thus, this implanted sensor assists in delivering signals of heart attack at an early stage by transmitting real-time data. These real-time troponin levels are collected and stored in EHR database for further analysis (Alexander & Wang, 2017).

2.1.3 Wireless detection

Smart devices like smartphones, wrist watches etc. wireless sensors can be utilized to acquire signal prior to a heart attack. If any software can be incorporated into these smart devices that can show the readings of EKG, this will alert the user by indicating abnormalities in EKG (Alexander & Wang, 2017). One research has mentioned a wrist watch with a heart attack detection sensor. That wristwatch has three subunits: a) The circuit, b) Analysis algorithm, and c) Bluetooth communication. In the watch, the ECG circuit captures signals from the heartbeat which are processed by a microcontroller unit that runs a heart attack algorithm. If any abnormal signal is sent by the circuit unit as well as by the microcontroller unit, a warning sign is provided to the user. At the moment of heart attack, the Bluetooth communication unit operates emergency calls for medical assistance (Kumar et al., 2014).

2.1.4 Telecardiology in heart attack prediction

Telecardiology is a system that diagnoses or evaluates cardiac activity from distance and enables precise therapeutic strategies for patients who reside in remote, rural areas using a telecommunication platform (Alexander & Wang, 2017; Hsieh et al., 2013). Telecardiology can benefit from "cloud computing" and large-scale medical data analysis. Cloud key features of "cloud computing" technology are high availability, accessibility, and scalability (Hsieh et al., 2013).

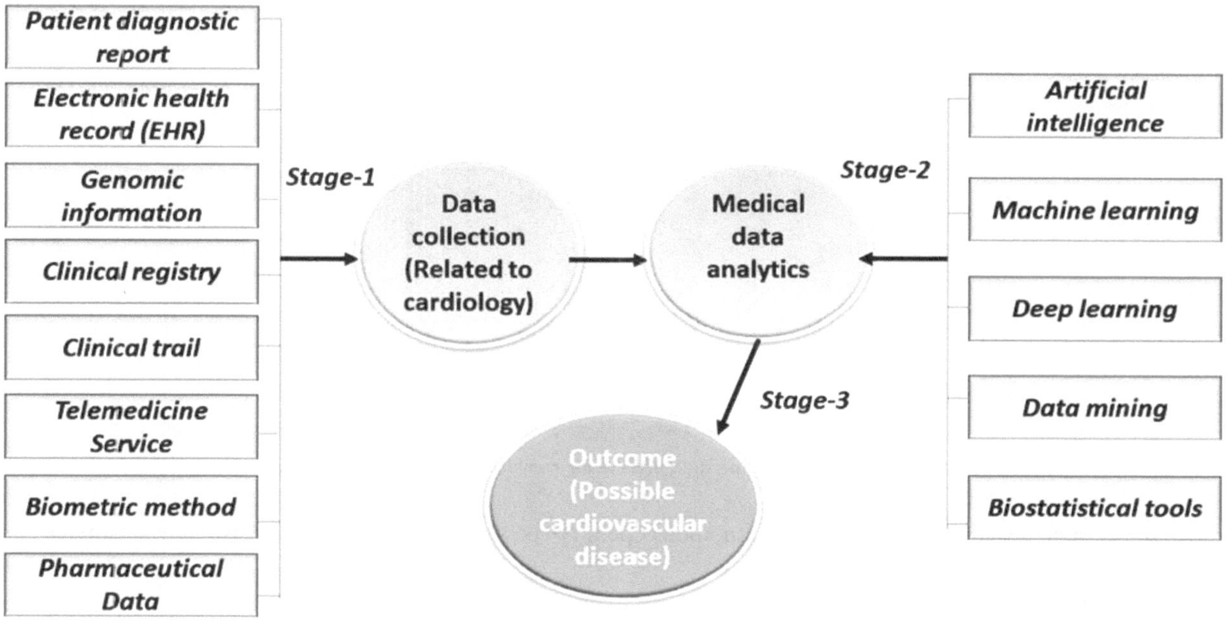

FIGURE 10.5 A scheme of big medical data analytics for improved cardiovascular diagnosis outcome.

Data mining is a technique that uses the existing big medical data to evaluate, predict, and suggest the best treatment model for patients. One research study has included some data mining tools like Decision trees (DT), C4.5, Artificial Neural Network (ANN), Naïve Bayes, Random Forest, and SVM, to assess cardiac data and predict heart disease. Among them, ANN, C4.5, and DT algorithms are used to examine ECG signals to capture any sign of cardiological disorder. That research work mentioned that the DT algorithm provides the best outcome among all other algorithms (Prerana et al., 2015).

Another research mentioned an open-source data mining tool Waikato Environment for Knowledge Analysis (WEKA). Some machine learning algorithms have been utilized to build a model for heart disease Alternating Decision Tree (ADTree), Random Tree, Random Forest, J48, J48graft, IB1, Naive Bayes, and meta–Cost Sensitive Classifier (listed by their WEKA denominations). The predictive models have gone through 10-fold cross-verification for investigating the validation. Among all the classifiers, the ADTree classifier produced the best result by predicting an 89% accuracy in-hospital mortality (Sladojević et al., 2015). Fig. 10.5 illustrates a scheme of big medical data analytics for improved cardiovascular diagnosis outcome.

2.2 Neurology

In the empire of medication, neurological problems are the most difficult to analyze, oversee, and screen because of the complex sensory system. Finding neurological disorders and their medicines require high exactness, commitment, and experience. There are in excess of 600 sicknesses of the sensory system, like epilepsy, dementias, Alzheimer's illness, and cerebrovascular infections including stroke, various sclerosis, Parkinson's infection, headache, neuro-contamination, brain tumors, and awful problems of the sensory system, for example, brain injury and physical imbalance (Siuly et al., 2011). Fig. 10.6 shows the involvement of specific causes to the combined burden of neurological diseases and disorders.

2.2.1 Epilepsy and epileptic seizure diagnosis

Epilepsy is quite possibly the most widely recognized and annihilating neurological illness in the world. Epilepsy is described by repetitive seizures (Siuly & Li, 2015). Seizures are characterized as abrupt changes in the electrical work of the brain, bringing about modified practices, like passing out, jerky developments, impermanent loss of breath, and cognitive decline. The EEG is a significant clinical apparatus which contains important data for understanding epilepsy (Siuly et al., 2015). A study was conducted in which the deep learning approach of data analytics associated with low power neuromorphic chip was used to predict seizures for patients with epilepsy. In this study, data was collected from intracranial electroencephalography which was processed using deep learning classifier and the deep learning model was verified for accuracy. This whole system was transferred into an ultralow power neuromorphic chip (TrueNorth chip) with

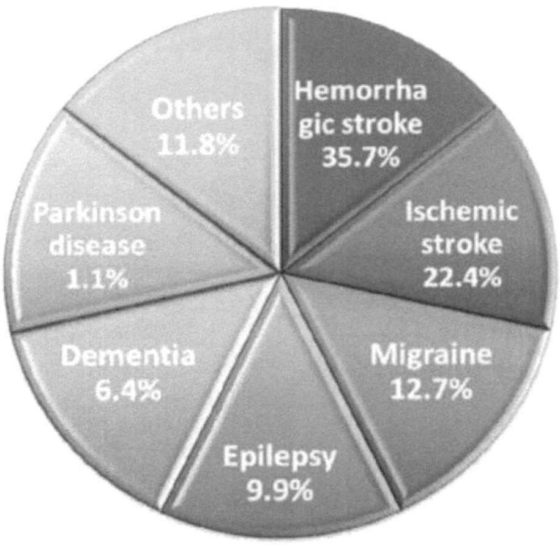

FIGURE 10.6 Involvement of specific causes to the combined burden of neurological diseases.

a view to developing a wearable device with autonomous operative power. The whole system showed a sensitivity of 69% (Kiral-Kornek et al., 2018).

2.2.2 Parkinson's disease diagnosis

One research study introduced a computerized system that uses big medical data for neurological disease diagnosis named "Computer-aided diagnosis (CAD)." This system involves three principal functions: 1) Data preprocessing, 2) Feature extraction, and 3) Data classification. In some diseases, CAD can assist expertise with higher accuracy and by reducing the cost for diagnosis, yet it is suggested in that research that an improved machine learning algorithm should be developed for making this system user friendly, which can assist in detecting many other intricate neural disorders (Siuly & Zhang, 2016).

Dinvo et al. (2016) highlighted in their research study that some ML approaches, adaptive boosting, support vector machines, etc., perform better for anticipating neural disorders. In this study, they have utilized Parkinson's Progression Markers Initiative (PPMI)—a heterogeneous data source. They concluded that several machine learning approaches were capable of predicting Parkinson's disease (using PPMI data) with more than 96% accuracy (by statistical n-fold cross-validation). In the case of disease diagnosis using the ML approaches, other parameters, e.g., Unified Parkinson's Disease Rating Scale scores (clinical parameter), cerebellum shape index (neuroimaging biomarker), rs34637584, and chr12 (genetics), were also included for making the prediction more reliable (Dinov et al., 2016).

An ML technique, Neural Network Construction (NNC), was introduced by Tsoulos et al. (2019) to diagnose PD that showed a promising outcome. In their research study, the objective was to differentiate between PD patients and healthy volunteers using an artificial intelligence (AI) platform (e.g., machine learning) and also capture various disease features of the PD patients. Data of the patients and volunteers were collected via mobile applications and classified by iMotor. iMotor is a cloud-based platform powered by an AI system showing high efficacy in classifying data. Classified data is then analyzed by ML technique NNC and achieved accuracy was 93.11% (Tsoulos et al., 2019). Fig. 10.7 shows a sample of the CAD system for neural disorder recognition/prediction.

2.2.3 Multiple sclerosis diagnosis

Multiple sclerosis (MS) is an autoimmune-medicated neural disorder which causes inflammation in the central nervous system causing severe physical or cognitive impairment (Ghasemi et al., 2017). Data analytics techniques—logistic regression (LR-a statistical tool) and support vector machine (SVM-a machine learning algorithm)—were highlighted by Zhao et al. (2017) in their research work for predicting MS using machine learning. Data including demographic, MRI data, and clinical data were analyzed by SVM tool and then the outcome is compared with LR analysis. SVM outperformed LR with a sensitivity and specificity of 71% and 68%, respectively (Zhao et al., 2017).

2.2.4 Stroke

Stroke is a life-threatening condition, also known as a Cerebro-Vascular Accident or CVA, which occurs due to blood flow disruption in the brain; blockages can disrupt the blood flow path, causing ischemic stroke, and another reason can be

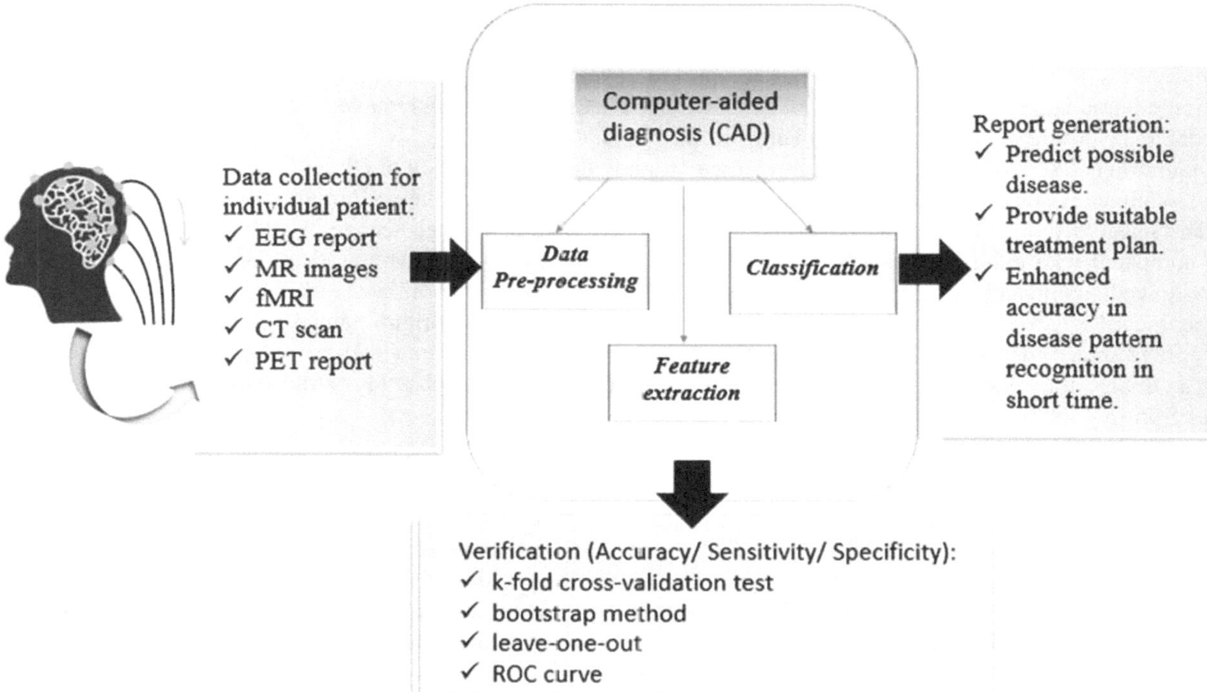

FIGURE 10.7 Computer-aided diagnosis (CAD) system for neural disorder recognition/prediction.

bursts of blood vessels causing hemorrhagic stroke. A research study mentioned the efficacy of an AI-based technique, ANN, which showed an accuracy of 95.15% in detecting the type of stroke and its further condition. By using k-fold cross-validation, the overall accuracy was 94.97%. The research work suggests data analytics tools as a promising feature for decision-making and treatment modeling activities (Masruriyah et al., 2019).

2.3 Ophthalmology

2.3.1 Deep learning in ophthalmology

Big medical data analytics has already created an influential impact on genomic analysis, targeted drug delivery, modeling treatment plans (Rahimy, 2018), real-time biomedical, and health monitoring systems (Dash et al., 2019) among many other healthcare fields. In ophthalmology, AI is already augmenting various diagnosis methods including imaging capabilities, early disease detection (Rahimy, 2018), assessment of diabetic retinopathy (DR), age-related macular degeneration (AMD) (Ting et al., 2019; Tufail et al., 2017), refractive error (Ting et al., 2019), and so on. The advancement of AI platforms is raising the hope to improve detection of other ophthalmic diseases including cataracts, corneal ectasia, and oculoplastic reconstruction after basal cell carcinoma excision (Rahimy, 2018).

The accuracy of predicted outcome using deep learning depends on the following factors: (a) advancement in central processing units, (b) advancement in graphics processing units, (c) availability of a huge amount of data, and d) developments in training algorithms (Shen et al., 2017). In the DL, each successive processing layer uses the output from the previous immediate layer and the last stage of the cascade delivers a diagnostic output (Rahimy, 2018).

2.3.2 Diabetic retinopathy

In a study by Tufail et al. (2017)etinal images were screened and analyzed by three different commercially available Automated Retinal Image Analysis Systems (ARIAS); they are (1) EyeArt (Eyenuk, Woodland Hills, California), (2) iGradingM (Medalytix Group Ltd, Manchester, UK), and (3) Retmarker (Retmarker SA, Taveiro, Portugal). A comparison was made with the manually graded same images, clearly indicating that EyeArt and Retmarker showed acceptable sensitivity and more cost-effective options for referable retinopathy compared with manual graders. The sensitivities estimated of the ARIAS were as follows: for retinopathy, EyeArt showed sensitivity of 94.7% (94.2%–95.2%), for referable retinopathy, the estimation was 93.8% (92.9%–94.6%), and for proliferative retinopathy, it was 99.6% (97.0%–99.9%); Retmarker system showed 73.0% (72.0 %-74.0%) for any retinopathy, for referable retinopathy, the sensitivity was 85.0% (83.6%–86.2%), and for proliferative retinopathy, Retmarker showed 97.9% (94.9%–99.1%) sensitivity. iGradingM served the result as all either having disease or being ungradable. The human grade result was either ungradable, or proliferative maculopathy (Tufail et al., 2017).

Abràmoff et al. (2016) demonstrated in their research study that incorporation of DL tool convolutional neural networks (CNNs) with an existing lesion-based DR detection algorithm has enhanced the performance of identification referable to DR. The sensitivity was detected at 96.8% and specificity was 87.0%. Though sensitivity did not show much difference when compared with published sensitivity of IDP (Iowa Detection Program - without deep learning components), specificity showed significantly better results than that of IDP specificity (Abràmoff et al., 2016).

Cheng et al. (2020) have mentioned in the research study that a DL algorithm named SELENA+ was authorized in Singapore to screen for DR. In that same study they have mentioned another example from Poplin et al. research work in which a DL algorithm was developed to successfully predict the risk factors related to cardiovascular diseases using retinal images from big medical data sources (Cheng et al., 2020).

2.3.3 Age-related macular degeneration

AMD is the deterioration of the retina which is one of the common disorders that cause elderly people to lose their vision, which has no cure (Burlina et al., 2017). The researchers tried to develop a DL algorithm for detecting AMD by means of automated investigation using existing fundus images. The outcome of deep CNNs (DL algorithm) which was trained to assess automated AMD and an alternative DL method (that used transfer learning, universal features, and a trained clinical grader) was compared. The deep CNN algorithm presented an accuracy of a range between 88.4% (SD, 0.5%) and 91.6% (SD, 0.1%). This outcome was pertinent to the standard dataset for Age-Related Eye Disease Study (AREDS) (Burlina et al., 2017; Rahimy, 2018).

Dong et al. (2021) mentioned in their study that the largest database, Age-Related Eye Disease Study (AREDS), which is a publicly available database, includes more than 130,000 fundus images. This database is widely used to diagnose AMD. Bhuiyan et al. mentioned that when a trained CNN-based algorithm was incorporated with AREDS database, an accuracy of 99.2% for detecting referable AMD was obtained (Dong et al., 2021).

2.3.4 Glaucoma

Glaucoma is the progressive degradation of optical nerves associated with diminished retinal ganglion cells as well as thinning of the retinal nerve fiber layer (Schuster et al., 2020). Asaoka et al. (2016) mentioned in their study that a DL tool named deep feed-forward neural network (FNN) can assist in differentiating visual fields (VFs) of preperimetric glaucoma from that of healthy VFs. This tool has produced higher area under the operating characteristic curve of 92.6% (95% confidence interval [CI]). Compared with any other machine learning systems, the FNN has provided the best outcome (Asaoka et al., 2016; Rahimy, 2018).

One study evaluates a computer vision–based hybrid deep learning method (HDLM), where the results are compared with optical coherence tomography (OCT) and VFs. The focus in this comparison was whether HDLM can distinguish eyes (which are already classified by some other evaluation process) in healthy or mild glaucoma categories. HDML protocol performs better than conventional OCT and VF outcomes with accuracy of approximately 63.7%–93.1%; on the other hand, the accuracy range for OCT and 24-2, 10-2 VF metrics was approximately 66.7%–87.3% (Muhammad et al., 2017). Fig. 10.8 presents an overview of big medical data analytics in ophthalmology for better diagnostic output.

2.4 Respiratory system

2.4.1 Big medical data in lung care purpose

Big medical data investigation which uses masses of dissimilar, organized, and unstructured data sources will assume a fundamental part in how medical services are drilled later on. One would already be able to see a range of investigations being used, supporting the dynamic and execution of medical care staff and patients in health care mentioned ably in respiratory and critical care medicine for the lungs as well (Panda et al., 2016).

2.4.2 Use of big medical data analytics to interpret COPD

The possibility of big medical data in the field of wellbeing explicitly in the lung care area is not just about the size of it, but it discovers normal understanding of the heterogeneous, complex, and longitudinal boundaries of data sets. Big medical

Big Medical Data Analytics in Ophthalmology

Diseases/ Disorder	Data Analytics Tools	Outcome
• Cataract • Diabetic Retinopathy • Age-related macular degeneration (AMD) • Glaucoma • Myopia • Hypermetropia • Corneal ectasia	• Deep learning tool • Convolutional neural networks (CNNs) • SELENA+ • Feed-forward neural network (FNN) • Hybrid deep learning method (HDLM) • EyeArt • iGradingM • Retmarker	• Early disease prediction • Increase regulatory compliance • Decrease diagnosis costs • Decrease decision-making times • Diagnose disease more precisely • Prescribe customized treatment model

FIGURE 10.8 An overview of big medical data analytics in ophthalmology for better diagnostic output.

data can be of gigantic benefit to the medical care industry, overflowing with the monstrous volume of data that should be approved and dissected.

A medical service proficient thinks that it's hard to recognize patients in high danger of having Chronic Obstructive Pulmonary Disease, yet information on the patient's clinical history may make it simple for them. Data mining is the way toward analyzing enormous datasets to remove the covered up and obscure examples, connections, and information that are truly challenging to relate to conventional factual techniques. Data mining in the medical care industry is an rising field for giving high significance to specialist conclusions in regards to how patients will recuperate from sickness and furthermore understanding further about clinical data (Panda et al., 2016).

2.4.3 Practice of big medical data in lung cancer

Big medical data certainly tosses dare on malignancy research in various conditions. The patterns of getting sorted out various stages and their discoveries make an intersection among various areas and estimation, which is eventually a stage toward a whole comprehension of the infection. The data remain alive of data on a few cellular breakdowns in the lungs patients used to analyze the impact of chemotherapy medicines in drawing out solidness time. Reiteration is a trait of data interaction, not a part of the model to fill the entire need productively (Alsunaidi et al., 2021).

2.4.4 Solicitation of big medical data to regulate the controlling of COVID-19 pandemic

The work of man-made consciousness close by data examination devices can help in the extraction and portrayal of data continuously in computerized early conclusion and visualization of a few illnesses overall, and COVID-19 explicitly has shown huge results. Essentially, a distant COVID-19 patient triaging framework likewise permits them to distantly check the patients.

The volume of data increments significantly after some time, particularly data produced on the worldwide pandemic brought about by COVID-19. Such a volume of data requires using big medical data examination instruments alongside AI strategies to sort out the pandemic and control its spread in an ideal way (Kumar & Singh, 2019). Fig. 10.9 shows big medical data analytics in lung care screening purposes.

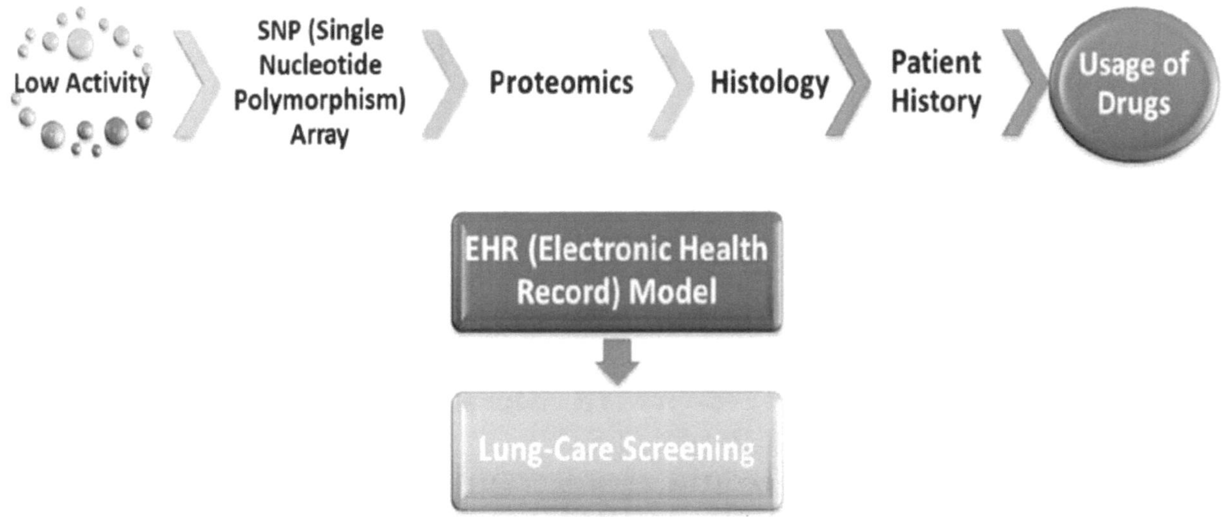

FIGURE 10.9 Big medical data analytics in lung care screening purposes.

3. Big medical data analytics tools/algorithms

3.1 Machine learning on big medical data analysis for diagnosis

Analytics of big data by means of machine learning (ML) provides the user with considerable benefits, including assimilation, analyzation, and evaluation of massive intricate data in the healthcare discipline (Ngiam & Khor, 2019). Among the subclasses of AI, ML is a self-learning−based tool that executes its learning process in accordance to the implemented algorithms. Supervised, unsupervised, and reinforcement learning are the prominent categories of ML. Algorithm that provides input database for training as well as testing is referred to as "Supervised learning." This learning is utilized to predict the outcomes when a huge dataset is given. The algorithm which is implemented to identify intricate data by means of formerly acquired knowledge and can further classify the class of data is termed as "Unsupervised learning." Reinforcement learning is an algorithm which is based on learning related to decision-making concepts; this learning acts to deliver valuable or desired accuracy in outcome (Sharma et al., 2021). Clinical datasets are often analyzed by ML tools using supervised learning algorithms. This approach of data analytics provides potential technological support in finding effective structural information from any given digital database. Unlike any clinical device, ML tools have a unique feature of continuously updating data and predicted outcomes through "incremental learning," where the AI system is connected using closed data feed-back loop to reestablish the predictive accuracy of the analysis through the repetitive retraining approach (Alexander & Hammer, 2016).

One study has stated the higher sensitivity of the ML algorithm in retinal diagnosis. IDx-DR, an ML tool, has finally been incorporated to detect current clinical problems. This tool is also the first FDA-approved ML tool which can provide screening decisions. This tool analyzes retinal images of the patient and delivers the result in two ways: (1) Positive (for more than mild DR) and (2) Negative (Lower or mind DR). The study also mentioned its high sensitivity and specificity, which are 87% and 91%, respectively (Ngiam & Khor, 2019).

In that study, they mentioned some machine learning approaches that can generate multilable read-outs. A deep neural network is such an example which analyzed images from ultrasound and was capable of labeling prostate cancer tumors into aggressive, less clinically significant and benign categories. In this regard, the sensitivity and specificity of the system was higher than 70% (Ngiam & Khor, 2019).

3.2 Data mining in big medical data analytics

Data mining on big medical data analytics can be modeled for detecting various diseases at an early stage. The researcher proposed a method termed as "Patient-customized Health System based on Hadoop with Text Mining (PHSHT)." This method is capable of producing accurate disease rules and can assist in decision-making. Patients get access to know current health conditions through the system so that any unexpected accidents can be avoided. The Hadoop platform is a text mining framework that it is designed to assess an individual's health condition by evaluating patient reports, then predict the disease (Alexander & Wang, 2017; Lee & Jeong, 2014).

Apache Hadoop is a prominent aspect in the field of medical data analytics which was developed by Yahoo. It is basically an open-source software platform that is built using Java and can process and store numerous datasets on computer clusters. Apache Hadoop's central core includes (i) a storage part - HDFS and (ii) a processing segment - Map Reduce. Copies of each data set are made by HDFS and this system further distributes the copies to a cluster for reliable access. The Hadoop framework divides big medical data into smaller parts to store it in a computer cluster (Ghadge et al., 2015).

The PHSHT, which is a Hadoop-based framework, is segmented into four modules as the following:

1. **Medical Data Collection Module (MDCM):** This module collects data from various sources and stores this data in Hbase. Hbase is the data storage and is used when engineers need any kind of data (real-time read and write access). The data collected from various sources by MDCM is separated into structured data (for instance, patient information, family history, medical reports, etc.) and unstructured data (for example, EHR, PACs - picture archiving and communication system, etc.) (Alexander & Wang, 2017; Lee & Jeong, 2014).
2. **Text Mining–based Hadoop Module (TMHM):** This module analyzes the assembled unstructured data through text mining and converts it into structured data (Lee & Jeong, 2014).
3. **Disease Rule Creation Module (DRCM):** In this module, the patient-specific disease rule is generated by combining the stored information in the Hbase and the Conditional Probability Set Theory algorithm (Lee & Jeong, 2014).
4. **Disease Management and Prediction Module (DMPM):** After analyzing the risk factors of an individual patient using his/her collected data and disease rules generated by DRCM, this module acts to notify the patient of a risk index resulting from disease prediction (Lee & Jeong, 2014).

3.3 The Internet of Things and disease prediction

Big medical data assembled from the Internet of Things (IoT) has dramatically influenced clinical informatics and telematics (Saheb & Izadi, 2019). IoT is an advanced technology that includes sensors/wearable devices, data acquisition algorithms, and network connectivity where subjects (i.e., patients and doctors) can remain connected to a remote service and can exchange data (Alexander & Wang, 2017; Dimitrov, 2016). Technologies that interact with physical systems effectively, e.g., Radio Frequency Identification (RFID) and Near Field Communication (NFC) devices, are intensively used in this IoT field (Dash et al., 2019).

A research work mentioned a big medical data analytics framework using IoT which facilitates the basic parameters of data analytics—volume and velocity (Rahman et al., 2019). The IoT can be used to predict diseases or can help in taking immediate measures in case of sudden health distress based on monitoring real-time data (Alexander & Wang, 2017). Now, engineering analytical solutions are making medicine participatory, personalized, predictive, and preventive (also termed as P4 medicine) using data collected from the medical Internet of Things (Dimitrov, 2016).

Dimitrov (2016) has mentioned in a study that many companies are trying to pile up this data to obtain control. For instance, Health Vault—an e-health safe—developed by Microsoft acts as an Electronic Medical Records. Another such platform is "HereIsMyData"—Radboud University Medical Center, Holland, collaborated with Philips and Salesforce to have developed this platform, which is actually a database that stores patient's health data and can control access (Dimitrov, 2016).

4. Challenges

Big medical data analytics is such a promising aspect that will advance the whole healthcare industry. This assists clinicians to take accurate decisions regarding equivocal conditions and decreases the length of time for making diagnostic decisions and curb down expenses on diagnosis. However, big medical data analytics include some challenges which may sometimes limit its efficacy (Rumsfeld et al., 2016). The challenges can be highlighted as follows:

- Big medical data analytics deals with massive heterogeneous clinical data. This data is then processed using AI techniques. Sometimes it is a challenge for the system to correlate between a standard treatment protocol using this huge heterogeneous data.
- Sometimes it becomes a matter of challenge to the system to understand intricate unstructured clinical notes to produce an appropriate context.
- Analyzing complex data (e.g., genomic data) computationally is an intensive, rigorous process. Merging the result from computational analysis and standard protocols requires the whole system to include more complex analytics layers (Alexander & Wang, 2017).

- Capturing behavioral data is another challenge in big medical data analytics as this data varies drastically from person to person. Developing an algorithm that can capture this type of data previously is really challenging.
- Sometimes, poor quality of medical images puts the analytics system at a stake. Clinical notes—that are given as an input to train analytic algorithms—sometimes demand an explanation. Therefore, providing worldwide accepted clinical notes requires extremely vigorous data reasonable or credible data collection process (Rumsfeld et al., 2016).
- Another biggest challenge in medical data analytics is the privacy of patient data, data security, and legal considerations (Rumsfeld et al., 2016).
- One challenging issue in this regard is the diagnosis of rare diseases. In the case of common diseases, the machine learning algorithms/software can be trained with a massive amount of data, but in the case of rare diseases, the software cannot be trained with adequate data, and thus diagnosing rare diseases using big medical data analytics remains a questionable issue (Ting et al., 2019).

5. Future scopes

Big medical data investigation in medication and medical services is an exceptionally encouraging cycle of incorporating, investigating, and breaking down enormous complex heterogeneous data. Reconciliation of such assorted data has raised the hope of improved fields such as bioinformatics, clinical imaging, sensor informatics, clinical informatics, wellbeing informatics, and computational biomedicine. Some mentionable future perspectives and opportunities are:

- To develop the dynamic cycle with the ongoing examination and to further progress patient-driven medical services and to upgrade customized medication.
- To help early discovery of illnesses and prognostic appraisal by anticipating plagues and pandemics, further developing infection observing, carrying out, and following wellbeing practices.
- To additionally improve data quality, construction, and openness by empowering the improvement of quick obtaining of enormous volumes and sorts of data, in a straightforward way.
- To work on the nature of care by further developing proficient wellbeing results, diminishing the misuse of assets, expanding efficiency and execution, advancing danger decrease, and enhancing measures the board.
- To give better structures to oversee populace wellbeing either through early location of illnesses or building up approaches to help wellbeing policymakers.

6. Conclusion

The medical field is enriched with complex, heterogeneous medical data. Big medical data analytics tools incorporated with existing treatment modalities using this huge data is overhauling medical service in such a way that was unimaginative once. By ousting intricate and time-consuming manual diagnosis procedures, these analytics is incessantly proving its promising role by delivering epigrammatic diagnosis outcomes, making doctors more aplomb in treatment planning. In this chapter, we have introduced some ML algorithms, deep learning techniques, and data mining tools that have proved to deliver diagnosis outcomes with higher accuracy, sensitivity, and specificity. In addition, advancing in any medical research using big medical data will surly be an effective way; achieving a realistic and credible result will be more easier without stretching out enormous methods/tools. However, this field of data analytics faces some challenges that sometimes constrain its promising role. To overcome the challenges, intensive delve is needed. The articulate research outcome will augment disease diagnosis techniques by developing more reasonable diagnosis algorithms or software.

References

Abràmoff, M. D., Lou, Y., Erginay, A., Clarida, W., Amelon, R., Folk, J. C., & Niemeijer, M. (2016). Improved automated detection of diabetic retinopathy on a publicly available dataset through integration of deep learning. *Investigative Ophthalmology & Visual Science, 57*(13), 5200–5206. https://doi.org/10.1167/iovs.16-19964

Alexander, G., & Hammer, B. (2016). Incremental learning algorithms and applications. In *European Symposium on Artificial Neural Networks (ESANN), Bruges, Belgium. ⟨hal-01418129⟩*.

Alexander, C., & Wang, L. (2017). Big data analytics in heart attack prediction. *Journal of Nursing & Care, 06*. https://doi.org/10.4172/2167-1168.1000393

Alsunaidi, S. J., Almuhaideb, A. M., Ibrahim, N. M., Shaikh, F. S., Alqudaihi, K. S., Alhaidari, F. A., … Alshahrani, M. S. (2021). Applications of big data analytics to control COVID-19 pandemic. *Sensors, 21*(7), 2282.

Antman, E. M., Cohen, M., Bernink, P. J. L. M., McCabe, C. H., Horacek, T., Papuchis, G., … Braunwald, E. (2000). The TIMI risk score for unstable Angina/non−ST elevation MI. *Journal of the American Medical Association, 284*(7), 835.

Asaoka, R., Murata, H., Iwase, A., & Araie, M. (2016). Detecting preperimetric glaucoma with standard automated perimetry using a deep learning classifier. *Ophthalmology, 123*(9), 1974−1980. https://doi.org/10.1016/j.ophtha.2016.05.029

Burlina, P. M., Joshi, N., Pekala, M., Pacheco, K. D., Freund, D. E., & Bressler, N. M. (2017). Automated grading of age-related macular degeneration from color fundus images using deep convolutional neural networks. *JAMA Ophthalmology, 135*(11), 1170−1176. https://doi.org/10.1001/jamaophthalmol.2017.3782

Cheng, C.-Y., Soh, Z. D., Shivani, M., Sahil, T., Rim, T. H., Tham, Y. C., & Wong, T. Y. (2020). Big data in ophthalmology. *Asia-Pacific Journal of Ophthalmology, 9*(4), 291−298. https://doi.org/10.1097/APO.0000000000000304

Dash, S., Shakyawar, S., Sharma, M. K., & Kaushik, S. (2019). Big data in healthcare: Management, analysis and future prospects. *Journal of Big Data, 6*, 1−25.

Dimitrov, D. V. (2016). Medical Internet of things and big data in healthcare. *Healthcare Informatics Research, 22*(3), 156−163. https://doi.org/10.4258/hir.2016.22.3.156

Dinov, I. D., Heavner, B., Tang, M., Glusman, G., Chard, K., Darcy, M., Madduri, R., Pa, J., Spino, C., Kesselman, C., Foster, I., Deutsch, E. W., Price, N. D., Van Horn, J. D., Ames, J., Clark, K., Hood, L., Hampstead, B. M., Dauer, W., & Toga, A. W. (2016). Predictive big data analytics: A study of Parkinson's disease using large, complex, heterogeneous, incongruent, multi-source and incomplete observations. *PLoS One, 11*(8), e0157077. https://doi.org/10.1371/journal.pone.0157077

Dong, L., Yang, Q., Zhang, R. H., & Wei, W. B. (2021). Artificial intelligence for the detection of age-related macular degeneration in color fundus photographs: A systematic review and meta-analysis. *EClinicalMedicine, 35*, 100875. https://doi.org/10.1016/j.eclinm.2021.100875

Ghadge, P., Girme, V., Kokane, K., & Deshmukh, P. (2015). Intelligent heart attack prediction system using big data. *International Journal of Recent Research in Mathematics Computer Science and Information Technology, 2*, 73−77.

Ghasemi, N., Razavi, S., & Nikzad, E. (2017). Multiple sclerosis: Pathogenesis, symptoms, diagnoses and cell-based therapy. *Cell Journal, 19*(1), 1−10. https://doi.org/10.22074/cellj.2016.4867

Hsieh, J. C., Li, A. H., & Yang, C. C. (2013). Mobile, cloud, and big data computing: Contributions, challenges, and new directions in telecardiology. *International Journal of Environmental Research and Public Health, 10*(11), 6131−6153. https://doi.org/10.3390/ijerph10116131

Khan, M., Uddin, M., & Gupta, N. (2014). *Seven V's of big data understanding big data to extract value*. https://doi.org/10.1109/ASEEZone1.2014.6820689

Kiral-Kornek, I., Roy, S., Nurse, E., Mashford, B., Karoly, P., Carroll, T., Payne, D., Saha, S., Baldassano, S., O'Brien, T., Grayden, D., Cook, M., Freestone, D., & Harrer, S. (2018). Epileptic seizure prediction using big data and deep learning: Toward a mobile system. *EBioMedicine, 27*, 103−111. https://doi.org/10.1016/j.ebiom.2017.11.032

Koh, H. C., & Tan, G. (2005). Data mining applications in healthcare. *Journal of Healthcare Information Management: JHIM, 19*(2), 64−72.

Kumar, K. G., Arvind, R., Keerthan, P. B., Kumar, S. A., & Dass, P. A (2014). Wireless methodology of heart attack detection. *International Journal for Scientific Research and Development, 2*(4), 673−676.

Kumar, S., & Singh, M. (2019). Big data analytics for healthcare industry: Impact, applications, and tools. *Big Data Mining and Analytics, 2*(1), 48−57. https://doi.org/10.26599/bdma.2018.9020031

Lee, B. K., & Jeong, E. H. (2014). A design of a Patient-customized healthcare system based on the Hadoop with text mining (PHSHT) for an efficient disease management and prediction. *International Journal of Software Engineering and its Applications, 8*, 131−150. https://doi.org/10.14257/ijseia.2014.8.8,13

Lip, G. Y. H., Nieuwlaat, R., Pisters, R., Lane, D. A., & Crijns, H. J. G. M. (2010). Refining clinical risk stratification for predicting stroke and thromboembolism in atrial fibrillation using a novel risk factor-based approach. *Chest, 137*(2), 263−272.

Masruriyah, A., Djatna, T., Hardhienata, M., Hikmayanti, H., & Wahiddin, D. (2019). *Predictive analytics for stroke disease* (pp. 1−4). https://doi.org/10.1109/ICIC47613.2019.8985716

Muhammad, H., Fuchs, T. J., De Cuir, N., De Moraes, C. G., Blumberg, D. M., Liebmann, J. M., Ritch, R., & Hood, D. C. (2017). Hybrid deep learning on single wide-field optical coherence tomography scans accurately classifies glaucoma suspects. *Journal of Glaucoma, 26*(12), 1086−1094. https://doi.org/10.1097/IJG.0000000000000765

Ngiam, K. Y., & Khor, I. W. (2019). Big data and machine learning algorithms for health-care delivery. *The Lancet Oncology, 20*(5), e262−e273. https://doi.org/10.1016/S1470-2045(19)30149-4

Panda, R. P., Barik, P. P., & Prusty, P. A. K. (2016). A review paper on big data in lung cancer big data analytics in lung cancer. *International Journal of Trend in Research and Development, 3*(5), 2394−9333.

Pastorino, R., De Vito, C., Migliara, G., Glocker, K , Binenbaum, I., Ricciardi, W., & Boccia, S. (2019). Benefits and challenges of big data in healthcare: An overview of the European initiatives. *The European Journal of Public Health, 29*(Suppl. 3), 23−27. https://doi.org/10.1093/eurpub/ckz168

Prerana, T. H. M., Shivaprakash, N. C., & Swetha, N. (2015). Prediction of heart disease using machine learning algorithms- Naïve Bayes, introduction to PAC algorithm, comparison of algorithms and HDPS. *International Journal of Science and Engineering, 3*, 90−99.

Raghupathi, W., & Raghupathi, V. (2014). Big data analytics in healthcare: Promise and potential. *Health Information Science and Systems, 2*, 3. https://doi.org/10.1186/2047-2501-2-3

Rahimy, E. (2018). Deep learning applications in ophthalmology. *Current Opinion in Ophthalmology, 29*(3), 254−260. https://doi.org/10.1097/ICU.0000000000000470

Rahman, Md, Chhowa, T., Paul, A., & Ahmmed, R. (2019). *A narrative analysis on deep learning in IoT based medical big data analysis with future perspectives*. https://doi.org/10.1109/ECACE.2019.8679200

Ristevski, B., & Chen, M. (2018). Big data analytics in medicine and healthcare. *Journal of Integrative Bioinformatics, 15*(3), 20170030. https://doi.org/10.1515/jib-2017-0030

Rumsfeld, J. S., Joynt, K. E., & Maddox, T. M. (2016). Big data analytics to improve cardiovascular care: Promise and challenges. *Nature Reviews. Cardiology, 13*(6), 350–359. https://doi.org/10.1038/nrcardio.2016.42

Saheb, T., & Izadi, L. (2019). The paradigm of IoT big data analytics in the healthcare industry: A review of scientific literature and mapping of research trends. *Telematics and Informatics, 41*. https://doi.org/10.1016/j.tele.2019.03.005

Schuster, A. K., Erb, C., Hoffmann, E. M., Dietlein, T., & Pfeiffer, N. (2020). The diagnosis and treatment of glaucoma. *Deutsches Arzteblatt International, 117*(13), 225–234. https://doi.org/10.3238/arztebl.2020.0225

Sharma, N., Sharma, R., & Jindal, N. (2021). Machine learning and deep learning applications-A vision. *Global Transitions Proceedings, 2*. https://doi.org/10.1016/j.gltp.2021.01.004

Shen, D., Wu, G., & Suk, H. I. (2017). Deep learning in medical image analysis. *Annual Review of Biomedical Engineering, 19*, 221–248. https://doi.org/10.1146/annurev-bioeng-071516-044442

Siuly, S., Kabir, E., Wang, H., & Zhang, Y. (2015). Exploring sampling in the detection of multi-category EEG signals. *Computational and Mathematical Methods in Medicine*, 576437. https://doi.org/10.1155/2015/576437

Siuly, S., & Li, Y. (2015). Designing a robust feature extraction method based on optimum allocation and principal component analysis for epileptic EEG signal classification. *Computer Methods and Programs in Biomedicine, 119*(1), 29–42.

Siuly, S., Li, Y., & Wen, P. (2011). Clustering technique-based least square support vector machine for EEG signal classification. *Computer Methods and Programs in Biomedicine, 104*(3), 358–372.

Siuly, S., & Zhang, Y. (2016). Medical big data: Neurological diseases diagnosis through medical data analysis. *Data Science and Engineering, 1*(2), 54–64.

Sladojević, M., Čanković, M., Čemerlić, S., Mihajlović, B., Ađić, F., & Jaraković, M. (2015). Data mining approach for in-hospital treatment outcome in patients with acute coronary syndrome. *Medicinski Pregled, 68*(5–6), 157–161. https://doi.org/10.2298/mpns1506157s

Sonnati, R. (2017). Improving healthcare using big data analytics. *International Journal of Scientific & Technology Research, 6*, 142–146.

Ting, D., Peng, L., Varadarajan, A. V., Keane, P. A., Burlina, P. M., Chiang, M. F., Schmetterer, L., Pasquale, L. R., Bressler, N. M., Webster, D. R., Abramoff, M., & Wong, T. Y. (2019). Deep learning in ophthalmology: The technical and clinical considerations. *Progress in Retinal and Eye Research, 72*, 100759. https://doi.org/10.1016/j.preteyeres.2019.04.003

Tsoulos, I., Mitsi, G., Stavrakoudis, A., & Papapetropoulos, S. (2019). Application of machine learning in a Parkinson's disease digital biomarker dataset using neural network construction (NNC) methodology discriminates patient motor status. *Frontiers in ICT, 6*. https://doi.org/10.3389/fict.2019.00010

Tufail, A., Rudisill, C., Egan, C., Kapetanakis, V. V., Salas-Vega, S., Owen, C. G., Lee, A., Louw, V., Anderson, J., Liew, G., Bolter, L., Srinivas, S., Nittala, M., Sadda, S., Taylor, P., & Rudnicka, A. R. (2017). Automated diabetic retinopathy image assessment software: Diagnostic accuracy and cost-effectiveness compared with human graders. *Ophthalmology, 124*(3), 343–351. https://doi.org/10.1016/j.ophtha.2016.11.014

Wanaskar, U. H., Ghadge, P., Girmev, V., Deshmukh, P., & Kokane, K. (2016). Intelligent Heart attack prediction system using big data. *International Journal of Advanced Research in Computer and Communication Engineering, 5*, 723–725.

Xiao, H., Ali, S., Zhang, Z., Sarfraz, M. S., Zhang, F., & Faisal, M. (2021). Big data, extracting insights, comprehension, and analytics in cardiology: An overview. *Journal of Healthcare Engineering, 2021*, 6635463. https://doi.org/10.1155/2021/6635463

Zhao, Y., Healy, B. C., Rotstein, D., Guttmann, C. R., Bakshi, R., Weiner, H. L., Brodley, C. E., & Chitnis, T. (2017). Exploration of machine learning techniques in predicting multiple sclerosis disease course. *PLoS One, 12*(4), e0174866. https://doi.org/10.1371/journal.pone.0174866

Chapter 11

Big data analytics and radiomics to discover diagnostics on different cancer types

Ebru Aydindag Bayrak[1] **and Pinar Kirci**[2]
[1]*Istanbul University-Cerrahpasa, Istanbul, Turkey;* [2]*Bursa Uludag University, Bursa, Turkey*

1. Introduction

The latest developments in image processing and the utility of digital imaging on data extend the boundaries of the radiomics and radiomics analysis approaches. Radiomics is used for diagnosis of diseases, evaluation of prognosis, calculation of survivability rate, and prediction of treatment response.

In this ever-developing field, the main aim of the chapter is to explain the basics of radiomics and big data analytics. Several studies that are based on the detection of cancer using both big data analytics and radiomics have been reviewed. This chapter highlights the similarities, differences, challenges of radiomics and big data analytics, and also the applications that are using radiomics together with big data analytics.

The presented chapter is organized as follows. In Section 2, radiomics is explained. In Section 3, the methodology of radiomics and variable definitions of the process of radiomics are given. In Section 4, the applications of radiomics on several kinds of cancer types such as lung cancer, head and neck cancer, breast cancer, cervical cancer, bladder cancer, pancreatic cancer, liver cancer, ovarian cancer, biliary tract cancer, etc., are explained briefly. In Section 5, the definition of big data and the components of big data are mentioned. In Section 6, big data analytics, the comparison of big data analytics, traditional analytics, and the brief history of the emergence of big data analytics are clarified. The similarities and differences of radiomics and big data analytics are explained in Section 6. In Section 7, the challenges of radiomics and big data analytics are given. In Section 8, the relationship between radiomics and big data analytics are represented. And finally, this chapter ends with discussion and conclusion sections.

2. Radiomics

Radiomics was first coined by Lambin et al. (2012) and explained as a process that converts standard of care medical images into mineable high-dimensional data. Radiomics focuses on improvements in medical image analysis, using automated high-throughput extraction of huge amounts (higher than 200) of quantitative features of medical images. It can be said that it is the latest innovation in the field of medical imaging analysis. The hypothesis about radiomics can be explained by quantitative analysis of medical image data through automatic or semiautomatic software of a given imaging modality that can supply more accurate information than that of an expert. This approach is assisted by the fact that patients exhibit differences in texture and tumor shape measurable by several medical imaging modalities (Lambin et al., 2012).

Radiomics is a combination of the words “radio,” which means medical images, and “omics,” which represents fields such as genomics and proteomics that help us to understand various medical conditions. Radiomics can be applied to various imaging techniques such as Computer Tomography (CT), Magnetic Resonance Imaging (MRI), Positron Emission Tomography (PET), X-ray, and ultrasonography (Taşlõçay, 2020).

Quantitative extraction of imaging features from medical imaging is called radiomics, which has been spotlighted in recent times by lots of researchers. The studies in the literature have highlighted the potential of radiomics that can be used

Big Data Analytics for Healthcare. https://doi.org/10.1016/B978-0-323-91907-4.00016-9

as computer-aid diagnosis, as well as for estimating the possibility of survival and their response to the treatment for patients. Radiomics is an attractive field that purpose full-field analysis of the lesion and tumors and is noninvasive and almost enables real-time results (Bianconi et al., 2020).

Radiomics can be explained by the process of creating a set of systematic data that is derived from the physical features of an object of interest. For instance, radiomics is taking a photograph of an apple and recording lots of features on that apple's photo, containing the shape, color, overall size, smoothness, and number of lobulations. This data can be analyzed with statistical or machine learning techniques to state with a large accuracy value that the object in the photo is an apple and not a car. If we think in advanced stage, we can also state that the apple is a Granny Smith apple, its ripeness, and whether it is a hybrid variant. The promise of radiomics is that a certain evaluation of a lesion's imaging phenotype is an accurate representation of the lesion's biological behavior and genotype. This is sometimes called "radiogenomics" or "imaging genomics" as the second denotation (Hassani, Varghese, Nieva, & Duddalwar, 2019).

Radiomics is data obtained by extracting many numerical parametric values (attributes) from radiographic medical images. These numerical radiomics data can reveal disease attributes invisible to the naked eye. The aim of radiomics is to extract and analyze as much and meaningful confidential digital imaging data as possible for use in disease detection (Yiğit, 2021).

Radiomics emerged as a field of science that studies the numerical properties of images obtained by radiographic imaging methods. For example, a multislice or three-dimensional image of a patient may contain millions of voxels. A voxel can be defined as an image component of a CT image. In addition, a found tumor is expressed with hundreds of features that define the tumor's structure, size, shape, and texture. All these data are attempted to be associated with a clinical outcome. Radiogenomics, on the other hand, is a field of science that tries to correlate radiomics data with genetic data at the same time, and its aim is to determine the relationship between the genotype of cancer and the imaging phenotype (Parlar, 2020).

Radiomics uses the high throughput of extraction improved quantitative features to objectively and quantitatively to explain tumor phenotypes. These features are called radiomic features, because they cannot be detected with the naked eye, they are extracted from medical images using advanced mathematical algorithms to reveal tumor characteristics. Radiomics could ensure a huge chance to catch important phenotypic information like intratumor heterogeneity, and this valuable information can be used for personalized treatment (Yip & Aerts, 2016).

In traditional radiology practice, except for a few measurements like size and volume, the medical imaging datasets are assessed visually or qualitatively in general. This approximation not only involves intra- and interobserver variability but also ignores the vast amount of hidden data in the medical images. A general clinical scenario for the explanation of radiomics would be possible by imagining two patients with tumors with several qualitative features like shape, borders, size, and heterogeneity. In this scenario, the survival of the patients will likely be distinctive although the tumors have similar features as histopathologically. If the early prediction of prognosis of the patients is provided before any treatment, the health management of the patients would be divergent. This approach is termed precision medicine. In precision medicine, patients that belong to different subtypes need to be searched for to obtain better outcomes for diseases. Radiomics can be identified as an objective way to achieve these aims. The main aim of radiomics is to extract more and significant hidden objective data used in decision support systems (Koçak, Durmaz, Ateş, & Kõlõçkesmez, 2019).

The main goal of Radiomics is to provide worthwhile information about diagnostic, prognostic, or predictive using biological or medical data. Radiomics intends to utilize the full potential of medical imaging by extracting and analyzing huge amounts of developed quantitative imaging components, with high throughput from digital medical images, obtained from MRI, PET, and CT, etc. It enables a more detailed quantification of tumor phenotypic features such as intensity, texture, shape, and intratumor heterogeneity. When this process is applied, medical images are converted into a high-dimensional mineable feature space (Scrivener et al., 2016).

The determination of subtype and genotype of tumors with radiomics applications is possible today. Radiomics applications have important advantages in histopathological diagnosis processes because they are noninvasive and allow to obtain information from the entire tissue (Özer, 2019).

3. The methodology of radiomics

The Radiomics workflow on the medical images was summarized by four steps. The first step involves the image acquisition of high quality and standardized medical imaging, for diagnostic or planning. In the second step, segmentation is performed to identify the tumor region. In the third step, from this region, the features are extracted, such as features based on tumor shape, texture, and intensity. And, the final step, these features are used for analysis because the features are evaluated for their prognostic power, gene expression, or linked with stage (Lambin et al., 2012).

There are variable descriptions in various studies related to the radiomics process. The descriptions or summarizing of the process of radiomics included in variable sources are the following:

The process of radiomics is grouped as the following (Gillies, Kinahan, & Hricak, 2016):

Image acquisition, Preprocessing (Volume of interest identification), Segmentation, Feature Extraction, Building Database, and Data analysis.

The process of radiomic cycle was summarized differently with a few stages by (Capobianco & Dominietto, 2020):

Data Acquisition, Mining, and Assimilation, Feature Extraction, Feature Ranking and/or Selection, Modeling, and Validation.

Kumar et al. (2012) divided the process of radiomics into five steps:

Image acquisition and reconstruction, Image segmentation and rendering, Feature extraction and feature qualification, Databases and data sharing, and Informatics analysis.

In this chapter, the process of radiomics or the workflow of radiomics is grouped into four steps: (1) image acquisition, (2) segmentation, (3) feature extraction, and (4) analysis.

3.1 Image acquisition

One of the main steps in the process of radiomics is to define one or several volumes of interest (the primary tumor, nodules, etc.) in diagnostic medical imaging (Scrivener et al., 2016). The radiological images are obtained from several noninvasive medical imaging modalities such as CT, US, MRI, and PET. These preprocessed medical images are provided that they are coherent, and uniformity is continued. Then, all medical images are gathered to form a big database (Acharya et al., 2018).

3.2 Segmentation

Segmentation is an essential step as highly distinctive features are obtained from the segmented area of the images and these features are used in the development of a model for automated screening of radiological images. The aim of segmentation is to simplify or to modify the image for more meaningful analysis (Aerts et al., 2014).

The function of selecting the region of interest (ROI) and removing other irrelevant regions is called segmentation. Segmentation process can be according to a threshold value, region, model, and pixels (Parlar, 2020).

3.3 Feature extraction

Feature extraction is a step after when region interest (ROI) is determined and segmented. It is the selection of valuable information to help in the characterization of normal and nonnormal radiological images. These features consist of the shape, intensity, texture, and size of an ROI determined from radiological images (Acharya et al., 2018).

Feature extraction, which we can also call data transformation, is to obtain the image data as quantitative data suitable for the structure of machine learning algorithms. Two radiomic features are extracted in radiomics as semantic and agnostic features. Semantic radiomic features are generally used for explaining lesions by radiologists. With the prior knowledge that semantic features are of prognostic value, by means of early research in radiomics, the researchers developed radiology glossary much the same as BI-RADS (Breast Imaging Reporting and Data System), PI-RADS (Prostate Imaging Reporting and Data System), and Lung-RADS (Lung Imaging Reporting and Data System). Agnostic radiomic features on an image are mathematically extracted quantitative descriptors, which are not part of the radiologist's glossary (Gillies et al., 2016).

Radiomic features catch lesion and texture characteristics such as shape and heterogeneity and they can, solo or in conjunction with histologic, demographic, proteomic, or genomic data, be evaluated for clinical problem solving. Radiomic features are not only associated with genomic data but also may ensure supplementary (extra) information about tumor heterogeneity across the whole tumor volume to advance the prediction of survival. This useful information can be seen as proof of the classification of sick and healthy patients (Mayerhoefer et al., 2020).

The main part of radiomics is the high throughput extraction of quantitative image features that characterize the volumes of interest. The quantity of features is huge. That is more than 1000 and complicated. This causes to increase the risk of overfitting (Scrivener et al., 2016).

3.4 Analysis

In the last step of radiomics methodology, the selected and statistically significant features are supported by classifiers for further analysis and evaluation. These extracted radiomics features are then examined together with clinical data to analyze the mutuality of radiomics and clinical features (Narang, Lehrer, Yang, Lee, & Rao, 2016).

Radiomics analysis generally comprises of two main steps (Rizzo et al., 2018):

1. Dimensionality reduction and feature selection. It is usually achieved using unsupervised approaches.
2. Association analysis with one or more specific results using supervised approaches.

The step of analysis consists of two separate steps: the first step can be called model building in which a classification and/or regression model is produced and the second step, where the model is used to make predictions about the case or cohort of patients under evaluation (Bianconi et al., 2020).

Machine learning and deep learning are mostly used analysis techniques in radiomics and radiogenomics. Machine learning uses several algorithms to learn the data, analyze the data, and estimate from the data. By means of the improvement and progress in the field of machine learning, deep learning has emerged as a subset of machine learning (Acharya et al., 2018).

Machine learning methods enable us to analyze existing data and obtain the existing relationships in the data set and the characteristics of important information. Also, it produces a computational model that will identify data (Maity & Das, 2017, pp. 1–9).

Two significant roles of machine learning in radiology are as follows: Firstly, the allowing of radiomics, the automation of repetitive works, and the interpretation of complicated patterns in medical imaging data are not understandable with the naked eye. Secondly, the exploration of new disease signs and indicator patterns both in imaging and clinical record data, and the association of these signs to prediction of treatment response and the course of disease (Langs et al., 2018).

Deep learning is a computational model that consists of multiprocessing layers for learning representations of data with multidegree of abstraction. Deep learning explores complex structures in huge datasets using the backpropagation algorithm. The fundamental point of deep learning is that these layers of features are not planned/designed by human engineers. They are learned from data that is wielded a general-purpose learning procedure (LeCun, Bengio, & Hinton, 2015).

Machine and deep learning algorithms provide strong modeling tools to mine the big image data available, reveal hidden complex biological mechanisms, and enable personalized precision cancer treatment planning and early diagnosis (Avanzo et al., 2020).

As a result of the above-mentioned stages, which are also shown in Fig. 11.1, the qualitative and quantitative data obtained from the examined lesion are compared with the data in a large database through statistical models, and helpful information about the lesion characterization is obtained.

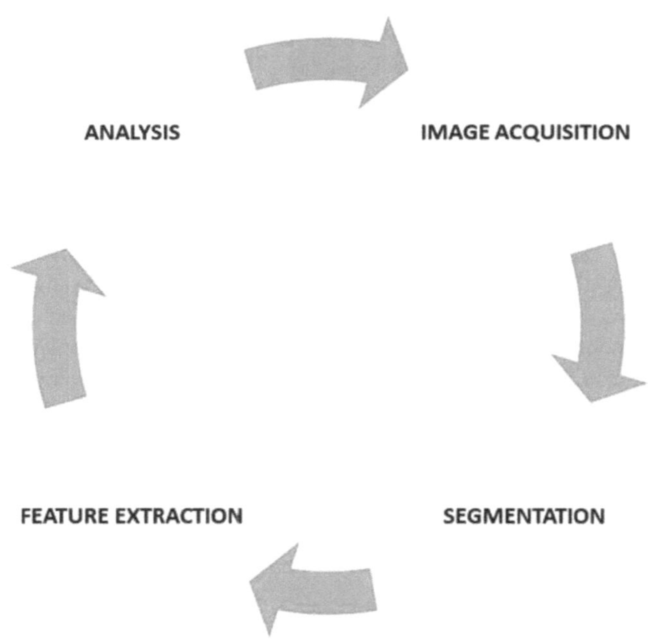

FIGURE 11.1 Overview of methodological processes in Radiomics.

4. The applications of radiomics on several kinds of cancer types

When reviewing the studies about radiomics and radiomics analysis, it is seen that a great number of them focused on oncological fields. O'connor (2017) made very good descriptions with his words about radiomic applications in cancer studies. "Radiomics uses computer algorithms to process the data collected by different medical imaging techniques and is becoming increasingly popular in cancer imaging research. One of its key characteristics is that radiomics recognizes that digital medical images are not only pictures—they are also complex data. Radiomic analyses extract and measure an array of 'features' that describe the image texture and distributions of individual voxel values—the units that make up a 3D image—within a tumor. Each voxel represents a tiny amount of tissue and contains around 105 to 107 neoplastic and stromal cells, depending on tumor type and voxel dimensions." (O'connor, 2017).

Below, studies on different types of cancer using radiomics and radiomics analysis techniques are briefly mentioned.

Ai, Zhu, Xie and Jin (2020) reviewed the latest clinical studies and future potential for the application of radiomics in the treatment of patients with cervical cancer. They concentrated on current and future potential of radiomics and how it can help to determine tumor stage, histological type, survival, metastasis, etc., in cervical cancer patients. Also, they discussed the existing difficulty and limitations of radiomics for oncology.

Conti, Duggento, Indovina, Guerrisi and Toschi (2021) reviewed the latest radiomics based on breast cancer research studies. The results showed that radiomics has a high potential to distinguish malign from benign breast lesions, classify breast cancer type, predict treatment response, and the risk of recurrence. They highlighted that radiomics can make a great contribution to early diagnosis, prognosis, prediction, and image-based diagnosis of breast cancer.

Gillies and Schabath (2020) studied how radiomics improved cancer screening and early detection. In particular, several studies about different cancer types such as cutaneous neoplasms, lung cancer, breast cancer, pancreatic cancer, prostate cancer, and liver cancer were reviewed to see the improvements of quantitative imaging approaches.

Mayerhoefer et al. (2020) intended to introduce radiomics with basic radiomics workflow. The studies about survival ability and treatment response of clinical applications in nuclear medicine based on PET radiomics are handled. Some selected articles on lung cancer, colorectal cancer, and gastric cancer are investigated in terms of application and limitations.

Sun et al. (2020) developed a model that evaluates axillary lymph node (ALN) metastasis status with deep learning (CNN), which is important in the treatment of breast cancer. They compared the CNN model with the model developed by classical radiomics analysis to predict ALN metastasis using mammography images. At the same time, three radiomics models were developed using the Random Forest (RF) machine learning algorithm. In the evaluated models, CNN models showed higher success in general.

Zhang et al. (2020) examined a radiomics model based on CT images for diagnosis and prediction of bladder cancer. Their study had good diagnostic performance. The AUC values of the suggested radiomics model were calculated at 0.95 and 0.86 for training and validation groups, respectively. Also, accuracy, sensitivity, specificity, positive prediction value, negative predictive value, and 95% confidence interval were calculated for both training and validation groups of bladder cancer.

Nougaret et al. (2019) explained the basics of radiomics, how to perform texture analysis as a form of radiomics, and its applications to ovarian cancer imaging in their study. They assessed that texture analysis could be difficult, but the result of the analysis was hopeful for tumor heterogeneity on CT and patient outcome.

Ji et al. (2019) suggested a radiomics-based model for predicting lymph node metastasis in biliary tract cancers and to identify its prognostic value for disease-specific and recurrence-free survival. Multivariable logistic regression analysis was applied to advance a model for predicting lymph node metastasis in the primary cohort. They evaluated the prognostic value of the radiomics model.

Sun et al. (2018) exercised to determine the effect of several machine learning and feature selection methods on prediction of overall survival for nonsmall cell lung cancer based on radiomics analysis. Spearman's linear correlation coefficient, Kendall's, Pearson's, Mutual information, and Concordance index were used as the filter-based feature selection methods to reduce the dimensions of radiomics features. The gradient boosting linear models based on Cox's partial likelihood method using the concordance index feature selection method showed the best performance.

Scrivener et al. (2016) studied a review about radiomics which was applied to lung cancer. The applications focused on radiomics in lung cancer are seen to become dense in two groups, as classification of lung nodules (diagnostic) and prognostication of established lung cancer (diagnostic). The advantages and disadvantages of radiomics in lung cancer were discussed and it is emphasized that radiomics enables new opportunities for precision medicine.

Wilson and Devaraj (2017) examined why radiomics analysis is suitable for interoperation of lung nodules. They reviewed several clinical applications about histological subtyping, predicting malignancy, posttreatment prognosis, and gene expression. It was explained that radiomics was cost-effective and noninvasive. It has a huge potential for diagnosis, survival ability, and treatment of lung cancer disease.

Cho, Clausi and Wong (2015) studied dermal radiomics framework for melanoma screening based on computer aid. They emphasized that radiomics increased the effectivity of distinguishing benign from malign melanoma. They calculated an 82.4% accuracy rate with RF classifier on 206 dermal radiomics features.

Hatt et al., 2015 executed texture feature analysis on PET images acquired from multiple cancer centers consisting of breast, cervical, NSCLC, esophageal, lung and head-and-neck tumors, and determined four prognostic radiomic features. Their results emphasize that the relationship and the level of correlation is not the same for all radiomics features.

Parmar et al. (2015) aimed to determine the best machine learning methods for the diagnosis of survival ability of head and neck cancer. They used 440 extracted radiomic features explaining shape, texture, and the first-order intensity statistics of the 3D tumor region on CT images of head and neck cancer. 13 feature selection methods based on filter approaches were used in their analysis. Also, 11 machine learning methods were applied to the images. RF, Bayesian, and Neural networks as machine learning methods showed great performance and stability for both cancer types.

Aerts (2016) investigated radiomic analysis of seven lung or head-and-neck cancer image data sets. They analyzed a large data set of 1019 lung and head-and-neck cancer patients, of extracted radiomic features from CT images. They found that numerous radiomic features have strong prognosis in independent datasets of lung and head-and-neck cancer patients, but many of them were not defined as significant marker previously. They showed that radiomic features based on capturing intratumor heterogeneity were a strong marker of prognosis and validated in three independent data sets of lung and head-and-neck cancer patients. Also, this result was affiliated with gene expression profiles.

Radiomics is a state-of-art approach that can provide a lot of information on the characteristics of tumors, and this promising approach can help to improve the early diagnosis, treatment, surveillance, the possibility of survivability, and prognosis of patients with several kinds of cancer types.

Radiomics enables to determine prognostic and predictive medical imaging biomarkers in noninvasive imaging experiments supplying so-called digital biopsies that can be obtained throughout the whole length of the treatment period of cancer. Radiomics can assist the results of biopsy techniques by detecting more doubtful locations by providing subsidiary information for cancer diagnosis, outcome prognosis, and prediction. Also, the combination of radiomics with other informative biomarkers can better promote clinical decision-making (Li et al., 2020).

The underlying hypothesis of radiomics is that improved image analysis on traditional and nouveau medical imaging could catch additional information not actually used, and more specifically, that genomic and proteomics models can be explained by using macroscopic image-based features. If it is verified, phenotypes or gene–protein signatures possibly containing prognostic information can be concluded from the quantitative analysis of medical image data (Lambin et al., 2012).

5. Big data

The term big data was first used in a study (Cox & Ellsworth, 1997). While explaining this concept, it was mentioned that the data sets are very large and fill the memory, disks, and even external disks of the computer system, and this problem encountered is called the "Big Data Problem" (Cox & Ellsworth, 1997).

Big data means data that is so huge, speedy, or complicated that it's hard to process using conventional methods. It is produced in several formats, fast and in huge volumes. As can be seen from the basic explanation of big data, it also brings new disadvantages in addition to its advantages (Bejarano & Erdoğan, 2020).

Electronic transactions, data traffic, applications, e-mails, texts, documents, videos, sounds, images, clickstreams, system logs, search queries, social network interactions, health records, scientific data, government and private sector records, sensors, and transactions on smartphones feed big data (Terzi, Sağõroğlu, & Demirezen, 2017).

Big data is the whole of structured, semistructured, and unstructured data produced at high volume, speed, and variety. Many industrial fields are sources of big data by generating new data or digitizing existing data. Information is an important production factor for organizations to gain a competitive advantage. At this point, the fact that big data is the raw material of information and therefore affects decision-making processes increases the importance of big data analytics.

The types of big data can be explained as the following (Gahi, Guennoun, & Mouftah, 2016):

5.1 Structured data

Structured data means all kinds of data that are easy to model, input, store, query, manipulate, and visualize. In general, it is presented in predefined fields of certain types and sizes and can be managed in relational databases or tables.

5.2 Semistructured data

Semistructured data includes models in which structurality is defined, as well as specific elements and different types of data. It also includes various meta models, such as tags and flags, which are used to define a hierarchical representation of fields. XML (Extensible Markup Language) and JSON (JavaScript Object Notation) programming languages are one of the best-known examples of semistructured data.

5.3 Unstructured data

Unstructured data are types of records that are presented and stored in other than a defined format. It consists of free formats such as documents, books, articles, e-mails, and media files (images, audio, and video). It is difficult to present this type of data in a strict manner, so NoSQL has emerged as a new mechanism (not only SQL) in data processing processes.

Demographic data of patients, medical history, active medical problems, vaccines, allergies, drugs, vital signs, laboratory and administrative and financial documents such as results from radiology tests, pathology reports, progress notes prepared by healthcare providers, health claims and billing records, electronic medical records (EMR), patient records, remote sensors, wearable devices, data from smart meters and sensors, data from vital signs devices, fingerprints of individuals, retina scans, Facebook, Twitter and other social media platforms and data including users' locations, health behaviors, emotions and social interactions, step counts that are showing their exercise levels, weight changes, diets, foods they consume, beneficial/harmful habits, etc., are given as examples of structured and unstructured big data.

Big data, which also expresses the ability to analyze data sets, has significant potential to better understand the needs of the healthcare system, optimize existing products and services, and create value (Altõndiş, 2018).

5.4 The components of big data

Big data is still a new view, and it has a great many descriptions from researchers and organizations. In 2001, Doung Laney, who was an industry analyst at Gartner company, introduced the description of big data components regarding in terms of three Vs: Volume, Velocity, and Variety. SAS (Statistical Analysis System) has added two additional components. They are Variability and Veracity. Then, Oracle has identified big data in terms of four Vs, i.e., Volume, Velocity, Variety, and Value. Furthermore, Oguntimilehin and Ademola (2014) explained big data in terms of five component V's Volume, Velocity, Variety, Variability, and Value. Data Science Central, Kirk Born, has asserted big data components in 10 Vs i.e., Volume, Variety, Velocity, Veracity, Validity, Value, Variability, Venue, Vocabulary, and Vagueness (Kapil, Agrawal, & Khan, 2016, pp. 1−4).

In the literature, among the studies of several researchers, components in the concept of big data have been explained as 3V, 4V, 5V, 6V, 7V, and 9V. Fig. 11.2 shows the several components of big data, known as the 9Vs, and mentioned in the literature. The 9V components of big data are explained in Table 11.1 (Owais & Hussein, 2016).

Some big data research centers were established for data-driven personalized treatments using collecting and analyzing cancer data. For example, In the United Kingdom, Oxford University has established Big Data Institute and the Chan Soon-Shiong Oxford Center for Molecular Medicine to gather and analyze huge anonymized medical datasets and improve data driven. In the United Kingdom, Public Health England and the National Cancer Intelligence Network have established the world's largest database of cancer patients to coordinate the data, improve data analysis and enhance oncology prevention, diagnosis, treatment, and results (Salas-Vega, Haimann, & Mossialos, 2016).

In Italy, IBM has partnered with the National Cancer Institute of Milan to leverage available data with the purpose of improving cancer care such as treatment of rare tumors, sarcomas, and cancers of the head and neck (Digital Health News. Analytics and Big Data Improve Cancer Treatment at Italian Institute, 2013).

Because of many therapeutic and diagnostic procedures in oncology and the ubiquity of imaging, cancer data can be said as big data. To make a calculation, in the past 10 years, roughly 140 million patients were diagnosed with cancer in about 100,000 hospitals in the whole of the world. If we think data volume is in the range of 0.1−10 Gb of data per patient, the total volume of cancer patient data in the world is predicted to be in the range 14−1400 of petabytes of data. Data in radiation oncology can be identified as big data. In addition, the characteristics of data in radiation oncology, such as the use of data-intensive imaging modalities, the imaging archives are increasing quickly, the growing of imaging and diagnostic modalities and evaluation and quality differs between care providers are associated with the components of big data, that are respectively volume, velocity, variety, and veracity (Lustberg et al., 2017).

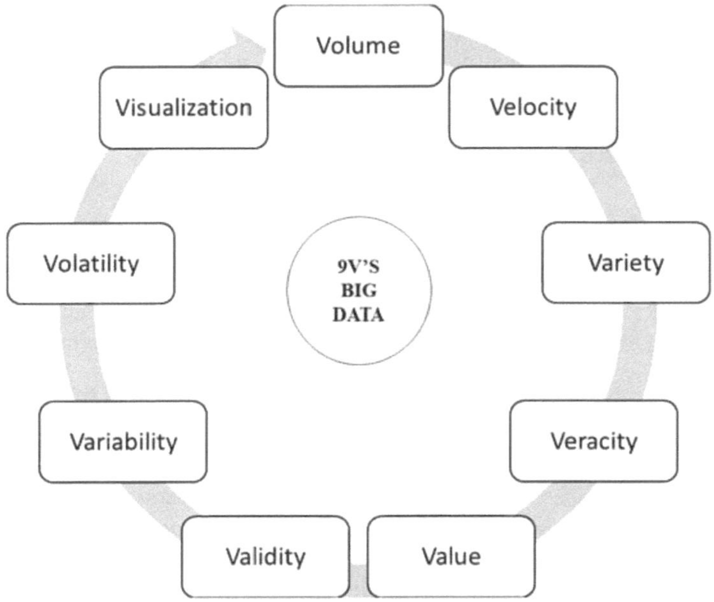

FIGURE 11.2 9V components of Big Data (Hackenberger, 2019).

TABLE 11.1 The 9V components of big data.

9V components	Explanation
Volume	It means the quantity of data that is continuously generated from several sources by every day.
Velocity	It means how fast the data is to be accessed.
Variety	It refers to basically type of data. It means different forms in a dataset such as structured, semistructured, and unstructured data.
Veracity	It means to the noises, biases, and abnormality in data.
Value	It is about the importance of data.
Validity	It refers to accuracy of big data used to extract result.
Variability	It refers to the meaning of the data.
Volatility	It means how long the stored big data is useful to the user.
Visualization	It refers to use graphs and charts to visualize huge amounts of data for more understand problem.

Modified From Owais, S. S. & Hussein, N. S. (2016). Extract five categories CPIVW from the 9V's characteristics of the big data. *International Journal of Advanced Computer Science and Applications, 7*(3), 254–258.

6. Big data analytics

There is a great increase in the number of smart devices used with the development of technology. Devices produce real-time event records (log) with the help of sensors. The rise in mobility, internet access, and social networks increase the diversity, speed, and volume of the data that surround us. This situation brings with it the problems of receiving, storing, and processing big data at the same speed. At this point, choosing the appropriate ones from big data analytics, structured corporate data, and unstructured data world such as video, audio, text file, provides access to information through its storage and processing (Aktan, 2018).

Big data analytics is the analysis of data in several formats and includes many kinds of content using advanced analytical and parallel techniques. It is difficult to apply these analyses and processes in the correct way. Because quickly changing and huge structural, semistructural and nonstructural data types are analyzed totally. The big data analytics process aims to extract important and worthy information from big data (Das, 2020).

Big data analytics is a technique used in huge datasets and can be explained through workflow in the overall process of valuable information extraction from big datasets. The basic process of big data analytics can be summarized in five steps. The first three steps are called data management and the last two steps are called analytics (Gandomi & Haider, 2015):

1. Data acquisition
2. Information extraction
3. Integration
4. Modeling and analysis
5. Interpretation

Although the concept of "big data" is comparatively new, the act of collecting and storing huge quantities of information for eventual data analysis goes a long way back. Companies that are active in different sectors, especially, have bigger dimensions and, with a greater volume of data, have enhanced solutions that are called business intelligence (BI) or traditional analytics to promote business management processes. BI is defined as using a set of methodologies, processes, structures, and technologies that transform a huge amount of raw data into useful information for making strategic decisions (Almeida, 2018). Fig. 11.3 shows a comparative analysis between the concept of BI (traditional analytics) and big data analytics.

The brief history of the emergence of big data analytics is shown in Fig. 11.4. For the origin of big data analytics, it can be said that it emerged in the 1970s or before, based on the development of machine learning and statistical computing. In the following decade, the scale and volume of data increased due to the advanced capability of automation and computing power. These huge datasets were named as "very large databases" (VLDBs) or "massive data" to separate from conventional data. In the 1990s, data mining, statistical learning, and knowledge discovery in databases stood out and this was named as the first wave of big data analytics. When we came in the 2000s, big data analytics has been successfully applied in many different fields, such as bioinformatics, health informatics and business analytics in business and management schools, etc. This period can be called the second wave (Tsui, Zhao, & Wang, 2019).

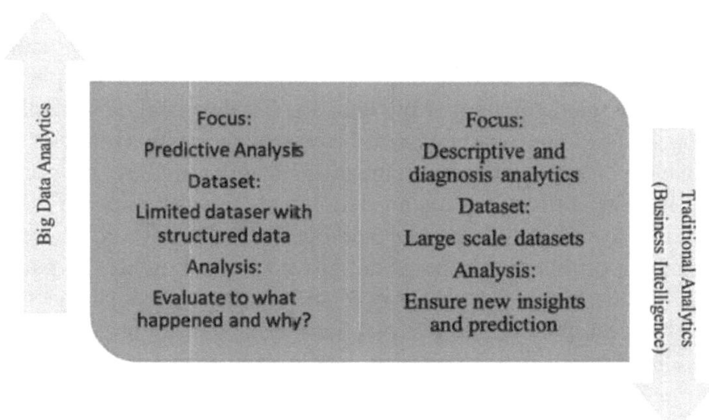

FIGURE 11.3 The comparison of Big Data Analytics and Traditional Analytics (Business Intelligence-BI) (Almeida, 2018).

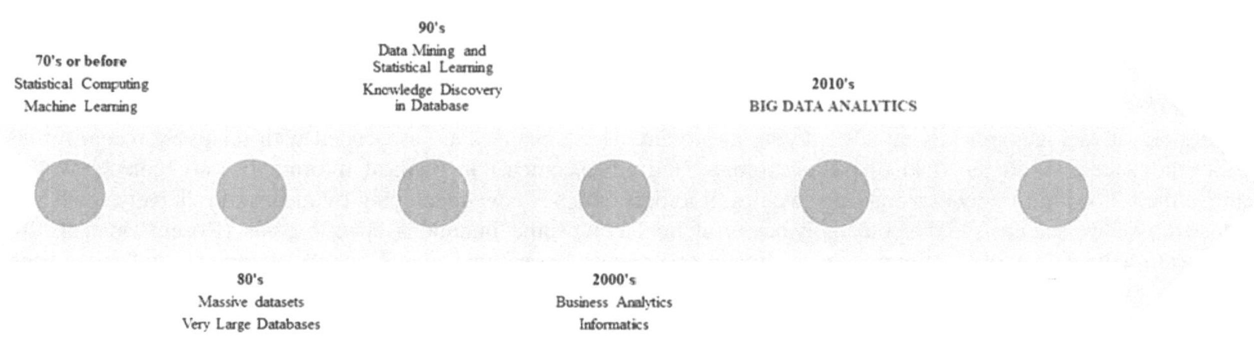

FIGURE 11.4 The brief history of the emergence of big data analytics (Tsui et al., 2019).

Big data analytics in healthcare includes the analysis of huge, defining clusters, and correlation between datasets, besides improving predictive models with the use of data mining and artificial intelligence techniques (Viceconti, Hunter, & Hose, 2015). Big data analytics in healthcare systems unify analysis of several scientific areas, such as health informatics, bioinformatics, medical imaging (radiology), sensor informatics, medical informatics, and computational biomedicine (Wang, Kung, Wang, & Cegielski, 2018).

The practices of big data analytics can enhance the patient-based service, produce new ideas about disease mechanisms, early detection of spreading diseases, monitor the quality of the medical and healthcare institutions, as well as ensure much better treatment methods (Agarwal, Adhil, & Talukder, 2015). Big data analytics can increase profits and economize on it. Moreover, it predicts epidemics, treats diseases, advances the quality of life, and decreases preventable deaths.

About the collection of big data, some hardships should be taken into consideration. Collecting high-throughput—omics data is related to the expense of experimental measurements. Concerning the heterogeneity of the data sources, the noise of the experimental—omics data, environmental conditions, the variety of the experimental techniques and biological nature should not be missed, before integration of these heterogeneous data and employing of the data mining methods. Several data mining techniques can be applied on these heterogeneous biomedical big data sets, such as anomaly detection, clustering, classification, association rules, etc., as well as summarization and visualization of those big data sets (Ristevski & Chen, 2018).

7. The similarities and differences of radiomics and big data analytics

Radiomics aims a large pool of medical imaging data that can be named big data with widening radiomics feature dimensions and growing cohort sizes (Parmar et al., 2015). In radiomics, a reliable result is based on enough data. By means of big and standardized clinical data, radiomics will be suitable in terms of clinical usage and application. However, accessing big data of researchers on radiomics needs to be easy as medical images are scattered in different hospitals or data centers or laboratories, and the capacity of the patient population is the basis of huge amounts of medical images (Liu et al., 2019). Radiomics enables quantitative (numerical) identifiers of the ROI that can be first-hand used for the design of big data analytics models to assist the clinical management of patients (Aiello et al., 2019).

As a result of the development of technology, information is an important unit of radiology, and accessible information based on it electronically exists in large amounts within the information systems at the center of every modern radiology department. It can be called the key parameter needed to improve big data analytics. Despite the existing treasure of digital medical imaging data in radiology, to see the impact of big data and big data analytics on clinical radiology, more analysis should be studied and developed. Big data analytics can be associated with computer vision algorithms to provide automated and quantitative voxel-by-voxel evaluation of medical imaging studies. As such, largely qualitative interpretation of medical imaging data is quite difficult for expert radiologists (Kansagra et al., 2016).

In the era of precision medicine, lots of data (gigabytes, terabytes, etc.) are picked up from each patient, and radiomics data can ensure an important element of this. The exponential growth in the numbers of patients and the data components are known as "big data." The studies about big data are goaled extraction from huge datasets that are not based on controlled experiments attentively. Even though, correlations between observations can be many and effortless to acquire, causality is much harder to evaluate, since it is an unclear and insufficient specified construct for complicated systems (Gillies et al., 2016).

8. The challenges of radiomics and big data analytics

Radiomics is an output of the era of big data. Adequate data features and database construction are pioneering the research of imaging radiomics. At present, a great number of radiomic studies have few sample sizes. Because of small data sets comprised of inadequate sample sizes, the accuracy of a model's prediction is decreased, and the risk of overfitting has increased (Meng et al., 2019).

The field of radiogenomics is rapidly varying at present. These changes are associated with relatively recent results of research advances within the field of radiogenomics, and advancements in medical informatics and biotechnology that facilitate the following of new exploration strategies. Radiogenomics is now developing by means of relatively small studies conducted by a few scientists to the potentially powerful, but having some limitations, era of big data (Rosenstein et al., 2014).

Several challenges about radiomics are technical complexity, overfitting of data, methodological challenges such as weak study design, and deficiency of standards for validating its results (Gillies et al., 2016). The usage of radiomics for confidential and fruitful assistance is a clinical decision-making in cancer treatment. It can be said that it remains largely immature with many challenges (Li et al., 2020).

9. The relationship between radiomics and big data analytics

The Mount Sinai Medical Center in the United States uses technologies of Ayasdi big data analysis company, for analyzing all genetic sequences of *Escherichia coli*, including over one million DNA variants, to learn why bacterial strains show resistance to antibiotics. HealthVault of Microsoft is a perfect application of medical big data released in 2007. The aim of the application is to conduct personal health information on individual and family medical equipment. In this system, health information of people can be entered on mobile smart devices and imported into personal medical information by a third party. In terms of the management and improvement of health information, it is a pretty useful application (Chen, Mao, Zhang, & Leung, 2014).

The applications of big data are seen in the emerging fields of radiomics and radiogenomics for determining new imaging features. These applications include extraction of quantitative imaging features related to functional parameters, image texture, and multiparametric imaging relationships and then radiomics features are examined to correlate with genetic, metabolomic, or proteomic markers. Extraction of quantitative medical imaging features can be simplified by automated and high-throughput image processing algorithms. The relationships that are revealed by these algorithms can be used to make a significant relationship between molecular diagnostics and diagnostic imaging (Kansagra et al., 2016).

The big data studies in radiology are at an early step, and in imaging, convenient solutions will have to be advanced for managing the signal to noise ratio. Also, a powerful basis in clinical trials and traditional validation techniques are essential to carry onward hypotheses formed by big data. Nevertheless, big data could still be beneficial in generating real-time data in clinical scenarios where more confirmed studies have not been executed and better knowledge does not exist (Morris, Saboury, Burkett, Gao, & Siegel, 2018).

In the process of big data analytics, using the clinical, laboratory, and imaging data for the discovery of new diagnostic radiological imaging markers is shown in Fig. 11.5.

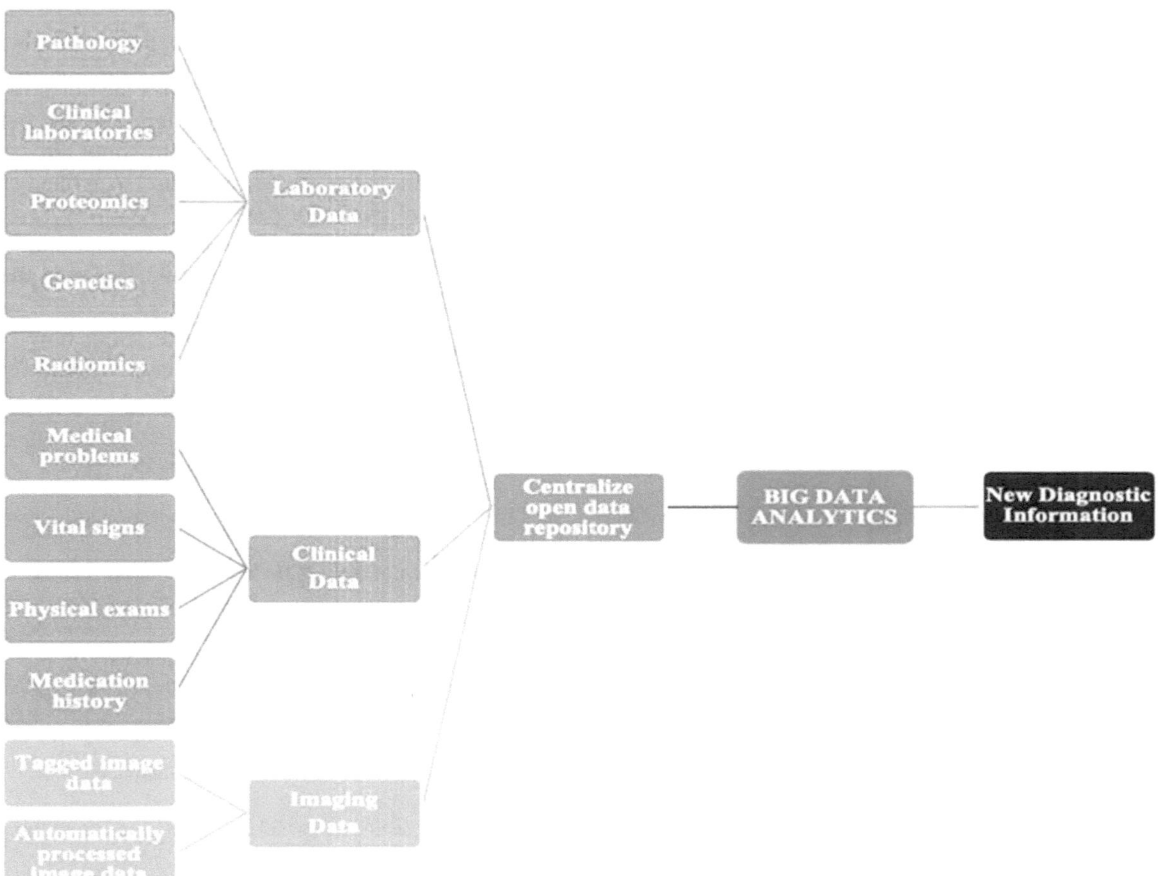

FIGURE 11.5 In the process of big data analytics, using the clinical, laboratory, and imaging data to the discovery of new diagnostic radiological imaging markers (Kansagra et al., 2016).

The field of big data analytics enables strong analytic tools for analyzing huge amounts of information, can give an opportunity to provide a better classification of patient cohorts in clinical trials, assists clinical decisions on treatment planning and adaption, enhances predictions of patients' treatment outcome (Peeken et al., 2018).

10. Discussion

This chapter is intended to present basic information to the researchers by examining the studies on big data analytics and radiomics in the field of healthcare systems. The application of radiomics and radiomics analysis in diagnosis of different cancer types (oncology) was reviewed. The most attractive of these studies are tried to be summarized. It is observed that studies of radiomics have been conducted on many different cancer types, which are breast cancer, head and neck cancer, colorectal cancer, lung cancer, etc. Especially, the radiomics studies concentrate on breast cancer and lung cancer research.

The chapter is organized as follows. The general information about what radiomics is explained. The methodology of radiomics and different definitions of the process of radiomics are expressed. The workflow of radiomics is summarized basically with four steps as image acquisition, segmentation, feature extraction, and analysis. Machine learning and deep learning are mostly used analysis techniques in radiomics and radiogenomics. The studies about radiomics on several kinds of cancer types are explained briefly. These studies are some review and research studies that apply radiomics analysis. With the definition of big data, the components of big data are mentioned in different sources. Big data analytics, the comparison of big data analytics, and traditional analytics, and the brief history of the emergence of big data analytics are clarified. The similarity and differences of radiomics and big data analytics are explained. Moreover, the relationship between radiomics and big data analytics is represented.

It is seen that big data analytics and radiomics are especially used in the healthcare system to obtain useful information about early diagnosis of any potential on several cancer disease, the survivability rate of cancer, and the rate of propagation of existing cancer.

11. Conclusion

The use of big data analytics and radiomics in the field of healthcare is increasing day by day, as does the development of technologies. The statistically important and useful results of the reviewed studies increased the interest in this field even more. Therefore, some limitations and challenges in big data analytics and radiomics can occur in some areas such as medical image analysis and radiology. In future, any advancement of big data analytics and radiomics as applied could be better for more accurate classification or early diagnosis of different types of cancer diseases.

When the reviewed studies are considered, big data analytics has a great potential to enable help and solutions for many challenges about complicated clinical and research problems in the radiology department. It should be noted that more studies need to be done if the potential is to be used properly.

As information and novelty in big data increases, departments of healthcare can get guidance about how big data analytics can be applied. In particular, radiomics and radiogenomics fields in radiology departments can be pioneered in the era of health informatics, big data, and data science, when useful and intelligent investment is applied to technology.

References

Acharya, U. R., Hagiwara, Y., Sudarshan, V. K., Chan, W. Y., & Ng, K. H. (2018). Towards precision medicine: From quantitative imaging to radiomics. *Journal of Zhejiang University - Science B, 19*(1), 6–24. https://doi.org/10.1631/jzus.B1700260

Aerts, H. J. W. L. (2016). The potential of radiomic-based phenotyping in precisionmedicine a review. *JAMA Oncology, 2*(12), 1636–1642. https://doi.org/10.1001/jamaoncol.2016.2631

Aerts, H. J. W. L., Velazquez, E. R., Leijenaar, R. T. H., Parmar, C., Grossmann, P., Carvalho, S., et al. (2014). Decoding tumour phenotype by noninvasive imaging using a quantitative radiomics approach. *Nature Communications, 5*. https://doi.org/10.1038/ncomms5006

Agarwal, M., Adhil, M., & Talukder, A. K. (2015). Multi-omics multi-scale big data analytics for cancer genomics. In *Lecture notes in computer science (including subseries lecture notes in artificial intelligence and lecture notes in bioinformatics)* (Vol. 9498, pp. 228–243). Springer Verlag. https://doi.org/10.1007/978-3-319-27057-9_16

Aiello, M., Cavaliere, C., D'Albore, A., & Salvatore, M. (2019). The challenges of diagnostic imaging in the era of big data. *Journal of Clinical Medicine, 316*. https://doi.org/10.3390/jcm8030316

Ai, Y., Zhu, H., Xie, C., & Jin, X. (2020). Radiomics in cervical cancer: Current applications and future potential. *Critical Reviews in Oncology, 152*, 102985. https://doi.org/10.1016/j.critrevonc.2020.102985

Aktan, E. (2018). Büyük veri: Uygulama alanlarõ, analitiği ve güvenlik boyutu. *Bilgi Yönetimi, 1*(1), 1–22. https://doi.org/10.33721/by.403010

Almeida, F. (2018). Big data: Concept, potentialities and vulnerabilities. *Emerging Science Journal, 2*(1), 1–10. https://doi.org/10.28991/esj-2018-01123

Altõndiş, S. (2018). Büyük verinin sağlõk hizmetleri kalitesindeki rolü. *Sakarya Medical Journal, 8*(2), 205–213. https://doi.org/10.31832/smj.423011

Avanzo, M., Wei, L., Stancanello, J., Vallieres, M., Rao, A., Morin, O., et al. (2020). Machine and deep learning methods for radiomics. *Medical Physics, 47*(5).

Bejarano, J. S., & Erdoğan, E. (2020). Big data and open data analytics: The applications and the path taken in Turkey. *Journal of Research in Business, 5*(2), 147–159. https://doi.org/10.35333/jrb.2020.278

Bianconi, F., Palumbo, I., Spanu, A., Nuvoli, S., Fravolini, M. L., & Palumbo, B. (2020). PET/CT radiomics in lung cancer: An overview. *Applied Sciences, 10*(5), 1718. https://doi.org/10.3390/app10051718

Capobianco, E., & Dominietto, M. (2020). From medical imaging to radiomics: Role of data science for advancing precision health. *Journal of Personalized Medicine, 10*(1). https://doi.org/10.3390/jpm10010015

Chen, M., Mao, S., Zhang, Y., & Leung, V. C. (2014). *Big data: Related technologies, challenges and future prospects.*

Cho, D., Clausi, D., & Wong, A. (2015). Dermal radiomics for melanoma screening. *Vision Letters, 1*(1). https://doi.org/10.15353/vsnl.v1i1.58

Conti, A., Duggento, A., Indovina, I., Guerrisi, M., & Toschi, N. (2021). Radiomics in breast cancer classification and prediction. *Seminars in Cancer Biology, 72*, 238–250. https://doi.org/10.1016/j.semcancer.2020.04.002

Cox, M., & Ellsworth, D. (1997). Application-controlled demand paging for out-of-core visualization. In *Proceedings of the IEEE visualization conference* (pp. 235–244). IEEE Comp Soc.

Das, B. (2020). An overview on big data: Characteristics, security and applications. *Journal of Network Communications and Emerging Technologies (JNCET), 9.*

Digital Health News. (2013). *Analytics and big data improve cancer treatment at Italian institute.* https://www.digitalhealthnews.eu/ibm/3519-analytics-and-big-data-improvecancer-treatment-at-italian-institute.

Gahi, Y., Guennoun, M., & Mouftah, H. T. (2016). Big data analytics: Security and privacy challenges. In *Proceedings - IEEE symposium on computers and communications* (Vols. 2016–, pp. 952–957). Institute of Electrical and Electronics Engineers Inc. https://doi.org/10.1109/ISCC.2016.7543859

Gandomi, A., & Haider, M. (2015). Beyond the hype: Big data concepts, methods, and analytics. *International Journal of Information Management, 35*(2), 137–144. https://doi.org/10.1016/j.ijinfomgt.2014.10.007

Gillies, R. J., Kinahan, P. E., & Hricak, H. (2016). Radiomics: Images are more than pictures, they are data. *Radiology, 278*(2), 563–577. https://doi.org/10.1148/radiol.2015151169

Gillies, R. J., & Schabath, M. B. (2020). Radiomics improves cancer screening and early detection. *Cancer Epidemiology, Biomarkers & Prevention, 29*(12), 2556–2567. https://doi.org/10.1158/1055-9965.EPI-20-0075

Hackenberger, B. K. (2019). Data by data, big data. *Croatian Medical Journal, 60*(3).

Hassani, C., Varghese, B. A., Nieva, J., & Duddalwar, V. (2019). Radiomics in pulmonary lesion imaging. *American Journal of Roentgenology, 212*(3), 497–504. https://doi.org/10.2214/AJR.18.20623

Hatt, M., Majdoub, M., Vallières, M., Tixier, F., Le Rest, C. C., Groheux, D., et al. (2015). 18F-FDG PET uptake characterization through texture analysis: Investigating the complementary nature of heterogeneity and functional tumor volume in a multi-cancer site patient cohort. *Journal of Nuclear Medicine, 56*(1), 38–44. https://doi.org/10.2967/jnumed.114.144055

Ji, G. W., Zhang, Y. D., Zhang, H., Zhu, F. P., Wang, K., Xia, Y. X., et al. (2019). Biliary tract cancer at CT: A radiomics-based model to predict lymph node metastasis and survival outcomes. *Radiology, 290*(1), 90–98. https://doi.org/10.1148/radiol.2018181408

Kansagra, A. P., Yu, J. P. J., Chatterjee, A. R., Lenchik, L., Chow, D. S., Prater, A. B., et al. (2016). Big data and the future of radiology informatics. *Academic Radiology, 23*(1), 30–42. https://doi.org/10.1016/j.acra.2015.10.004

Kapil, G., Agrawal, A., & Khan, R. A. (2016). *A study of big data characteristics.*

Koçak, B., Durmaz, E.Ş., Ateş, E., & Kõlõçkesmez, Ö. (2019). Radiomics with artificial intelligence: A practical guide for beginners. *Diagnostic and interventional radiology, 25*(6), 485–495. https://doi.org/10.5152/dir.2019.19321

Kumar, V., Gu, Y., Basu, S., Berglund, A., Eschrich, S. A., Schabath, M. B., et al. (2012). Radiomics: The process and the challenges. *Magnetic Resonance Imaging, 30*(9), 1234–1248. https://doi.org/10.1016/j.mri.2012.06.010

Lambin, P., Rios-Velazquez, E., Leijenaar, R., Carvalho, S., Van Stiphout, R. G. P. M., Granton, P., et al. (2012). Radiomics: Extracting more information from medical images using advanced feature analysis. *European Journal of Cancer, 48*(4), 441–446. https://doi.org/10.1016/j.ejca.2011.11.036

Langs, G., Röhrich, S., Hofmanninger, J., Prayer, F., Pan, J., Herold, C., et al. (2018). Machine learning: From radiomics to discovery and routine. *Radiologe, Der, 58*, 1–6. https://doi.org/10.1007/s00117-018-0407-3

LeCun, Y., Bengio, Y., & Hinton, G. (2015). Deep learning. *Nature, 521*(7553), 436–444. https://doi.org/10.1038/nature14539

Li, H., El Naqa, I., & Rong, Y. (2020). Current status of Radiomics for cancer management: Challenges versus opportunities for clinical practice. *Journal of Applied Clinical Medical Physics, 21*(7), 7–10. https://doi.org/10.1002/acm2.12982

Liu, Z., Wang, S., Dong, D., Wei, J., Fang, C., Zhou, X., et al. (2019). The applications of radiomics in precision diagnosis and treatment of oncology: Opportunities and challenges. *Theranostics, 9*(5), 1303–1322. https://doi.org/10.7150/thno.30309

Lustberg, T., Soest, Jochems, A., Deist, T., Wijk, Walsh, S., et al. (2017). Big data in radiation therapy: Challenges and opportunities. *British Journal of Radiology, 90.*

Maity, N. G., & Das, S. (2017). *Machine learning for improved diagnosis and prognosis in healthcare.*

Mayerhoefer, M. E., Materka, A., Langs, G., Häggström, I., Szczypiński, P., Gibbs, P., et al. (2020). Introduction to radiomics. *Journal of Nuclear Medicine, 61*(4), 488–495. https://doi.org/10.2967/JNUMED.118.222893

Meng, Y., Sun, J., Qu, N., Zhang, G., Yu, T., & Piao, H. (2019). Application of radiomics for personalized treatment of cancer patients. *Cancer Management and Research, 11*, 10851–10858. https://doi.org/10.2147/CMAR.S232473

Morris, M. A., Saboury, B., Burkett, B., Gao, J., & Siegel, E. L. (2018). Reinventing radiology: Big data and the future of medical imaging. In *Journal of thoracic imaging* (Vol. 33, pp. 4–16). Lippincott Williams and Wilkins. https://doi.org/10.1097/RTI.0000000000000311. Issue 1.

Narang, S., Lehrer, M., Yang, D., Lee, J., & Rao, A. (2016). Radiomics in glioblastoma: Current status, challenges and potential opportunities. *Translational Cancer Research, 5*(4), 383–397. https://doi.org/10.21037/tcr.2016.06.31

Nougaret, S., Tardieu, M., Vargas, H. A., Reinhold, C., Vande Perre, S., Bonanno, N., et al. (2019). Ovarian cancer: An update on imaging in the era of radiomics. *Diagnostic and Interventional Imaging, 100*(10), 647–655. https://doi.org/10.1016/j.diii.2018.11.007

O'connor, J. P. B. (2017). Rethinking the role of clinical imaging. *ELife, 6*. https://doi.org/10.7554/eLife.30563

Oguntimilehin, A., & Ademola, E. O. (2014). A review of big data management, benefits and challenges. *Journal of Emerging Trends in Computing and Information Sciences, 5*(6), 1–7.

Owais, S. S., & Hussein, N. S. (2016). Extract five categories CPIVW from the 9V's characteristics of the big data. *International Journal of Advanced Computer Science and Applications, 7*(3), 254–258.

Özer, T. (2019). İskemik inme hastalarõnõn erken radyolojik işaret ve bulgu saptanmayan kontrastsõz kranial bilgisayarlõ tomografi görüntülerinin karşõ taraf normal beyin parankimi ile "radiomics" parametreleri üzerinden karşõlaştõrõlmasõ. *Master Thesis, Kocaeli University, Radiology Department*. Kocaeli University.

Parlar, T. (2020). Meme kanseri teşhis ve prognozunda radiomics ile yapay zeka yöntemleri kullanõmõ hakkõnda bir İnceleme. *European Journal of Science and Technology*, 300–306. https://doi.org/10.31590/ejosat.780052

Parmar, C., Grossmann, P., Rietveld, D., Rietbergen, M. M., Lambin, P., & Aerts, H. J. W. L. (2015). Radiomic machine-learning classifiers for prognostic biomarkers of head and neck cancer. *Frontiers in Oncology, 5*. https://doi.org/10.3389/fonc.2015.00272

Peeken, J. C., Bernhofer, M., Wiestler, B., Goldberg, T., Cremers, D., Rost, B., et al. (2018). Radiomics in radiooncology – challenging the medical physicist. *Physica Medica, 48*, 27–36. https://doi.org/10.1016/j.ejmp.2018.03.012

Ristevski, B., & Chen, M. (2018). Big data analytics in medicine and healthcare. *Journal of Integrative Bioinformatics, 15*(3). https://doi.org/10.1515/jib-2017-0030

Rizzo, S., Botta, F., Raimondi, S., Origgi, D., Fanciullo, C., Morganti, A. G., et al. (2018). Radiomics: The facts and the challenges of image analysis. *European Radiology Experimental, 2*(1). https://doi.org/10.1186/s41747-018-0068-z

Rosenstein, B. S., West, C. M., Bentzen, S. M., Alsner, J., Andreassen, C. N., Azria, D., et al. (2014). Radiogenomics: Radiobiology enters the era of big data and team science. *International Journal of Radiation Oncology, Biology, Physics, 89*(4), 709–713. https://doi.org/10.1016/j.ijrobp.2014.03.009

Salas-Vega, S., Haimann, A., & Mossialos, E. (2016). Big data and health care: Challenges and opportunities for coordinated policy development in the EU. *Health Systems & Reform, 1*(4), 285–300. https://doi.org/10.1080/23288604.2015.1091538

Scrivener, M., de Jong, E. E. C., van Timmeren, J. E., Pieters, T., Ghaye, B., & Geets, X. (2016). Radiomics applied to lung cancer: A review. *Translational Cancer Research, 5*(4), 398–409. https://doi.org/10.21037/tcr.2016.06.18

Sun, Q., Lin, X., Zhao, Y., Li, L., Yan, K., Liang, D., et al. (2020). Deep learning vs. Radiomics for predicting axillary lymph node metastasis of breast cancer using ultrasound images: Don't forget the peritumoral region. *Frontiers in Oncology, 10*. https://doi.org/10.3389/fonc.2020.00053

Sun, W., Jiang, M., Dang, J., Chang, P., & Yin, F.-F. (2018). Effect of machine learning methods on predicting NSCLC overall survival time based on Radiomics analysis. *Radiation Oncology, 13*, Article 197. https://doi.org/10.1186/s13014-018-1140-9

Taşlõçay, A. C. (2020). *Konvansiyonel manyetik rezonans görüntülemenin ve radiomiks tabanlõ makina öğrenmesinin menenjiom hastalarõnda pre-operatif grade, histolojik subtip ve surveyansõ öngörmeye katkõsõ.*

Terzi, R., Sağõroğlu, S., & Demirezen, U. (2017). *Büyük Veri ve Açõk Veri: Temel Kavramlar.*

Tsui, K. L., Zhao, Y., & Wang, D. (2019). Big data opportunities: System health monitoring and management. *IEEE Access, 7*, 68853–68867. https://doi.org/10.1109/ACCESS.2019.2917891

Viceconti, M., Hunter, P., & Hose, R. (2015). Big data, big knowledge: Big data for personalized healthcare. *IEEE Journal of Biomedical and Health Informatics, 19*(4), 1209–1215. https://doi.org/10.1109/JBHI.2015.2406883

Wang, Y., Kung, L., Wang, W. Y. C., & Cegielski, C. G. (2018). An integrated big data analytics-enabled transformation model: Application to health care. *Information & Management, 55*(1), 64–79. https://doi.org/10.1016/j.im.2017.04.001

Wilson, R., & Devaraj, A. (2017). Radiomics of pulmonary nodules and lung cancer. *Translational Lung Cancer Research, 6*(1), 86–91. https://doi.org/10.21037/tlcr.2017.01.04

Yiğit, F. (2021). *Endometrial kanserin ameliyat öncesi bt görüntülerinde elde edilen radiomics verileri kullanõlarak makine öğrenmesi teknikleriyle kitle için yüksek risk değerlendirmesi yöntemi. Fen Bilimleri Enstitüsü.*

Yip, S. S. F., & Aerts, H. J. W. L. (2016). Applications and limitations of radiomics. *Physics in Medicine and Biology, 61*(13), R150–R166. https://doi.org/10.1088/0031-9155/61/13/R150

Zhang, G., Xu, L., Zhao, L., Mao, L., Li, X., Jin, Z., et al. (2020). CT-based radiomics to predict the pathological grade of bladder cancer. *European Radiology, 30*(12), 6749–6756. https://doi.org/10.1007/s00330-020-06893-8

Chapter 12

Big medical data, cloud computing, and artificial intelligence for improving diagnosis in healthcare

Mustafa Asim Kazancigil[1,2,3]
[1]Department of Management Information Systems, Yeditepe University, Istanbul, Turkey; [2]Department of Information Systems and Technologies, Yeditepe University, Istanbul, Turkey; [3]Department of Information Security Technology, Yeditepe University, Istanbul, Turkey

1. Introduction

In recent years, new methods have become available for integrating data obtained from mobile medical apps and IoT devices into the cloud-based data warehouses of online hospital information systems (HIS). The common use and widespread presence of mobile computing devices such as smartphones, smartwatches, and tablets, which are today equipped with advanced digital cameras, touchscreen electronic visual displays, and sensors, have enabled software developers to apply new methods for the creation of multipurpose medical apps which can perform tests for diagnosing and monitoring a large variety of diseases. The data warehouses of HIS are also being upgraded to allow the use of big data collected in cloud-based repositories and obtained from a vast array of sources, including medical apps and IoT devices. Today, various artificial intelligence (AI) methods are used by clinical decision support systems (CDSS) in hospitals worldwide for assisting physicians in accurately diagnosing diseases. Through the use of these devices and systems, physicians today can continuously monitor the treatment process of their patients from remote locations.

There are numerous sources which generate big data in the healthcare industry, such as the medical records of patients, results of medical examinations, medical data sent by IoT devices, and medical apps installed on mobile computing devices. To efficiently use the vast amount of medical data collected in the big data repositories of HIS and to process it into useful information, proper data management, analysis, and online analytical processing methods are required (Dash et al., 2019).

AI techniques must be applied by CDSS for correctly diagnosing diseases. The main applications of AI in healthcare today include diagnosis, treatment recommendations, patient engagement and adherence, and administrative activities (Davenport & Kalakota, 2019). Recent studies have shown that in some cases, AI has managed to perform healthcare tasks such as diagnosing medical disorders as accurately as human physicians (Davenport & Kalakota, 2019). However, the main goal and purpose of employing AI in healthcare is to assist physicians in making decisions, not to eventually replace them (Davenport & Kalakota, 2019). As AI systems, platforms, and devices are becoming more advanced and widespread, ethical issues and concerns regarding their use in healthcare are also emerging, such as the privacy of personal information and the possible security loopholes in information systems for preventing its unauthorized transmission from one device or system to the other (Davenport & Kalakota, 2019). Nevertheless, the use and application of AI for clinical decision-making and remote patient monitoring will continue to increase in the future (Leggat & Yap, 2020).

This chapter starts with introduction, followed by the methods for retrieving patient data from medical apps. Afterward, collecting patient data into cloud-based big data repositories is explained. Then, using AI techniques for improving diagnosis is mentioned. Finally, the chapter is wrapped up with conclusion.

Big Data Analytics for Healthcare. https://doi.org/10.1016/B978-0-323-91907-4.00021-2

2. Retrieving patient data from medical apps

Medical apps installed on smartphones, smartwatches, and tablets can be used for testing, diagnosing, and monitoring numerous medical disorders (Kazancigil, 2019), including skin cancer, cutaneous health disorders, cancerous tissues, blood pressure (BP), cardiovascular disorders, blood glucose levels, diabetes, ocular health disorders, neurological health disorders, urinalysis, kidney, and urinary tract diseases, among others (Kazancigil, 2021). In 2019, Watson et al. identified four main decision support modalities: Camera-based apps, guideline provision/algorithm apps, predictive modeling apps, and sensor-linked apps (Watson et al., 2019).

2.1 Medical apps for cutaneous disorders

In 2019, a team of students at Yeditepe University developed a medical app for testing and diagnosing cutaneous health disorders, by using images obtained via smartphone digital cameras and comparing them with the images in their dataset (Fig. 12.1). The images were tagged with the disease names and were used for training the computer vision algorithms (Aydin & Ermertcan, 2019).

The methods of *convolution* and *max pooling* were used in digital image processing as shown in Fig. 12.2 (Aydin & Ermertcan, 2019). A *convolution* is considered as sum of weighted inputs, which is computed for each pixel of an image. It is the process of adding each element of the image to its local neighbors, weighted by the kernel (Kazancigil, 2021).

$$\text{result} = \sum (k\,[n,\ p] \times I\,[x,\ y])$$

Max pooling is a sample-based discretization process which aims to down-sample an image by reducing its dimensionality and allowing for assumptions to be made about features contained in the subregions that are binned (Kazancigil, 2021).

To optimize the diagnosis (Aydin & Ermertcan, 2019), the *thresholding* method of image segmentation is applied for creating binary (black and white) images from grayscale images (Fig. 12.3).

Other popular mobile apps for the detection of skin cancers and cutaneous disorders include *SkinVision* developed in the Netherlands (SkinVision, n.d.); *UMSkinCheck* developed by the University of Michigan (*Rogel Cancer Center: UMSkinCheck App*, n.d.); *Miiskin* developed in Denmark (Miiskin, n.d.); and *MoleScope* developed in Canada (MoleScope, n.d.). *SkinVision* uses a machine learning algorithm to analyze spots on the skin (SkinVision, n.d.). *Miiskin* is an app which enables users to take HD photos of their skin and store the images in an online database. The app uses AI for making comparisons with the follow-up photos in order to identify any changes that may indicate the existence of a cutaneous disorder (Miiskin, n.d.).

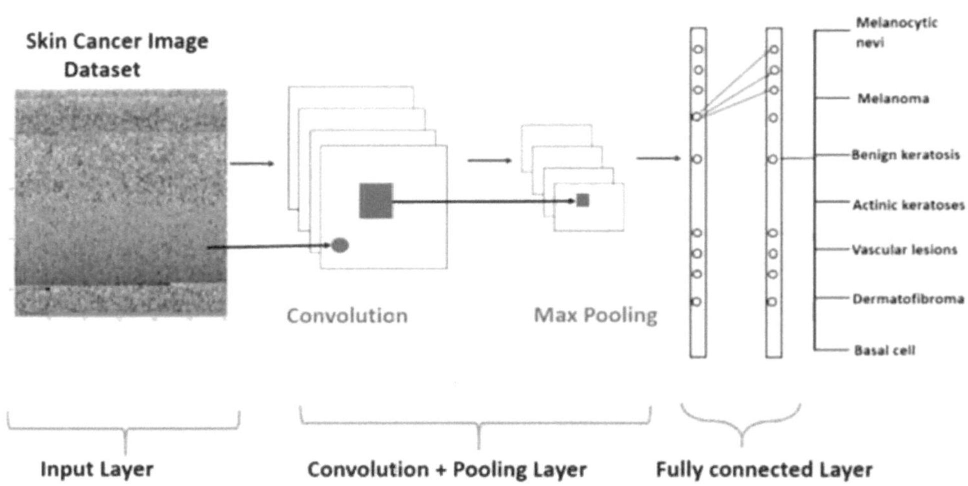

FIGURE 12.1 Methodology used in the medical app developed by Aydin and Ermertcan (Yeditepe University, 2019) for testing and diagnosing cutaneous disorders.

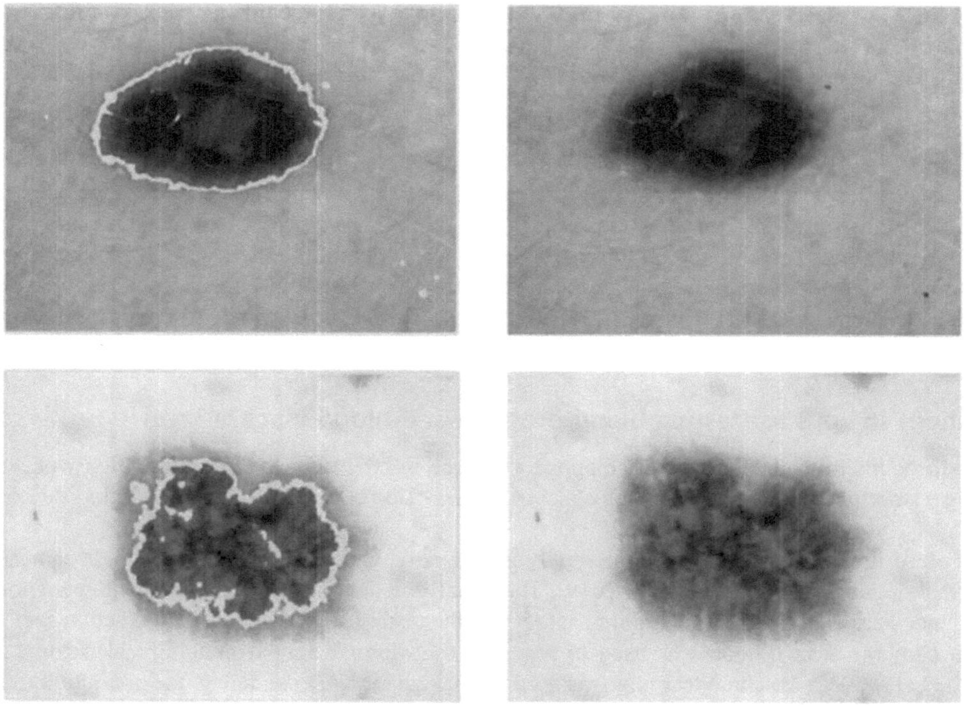

FIGURE 12.2 Application of the *convolution* and *max pooling* methods on the images for diagnosing cutaneous disorders.

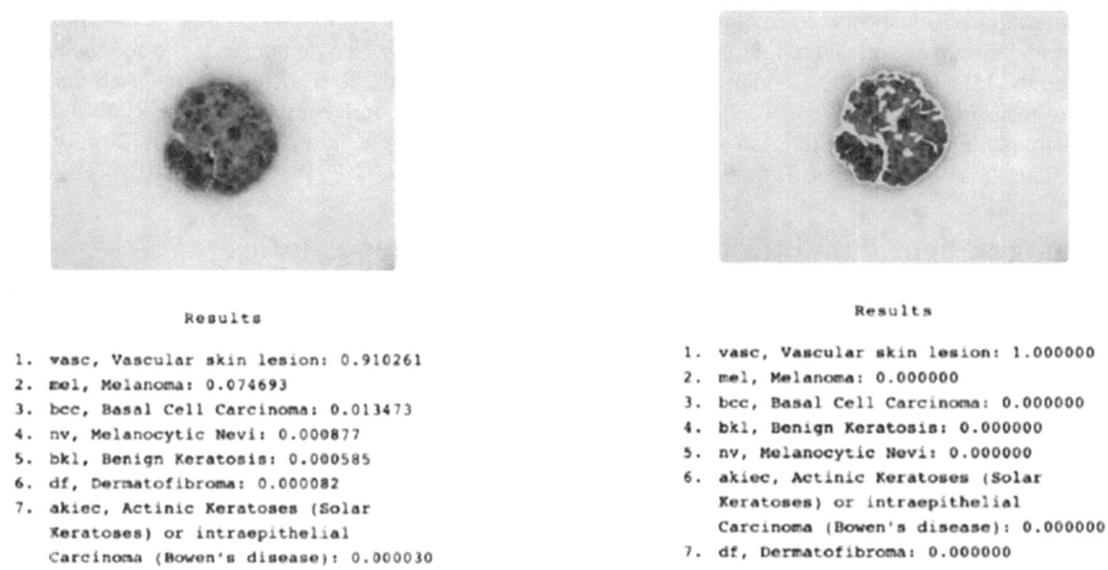

FIGURE 12.3 Improved diagnosis after the *thresholding* method of image segmentation.

2.2 Medical apps for cardiovascular diseases

In 2015, Muhlestein et al. demonstrated that a smartphone can be used to obtain similar results with a 12-lead ECG (electrocardiography) device for the initial evaluation of myocardial ischemia (Muhlestein et al., 2015). The tests revealed that the 12-lead ECG outputs generated from the two wires of *AliveCor KardiaMobile* corresponded to those obtained from a standard 12-lead ECG device used in hospitals (Muhlestein et al., 2015). To reach a similar level of accuracy, the two wires of *AliveCor KardiaMobile* are moved around the bodies of the patients to examine all 12 parts (Muhlestein et al., 2015).

Approved by the FDA in 2017, *AliveCor KardiaBand* for Apple Watch records an electrocardiogram and checks the pulses to determine the user's heart rate to make sure the upper and lower chambers of the heart are in rhythm (AliveCor KardiaBand, n.d.). If they are out of rhythm, this may indicate atrial fibrillation (AliveCor KardiaBand, n.d.).

2.3 Medical apps for visual and cognitive disorders

PupilScreen, which enables a smartphone to test for concussion and other brain injuries, was developed by researchers at the University of Washington in 2017 (Mariakakis et al., 2017). *PupilScreen* can detect changes in a pupil's response to light by using a smartphone's camera and applying AI techniques to determine the results (Mariakakis et al., 2017). The app works by stimulating the patient's eyes using the smartphone's flashlight and records the pupil's response using the smartphone's video camera (Mariakakis et al., 2017). The *PupilScreen* box, which resembles a head-mounted virtual reality display, controls the eyes' exposure to light (Mariakakis et al., 2017).

2.4 New methods in apps for testing blood pressure and blood glucose levels

Two major breakthroughs in medical smartphone apps took place in 2019: For the first time, highly accurate results were obtained by using a smartphone's digital camera for measuring BP (Luo et al., 2019) and blood glucose levels (Wang et al., 2019).

Hong Luo et al. of the Hangzhou Normal University in Zhejiang, China, used a smartphone's camera to measure BP through transdermal optical imaging (Luo et al., 2019). They analyzed data from 1328 adults who were normotensive (Luo et al., 2019). Patients were either part of the training set (70%), the testing set (15%), or the validation set (15%) (Luo et al., 2019). The front camera of an iPhone was used to record a transdermal optical imaging video for 2 min, in order to measure BP (Luo et al., 2019). Machine learning was used to analyze the video and generate prediction models for systolic BP, diastolic BP, and pulse pressure (Luo et al., 2019). The average accuracy rate for predicting systolic BP was 94.81%, while the figure was 95.71% for diastolic BP and 95.75% for pulse pressure (Luo et al., 2019).

Hung-Chih Wang et al. (2019) introduced an integrated blood glucose detection device (IBGDD) that uses the digital camera of a smartphone to inspect colorimetric blood strips. The IBGDD consists of a blood glucose test site, a disposable lancet, a cover and baseplate set, and a light guide channel (Wang et al., 2019). To demonstrate the accuracy conformance of the device to the ISO 15197:2013 standard for blood glucose measurement, 20 diabetes patients used the IBGDD with smartphones to measure their blood glucose levels (Wang et al., 2019). The uniformity values for RGB signals from five separate measurements were all higher than 94.5% (Wang et al., 2019). The values of G signal uniformity were significantly higher than those of the R and B signals, with an average value of 97.4% (Wang et al., 2019).

3. Collecting patient data into cloud-based big data repositories

Large amounts of data which are unmanageable using traditional software and surpass the normally used amount of storage, processing, and analytical power are called big data (Dash et al., 2019). The most commonly accepted definition was given by Douglas B. Laney, who observed that data was growing in three different dimensions, namely "volume, velocity, and variety," often abbreviated as the "3 Vs" (Laney, 2001). *Volume* refers to the large size of big data; *velocity* refers to the speed of data collection and making it available for analysis; while *variety* refers to the different types of organized and unorganized (structured and unstructured) data that can be collected (Laney, 2001). The most accepted fourth V remains "veracity," while some authors add "value" as the fifth V (Combi & Pozzi, 2019). Primary sources of big data in healthcare (NEJM Catalyst, 2018) are shown in Fig. 12.4.

3.1 Big data repositories in healthcare

In 2003, the Institute of Medicine chose the term "electronic health records" (EHRs) to define records maintained by the healthcare sector regarding patients and clinicians (Dash et al., 2019). Murphy et al. (1999) defined EHR as "computerized medical records for patients, recording any information relating to the past, present, or future physical/mental health or condition of an individual which resides in electronic system(s) used to capture, transmit, receive, store, retrieve, link, and manipulate multimedia data for the primary purpose of providing healthcare and health-related services" (Dash et al., 2019; Murphy et al., 1999; Reisman, 2017).

EHRs enable key healthcare indicators to be rapidly provided to organizations. They also improve public health surveillance by immediately reporting outbreaks of diseases (Dash et al., 2019). The use of EHRs has grown substantially since 2008 (Reisman, 2017). By the year 2015, 96% of the hospitals in the United States had a federally tested EHR program, a ninefold increase in the period between 2008 and 2015 (Henry et al., 2016; Reisman, 2017).

FIGURE 12.4 Primary sources of big data in healthcare.

3.1.1 *IoT in healthcare*

Thanks to IoT, physicians can measure and monitor various parameters from their clients in remote locations, which significantly reduces costs in healthcare expenses (Dash et al., 2019). IoT used in healthcare includes health-tracking wearable devices for monitoring vital signs, which generate a large amount of data (Dash et al., 2019; Kazancigil, 2019, 2021). The real-time analysis of data from IoT requires advanced hardware and software applications and network operating systems (Dash et al., 2019; Kazancigil, 2019, 2021).

3.2 Management and analysis of big data in healthcare

Hadoop and Apache are among the most commonly used platforms for working with big data (Dash et al., 2019). The logical approach for analyzing large volumes of complex big data is to distribute and process it in parallel on multiple computing devices (nodes) on a network (Dash et al., 2019). The large size of data requires the combined CPUs of thousands of computers to distribute and process it in the shortest possible amount of time (Dash et al., 2019). Using thousands of nodes simultaneously brings forth issues like how to parallelize the computation, distribute the data, and handle failures (Dash et al., 2019).

Hadoop is among the most popular open-source distributed applications for the parallel processing of big data (Shvachko et al., 2010). Hadoop implements the MapReduce algorithm for processing and generating large datasets. MapReduce uses maps and reduces primitives to map each logical record into a set of intermediate key—value pairs, and reduces operations that combine all the values shared by the same key (Dean & Ghemawat, 2008). It efficiently parallelizes the computation, handles failures, and schedules intermachine communication across large-scale clusters of nodes (Dash et al., 2019).

Apache Spark is a unified engine for distributed data processing that includes higher-level libraries for supporting SQL queries, streaming data, machine learning, and graph processing (Zaharia et al., 2016). The programming interface of these libraries requires less coding efforts and can be easily combined to create more types of complex computations (Zaharia et al., 2016). In-memory processing of data becomes available in Spark when the Resilient Distributed Datasets are implemented, which enables it to become about 100 times faster than Hadoop in multipass analytics on small datasets (Ahmed et al., 2016; Gopalani & Arora, 2015). Due to its relatively higher performance and use of an application programming interface, Spark has become more popular than the MapReduce framework in recent years (Ahmed et al., 2020). In both frameworks, the combination of more than 150 parameters has a considerable impact on cluster performance, which largely depends on input data size and the correct selection of the parameters (Ahmed et al., 2020). When data sets are small, Spark has a significantly better performance compared to Hadoop (Ahmed et al., 2020).

3.3 Commercial platforms for healthcare data analytics

3.3.1 Linguamatics

Linguamatics is a natural language processing (NLP)—based algorithm that relies on I2E, an interactive text mining algorithm (Dash et al., 2019). I2E can extract and analyze a wide array of textual information. Results obtained by using this technique can be up to 10 times faster than those obtained through other tools, and I2E does not require expert knowledge for data interpretation (Dash et al., 2019). When integrated into EHRs, NLP can facilitate the extraction of clean and structured information that often remains hidden in unstructured input data (Dash et al., 2019).

3.3.2 IBM Watson

IBM Watson uses ML and AI-based algorithms with the purpose of extracting the maximum amount of information from minimal data input (Dash et al., 2019). It has been used to predict specific types of diseases, such as cancer, through the analysis of gene expression profiles obtained from various large datasets (Dash et al., 2019). It is also used in pharmaceutical research programs by integrating curated literature and forming network maps to provide detailed overviews of the molecular structures and environments in specific disease models (Dash et al., 2019).

Healthcare analytics can be divided into four main categories: descriptive, diagnostic, predictive, and prescriptive (Dash et al., 2019). *Descriptive analytics* refers to the definition of a present medical situation, whereas *diagnostic analysis* tries to identify the reasons for the occurrence of symptoms (Dash et al., 2019). *Predictive analytics* tries to forecast future outcomes by determining the probabilities, while *prescriptive analytics* aims to propose optimal decisions for the treatment process, if deemed necessary (Dash et al., 2019).

4. Using artificial intelligence techniques for improving diagnosis

4.1 Clinical Information Systems and clinical decision support systems

Clinical Information Systems (CIS) are designed to respond to the informational needs regarding clinical activities, such as patient data (admission, discharge, transfer), management of the posttreatment follow-up, and disease prevention (Combi & Pozzi, 2019; Marin et al., 2016).

The use of a CDSS is particularly important in Emergency Departments (Combi & Pozzi, 2019; Damiani et al., 2014; Kazancigil, 2013). Preserving the privacy of clinical data is a common problem that needs to be addressed by the developers of CDSSs (Rahulamathavan et al., 2014).

Yoon et al. (2017) have studied the methods for predicting the evolution of the disease of a patient, in order to suggest the optimal therapy. They propose a discovery engine which uses the patient's data stored in the CIS to perform a personalized forecast (Yoon et al., 2017).

4.2 AI methods used in healthcare

4.2.1 Machine learning, neural networks, and deep learning in healthcare

Machine learning is a statistical technique for fitting models to data and to "learn" by training models with data (Davenport & Kalakota, 2019). According to a 2018 Deloitte survey, 63% of the 1100 managers who participated were employing machine learning in their businesses (Deloitte Insights, 2018). It is one of the core AI techniques, with numerous types (Davenport & Kalakota, 2019).

The most common use of machine learning in healthcare is precision medicine, i.e., predicting what treatment protocols are likely to succeed on a patient (Lee et al., 2018). A high percentage of machine learning and precision medicine applications require a training dataset with a known outcome variable (Davenport & Kalakota, 2019). This method is called supervised learning (Davenport & Kalakota, 2019).

The neural network is a more complex form of machine learning which was originally conceived in the 1960s and has been used in healthcare applications like determining whether a patient will acquire a particular disease (Sordo, 2002). The most complex forms involve deep learning or neural network models with many levels of features or variables that predict outcomes (Davenport & Kalakota, 2019), e.g., for potentially cancerous lesions in radiology images (Aydin & Ermertcan, 2019; Kazancigil, 2021; Fakoor et al., 2013). Speech recognition is another area where deep learning is used, which makes it a form of NLP (Davenport and Kalakota, 2019).

4.2.2 Natural language processing in healthcare

NLP includes applications such as speech recognition, text analysis, translation, and other goals related to language (Davenport & Kalakota, 2019). There are two main approaches to it: statistical and semantic NLP (Davenport & Kalakota, 2019). In healthcare, NLP is mainly used in the creation, analysis, and classification of clinical documentation and published research (Davenport & Kalakota, 2019). NLP systems can analyze unstructured clinical notes on patients, document patient interactions, conduct AI conversations, and prepare reports (Davenport & Kalakota, 2019).

As numerous kinds of clinical data and information are collected in an unstructured or semistructured form, NLP becomes necessary to manage clinical information (Combi & Pozzi, 2019). One of the goals of NLP is to extract knowledge from natural language texts coming from different sources like medical records, reports, or social media (Combi & Pozzi, 2019).

Kreimeyer et al. (2017) have studied the current NLP systems developed for clinical domains. The analyzed systems allow the extraction of structured information from unstructured free texts (Kreimeyer et al., 2017). Ford et al. (2016) have analyzed the role of electronic medical records in health-related research. Wang et al. (2015) have studied the use of NLP to process EHRs of congestive heart failure patients. Agarwal et al. (2018) have suggested that hospital readmission rates should be monitored by healthcare institutions. Their work focuses on the use of unstructured clinical notes to statistically predict the patients most in danger of readmission (Agarwal et al., 2018). A framework is proposed which uses NLP for the analysis of clinical notes (Agarwal et al., 2018). It selects the most suitable algorithms within the field of data mining and machine learning for predicting readmissions (Agarwal et al., 2018).

4.2.3 Process mining and pathway identification in healthcare

Care pathways (CPs) are the mutually agreed frameworks for the decision-making and organization of healthcare processes for a group of patients during a given period (Combi & Pozzi, 2019). They are often characterized by elaborate decision-making tasks and data-intensive activities which need to be represented, designed, managed, analyzed, and discovered (Combi et al., 2014, 2017).

Rojas et al. (2016) provided a survey of healthcare process mining, which consists of deriving knowledge from data processed and stored in HIS, to analyze the applied methods. Huang et al. (2014) have focused on the discovery of CP patterns through clinical event logs, which record various treatment activities. Gotz et al. (2014) devised a method for interactive pattern mining and analysis using past clinical patient data. Zhang et al. (2015) have also based their methodology on mining and visualizing CPs from EHR data and proposed a practice-based CP development process and a data-driven methodology for deriving common clinical pathways.

4.2.4 Rule-based expert systems in healthcare

Expert systems built upon collections of "if-then" statements were the most common AI systems used in the 1980s and were also widely used in later periods (Davenport & Kalakota, 2019). In healthcare, they have been commonly used in CDSS applications (Vial et al., 2018). EHR content creators usually provide a set of rules with their systems (Davenport & Kalakota, 2019).

Expert systems require human experts and knowledge engineers to devise a series of algorithms and rules (Davenport & Kalakota, 2019). They usually work well and are easy to understand, except for when there are too many rules (over several thousand), which eventually begin to conflict with each other, which causes the system to malfunction (Davenport & Kalakota, 2019). They are being replaced in healthcare by approaches that are based on data and machine learning algorithms (Davenport & Kalakota, 2019).

4.2.5 Robots in healthcare

Robots perform predefined tasks like lifting, repositioning, or assembling objects in places like factories and warehouses, and delivering medical supplies in hospitals (Davenport & Kalakota, 2019; Hussain et al., 2014). More recently, robots and androids with advanced levels of AI and more complex operating systems have become more collaborative with humans and can be trained through a given duty (Davenport & Kalakota, 2019; Hussain et al., 2014).

Embedded knowledge systems and surgical robots have significantly increased the capabilities of surgeons by improving their ability to diagnose, see, and precisely operate within microscopic distances in difficult tasks such as gynecologic surgery, prostate surgery, head and neck surgery, etc (Hussain et al., 2014), though the most critical decisions are still made by surgeons (Davenport & Kalakota, 2019). Because overreliance on computerized knowledge can easily lead to mistakes, these embedded knowledge systems should provide physicians with recommendations, not commands (Davenport & Glaser, 2002). The main purpose should be the combination of the knowledge and skills of the physicians with those of the embedded knowledge systems and surgical robots (Davenport & Glaser, 2002).

4.2.6 Robotic process automation in healthcare

Robotic Process Automation (RPA) does not really involve physical robots; it is executed by computer programs on servers (Davenport & Kalakota, 2019). Information systems can perform structured digital tasks for administrative purposes as if they were a human user, following an algorithm of procedures and rules (Davenport & Kalakota, 2019). RPA works through a presentation layer that is combined with a workflow of business rules and is integrated with healthcare information systems to act like a semiintelligent user (Davenport & Kalakota, 2019). In HIS, they are used for repetitive tasks such as priority authorization and generating patient records and receipts (Davenport & Kalakota, 2019). When combined with technologies like image recognition, they can be used to extract data from images to be used as inputs for the transactional processing systems of hospitals (Hussain et al., 2014).

4.2.7 The use of AI by hospital information systems in decision-making

AI decision-making methods (Leggat & Yap, 2020) in CDSS are shown in Fig. 12.5.

There are three main categories of AI decision-making methods: (1) knowledge-based decision support, (2) data-driven decision support, and (3) probabilistic reasoning (Leggat & Yap, 2020).

4.2.7.1 Knowledge-based decision support in AI for healthcare

Most of the knowledge-based applications for strategic decision-making in healthcare were constructed using a rules-based design (Leggat & Yap, 2020). Starting from the late 1990s, applications began to gather information from existing healthcare databases for CDSSs (Abidi, 1999; Forgionne & Kohli, 1996; Ramani, 2004). Hospital Management Support Systems enabled greater maturity in decision-making (Forgionne & Kohli, 1996).

SOMAS (Service-Oriented Multi-Agent Systems) was a knowledge-based application using organizational information that provided service matching more effectively and efficiently than human processing (Fernández & Ossowski, 2008). Fala et al. (1995) described four expert systems that they suggested were useful for health services, comprising INFER, PsychINFER, Procedure Necessity, and Alternatives to Non-Surgical Admissions. These expert systems were developed using knowledge engineering (Fala et al., 1995).

4.2.7.2 Data-driven decision support in AI for healthcare

Erdoğan et al. (2019) described a spreadsheet-based decision support system and a search algorithm that accessed GIS data which the authors used to plan maternity service sites for a UK hospital network (Erdoğan et al., 2019; Leggat & Yap, 2020). Since 2011, greater focus is given on the application of artificial neural networks (ANNs) (Leggat & Yap, 2020). A 2019 scoping review found the majority of the ANN published applications were related to clinical decision-making, with only six applications that might have been related to organizational strategic decision-making (Shahid et al., 2019). There were also studies on clinical decisions (Atoui et al., 2011; Berardi & Zhang, 1999) or management of operations, such as

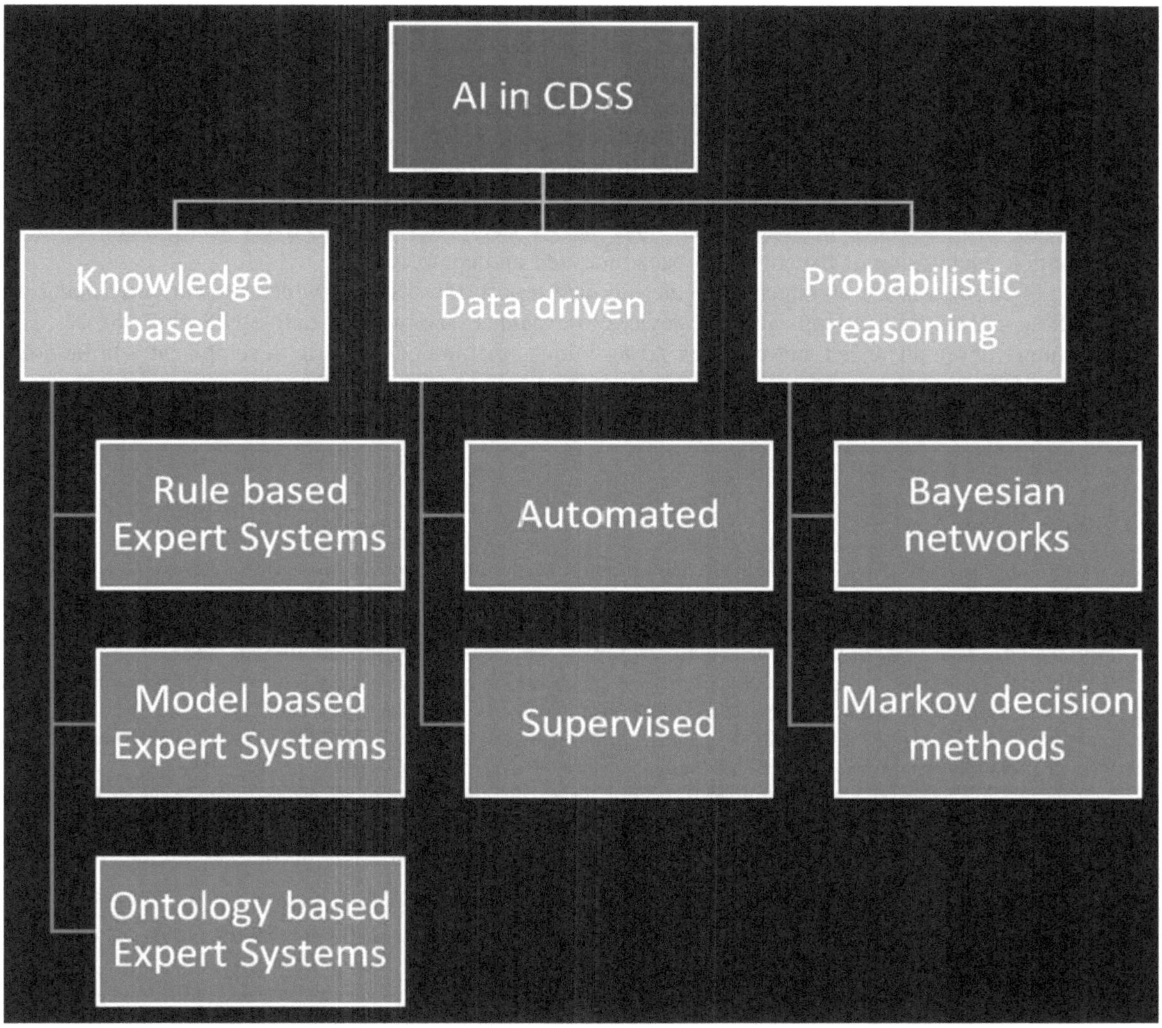

FIGURE 12.5 AI decision-making methods in Clinical Decision Support Systems (CDSSs).

adoption of radio frequency identification technology adoption in a clinical setting (Chong et al., 2015) and evaluating the effect of hospital employee motivation on patient satisfaction (Hanafizadeh et al., 2010). Two recent applications were focused on the analysis of text-based clinical data to address patient harm, and the ANNs were found to outperform human analysis of the same data (Cohan et al., 2017; Tafti et al., 2017). Another application used ANNs to predict hospital readmissions and was found to perform better than the existing practice at the hospital (Wang et al., 2018).

4.2.7.3 Probabilistic reasoning in AI for healthcare

A private hospital in Turkey constructed a Bayesian network to track resource utilization and to identify strategies to improve efficiency using radiology data (Aktaş et al., 2007). The authors illustrated how the CDSS could be used to improve strategic decision-making (Aktaş et al., 2007). A probabilistic model using NLP that was applied at a Chinese hospital was found to be effective at designing treatment plans (Sun & Medaglia, 2019). Difficulties in the implementation of this model included the reluctance to share data among hospitals and the lack of trust for AI decisions by health professionals (Sun & Medaglia, 2019). McClean and Millard conceived a Markov analysis that calculated the costs of possible treatment options for senior citizens (McClean & Millard, 2007).

5. Conclusions

New methods have become available in recent years for integrating the data obtained from mobile medical apps and IoT devices into the cloud-based data warehouses of online HIS. The common use and increasing features and capabilities of mobile computing devices such as smartphones and smartwatches are enabling software developers to apply new methods for the creation of medical apps. These apps can perform tests for diagnosing a large variety of diseases with increasing accuracy. As these apps and numerous IoT devices have started to yield highly accurate testing and diagnosis results, some of them receiving FDA approval, the opportunity of integrating their data into HIS has emerged. Medical data collected in the data warehouses of hospitals can be used by the CDSS for aiding physicians in more accurately diagnosing diseases and remotely monitoring the treatment process of their patients in real time.

In this research, the current and future trends and methods for collecting data from mobile apps and IoT devices into the data warehouses of hospitals have been identified, and the AI techniques for effectively using medical data for the diagnosis and remote monitoring of patients have been analyzed and compared.

Another area of focus was the architecture of the big data repositories of HIS, which are currently being upgraded worldwide to allow mobile medical apps and IoT devices to exchange data with an online HIS or CDSS.

In the near future, more advanced and complex AI techniques that are currently in development will be used by the CDSS for further improving the accuracy of the decisions made by physicians. Technological advances in the field of robotics and the advent of more capable medical robots are set to assist physicians in perfecting their surgical operation skills.

References

Abidi, S. S. R. (1999). Applying data mining in healthcare: an info-structure for delivering 'data-driven' strategic services. *Studies in Health Technology and Informatics, 68*(453–456), 453–456. https://doi.org/10.3233/978-1-60750-912-7-453

Agarwal, A., Baechle, C., Behara, R., & Zhu, X. (2018). A natural language processing framework for assessing hospital readmissions for patients with COPD. *IEEE Journal of Biomedical and Health Informatics, 22*(2), 588–596. https://doi.org/10.1109/JBHI.2017.2684121

Ahmed, N., Barczak, A. L. C., Susnjak, T., & Rashid, M. A. (2020). A comprehensive performance analysis of Apache Hadoop and Apache Spark for large scale data sets using HiBench. *Journal of Big Data, 7*(110). https://doi.org/10.1186/s40537-020-00388-5

Ahmed, H., Ismail, M. A., Hyder, M. F., Sheraz, S. M., & Fouq, N. (2016). Performance comparison of spark clusters configured conventionally and a cloud service. *Procedia Computer Science, 82*, 99–106. https://doi.org/10.1016/j.procs.2016.04.014

Aktaş, E., Ülengin, F., & Şahin, Ş.Ö. (2007). A decision support system to improve the efficiency of resource allocation in healthcare management. *Socio-Economic Planning Sciences, 41*(2), 130–146. https://doi.org/10.1016/j.seps.2005.10.008

AliveCor KardiaBand. (n.d.). Retrieved August 29, 2021, from https://www.alivecor.com/press/press_release/fda-clears-first-medical-device-for-apple-watch.

Atoui, H., Télisson, D., Fyan, J., & Rubel, P. (2011). Ambient intelligence and pervasive architecture designed within the EPI-MEDICS personal ECG monitor. In J. Tan (Ed.), *Developments in healthcare information systems and technologies: models and methods* (pp. 302–311). IGI Global. http://doi:10.4018/978-1-61692-002-9.ch021.

Aydin, R., & Ermertcan, M. K. (2019). *Gradual approach to skin cancer classification with artificial intelligence and OpenCV draw contouring*. Yeditepe University.

Berardi, V. L., & Zhang, G. P. (1999). The effect of misclassification costs on neural network classifiers. *Decision Sciences, 30*(3), 659–682. https://doi.org/10.1111/j.1540-5915.1999.tb00902.x

Chong, A. Y.-L., Liu, M. J., Luo, J., & Keng-Boon, O. (2015) Predicting RFID adoption in healthcare supply chain from the perspectives of users. *International Journal of Production Economics, 159*, 66–75. https://doi.org/10.1016/j.ijpe.2014.09.034

Cohan, A., Fong, A., Ratwani, R. M., & Goharian, N. (2017). Identifying harm events in clinical care through medical narratives. In *ACM-BCB' 17: proceedings of the 8th ACM international conference on bioinformatics, computational biology, and health informatics* (pp. 52–59). Association for Computing Machinery. https://doi.org/10.1145/3107411.3107485

Combi, C., Gambini, M., Migliorini, S., & Posenato, R. (2014). Representing business processes through a temporal data-centric workflow modeling language: an application to the management of clinical pathways. *IEEE Transactions on Systems, Man, and Cybernetics: Systems, 44*(9), 1182–1203. https://doi.org/10.1109/TSMC.2014.2300055

Combi, C., Oliboni, B., Zardini, A., & Zerbato, F. (2017). A methodological framework for the integrated design of decision-intensive care pathways—an application to the management of COPD patients. *Journal of Healthcare Informatics Research, 1*, 157–217. https://doi.org/10.1007/s41666-017-0007-4

Combi, C., & Pozzi, G. (2019). Clinical information systems and artificial intelligence: recent research trends. In (1st ed., *Vol. 28. Yearbook of medical informatics 2019, section 3: clinical information systems survey* (pp. 83–94). Georg Thieme Verlag KG Stuttgart. https://doi.org/10.1055/s-0039-1677915

Damiani, E., Kazancigil, M. A., Frati, F., Birregah, B., Knauf, R., & Tsuruta, S. (2014). Disaster early warning and relief: a human-centered approach. In H.-N. Teodorescu, A. Kirschenbaum, S. Cojocaru, & C. Bruderlein (Eds.), *Improving disaster resilience and mitigation-IT means and tools* (pp. 135–151). Springer. https://doi.org/10.1007/978-94-017-9136-6_9

Dash, S., Shakyawar, S. K., Sharma, M., & Kaushik, S. (2019). Big data in healthcare: management, analysis and future prospects. *Journal of Big Data, 6*(54), 1–25. https://doi.org/10.1186/s40537-019-0217-0

Davenport, T. H., & Glaser, J. (2002). Just-in-time delivery comes to knowledge management. *Harvard Business Review*. https://hbr.org/2002/07/just-in-time-delivery-comes-to-knowledge-management.

Davenport, T., & Kalakota, R. (2019). The potential for artificial intelligence in healthcare. *Future Healthcare Journal, 6*(2), 94−98. https://doi.org/10.7861/futurehosp.6-2-94

Dean, J., & Ghemawat, S. (2008). MapReduce: simplified data processing on large clusters. *Communications of the ACM, 51*(1), 107−113. https://doi.org/10.1145/1327452.1327492

Deloitte Insights. (2018). *State of AI in the enterprise-2nd annual survey highlights*. https://www2.deloitte.com/content/dam/insights/us/articles/4780_State-of-AI-in-the-enterprise/AICognitiveSurvey2018_Infographic.pdf.

Erdoğan, G., Stylianou, N., & Vasilakis, C. (2019). An open source decision support system for facility location analysis. *Decision Support Systems, 125*. https://doi.org/10.1016/j.dss.2019.113116

Fakoor, R., Ladhak, F., Nazi, A., & Huber, M. (2013). Using deep learning to enhance cancer diagnosis and classification. In *Proceedings of the ICML workshop on the role of machine learning in transforming healthcare*. https://www.researchgate.net/publication/281857285_Using_deep_learning_to_enhance_cancer_diagnosis_and_classification.

Fala, G. J., Clayton, K. T., & Masciantonio, D. M. (1995). Applying expert systems to health care management. In *SAC '95: Proceedings of the 1995 ACM symposium on applied computing* (pp. 237−241). Association for Computing Machinery. https://doi.org/10.1145/315891.315968

Fernández, A., & Ossowski, S. (2008). Exploiting organisational information for service coordination in multiagent systems. In *AAMAS '08: proceedings of the 7th international joint conference on autonomous agents and multiagent systems* (Vol. 1, pp. 257−264). International Foundation for Autonomous Agents and Multiagent Systems. https://dl.acm.org/doi/abs/10.5555/1402383.1402423.

Ford, E., Carroll, J. A., Smith, H. E., Scott, D., & Cassell, J. A. (2016). Extracting information from the text of electronic medical records to improve case detection: A systematic review. *Journal of the American Medical Informatics Association, 23*(5), 1007−1015. https://doi.org/10.1093/jamia/ocv180

Forgionne, G. A., & Kohli, R. (1996). HMSS: a management support system for concurrent hospital decision making. *Decision Support Systems, 16*(3), 209−229. https://doi.org/10.1016/0167-9236(95)00011-9

Gopalani, S., & Arora, R. (2015). Comparing Apache Spark and map reduce with performance analysis using K-means. *International Journal of Computer Application, 113*(1), 8−11. https://doi.org/10.5120/19788-0531

Gotz, D., Wang, F., & Perer, A. (2014). A methodology for interactive mining and visual analysis of clinical event patterns using electronic health record data. *Journal of Biomedical Informatics, 48*, 148−159. https://doi.org/10.1016/j.jbi.2014.01.007

Hanafizadeh, P., Paydar, N. R., & Aliabadi, N. (2010). Neural network-based evaluation of the effect of the motivation of hospital employees on patients' satisfaction. *International Journal of Healthcare Information Systems and Informatics, 5*(4), 1−19. https://doi.org/10.4018/jhisi.2010100101

Henry, J., Pylypchuk, Y., Searcy, T., & Patel, V. (2016). Adoption of electronic health record systems among U.S. Non-Federal Acute Care Hospitals: 2008−2015. In *ONC data brief, no. 35, May 2016. The office of the national coordinator for health information technology*. https://www.healthit.gov/sites/default/files/briefs/2015_hospital_adoption_db_v17.pdf.

Huang, Z., Dong, W., Ji, L., Gan, C., Lu, X., & Duan, H. (2014). Discovery of clinical pathway patterns from event logs using probabilistic topic models. *Journal of Biomedical Informatics, 47*, 39−57. https://doi.org/10.1016/j.jbi.2013.09.003

Hussain, A., Malik, A., Halim, M. U., & Ali, A. M. (2014). The use of robotics in surgery: a review. *International Journal of Clinical Practice, 68*(11), 1376−1382. https://doi.org/10.1111/ijcp.12492

Kazancigil, M. A. (2013). Xlet-based applications for seismic early warning and emergency services in the IDTV environment. In *2013 international conference on collaboration technologies and systems (CTS)* (pp. 273−280). IEEE. https://doi.org/10.1109/CTS.2013.6567241

Kazancigil, M. A. (2019). Innovations and convergence in mobile medical applications and cloud-based hospital information systems for the real-time monitoring of patients and early warning of diseases. In *2019 IEEE World Congress on Services (SERVICES)* (pp. 301−306). IEEE. https://doi.org/10.1109/SERVICES.2019.00085

Kazancigil, M. A. (2021). Innovations in medical apps and the integration of their data into the big data repositories of hospital information systems for improved diagnosis and treatment in healthcare. In A. Zimmermann, R. J. Howlett, & L. C. Jain (Eds.), *Smart innovation, systems and technologies* (Vol. 189, pp. 183−192). Springer. https://doi.org/10.1007/978-981-15-5784-2_15

Kreimeyer, K., Foster, M., Pandey, A., Arya, N., Halford, G., Jones, S. F., Forshee, R., Walderhaug, M., & Botsis, T. (2017). Natural language processing systems for capturing and standardizing unstructured clinical information: a systematic review. *Journal of Biomedical Informatics, 73*, 14−29. https://doi.org/10.1016/j.jbi.2017.07.012

Laney, D. (2001). *3D data management: controlling data volume, velocity, and variety*. Application Delivery Strategies, META Group.

Lee, S.-I., Celik, S., Logsdon, B. A., Lundberg, S. M., Martins, T. J., Oehler, V. G., Estey, E. H., Miller, C. P., Chien, S., Dai, J., Saxena, A., Blau, C. A., & Becker, P. S. (2018). A machine learning approach to integrate big data for precision medicine in acute myeloid leukemia. *Nature Communications, 9*(42). https://doi.org/10.1038/s41467-017-02465-5

Leggat, S. G., & Yap, K. (2020). How are hospitals using artificial intelligence in strategic decision- making?—a scoping review. *Journal of Hospital Management and Health Policy, 4*, 39. https://doi.org/10.21037/jhmhp-20-92

Luo, H., Yang, D., Barszczyk, A., Vempala, N., Wei, J., Wu, S. J., Zheng, P. P., Fu, G., Lee, K., & Feng, Z.-P. (2019). Smartphone-based blood pressure measurement using transdermal optical imaging technology. *Circulation: Cardiovascular Imaging, 12*(8). https://doi.org/10.1161/CIRCIMAGING.119.008857

Mariakakis, A., Baudin, J., Whitmire, E., Mehta, V., Banks, M. A., Law, A., McGrath, L., & Patel, S. N. (2017). PupilScreen: using smartphones to assess traumatic brain injury. In, *Vol. 1 (3). Proceedings of the ACM on interactive, mobile, wearable and ubiquitous technologies* (pp. 1−27). Association for Computing Machinery. https://doi.org/10.1145/3131896

Marin, H., Massad, E., Gutierrez, M. A., Rodrigues, R. J., & Sigulem, D. (Eds.). (2016). *Global health informatics: how information technology can change our lives in a globalized world* (1st ed.). Elsevier https://www.elsevier.com/books/global-health-informatics/marin/978-0-12-804591-6.

McClean, S., & Millard, P. (2007). Where to treat the older patient? can Markov models help us better understand the relationship between hospital and community care? *Journal of the Operational Research Society, 58*(2), 255–261. https://doi.org/10.1057/palgrave.jors.2602173

Miiskin. (n.d.). Retrieved August 28, 2021, from https://miiskin.com/app/.

MoleScope. (n.d.). Retrieved August 28, 2021, from https://www.molescope.com.

Muhlestein, J. B., Le, V., Albert, D., Moreno, F. L., Anderson, J. L., Yanowitz, F., Vranian, R. B., Barsness, G. W., Bethea, C. F., Severance, H. W., Ramo, B., Pierce, J., Barbagelata, A., & Muhlestein, J. B. (2015). Smartphone ECG for evaluation of STEMI: results of the ST LEUIS pilot study. *Journal of Electrocardiology, 48*(2), 249–259. https://doi.org/10.1016/j.jelectrocard.2014.11.005

Murphy, G. F., Hanken, M. A., & Waters, K. A. (1999). *Electronic health records: changing the vision* (1st ed.). W. B. Saunders Company https://www.amazon.com/Electronic-Health-Records-Changing-Macintosh/dp/0721673864.

NEJM Catalyst. (2018). Healthcare big data and the promise of value-based care. *NEJM Catalyst, Innovations in Care Delivery*. https://catalyst.nejm.org/doi/full/10.1056/CAT.18.0290.

Rahulamathavan, Y., Veluru, S., Phan, R. C.-W., Chambers, J. A., & Rajarajan, M. (2014). Privacy-preserving clinical decision support system using Gaussian kernel-based classification. *IEEE Journal of Biomedical and Health Informatics, 18*(1), 56–66. https://doi.org/10.1109/JBHI.2013.2274899

Ramani, K. V. (2004). A management information system to plan and monitor the delivery of health-care services in government hospitals in India. *Journal of Health Organization and Management, 18*(3), 207–220. https://doi.org/10.1108/14777260410548446

Reisman, M. (2017). EHRs: the challenge of making electronic data useable and interoperable. *Pharmacy and Therapeutics, 42*(9), 572–575. https://www.ncbi.nlm.nih.gov/pmc/articles/PMC5565131/.

Rogel Cancer Center: UMSkinCheck App. (n.d.). Retrieved August 28, 2021, from https://www.rogelcancercenter.org/skin-cancer/melanoma/prevention/app.

Rojas, E., Munoz-Gama, J., Sepúlveda, M., & Capurro, D. (2016). Process mining in healthcare: A literature review. *Journal of Biomedical Informatics, 61*, 224–236. https://doi.org/10.1016/j.jbi.2016.04.007

Shahid, N., Rappon, T., & Berta, W. (2019). Applications of artificial neural networks in health care organizational decision-making: a scoping review. *PLoS One, 14*(2), e0212356. https://doi.org/10.1371/journal.pone.0212356

Shvachko, K., Kuang, H., Radia, S., & Chansler, R. (2010). The Hadoop distributed file system. In *2010 IEEE 26th symposium on mass storage systems and technologies (MSST)* (pp. 1–10). IEEE. https://doi.org/10.1109/MSST.2010.5496972

SkinVision. (n.d.). Retrieved August 28, 2021, from https://www.skinvision.com.

Sordo, M. (2002). Introduction to neural networks in healthcare. *Open Clinical Document*. https://www.academia.edu/20719514/Introduction_to_neural_networks_in_healthcare.

Sun, T. Q., & Medaglia, R. (2019). Mapping the challenges of artificial intelligence in the public sector: evidence from public healthcare. *Government Information Quarterly, 36*(2), 368–383. https://doi.org/10.1016/j.giq.2018.09.008

Tafti, A. P., Badger, J., LaRose, E., Shirzadi, E., Mahnke, A., Mayer, J., Ye, Z., Page, D., & Peissig, P. (2017). Adverse drug event discovery using biomedical literature: a big data neural network adventure. *JMIR Medical Informatics, 5*(4), e51. https://doi.org/10.2196/medinform.9170

Vial, A., Stirling, D., Field, M., Ros, M., Ritz, C., Carolan, M., Holloway, L., & Miller, A. A. (2018). The role of deep learning and radiomic feature extraction in cancer-specific predictive modelling: a review. *Translational Cancer Research, 7*(3), 803–816. https://doi.org/10.21037/tcr.2018.05.02

Wang, H.-C., Chang, F.-Y., Tsai, T.-M., Chen, C.-H., & Chen, Y.-Y. (2019). Design, fabrication, and feasibility analysis of a colorimetric detection system with a smartphone for self-monitoring blood glucose. *Journal of Biomedical Optics, 24*(2). https://doi.org/10.1117/1.JBO.24.2.027002

Wang, H., Cui, Z., Chen, Y., Avidan, M., Abdallah, A. B., & Kronzer, A. (2018). Predicting hospital readmission via cost-sensitive deep learning. *IEEE/ACM Transactions on Computational Biology and Bioinformatics, 15*(6), 1968–1978. https://doi.org/10.1109/TCBB.2018.2827029

Wang, Y., Luo, J., Hao, S., Xu, H., Shin, A. Y., Jin, B., Liu, R., Deng, X., Wang, L., Zheng, L., Zhao, Y., Zhu, C., Hu, Z., Fu, C., Hao, Y., Zhao, Y., Jiang, Y., Dai, D., Culver, D. S., … Ling, X. B. (2015). NLP based congestive heart failure case finding: a prospective analysis on statewide electronic medical records. *International Journal of Medical Informatics, 84*(12), 1039–1047. https://doi.org/10.1016/j.ijmedinf.2015.06.007

Watson, H. A., Tribe, R. M., & Shennan, A. H. (2019). The role of medical smartphone apps in clinical decision-support: a literature review. *Artificial Intelligence in Medicine, 100*. https://doi.org/10.1016/j.artmed.2019.101707

Yoon, J., Davtyan, C., & van der Schaar, M. (2017). Discovery and clinical decision support for personalized healthcare. *IEEE Journal of Biomedical and Health Informatics, 21*(4), 1133–1145. https://doi.org/10.1109/JBHI.2016.2574857

Zaharia, M., Xin, R. S., Wendell, P., Das, T., Armbrust, M., Dave, A., Meng, X., Rosen, J., Venkataraman, S., Franklin, M. J., Ghodsi, A., Gonzalez, J., Shenker, S., & Stoica, I. (2016). Apache Spark: a unified engine for big data processing. *Communications of the ACM, 59*(11), 56–65. https://doi.org/10.1145/2934664

Zhang, Y., Padman, R., & Patel, N. (2015). Paving the COWpath: learning and visualizing clinical pathways from electronic health record data. *Journal of Biomedical Informatics, 58*, 186–197. https://doi.org/10.1016/j.jbi.2015.09.009

Section IV

Prediction: Big data analytical techniques, datasets, life cycles, managements, and applications for prediction

Chapter 13

Use of artificial intelligence for predicting infectious disease

Suna Kang[1] and Donghyun Lee[2]
[1]*Korea Environment Institute, Sicheong-daero, Sejong-si, Republic of Korea;* [2]*Department of Business Administration, Tech University of Korea, Gyeonggi-do, Republic of Korea*

1. Introduction

Infectious diseases are caused by organisms such as bacteria, viruses, fungi, or parasites. They can directly or indirectly spread from one person to another, and according to the WHO (n.d.), they can be grouped into three categories: diseases that cause high levels of mortality, diseases that place heavy burdens on disabled populations, and diseases that have severe global repercussions, owning to the rapid and unexpected nature of their spread (WHO, n.d.) According to WHO's (n.d.) annual estimate, there are 229 million malaria cases and 409,000 deaths caused by malaria worldwide. In addition, there are 376 million STD cases, including syphilis, gonorrhea, chlamydia, and trichomoniasis, 37.7 million (30.2−45.1 million) HIV/AIDS cases, and 1.3−4 million cholera cases (WHO, n.d.). COVID-19 is caused by SARS-CoV-2, and it started to appear in December 2019, before spreading worldwide. Infectious diseases have killed at least tens of people, and as many as tens of millions of people. The history of infectious diseases is presented in Table 13.1 (Bean, 2020; Jonhs Hopkins University, 2021).

Infectious diseases threaten the lives of the entire global population. Some diseases such as SARS and COVID-19 trigger pandemics and spread from country to country, whereas diseases such as smallpox and chikungunya only spread to a few countries. A pandemic-level infectious disease has severe adverse effects on the medical system such as shortages in medical professionals and equipment, financial burden, and death. Therefore, it is crucial to predict and respond to the spread of infectious diseases. Accordingly, we analyzed studies related to the prediction models for the spread of infectious diseases. A research was comprehensively conducted, based on various methodologies such as conventional mathematical models (SIR and SEIR models), agent-based models (ABMs), and artificial intelligence methodologies, including big data and machine learning methodologies (Kermack & McKendrick, 1927). We conducted a research that performs categorizations and analyses based on these methodologies.

This chapter is structured as follows. In Section 2, the mathematical modeling of infectious diseases and their development are introduced. In Section 3, models that predict infectious diseases using artificial intelligence are analyzed. Finally, in Section 4, a conclusion is drawn.

2. Mathematical modeling of infectious diseases and their development

2.1 SIR and SEIR

Conventional prediction models for infectious diseases include SIR and SEIR models. The SIR model was developed in 1927 by Kermack and McKendrick, and with its mathematical approach to the spread of infectious diseases, it became the basis for other models. In the SIR model, "S" represents the "susceptible" infection target group and the group that can be infected in the entire population, "I" denotes the "infected" group in the infection target group, and "R" stands for the "removed" group that died or recovered after infection, i.e., the group with no possibility of an infection. This model estimates the spread and increase of infectious diseases based on the assumption that there is no incubation period until infection, and that reinfection does not occur after recovering from a disease. The SIR model was the first mathematical

Big Data Analytics for Healthcare. https://doi.org/10.1016/B978-0-323-91907-4.0000[illegible]-7

TABLE 13.1 History of infectious diseases.

Year	Disease	Location	Deaths
430 BCE	Plague of Athens	Greece, Libya, Egypt, Ethiopia	Approximately100,000
541	Plague of Justinian	Europe and West Asia	30–50 million
1340s	Black Death	Worldwide	50 million
1494	Syphilis		More than 50,000
1520	Smallpox	Mexico	Approximately 3.5 million
1793–1798	Yellow fever	Philadelphia, United States	Approximately 25,000
1832	Cholera pandemic	Asia, Europe	Approximately 18,402
1918, 1957, 1968, 2009	Spanish flu	Worldwide	Approximately 50 million
1976–2020	Ebola	29 epidemics	15,258
1981	HIV/AIDS	Worldwide	Approximately 37 million
2002	SARS	Worldwide	813
2009	H1N1 "swine flu"	Worldwide	284,000
2014	Chikungunya	Americas	183
2015	Zika	Worldwide	53
2019-present	COVID-19	Worldwide	4.5 million+ (as of 30 August, 2021)

model (Kermack & McKendrick, 1927), and advancements have been steadily made based on this model. SEIR is a model that considers the incubation period in SIR, and its equations are as follows:

$$\mathrm{S+E+I+R} = 1. \tag{13.1}$$

$$\mathrm{NS+NE+NI+NR} = \mathrm{N}. \tag{13.2}$$

$$\frac{dS}{dt} = -\beta SI, \tag{13.3}$$

$$\frac{dE}{dt} = \beta SI - aE, \tag{13.4}$$

$$\frac{dI}{dt} = aE - \gamma I, \tag{13.5}$$

$$\frac{dR}{dt} = I. \tag{13.6}$$

In SEIR, "E" stands for "exposed" group, and it represents the period when a very small number of viruses invade and actively proliferate the body, owing to the absence of an immune response that occurs. During this period, the virus is not infectious; hence, it does not belong to the S or I group. SEIR belongs to the nonlinear system of the ordinary differential equation. In this equation, t and β denote the time (days) and infection rate, respectively. In addition, γ and a, respectively, represent the recovery rate and average latency (Neuwirth & Arganbright, 2003).

Lloyd-Smith, Galvani and Getz (2003) presented a probabilistic model of SARS outbreaks that occurred in communities and hospitals, because SARS is transmitted within hospitals, and healthcare workers constitute a significant proportion of SARS cases worldwide. Their analysis indicated that contact tracing and quarantine contribute to preventing the spread of an outbreak to a certain degree; however, inadequate quarantine facilities increase the spread of the outbreak. It was verified that if an individual is not quarantined by 5 days after exposure, owing to delayed contact tracing, the contribution of quarantine significantly decreased, and if quarantine or the initiation of quarantine is delayed, the effectiveness of other measures decreases significantly. Healthcare workers are exposed to a significantly higher prevalence than the rest of the community, and measures to reduce in-hospital transmission exert the most significant impact on the R_0

value of infectious diseases. Combining contact tracing and case management measures (quarantine) has been demonstrated to inhibit SARS outbreaks by 85%. Nishiura et al. (2004) evaluated the effects of interventions on SARS via mathematical modeling. This study estimated the initial attack size triggered by the quarantine failure. The analysis indicated that 100% effective preventive public health measures or quarantines reduced the number of cases, and their combination linearly reduced the R_0 value, as opposed to quarantine practices. In the absence of preventive public health measures, the epidemic should be contained by isolating at least 66.7% of those who may be infected. A high proportion of vulnerable people (75% or 90%) suggests that precautions should be taken to reduce the number of newly infected cases in the absence of quarantine.

Various SIR and SEIR studies related to the spread of coronavirus have been conducted recently. On February 19, 2020, via a combination of strict preventive and control measures, Car, Baressi Šegota, Andjelić, Lorencin and Mrzljak (2020) modeled the spread of COVID-19 using the SEIR model with the highest incidence of approximately 50,000 cases in Hubei (isolation, physical distancing). The study argued that without preventive and control measures, twice as many people would be infected, and the peak infection rate renewal would be faster and higher, thereby resulting in the loss of many. Moreover, assuming that the quarantine rate has dropped to 0.6, it is expected that the maximum number of cases will double, compared to maintaining full preventive and control measures. Fang, Nie and Penny (2020) also adopted the SEIR model to model the spread of COVID-19, using the case data published by Chinese authorities and official media. The study pointed out that stringent government measures are effective in stopping the spread of COVID-19; and these measures include early detection, isolation and quarantine, sufficient medical equipment, inpatients in hospitals, and treatment strategies. More stringent government-controlled policies are associated with slower growth in the infected population, while quarantine and protection procedures are less effective as more cases occur, thus stressing the importance of optimizing treatment plans and developing specific drugs. Geng et al. (2020) employed the SEIR model to verify that reducing contact with COVID-19 patients via travel restrictions (community isolation, and permitting interactions with people who can only live in certain areas), as well as work and school lockdowns, will slow the outbreak of the epidemic. Travel restrictions and workplace and school lockdowns reduced the exposure to the virus and its infection by 45.71% and 29.90%, respectively. Hou et al. (2020) analyzed the spread of COVID-19 using well-mixed SEIR. It was confirmed that interventions like quarantine can effectively reduce the maximum number of COVID-19 infection cases by reducing the contact rate, as well as delay the maximum time of infection. Pandey, Subedee, Khanal, & Koirala (2020) modeled the spread of COVID-19 using the age structure SEIR. The study pointed out that unless special measures are taken, the spread will peak within 100 days from March 24, and the demand for ICU beds will exceed the available supply for Kathmandu, Nepal, by 25 times. In addition, it was analyzed that if social distancing is maintained for 1 month and for 1 year to lower the contact rate to 35%, the mortality rate will decrease by 33%, while the need for ICU beds will decrease by 63%. A control strategy that focuses on isolating contacts and infected individuals for 1 year after lockdown for a period of 1 month is expected to reduce mortality by 27% and reduce health care demand by 50%. Combining social distancing and investigation with quarantine is expected to reduce the total expected death toll by 99.6% after 1 month of social lockdown, as well as reduce medical demand to a similar level. Semenova et al. (2020) simulated the COVID-19 cases and mortality rates in Kazakhstan using the SEIR model. The simulation showed that without quarantine measures, there will be 2.04 million infections, 15,740 deaths, and 156,000 patients hospitalized in Kazakhstan. The application of quarantine measures would result in 188,983 cases, with a total decrease in death of 3750 at the peak, and hospitalization is expected to decrease to 931,000 at its peak. Tang et al. (2020) simulated the SEIR model to predict the spread of COVID-19 in China. This study posited that reducing contact via isolation reduces the peak value; however, it only delays the peak. Furthermore, if the quarantine rate is increased by 10–20 times, the peak is 6.5–9 days earlier, and the peak number of infected people decreases by 87% or 93%. This indicates that strengthening quarantine after contact tracing, and reducing the contact rate, can significantly lower the peak and reduce the cumulative number of reported cases. Owing to travel restrictions in Wuhan, the number of people infected in Beijing within 7 days would fall by 88.9%, only if the quarantine rate increases by 100,000 times. This implies that the effect of Wuhan's travel restrictions on Beijing's infection is almost equivalent to increasing quarantine by a threshold of 100,000. Su et al. (2020) developed a COVID-19 spread model using SEIR with data reported from January 24, 2020, to February 23, 2020. The analysis indicated that reducing the proportion of quarantined individuals (0.8q, 0.6q) increased the peak value and delayed the peak time. However, the peak time occurred earlier as the peak value decreased, and the isolation rate of exposed individuals was higher. Sjödin, Wilder-Smith, Osman, Farooq and Rocklöv (2020) developed an SEIR to model the spread of COVID-19 in regions in Italy, and continuously modeled the outbreak progression as a Markov process. This model elucidates the importance of probability in small towns and individual-based processes within the home. Based on published data, this model parameterized the incubation period, infection period, infection period of asymptomatic people, asymptomatic rate, contact rate at home, and contact rate in public places. The study was modeled as a scenario in which 0.1% of the quarantined village population was in the incubation period when the quarantine policy was implemented on February 22. Owing to modeling, the small quarantine units and degree of policy compliance help to minimize infection cases for 14 days, and latent and infection cases are also minimized at the end of the lockdown. A less stringent quarantine also contributes to a longer lockdown period. By modeling a two-person household by dividing community isolation into complete, near-complete, moderate, and noncommunity isolation levels, 3, 4, 7, and 11 secondary infections are expected to occur, respectively. For an average household size of 3, 7, 8, 12, and 20 secondary infections are expected, respectively. The lockdown suggests that transmission will continue unless quarantine is taken at the strongest community level, with smaller households or smaller isolation groups having fewer secondary cases. A literature analysis was performed on mathematical modeling to simulate the spread of COVID-19. Mathematical modeling was suitable in understanding the effectiveness of government policies, or the effects caused by reducing interpersonal contact while altering isolation and contact rates. Therefore, in the mathematical modeling process, human-to-human contact and the medical system may be the most important factors among other variables. There are only approximately 11 cases of COVID-19-related mathematical modeling that we have reviewed so far. A common argument from the 11 cases is that social distancing, lockdown, and isolation are important factors in reducing the spread and mortality of COVID-19. Pandey, Chaudhary, Gupta, Pal (2020) attempted to predict the number of cases for the next 2 weeks in India up to March 30, 2020. Using the SEIR and regression models, predictions were made based on data provided by Johns Hopkins from January 30, 2020, to March 30, 2020. Based on the analysis, the root mean squared log error (RMSLE) values of the SEIR and regression models were 1.52 and 1.75, respectively. The RMSLE error ratio between the SEIR and the regression model was 2.01.

2.2 Agent-based model

Mathematical modeling is limited because it is difficult to reflect individual behavioral patterns and detailed real world scenarios. To address this limitation, an ABM that can reflect individual behavior has been developed. The ABM is a model that considers the interaction and heterogeneity between agents covering countries, individuals, and regions. Hence, it is a model that can capture unexpected diffusion phenomena triggered by individual actions. Three important components of ABM are the population, the social contact network among individuals within the population, and an appropriate disease spread model (Eubank et al., 2004). The framework for reconstructing epidemic dynamics is an ABM, which starts with the assumption that the spread of the influenza A virus (H1N1) follows a congestion pattern within the population, and that this pattern is partially affected by regional factors, including population distribution, age, household size, and employment status. In the FRED model, each agent contains information such as demographic information, health information, activity radius, and health-related behavior, and based on this information, it ascertains whether agents change their intention when exhibiting health-related behavior. In addition to the agents' personal information, external conditions such as vaccine availability influence the final decision. The FRED model simulated the impact of school closures during influenza epidemics, and was adopted to identify the impact of employment-related health policies. This model suggests that it is important to consider individual health-related behaviors and heterogeneity in the workplace environment to model disease spread (Grefenstette et al., 2013). The FRED model was later released as a scenario via the red.publichealth.pitt.edu Website, and it was opened for use by the government and private sector. This website allows the user to run influenza simulations with various combinations of epidemic parameters and controls, etc. In addition to cases, prevalence, and attack rate curves, it provides services such as maps and images to visualize the results. Merler et al. (2015) simulated the outbreak of the Ebola virus in Liberia using a spatial ABM. In this model, contacts in hospitals, homes, and funerals were considered. The model developed by Merler et al. (2015) can be employed to estimate Ebola virus transmission parameters in West Africa, and investigate the availability of Ebola treatment devices. Peak, Childs, Grad and Buckee (2017) argued that there are no drugs or vaccines available to contain the outbreak of emerging infectious diseases; hence, mitigation efforts rely on quarantine measures and the epidemiological characteristics of the infection. However, no systematic framework currently exists to evaluate the relationship between different isolation strategies and the natural history and epidemiology of pathogens. Therefore, we compared the effectiveness of isolation and symptom monitoring implemented via contact tracing when controlling an epidemic with an ABM. In this study, seven diseases, including Ebola, influenza A, and SARS, were investigated. The results of the study verified that the comparative effectiveness of symptom monitoring and quarantine is significantly dependent on the natural history of the infectious disease, its inherent contagiousness, and the likelihood of intervention in a particular medical setting. The benefits of isolation over symptom monitoring are generally maximized in fast-path diseases (diseases with shorter incubation periods than periods of infection and short incubation periods) and in environments where isolation is highly effective or with high contact.

Pourbohloul et al. (2005) compared intervention strategies for communicable diseases, such as SARS and smallpox, using contact network dynamics. To perform contact network modeling, all areas where contact can be made, such as homes, schools, workplaces, hospitals, and other public places, were considered. In this model, each person is represented by a vertex in the network, and each contact between two people is represented by an edge connecting the vertices. This study established a city contact network model based on the demographic information of Vancouver, Canada. Studies have shown that for mild communicable diseases, outbreaks were controlled via a combination of isolation, which shortens the duration of infection by 25%, and successful isolation of 30% of all patient contacts. More contagious diseases require significantly stricter isolation. Zhang et al. (2017) performed transmission dynamics modeling for MERS, which spread in Korea in 2015. The MERS outbreak in Korea began on May 20, 2015, by a traveler from the Middle East, and there were 186 cases of this outbreak, including 38 deaths. Cases were scattered across the country, and these 186 cases included asymptomatic individuals. Based on the transmission dynamics modeling, isolating close contacts and informing the public of the actual occurrence can be primary countermeasures. The most effective combination of interventions is characterized by increased quarantine in designated hospitals, self-protection of Iranians to reduce contacts rates, and rapid response to symptom onset for confirmatory testing by implementing appropriate quarantine procedures. Hoertel et al. (2020) performed a stochastic agent-based microsimulation modeling analysis of COVID-19 in New York. For all New Yorkers, quarantine measures were very effective in containing the spread of the virus; however, they were insufficient in preventing a second peak after the policy was lifted. Moreover, the period of quarantine (4–16 weeks) did not appear to have any significant effect on suppressing the spread. The suspension of the second stage of the quarantine according to age, i.e., 3 weeks of isolation for individuals under the age of 70 and an additional 8 weeks of isolation for those over the age of 70, was determined to lower the cumulative incidence by 23%, and reduce the cumulative mortality rate. Without quarantine, the model estimated that approximately 30,000 deaths would occur in New York. Koo et al. (2020) simulated COVID-19 confirmed cases in the Singaporean population and adopted an influenza epidemic simulation model to estimate the possibility of human-to-human transmission. Based on the analysis, it determined that the isolation of the infected and family isolation reduced the number of infected people by 95.8% compared to the baseline scenario; in addition, isolations, school lockdowns, and social distancing reduced the central cumulative number of infections by 96.4%. Kucharski et al. (2020) modeled the spread of COVID-19 on 40,162 people from the British population, using an individual-level transmission model. The analysis scenarios included no control (default), weekly mass randomized testing of 5% of the population, isolation of suspected cases at home, self-isolation outside the household, self-isolation + home isolation, self-isolation + home isolation + contact tracing at work and school, self-quarantine + home quarantine + all contact tracking, self-isolation + home quarantine + acquaintance-oriented contact tracking, self-isolation + home quarantine + app-based contact tracking, self-isolation + home quarantine + acquaintance-oriented contact tracking + limiting contact with other individuals daily, and self-quarantine – home quarantine + contact tracing centered on acquaintances + limiting contact with other individuals to four daily contacts. The results obtained from the analysis are presented in Table 13.2.

TABLE 13.2 Model result about spread of COVID-19.

Item	Changes in percentage
No control (default)	0% decrease
Weekly mass randomized testing of 5% of the population	2% decrease
Isolation of suspected cases at home: 29% decrease	29% decrease
Self-isolation outside the household	35% decrease
Self-isolation + home isolation	37% decrease
Self-isolation + home isolation + contact tracing at work and school	53% decrease
Self-quarantine + home quarantine + all contact tracking	64% decrease
Self-isolation + home quarantine + acquaintance-oriented contact tracking	57% decrease
Self-isolation + home quarantine + app-based contact tracking	47% decrease
Self-isolation + home quarantine + acquaintance-oriented contact tracking + limiting contact with other individuals daily	64% decrease
Self-quarantine + home quarantine + contact tracing centered on acquaintances + limiting contact with other individuals to 4 daily contacts	66% decrease

3. Predicting infectious diseases using artificial intelligence

3.1 Big data

Search terms started properly with Google flu trends (GFT) in 2008 can be employed in predicting infectious diseases (Ginsberg et al., 2009). GFT predicted flu epidemics regionally in the United States, based on hundreds of billions of individual search terms in Google search logs. This model is developed based on the fact that people search for flu-related terms when they get the flu.

The equation for GFT is expressed as follows:

$$\text{log}it\ (I(t)) = \alpha \times \text{log}it(Q(t)) + \varepsilon \tag{13.7}$$

where $I(t)$, $Q(t)$, α, and ε denote the rate of doctor visits for influenza-like illnesses (ILIs), rate of ILI-related queries at time t, the multiplication coefficients, and error term, respectively. GFT tests of the 50 million search terms entered each week in the United States with a Q from 2003 to 2008 were considered to ensure that the results calculated from a single search match the ILI data from the Center for Disease Control and Prevention (CDC). Via this process, a list of 45 top queries with high correlation with the CDC ILI data was generated as shown in Table 13.3.

Using the ILI-related query rate as an explanatory variable, the weekly ILI percentage (from 2003 to 2007) and a linear model were assumed, and the coefficients were derived. This model exhibited an outstanding performance with a correlation of 0.90 with the ILI percentage announced by the CDC. Moreover, GFT's predictions were more accurate than the CDC's existing prediction system by approximately 2 weeks. The CDC report is later than GFT, where real-time data is available, because it predicts the spread of the flu after collecting data from multiple sources, including health care providers and medical records. However, the GFT did not detect the 2009 swine influenza (N1H1) epidemic prediction. Furthermore, 100 out of 108 weeks in 2011 were predicted to be higher than the actual flu outbreak (Lazer, Kennedy, King, & Vespignani, 2014). It was deduced that it would be difficult to replace the existing epidemiological survey because it predicted that influenza would be more prevalent in 2013 than the actual outbreak (Butler, 2013).

Search terms and expressions used online cannot replace the patient's health status; however, they can complement existing epidemiological methods, as several studies have confirmed that there is a high correlation between search terms and the occurrence of infectious diseases, especially influenza. Yuan et al. (2013) predicted the flu outbreak using search query data from Baidu, China, and verified that the correlation coefficient between the search index and the flu outbreak

TABLE 13.3 List of 45 search queries that are highly correlated with CDC ILI data.

	Top 45 queries	
Search query	**N**	**Weighted**
Influenza complication	11	18.15
Cold/flu remedy	8	5.05
General influenza symptoms	5	2.60
Term for influenza	4	3.74
Specific influenza symptom	4	2.54
Symptoms of influenza complication	4	2.21
Antibiotic medication	3	6.23
General influenza remedies	2	0.18
Symptoms of a related disease	2	1.66
Antiviral medication	1	0.39
Related disease	1	6.66
Unrelated to influenza	0	0.00
Total	45	49.40

Reproduced from Ginsberg, J., Mohebbi, M. H., Patel, R. S., Brammer, L., Smolinski, M. S., & Brilliant, L. (2009). Detecting influenza epidemics using search engine query data. *Nature, 457*(7232), 1012–1014.

was 0.96. In addition, it was confirmed that the search index is an important signal for influenza epidemics, as it can identify the peak and trough of the flu time series curve. Culotta (2010) proposed several regression analysis methods to identify messages related to ILI by collecting 500,000 Twitter messages written over 10 weeks from February 12, 2020, to April 24, 2010. Among them, it was confirmed that there was a correlation of 0.78 with the CDC statistics in the regression analysis exhibiting the best performance. Chan, Sahai, Conrad and Brownstein (2011) analyzed the relationship between the daily search volume of Google Trends in Bolivia, Brazil, India, Indonesia, and Singapore, including the number of monthly dengue cases from 2003 to 2010, using the linear model:

$$O = \beta_0 + \beta_1 S + \varepsilon \tag{13.8}$$

where O and S denote the number of cases per dengue, and percentage of Google search terms related to dengue, respectively. Based on the analysis, it was confirmed that the predicted epidemic curve coincided with the official number of dengue cases, and the correlation coefficient between the two relationships was significantly high (from 0.82 to 0.99).

3.2 AI

Recently, infectious disease spread models using machine learning and deep learning are emerging. The main studies that predicted the spread of infectious diseases by applying machine learning and deep learning for each infectious disease are considered.

3.2.1 Influenza

Several studies have been conducted to predict ILI using machine learning and deep learning. Xu et al. (2017) used weather data such as Google search data, average temperature, and atmospheric pressure as input variables to predict influenza ILI cases from 2011 to 2016, and modeled it using a generalized linear model, least absolute shrinkage and selection operator, auto-regressive integrated moving average (ARIMA), and feed-forward neural network. Based on the analysis, the prediction performance of the FNN methodology was the best; however, it was underestimated compared to the actual value, and the prediction accuracy of the influenza epidemic period, the period was insufficient. In the ARIMA case, although the value was predicted close to that of the ILI, there was a tendency to predict by delaying the peak point.

Hu et al. (2018) developed an artificial tree algorithm to predict ILI using CDC and Twitter data for 10 regions in the United States. Based on the analysis, the average mean squared errors of BP neural network (BPNN), artificial tree-BPNN (AT-BPNN), and IAT-BPNN (a developed model that optimized the initial parameters of BPNN) for the 10 regions were 0.1542, 0.0953, and 0.0495, respectively. Zhu et al. (2019) developed a model for predicting ILI in Guangzhou, China, using an attention-based recurrent neural network (RNN). After allowing the model to remember the data for 6, 8, 10, 12, and 14 weeks, the mean absolute percentage error (MAPE) was measured and the obtained results were 0.107, 0.092, 0.086, 0.106, and 0.109, respectively. This result is improved from the performance obtained using long short-term memory (LSTM) and RNN, which were 0.118 and 0.132, respectively. Liu, Han, Zhou and Wang (2018) developed an LSTM model to predict ILI using air pollution (PM2.5, CO, Pb, NO2, PM10, SO2), meteorological data (minimum temperature, maximum temperature, average temperature), and Google trend search volume (flu shot, flu vaccine). Based on this analysis, the RMSE was improved from 0.017 to 0.015 when both air pollution and meteorological data were adopted, compared to the analysis result obtained with the Google Trend search volume.

3.2.2 Skin diseases

Obeidat, Alsmadi, Bani Bakr and Obeidat (2020) modeled the relationship between the number of search keywords in Google Trends and the monthly number of skin diseases (rubella, measles) provided by the CDC using a support vector machine (SVM), logistic regression (LR), and decision tree (DT). Data on monthly skin disease occurrence cases were for the United States, obtained from 2004 to 2018, and the initial set of disease-related keywords was the monthly cumulative amount of Google Trends data. The prediction of each disease occurrence was evaluated using the SVM model, and the influence of keywords that triggered the occurrence of the epidemic class was confirmed using LR and DT. Here, the epidemic class is classified as "1" if the epidemic occurs, and increases for three consecutive months, otherwise it is "0." Based on this analysis, it was verified that the number of search keywords for rubella and measles was related to the increase in the monthly number of diseases announced by the CDC.

3.2.3 Malaria

Mohapatra, Tripathi, Pal and Shrestha (2021) developed a machine learning model to predict malaria using rainfall, relative humidity, and maximum temperature data in Sundargarh, Odisha, which records the highest number of deaths from malaria. By adopting J48 (a random forest model) and multilayer perceptron (MLP), it was deduced that the performance of the J48 model was almost similar to that of MLP; however, J48 was slightly better than MLP. Chae, Kwon and Lee (2018) attempted to predict the spread of malaria in Korea using LSTM deep learning and query data. Wang et al. (2019) developed malaria predictive modeling using ARIMA, BPNN, LSTM, and stacking with the monthly number of malaria cases in China from 2011 to 2017. Based on this analysis, the RMSE value of each modeling was 13.176, 9.571, 7.208, and 6.810, respectively, thereby confirming that the stacking technique was the best.

The infectious disease spread model has been developed and applied to various methodologies from SIR and SEIR to deep learning. Simultaneously, the obtained data has also been refined. As a previous approach, an infectious disease spreads in a series of processes, including exposure, infection, and recovery. In the past 10 years, it was confirmed that the spread of infectious diseases is predicted by considering various factors such as human behavior, decision-making process, information acquisition, and search terms.

3.2.4 COVID-19

Yang et al. (2020) derived the prevalence curve by integrating the population movement (interregional inflow and outflow) data, before and after January 2020, into the SEIR model. In addition, they adopted the LSTM technique trained with the 2003 SARS data. Accordingly, the pandemic was predicted. Based on this analysis, it was deduced that SEIR is an effective methodology for predicting the peak and magnitude of the COVID-19 pandemic, and it was determined that the actual number of new positive cases and LSTM prediction curve are relatively similar. Car et al. (2020) developed a COVID-19 infection spread modeling using the MLP algorithm with the COVID-19 case data provided by John Hopkins CSSE. The data were divided into infection, recovery, and death, and geographic distribution information of infected patients at various time points was reflected in the modeling. In this study, the input variables were latitude, longitude, and the number of days after infection. In addition, modeling was performed using 406 location information for 51 days. Based on this analysis, the R^2 factor of each model for infection, death, and recovery trends were 0.98, 0.99, and 0.97, respectively. However, in the cross-validation (fivefold) process, the R^2 factors of each model for the models were 0.94, 0.986, and 0.781, respectively. This model is beneficial because it created a COVID-19 infection spread model by considering spatiotemporal data. However, the robustness of the model for estimating recovered patients was lower than that of the model for identifying infection and death trends. Arora, Kumar and Panigrahi (2020) adopted LSTM to predict the number of positive cases of COVID-19 in 32 Indian states. The analysis data include COVID-19 positive cases for the period from March 14, 2020, to May 14, 2020. The data from March 14, 2020, to May 8, 2020, were adopted as the training data set, and the data from May 9, 202,0 to May 14, 2020, which a later period, were adopted as the test data set. In this study, the severity of COVID-19 was expressed in a spreadsheet independent of the prediction, and the severity was divided into three categories based on the number of positive COVID-19 cases and daily increase rate. A mild zone represents a state where the total number of positive COVID-19 cases is less than 200, with a daily increase rate of less than 2%, and a moderate zone is a state where the total number of COVID-19 positive cases is between 200 and 2000 cases, with a daily increase rate less than 5%. Finally, a severe zone is a state in which the number of positive COVID-19 cases was more than 2000, with a daily increase rate of more than 5%. Stacked LSTM, bidirection LSTM, and convolutional LSTM were employed as models. Based on this analysis, it was deduced that the predictive performance of the bidirection LSTM was the best among the three modified LSTM models, as it predicted the actual number of cases closely. It was determined that the MAPE of the daily forecast of this model was within 3%, and the MAPE of the weekly forecast was in the range of 4%–8%. Furthermore, it exhibited substantially accurate results in short-term predictions from 1 to 3 days. Chimmula and Zhang (2020) also adopted LSTM techniques to predict COVID-19 infection in Canada. In this study, a COVID-19 prediction model was developed using data from two countries, Canada and Italy. First, a model was developed using Candida's COVID-19 infection data until March 31, 2020. In the model developed using data obtained from Canada, the RMSE of the training dataset was 34.83 and the short-term prediction accuracy was 93.4%. The RMSE of the validation and test datasets was 45.70, and the accuracy of long-term prediction was 92.67%. The short-term prediction RMSE of the model using the data from Italy was 51.46, which was lower than the model developed using the data from Canada. However, this study is limited, as it was developed using a data set for a short time. Punn et al. (2020) employed machine and deep learning for the epidemiologic analysis of COVID-19. The daily number of COVID-19 cases provided by Johns Hopkins from January 22, 2020, to April 1, 2020, was adopted as input data, and the adopted methodologies include support vector regression (SVR), polynomial regression (PR), DNN, and LSTM. The study predicted the number of confirmed cases, deaths, and recovery of COVID-19 over the next 10 days, worldwide. Based on this analysis, it was confirmed that the prediction performance of SVR and PR was better than that of DNN and LSTM in deep learning. The RMSEs of the SVR, DNN LSTM, and PR models after 10 days were 1,970,860, 211,213, 1,002,543, and 2,156,540, respectively. After 10 days, the RMSEs of the mortality prediction model were 93,112, 7149, 50,362, and 124,021, respectively. Finally, the RMSEs of the model for predicting the number of recoveries after 10 days were 422,740, 93,476, 206,916, and 557,125, respectively. Zeroual, Harrou, Dairi and Sun (2020) performed a comparative study on five deep learning methodologies to predict confirmed and recovery COVID-19 cases. Specifically, RNN, LSTM, bi-LSTM, gated recurrent units (GRUs), and variational auto-encoders (VAEs) algorithms were employed. The study modeled the daily number of confirmed and recovery cases in Italy, Spain, France, China, the United States, and Australia. From January 22, 2020, to May 31, 2020, confirmed and recovery COVID-19 cases were adopted as the training data set, and from June 1, 2020, to June 17, 2020, as the test data set. Based on this prediction, it was verified that VAE exhibited the best performance in the prediction model for confirmed COVID-19 cases. Although the prediction model for the recovery cases exhibits a lower performance than that of the confirmed cases, it can be inferred that the VAE performance is the best.

4. Conclusion

The research on infectious disease models has been progressing steadily since 1920. Owing to the development of geographic information system (GIS) techniques and digitization, various big data such as human movement, epidemiological, and medical data have become available. Moreover, the combination of SEIR, a mathematical modeling technique, and LSTM, a deep learning technique, increases the spread and prediction accuracy of infectious diseases, which is substantially beneficial in preventing and controlling infectious diseases (Yang et al., 2020).

Differential equations for SIR and SEIR (existing mathematical modeling techniques) represent the regression of infectious diseases. In the SIR model, recovered individuals develop immune antibodies to the pathogen, and in the SEIR model, an individual goes through an incubation period for a certain time period after exposure to the pathogen (Yadav & Akhter, 2021). In addition, SIR and SEIR can determine the effect of suppressing the spread of infectious diseases. Geng et al. (2020) verified that travel restrictions and lockdowns of workplaces and schools reduced COVID-19 exposure and the degree of infection by 45.71% and 29.90%, respectively. Hou et al. (2020) verified that by reducing quarantine and contact rates, it is possible to effectively reduce the maximum number of cases of COVID-19 infection and delay the maximum time of infection. Pandey et al. (2020) deduced that maintaining a 1-month social lockdown and 1-year social distancing to lower the contact rate to 35% reduced mortality by 33%, and reduced the need for ICU beds by 63%. The ABM model is a model that considers the interaction and heterogeneity between agents covering countries, individuals, and regions, and it reflects individual characteristics such as national differences, population distribution, and age (Hoertel et al., 2020; Koo et al., 2020; Kucharski et al., 2020; Merler et al., 2015; Peak et al., 2017; Pourbohloul et al., 2005).

Studies using big data and artificial intelligence were modeled with search queries that can reflect the number of cases, deaths, spread, weather data, and individual behavioral patterns. Machine and deep learning analyses were determined to be highly accurate, up to a 90% accuracy (Chimmula & Zhang, 2020). However, deep learning techniques such as DNN, LSTM, and GRU contain black boxes inside; hence, it is difficult to interpret the results. Furthermore, because it is not an epidemiological model like SIR, SEIR, and ABM modeling, it is difficult to determine the preventive effect of national and regional measures.

During a public health emergency response, decision-makers are required to adopt modeling results to make several crucial decisions. Public risk must be quantified, policy priorities determined, and flexibility maintained in a variety of situations (Fischer et al., 2016; Lutz et al., 2019). However, these decisions are often made based on unavailable or uncertain information (Wernstedt, Roberts, Arvai, & Redmond, 2019). For decision-makers to gain more insight, it is necessary to combine useful information and extract relevant information from various data sources, including monitoring data and social media provided by modelers (Fischer et al., 2016). Furthermore, decision-makers should make decisions by considering the limitations of infectious disease modeling.

First, the limitations of the data used in infectious disease modeling should be considered. The data adopted in the modeling are significantly similar to SIR, SEIR, and artificial intelligence techniques in terms of changes in the infectious disease population, disease incubation period, and disease transmission path. Although big data and artificial intelligence techniques are currently being developed, it is difficult to quantify the epidemiologic parameters of infectious disease in the real world, and the accuracy and sensitivity of the model are inconsistent because each country undergoes different conditions such as social environment, political climate, and economic situations. Therefore, methodologies suitable for national and social environments should be considered, and interactions between individuals and pathogens should be thoroughly considered (Lutz et al., 2019).

Second, the modeling results of infectious disease should be interpreted cautiously. Although mathematical modeling and artificial intelligence techniques for predicting infectious diseases are theoretically transparent, the complexities of the models make it difficult for decision-makers to comprehensively interpret the results. The modeling itself is not designed to help decision-making; hence, it is difficult to adapt it to key policy decisions. In particular, deep learning contains a black box; hence, it is difficult to interpret its results. Therefore, modelers should transparently provide data collection, coding, and modeling processes, as well as information on model uncertainty to help decision-makers make policy decisions (Knight et al., 2016).

Decision-makers should refer to epidemiologic data and modeling results to make scientifically sound decisions. Furthermore, they should make rational decisions based on evidence, considering GIS and interpersonal interactions, as well as national and social environments.

References

Arora, P., Kumar, H., & Panigrahi, B. K. (2020). Prediction and analysis of COVID-19 positive cases using deep learning models: A descriptive case study of India. *Chaos, Solitons & Fractals, 139*, 110017.

Bean, M. (2020). A timeline of emerging infectious diseases in history. https://www.beckershospitalreview.com/public-health/a-timeline-of-emerging-infectious-diseases-in-history.html. (Accessed 16 July 2021).

Butler, D. (2013). When Google got flu wrong. *Nature News, 494*(7436), 155.

Car, Z., Baressi Šegota, S., Andjelić, N., Lorencin, I., & Mrzljak, V. (2020). Modeling the spread of COVID-19 infection using a multilayer perceptron. *Computational and mathematical methods in medicine, 2020*.

Chae, S., Kwon, S., & Lee, D. (2018). Predicting infectious disease using deep learning and big data. *International Journal of Environmental Research and Public Health, 15*(8), 1596.

Chan, E. H., Sahai, V., Conrad, C., & Brownstein, J. S. (2011). Using web search query data to monitor dengue epidemics: A new model for neglected tropical disease surveillance. *PLoS Neglected Tropical Diseases, 5*(5), e1206.

Chimmula, V. K. R., & Zhang, L. (2020). Time series forecasting of COVID-19 transmission in Canada using LSTM networks. *Chaos, Solitons & Fractals, 135*, 109864.

Culotta, A. (2010). Towards detecting influenza epidemics by analyzing Twitter messages. *Proceedings of the first workshop on social media analytics*, 115–122.

Eubank, S., Guclu, H., Kumar, V. A., Marathe, M. V., Srinivasan, A., Toroczkai, Z., et al. (2004). Modeling disease outbreaks in realistic urban social networks. *Nature, 429*(6988), 180–184.

Fang, Y., Nie, Y., & Penny, M. (2020). Transmission dynamics of the COVID-19 outbreak and effectiveness of government interventions: A data-driven analysis. *Journal of Medical Virology, 92*(6), 645–659.

Fischer, L. S., Santibanez, S., Hatchett, R. J., Jernigan, D. B., Meyers, L. A., Thorpe, P. G., et al. (2016). CDC grand rounds: Modeling and public health decision-making. *Morbidity and Mortality Weekly Report, 65*(48), 1374–1377.

Geng, H., Xu, A., Wang, X., Zhang, Y., Yin, X., & Mao, M. A. (2020). Analysis of the role of current prevention and control measures in the epidemic of new coronavirus based on SEIR model. *Journal of Jinan University (Natural Science & Medicine Edition), 41*(2), 1–7.

Ginsberg, J., Mohebbi, M. H., Patel, R. S., Brammer, L., Smolinski, M. S., & Brilliant, L. (2009). Detecting influenza epidemics using search engine query data. *Nature, 457*(7232), 1012–1014.

Grefenstette, J. J., Brown, S. T., Rosenfeld, R., DePasse, J., Stone, N. T., Cooley, P. C., et al. (2013). FRED (A Framework for Reconstructing Epidemic Dynamics): An open-source software system for modeling infectious diseases and control strategies using census-based populations. *BMC Public Health, 13*(1), 1–14.

Hoertel, N., Blachier, M., Blanco, C., Olfson, M., Massetti, M., Limosin, F., et al. (2020). Facing the COVID-19 epidemic in NYC: A stochastic agent-based model of various intervention strategies. *MedRxiv*.

Hou, C., Chen, J., Zhou, Y., Hua, L., Yuan, J., He, S., et al. (2020). The effectiveness of quarantine of Wuhan city against the Corona virus disease 2019 (COVID-19): A well-mixed SEIR model analysis. *Journal of Medical Virology, 92*(7), 841–848.

Hu, H., Wang, H., Wang, F., Langley, D., Avram, A., & Liu, M. (2018). Prediction of influenza-like illness based on the improved artificial tree algorithm and artificial neural network. *Scientific Reports, 8*(1), 1–8.

Jonhs Hopkins University. (2021). *COVID-19 Dashboard by the Center for Systems Science and Engineering (CSSE)*. Johns Hopkins University. https://coronavirus.jhu.edu/map.html. (Accessed 30 August 2021).

Kermack, W. O., & McKendrick, A. G. (1927). A contribution to the mathematical theory of epidemics. *Proceedings of the Royal Society of London. Series A, Containing Papers of a Mathematical and Physical Character, 115*(772), 700–721.

Knight, G. M., Dharan, N. J., Fox, G. J., Stennis, N., Zwerling, A., Khurana, R., et al. (2016). Bridging the gap between evidence and policy for infectious diseases: How models can aid public health decision-making. *International Journal of Infectious Diseases, 42*, 17–23.

Koo, J. R., Cook, A. R., Park, M., Sun, Y., Sun, H., Lim, J. T., et al. (2020). Interventions to mitigate the early spread of SARS-CoV-2 in Singapore: A modeling study. *The Lancet Infectious Diseases, 20*(6), 678–688.

Kucharski, A. J., Klepac, P., Conlan, A. J., Kissler, S. M., Tang, M. L., Fry, H., et al. (2020). Effectiveness of isolation, testing, contact tracing, and physical distancing on reducing transmission of SARS-CoV-2 in different settings: A mathematical modeling study. *The Lancet Infectious Diseases, 20*(10), 1151–1160.

Lazer, D., Kennedy, R., King, G., & Vespignani, A. (2014). The parable of Google Flu: Traps in big data analysis. *Science, 343*(6176), 1203–1205.

Liu, L., Han, M., Zhou, Y., & Wang, Y. (2018). Lstm recurrent neural networks for influenza trends prediction. *International Symposium on Bioinformatics Research and Applications*, 259–264.

Lloyd-Smith, J. O , Galvani, A. P., & Getz, W. M. (2003). Curtailing transmission of the severe acute respiratory syndrome within a community and its hospital. *Proceedings of the Royal Society of London - Series B: Biological Sciences, 270*(1528), 1979–1989.

Lutz, C. S., Huynh, M. P., Schroeder, M., Anyatonwu, S., Dahlgren, F. S., Danyluk, G., et al. (2019). Applying infectious disease forecasting to public health: A path forward using influenza forecasting examples. *BMC Public Health, 19*(1), 1–12.

Merler, S., Ajello, M., Fumanelli, L., Gomes, M. F., y Piontti, A. P., Rossi, L., et al. (2015). Spatiotemporal spread of the 2014 outbreak of Ebola virus disease in Liberia and the effectiveness of non-pharmaceutical interventions: A computational modeling analysis. *The Lancet Infectious Diseases, 15*(2), 204–211.

Mohapatra, P., Tripathi, N. K., Pal, I., & Shrestha, S. (2021). Determining suitable machine learning classifier technique for prediction of malaria incidents attributed to the climate of Odisha. *International Journal of Environmental Health Research*, 1–17.

Neuwirth, E., & Arganbright, D. (2003). *The active modeler: Mathematical modeling with Microsoft Excel.* Duxbury Press.

Nishiura, H., Patanarapelert, K., Sriprom, M., Sarakorn, W., Sriyab, S , & Tang, I. M. (2004). Modeling potential responses to the severe acute respiratory syndrome in Japan: The role of initial attack size, precaution, and quarantine. *Journal of Epidemiology & Community Health, 58*(3), 186–191.

Obeidat, R., Alsmadi, I., Bani Bakr, Q., & Obeidat, L. (2020). Can users search trends predict people scares or disease breakout? An examination of infectious skin diseases in the United States. *Infectious Diseases: Research and Treatment, 13*, 1178633720928356.

Pandey, G., Chaudhary, P., Gupta, R., & Pal, S. (2020). *SEIR and Regression Model based COVID-19 outbreak predictions in India.* arXiv preprint arXiv:2004.00958.

Pandey, K. R., Subedee, A., Khanal, B., & Koirala, B. (2020). COVID-19 control strategies and intervention effects in resource-limited settings: A modeling study. *medRxiv.*

Peak, C. M., Childs, L. M., Grad, Y. H., & Buckee, C. O. (2017). Comparing nonpharmaceutical interventions for containing emerging epidemics. *Proceedings of the National Academy of Sciences, 114*(15), 4023–4028.

Pourbohloul, B., Meyers, L. A., Skowronski, D. M., Krajden, M., Patrick, D. M., & Brunham, R. C. (2005). Modeling control strategies of respiratory pathogens. *Emerging Infectious Diseases, 11*(8), 1249.

Punn, N. S., Sonbhadra, S. K., & Agarwal, S. (2020). COVID-19 epidemic analysis using machine learning and deep learning algorithms. *MedRxiv.*

Semenova, Y., Glushkova, N., Pivina, L., Khismetova, Z., Zhunussov, Y., Sandybaev, M., et al. (2020). Epidemiological characteristics and forecast of COVID-19 outbreak in the Republic of Kazakhstan. *Journal of Korean Medical Science, 35*(24).

Sjödin, H., Wilder-Smith, A., Osman, S., Farooq, Z., & Rocklöv, J. (2020). Only strict quarantine measures can curb the coronavirus disease (COVID-19) outbreak in Italy, 2020. *Euro Surveillance, 25*(13), 2000280.

Su, L., Hong, N., Zhou, X., He, J., Ma, Y., Jiang, H., et al. (2020). Evaluation of the secondary transmission pattern and epidemic prediction of COVID-19 in the four metropolitan areas of China. *Frontiers of Medicine, 7.*

Tang, B., Wang, X., Li, Q., Bragazzi, N. L., Tang, S., Xiao, Y., et al. (2020). Estimation of the transmission risk of the 2019-nCoV and its implication for public health interventions. *Journal of Clinical Medicine, 9*(2), 462.

Wang, M., Wang, H., Wang, J., Liu, H., Lu, R., Duan, T., et al. (2019). A novel model for malaria prediction based on ensemble algorithms. *PLoS One, 14*(12), e0226910.

Wernstedt, K., Roberts, P. S., Arvai, J., & Redmond, K. (2019). How emergency managers (mis?) interpret forecasts. *Disasters, 43*(1), 88–109.

WHO. (n.d.). Infectious diseases. World Health Organization. http://www.emro.who.int/health-topics/infectious-diseases/index.html [Accessed 16 July 2021].

Xu, Q., Gel, Y. R., Ramirez Ramirez, L. L., Nezafati, K., Zhang, Q., & Tsui, K.-L. (2017). Forecasting influenza in Hong Kong with Google search queries and statistical model fusion. *PLoS One, 12*(5), e0176690.

Yadav, S. K., & Akhter, Y. (2021). Statistical modeling for the prediction of infectious disease dissemination with special reference to COVID-19 spread. *Frontiers in Public Health, 9.*

Yang, Z., Zeng, Z., Wang, K., Wong, S.-S., Liang, W., Zanin, M., et al. (2020). Modified SEIR and AI prediction of the epidemics trend of COVID-19 in China under public health interventions. *Journal of Thoracic Disease, 12*(3), 165.

Yuan, Q., Nsoesie, E. O., Lv, B., Peng, G., Chunara, R., & Brownstein, J. S. (2013). Monitoring influenza epidemics in China with search query from Baidu. *PLoS One, 8*(5), e64323.

Zeroual, A., Harrou, F., Dairi, A., & Sun, Y. (2020). Deep learning methods for forecasting COVID-19 time-series data: A comparative study. *Chaos, Solitons & Fractals, 140*, 110121.

Zhang, X.-S., Pebody, R., Charlett, A., De Angelis, D., Birrell, P., Kang, H., et al. (2017). Estimating and modeling the transmissibility of Middle East respiratory syndrome CoronaVirus during the 2015 outbreak in the Republic of Korea. *Influenza and other respiratory viruses, 11*(5), 434–444.

Zhu, X., Fu, B., Yang, Y., Ma, Y., Hao, J., Chen, S., et al. (2019). Attention-based recurrent neural network for influenza epidemic prediction. *BMC Bioinformatics, 20*(18), 1–10.

Chapter 14

Hospital data analytics system for tracking and predicting obese patients' lifestyle habits

Liew Set Yee and Pantea Keikhosrokiani
School of Computer Sciences, Universiti Sains Malaysia, Minden, Penang, Malaysia

1. Introduction

With the emergence of new technologies, large amounts of data (structured and unstructured data) are being generated by various Internet of Things devices, sensors, applications, and web-based systems. Recently, the healthcare industry has also generated large amounts of data, such as patient profile data, patient historical data, medical data, behavioral data, prescriptions, and so forth (Keikhosrokiani, 2019, 2021a, 2021b). Big medical data analytical techniques can be used to analyze a patient's symptoms, predict the patient's disease, and enhance the improvement of the diagnosis (Raghupathi & Raghupathi, 2014). A hospital can detect a patient's disease at an earlier stage to save him/her from unexpected death. Therefore, the healthcare industry can utilize big medical data effectively for providing better healthcare services and for better decision-making.

According to the World Health Organization (WHO), Malaysia is among the Asian countries with the highest rate of obesity and overweight cases. WHO has stated that 64% of males and 65% of the female population are obese or overweight (Ying, 2019). Obesity can affect the human major organ system and cause serious chronic diseases such as cardiovascular disease, type II diabetes mellitus, hypertension, breast cancer, and so on (Aronne & Havas, 2009; Chan et al., 2017; Guh et al., 2009). One of the main causes of obesity is bad habits such as unhealthy eating habits, sedentary behavior, low physical activity, as well as individual susceptibility (Al-Nakeeb, Lyons, Dodd, & Al-Nuaim, 2015; Keikhosrokiani, 2020; Wilbur, Chandler, Dancy, Choi, & Plonczynski, 2002). Therefore, this chapter focuses on developing a web-based system to monitor obese patients' lifestyle habits related to diet, exercise, and sleep as well as patient's physiological data such as heart rate. The proposed system is called Hospital Data Analytics System (HDAS) which aims to monitor and predict obese patient's life style habit using machine learning. Based on the predictive results, doctor and nutritionist can advise proper prescriptions to prevent patient from the bad lifestyle habits related to diet and exercise. Furthermore, if patient is aware that his/her habits are under monitoring, he/she will try to follow healthier habit and lifestyle. In order to test HDAS functionality, data is collected from an obese patient using smartwatch and mobile application. Patient's lifestyle habit was monitored for few months and was analyzed using machine learning to predict patient future habit.

This chapter introduces a hospital data analytics system which monitors, tracks, and predict obese patient's lifestyle habits related to diet, exercise, sleep, and biomedical data. Existing habit tracking systems and applications are reviewed in the first section. Then, the development methodology for the proposed HDAS is added followed by system design and implementation. Afterward, data analytics, results, and system user interface (UI) are added. Finally, the chapter is wrapped up with discussion and conclusion.

Big Data Analytics for Healthcare. https://doi.org/10.1016/B978-0-323-91907-4.00004-2

2. Related works

Various studies have been carried on which are related big data analytics systems in healthcare. Although there are many available habit tracker applications in current market, many of them are not able to analyze a user's future habit change or behavior based on the user's historical data. Thus, some of the existing big data analytics systems used in healthcare industry are introduced in this section.

2.1 Existing habit-based healthcare systems with analytical features

BeHabit is an emotional-persuasive habit change support mobile application which is developed to improve heart disease patients' lifestyles (Ravichandran & Keikhosrokiani, 2021). BeHabit implements persuasive and emotional features to persuade patients for changing their bad habits. This application applied a point collecting system known as BeHabit point and utilizes dialogue support, credibility support, and primary task to support the persuasion context. Moreover, the app tracks of the user's mood before and after an activity. Finally, BeHabit shows a range of emoticons, pictures, and texts to define how the user feels.

Doctive is a habit change support web-based system with big data analytical features for hospitals (Augustine & Keikhosrokiani, 2021). Doctive is targeted for hospital authorities to monitor patients and their habits and to prescribe medication and advice based on patients' habits and gathered information. Based on the patient historical data related to exercise, calories intake and burns calories, and mood, Doctive creates a decision tree for further actions. Doctors or health care providers can advise users or patients based on the decision tree.

Momentum habit tracker (Maehlum, 2020) is a powerful habit tracker that allows users to track their daily habits for accomplishing their goals. User can create a daily routine on their own and user can get motivation from the streaks in the application. Other than that, this application will integrate with iCloud sync. Thus, the user can view their habits using other apple products. The application is only applicable to apple devices.

Habitica (HabitRPG, 2021) is a game-based habit tracker application that is inspired by role-playing video game. Users need to input their habits, set their daily goals, to-do-list, and create a custom avatar. Users need to clear their daily goals in order to level up their avatar and unlock features like armor, pet, etc., in the game. Users can join with their friends to complete quests and missions (e.g., going to gym every day) in the game.

Balanced (Play, 2021) is an application developed to help people change their behavior for improving their health. This application is using latest scientific evidence to change users' behavior and measure their sleep quality, exercise level, and time spent by a person to sit. This application will provide tips and proven strategies to improve a user's behaviors.

2.2 Big data and predictive analytics in healthcare

As big data is growing fast in healthcare industry, predictive analytics using machine learning and deep learning can assist healthcare providers to harness large volume datasets and analyze a wide variety of data. The results can assist doctors to improve diagnosis, make accurate and proper decision for treatment, and inform preventative medicine practices (Hassan, Dhali, Zaman, & Tanveer, 2021; Keikhosrokiani, 2021b; Teoh Yi Zhe & Keikhosrokiani, 2020).

Although predictive analytics prove great promise in healthcare, they encounter serious obstacles for extensive adoption. Healthcare systems with predictive analytics capabilities provide actionable processes that encourage prevention and minimize health risk (Dhar, 2014; Nijjer, Saurabh, & Raj, 2020). Predictive analytics can reveal patient's medical histories for a doctor to review and predict a patient's future result. For instance, it can be predicted what disease might be encountered by the patient, so that the doctor could take action immediately to prevent this phenomenon to occur.

2.3 Big data and Clinical Decision Support Systems

Clinical Decision Support Systems (CDSS) are computerized systems that utilize data analytics within electronic health records to provide prompts and reminders for assisting healthcare providers. As the volume of data in healthcare industry is increasing, CDSS become an essential tool for healthcare providers to deliver valuable care and services (Wasylewicz & Scheepers-Hoeks, 2019). With emergence of big data in healthcare, analytical techniques can be integrated into CDSS to support better decision-making such as chronic disease management (Dagliati et al., 2018). Therefore, CDSS can analyze a patient medical data that sent from medical device on the spot, then providing the patient's condition to a doctor so the doctor can make prescriptive decisions for the patient immediately.

3. Development methodology

For this study, agile development methodology (iteration model) is used. Agile development methodology is also known as adaptive approach. When there are some new requirements or changes that are needed to add to the project, agile development methodology is able to adapt and add in the changes. Unlike the Waterfall model, Agile is a methodology that allows developers to update or adapt to new changes despite the project under progress (Bhatt, 2021).

The system development is started by analyzing the requirements, scope, project user interface (UI), and system functionality. Existing habit-related applications and systems are being reviewed and studied in order to gain a better understanding of why habit change data analysis should be implemented. Most of the existing systems or applications are focusing on tracking habits; thus, it is hard to find a habit change analytics system in current market. It is possible for this project to have changes from time to time during project development. Rapid change of a system is to help the system deal with different users. Therefore, agile approach is implemented to ensure changes can be made during the project development.

In System Development Life Cycle (SDLC), six processes are involved including (1) planning, (2) analysis, (3) design, (4) system development and (5) testing, and (6) closing. The work breakdown structure of HDAS system is illustrated in Fig. 14.1. Iteration of SDLC involves these five processes. System requirements are gathered and functionality of the project is defined in planning stage. Further analysis on related system details is done at analysis stage, whereas the system is developed at development stage. System testing is done on the system and debug process is happening at the development stage. System design is the stage to design system architecture or system functionalities. The closing stage is the final process that the system is well developed and done.

FIGURE 14.1 Work breakdown structure of HDAS system.

Agile approach allows a developer to assist previous progress in order to reduce the number of errors and to make improvements and updating on previous work. The quality of the system is guaranteed before the system is launched for users to use. Since agile approach is using iteration as a lifecycle of a project, then every iteration will go through all the core activities. Each iteration is concentrating on different activities in the core activity area. As the first iteration is completed without any error, the second iteration will be started by using agile approach as well.

A survey using questionnaires was conducted to gather information for the requirement of this project. Information gathering is an important process to seek a user's requirements. For this study, 30 users were selected to participate in the survey for the system requirement and system testing. Based on the survey results, 56.66% of the respondents are agree that the occurrence of health diseases like obesity or heart disease can be reduced by having a habit change analytics system in healthcare industry. Furthermore, the majority of the respondents (83.33%) think that one's habit will affect their health condition. It is undeniable that one's healthy living habit is important to avoid themselves from health diseases. Among all respondents, only 10 of them have installed habit tracker applications in their mobile or laptop, while 20 respondents never used any habit tracker application. Therefore, we can conclude that among the respondents, not many of them are taking care of their living habits. Among all respondents, 53.33% of them think that habit tracker application with habit change analytics techniques is attractive. Finally, 60% of the respondents support the fact that habit change analytics system could help the healthcare industry to monitor a patient's health condition.

4. System design and implementation

4.1 System modules and use case diagram

This chapter focuses on the development of a web-based system called "Hospital Data Analytics System (HDAS)" that enables healthcare professional to retrieve patient's personal details, keep track of medical data from patient and doctor's prescriptions, nutritionist's comment, and predict patient's future lifestyle habit or behavior. Hence, predictive analytics is implemented and integrated into the system in order to predict a patient's future lifestyle habit. In order to perform predictive analytics, machine learning techniques and big data analytics techniques are used.

Fig. 14.2 shows HDAS which consists of five main modules which are patient profile module, medical and habit data module, doctor/nutritionist's module, appointment and meeting module, and big data analytics (data prediction) module. Patient profile module is used to retrieve the personal details of a patient such as patient's name, age, and patient's personal details. System user (doctor, nurse, etc.) is able to review and update patient's details. New patient's data can be added by using this module.

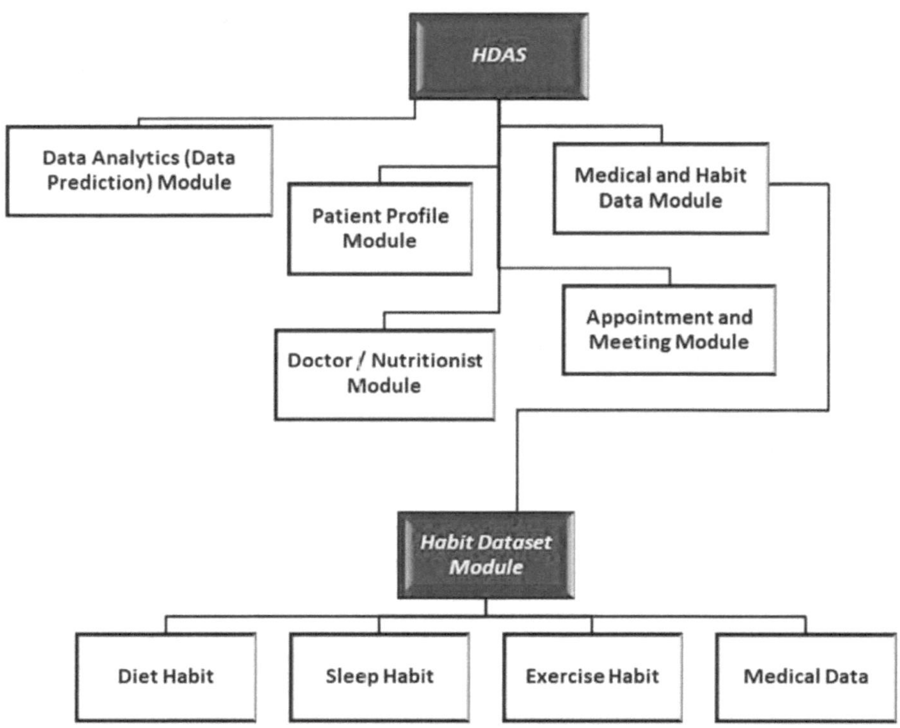

FIGURE 14.2 Module diagram for HDAS.

Medical and habit data module is a module that records all patient's medical data and their lifestyle habit data related to diet, sleep, and exercise. System users like doctor and nurse are able to edit, add, and delete the record of a patient if required.

Data prediction module focuses on predicting patient's future lifestyle habit. After analyzing all historical data relevant to a patient's habit, the system should be able to predict the patient future habit data. System users need to enter prediction period to let the prediction module to start functioning. System users are able to predict a patient's future heartbeat rate, daily walking steps, and daily calories intake.

Doctor/nutritionist's module is another feature that records the history of prescription and advice given by doctor/nutritionist to a patient. Doctor can keep track of patient's condition by reviewing the prescription given by him/her. Doctor/nutritionist can also review and give any new advice to the patients using this module.

Lastly, appointment and meeting module is a module that manages an appointment/meeting between a doctor/nutritionist and a patient or meeting with hospital staff. Doctor or nutritionist can retrieve an appointment date with a patient and manage their appointment details. They can also create a meeting agenda on this meeting module.

Use case diagram for HDAS is shown in Fig. 14.3 which includes the details of the activities explained in module diagram. This figure shows the users involvement in various activities.

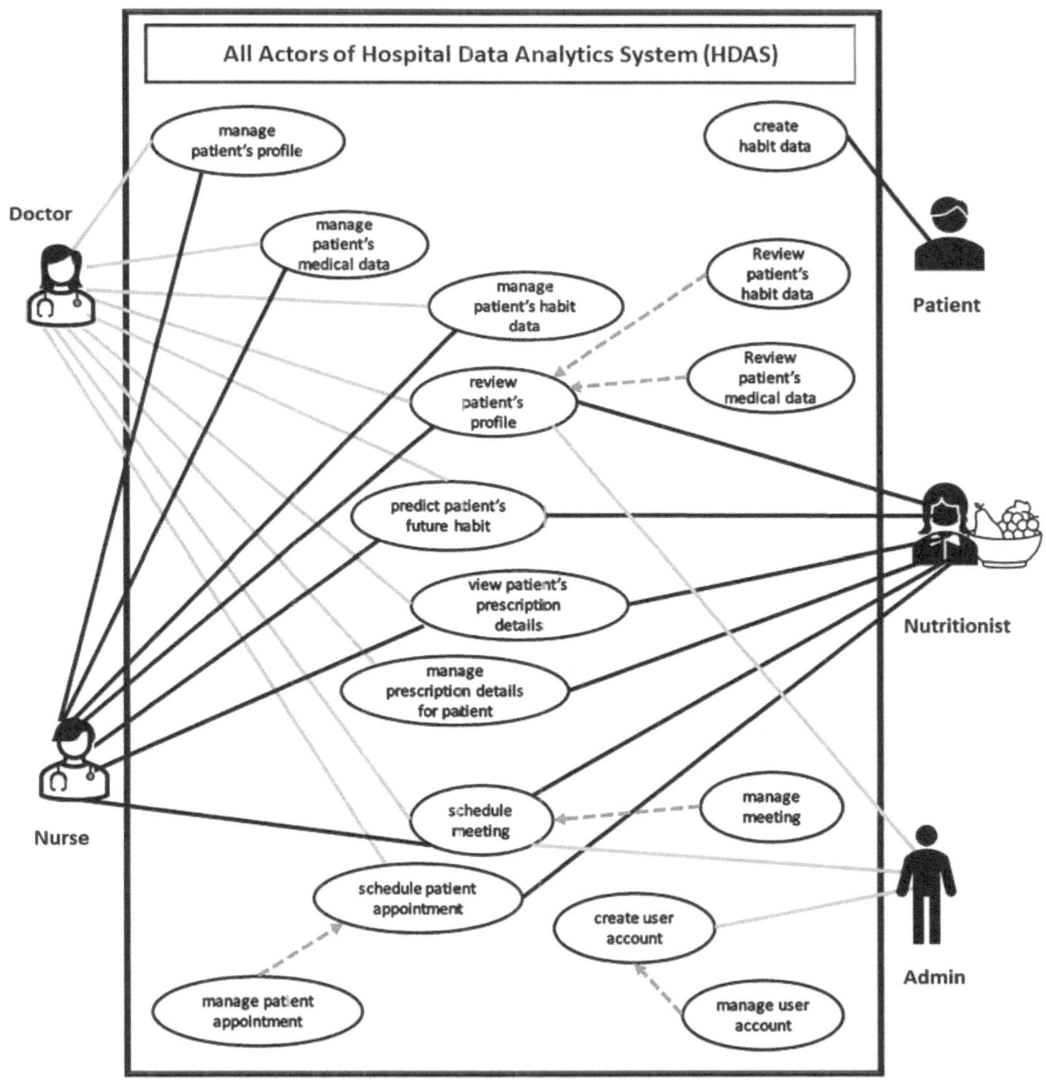

FIGURE 14.3 Use case diagram for HDAS.

4.2 System architecture design and predictive analytics

The system architecture diagram for HDAS is illustrated in Fig. 14.4. All patient data including patient's profile, medical data, and lifestyle habit data will be collected using smartwatch and mobile application and imported into HDAS's database and SQL Server.

A patient's habit data and medical data are used as the dataset by HDAS to predict patient's habit. Therefore, collection of patient's habit data needs to be done before performing data prediction. A patient's collected lifestyle habit dataset is divided into four categories which are medical data, diet habit, sleep habit, and exercise habit. Medical data such as heart rate is the data that received from a smartwatch and will be stored in SQL Server. Diet habit is a dataset related to a patient's daily diet intake such as intake of vegetables, fruits, carbohydrates, protein, etc. Exercise habit refers to patient's exercise time, step counts, type of exercise, etc. The last dataset is related to patient's sleep habit. Having good quality sleep can help to protect one's mental health, physical health, and quality of life. Examples of the dataset for sleep habit are time to sleep, time to wake up, sleep categories such as awake, light, deep, and Rapid Eye Movement (REM), etc.

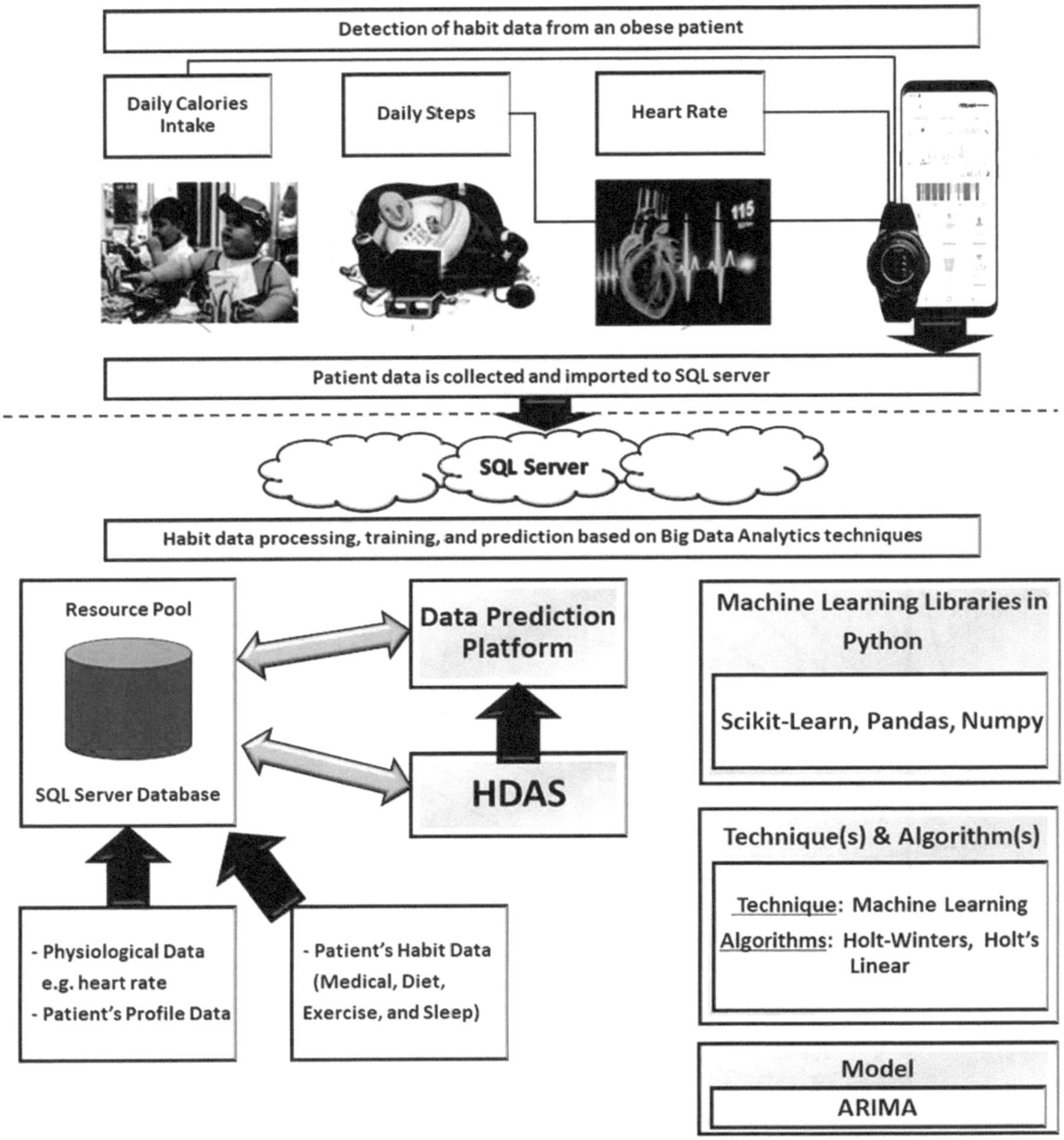

FIGURE 14.4 System architecture diagram for HDAS.

4.3 Implementation strategy

The implementation strategy used in HDAS is the top-down approach. The top-down strategy is used because it breaks a huge module into a small submodule in a reverse engineering fashion which can reduce the complication of the implementation process. For example, the patient—profile module can be segmented into the interface of the patient profile page, add a patient profile, update the patient profile, and delete the patient profile.

Since the agile development approach (Bhatt, 2021) is applied to build HDAS, the top-down strategy is used to produce working prototypes and different versions of programs. For instance, the first prototype developed in HDAS is the patient profile module where it is first developed with UI design, followed by the logic to be implemented to the module. The same processes are repeated throughout the entire system development project until the proposed system is completed.

4.4 Testing strategy

Testing has been executed for HDAS to ensure that the system is working fine and well. Other than the system is performing well, testing also is a way to ensure that system requirement and users' expectations are achieved. Four testing strategies are used to test the system, which are (1) unit testing, (2) integration testing, (3) system testing, and (4) acceptance testing techniques.

Unit testing is the process of testing individual modules or functions before the system is integrated. Therefore, every unit and component of HDAS modules are tested to ensure that there is no defect in writing the program code. If any defect is found during the unit testing process, the system developer can check on the module on the spot and the debugging time used in integration testing can be reduced. Each function in the module is tested before the integration process begins. In short, unit testing is important to improve the quality of the logic implemented and fixed all the defects at the early stage of system development. For example, create functions in the patient profile module are tested to make sure it is functioning well.

Integration testing is performed after each module or function is combined. All the small components in a module are combined into a single module and then will be further combined into a complete system. The performance and behavior of the system are verified and validated using the integration testing strategy. For example, integration testing is being tested on the data prediction module because it is involving integration between a Python script and C# script to preform data prediction function. This scenario is tested to determine whether all the variables between these two scripts are a success.

The next testing strategy is system testing. System testing is performed after integration testing. In this system testing, the entire system is tested in an actual flow of a specific user after he/she has logged in to the system. The purpose of system testing is to verify and validate whether the system meets the functional and nonfunctional requirements stated in Tables 14.1 and 14.2 respectively. Therefore, in system testing, system developers are testing the entire system through the GUI of the system and to ensure that the system is performing all functions in a normal way.

The last testing strategy is acceptance testing. Acceptance testing is tested by the actual system user after the system is deployed to relevant organizations. This strategy is used to determine whether the system is fulfilling the user's need and expectations.

The testing of HDAS is conducted during the entire system development process. The system is tested using debugging mode in coding IDE and running it in Google Chrome. By having a system testing phase, all of the defects that are found in the early phase are solved immediately without pending until the system integration process starts. Since all of the test cases of HDAS are passed, the system is developed by filling all the functional and nonfunctional requirements. In short, HDAS is satisfying because the system can perform all the required functionalities as expected.

5. Data analytics, results, and user interface

5.1 Dataset

The datasets for HDAS are from medical data, diet habit, sleep habit, and exercise habit which are collected from user's smartwatch and mobile applications. HDAS is predicting patient's future lifestyle habit from their daily meal intake calories, heart rate, sleep, and daily walking steps. Diet habit dataset is recording a patient's daily food intake. "Medical Data," "Diet Habit," "Exercise Habit," and "Sleep Habit" are added into the database to be used as the main datasets for HDAS.

Medical data is dataset that records a patient biomedical data such as heart rate and cadence values collected from smartwatch. Diet habit data is a set of datasets that are used to record a patient's daily meal information like daily calories,

TABLE 14.1 Functional requirements for HDAS.

Functional ID	Functional requirement
F01	The system should able to retrieve patient's profile for hospital's users.
F02	The system should able to allow users to manage (CRUD) patient's profile data.
F03	The system should allow users to retrieve a patient's medical records.
F04	The system should able to allow users to manage (CRUD) patient's medical data.
F05	The system should allow users to retrieve a patient's diet records.
F06	The system should able to allow users to manage (CRUD) patient's diet data.
F07	The system should allow users to retrieve a patient's exercise records.
F08	The system should able to allow users to manage (CRUD) patient's exercise data.
F09	The system should allow users to retrieve a patient's sleep records.
F10	The system should able to allow users to manage (CRUD) patient's sleep data.
F11	The system should allow users to retrieve a patient's prescription records.
F12	The system should able to allow users to manage (CRUD) patient's prescription data.
F13	The system should allow users to retrieve account user records.
F14	The system should able to allow users to manage (CRUD) account user data.
F15	The system should allow users to retrieve appointment details.
F16	The system should able to allow users to manage (CRUD) appointment details.
F17	The system should allow users to retrieve meeting details.
F18	The system should able to allow users to manage (CRUD) meeting's details.
F19	The system must able to predict patient's future habit data

TABLE 14.2 Nonfunctional requirements for HDAS.

Nonfunctional ID	Functionality	All the functions or requirements in user's requirements should be fulfilled
NF01	**Reliability**	The system should be able to function at optimal level at all times unless there is no Internet connection or poor Internet connection.
NF02	**Usability**	The system should response to user's request such as user presses a button to review patient's profile details.
NF03	**Efficiency**	The system should be able to predict and output a patient's future habit data once the user is requesting to do so.
NF04	**Maintainability**	The system should be able to update or modify without rebuilding it again.
NF05	**Security**	Every user is required to login the system by entering their password.
		Patient's profile data should be secured and protected since those data are privacy.
NF06	**Time-bound**	The system was completed and tested on June 1, 2020.

meal taken time, potassium amount, etc. Exercise dataset is recording a patient's exercise information like their exercise working hours, daily working steps, calories burned in exercise, type of exercise activity, and so on. The last dataset is a dataset that records a patient's sleep data like time to wake up, time to sleep, sleep categories such as awake, light, deep, and REM, etc.

5.2 Predictive analytics using machine learning

5.2.1 Predictive analytical models

5.2.1.1 Holt–Winters forecasting algorithm

Holt–Winters is a method used to model and predict the behavior of a sequence of values over time (Arceda, Laura, & Arceda, 2021; Bhalla, Srivastava, & Gosain, 2021). It is one of the popular time-series forecasting algorithms. The time series algorithm is the algorithm that is able to extract and analyze data and characterize results to produce more accurate prediction results based on historical data. Holt–Winters is using an exponential smoothing technique to encode all the historical values and uses those values to predict "typical" values of either future or past values. Holt–Winters is an algorithm that allows users to smooth time series and use those data to forecast the values of interest areas. The exponential smoothing technique assigns decreasing weight and values exponentially from the historical data in order to reduce the value of the weight from the past historical data. The more recent historical data is assigned to Holt–Winters algorithm, the more weight value in forecasting results as compared to the older results. The advantage of using the Holt–Winters algorithm is to produce a smooth result for the prediction.

5.2.1.2 Holt's linear forecasting model

Holt Linear algorithm is also known as the Double Exponential Smoothing algorithm (Poornima, Pushpalatha, & Sujit Shankar, 2019). This method consists of forecasting value with the levels and trends of data pattern. It computes a trend equation using a special weighting function. This weighting function is calculated by placing the greatest emphasis on the most recent time periods. It is using a local trend equation rather than a global trend equation. The trend equation is improved and modified from time to time. The forecasting equation also changes from period to period.

5.2.1.3 ARIMA model

AutoRegressive Integrated Moving Average (ARIMA) is a statistical analysis model that uses time series historical data to predict future trends (Arceda et al., 2021; Sharma & Soni, 2021). AutoRegressive (AR) means that it is a model that uses the dependent relationship between observation and lagged observations. The meaning of lagged observations is a fixed amount of passing time values. While integrated (I) gives the meaning that the model is using a differencing method on raw observations in order to make the time series values stationary, the meaning of Moving Average (MA) is applying the dependency between an observation and a residual error from a moving average to lagged observations. Each of the mentioned components is used in the ARIMA model and the standard notation of ARIMA is in (p, d, q) where the values of p, d, and q are substituted with integer values.

p stands for the number of lag observations included in the model.

d stands for the number of times that raw observations are differenced.

q stands for the size of the moving average window.

"0" can be used as a parameter with the meaning of the model not to use the element for the model. Via this method, the ARIMA model can be configured to simple AR, I, or MA model to perform as the ARIMA model does.

5.2.2 Prediction module for HDAS

All the collected data is integrated with HDAS. All the patient's information is stored in SQL Server, an SQL-based database. HDAS is able to manage and read data from SQL Server database. In HDAS, there is big data analytics (data prediction) platform to predict patient's future lifestyle habit. Therefore, system users are able to preview a patient's future lifestyle habit by executing prediction function

Generally, machine learning library in python is used to process and train data. For example, Pandas is used to retrieve and process data retrieved from SQL Server. Thus, the machine learning model is integrated with HDAS web application to perform data prediction function. The technique used in HDAS is machine learning predictive analytics technique. Hence, prediction algorithms such as Holt–Winters and Holt's linear are used to predict patient's lifestyle habit. Besides, a predictive model, ARIMA, is implemented to predict a patient's future lifestyle habit.

When the system user is clicking in the data prediction page on HDAS and selected all the required data inputs, HDAS will transmit all the data value required for data prediction via the application server to the data prediction python script. Python.exe will be launched by HDAS in the background to execute the python script. Python.exe will get all the training data required for data prediction from SQL Server directly and starts performing data training and prediction process. Next, the prediction results will be sent back to the application server from python EXE. All the prediction results will be retrieved on HDAS's data prediction page for users to review. Fig. 14.5 shows the system architecture for the data prediction module.

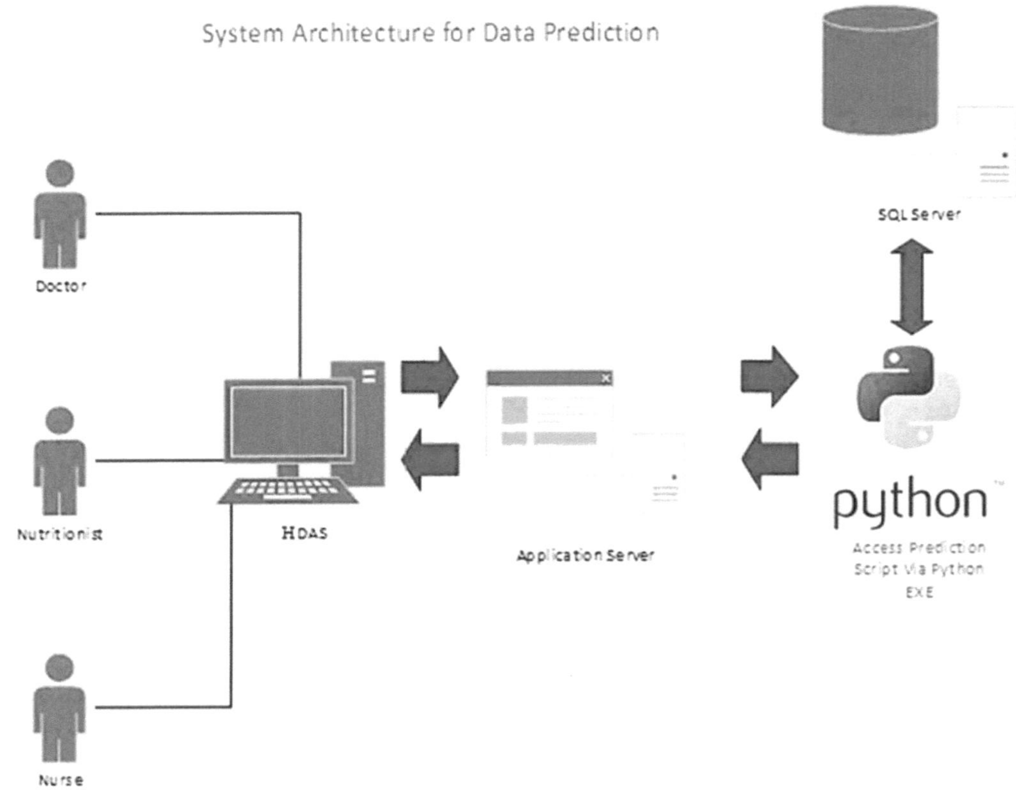

FIGURE 14.5 System architecture for data prediction module.

5.2.3 Sample results for predictive analytics in HDAS

The data was collected form the selected patient from October 2019 until January 2020. All the prediction results are done from January 31, 2020 to June 1, 2020. The graph in Fig. 14.6 shows the record of the selected patient's calorie intake per day. All data related to calorie intake for the selected patient are transformed into a line graph format. From this graph, the system user can review the selected patient's average calories records from October 2019 until January 2020.

The graph illustrated in Fig. 14.7 shows the data prediction result for the selected patient's future calorie intake amount predicted by ARIMA model. The predicted results for Feb 2020 to Jun 2020 are very consistent. Based on the predicted result, we can conclude that the calorie intake habit for this selected patient is good and healthy since the predicted results are not exceeding the basement line of the target calories intake. The Root mean squared error (RMSE) value of the predicted result using ARIMA model is around 0.3. The lower the value of RMSE, the better it is.

Fig. 14.8 shows the prediction result for the selected patient's future diet habits related to calorie intake using Holt–Winters forecasting model. The prediction results show the calories taken amount of the selected patient is increasing per day, but it is not achieving the target calorie intake amount yet. Therefore, the results show the future diet habit for the selected patient is considered as healthy as the patient's calorie intake does not exceed the target calorie intake amount per day. The RMSE value of the predicted result using Holt–Winters forecasting model is around 0.5.

Fig. 14.9 illustrates the data of future diet habits prediction results using the Holt's linear model. The future diet habits prediction results by Holt's linear model are different from the result by ARIMA model and Holt–Winters forecasting algorithm. The predicted result for this Holt's linear forecasting algorithm is having the highest RMSE around 0.8. The results show that the future calorie intake by the patient is decreasing below 500 kcal. Therefore, the doctor or nutritionist needs to give advice to the patient to take more calories but not more than 2000 kcal.

Since all the prediction results for calories intake amount are different, a doctor or nutritionist needs to review the predicted result with the lowest RMSE value to give better advice or prescription to the selected patient. For example, the RMSE value for ARIMA model is 0.3, RMSE value for Holt–Winters Forecasting model is 0.5, and for Holt's linear model is 0.8. Therefore, a doctor or nutritionist is recommended to review the predicted result of ARIMA model since it is having the lowest RMSE value.

FIGURE 14.6 Calorie intake per day by an obese patient.

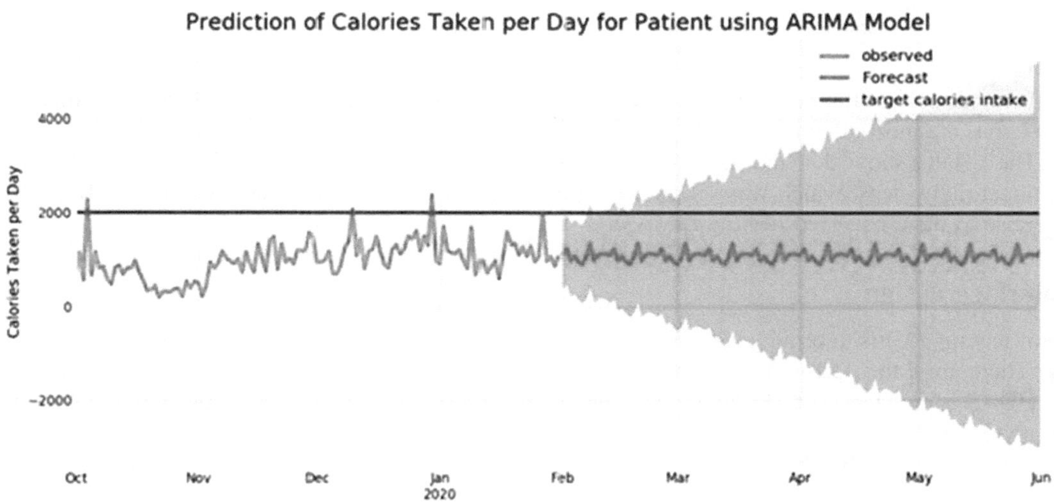

FIGURE 14.7 Prediction of Obese Patient's Future Habits related to Calorie Intake Using ARIMA Model.

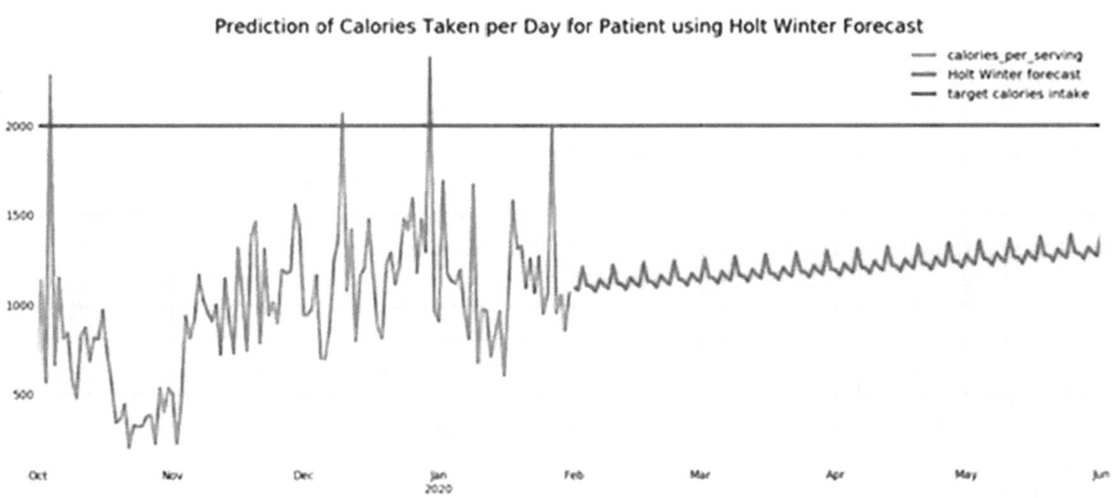

FIGURE 14.8 Prediction of Obese Patient's Future Habits related to Calorie Intake Using Holt–Winters Forecasting Model.

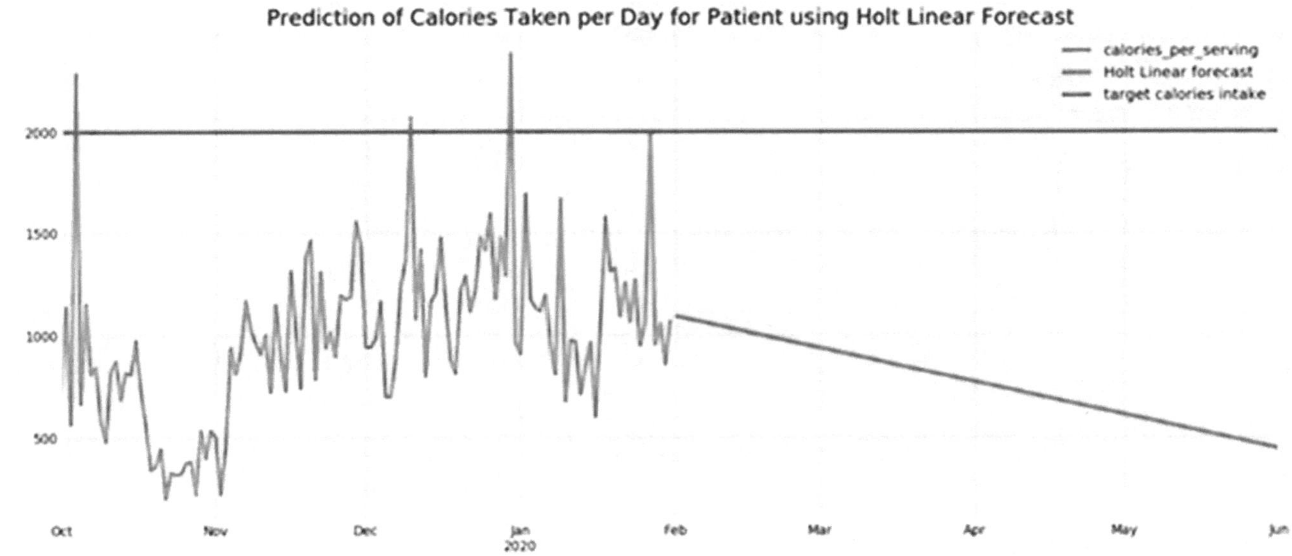

FIGURE 14.9 Prediction of Obese Patient's Future Habits related to Calorie Intake Using Holt's Linear Model.

Similar to the prediction of future diet habit, habit prediction for exercise was done. Based on the prediction results for future exercise habit, the most effective model with highest accuracy was Holt's linear forecasting algorithm with RMSE value of 0.4. The results show that the daily steps of the selected patient are decreasing significantly and not event achieving the target daily steps, which was set on 6000 steps per day. Therefore, the doctor should advice the patient to have more exercise to have balanced healthy lifestyle.

5.3 User interface design

The objective of having a UI is to provide a convenient way for the system user to manipulate the information and data in an easier way. There are a few factors that should be considered when designing a UI such as user-friendly, simple, and consistent. As HDAS is a system that will be implemented in hospitals, we tried to use a simple and user-friendly interface for hospital staff to use (Fig. 14.10). The navigation tab is shown in a clear way for users to navigate to their desired section. Besides, the design of HDAS's interface is consistent throughout the web application. For example, HDAS aims to design an easy UI, and the interfaces designed for each module are in the same in terms of layout design, button color, and also the webpage's pattern. The entire system is designed in green, blue, and white color. It can avoid users to feel confusing when they are using the system. By implementing consistent layout and design, the accessibility of HDAS is improved.

6. Discussion and conclusion

One of the main causes of obesity and chronic disease is bad lifestyle habits such as abnormal eating habits, low physical activities, sedentary behavior, bad sleeping habits, and individual susceptibility (Al-Nakeeb et al., 2015; Keikhosrokiani, 2020; Wilbur et al., 2002). Individual's bad health behavior or lifestyle habit might increase the chance of chronic disease such as heart disease. Therefore, a system is required to track patient's lifestyle habits and to predict patient's future lifestyle habit for assisting healthcare practitioners to prevent rises in the number of chronic diseases. Therefore, HDAS is introduced in this chapter with the objective to monitor patient's lifestyle habit and to predict patient's future behavior for preventing unexpected circumstances related to chronic disease. Moreover, with the implementation of HDAS, health practitioners are able to review patients' habits and medical data. HDAS is able to predict patient lifestyle habit data for heart rate, steps, and calories intake using machine learning techniques. The predictive analytical models (ARIMA model, Holt–Winters, and Holt's linear forecasting model) for analyzing and predicting future lifestyle habit are integrated to the web-based system. All the stated requirements have been achieved by HDAS and each requirement is performing well. The system is developed and tested successfully. In addition, the system is evaluated by users during the prototype presentation. Then, the system is improved and enhanced according to users' feedbacks and comments.

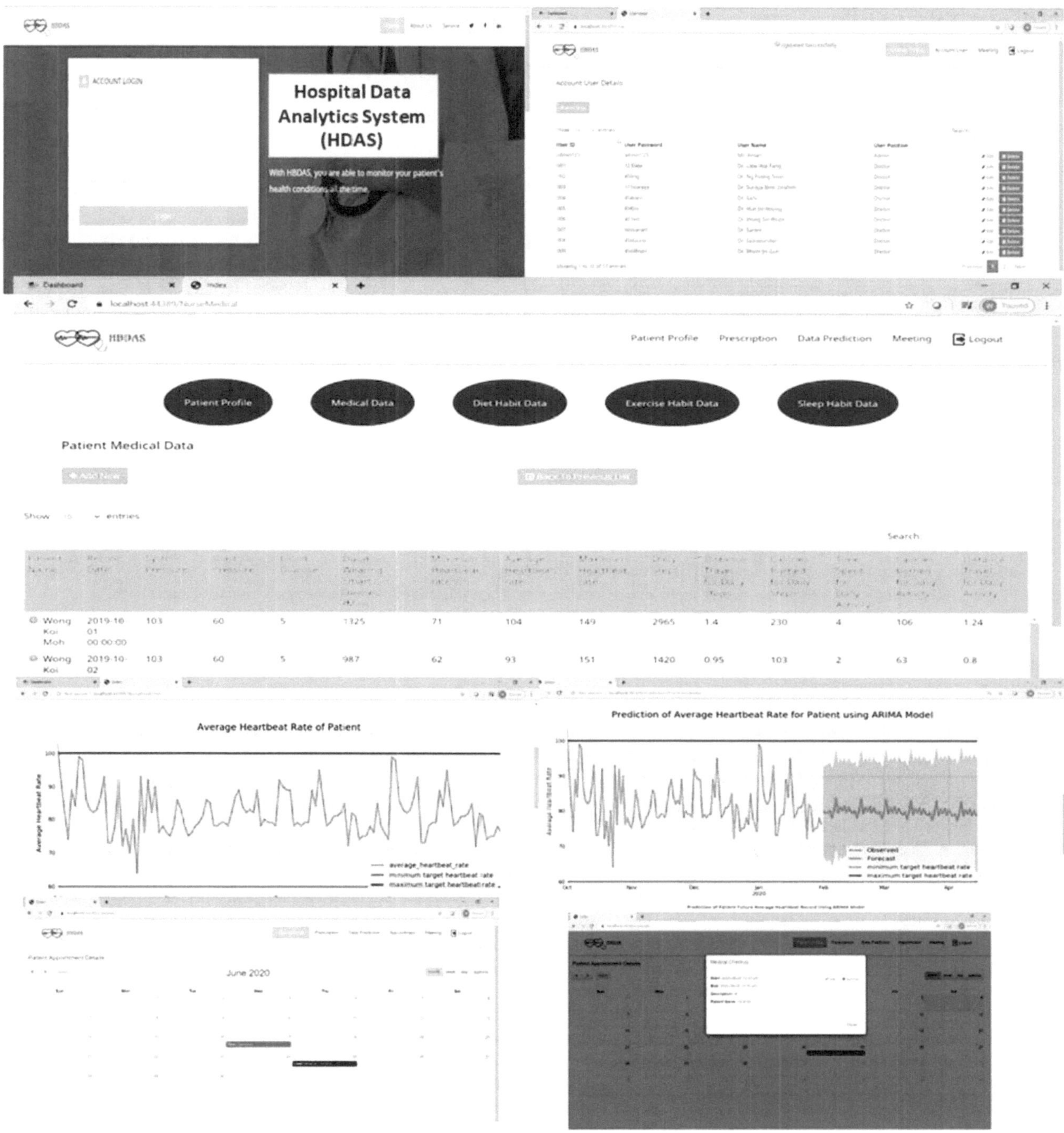

FIGURE 14.10 Sample user interface for HDAS.

HDAS can be useful for the healthcare providers to keep track of their patient's behavior for preventing them from chronic diseases. This system has entered the project closing stage, but there are still a lot of improvements and enhancements that can be added to the existing system in the future. The first enhancement of HDAS is the integration of the system with Habit-Change Support Mobile Application (HCSmApp). HCSmApp is an application that used to collect all patient's lifestyle habit data. Hence, this application is also connecting with a medical sensor like Samsung smartwatch to read and record a patient's medical reading such as heartbeat rate, etc. The second improvement is connecting the patient appointment module between HCSmApp and HDAS. Finally, the machine learning classification techniques can be implemented in this system for a doctor to classify the health condition of their patient. This feature can assist a doctor to know their patient's condition well before offering any prescription and advice.

Acknowledgments

The authors are thankful to the School of Computer Sciences, and Division of Research and Innovation, USM, for providing financial support from Short Term Grant (304/PKOMP/6315435) granted to Dr. Pantea Keikhosrokiani.

References

Al-Nakeeb, Y., Lyons, M., Dodd, L. J., & Al-Nuaim, A. (2015). An investigation into the lifestyle, health habits and risk factors of young adults. *International Journal of Environmental Research and Public Health, 12*(4), 4380–4394. https://www.mdpi.com/1660-4601/12/4/4380.

Arceda, M. A. M., Laura, P. C. L., & Arceda, V. E. M. (2021). Forecasting time series with multiplicative trend exponential smoothing and LSTM: COVID-19 case study. In K. Arai, S. Kapoor, & R. Bhatia (Eds.), *Proceedings of the future technologies conference (FTC) 2020* (Vol. 2) (Cham).

Aronne, L. J., & Havas, S. (2009). The obesity epidemic: Strategies in reducing cardiometabolic risk. *The American Journal of Medicine, 122*(4 Suppl. 1).

Augustine, C. A., & Keikhosrokiani, P. (2021). A habit-change support web-based system with big data analytical features for hospitals (doctive). In F. Saeed, F. Mohammed, & A. Al-Nahari (Eds.), *Innovative systems for intelligent health informatics* (pp. 91–101). Springer International Publishing. https://doi.org/10.1007/978-3-030-70713-2_10

Bhalla, K., Srivastava, S., & Gosain, A. (2021). Systematic analysis and prediction of air quality index in Delhi. In D. Gupta, A. Khanna, S. Bhattacharyya, A. E. Hassanien, S. Anand, & A. Jaiswal (Eds.), *International conference on innovative computing and communications Singapore*.

Bhatt, P. C. P. (2021). *Software design, architecture and engineering: Concepts and practice*. PHI Learning Pvt. Ltd.

Chan, Y. Y., Lim, K. K., Lim, K. H., Teh, C. H., Kee, C. C., Cheong, S. M., et al. (2017). Physical activity and overweight/obesity among Malaysian adults: Findings from the 2015 national health and morbidity survey (NHMS). *BMC Public Health, 17*(1), 1–12.

Dagliati, A., Tibollo, V., Sacchi, L., Malovini, A., Limongelli, I., Gabetta, M., et al. (2018). Big data as a driver for clinical decision support systems: A learning health systems perspective [perspective]. *Frontiers in Digital Humanities, 5*(8). https://doi.org/10.3389/fdigh.2018.00008

Dhar, V. (2014). Big data and predictive analytics in health care. *Big Data, 2*(3), 113–116. https://doi.org/10.1089/big.2014.1525

Guh, D. P., Zhang, W., Bansback, N., Amarsi, Z., Birmingham, C. L., & Anis, A. H. (2009). The incidence of co-morbidities related to obesity and overweight: A systematic review and meta-analysis. *BMC Public Health, 9*(1), 1–20.

HabitRPG, I. (2021). *Habitica: Gamify your tasks*. https://play.google.com/store/apps/details?id=com.habitrpg.android.habitica&hl=en.

Hassan, S., Dhali, M., Zaman, F., & Tanveer, M. (2021). Big data and predictive analytics in healthcare in Bangladesh: Regulatory challenges. *Heliyon, 7*(6), e07179. https://doi.org/10.1016/j.heliyon.2021.e07179

Keikhosrokiani, P. (2019). *Perspectives in the development of mobile medical information systems: Life Cycle, management, methodological approach and application*. Academic Press.

Keikhosrokiani, P. (2020). Chapter 6 - emotional-persuasive and habit-change assessment of mobile medical information Systems (mMIS). In P. Keikhosrokiani (Ed.), *Perspectives in the development of mobile medical information systems: Life cycle, management, methodological approach and application* (pp. 101–109). Academic Press. https://doi.org/10.1016/B978-0-12-817657-3.00006-7

Keikhosrokiani, P. (2021a). IoT for enhanced decision-making in medical information systems: A systematic review. In G. Marques, A. Kumar Bhoi, I. de la Torre Díez, & B. Garcia-Zapirain (Eds.), *Enhanced telemedicine and e-health: Advanced IoT enabled soft computing framework* (pp. 119–140). Springer International Publishing. https://doi.org/10.1007/978-3-030-70111-6_6

Keikhosrokiani, P. (2021b). Predicating smartphone users' behaviour towards a location-aware IoMT-based information system: An empirical study. *International Journal of E-Adoption, 13*(2), 52–77. https://doi.org/10.4018/IJEA.2021070104

Maehlum, M. (2020). *Momentum habit tracker - routines, goals & rituals. App store*. https://apps.apple.com/us/app/momentum-habit-tracker-routines-goals-rituals/id946923599.

Nijjer, S., Saurabh, K., & Raj, S. (2020). Predictive big data analytics in healthcare. In P. Tanwar, V. Jain, C.-M. Liu, & V. Goyal (Eds.), *Big data analytics and intelligence: A perspective for health care* (pp. 75–91). Emerald Publishing Limited. https://doi.org/10.1108/978-1-83909-099-820201009

Play, G. (2021). *Balanced*. https://play.google.com/store/apps/details?id=au.com.headjam.balanced&hl=en.

Poornima, S., Pushpalatha, M., & Sujit Shankar, J. (2019). Analysis of weather data using forecasting algorithms. In N. K. Verma, & A. K. Ghosh (Eds.), *Computational intelligence: Theories, applications and future directions - volume I Singapore*.

Raghupathi, W., & Raghupathi, V. (2014). Big data analytics in healthcare: Promise and potential. *Health Information Science and Systems, 2*(1), 1–10.

Ravichandran, B. D., & Keikhosrokiani, P. (2021). An emotional-persuasive habit-change support mobile application for heart disease patients (BeHabit). In F. Saeed, F. Mohammed, & A. Al-Nahari (Eds.), *Innovative systems for intelligent health informatics* (pp. 252–262). Springer International Publishing. https://doi.org/10.1007/978-3-030-70713-2_25

Sharma, S., & Soni, H. K. (2021). An unemployment prediction rate for Indian youth through time series forecasting. In S. Agrawal, K. Kumar Gupta, J. H. Chan, J. Agrawal, & M. Gupta (Eds.), *Machine intelligence and smart systems Singapore*.

Teoh Yi Zhe, I., & Keikhosrokiani, P. (2020). *Knowledge workers mental workload prediction using optimised ELANFIS*. Applied Intelligence. https://doi.org/10.1007/s10489-020-01928-5

Wasylewicz, A. T. M., & Scheepers-Hoeks, A. M. J. W. (2019). Fundamentals of clinical data science. In P. Kubben, M. Dumontier, & A. Dekker (Eds.), *Clinical decision support systems*. Springer International Publishing. https://doi.org/10.1007/978-3-319-99713-1

Wilbur, J., Chandler, P., Dancy, B., Choi, J., & Plonczynski, D. (2002). Environmental, policy, and cultural factors related to physical activity in urban, African American women. *Women & Health, 36*(2), 17–28.

Ying, Y. (2019). *Malaysia and WHO call for more investment in primary health care the 21st century*. World Health Organization (WHO). https://www.who.int/malaysia/news/detail/08-04-2019-malaysia-and-who-call-for-more-investment-in-primary-health-care-the-21st-century.

Chapter 15

Predictions on diabetic patient datasets using big data analytics and machine learning techniques

Pratiyush Guleria
National Institute of Electronics and Information Technology (NIELIT) Shimla, Shimla, Himachal Pradesh, India

1. Introduction

Big Data is one of the trending technologies of emerging times. The technologies like internet of things (IoT), machine learning, and cloud-enabled technologies are collaborating with each other, especially in healthcare sector. Huge volume of data is collected every second, which requires big data analytics (BDA) to extract the meaningful and desired information. The digitized data in the Electronic Health Records (EHRs) is structured in nature. For example, the receipt obtained by the patient on the enquiry counter which includes the patients' name, date of birth, doctor name, hospital, etc., is structured information, handled by automated databases and can be easily coded (Raghupathi & Raghupathi, 2014a, 2014b). According to the authors, EHR keeps the patient health-related information in the computerized form (Murphy et al., 1999). The data in the electronic form act as the primary source for providing health-related services (Reisman, 2017). BDA leverage the gap within structured and unstructured data sources and Data Science gets insight from this data to extract meaningful information and make predictions. Along with a huge collection of data, the sources of emitting data are also growing at an alarming rate. The sources of data include social networking sites, web sources, blogs, surveys, Google Forms, and Multimedia data, etc. With an increase in the volume and velocity of data, the variety of data also comes into focus. The demand for the data varies as per the requirement of the business by different organizations. Big data has few characteristics like volume, velocity, variety, and veracity.

BDA and IoT are contributing in healthcare areas which include patient monitoring, medical resource allocation, personalized healthcare, predicting and diagnosing diseases, healthcare data analysis, EHR maintenance, telemedicine, etc. BDA is important for healthcare for improving patient health management and providing diagnostic support to patients. Machine learning and big data analytical techniques help exploit clinical data, patient diseases predictions, analysis of the past medical history of patients, and monitoring patient health (Galetsi & Katsaliaki, 2020). The 3 Vs, i.e., Volume, Velocity, and Variety, are the important characteristics of big data in the healthcare sector (Raghupathi & Raghupathi, 2014a, 2014b). Here 'Volume' shows the enormous growth of data, 'Velocity' represents the rapid accumulation of data, and finally, 'Variety' represents the format of data which may be structured, semistructured, or unstructured.

The "Analytics" term in BDA is categorized into the following by Wang et al. (2016):

(1) Descriptive Analytics: It works upon finding problems and trends in already existing processes.

(2) Predictive Analytics: It implements mathematical formulations and techniques to extract predictive trends. Machine learning also plays an important role in predictive analytics.

(3) Prescriptive Analytics: It helps in decision-making, with the objective of improvement and performance enhancement.

The potential benefits of big data in healthcare are detecting diseases at earlier stages, analyzing patient characteristics, cost-effective treatments, etc., (Raghupathi & Raghupathi, 2014a, 2014b). Big data analytical techniques help in analyzing a variety of healthcare data, i.e., semistructured and unstructured data which includes Electronic Medical Records,

Big Data Analytics for Healthcare. https://doi.org/10.1016/B978-0-323-91907-4.00018-2

TABLE 15.1 Big data common tools and platforms.

Tool/Platform name	Description
Hadoop	Hadoop is a framework for assigned storage and deals with big data using the MapReduce programming model. MapReduce consists of map and reduce functions. In map, cleaning and sorting of data are done, whereas in reduce function, summary operations are performed.
Pig	Pig is a tool to analyze and handle large datasets by creating programs in Pig Latin language and run them on Apache hadoop.
Hive	Hive is used for querying and analyzing large datasets stored in hadoop files. Hive is an SQL (structured query language) like query language (Bhardwaj, Kumar, Narayan, & Kumar, 2015).
Zookeeper	ZooKeeper is an open-source server for distributed environments and services (Junqueira & Reed, 2013).
HBase	HBase is open-source architecture for nonrelational databases and runs on top of the hadoop Distributed File System (HDFS). HBase is efficient in handling large datasets, i.e., real-time access to petabytes of data (Chrimes & Zamani, 2017).
Cassandra	Cassandra is an open-source, distributed, and NoSQL database management system to handle large data across many commodity servers. In Cassandra, data is distributed across the clusters, supports replication, scalability, fault-tolerance, supports MapReduce, and introduced CQL (Cassandra Query Language) as an alternative to SQL (Chebotko, Kashlev, & Lu, 2015).
Mahout	Apache mahout, a project of Apache Software Foundation is written in java, scala and is primarily focused on writing machine learning algorithms.
Oozie	Apache Oozie is a java web application for scheduling Apache hadoop jobs.
Avro	Avro is a data serialization framework developed within Apache hadoop project.
Jaql	Jaql is a JSON (JavaScript Object Notation) query language for query processing on big data.

Medicine Prescriptions, Operational data, Clinical data, and other paper documents to match medication with the result, predict patients at risk, and yield more adequate care (Cottle et al., 2013).

Big data platforms and tools play an important role in performing BDA on transformed data from the raw data. The Big Data sources consist of data from multiple platforms, locations, applications, etc. The raw data is transferred for the big data transformation phase. The big data platform and tools are briefly discussed in Table 15.1.

1.1 Challenges of healthcare data

Medical image data requires huge storage which can range from a few megabytes to hundreds of megabytes like in the case of thin slice Computerized Tomography (CT) scan studies (Seibert, 2009).

The biggest challenge of the BDA is the collection of a huge volume of medical data collected across heterogeneous platforms and their integration implementation (Dash, Shakyawar, Sharma, & Kaushik, 2019).

The complexity of data and deriving meaningful information from it is another challenge.

Extracting and performing pattern analysis from images, published articles, and textual data to get new insight is also one of the challenges. Medical images including Magnetic Resonance Imaging, CT scans, X-rays, etc., are an important source of data for diagnosis (Ritter et al., 2011).

Handling new data center workload and the performance of data along with Data Quality Assurance is another task of Big Data. The New Data Center workloads result in new infrastructure demands.

Another major challenge is difficulty in data capturing, storage, analysis, and visualization, etc., (Chen & Zhang, 2014).

2. Big data analytics using mapreduce, Pig, Hive, and Spark

Hadoop using MapReduce Framework, Apache Pig, Apache Hive, Apache Spark, etc., are some solutions for analyzing big data and are performed for experimentation on healthcare datasets in the proposed work. In big data, the processing issue of the original raw data stored only using a grid is one of the challenges. The data is collected, appended into it, and cannot explore the integrity of raw data. Another major challenge is, when the data is moved for computation to Extract, Transform, and Load (ETL) compute grid, it does not scale. The data after ETL phase is followed with Relational Database

Management System, i.e., Aggregated Data and only a meager 10% of the metadata remains available for Business Intelligence Reports and Interactive Apps. In some cases, the data does not process well and results into loss of data, and sometimes, complete data does not archive.

2.1 Hadoop MapReduce framework

It is an open-source framework for storing data and running applications on clusters of commodity hardware with the help of the MapReduce programming model. Hadoop as a solution has a storage layer, i.e., a distributed file system that can store a huge amount of data in multiple machines instead of a central server which makes it highly decisive, fault-tolerant, scattered for parallel processing, and extensible. Hadoop has two core components, which are Hadoop Distributed File System (HDFS) and implements the MapReduce computing model.

Hadoop as a key has a storage layer, i.e., a distributed file system that can store a huge amount of data in multiple machines instead of a central server. It imitates the data over multiple hosts and provides access to data across multiple Hadoop Clusters. Hadoop works on Master−Slave Architecture, i.e., NameNode is the Master and DataNodes acts as the Slave. An HDFS cluster consists of a single NameNode, a master server that conducts the file system namespace, and classifies access to files by clients. It also resolves the outline of blocks on Datanodes. The workflow of MapReduce Framework is shown in Fig. 15.1.

2.2 Apache Pig

Apache Pig, originally developed by Yahoo, is a platform for interpreting large data sets. It consists of a high-level language, i.e., Pig Latin for declaring data analysis programs. Pig analyzes the large datasets using simple lines of codes instead of writing java programs like in the case of Hadoop.

It is a large-scale data processing system and focuses on data transformations. Apache Pig consists of Grunt Shell and Pig Server followed with Parser, Optimizer, and Compiler for logical transformation and the Execution Engine to execute the query. The Pig Engine converts the queries into MapReduce Jobs and is needed to run the programs. The queries on the dataset files can be performed using the Grunt shell, only when the files are first transferred into the HDFS. The architecture of the Apache Pig is shown in Fig. 15.2.

2.3 Apache Hive

Hive developed by Facebook is a Data Warehousing package built on the top of Hadoop and is mainly used for data analysis. It is similar to SQL and is called Hive Query Language (HiveQL). It is for managing and querying structured data. The major advantage of HiveQL is that it abstracts the complexity of Hadoop and there is no such need to learn java programming. In companies like Facebook, the challenge is to analyze the huge volume of data and here Hive is the solution. In HiveQL, the tables can be partitioned and bucketed. There is schema flexibility and easy to plug-in customized mapper and reducer codes availability. Hive tables can be defined directly on HDFS and having extensible types, formats, functions, and scripts. The advantage of using Hive is that it provides tools to enable easy ETL operations.

It is extensible, scalable, and supports any client applications in Java, PHP, Python, C++, etc., languages. Hive applications are used in Data Mining, Log Processing, Document Indexing, Business Intelligence, and Predictive Modeling techniques. The architecture of Apache Hive is shown in Fig. 15.3. In the Hive Clients phase, Apache Thrift serves the request from the programming languages that support Thrift. Hive allows Java applications to connect to it using the Java Database Connectivity (JDBC) driver. In Open Database Connectivity (ODBC) clients, the Hive ODBC Driver allows applications that support the ODBC Protocol. The Hive Services consists of Hive CLI (Command Line Interface) which is the default shell provided by the Hive to execute Hive queries and commands directly. Hive Web interface is a GUI for

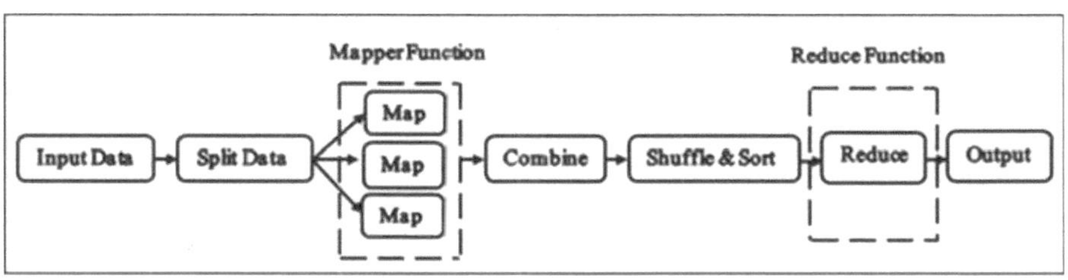

FIGURE 15.1 Workflow of MapReduce framework.

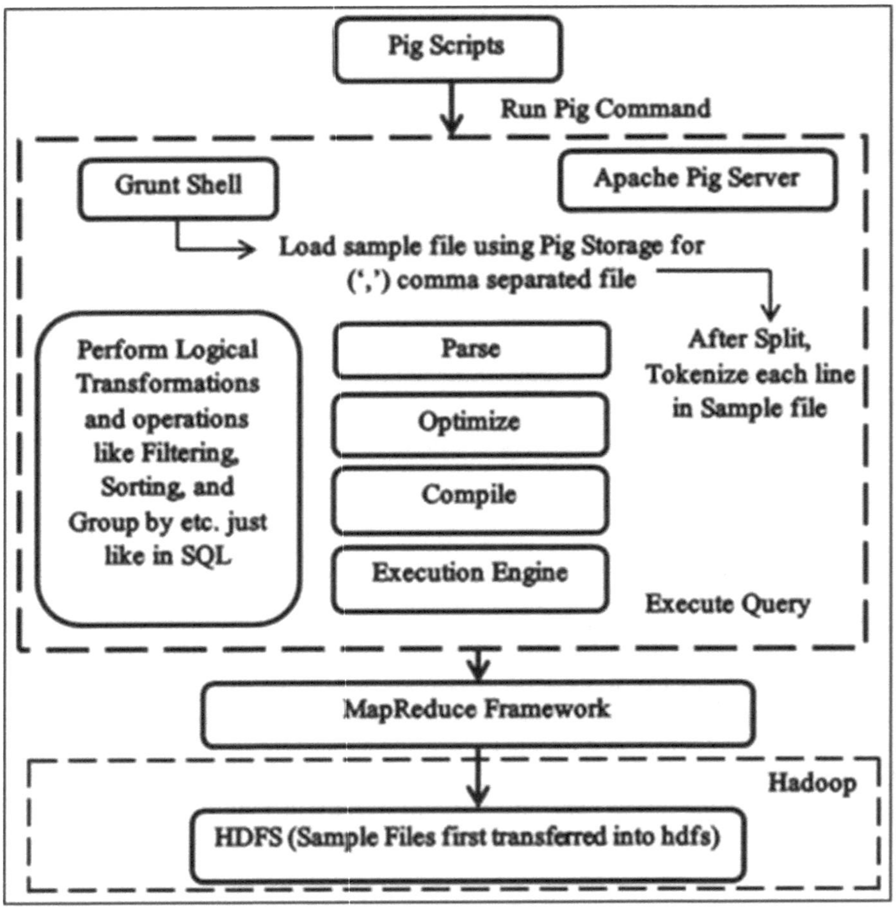

FIGURE 15.2 Apache Pig architecture.

executing Hive Queries and Commands. Hive Server is an Apache Thrift Server and allows different clients to submit requests to Hive and retrieve the final result, whereas Apache Hive Driver is responsible for receiving the queries submitted through the CLI, Web UI, JDBC, and ODBC Drivers. In Hive Server, Compiler, Optimizer, and Executor work and perform parsing, type checking, and semantic analysis takes place with the help of databases in metastore. In metastore, the metadata information like table structure, column partitions, and their type is stored. In the next phase, the roles of resource manager, i.e., YARN and MapReduce, and HDFS tasks are involved. In the final phase, the execution engine executes these tasks in the order of their dependencies using Hadoop.

2.4 Apache Spark

Apache Spark is an analytical engine for big data and machine learning. It is an open-source project for refining massive data used by companies like Netflix, Yahoo, etc., for analysis of customer preferences.

Spark platform provides in-memory computing competence to deliver speed, a generalized execution engine to support a wide variety of applications, and Java, Scala, and Python APIs for ease of development. Spark performs faster than Hadoop for large-scale data processing. It acts as a consolidated engine with higher-level libraries, including support for SQL queries, emerging data, machine learning, and graph processing. There is real-time data processing in Spark and Spark overcomes the time lag issue. The Spark component consists of Spark SQL, Spark Streaming, Spark MLlib, GraphX, and SparkR. Resilient Distributed Datasets (RDDs) are the building blocks of any Spark application. RDD is fault tolerant and has the capability of rebuilding data on failure distributing data among the multiple nodes in a cluster. The two types of operations performed by RDD include transformations and actions that are applied on an RDD to instruct Spark to apply computation (Salloum, Dautov, Chen, Peng, & Huang, 2016). The architecture of Apache Spark is shown in Fig. 15.4.

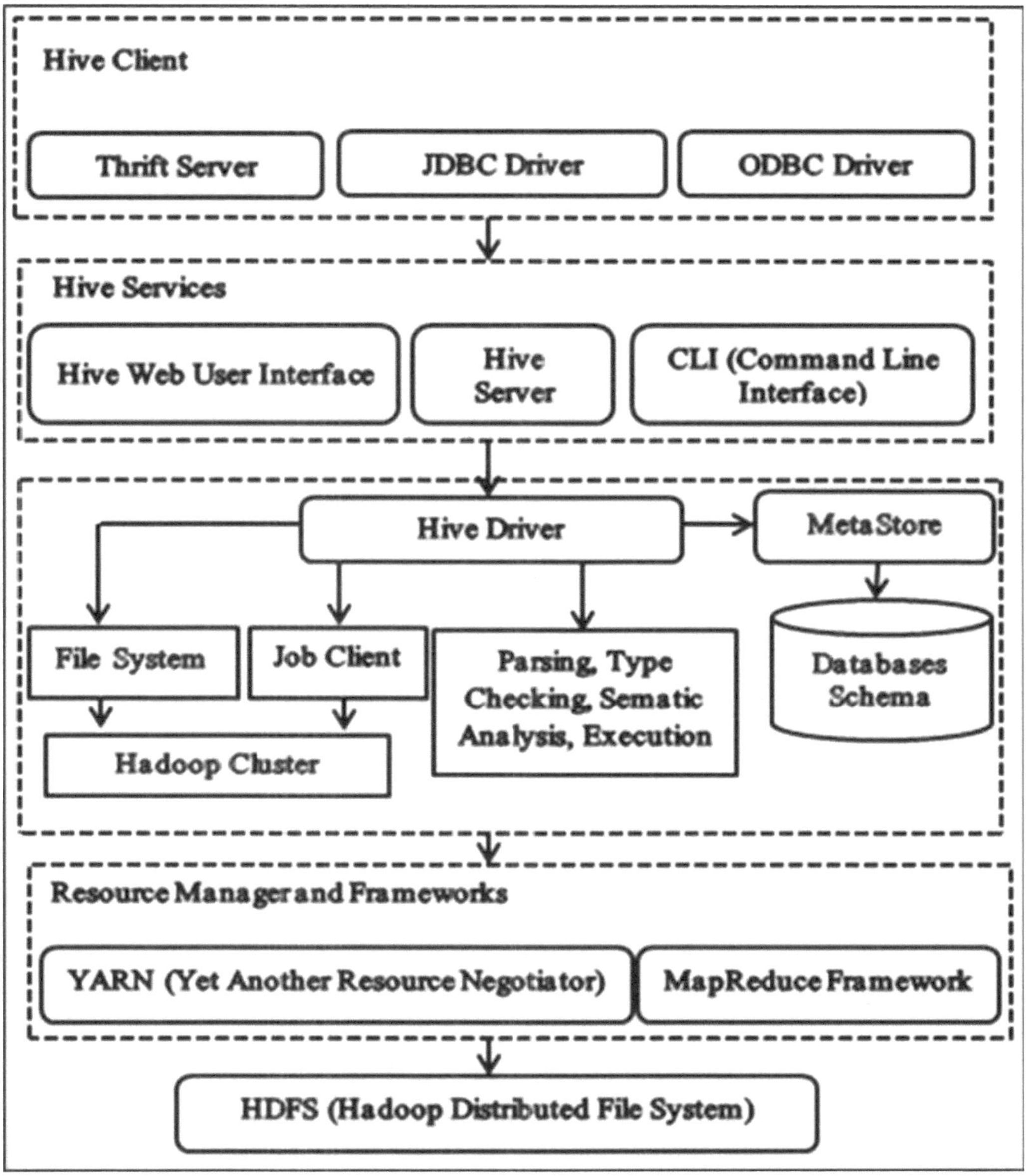

FIGURE 15.3 Apache Hive architecture.

3. Methodology adopted

In the proposed work, experimentation is performed on the diabetic patient's dataset. The dataset taken in the proposed work is available in the public domain (archive). The dataset contains the sign and symptoms of a newly diabetic or would-be diabetic patient and has been collected using a direct survey from the patients of Sylhet Diabetes Hospital in Sylhet, Bangladesh. The dataset constitutes 520 instances and the number of attributes is 17. The dataset characteristics are of multivariate type. For the experimentation purpose, Cloudera open-source platform, i.e., distribution of Hadoop virtual machine is run on VMware workstation. The sample dataset of a diabetic patient is first converted into HDFS. The sample dataset is shown in Table 15.2.

The results after analyzing the data through MapReduce are shown in Fig. 15.5. The input data shown in Table 15.2 is first stored on HDFS, and then, the input data get split. The record reader reads the data using an input key value pair and passed it to Mapper. The intermediate key−value pairs are passed to the combiner phase for further partitioning using partitioner phase. The values fetched from partitioner are shuffled and sorted. The final stage is to pass the data through

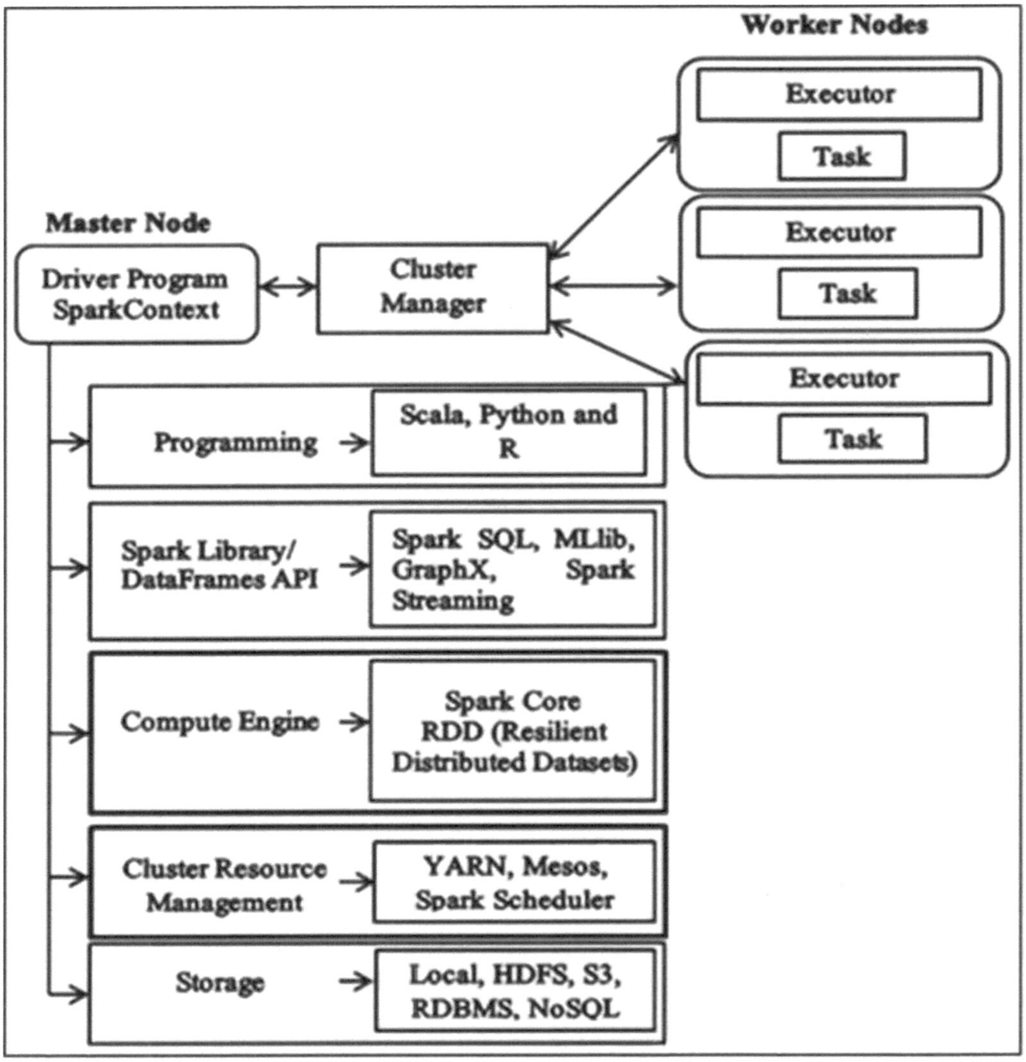

FIGURE 15.4 Apache spark architecture.

reducer. The output obtained from the reducer phase will be stored on HDFS. After MapReduce, the data shown in Table 15.2 is analyzed using Apache Pig Latin. The input dataset is converted into HDFS before running the Apache Pig Grunt Shell. The data analyzed using Pig Grunt Shell is shown in Fig. 15.6 and the job statistical report of Apache Grunt Shell is shown in Fig. 15.7.

The diabetic patient data is then analyzed using Apache Hive. In Apache Hive, the SQL-like queries are executed and perform faster data analyses compared to Apache Pig Latin. The table is created in Apache Hive and the data type of the attributes is taken as integer and string. The time taken for creating the table by Apache Hive is 0.467 s. The dataset is first loaded into HDFS before executing the Hive queries in Apache Hive shell. The Hive services consist of Hive Server, CLI, Web UI for running the queries and using Hive Driver, type checking and semantic analysis are performed and are connected to metastore. Metastore is the central repository for databases like Derby, MySql, etc., and contains the database structure. The Hive shell, where the Data Definition Language and Data Manipulation Language commands are executed, is shown in Figs. 15.8 and 15.9.

The dataset is loaded externally into the table “patients” using the command as shown in Fig. 15.10. A HiveQL query is shown in Figs. 15.11 and 15.12 for fetching the data from a table using where clause.

The data after using Apache Hive is analyzed using Apache Spark. The data stored in Hadoop is processed over time, whereas, in Apache Spark, it performs real-time data processing and overcomes the time lag issue. Apache Spark has an in-

TABLE 15.2 Sample dataset of newly diabetic or would–be diabetic patients.

Age	Gender	Polyuria	Polydipsia	Sudden weight loss	Weakness	Polyphagia	Genital thrush	Visual blurring	Itching	Irritability	Delayed healing	Partial paresis	Muscle stiffness	Alopecia	Obesity	Class
31	Male	Yes	No	No	No	Yes	No	Yes	No	No	No	Yes	No	Yes	No	Positive
66	Male	No	No	No	No	Yes	No	Yes	No	No	No	Yes	No	Yes	No	Positive
61	Female	Yes	No	No	No	Yes	No	No	No	Yes	No	No	No	Yes	No	Positive
58	Female	Yes	No	Yes	No	Yes	No	No	No	Yes	No	No	Yes	No	Yes	Positive
69	Female	Yes	Yes	Yes	Yes	No	No	Yes	Yes	Yes	No	No	Yes	No	Yes	Positive
40	Male	No	Yes	Yes	Yes	No	No	Yes	Yes	No	No	Yes	Yes	No	No	Negative

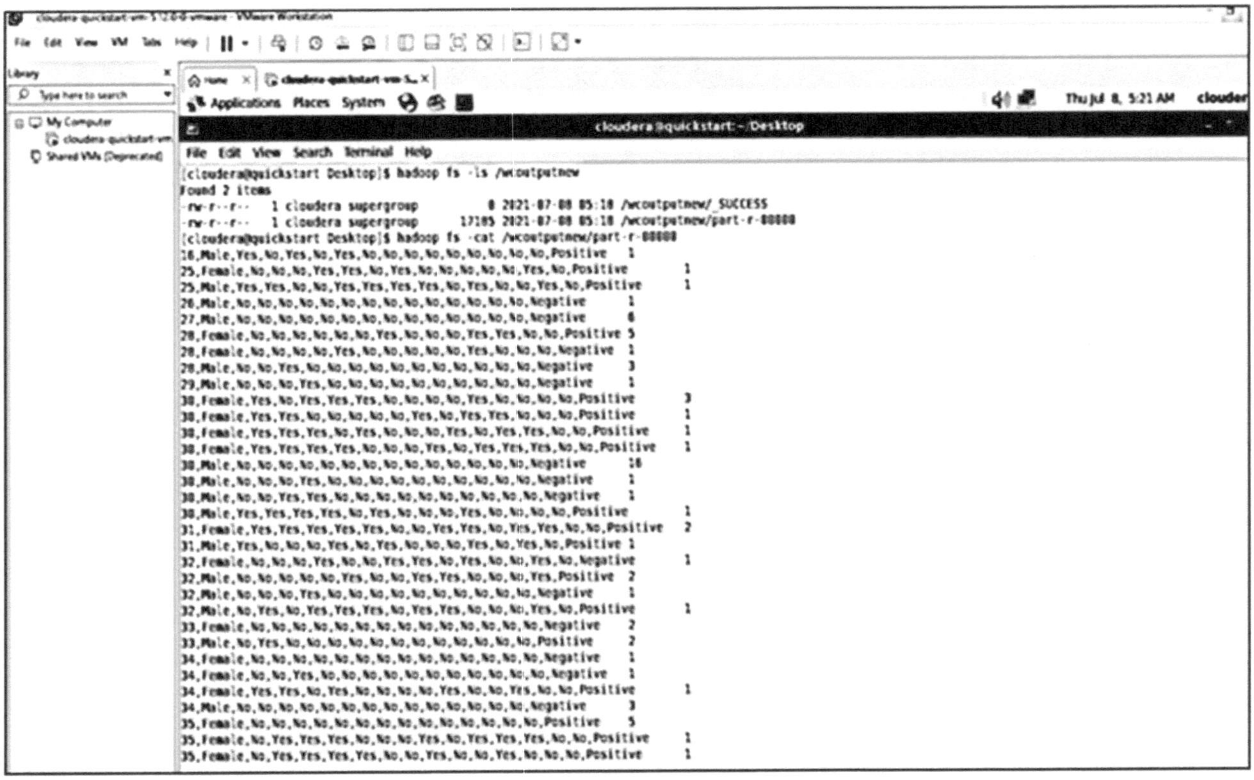

FIGURE 15.5 Data analyzed using MapReduce framework.

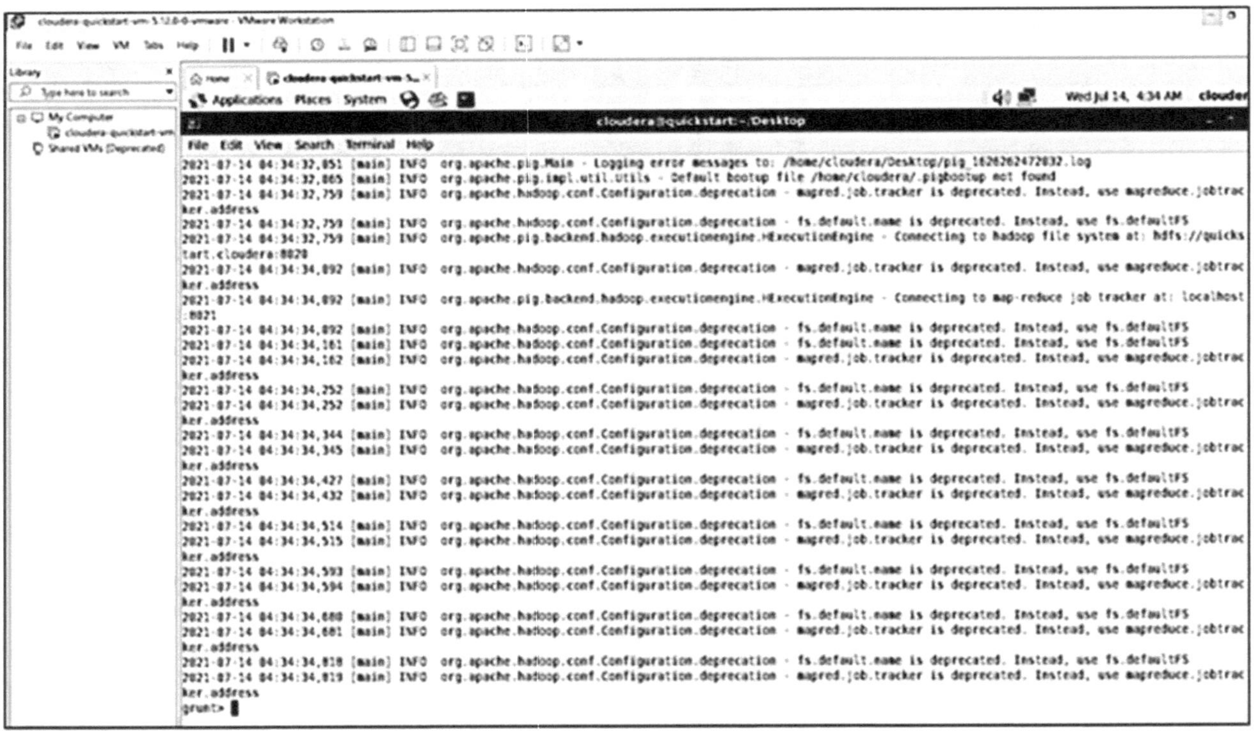

FIGURE 15.6 Apache Pig grunt shell.

```
HadoopVersion   PigVersion      UserId  StartedAt       FinishedAt      Features
2.6.0-cdh5.12.0 0.12.0-cdh5.12.0        cloudera        2021-07-14 04:48:35     2021-07-14 04:49:04     GROUP_BY

Success!

Job Stats (time in seconds):
JobId   Maps    Reduces MaxMapTime      MinMapTIme      AvgMapTime      MedianMapTime   MaxReduceTime   MinReduceTime   AvgReduceTime   MedianReducetime
Alias   Feature Outputs
job_1626261892714_0003  1       1       4       4       4       4       5       5       5       5       A,B,C,D GROUP_BY,COMBINER       hdfs://quickstar
t.cloudera:8020/tmp/temp-1163216028/tmp-203905407,

Input(s):
Successfully read 520 records (34850 bytes) from: "/diabetes.csv"

Output(s):
Successfully stored 2 records (36 bytes) in: "hdfs://quickstart.cloudera:8020/tmp/temp-1163216028/tmp-203905407"

Counters:
Total records written : 2
Total bytes written : 36
Spillable Memory Manager spill count : 0
Total bags proactively spilled: 0
Total records proactively spilled: 0

Job DAG:
job_1626261892714_0003


2021-07-14 04:49:04,291 [main] INFO  org.apache.pig.backend.hadoop.executionengine.mapReduceLayer.MapReduceLauncher - Success!
2021-07-14 04:49:04,292 [main] INFO  org.apache.hadoop.conf.Configuration.deprecation - fs.default.name is deprecated. Instead, use fs.defaultFS
2021-07-14 04:49:04,292 [main] INFO  org.apache.hadoop.conf.Configuration.deprecation - mapred.job.tracker is deprecated. Instead, use mapreduce.jobtrac
ker.address
2021-07-14 04:49:04,292 [main] INFO  org.apache.pig.data.SchemaTupleBackend - Key [pig.schematuple] was not set... will not generate code.
2021-07-14 04:49:04,299 [main] INFO  org.apache.hadoop.mapreduce.lib.input.FileInputFormat - Total input paths to process : 1
2021-07-14 04:49:04,299 [main] INFO  org.apache.pig.backend.hadoop.executionengine.util.MapRedUtil - Total input paths to process : 1
(Negative,200)
(Positive,320)
grunt>
```

FIGURE 15.7 Job statistics repcrt of Apache Pig grunt shell.

```
hive> create database diabetes;
OK
Time taken: 11.822 seconds
hive> use diabetes;
OK
Time taken: 0.08 seconds
hive> create table patient(Age int,Gender string,Polyuria string,Polydipsia string,suddenweightloss string,weakness string,Polyphagia string,Genitalthru
ng string,Itching string,Irritability string,delayedhealing string,partialparesis string,musclestiffness string,Alopecia string,Obesity string,class str
OK
Time taken: 0.467 seconds
hive>
```

FIGURE 15.8 Table creation in Apache Hive shell.

```
hive> create table patients(Age int,Gender string,Polyuria string,Polydipsia string,suddenweightloss string,weakness string,Polyphagia string,Genitalthr
ush string,visualblurring string,Itching string,Irritability string,delayedhealing string,partialparesis string,musclestiffness string,Alopecia string,O
besity string,class string)row format delimited fields terminated by ',';
OK
Time taken: 0.123 seconds
hive> describe patients;
OK
age                     int
gender                  string
polyuria                string
polydipsia              string
suddenweightloss        string
weakness                string
polyphagia              string
genitalthrush           string
visualblurring          string
itching                 string
irritability            string
delayedhealing          string
partialparesis          string
musclestiffness         string
alopecia                string
obesity                 string
class                   string
Time taken: 0.105 seconds, Fetched: 17 row(s)
```

FIGURE 15.9 Table structure of diabetic patients in Apache Hive shell.

```
hive> load data inpath '/diabetes.txt' into table patients;
Loading data to table diabetes.patients
Table diabetes.patients stats: [numFiles=1, totalSize=34487]
OK
Time taken: 0.351 seconds
hive>
```

FIGURE 15.10 Loading data externally into a table in Apache Hive.

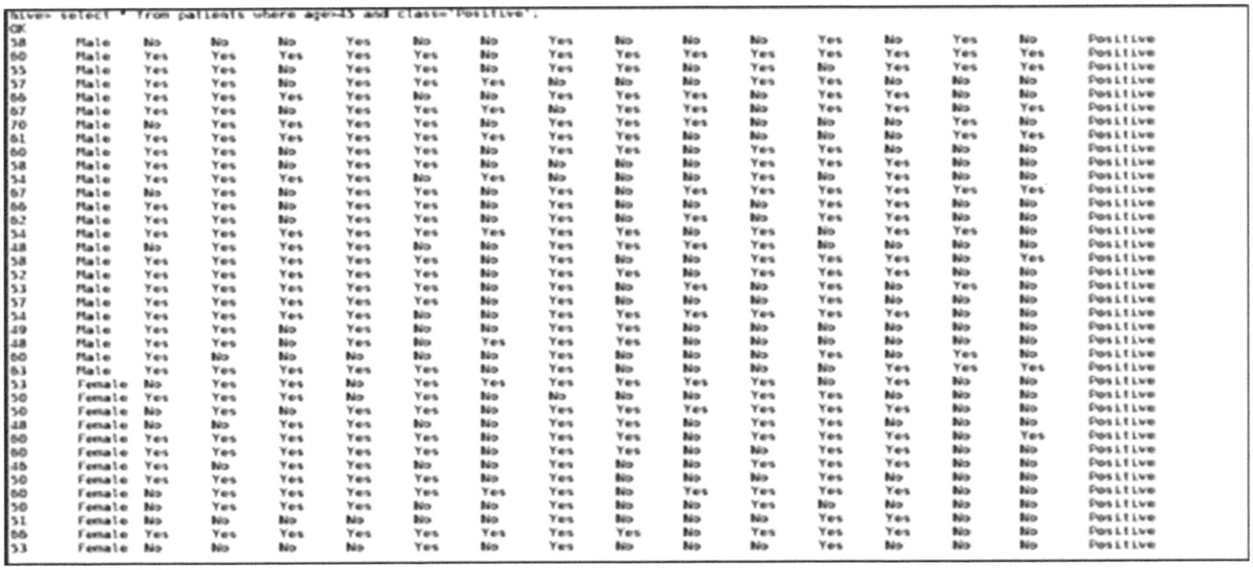

FIGURE 15.11 Fetching data from a table using where clause in Hive.

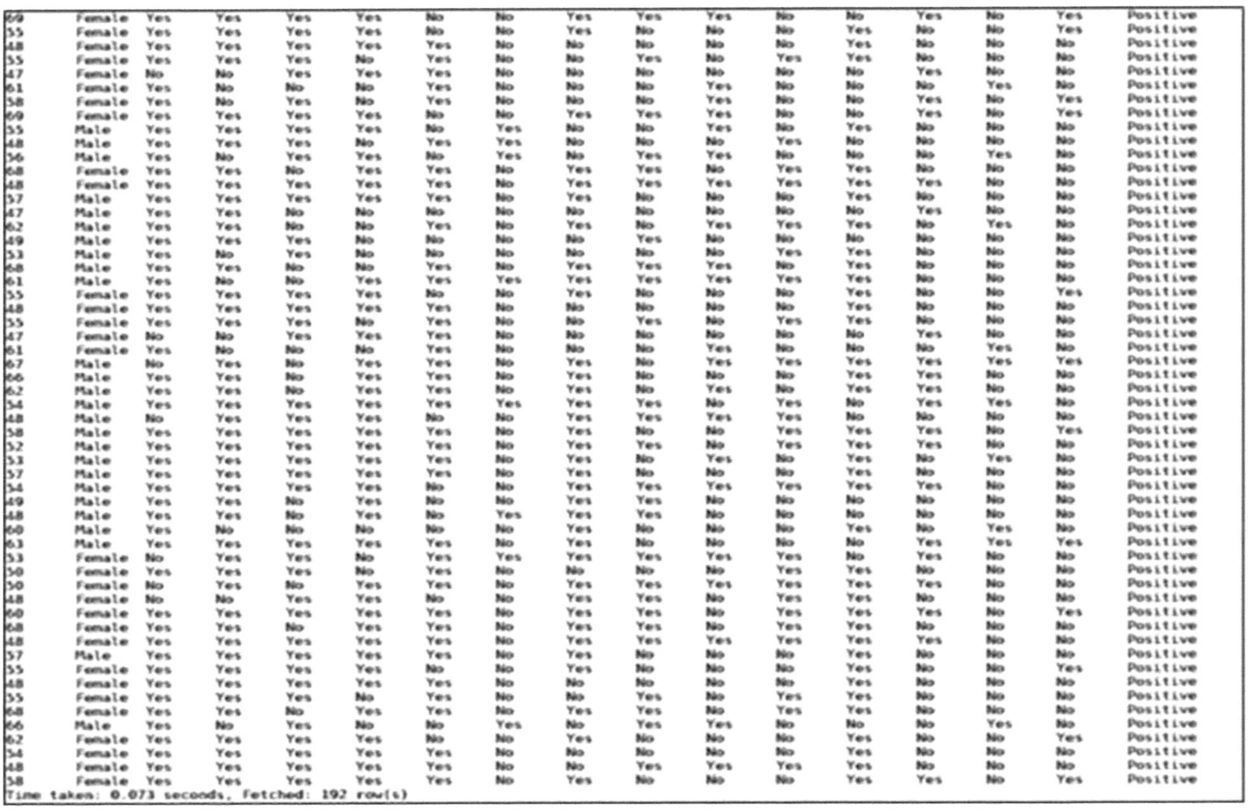

FIGURE 15.12 Total number of records fetched.

memory cluster computing paradigm that enhances the processing speed of an application. The diabetic patients' dataset is first loaded into HDFS and then Apache Spark shell version 1.6.8 is opened for dataset processing as shown in Fig. 15.13. The Apache Spark Data Flow pattern is shown in Fig. 15.14 where RDD plays an important role and is the main feature for any Spark application. It is fault tolerant and is competent in fixing data on failure. The data is distributed on multiple

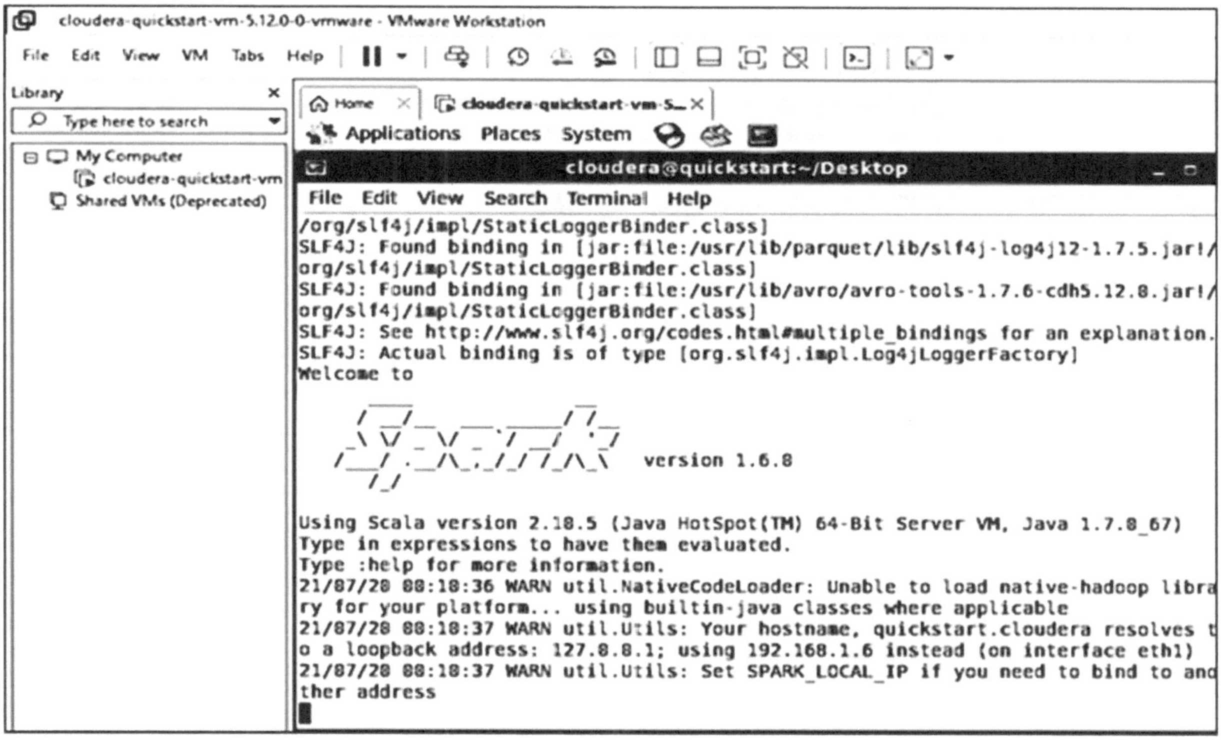

FIGURE 15.13 Apache spark shell.

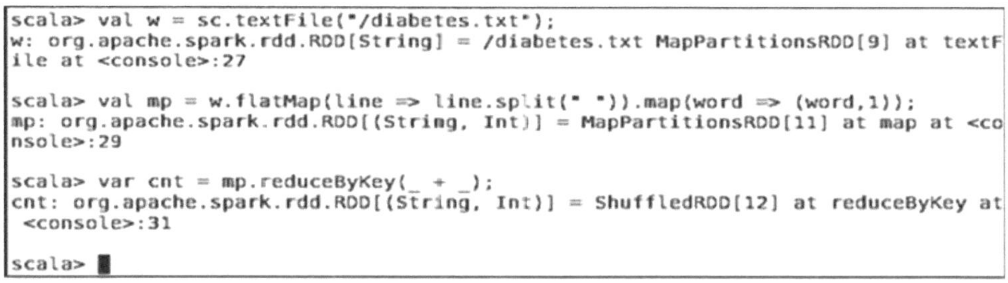

FIGURE 15.14 Spark mapreduce data flow pattern.

nodes in a cluster and the queries are run in parallel. In RDD, dataset is the collection of distributed data with values. The Apache Spark RDD operations and transformations are performed on the diabetic patients' dataset, and then, the count of patients' features and patient outcome class is shown in Fig. 15.15.

3.1 Big data and machine learning techniques for healthcare

Big data and machine learning techniques are promising fields to gain meaningful insight and decisive knowledge, information, and patterns from the data which may be in structured, unstructured, or semistructured form. Machine learning algorithms are applied to the training datasets to train the models for analyzing data, effective decision-making, and performing predictions. In the proposed work, the diabetic dataset of the female patients is considered for data analysis using machine learning techniques in Matlab R2021a. The sample dataset shown in Table 15.3 contains the data of female patients and at least 21 years old of Pima Indian heritage. The dataset is available in the public domain and is obtained from Kaggle (kaggle). The dataset is preprocessed to remove the outliers and then machine learning techniques are implemented on the dataset to predict whether the patient is diabetic or not based on certain diagnostic measurements included in the dataset. The dataset consists of eight attributes that act as an independent variable and the 'outcome' attribute is considered as the target, i.e., outcome variable. A linear regression is one of the simplest Machine Learning and Statistical Technique.

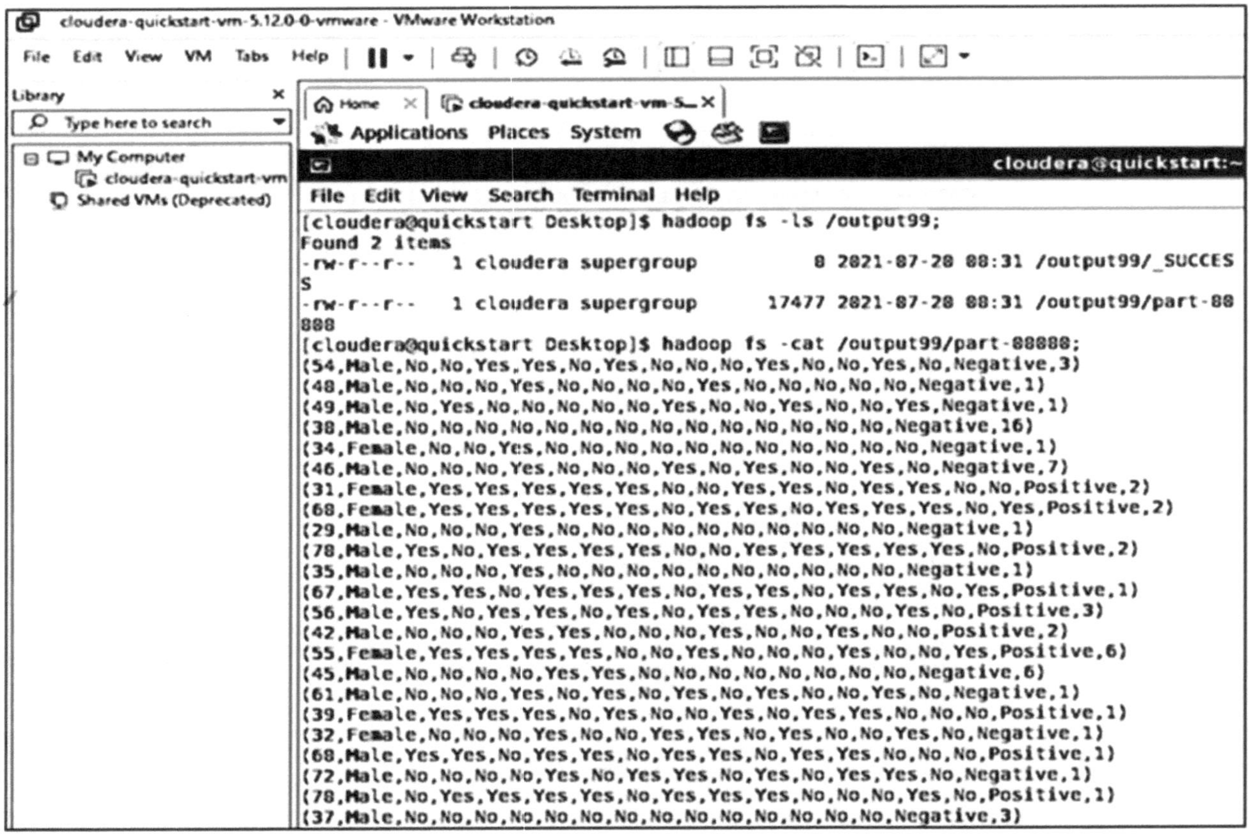

FIGURE 15.15 Diabetic patients' data and count of outcome class, i.e., "Positive" or "Negative" displayed on the terminal after Apache Spark RDD operations.

TABLE 15.3 Sample dataset of female diabetic patients.

Pregnancies	Glucose	Blood Pressure	Skin Thickness	Insulin	BMI	Diabetes Pedigree Function	Age	Outcome
6	148	72	35	0	33.6	0.627	50	1
1	85	66	29	0	26.6	0.351	31	0
8	183	64	0	0	23.3	0.672	32	1
1	89	66	23	94	28.1	0.167	21	0
0	137	40	35	168	43.1	2.288	33	1
5	116	74	0	0	25.6	0.201	30	0

It is a model for interpreting the analogy between independent and dependent numerical variables (Maulud & Abdulazeez, 2020). A linear regression equation in the form of a model is shown in Eq. (15.1).

$$b_{out} = \gamma_0 + \gamma_1 a_{inp} \tag{15.1}$$

Here, b_{out} is the outcome variable, i.e., the predicted value, whereas a_{inp} is the input variable taken. γ_0 and γ_1 refer to the coefficient values. γ_0 is the intercept line, i.e., b_{out} of the estimated regression line and γ_1 is the slope.

The ML algorithms implemented in the proposed work for performing predictions on the dataset shown in Table 15.3 are KNN (K-Nearest Neighbor), Decision Tree, and Ensembling Method, i.e., Bagged Trees.

3.1.1 K-nearest neighbor

KNN is a machine learning technique for classification and regression. It is based on feature similarity and finds the k the closest training examples in the dataset using the distance function (Hu, Huang, Ke, & Tsai, 2016). In KNN, for K number of the nearest neighbors, the distance between the query examples and all the training cases is computed using Euclidean distance for calculating the distance of unknown data from all the data points as shown in Eq. (15.2).

$$dt = \sqrt{\left([\![(x_1 - x_2)]\!]^2 + [\![(y_1 - y_2)]\!]^2 \right)} \tag{15.2}$$

Here, dt is the distance, and x_1, x_2, y_1, and y_2 are the Cartesian coordinates and the distance between x and y is calculated as shown in the equation. After calculating the distance, the new data point will be assigned to the category for which the number of neighbors is maximal. The correct and incorrect model predictions using the KNN algorithm taking 10 neighbors for the attributes 'Age' versus 'Body Mass Index (BMI)," "Age" versus "Blood Pressure," and "Blood Pressure" versus "Glucose" are shown in Figs. 15.16–15.18.

3.1.2 Decision trees

Decision trees are one of the most popular machine learning approaches for representing classifiers. In a decision tree, each internal node divides the instance space into two or more subspaces according to a certain feature of the input attribute values. Here, each leaf node is assigned to one class representing the most appropriate target value (Rokach & Maimon, 2005a, 2005b). The decision tree algorithm works in a top-down and chooses a variable at each step that best splits the set of items (Rokach & Maimon, 2005a, 2005b). In Classification and Regression Trees, i.e., CART, Gini Impurity measure is calculated as the probability of misclassification of an observation in the training dataset (Khemphila & Boonjing, 2010). The Gini Impurity, i.e., g for n total classes, is calculated as shown in Eq. (15.3).

$$g = \sum_{i=1}^{n} pb(i) * (1 - pb(i)) \tag{15.3}$$

Here $pb(i)$ is the probability of randomly choosing an element of class i and incorrectly classifying the randomly chosen element. In decision trees, the node attaining the highest information gain is considered as the root node. Information gain is based on the concept of entropy. Entropy is used to measure impurity, i.e., disorder in the outcome variable which means

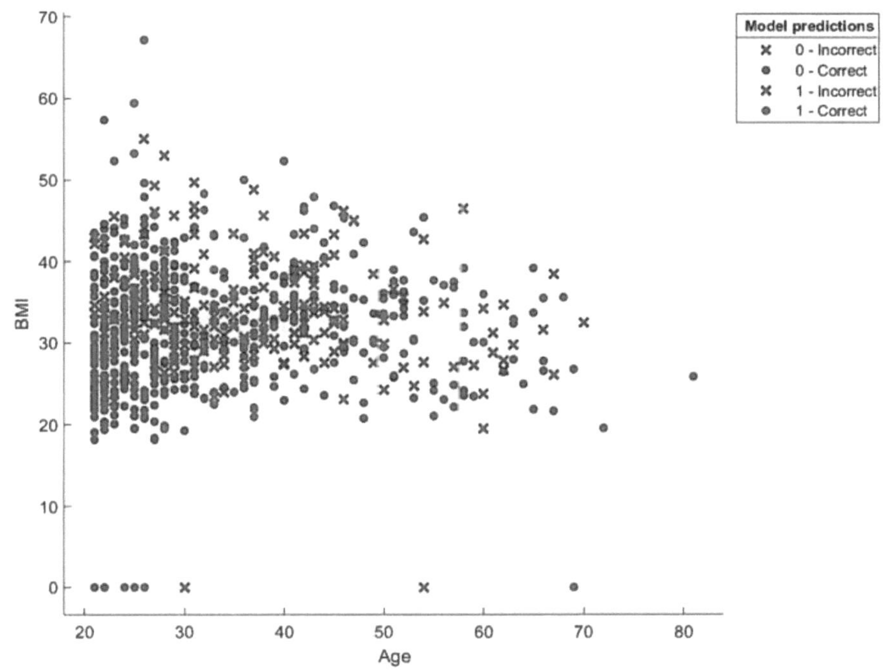

FIGURE 15.16 KNN model predictions "Age" versus "BMI."

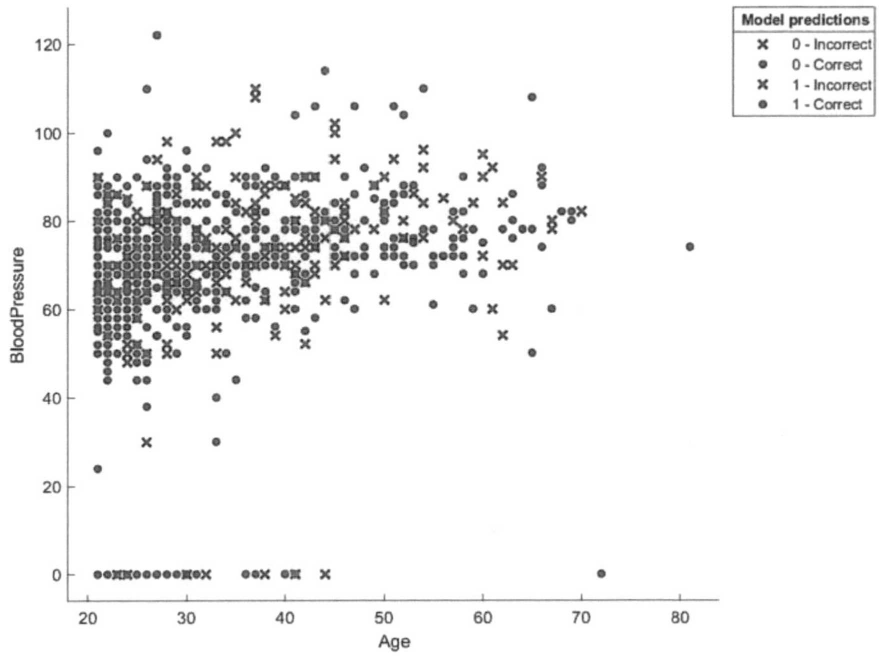

FIGURE 15.17 KNN model predictions "Age" versus "Blood Pressure."

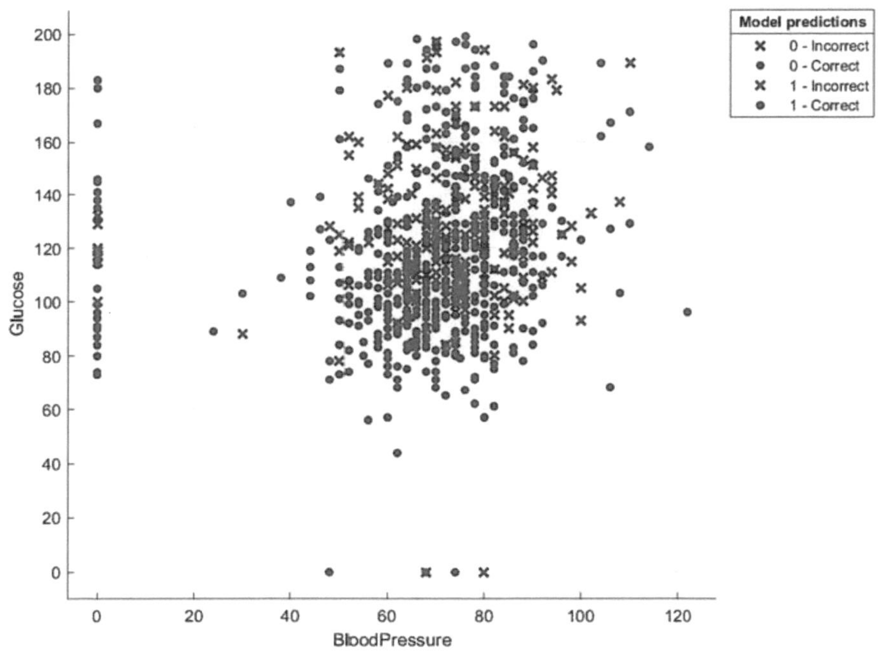

FIGURE 15.18 KNN model predictions "Blood Pressure" versus "Glucose."

value may be 0 or 1. The formula of entropy for n classes is shown in Eq. (15.4) and the information gain is calculated as shown in Eq. (15.5) (Tangirala, 2020).

$$e = -\sum_{i=1}^{n} p(x_i) log_2\, p(x_i) \tag{15.4}$$

$$i_g(t_v,\ i_v) = e(\bar{t}_v) - \sum V\ i_v \frac{|t_{vV}|}{t_v}.e(t_{vV}) \tag{15.5}$$

Here in Eq. (15.5), t_v is the target variable, i_v is the independent variable selected for testing purposes, and V refers to each value in i_v. The correct and incorrect model predictions using decision tree for the attributes 'Age' versus 'BMI' 'Age' versus 'Blood Pressure' and 'Blood Pressure' versus 'Glucose' are shown in Figs. 15.19–15.21.

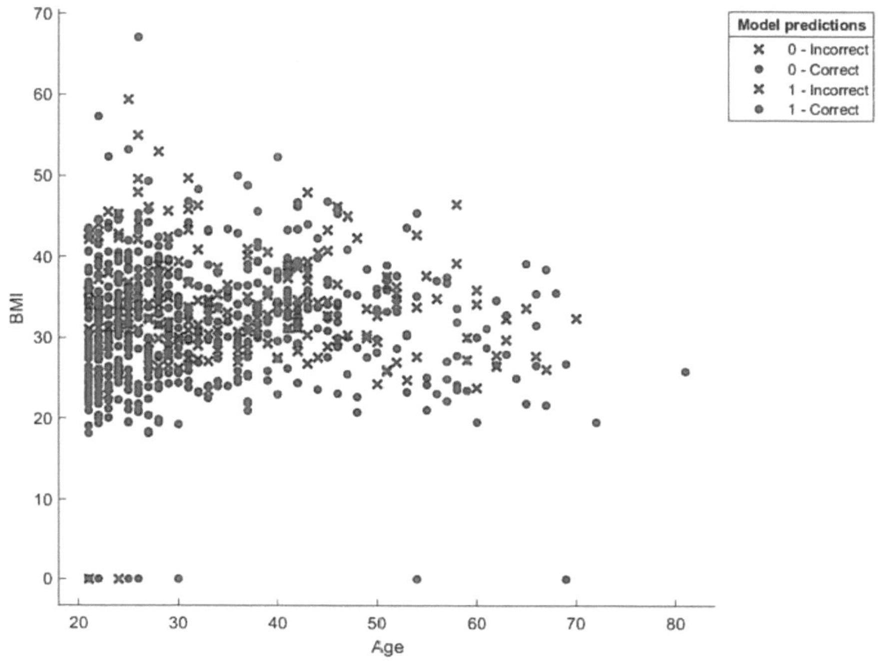

FIGURE 15.19 Decision Tree Model Predictions "Age" versus "BMI."

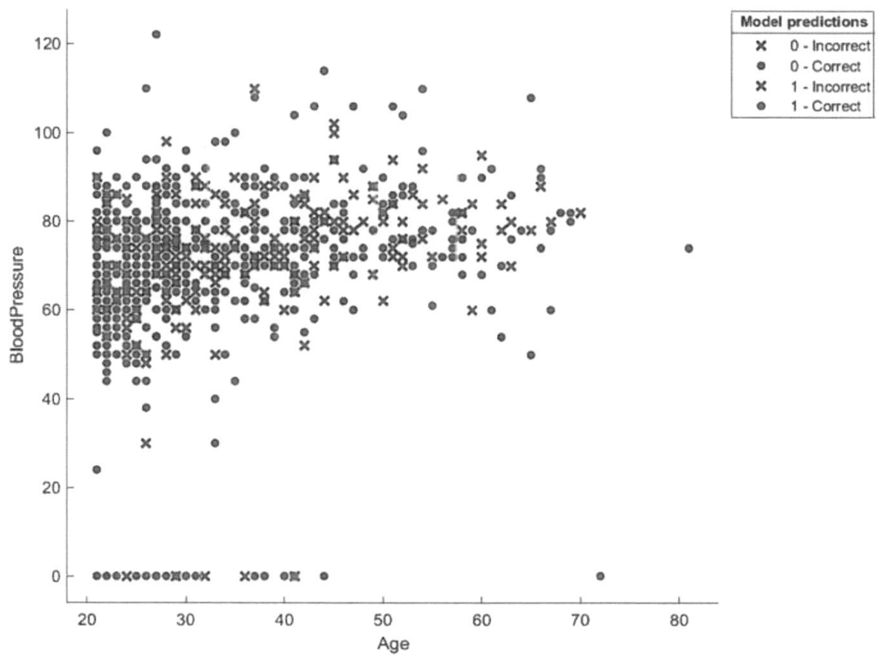

FIGURE 15.20 Decision tree model predictions "Age" versus "Blood Pressure."

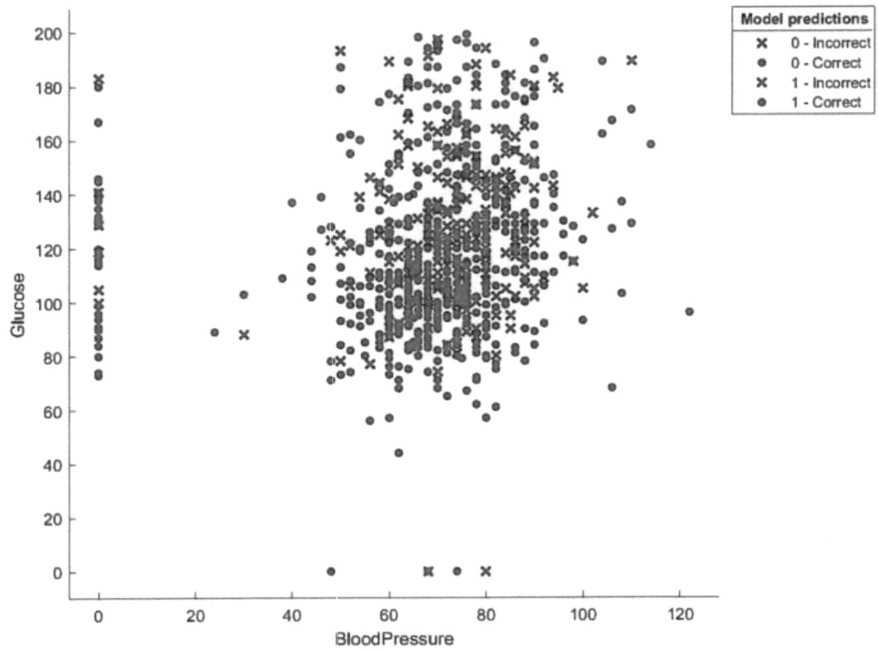

FIGURE 15.21 Decision tree model predictions "Blood Pressure" versus "Glucose."

As per decision tree results, the patients having glucose levels above 120 and blood pressure values between 50 and 115 are diabetic, whereas the patients whose glucose levels are below 115 are not diabetic. The results for 'age' and 'BMI' are somewhere similar to KNN. The females above age 25 and BMI above 25 are positive and females above age 35 and blood pressure values above 55 are also shown diabetic by ML Model, whereas females below age 25 are not diabetic.

3.1.3 Bagged trees

Random Forests first created by Ho (Ho, 1995) using the random subspace method (Ho, 1998) are the ensembling methods for classification and regression techniques. In random forest, for classification, the output of the random forest is the class selected by the most trees whereas, for regression techniques, the mean or average prediction of the individual trees is there. The Random forest applies the technique of Bootstrap aggregating, i.e., known as Bagging and aggregates the individual regression trees. In Bagging, for a training dataset $X = x_1, x_2 \ldots\ldots, x_n$ with response variable $Y = y_1, y_2, \ldots\ldots, y_n$, it selects random sample values of the training set and fits trees to these samples. In Bagging, predictions are performed by taking the average of the predictions from all the individual regression trees on x' samples as shown in Eq. (15.6).

$$\widehat{f} = \frac{1}{N}\sum_{b=1}^{N} f_b(x') \tag{15.6}$$

Here, f_b is the classification, and the regression trees trained on X_b training dataset with responses Y_b, bagging b for N number of times, and the majority vote is considered for classification (González, Garcí, Del Ser, Rokach, & Herrera, 2020).

The results of bagged tree for 30 learners are somewhere similar to decision trees and KNN. The females having a body mass index of nearly 30 and above age 20 have shown positive class results for diabetes and the females above age 28 and blood pressure values above 60 are showing signs of diabetes. The female patients below age 30 and blood pressure values from 40 to 85 are mainly nondiabetic. The glucose level predicted by the model for diabetic females is above 115 and the blood pressure value above 55. The results of the bagged trees for attributes 'Age' versus 'BMI' 'Age' versus 'Blood Pressure' and 'Blood Pressure' versus 'Glucose' are shown in Figs. 15.22−15.24.

The Confusion Matrix of all the three algorithms KNN, Decision Tree, and Bagged Trees implemented in the proposed work is shown in Table 15.4. The confusion matrix shows the number of observations, like True Positive (*tp*), False Positive (*fp*), True Negative (*tn*), and False Negative (*fn*). The performance metrics achieved by the ML Models, like

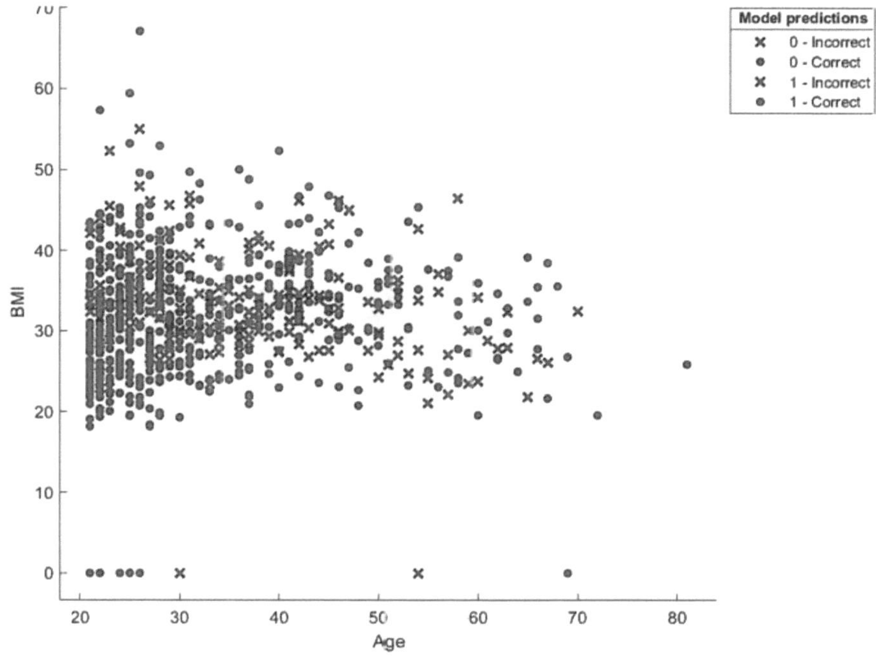

FIGURE 15.22 Bagged trees model predictions “Age” versus “BMI.”

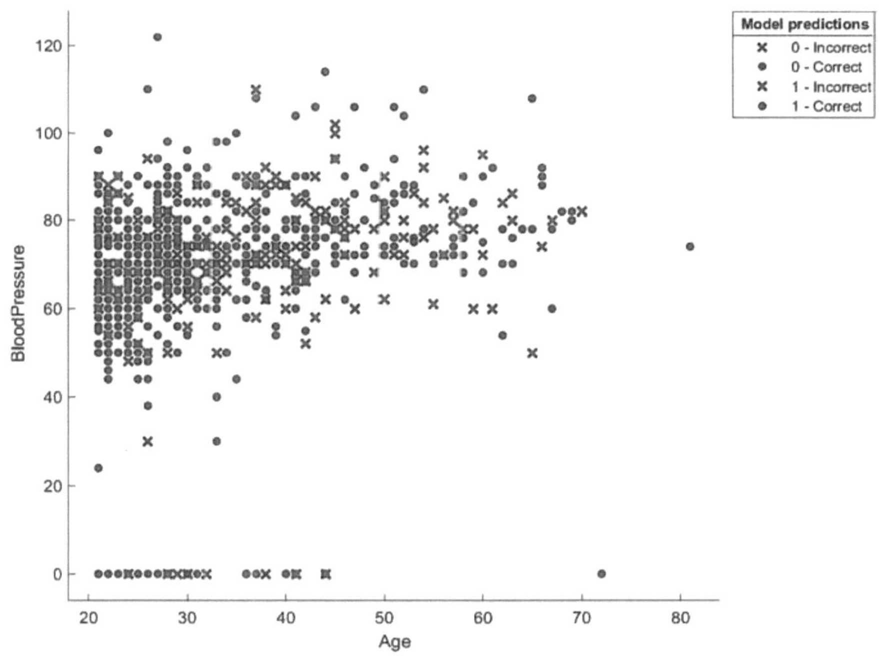

FIGURE 15.23 Bagged trees model predictions “Age” versus “Blood Pressure.”

Sensitivity, i.e., True Positive Rate, Specificity, i.e., True Negative Rate, Precision, Accuracy, False Positive Rate, False Negative Rate, etc., are shown in Table 15.5.

The highest sensitivity and specificity value achieved by ML models, i.e., decision tree is 61.2% and KNN is 89.2%. Sensitivity means that the model has correctly identified the female patients with diseases, i.e., diabetic, whereas specificity means the model has correctly identified the female patients without diabetes. The positive predictive value (*ppv*) of the KNN model is highest, i.e., 69.5% which is the probability of females’ tests truly with diseases, i.e., positive for diabetes

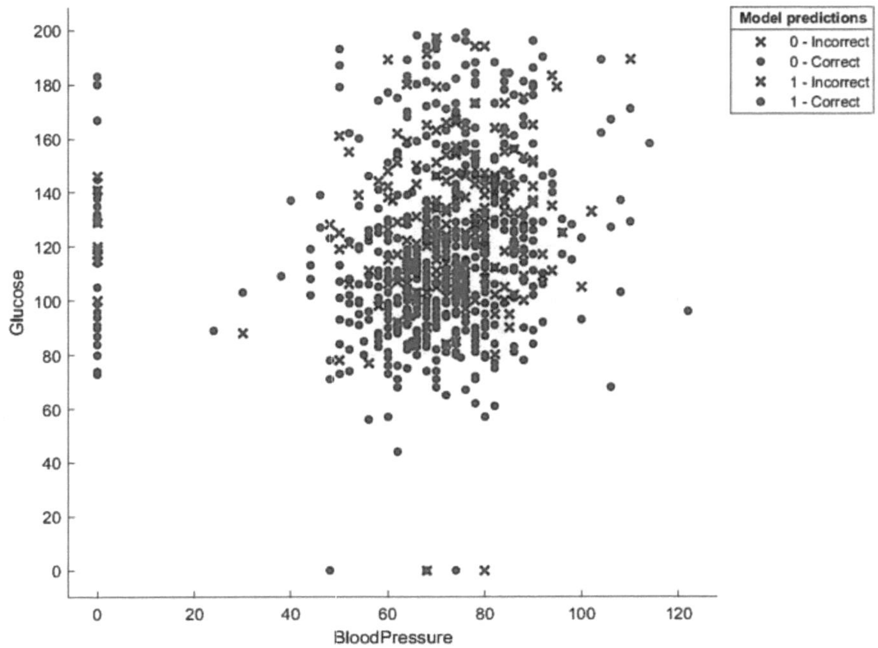

FIGURE 15.24 Bagged trees model predictions "Blood Pressure" versus "Glucose."

TABLE 15.4 Confusion matrix of ML classifiers.

Model	True negative (TN)	False negative (FN)	True positive (TP)	False positive (FP)
KNN	446	145	123	54
Decision tree	400	104	164	100
Bagged tree	424	116	152	76

TABLE 15.5 Performance metrics of machine learning models.

Model	Sensitivity or true positive rate or recall (tpr) (%)	Specificity or true negative rate (tnr) (%)	Positive predictive value or precision (ppv) (%)	Negative predictive value (npv) (%)	False positive rate (fpr) (%)	False negative rate (fnr) (%)	Accuracy (A)	Training time (sec)
Formula	tpr = tp/(tp + fn)	tnr = tn/(tn + fp)	ppv = tp/(tp + fp)	npv = tn/(tn + fn)	fpr = fp/(fp + tn)	fnr = fn/(fn + tp)	accuracy = (tp + tn) /(tp + tn + fp + fn)	
KNN	45.9	89.2	69.5	75.5	10.8	54.1	74.1	1.261
Decision tree	61.2	80	62.1	79.4	20	38.8	73.4	1.261
Bagged tree	56.7	84.8	66.7	78.5	15.2	43.3	75	3.343

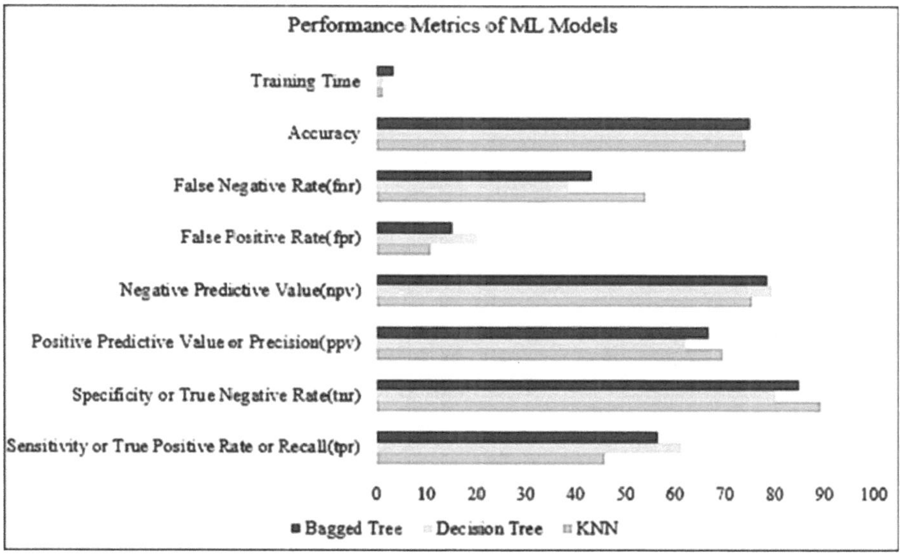

FIGURE 15.25 ML model metrics.

and negative predictive value (*npv*) of the decision tree is highest, i.e., 79.4% which is the probability of females' tests truly without diseases, i.e., negative. The performance metrics of ML Models shown in Table 15.5 are visualized in Fig. 15.25.

4. Conclusion

BDA and machine learning are emerging technologies with an effective presence in medicine. The confluence of both these technologies analyzes the healthcare data, provides personalized healthcare to patients, accurate diagnosis, prognosis, and makes effective decisions. BDA techniques are capable of analyzing a huge volume of data effectively in less time. In the proposed work, the data analysis is done using big data analytical techniques and their architectures are explored. Machine learning algorithms are implemented on the diabetic patients' dataset to attain predictive results. ML techniques are helpful for trend analysis related to personalized healthcare. BDA and ML techniques are being implemented in telemedicine and are blessings for patients who need immediate diagnosis at the doorstep. The work in this direction can further be explored on different datasets with a huge volume of data related to health to understand the trends and transform them into meaningful information for effective decision-making. The upcoming emerging areas like IoT, deep learning, and cloud computing can be explored along with BDA and machine learning to find new correlations from healthcare datasets to make better decisions in the service of society with these latest technologies. The abbreviations for this chapter are listed in Table 15.6.

TABLE 15.6 Abbreviations.

BDA	Big data Analytics
BMI	Body Mass Index
CART	Classification and Regression Trees
CLI	Command Line Interface
CT	Computerized Tomography
CQL	Cassandra Query Language
DDL	Data Definition Language
DML	Data Manipulation Language

Continued

TABLE 15.6 Abbreviations.—cont'd

EHR	Electronic Health Record
EMR	Electronic Medical Record
ETL	Extract, Transform, and Load
HDFS	Hadoop Distributed File System
FP	False Positive
FN	False Negative
FPR	False Positive Rate
FNR	False Negative Rate
HIVEQL	Hive Query Language
IoT	Internet of Things
JDBC	Java Database Connectivity
JSON	JavaScript Object Notations
KNN	K-Nearest Neighbor
ML	Machine Learning
MRI	Magnetic Resonance Imaging
NPV	Negative Predictive Value
ODBC	Open Database Connectivity
PPV	Positive Predictive Value
RDD	Resilient Distributed Datasets
RDBMS	Relational Database Management System
SQL	Structured Query Language
TN	True Negative
TPR	True Positive Rate
TNR	True Negative Rate
TP	True Positive
YARN	Yet Another Resource Negotiator

References

Bhardwaj, A., Kumar, A., Narayan, Y., & Kumar, P. (2015). Big data emerging technologies: A casestudy with analyzing twitter data using Apache hive. In *2015 2nd international conference on recent advances in engineering & computational sciences (RAECS)* (pp. 1–6). IEEE.

Chebotko, A., Kashlev, A., & Lu, S. (2015). A big data modeling methodology for Apache Cassandra. In *2015 IEEE international congress on big data* (pp. 238–245). IEEE.

Chen, C. P., & Zhang, C. Y. (2014). Data-intensive applications, challenges, techniques and technologies: a survey on big data. *Information Sciences, 275*, 314–347.

Chrimes, D., & Zamani, H. (2017). *Using distributed data over HBase in big data analytics platform for clinical services. Computational and mathematical methods in medicine*, 2017.

Cottle, M., Hoover, W., Kanwal, S., Kohn, M., Strome, T., & Treister, N. (2013). *Transforming Health Care through Big Data Strategies for leveraging big data in the health care industry*. Institute for Health Technology Transformation. http://ihealthtran.com/big-data-in-healthcare.

Dash, S., Shakyawar, S. K., Sharma, M., & Kaushik, S. (2019). Big data in healthcare: Management, analysis and future prospects. *Journal of Big Data, 6*(1), 1–25.

Galetsi, P., & Katsaliaki, K. (2020). A review of the literature on big data analytics in healthcare. *Journal of the Operational Research Society, 71*(10), 1511–1529.

González, S., García, S., Del Ser, J., Rokach, L., & Herrera, F. (2020). A practical tutorial on bagging and boosting based ensembles for machine learning: Algorithms, software tools, performance study, practical perspectives and opportunities. *Information Fusion, 64*, 205–237.

Ho, Tin Kam (1995). Random decision forests (PDF). In *Proceedings of the 3rd international conference on document analysis and recognition, montreal, QC, 14–16 august 1995* (pp. 278–282). Archived from the original (PDF) on 17 April 2016. Retrieved 5 June 2016.

Ho, T. K. (1998). "The random subspace method for constructing decision forests" (PDF). *IEEE Transactions on Pattern Analysis and Machine Intelligence, 20*(8), 832–844. https://doi.org/10.1109/34.709601

https://archive.ics.uci.edu/ml/datasets/Early%20stage%20diabetes%20risk%20prediction%20dataset.

https://www.kaggle.com/uciml/pima-indians-diabetes-database.

Hu, L. Y., Huang, M. W., Ke, S. W., & Tsai, C. F. (2016). The distance function effect on k-nearest neighbor classification for medical datasets. *SpringerPlus, 5*(1), 1–9.

Junqueira, F., & Reed, B. (2013). *ZooKeeper: Distributed process coordination*. O'Reilly Media, Inc.

Khemphila, A., & Boonjing, V. (2010). Comparing performances of logistic regression, decision trees, and neural networks for classifying heart disease patients. In *2010 international conference on computer information systems and industrial management applications (CISIM)* (pp. 193–198). IEEE.

Maulud, D., & Abdulazeez, A. M. (2020). A review on linear regression comprehensive in machine learning. *Journal of Applied Science and Technology Trends, 1*(4), 140–147.

Murphy, G. F., Hanken, A. M., & Waters, K. A. (Eds.). (1999). *Electronic health records: Changing the vision*. WB Saunders Company.

Raghupathi, W., & Raghupathi, V. (2014a). Big data analytics in healthcare: Promise and potential. *Health Information Science and Systems, 2*(1), 1–10.

Raghupathi, W., & Raghupathi, V. (2014b). Big data analytics in healthcare: Promise and potential. *Health Information Science and Systems, 2*(1), 1–10.

Reisman, M. (2017). EHRs: The challenge of making electronic data useable and interoperable. *Pharmacy and Therapeutics, 42*(9), 572.

Ritter, F., Boskamp, T., Homeyer, A., Laue, H., Schwier, M., Link, F., & Peitgen, H. O. (2011). Medical image analysis. *IEEE pulse, 2*(6), 60–70.

Rokach, L., & Maimon, O. (2005a). Decision trees. In *Data mining and knowledge discovery handbook* (pp. 165–192). Boston, MA: Springer.

Rokach, L., & Maimon, O. (2005b). Top-down induction of decision trees classifiers-a survey. *IEEE Transactions on Systems, Man, and Cybernetics, Part C (Applications and Reviews), 35*(4), 476–487.

Salloum, S., Dautov, R., Chen, X., Peng, P. X., & Huang, J. Z. (2016). Big data analytics on Apache Spark. *International Journal of Data Science and Analytics, 1*(3), 145–164.

Seibert, J. A. (2009). Modalities and data acquisition. In *Practical imaging informatics* (pp. 49–66). New York, NY: Springer.

Tangirala, S. (2020). Evaluating the impact of GINI index and information gain on classification using decision tree classifier algorithm. *International Journal of Advanced Computer Science and Applications, 11*(2), 612–619.

Wang, G., Gunasekaran, A., Ngai, E. W., & Papadopoulos, T. (2016). Big data analytics in logistics and supply chain management: Certain investigations for research and applications. *International Journal of Production Economics, 176*, 98–110.

Chapter 16

Skin cancer prediction using big data analytics and AI techniques

Piyush Kumar[1], Rishi Chauhan[1], Radhika Goyal[1], Nishi Bhati[2], Shubham Garg[1] and Shuchi Mala[1]
[1]*Amity University, Department of Computer Science and Engineering, Noida, Uttar Pradesh, India;* [2]*Zuora, Chennai, Tamil Nadu, India*

1. Introduction

In this 21st century, every human being is circumvented by multiple kinds of information. In other words, it can be said that, "every living person on this planet is surrounded by big data." The term big data, as spoken, consists of two words, "big" and "data." Data is a piece of information that gives useful insights. Big data is basically data which is huge in number. Earlier data were stored in terms of numerical values and names. But today, there are numerous types of data. The domain of data types has increased over the years and is continuously becoming huge. Today, every small activty which is done by human, can be used as data. Thus, it is not wrong to say that every action of a human being is a huge data source itself.

If the data are in the form of a web page, then the average size of a webpage can lie between 1.6 and 2 MB. An e-book, with 250−300 pages, average size is 1−5 MB, while a size of a song may be between 3.5 and 5.8 MB and so on (Wu et al., 2016). The mankind is still not aware about the size of the big data. It is said that every minute American people generate almost three million internet traffic alone, while Asia accounts for the majority of internet users with approximately 2 billion users in 2021 (Key Internet Statistics to know in 2021 include Mobile, 2021). Keeping internet traffic as a measure, the volume of big data could lie between terabyte, i.e., 10^{12} to zettabyte, i.e., 10^{21} in range (Wu et al., 2016). Thus, the volume of big data is not yet defined.

The core objective of the chapter is to predict skin cancer using both big data analytics and artificial intelligence (AI) techniques. There are four models which have been proposed in this chapter, out of which three are trained using the pretrained models by applying state-of-the-art algorithms.

1.1 Dimensions of big data

Most often, dimensions of 3Vs. These Vs were given by Gartner and are also termed as Gartner's interpretation. These Vs include volume, variety, and velocity (Wu et al., 2016). Fig. 16.1 represents the 3Vs of big data.

1. Volume means that the data should be in huge amounts, like in petabytes, or terabytes.
2. Variety, the data should be in different data structures or formats.
3. Velocity means at what pace the data are being collected and used.

IBM, on the other hand, added another dimension to the 3V, making it 4V. The term IBM introduced was "veracity" (Wu et al., 2016). It can be seen in Fig. 16.2.

1. Volume means size of the data.
2. Variety means data in a different format.
3. Velocity means at what pace the data are being collected.
4. Veracity shows the uncertainty of data.

Big Data Analytics for Healthcare. https://doi.org/10.1016/B978-0-323-91907-4.00011-X

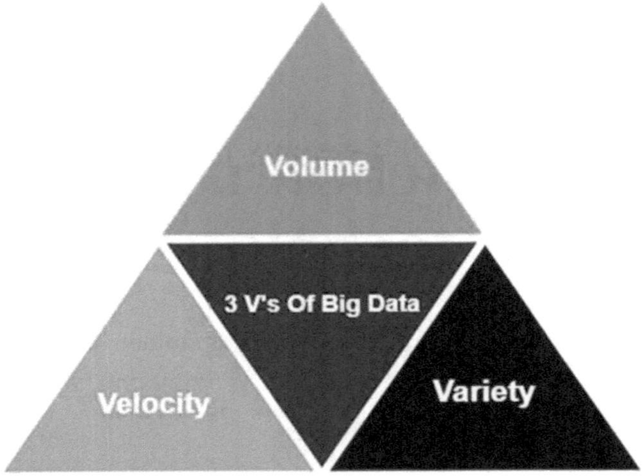

FIGURE 16.1 Represents the 3Vs of big data proposed by Gartner.

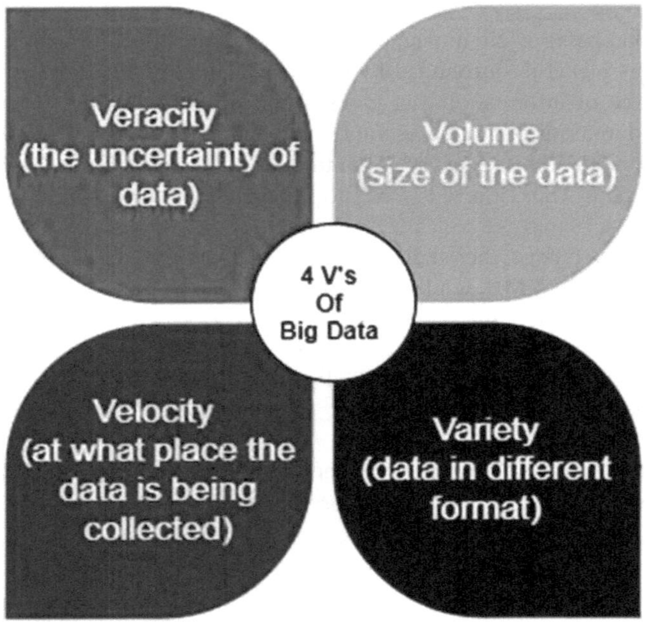

FIGURE 16.2 Represents the 4Vs of big data.

Moreover, Microsoft, for the sake of business purposes, introduced two more different attributes of big data, thus making it 6Vs (Wu et al., 2016). These were variability and visibility. Fig. 16.3 represents the 6Vs proposed by Microsoft.

1. Volume means size of the data.
2. Variety means data in a different format.
3. Velocity means at what pace the data are being collected.
4. Veracity shows the uncertainty of data.
5. Variability is defined as the complexity of the dataset.
6. Visibility refers to a clear image of data to make a decision.

Currently, there are more than 6Vs of big data. They can be either 9Vs or 11Vs and so on. Thus, big data may be described as data that is voluminous, complex, which is continuously growing at an exponential rate, thus making it difficult to store, that can be managed efficiently, processed and analyzed using traditional methods.

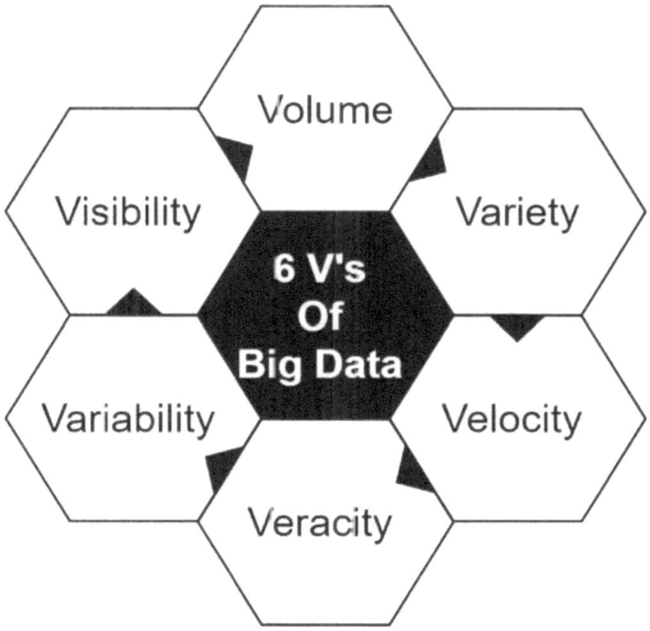

FIGURE 16.3 Represents the 6Vs of big data.

1.2 Types of big data

Big data is widely classified in three different forms (Types of Big Data, 2016). These can be seen in Fig. 16.4.

a. **Structured data**: The type of data which is already stored in the databases. It can be said that all the previously recorded data can be termed as structural data. As said earlier, every activity or action of a human being can be used as data. Thus, humans are a source of structured data. Every click made on the internet, the GPS data, feeding personal details on a website, etc., can be used as structured data.
b. **Semi-structured data**: The semi-structured data are those which are not traditionally stored in a database but can provide properties which make it easier to process. There is a very thin line between semi-structured and unstructured data. Most of the semi-structured data are based on RDF and XML.
c. **Unstructured data**: The unstructured data do not have a clear format of data but constitute about 80% of the total data stored. Most of the data are unstructured. The source of this type of data can be either machine generated or human generated. Most of the social media data, mobile data, and website content are unstructured in nature. These also include the videos people watch on YouTube, the pictures they upload on Facebook and Instagram, etc.

1.3 Big data analytics

Big data analytics can be applied using machine learning (ML) algorithms and AI. Over the years, there have been subsequent advancements in ML and AI. ML and AI together have resolved most human problems and eased life. But there still remains the potential to grow. With the assistance of ML and AI, the machine is able to train itself and give accurate results, thus becoming knowledgeable. Big data analytics is incomplete without ML or AI. The framework of big data supports the ML processes. Thus, ML is the root of big data analytics.

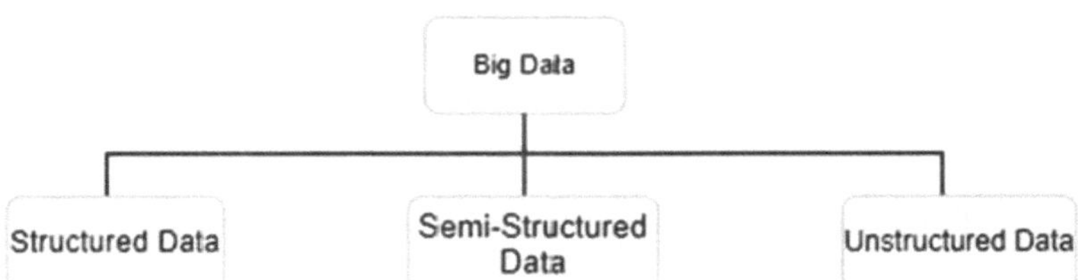

FIGURE 16.4 Represents the types of big data.

1.4 Platforms of big data analytics

Over the years, there have been numerous platforms to perform big data analytics and analyze the predictions made out of it.

2. Hadoop

Hadoop is the most common platform to perform big data analytics. The platform is designed using Java and it is linearly scalable and fault tolerant. Most of the data analysts prefer to use Hadoop. Moreover, Hadoop is good if the dataset is diversified in nature and it can store huge amounts of data in tens of TB. The objective of the Hadoop framework is to influence the commodity hardware for multiscale workload processing. The platform is open source in nature (Wu et al., 2016). There are different modules of the Hadoop framework. These include (Ishwarappa & Anuradha, 2015):

I. Hadoop distributed file system (HDFS) generally delivers high-throughput access to the application. It works on the principle of a master/slave structure where multiple devices or slave devices are controlled by one master's computer.
II. Hadoop Yarn/MapReduce is basically used for job scheduling and resource management. It processes a large amount of data in a distributed as well as parallel environment in a cluster.
III. HBase is a database that is scalable in nature and for the storage purpose of large tables, structured data storage is supported. It also allows transactional capabilities, thus providing features like UPDATES, INSERT, DELETION, etc. It allows real-time read and write access to big data.
IV. Pig is a high-level data-flow language and execution framework for parallel computation. It is basically a scripting language that provides the users writing complex MapReduce transformations. Pig is used for writing scripts for summarizing, sorting, joining, aggregation, etc.
V. Hive is a data warehouse that provides summarization and ad-hoc querying. HiveQL is a query language used to summarize, manage, write queries, and analyze datasets for tens of terabytes of data.
VI. Zookeeper provides operational services in the Hadoop framework. Thus, it is a coordination service for distributed systems or HDFS.

3. Spark

Spark is a fast computer engine for big data. It provides graphical computations, ML, and system processes like applications. It is faster than Hadoop MapReduce (Ishwarappa & Anuradha, 2015). Even Spark provides an application programming interface (API) which can directly be used in a python notebook using SparkMLib for classification and performance and scalability.

The Spark streaming is an extension of the Spark framework used for real-time analysis and processing with high-throughput, fault tolerant processing of live data. It generates a Dstream or discretized stream as a continuous stream of data. Dstream is nothing but represented as an RDD or resilient distributed database. It receives live input from a receiver and divides the data into microbatches. The Dstreams can be emitted straightway from the input data source or by passing RDDs from other Dstream outputs (Milosevic et al., 2016).

There are various other tools for big data analytics. These are Microsoft HDInsight, Skytree, Improvado, Xplenty, IBM SPSS Modeler, etc. (10 Best Data Analytics Tools for Big Data Analysis (2021), 2021).

Applications of big data in healthcare and medicine

Healthcare and medicine are another discipline after social media, finance, and business, where big data analytics has shown great impact. Today, the trend is Internet-of-Things (IOTs) and wearable devices. Hence, nowadays, collecting medical data using devices has become easier. Smartphones, health tracking apps, and smartwatches have made personal data collection smooth (Bora, 2019). With the assistance of IoT devices, one can even keep track of mental illness. Humans are aware of mental illness where there hasn't been any specific treatment. Thus, this part of the healthcare industry also needs attention (Kumar et al., 2021). Mental illness is treated in closed rooms and inmate level of care. Due to long-lasting care in a significant number of patients, the quantity of data available is huge. Moreover, secondary data generated from organizational databases are also a benefit to mental health. Electronic medical records (EMRs) are used by most of the psychiatrists and healthcare departments to organize records (Gonçalves-Pinho & Freitas, 2021).

With the advancement in technology and IoT devices, telepsychiatry can also be conducted using video calls, phone calls, etc. Long-distance patients and patients living in low-income countries who cannot afford psychiatrists can have telepsychiatry to get treatment. Traditional deep learning and ML algorithms like SVM, random forest, k-NN, etc., can be applied to the big data to perform analytics (Kumar et al., 2021; Wang & Alexander, 2021, pp. 35–49).

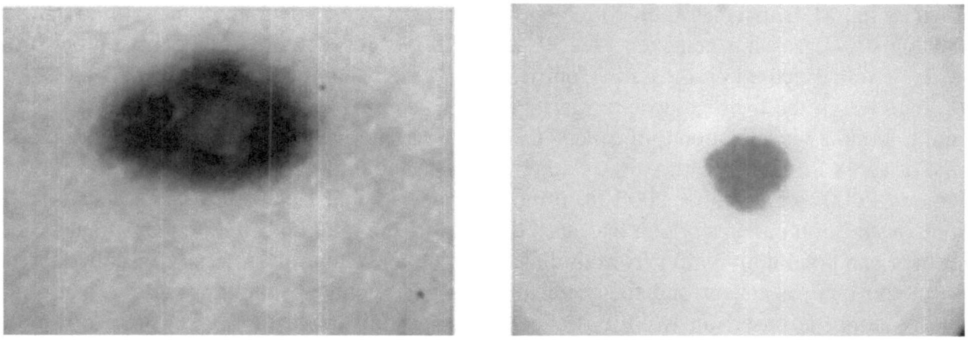

FIGURE 16.5 Skin cancer lesions having multiple color spots on the patient's skin. *Source: (Rotemberg et al., 2021).*

Medical images are produced in bulk and very delicate in nature as doctors make appropriate decisions based on those images. Proper predictions of the disease need a comprehensive approach for better perception of the disease state. Logical Observation Identifiers Names and Codes (LOINC) is a database source and universal standard for identifying medical laboratory observations which produce structural healthcare data. The pathology reports, doctors' prescriptions, and radiology reports can be considered as unstructured data.

Different types of medical images include computed tomography (CT), magnetic resource imaging (MRI), molecular imaging, photoacoustic imaging, etc. Hence, the medicinal image processing paradigm has a huge role in determining accurate and effective big data analysis (Bora, 2019).

Skin cancer is one such domain of disease which produces a huge number of medical images for analysis. Skin cancer occurs due to abnormal growth of skin cells. There are mainly two types of skin cancer. These include melanoma and nonmelanoma. Nonmelanoma is subdivided into basal cell carcinoma (BCC) and squamous cell carcinoma (SCC). Melanoma is the deadliest skin cancer among all other types. When a person suffers from melanoma, the pigment cells of the skin change. This produces *melanin* pigment which can be of multiple colors. The pigment grows continuously and the borders are irregular in nature. The crux of skin cancer is to be detected at an early stage so that it can be prevented before it spreads all over the body (Senan & Jadhav, 2021). There are approximately 5.4 million new cases of skin cancer every year. This statistic stands alone for the USA. Further, mortality is expected to increase by the end of this decade. If diagnosed during later stages, the survival rate is 14% or less (Kadampur & Al Riyaee, 2020). The global diagnostic imaging market was predicted to achieve or so 36.43 Billion USD in 2021 as of 26.53 Billion USD during 2016, at a pace of growth of 6.6% (Rastogi et al., 2018). Fig. 16.5 displayed below shows skin cancer images. The affected skin gets either red, purple, or brown.

Traditional methods to detect melanoma are through the ABCD rule, where A stands for asymmetry, B for border, C for color, and D for diameter. The detection of nonmelanoma cancer like BCC is done mostly through sonography and confocal microscopy. Optical coherence tomography is mostly done to detect SCC. Hence, the objective of this chapter is to compare the different receiver operating characteristic (ROC) curve of different models which predicts melanoma disease.

The rest of the chapter is prepared as follows: A review of previous related works, and motivations are presented in Section 2. A full-fledged explanation of methodology dataset, preprocessing steps, models applied during the research work is intended in Section 3, followed by a few results and discussion of relative studies in Section 4, and lastly, conclusive studies in Section 5.

4. Literature review

Researchers used a hybrid approach for computing in the cloud for skin cancer detection (Richter & Khoshgoftaar, 2019). Their approach can be broadly divided into distributed and nondistributed systems. They used a distributed approach for preprocessing and tagging the input using Apache Spark and a nondistributed approach for training various algorithms like random forest, logistic regression, and XGBoost using scikit-learn. The dataset used in this study was Modernizing Analytics for Melanoma (MAMEL) dataset. The dataset contains over a hundred thousand structured data points from over 4,000000 patients. Out of over four million patients, only 10,129 were there who were diagnosed with melanoma. The researchers used Amazon Web Services (AWS) for their work. They used services like the AWS Hadoop Cluster and Apache Spark engine for data preprocessing which was then stored as a sparse matrix for further computation. The best accuracy was shown by the XGBoost classifier, which was about 79.91% on a dataset of one million dataset samples, while random forest and logistic regression achieved 74.15% and 76.51%, respectively. XGBoost outperforms the other two classifiers even when it was executed on the entire four million datasets, having an accuracy of 79.88%, while for random forest and logistic regression, the average accuracy was 69.49% and 76.17%, respectively.

The authors aim to build a visualization tool called "Cancer Associations Map Animation" tool to map and compute the relation of nine major types of cancer with various other diseases (Iqbal et al., 2016). The dataset used for this tool was collected from January 2000 to December 2002 from the Taiwan National Health Insurance Database. The dataset contained data of about 782 million patients which was used to compute the relation between the patient's medical history and the type of cancer they can potentially suffer from in the coming years. The tool can easily visualize the above-mentioned relationship between the type of cancer and the medical history of a patient among people of various age groups and gender. The proposed study is based on two steps. Firstly, the establishment of the "Disease to Disease Association" database, and secondly, visualization of the computed association between diseases. The dataset consisted of 9.73 million males and 10.29 million females, respectively. The study covers nine major types of cancer, i.e., prostate cancer, breast cancer, lung cancer, liver cancer, stomach cancer, colorectal cancer, rectum rectosigmoid junction cancer, skin cancer, and cervical cancer.

The authors proposed a framework to use the IoMT technology to remotely monitor the health of elderly people across 12 different types of physical activities (Syed et al., 2019). The dataset used to train the proposed model was the MHEALTH big dataset. The dataset consists of data tracking 12 different physical activities. Namely, knee bending, sitting, cycling, lying down, climbing stairs, jogging, standing still, frontal elevation of arms, running, walking, and relaxing, waist bends forward and jumping front and back. The 12 mentioned activities were performed by 10 individuals who wore three sensors on each on them. The proposed model consisted of three major layers, i.e., first, perception layer; second, integrated cloud layer; third, the data analysis and visualization layer. The sensors were placed on the chest, right wrist, and left ankle to efficiently measure the movement experienced by different body parts. The authors used the AWS cloud for their study and huge amounts of data were processed with the help of Hadoop MapReduce. The complete dataset was divided in into a 70:30 ratio, out of which 70% was used for training and 30% for testing. A multidimensional Naïve Bayes is used on the training data. The study was conducted on 33,629 records extracted from the MHEALTH dataset and the model performed quite well with a classification accuracy of 97.1%. Compared to other models like the authors mentioned in previous works, the multidimensional Naïve Bayes performed far better than any other algorithm and classified all the 10 out of 12 activities with minimal to no confusion and returned relevant predictions.

The authors used both spectral and spatial techniques to boost the predictions made by convolutional neural networks (CNNs) or ConvNet in their study (Pölönen et al., 2019). The authors compared five different types of ConvNet architectures for the purpose of skin cancer detection. The dataset used in the study consisted of 61 hyperspectral images. For each image, annotated areas were defined, which were either lesions, healthy skin, or a marker. For training purposes, from each image's annotated areas, 1000 data points were selected. The researchers experimented with three different types of ConvNet learning structures, namely 1D CovNet, 2D ConvNet, and 3D ConvNet. The models achieved some very good results as all 15 melanoma patients were classified correctly using the 2D and 1D architecture. The 3D and the other two combinations were also able to identify 14 out of 15 melanoma cases correctly.

The authors have used big data analytics to analyze biomedical images in their study (Tchagna Kouanou et al., 2018). The paper has a comprehensive outline of big data analytics to understand the data, to sort the data, and to analyze the data. Two popular technologies of big data analytics, i.e., Hadoop and spark, are very efficient for biomedical images. In this paper, the researchers have proposed a roadmap using big data analytics tools for the management and analysis of biomedical images. The authors have used both popular techniques in this paper. As a result, the spark framework is the most thorough framework in terms of accuracy, simplicity, efficiency, etc. The embedded libraries in spark make it stand out among all. Spark architecture also supports in developing efficient and organized methods, and this power helps it to grasp classification of large numbers of images.

The researchers have focused on the three main domains of healthcare (Raj et al., 2019). The three domains are imaging, genomics, and electronic health records (EHRs). In the imaging domain, they have used algorithms like CNN, U-Net, V-Net, transfer learning, etc. In the second domain, genomics, the authors have used algorithms like DEEP, predictive enhancers with deep learning algorithms (PEDLAs), etc. Finally, in the third domain, i.e., EHRs, the researchers have used neural networks like CNN, recurrent neural network, etc. They concluded that, convolutional networks perform well in the image dataset and on the temporal component, long short-term memory (LSTM) and gated recurrent units perform very well in the data.

A study is conducted by researcher in which the main motive is to make the data analytics process less time-consuming and smooth (Peneti et al., 2021). A patient can easily upload a picture of the affected skin cancer area and can get prescriptions online only. In this paper the authors used the dataset which contains about 3000 skin cancer images. The authors have used the Keras model of python which helps to upload the dataset, preprocess the data, i.e., build the model, perform data augmentation, train the model, etc. The K-means algorithm has been used in this paper and the researchers have also built the 2D conventional neural network layer.

The authors have predicted infectious diseases with the help of the optimization of parameters using deep learning algorithms in their study (Chae et al., 2018). In this paper, the authors have used four learning models, i.e., deep neural network (DNN), LSTM, autoregressive integrated moving average (ARIMA), and ordinary least squares (OLSs). Data were collected on a daily basis for 576 days. Between the researchers started collecting data from January 1, 2016 to July 29, 2017. Three major diseases, i.e., chickenpox, scarlet fever, and malaria were used in case datasets. When the proposed models were applied on the dataset, then the deep learning models, like DNN and LSTM, outperformed the ARIMA and OLS models in every infectious disease scenario. On an average, the DNN model had the leading performance among all. On the contrary, when the infectious disease was spreading, LSTM made more precise predictions. In addition to that, the authors found one more characteristic of DNN and LSTM is that the DNN model has smaller values as compared to LSTM.

In another study, the authors proposed classification of images using a deep learning framework (Ashraf et al., 2020). In this paper, the authors have used publicly available datasets containing different classes of human body parts. There were 12 different classes out of which the dataset of 11 classes were taken from the publicly available dataset and the remaining one was taken from Messidor for knee images. The dataset has a total of 3600 images, each class has 300 images. For each class, 210 images were used for training proposals and 90 images for testing purposes. They have used pretrained deep network to classify the images. For classification, the authors have used deep CNNs. In the end, fine-tuning was applied to the models to increase accuracy. As a result, prostate cancer and brain cancer was detected with 100% accuracy followed by chest cancer, breast cancer, pancreas cancer, colon cancer, soft tissue cancer, and esophagus cancer as 99.9%, 98.8%, 99.8%, 97.8%, 98.6%, and 99.4%, respectively. The execution time of the proposed method is 682 min 10 s.

5. Methodology

For prediction of skin cancer, state of the algorithms and deep learning models have been used. The deep learning models include transfer learning algorithms like VGG19, MobileNet SSD, InceptionResNetV2, etc. Apart from this, a newly designed MelCONVO2d CNN is being proposed in this chapter which is able to predict cancer accurately. The complete workflow for this chapter is as follows and is represented in Fig. 16.6.

1. **Data acquisition**: The dataset was extracted from the International Skin Imaging Collaboration (ISIC) archive. It is used to facilitate the application of digital skin imaging to assist in reducing melanoma mortality. The objective of ISIC is to achieve certain goals by developing and promoting digital skin imaging and by appealing to the dermatology and computer science communities toward better-quality diagnostics.
2. **Data preprocessing**: The metadata for both train and test data was cleaned by removing null values from the dataset. The dataset was biased toward benign class; hence a sample dataset of 1000 was taken initially. One hot-encoding was also done and dummies were created wherever necessary. PySpark was used during the preprocessing step. The API for Apache spark was installed using pip install Pyspark and then the spark was in the background.
3. **Data visualization**: The cleaned data were used to perform visualization, which is mentioned in detail in the results and discussion section. The visualization provided quite insightful information of the skin cancer patients.
4. **Image resizing**: Since the dataset is image data, the images are of multiple sizes. Hence, based on the ease of modeling, the images were resized. The common size of images that were taken into consideration is 75 × 75, 256 × 256, etc.
5. **Model training**: Various models were trained, like VGG19, MobileNet SSD, InceptionResNetV2, etc. This is discussed in detail below.

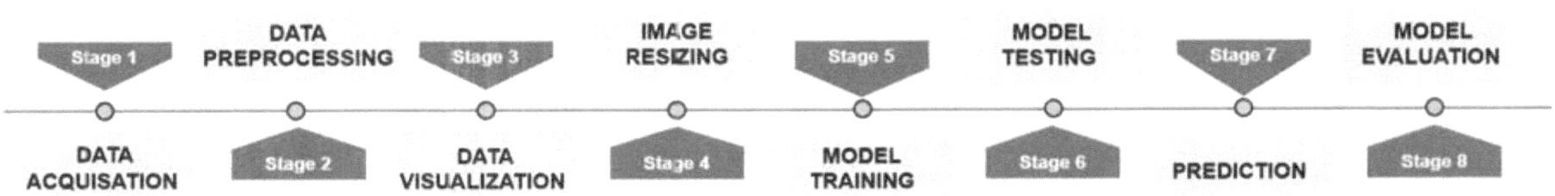

FIGURE 16.6 Represents the complete workflow of this chapter.

6. **Model testing**: Model testing was done based on the training of models. Accuracy was taken as the metrics to test the model.
7. **Prediction**: Prediction of skin cancer was made based on the testing data models.
8. **Evaluation**: The model was evaluated at the end; the ROC curve of all models was plotted and compared at the end.

5.1 Dataset

The dataset used for predicting skin cancer in this chapter is taken from the ISIC-2020 challenge. The dataset contains both images[3] and metadata. In total, there are 44,000 dermoscopic images of benign and malignant for over 2000 patients. The dataset is divided into trains and tests, where around 33,126 images are there in the train and 11,000 images are there for the test. All malignant diagnoses have been confirmed via histopathology, and benign diagnoses have been confirmed using either expert agreement, longitudinal follow-up, or histopathology (Rotemberg et al., 2021).

5.2 Device/platform used

Multiple devices and platforms were used for the prediction of skin cancer as follows:

1. ASUS—ROG Zephyrus G15, 15.6″ 165 Hz. WQHD gaming laptop with AMD Ryzen—9 of 16 GB memory with NVIDIA GeForce RTX 3070 and 1 TB SSD.
2. HP—Pavilion gaming laptop 15-ec0xxx with AMD Ryzen 5 3350H Radeon Vega Mobile Gfx microprocessor and 8 GB of RAM NVIDIA GeForce GTX 1050 was used.

Jupyter notebook and Google Collaboratory Pro were used as a platform to run the models, train the models, and predict kinds of skin cancer.

5.3 Techniques/models/algorithms

In this section, different models, algorithms, and techniques are discussed in detail which are used for making predictions of skin cancer detections.

5.4 Logistic regression

A simple logistic regression uses a sigmoid function. If the dataset contains values belonging to categories, like, Yes or No, or whether the cancer is benign or malignant, in that case, logistic regression is preferred. The value ranges between 0 and 1 only (Swaminathan, 2018) as shown in eq. 16.1.

$$sig(x) = \frac{1}{1 + e^{-x}} \tag{16.1}$$

The logistic regression can be either binary, multinominal, or ordinal type. In this chapter, binary logistic regression is used as the dataset had only two outcomes, i.e., benign or malignant.

5.5 Support vector machine

Support vector machine (SVM) is slightly different from logistic regression. In SVM, the purpose is to find a hyperplane with N-dimensional features. Unlike logistic regression, SVM can also be used for both multiclass and binary class predictions. If there are x feature vectors that represent unique points in space, then (Gandhi, 2018):

$$x \in R^d \tag{16.2}$$

where d is the dimension and Rd is the vector space as shown in eq. 16.2. For a hyperplane on a 2D plane, the equation is mentioned at 16.3 (Kunchhal, 2020):

$$H: w^T x + C = 0 \tag{16.3}$$

where C is the intercept of line. In this chapter, since the dataset is binary, linear SVM is used.

3. https://challenge2020.isic-archive.com/.

5.6 Gradient boosting

Gradient boosting is done for converting weak learning parameters to strong learning parameters. Each tree becomes a modified version of the original dataset. Gradient boosting trains the models in a steady, preservative, and chronological manner. Hence, this was applied to make better predictions (Singh, 2018).

A model with the combination of logistic regression, SVM, and gradient boosting was made to evaluate skin cancer. It is shown in Fig. 16.7.

5.7 VGG19

Unlike other models, VGG19 is also a traditional CNN model used to classify images. The model size is 549 MB. The top accuracy of the model ranges from 71.3% to 90% when the model was trained over on an ImageNet validation dataset. The model has 143 million parameters with a depth of 26 layers. The convolutional layers are of kernel 3 × 3 with a stride size of 1 pixel. Spatial padding is done to preserve the spatial resolution of the image. Between the layers, max pooling is performed over 2 × 2-pixel window with a stride size of 2. Followed by rectified linear unit (ReLU) layers to make classification quality better and improve computational time. In the end, three fully connected layers, FCN, were applied with the first two layers of size 4096 and the last layer with 1000 channels was made, followed by the final layer of SoftMax function (Keras Applications, n.d.; Understanding the VGG19 Architecture, n.d.).

In this model, extra layers are added to the VGG19 model. Fig. 16.8 represents the new architecture using the VGG19 model. The last layer in the VGG19 model, global average pooling 2D, is added and feeds them into a dropout layer with a rate of 0.5. This layer is then connected with a fully connected layer. FCN or dense layer, of stride 1 and activation function as Sigmoid.

5.8 InceptionResNetV2

InceptionResNetV2 is a pretrained deep learning CNN architecture. It is pretrained on a humongous set of images from the ImageNet dataset. It can classify images into a 1000 classes, such as elephant, mouse, tiger, etc. The model consists of 164 ConvNet layers and has 55,873,736 parameters. The model's default input image size is 299 × 299 × 3 and it outputs a list of predicted class probabilities. InceptionResNetV2 can be thought of as a combination of the Inception Net and the ResNet models. It consists of inception structures with residual connections. Residual connections do not only help with degradation issues caused by the deep layers but it also significantly reduces the training time. A flattened layer and a dense layer is added to the existing model (Elhamraoui, 2020). This can be seen in Fig. 16.9.

5.9 MobileNet SSD

For the proposed model, the MobileNet feature extraction module is used as a component of the CNN. Mobile Net is a simple architecture that is separable and uses a depth-wise CNN classification to lightweight DNN for the applications that have mobile application vision (Velasco et al., 2019; Wibowo et al., 2020). As shown in Fig. 16.10, a bottleneck layer is used to improve the feature extraction using SSD and classifier for input object detection.

FIGURE 16.7 Represents the model 1 which is a combination of logistic regression, SVM, and Gradient Descent.

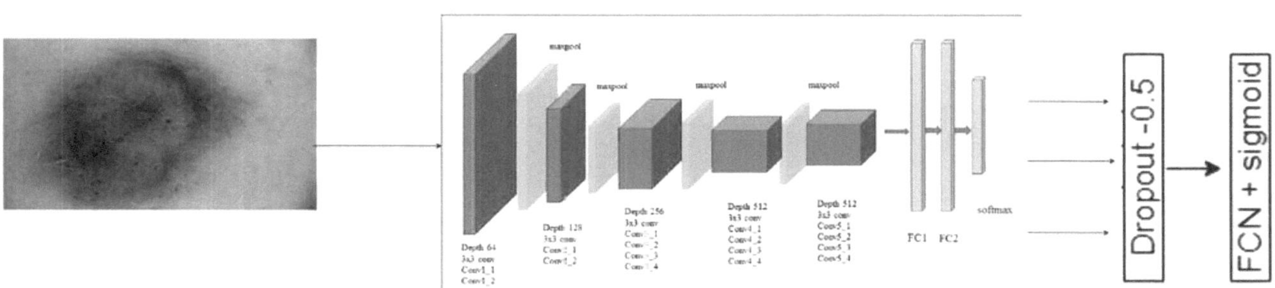

FIGURE 16.8 Represents the model using VGG19 architecture. *Source: https://miro.medium.com/max/1192/1*Q_bg1E3trWcjdk9_jnVGwg.png.*

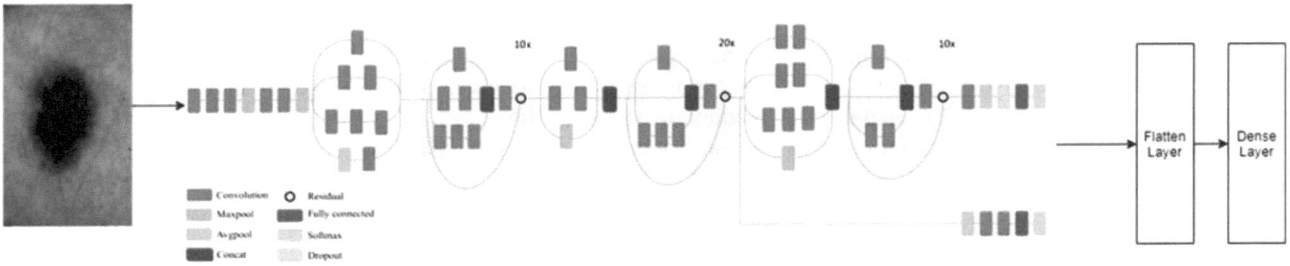

FIGURE 16.9 Represents the model using InceptionResNetV2 architecture. *Source: https://www.researchgate.net/figure/Schematic-diagram-of-InceptionResNetV2-model-compressed-view_fig9_326421398.*

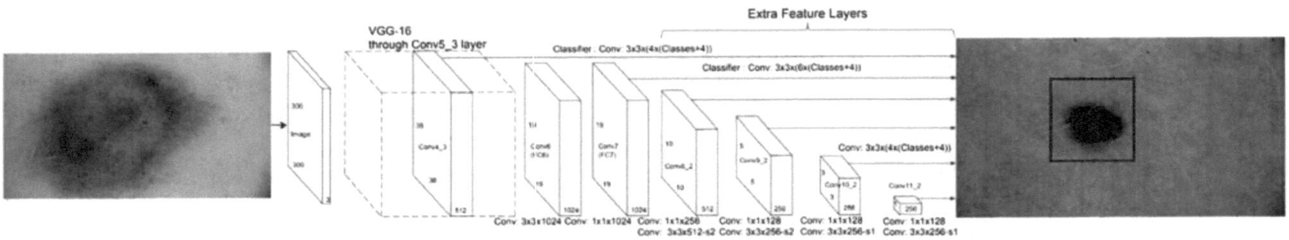

FIGURE 16.10 Represents the model using MobileNet SSD architecture. *Source: https://i.stack.imgur.com/g30dc.png.*

5.10 MelConvo2d

MelConvo2d is a model that is built using two-dimensional CNNs. It has a depth of 14 layers and contains a combination of conv2d, max_pooling2d, dropout, flatten and dense layers. The total number of parameters in the model is 494,337. The kernel size of all the Conv2D layers was set as 3 × 3 and had a ReLU activation function around them all. The pool size for the maxpool2d layers was set as 2 × 2. All dropout layers had a rate of 0.25. The first dense layer had ReLU as its activation function and the last dense layer had a sigmoid activation function around it. This was done to restrict the output or predictions made by the model to 0 and 1 for benign and malignant, respectively. The model is represented below in Fig. 16.11.

6. Data visualization and analysis

Fig. 16.12 represents a bar graph of gender against the count. By observation, it can be clearly seen that the male population is more prone to being affected by skin cancer as compared to females. According to this graph, the female count is slightly more than 15,000 and the male count is approximately around 17,000 to 18,000.

The histogram in Fig. 16.13 is made between age of the cancer patient and the number of total patients The histogram is normally distributed and is symmetric in nature. It can be observed that at the age of 45 to 55 years, people are more prone to have skin cancer. Infants have much less chance of being affected by skin cancer. Moreover, till the age of 15 or 17 years, there are fewer chances of pervasiveness of skin cancer. Apart from this, for people belonging to the age group of 77 or above, there are fewer chances of getting affected by skin cancer. This is explained in more detail in the next figure.

Fig. 16.14 shows the histogram with the age of skin cancer patients with respect to the count and sex of patient. According to this graph, it can be observed that patients belonging to the age group of 45–55 years old are more prone to

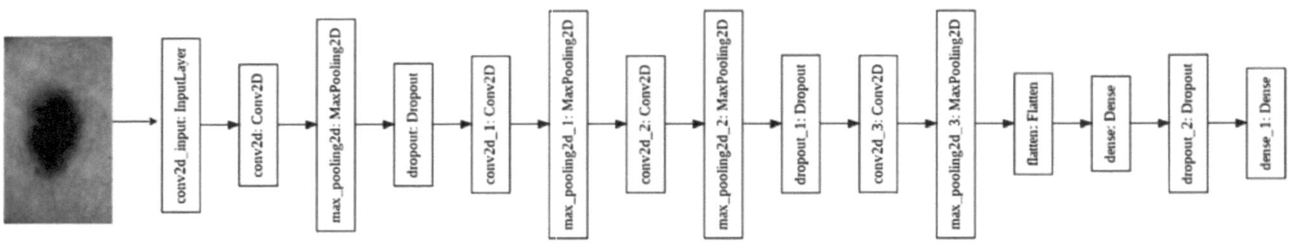

FIGURE 16.11 Represents the proposed model of MelConvo2D architecture.

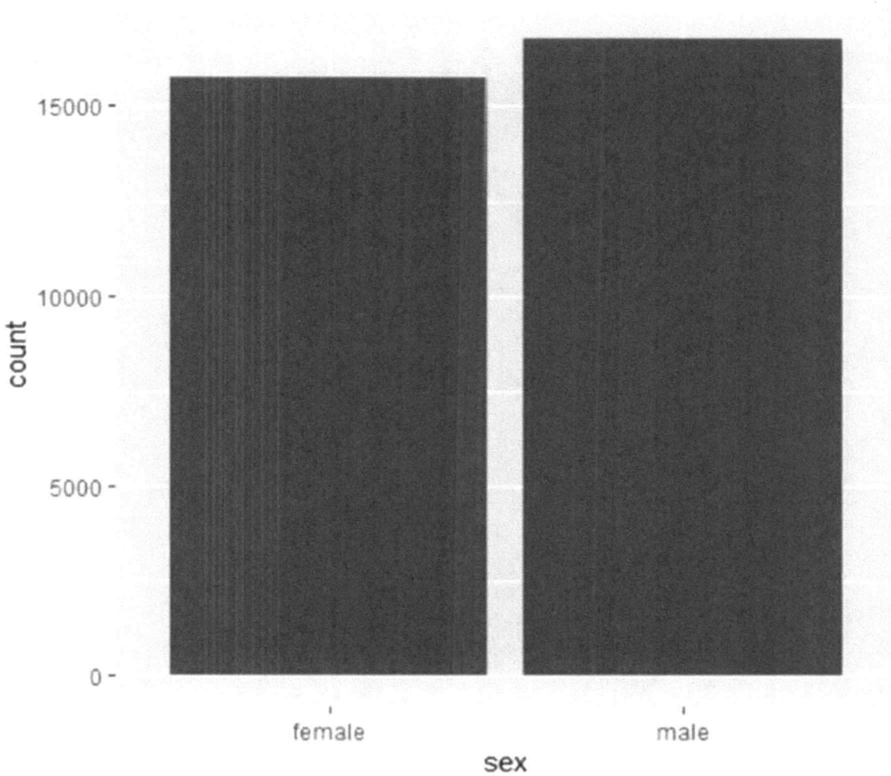

FIGURE 16.12 Represents the bar graph using gender.

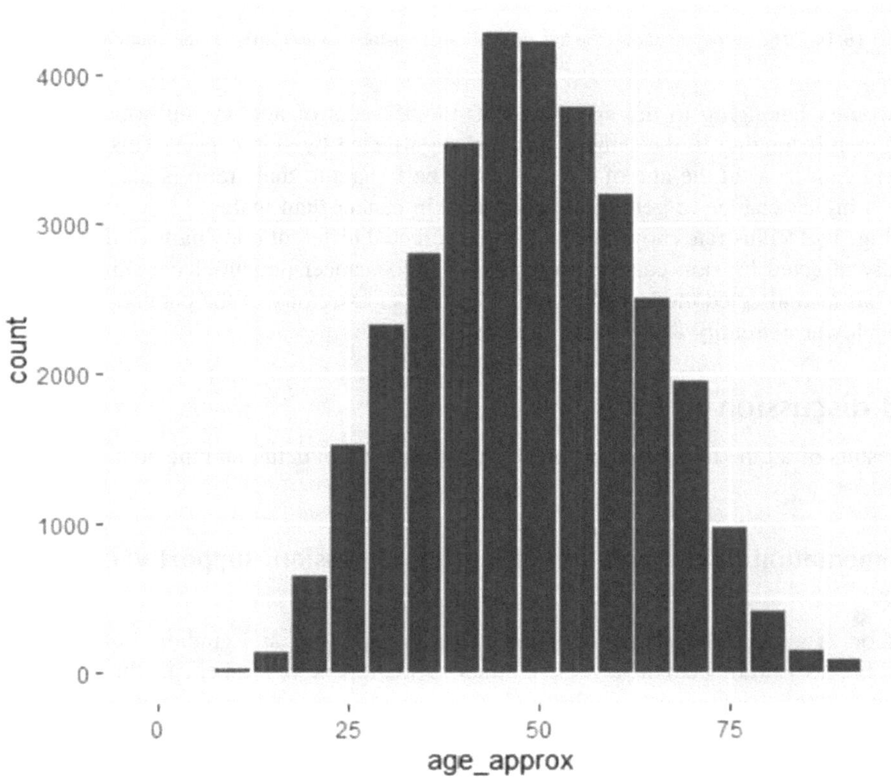

FIGURE 16.13 Represents the histogram of age of the cancer patients.

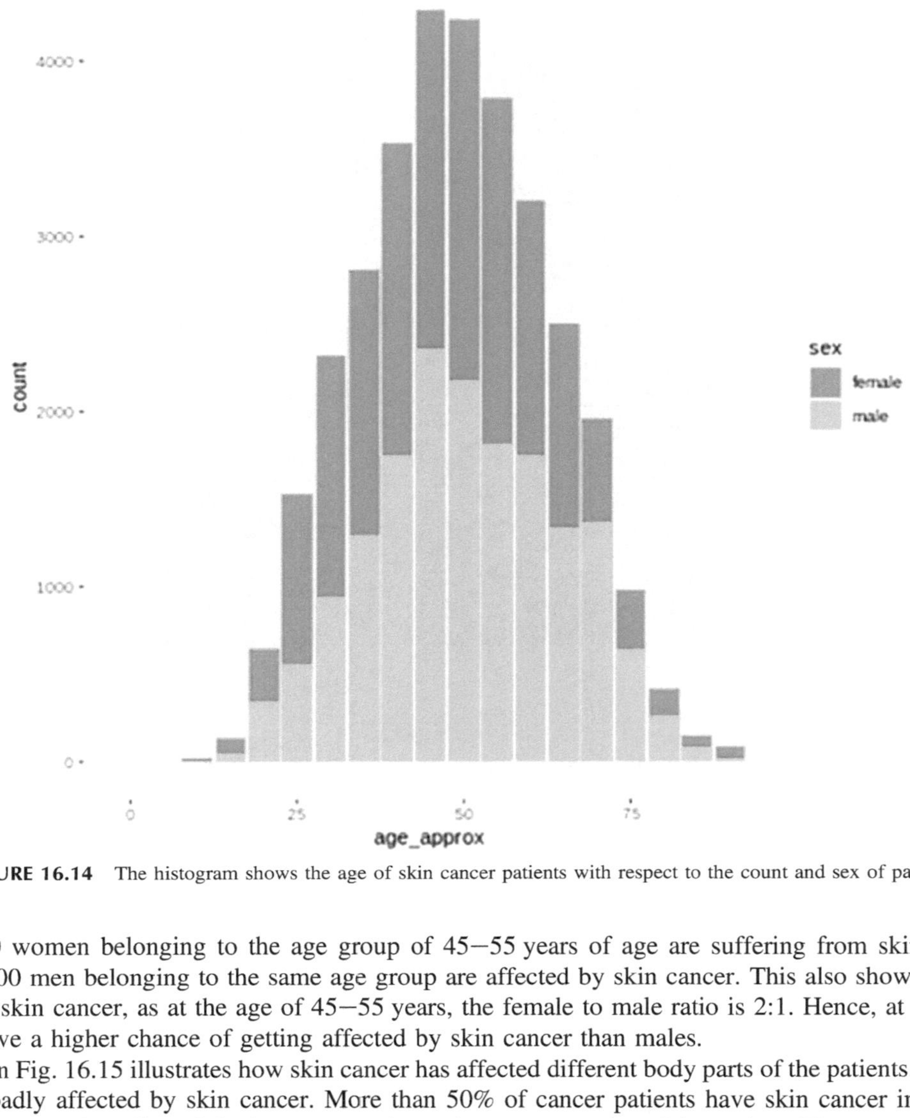

FIGURE 16.14 The histogram shows the age of skin cancer patients with respect to the count and sex of patient.

skin cancer. 4000 women belonging to the age group of 45–55 years of age are suffering from skin cancer, whereas approximately 2000 men belonging to the same age group are affected by skin cancer. This also shows the sex which is more disposed to skin cancer, as at the age of 45–55 years, the female to male ratio is 2:1. Hence, at this particular age range, females have a higher chance of getting affected by skin cancer than males.

The pie chart in Fig. 16.15 illustrates how skin cancer has affected different body parts of the patients. As it can be seen, that the torso is badly affected by skin cancer. More than 50% of cancer patients have skin cancer in the torso region. Further, skin cancer has also affected the lower extremity and upper extremity of the patient. The cancer has affected 25% of the people in their lower extremity and 16% in the upper extremity.

7. Results and discussion

In this section, the results of all the five proposed models are discussed in detail and the area under curve of deep learning models are compared.

7.1 Model implementation of combination of logistic regression, support vector machine, and gradient boosting

For the implementation of a model consisting of logistic regression, SVM, and gradient boosting, Pyspark was applied. Since the data were biased toward benign, a sample equal to malignant was taken. In the early phase, dummies were created in the column "anatom_site_general_challenge." The variables were taken as x while the "target" variable was set as y. The dataset was then split into the train and test ratio. Logistic regression, SVM, and gradient boosting were applied. It was found that logistic regression gave an accuracy of 63.66%, SVM gave an accuracy of 63.40%, and gradient boosting gave an accuracy of 63.48%. This can be seen in Fig. 16.16.

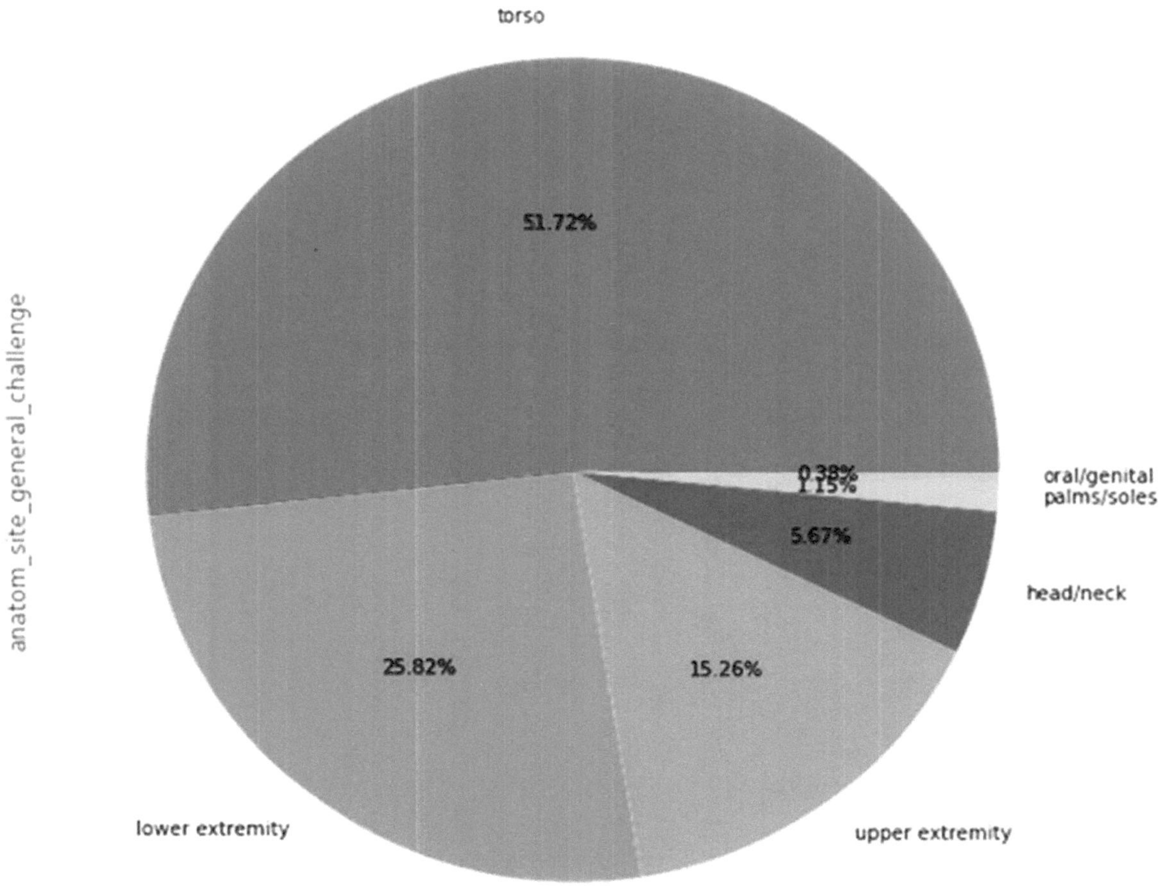

FIGURE 16.15 Represents the pie chart of affected area of body due to cancer.

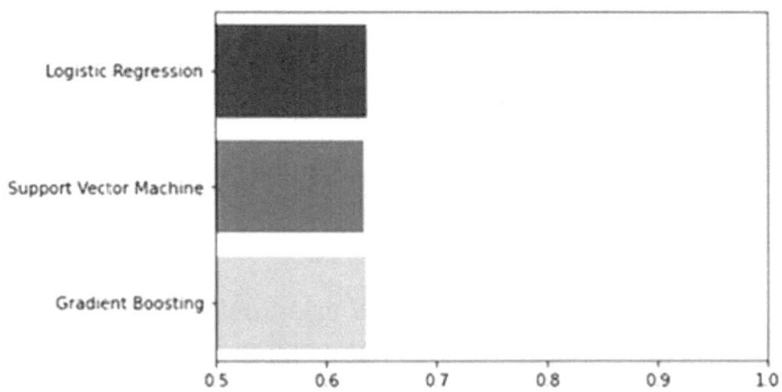

FIGURE 16.16 Represents the training graph of all the three different algorithms.

The same model was executed for the test image. It was found that gradient boosting outperformed logistic regression and supported machines (SVM). Logistic regression gave an accuracy of 53% on the test data, SVM gave an accuracy of 64.5%, whereas the gradient boosting gave an accuracy of 68%. It can be seen in Fig. 16.17.

7.2 Model implementation using VGG19 architecture

Since the dataset is biased toward benign, 1000 samples of benign were taken and all the 584 images of melanoma were taken for model training, testing, prediction, and evaluation purposes. The metadata was then mapped to the train image folder with their respective names. After the mapping was done, the dataset of 1584 was split into training and validation purposes at the ratio of 80:20. 80% of the data was used for training purposes, whereas 20% of the image was used for the testing images.

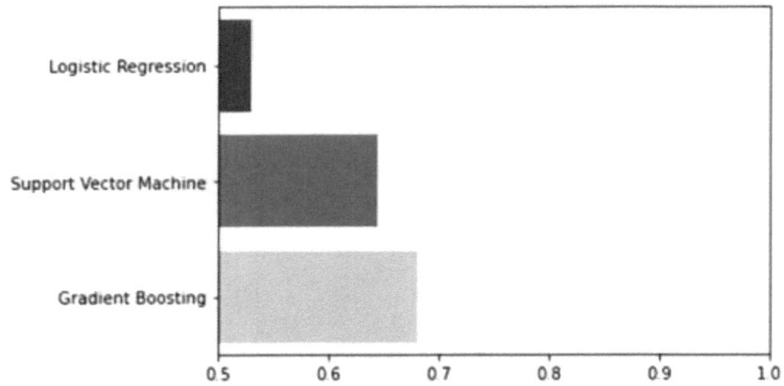

FIGURE 16.17 Represents the graph showing validation accuracy of the three models.

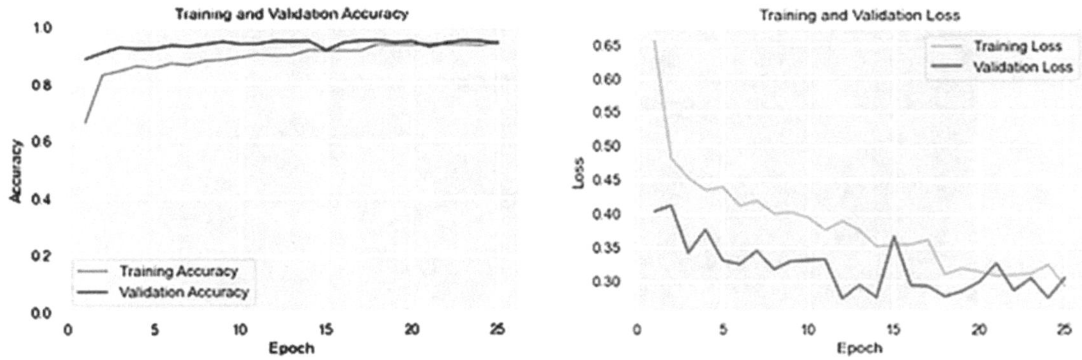

FIGURE 16.18 Shows the training and validation accuracy and loss of the VGG19 architecture.

The training and testing images were rescaled. Then, the training images were then augmented with a rotation range of 20, with a shift of 20%, a height shift of 20%, and the images were horizontally flipped. The target image size for both training and validation, in this case, was taken as 256 × 256. Batch size was taken as 8 and class mode was "raw," which gives the NumPy array of values present in the y_column, which in this case was "target."

Then the model using VGG19 architecture was designed. The Adam optimizer was used with a loss function like binary cross-entropy and metrics as accuracy was applied. Callbacks were initiated and the model executed for 25 epochs. The weights were saved in a file where there was improvement in validation accuracy. It was found that the model reached a training accuracy of 91.48% and a validation accuracy of 94.09%. Fig. 16.18 represents the graph of training and validation accuracy and loss against number of epochs.

7.3 Model implementation of InceptionResNetV2

The skin cancer images were taken, and the model was trained using them. The shape of the input dataset was taken as 256 × 256 × 3, where 3 represents the color channel RGB. Adam optimizer was applied to the model with a learning rate of 0.00001. The loss function used for the model was BinaryFocalLoss. The model was trained on 1584 images from the dataset to eliminate bias. These were then divided into two parts of 80% and 20% for training and validation purposes, respectively. The model was trained for 100 epochs and achieved a training accuracy of 92.97% and a validation accuracy of 98.08%. Fig. 16.19 depicts the accuracy and loss curves of the above model.

7.4 Model implementation of MobileNet SSD

Here, two categories of skin cancer are used: benign and malignant. After this, the data are divided into train, test, and validation sets. Then, model training for object detection and classification is done. Adam optimizer is used with a learning rate of 0.00005. The model was compiled using a loss function like binary cross-entropy and metrics such as "accuracy." The model was executed for 25 epochs with a batch size of 8. The target image was 256 × 256. The model achieved training accuracy of 92.59% and validation accuracy of 90.95%.

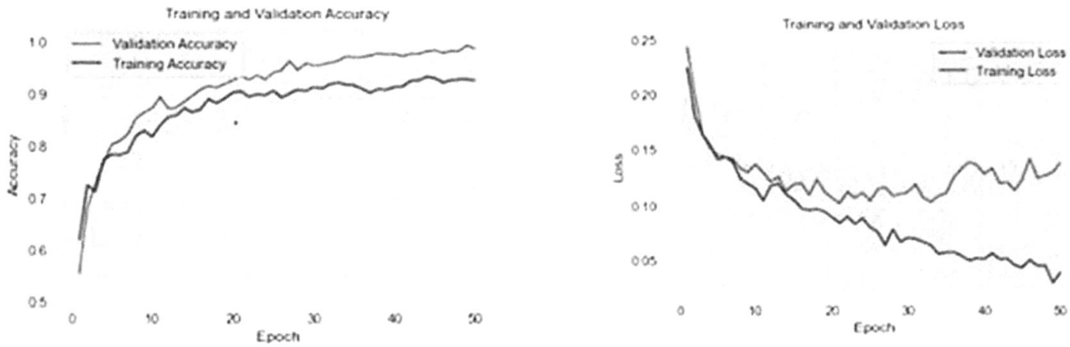

FIGURE 16.19 Shows the training and validation accuracy and loss of the InceptionResNetV2 architecture.

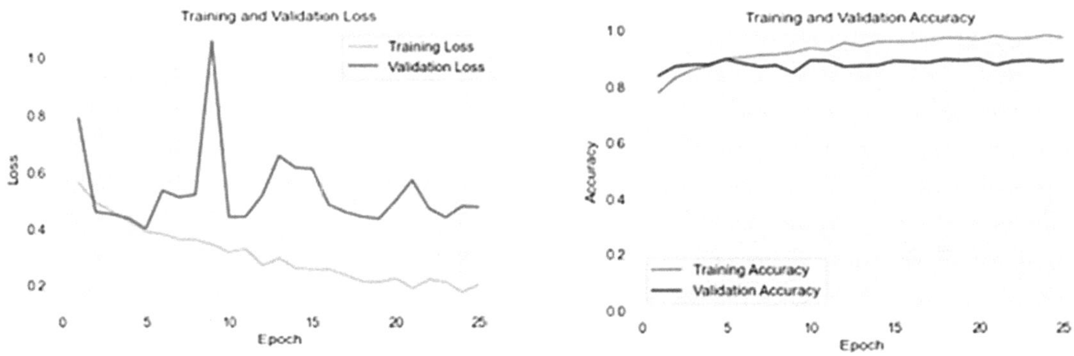

FIGURE 16.20 Shows the training and validation accuracy and loss of the MobileNetSSD architecture.

The two significant parameters, i.e., training loss and validation loss are important to determine the exactness of the proposed model. Whereas, two parameters that are evaluated against the loss parameters are training and validation accuracy as shown in Fig. 16.20.

7.5 Model implementation MelConvo2D

MelConvo2d was trained on a set of 1584 out of 33,136 (1000 benign and 584 melanoma) images out of which 80% were used for training and 20% for validation purposes. This was done to eliminate bias that might have been caused by the huge difference in the number of benign (98.3%) and melanoma (1.7%) images. The optimizer used for the model was Adam with a learning rate of 0.001. The model was trained for 100 epochs, and it achieved an accuracy of 92.65% and a validation accuracy of 95.10%. The models' accuracy and loss curves are shown in Fig. 16.21.

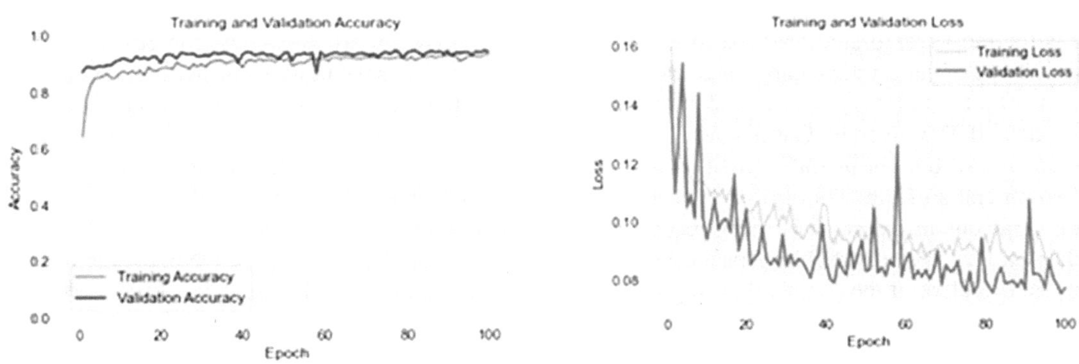

FIGURE 16.21 Shows the training and validation accuracy and loss of the MelConvo2d architecture.

TABLE 16.1 Represents the area under the ROC curve (AUC) of the models proposed in this chapter.

Sl. No.	Model/algorithms used	Training AUC	Validation AUC
1.	Logistic regression, SVM, and gradient boosting	63% - Accuracy	68% (Accuracy)—gradient boosting
2.	VGG19	91.48%	94.09%
3.	InceptionResNetV2	92.97%	98.08%
4.	MobileNet SSD	92.59%	90.95%
5.	MelConvo2D	92.65%	95.10%

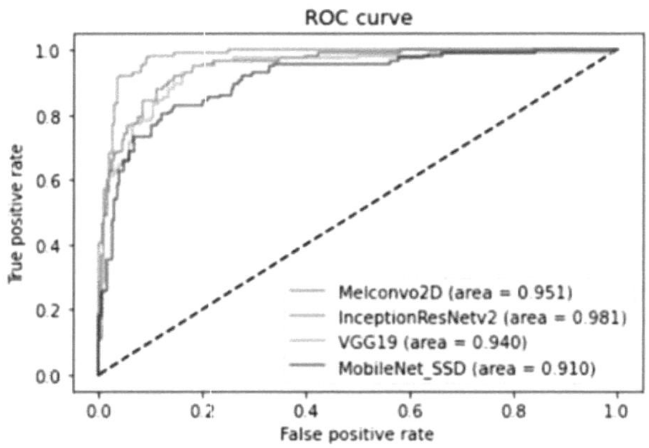

FIGURE 16.22 Shows the ROC curve of the deep learning models used in this chapter.

As mentioned above, different algorithms and models gave different area under ROC curve and accuracy toward the prediction of skin cancer (Table 16.1).

Since the dataset was highly biased toward the benign class and the melanoma class had just 584 images, making predictions become difficult. After preprocessing and cleaning the dataset, the various models were trained. All the models successfully crossed the 90% mark while training. None of the models were in overfitting and underfitting conditions, since the dataset was cleaned thoroughly.

In Fig. 16.22, the ROC curve is shown for all the four deep learning models. This shows the area under the curve. And, the graph is plotted between the false and true positive rates. It can be seen that InceptionResNetV2 shows validation accuracy of 98% as shown in orange. Now, the ROC curve is quite insightful in the medical field. Irrespective of the class of benign or melanoma, it shows the detection of skin cancer as a whole. In other words, it can be said that if the dataset is balanced and is in form of binary, i.e., benign and malignant, the InceptionResNetv2 performed exceptionally well.

8. Conclusion

Skin cancer is the most feared and deadliest disease which takes the lives of around 10 million people across the globe. Detection of the type of cancer at an early stage can be very crucial and can save millions of lives. The dataset used in this chapter consists of a total of around 44,000 skin cancer images. Thus, it can be said that skin cancer disease is one of the sources of big data. If 3Vs given by Gartner are applied, then the skin cancer data are voluminous in nature. It has a variety of data that consists of data in picture format as well as the data of cancer patients like their age, area of skin affected, gender, and so on and so forth. Thirdly, since cancer is affecting more than 10 million people every year, thus, the data generated are veracious in nature. It is being recorded at a faster pace.

In this chapter, the API provided by Apache Spark, i.e., PySpark is used as well as the DNN for the detection of skin cancer. The core objective of the chapter was to predict skin cancer using both big data analytics and AI techniques. There are four models which have been proposed in this chapter, out of which three are trained using the pretrained models by applying state-of-the-art algorithms. A newly proposed model, i.e., MelConvo2D is proposed in this chapter, which has a depth of 14 layers and has around four lakh parameters. All the deep learning models reached accuracy above 90% with InceptionResNetV2 showing accuracy of around 98%. Handling the biased data with its variety was a huge challenge during the process of making predictions and evaluations. The cloud is a good platform to execute huge amounts of data. Hence, clouds can be used for making predictions of skin cancer in the near future.

References

10 Best Data Analytics Tools for Big Data Analysis (2021). (2021). https://www.guru99.com/big-data-analytics-tools.html.

Ashraf, R., Habib, M. A., Akram, M., Latif, M. A., Malik, M. S. A., Awais, M., Dar, S. H., Mahmood, T., Yasir, M., & Abbas, Z. (2020). Deep convolution neural network for big data medical image classification. *IEEE Access, 8*, 105659–105670. https://doi.org/10.1109/ACCESS.2020.2998808

Bora, D. J. (2019). *Big data analytics in healthcare: A critical analysis* (pp. 43–57). Elsevier BV. https://doi.org/10.1016/b978-0-12-818146-1.00003-9

Chae, S., Kwon, S., & Lee, D. (2018). Predicting infectious disease using deep learning and big data. *International Journal of Environmental Research and Public Health, 15*(8). https://doi.org/10.3390/ijerph15081596

Elhamraoui, Z. (2020). *InceptionResNetV2 simple introduction*. https://medium.com/@zahraelhamraoui1997/inceptionresnetv2-simple-introduction-9a2000edcdb6#:~:text=Inception-ResNet-v2 is a,%2C pencil%2C and many animals.

Gandhi, R. (2018). Support vector machine—introduction to machine learning algorithms. *Data Science*. https://towardsdatascience.com/support-vector-machine-introduction-to-machine-learning-algorithms-934a444fca47.

Gonçalves-Pinho, M., & Freitas, A. (2021). *The use of Big Data in Psychiatry—the role of administrative databases* (pp. 155–165). Elsevier BV. https://doi.org/10.1016/b978-0-12-822884-5.00009-x

Iqbal, U., Hsu, C. K., Nguyen, P. A., Clinciu, D. L., Lu, R., Syed-Abdul, S., Yang, H. C., Wang, Y. C., Huang, C. Y., Huang, C. W., Chang, Y. C., Hsu, M. H., Jian, W. S., & Li, Y. C. (2016). Cancer-disease associations: A visualization and animation through medical big data. *Computer Methods and Programs in Biomedicine, 127*, 44–51. https://doi.org/10.1016/j.cmpb.2016.01.009

Ishwarappa, & Anuradha, J. (2015). A brief introduction on big data 5Vs characteristics and hadoop technology. In *Procedia computer science* (Vol. 48, pp. 319–324). Elsevier B.V. https://doi.org/10.1016/j.procs.2015.04.188. Issue C.

Kadampur, M. A., & Al Riyaee, S. (2020). Skin cancer detection: Applying a deep learning based model driven architecture in the cloud for classifying dermal cell images. *Informatics in Medicine Unlocked, 18*. https://doi.org/10.1016/j.imu.2019.100282

Keras Applications. (n.d.). https://keras.io/api/applications/.

Key Internet Statistics to know in 2021 (include Mobile). *Broadband Search*, (2021). https://www.broadbandsearch.net/blog/internet-statistics.

Kumar, P., Chauhan, R., Stephan, T., Shankar, A., & Thakur, S. (2021). A machine learning implementation for mental health care. Application: Smart watch for depression detection. In *Proceedings of the confluence 2021: 11th international conference on cloud computing, data science and engineering* (pp. 568–574). Institute of Electrical and Electronics Engineers Inc. https://doi.org/10.1109/Confluence51648.2021.9377199

Kunchhal, R. (2020). *The mathematics behind support vector machine algorithm (SVM)*. https://www.analyticsvidhya.com/blog/2020/10/the-mathematics-behind-svm/.

Milosevic, Z., Chen, W., Berry, A., & Rabhi, F. A. (2016). Real-time analytics. In *Big data: Principles and paradigms* (pp. 39–61). Elsevier Inc. https://doi.org/10.1016/B978-0-12-805394-2.00002-7

Peneti, P. S., Sri, A. R., Krishna, U. M. G., Alekhya, M., & Manikandhara, G. (2021). Skin cancer predictor by image processing using big data techniques. In *Proceedings - 5th International Conference on Intelligent Computing and Control Systems, ICICCS 2021* (pp. 913–916). Institute of Electrical and Electronics Engineers Inc. https://doi.org/10.1109/ICICCS51141.2021.9432213

Pölönen, I., Rahkonen, S., Annala, L., & Neittaanmäki, N. (2019). Convolutional neural networks in skin cancer detection using spatial and spectral domain. In *Progress in biomedical optics and imaging - proceedings of SPIE* (Vol. 10851)SPIE. https://doi.org/10.1117/12.2509871

Raj, D. S. S., Vijayakumar, V., Rawal, B., & Yang, L. (2019). *Analysis of big data technology for health care services. ArXiv*. https://arxiv.org.

Rastogi, P., Singh, V., & Yadav, M. (2018). Deep learning and big datatechnologies in medical image analysis. In *PDGC 2018 - 2018 5th International Conference on Parallel, Distributed and Grid Computing* (pp. 60–63). Institute of Electrical and Electronics Engineers Inc. https://doi.org/10.1109/PDGC.2018.8745750

Richter, A. N., & Khoshgoftaar, T. M. (2019). Efficient learning from big data for cancer risk modeling: A case study with melanoma. *Computers in Biology and Medicine, 110*, 29–39. https://doi.org/10.1016/j.compbiomed.2019.04.039

Rotemberg, V., Kurtansky, N., Betz-Stablein, B., Caffery, L., Chousakos, E., Codella, N., Combalia, M., Dusza, S., Guitera, P., Gutman, D., Halpern, A., Helba, B., Kittler, H., Kose, K., Langer, S., Lioprys, K., Malvehy, J., Musthaq, S., Nanda, J., ... Soyer, H. P. (2021). A patient-centric dataset of images and metadata for identifying melanomas using clinical context. *Scientific Data, 8*(1). https://doi.org/10.1038/s41597-021-00815-z

Senan, E. M., & Jadhav, M. E. (2021). Analysis of dermoscopy images by using ABCD rule for early detection of skin cancer. *Global Transitions Proceedings, 2*(1), 1–7. https://doi.org/10.1016/j.gltp.2021.01.001

Singh, H. (2018). *Understanding gradient boosting machines*. https://towardsdatascience.com/understanding-gradient-boosting-machines-9be756fe76ab.

Swaminathan, S. (2018). Logistic regression — detailed overview. *Data Science*.

Syed, L., Jabeen, S., Manimala, S., & Alsaeedi, A. (2019). Smart healthcare framework for ambient assisted living using IoMT and big data analytics techniques. *Future Generation Computer Systems, 101*, 136–151. https //doi.org/10.1016/j.future.2019.06.004

Tchagna Kouanou, A., Tchiotsop, D., Kengne, R., Zephirin, D. T., Adele Armele, N. M., & Tchinda, R. (2018). An optimal big data workflow for biomedical image analysis. *Informatics in Medicine Unlocked, 11*, 68–74. https://doi.org/10.1016/j.imu.2018.05.001

Types of Big Data. (2016). https://www.knowledgehut.com/blog/big-data/types-of-big-data.

Understanding the VGG19 Architecture. (n.d.). *In OpenGenus IQ: Computing expertise & legacy.*

Velasco, J., Pascion, C., Alberio, J. W., Apuang, J., Cruz, J. S., Gomez, M. A., Molina, B., Tuala, L., Thio-Ac, A., & Jorda, R. (2019). A smartphone-based skin disease classification using mobilenet CNN. *International Journal of Advanced Trends in Computer Science and Engineering, 8*(5), 2632–2637. https://doi.org/10.30534/ijatcse/2019/116852019

Wang, L., & Alexander, C. (2021). *Big data in personalized healthcare* (pp. 35–49). Elsevier BV. https://doi.org/10.1016/b978-0-12-822884-5.00017-9

Wibowo, A., Adhi Hartanto, C., & Wisnu Wirawan, P. (2020). Android skin cancer detection and classification based on MobileNet v2 model. *International Journal of Advances in Intelligent Informatics, 6*(2), 135. https://doi.org/10.26555/ijain.v6i2.492

Wu, C., Buyya, R., & Ramamohanarao, K. (2016). Big data analytics = machine learning + cloud computing. In *Big data: Principles and paradigms* (pp. 3–38). Elsevier Inc. https://doi.org/10.1016/B978-0-12-805394-2.00001-5

Section V

Big medical fake news analytics for preventing medical misinformation and myths

Chapter 17

COVID-19 fake news analytics from social media using topic modeling and clustering

Sherrylin Anak John and Pantea Keikhosrokiani
School of Computer Sciences, Universiti Sains Malaysia, Minden, Penang, Malaysia

1. Introduction

During COVID-19 pandemic, people are exposed to the relevant news easily due to the availability of social media such as Twitter, Facebook, Instagram, and WhatsApp. These social media platforms play a significant role where people could share the news, opinion, or up-to-date information globally. Therefore, misinformation and fake news related to COVID-19 has become rampant in the online world. The Communications and Multimedia Minister of Malaysia states that the COVID-19 misinformation needs to be monitored and quickly countered as it is believed that this fake news could cause public distress. Tasnim et al. (2020) mentioned that the abundance of the news related to COVID-19 could lead to media fatigue where it results in poor physical and mental health issues. Furthermore, it was stated that the spreading of fake news could cost lives because most of the victims believe and followed the myths or traditional treatment without having a consultation with the medical staff.

Consequently, as fake news spreading faster than COVID-19, the users might find difficulties in checking the validity of the news as they could not differentiate which one is the authorized news (O'Connor & Murphy, 2020). Thus, it is too risky that the people could easily sway by believing the news without knowing the validity of the news. Therefore, this chapter aims to focus on COVID-19 fake news analytics from social media using topic modeling. This kind of study can increase the awareness among social media users on the dangers of believing and sharing the misinformation that is related to COVID-19 (Bunker, 2020). After introducing the concept, this chapter reviewed studies related to misinformation and fake news. Afterward, a data science life cycle is designed to show the process of methodology. Then the steps of data analysis and the results are mentioned. Finally, the study is wrapped up with concluding remarks.

2. Background and related work

During this epidemic, the overabundance of information related to COVID-19 has become a serious problem where people find difficulties in trusting the sources and relying on guidance when they need it. Therefore, Tangcharoensathien et al. (2020) has taken an alternative way to hold a World Health Organization (WHO) consultation responding to these problems and crowdsource ideas to form a novel COVID-19 infodemic response framework. The consultation managed to submit the first version of the framework which consists of five action areas (Identity evidence, Science and knowledge translation, Amplify impact, Quantity impact and Coordination, Standards, and Governance). Meanwhile, Okan et al. (2020) have further studies focusing on health literacy related to COVID-19 infodemic among adults in Germany. They conducted a cross-sectional survey and found out that people with "inadequate" and "problematic" health literacy were more likely to mix up by the coronavirus information (Okan et al., 2020). This section covers the fake news concept, the related studies on misinformation, and fake news on social media related to COVID-19.

Big Data Analytics for Healthcare. https://doi.org/10.1016/B978-0-323-91907-4.00003-0

2.1 Misinformation and fake news

Research on misinformation and fake news has attempted to conceptualize these concepts variously with the same definition. McGonagle (2017) claimed that "fake news" is a piece of information that is intentionally fabricated which could deceive and mislead the individuals into trusting about the half-truths and the uncertain verifiable facts. Duffy et al. (2019) believe that fake news is information mimicking the verified news to enhance social cohesion even though the content of the news is false and misleading. Based on these definitions, some studies realize that there is a connection between fake news and social media platforms.

The existence of social media platforms allows creating and spreading of misleading information rapidly resulting in widespread real-world impact (Aldwairi & Alwahedi, 2018). At the same time, Bergström and Jervelycke Belfrage (2018) have proved that news consumption through social network sites is relatively widespread, while Schifferes et al. (2014) have further studies responding to the increasing concerns about the reliability of news on a social network such as Twitter and Facebook.

2.2 Related studies of misinformation and medical fake news on social media related to COVID-19

Studies related to the proliferation of false news are rising in the age of the COVID-19 pandemic. Some studies have tried to prove and realize the connection between social media and misinformation in this era of COVID-19 infodemic. Social media platforms allow people to share the news rapidly which could cause social media fatigue and the sharing of unproven information during this COVID-19 pandemic (Islam et al., 2020). Consistent with this finding, Aldwairi and Alwahedi (2018) believe that social media and news outlets emerge fake news or misinformation to increase the readers as for making a profit through clickbait.

There are high possibilities that the falsehood related to COVID-19 is shared far more than the evidence-based information in social media (Pulido et al., 2020). Risk communication has been ineffective during the COVID-19 pandemic (Hartley & Vu, 2020). This pandemic not only caused challenges for the health system but at the same time dealing with the fake news that is spreading more rapidly in social media instead of the reliable and trusted sources (Tasnim et al., 2020). This caused the authenticity balance of the news ecosystem to become damaged.

During the COVID-19 outbreak in India, social media has been misused for spreading false news, hatred, and creating racism which led to negative impacts such as stock out of masks and sanitizers from the market (Kadam & Atre, 2020). This act or behavior change is called panic buying where people buy large amounts of products in anticipation of past major disasters or health crises (Yuen et al., 2020).

3. Methodology

Fig. 17.1 shows the data science life cycle for this study, which includes six main steps. The first step focuses on exploring misinformation, fake news, and myth related to COVID-19. The second step concentrates on data collection and finding proper dataset which is related to COVID-19 fake news and collected from social media. After selecting proper dataset, data cleaning and data preprocessing are done. Then initial descriptive analysis and data exploration are performed to show the overview of the data. Afterward, topic modeling using Latent Dirichlet Allocation (LDA) is utilized to extract the proper topics from fake and real news. Finally, the results are interpreted, justified, and discussed. Some steps of the life cycle are explained in methodology section and some in the results and analysis section.

3.1 Data collection

In this study, the dataset related to COVID-19 healthcare misinformation collected from social media is used to analyze and classify the news. The dataset is collected from the Github website titled CoAID (COVID-19 healthcare misinformation dataset). The study is conducted to help the researchers combat the COVID-19 health misinformation (Cui & Lee, 2020). The dataset was collected on January 5, 2020 which consists of 1802 news related to COVID-19. This dataset includes both real and fake news related to COVID-19 which mainly focused on the English language community. However, there were only a few attributes that are being used from the datasets which are a type of the news, URL, title of the news, label of the news, and the source of the news. In this study, the classification of the COVID-19 news focuses on the title of the news instead of the content of the news.

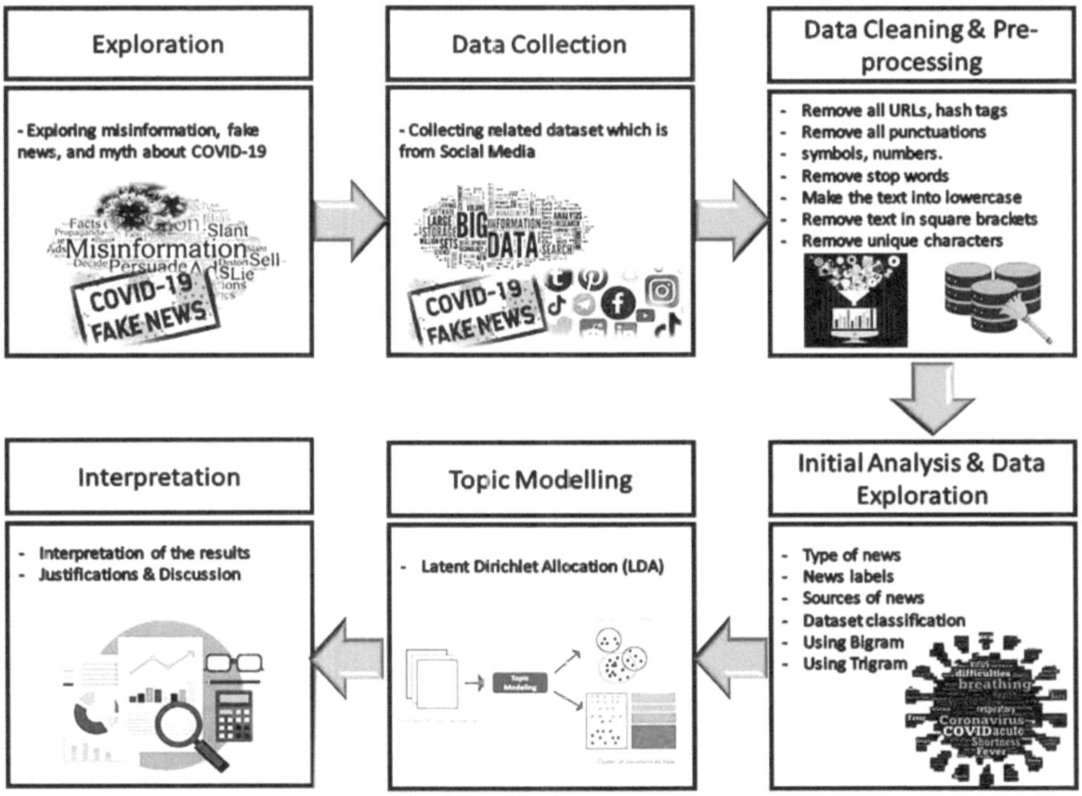

FIGURE 17.1 Data science life cycle.

3.2 Topic modeling

For the COVID-19 fake news classification, an LDA topic modeling method is used in this study. Topic modeling method is a machine learning and natural language processing technique where it automatically discovers the abstract "topics" that occur for a set of documents (Ying et al., 2021). In the previous work, Olowookere et al. (2015) have proposed the use of the topic modeling-based framework for data mining on document collections of the digital library to discover the topical structure of the document. Meanwhile, Mutanga and Abayomi (2020) have applied the LDA algorithm to extract the noteworthy topics obtained from the word cloud indication of the trending words relating to the COVID-19 pandemic in South Africa through Twitter messages. Therefore, LDA algorithm is used in this study to classify the COVID-19 news into particular topics.

3.3 Programming tools

There are several programming tools that are used in this research study. For instance, Google Colab which is a computer program used for data science and machine learning application is utilized in this study. Furthermore, Python, which is an interpreted high-level general-purpose programming language for data mining and data analytics, is used for data analytics purposes.

4. Data analysis and results (COVID-19 news classification)

4.1 COVID-19 news dataset

Based on the dataset, there are nine columns that are included in each fake and real news dataset which consists of a type of news, the fact checks URL, the news URL, source of the news, news title, content, abstract, publish date, and labels of news. Table 17.1 shows the details of the column included in the dataset. The dataset is separated into two datasets which are fake news and real news in which 572 of the news are fake news and 1230 of them are the real news.

TABLE 17.1 Dataset description.

Column	Description
Type of news	Type of the news collected either is from social media post, news article, or website article
Fact checks URL	The URL of the website to check the fact of the news
News URL	The URL of the news posted or published either is from social media post, news article, or website article
Source of news	The source name of the news from which the news is collected such as Facebook, twitter
News title	The title of the news
Content	The content of the news
Abstract	The summary and the overview of the news
Publish date	The publish date of the news
Labels of news	The labels of the news, either it is fake or real news

4.2 Data cleaning and data preprocessing

Before starting the process of news classification, data cleaning and preprocessing are performed as the raw data from the dataset might have inconsistency and redundancy. Even though there are nine columns in the dataset, this study only used three columns related to a source of news, news title, and label of the news. Meanwhile, during the data preprocessing, the unused columns are dropped before the classification of the news. In this study, the news title is used to classify the news that is related to the COVID-19. After the process of data cleaning, both datasets related to fake and real news are merged into one dataset which includes 1802 rows and 3 columns. Data preprocessing in this study includes the following steps: (1) remove all URLs and hashtags, (2) remove all punctuations, symbols, and numbers, (3) remove stop words, (4) make the text into lowercase, (5) remove text in square brackets, and (6) remove unique characters.

4.3 Initial analysis and data exploration

As shown in Fig. 17.2, the dataset for this study includes 572 fake news and 1230 true news which are labeled as 0 for real news and 1 for the fake news. The most reliable news is collected from a news website and the most unreliable news is collected from social media such as Facebook, Twitter, etc.

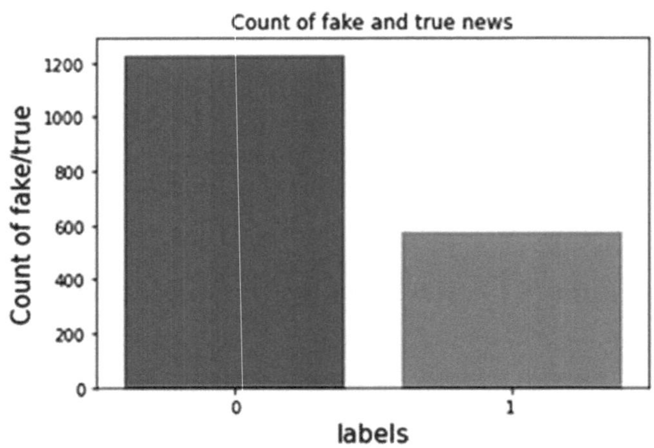

FIGURE 17.2 Dataset details.

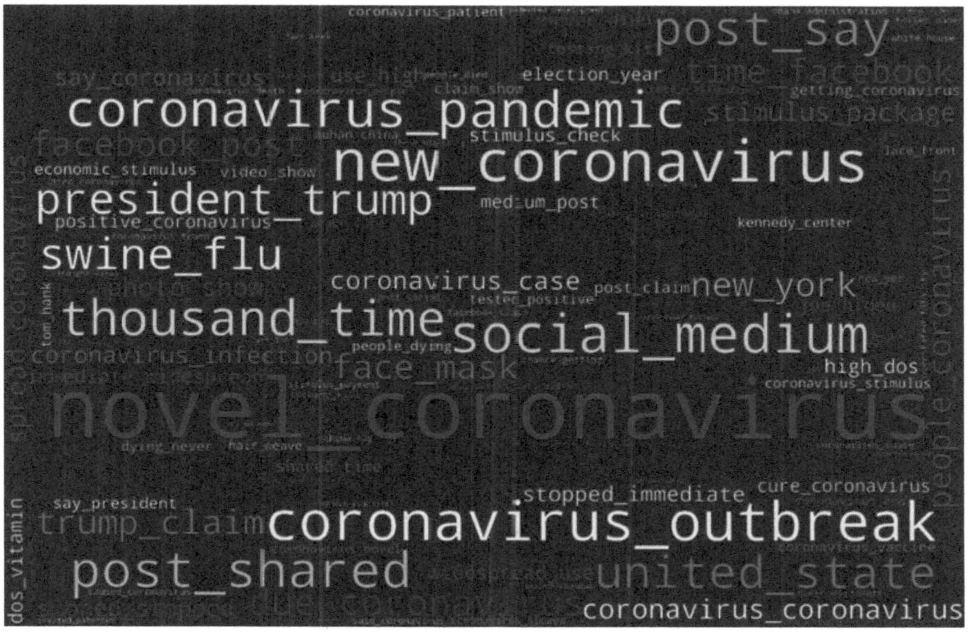

FIGURE 17.3 Bigram word clouds for the fake news.

For further exploration of the dataset, several word clouds of bigram and trigram were generated based on the fake and real news. Bigrams are two words that frequently occur in the document and trigrams are three words that frequently occur in the document (Malik et al., 2021). Figs. 17.3 and 17.4 illustrate the bigrams word clouds for both fake and real news, respectively, meanwhile Figs. 17.5 and 17.6 show the trigrams word clouds. Real news refer to the news which are from verified sources and give useful information related to COVID-19, whereas fake news make claims, myths, and speculations about COVID-19 which are verified that they are not true.

FIGURE 17.4 Bigram word clouds for the real news.

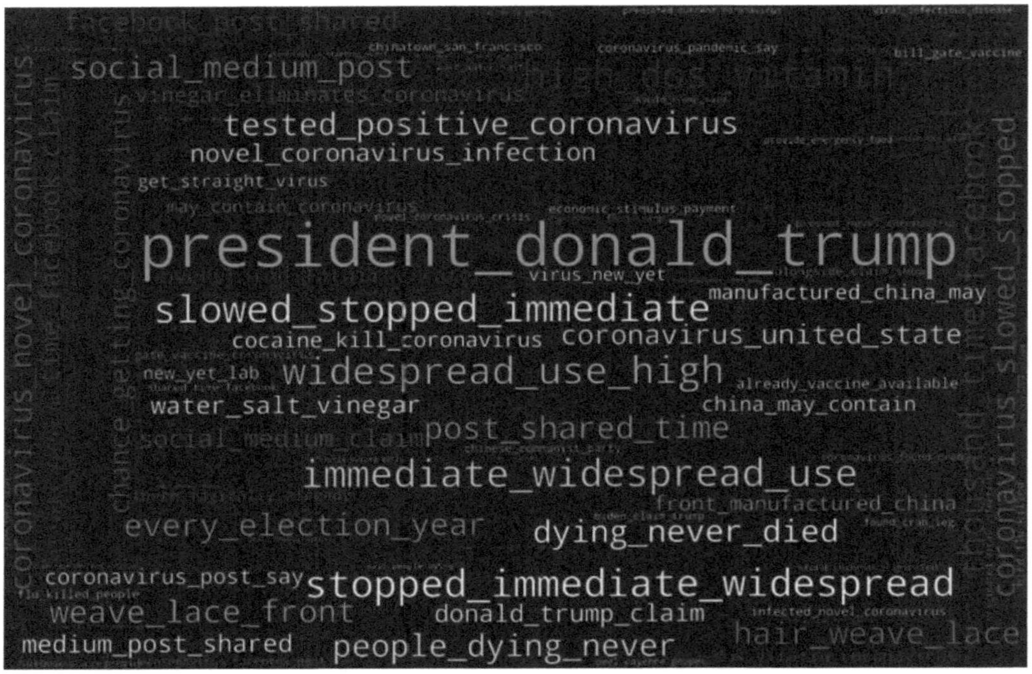

FIGURE 17.5 Trigram word clouds for fake news.

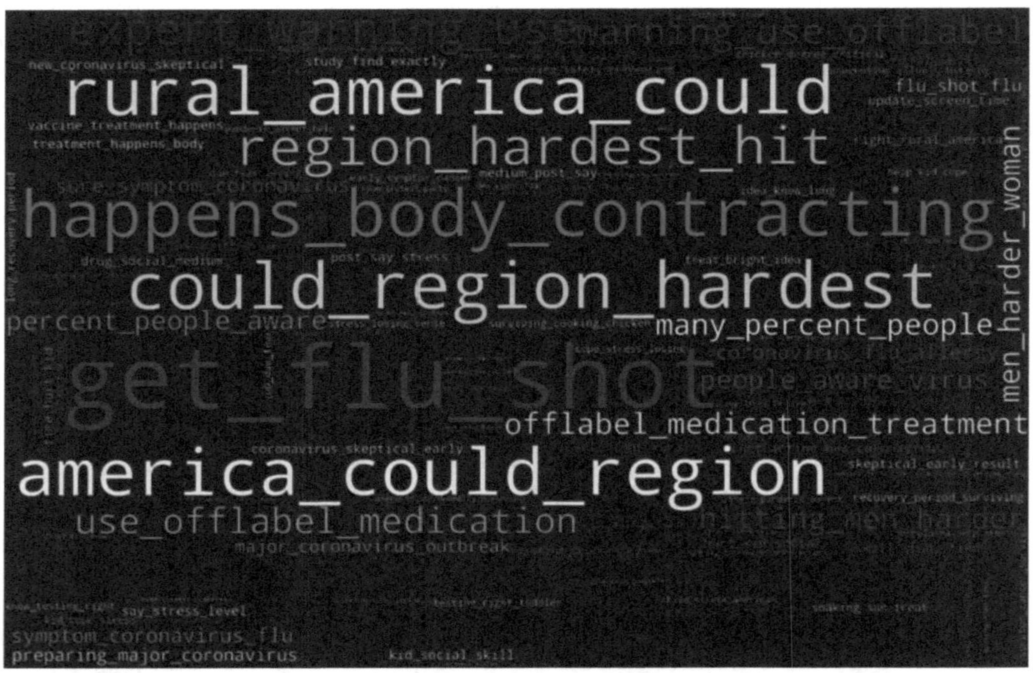

FIGURE 17.6 Trigram word clouds for real news.

Fig. 17.3 shows the bigrams word frequently used in COVID-19 news from the fake news dataset. The most frequently used words are "coronavirus_pandemic," "novel_coronavirus," "coronavirus_outbreak," "post_shared," "swine_flu," etc. In contrast, from Fig. 17.4, we can see that real news is much concerned about "know_coronavirus," "get_flu," "flu_season," "social_distancing," "face_mask," "vaccine_treatment," "expert_warning," etc. We could conclude that real news is more focused about the spread of COVID-19, warning about the precautions step, as well as medical treatment.

Fig. 17.5 shows the trigrams word clouds related to fake news that focuses on "tested_positive_coronavirus," "novel_coronavirus_infection," "stopped_immediate_widespread," "water_salt_vinegar," "cocaine_kill_coronavirus," etc. Fig. 17.6 illustrates the most frequent trigrams related to real news which are "expert_warning_use," "rural_america_could," "get_flu_shot," "exactly_vaccine_treatment," "off_label_medication_treatment," etc.

As shown on both bigram and trigram word clouds, there is a significant overlap of important words across fake news and real news. For example, for fake news, the top words mostly are "coronavirus," "post shared," "Facebook," and "shared thousand." Looking into the texts of the fake news, we could conclude that most of the COVID-19 news is related to the social media post which is Facebook. However, in the real news, the top words for both bigram and trigrams are "vaccine," "coronavirus," "flu," "expert warning," "medication," etc. This consists of the fact that the news is related to the treatment of COVID-19 by using medical treatments such as vaccines.

4.4 LDA topic modeling

In natural language processing, there is a generative statistical model called LDA which allows sets of observations to be explained by unobserved groups that explain why some parts of the data are similar. LDA is particularly very useful in finding the accuracy mixture of the topics within a given topic of the document set. In this study, LDA is used to perform topic modeling. Therefore, LDA topic modeling is performed using Python's Gensim package.

The first process is to import all the packages and libraries that will be used in the LDA topic modeling. The stop words are then downloaded and prepared. Each title of the news is then being tokenized into a list of words and the data is clean up by removing the punctuations and the unnecessary characters. The main input of the LDA model is dictionary and corpus; therefore, in order to train the model, the dictionary and the corpus must be created first.

4.4.1 Topics from LDA model

In this section, the keywords, relevant terms, and the word frequency are discussed. Tables 17.2 and 17.3 illustrated five examples of the topics that are generated from the LDA model Gensim with relevant terms and their word frequency for the fake and real news, respectively. The topics are selected based on the coherence score. Therefore, as shown in Table 17.2, topics 14, 11, 21, 2, and 11 are selected based on the coherence score each of which consists of their relevant terms and word frequency. For example, in topic 21, the relevant terms consist of keywords "virus" with the highest word frequency at "0.014" which means the word "virus" is the most probable word to appear in topic 21. In topic 21, there are 10 most

TABLE 17.2 Relevant topics, terms, and word frequency based on fake news.

Topic	Keywords/relevant terms and word frequency based on fake news	Topic content
14	'0.009*"**employee**" + 0.008*"**ban**" + 0.008*"**video**" + 0.007*"**sale**" + 0.007*"**treatment**" + 0.006*"**fatality**" + 0.005*"**warfare**" + 0.005*"**rate**" + 0.005*"**conspiracy**" + 0.005*"**company**"'	Organization/Company
16	'0.007*"**school**" + 0.006*"**manipulate**" + 0.006*"**rate**" – 0.006*"**quarantine**" + 0.006*"**cost**" + 0.005*"**folk**" + 0.005*"**claim**" – 0.005*"**beer**" + 0.005*"**lay**" + 0.005*"**mortality**"'	Community
21	'0.014*"**virus**" + 0.007*"**people**" + 0.006*"**wear**" + 0.006*"**write**" + 0.006*"**mask**" + 0.006*"**pandemic**" + 0.005*"**home**" + 0.005*"**raise**" + 0.005*"**originate**" + 0.005*"**product**"'	Standard operating procedures
2	'0.018*"**die**" + 0.011*"**death**" + 0.008*"**government**" + 0.007*"**people**" + 0.007*"**coronavirus**" + 0.007*"**control**" + 0.007*"**photo**" + 0.007*"**drug**" + 0.007*"**breaking**" + 0.007*"**win**"'	Mortality rate
11	'0.008*"**virus**" + 0.008*"**patent**" + 0.006*"**expire**" + 0.006*"**aide**" + 0.006*"**clip**" + 0.005*"**claim**" + 0.005*"**guard**" + 0.005*"**create**" + 0.005*"**order**" + 0.005*"**about**"'	Government

TABLE 17.3 Relevant topics, terms, and word frequency based on real news.

Topic	Keywords/relevant terms and word frequency based on real news	Topic content
11	'0.014*"**know**" + 0.011*"**people**" + 0.008*"**disinfect**" + 0.007*"**face**" + 0.007*"**symptom**" + 0.006*"**communication**" + 0.006*"**guide**" + 0.006*"**release**" + 0.006*"**recovery**" + 0.006*"**home**"'	COVID-19 outbreak
13	"0.015*"**drug**" + 0.011*"**contagious**" + 0.010*"**flu**" + 0.009*"**antibody**" + 0.008*"**death**" + 0.006*"**allergy**" + 0.006*"**inhibitor**" + 0.006*"**implication**" + 0.006*"**crisis**" + 0.006*"**population**"'	The symptoms
20	'0.015*"**health**" + 0.013*"**week**" + 0.009*"**drive**" + 0.009*"**outbreak**" + 0.008*"**lung**" + 0.008*"**cardiology**" + 0.008*"**asthma**" + 0.008*"**testing**" + 0.007*"**body**" + 0.006*"**novel**"'	Health condition
18	'0.009*"**help**" + 0.008*"**battle**" + 0.007*"**woman**" + 0.007*"**drug**" + 0.006*"**sign**" + 0.006*"**trial**" + 0.006*"**country**" + 0.006*"**video**" + 0.006*"**know**" + 0.006*"**fight**"'	COVID-19 battle
25	'0.007*"**plateau**" + 0.007*"**asthma**" + 0.007*"**pregnancy**" + 0.007*"**month**" + 0.006*"**swamp**" + 0.006*"**pandemic**" + 0.006*"**group**" + 0.005*"**effort**" + 0.005*"**foreshadow**" + 0.005*"**airline**"'	–

probable words that appear in the topic which are virus, people, wear, write, mask, pandemic, home, raise, originate, and product. Based on the expert opinion, we could conclude that this topic might be related to the "Standard Operating Procedure (SOP)."

In contrast, as shown in Table 17.3, in topic 25, the most probable words are plateau, asthma, pregnancy, month, swamp, pandemic, group, effort, foreshadow, and airline. Even though the words are not very relevant, it can be concluded that this topic is about the effect of COVID-19 on the some diseases such as asthma and also on the pregnant women.

4.4.2 pyLDAvis interpretation

Figs. 17.7 and 17.8 illustrate the pyLDAvis model for both fake and real news, respectively. These models are designed to interpret the topics in the topic modeling which are fit to the corpus of text data. Based on the figures, 22 topics are formed for the fake news and 28 topics for the real news. The term saliency refers to a measure of how much the term tells you about the topics. Relevance means a weighted average of the probability of the word which is given the topic and the word given the topic which is normalized by the probability of the topic. The size of the bubble measures the importance of the topics that are relative to the data.

4.4.3 LDA topic clustering

Figs. 17.9 and 17.10 show the topic clustering based on real and fake news, respectively. Fig. 17.9 illustrates eight clusters which are shown by different colors. The eight clusters are related to what people say about coronavirus, pandemic outbreak stimulus, the death virus, Facebook shared posts, Donald Trump president, flu swine government, people China door, and vaccine Senegal children. Among all clusters, the topic "coronavirus people says" is the largest cluster.

Fig. 17.10 also shows eight clusters which are coronavirus novel Facebook, coronavirus people say, coronavirus pandemic shows, coronavirus says states, coronavirus Trump president, coronavirus water people, coronavirus people say, and coronavirus new election. Most of the clusters involve the topics "coronavirus novel Facebook" and "coronavirus people say." Thus, in the fake news dataset, most of the topics are related to the spreading of the COVID-19 news through social media posts such as Facebook.

FIGURE 17.7 Final LDA model of fake news by pyLDAvis.

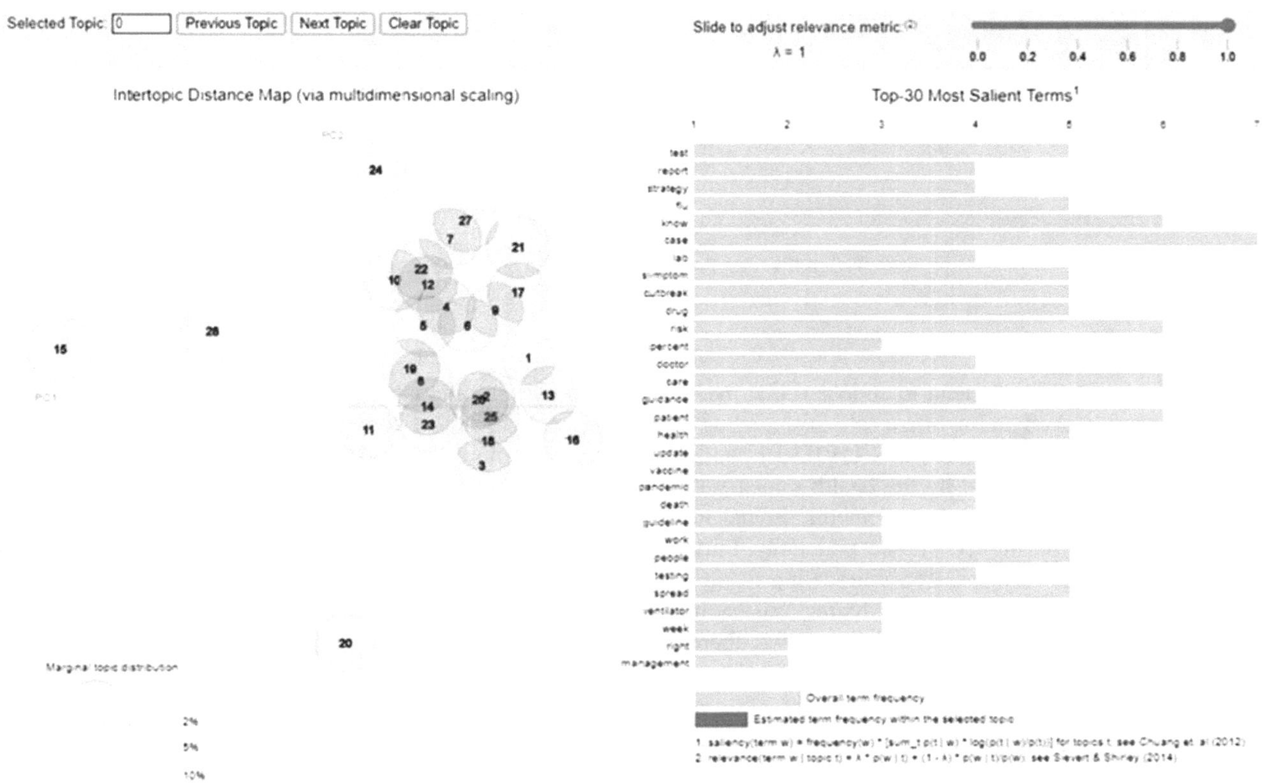

FIGURE 17.8 Final LDA model of true news by pyLDAvis.

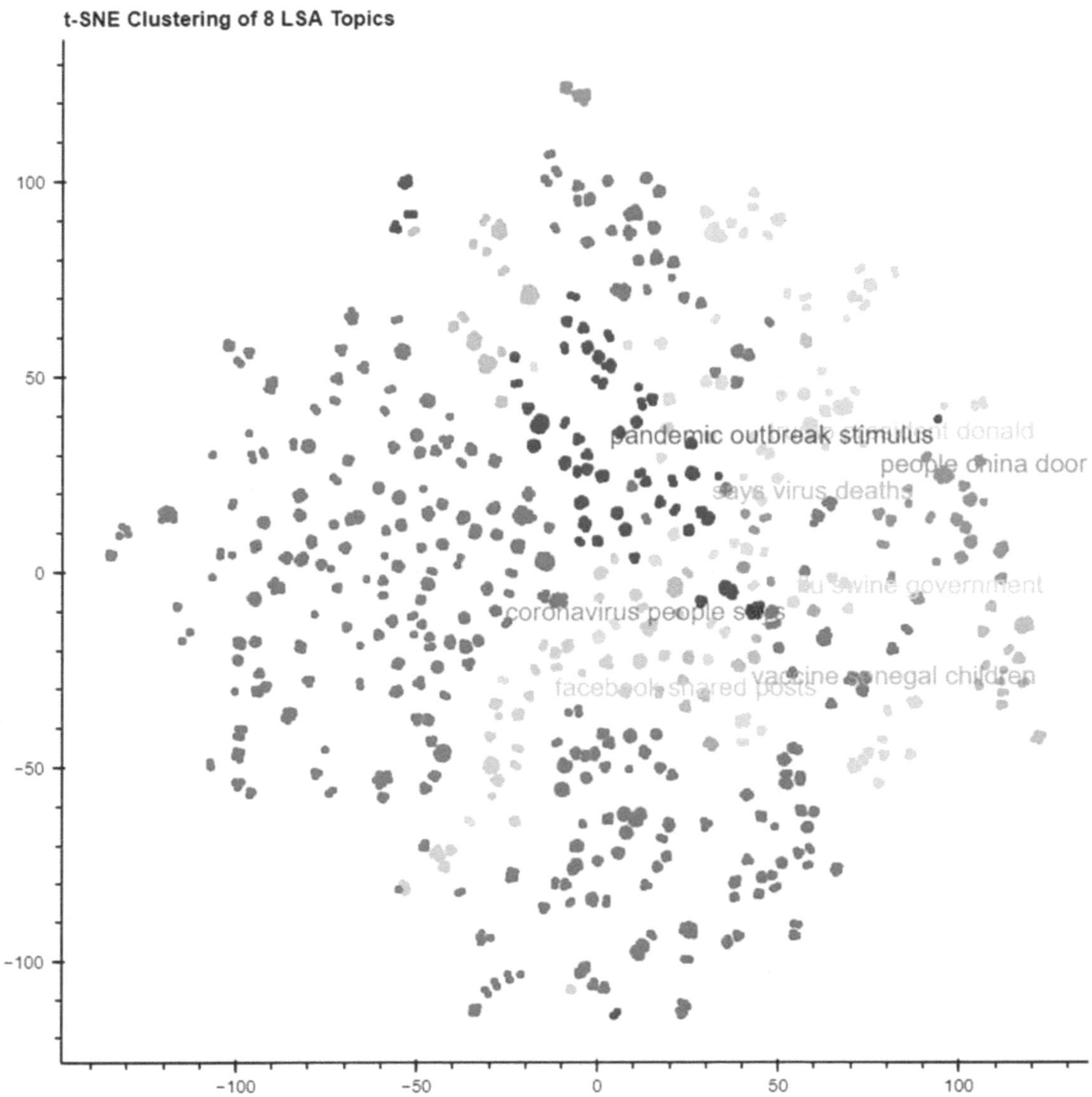

FIGURE 17.9 Topic clustering based on real news.

5. Conclusion

Over the last decade, people tend to choose social media platforms over traditional media such as newspapers, radio, and television as they played an important role in spreading the news quickly in a more convenient way. With the abundance of social media options and because of COVID-19 pandemic, people are more exposed to the news related to COVID-19 which is not being authorized by the health ministry during this pandemic. This study is useful in increasing awareness about disinformation spread in social media. Social media users must gain knowledge regarding fake news and misinformation especially during COVID-19 pandemic. Furthermore, the responsible parties should take serious actions and be aware of the COVID-19 news. Topic modeling results can assist the relevant parties to provide awareness about misinformation and fake to people for reducing misleading beliefs. Even though this study provides insight to increase awareness toward misinformation and fake news, there is still more information to be discovered.

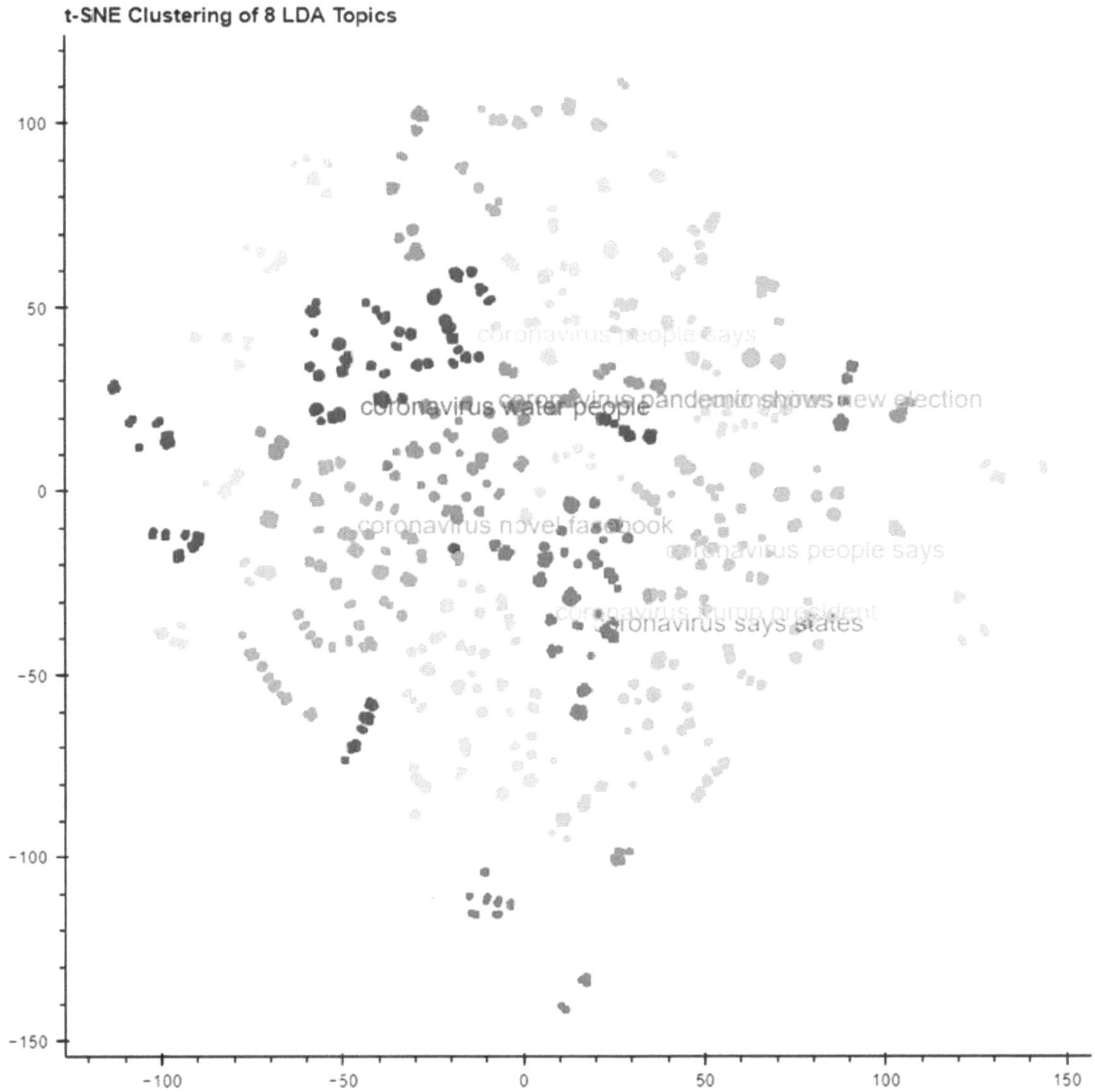

FIGURE 17.10 Topic clustering based on fake news.

Acknowledgments

The authors are thankful to School of Computer Sciences, and Division of Research and Innovation, USM, for providing financial support from Short Term Grant (304/PKOMP/6315435).

References

Aldwairi, M., & Alwahedi, A. (2018). Detecting fake news in social media networks. *Procedia Computer Science, 141*, 215–222. https://doi.org/10.1016/j.procs.2018.10.171

Bergström, A., & Jervelycke Belfrage, M. (2018). News in social media: Incidental consumption and the role of opinion leaders. *Digital Journalism, 6*(5), 583–598. https://doi.org/10.1080/21670811.2018.1423625

Bunker, D. (2020). Who do you trust? The digital destruction of shared situational awareness and the COVID-19 infodemic. *International Journal of Information Management, 55*(July), 102201. https://doi.org/10.1016/j.ijinfomgt.2020.102201

Cui, L., & Lee, D. (2020). Coaid: Covid-19 healthcare misinformation dataset. *arXiv*. preprint arXiv:2006.00885.

Duffy, A., Tandoc, E., & Ling, R. (2019). Too good to be true, too good not to share: The social utility of fake news. *Information, Communication & Society, 0*(0), 1–15. https://doi.org/10.1080/1369118X.2019.1623904

Hartley, K., & Vu, M. K. (2020). Fighting fake news in the COVID-19 era: Policy insights from an equilibrium model. *Policy Sciences, 53*(4), 735–758. https://doi.org/10.1007/s11077-020-09405-z

Islam, A. K. M. N., Laato, S., Talukder, S., & Sutinen, E. (2020). Misinformation sharing and social media fatigue during COVID-19: An affordance and cognitive load perspective. *Technological Forecasting and Social Change, 159*(July), 120201. https://doi.org/10.1016/j.techfore.2020.120201

Kadam, A. B., & Atre, S. R. (2020). Negative impact of social media panic during the COVID-19 outbreak in India. *Journal of Travel Medicine, 27*(3), 1–2. https://doi.org/10.1093/jtm/taaa057

Malik, E. F., Keikhosrokiani, P., & Asl, M. P. (2021). Text mining life cycle for a spatial reading of Viet Thanh Nguyen's the refugees (2017). In *2021 International congress of advanced technology and engineering (ICOTEN)*.

McGonagle, T. (2017). "Fake news": False fears or real concerns? *Netherlands Quarterly of Human Rights, 35*(4), 203–209. https://doi.org/10.1177/0924051917738685

Mutanga, M. B., & Abayomi, A. (2020). Tweeting on COVID-19 pandemic in South Africa: LDA-based topic modelling approach. *African Journal of Science, Technology, Innovation and Development, 0*(0), 1–10. https://doi.org/10.1080/20421338.2020.1817262

O'Connor, C., & Murphy, M. (2020). Going viral: Doctors must tackle fake news in the covid-19 pandemic. *BMJ, 369*, m1587. https://doi.org/10.1136/bmj.m1587

Okan, O., Bollweg, T. M., Berens, E. M., Hurrelmann, K., Bauer, U., & Schaeffer, D. (2020). Coronavirus-related health literacy: A cross-sectional study in adults during the COVID-19 infodemic in Germany. *International Journal of Environmental Research and Public Health, 17*(15), 1–20. https://doi.org/10.3390/ijerph17155503

Olowookere, T. A., Eke, B. O., & Oghenekaro, L. U. (2015). A Topic modelling-based framework for mining digital library's text documents. *IEEE African Journal of Computing and ICTs, Nigeria, 8*(4).

Pulido, C. M., Villarejo-Carballido, B., Redondo-Sama, G., & Gómez, A. (2020). COVID-19 infodemic: More retweets for science-based information on coronavirus than for false information. *International Sociology, 35*(4), 377–392. https://doi.org/10.1177/0268580920914755

Schifferes, S., Newman, N., Thurman, N., Corney, D., Göker, A., & Martin, C. (2014). Identifying and verifying news through social media: Developing a user-centred tool for professional journalists. *Digital Journalism, 2*(3), 406–418. https://doi.org/10.1080/21670811.2014.892747

Tangcharoensathien, V., Calleja, N., Nguyen, T., Purnat, T., D'Agostino, M., Garcia-Saiso, S., Landry, M., Rashidian, A., Hamilton, C., AbdAllah, A., Ghiga, I., Hill, A., Hougendobler, D., van Andel, J., Nunn, M., Brooks, I., Sacco, P. L., de Domenico, M., Mai, P., … Briand, S. (2020). Framework for managing the COVID-19 infodemic: Methods and results of an online, crowdsourced who technical consultation. *Journal of Medical Internet Research, 22*(6), 1–8. https://doi.org/10.2196/19659

Tasnim, S., Hossain, M. M., & Mazumder, H. (2020). Impact of rumors and misinformation on COVID-19 in social media. *Journal of preventive medicine and public health, 53*(3), 171–174. https://doi.org/10.3961/jpmph.20.094

Ying, S. Y., Keikhosrokiani, P., & Asl, M. P. (2021). Comparison of data analytic techniques for a spatial opinion mining in literary works: A review paper. In F. Saeed, F. Mohammed, & A. Al-Nahari (Eds.), *Innovative systems for intelligent health informatics* (pp. 523–535). Springer International Publishing. https://doi.org/10.1007/978-3-030-70713-2_49

Yuen, K. F., Wang, X., Ma, F., & Li, K. X. (2020). The psychological causes of panic buying following a health crisis. *International Journal of Environmental Research and Public Health, 17*(10). https://doi.org/10.3390/ijerph17103513

Chapter 18

Big medical data mining system (BigMed) for the detection and classification of COVID-19 misinformation

Nurul Husna Binti Rosli and Pantea Keikhosrokiani
School of Computer Sciences, Universiti Sains Malaysia, Minden, Penang, Malaysia

1. Introduction

Misinformation and disinformation regarding COVID-19 disease has spread on social media causing the public to feel insecure (Alahdal et al., 2020). This had caused anxiety among the public especially elderly since they are more exposed to the risk. Moreover, the rapid growth infection of COVID-19 in public causes the people to panic and become more cautious (Islam et al., 2020). The public should be updated with genuine and authorized information to avoid unnecessary panic.

The COVID-19 pandemic impacted people mentally and physiologically (Sood, 2020). The uncertainty of this disease had left the public feeling fear and anxiety. The disease was new and not enough information was provided. This leads to discrimination and prejudice driven by fear which have been flowing globally regardless of ages and races. Therefore, this chapter focuses on developing a big medical data mining system called BigMed which detects and classifies fake news related to COVID-19. BigMed system detects and analyzes news related to COVID-19 by using passive-aggressive classifier. Moreover, the BigMed system comes with several other functionalities which are providing up-to-date and genuine information related COVID-19, chatting options for authority and users to verify and validate news and improve their knowledge regarding COVID-19 disease.

2. Background and related works

The massive amount of fake news and misinformation of COVID-19 had spread rapidly especially with the use of social media platform (Scerri & Grech, 2020). Many people tend to share information through their social media without thinking how accurate the contents are and how they may affect others. Sharing misinformation and fake news on social medial becomes a global concern as this may intensify racism, fears, and stigma to the public. Specially during COVID-19 pandemic, the general public knowledge on COVID-19 disease is relatively low which is causing misconception (Wong et al., 2020). Therefore, the health information should be improvised to educate the public and increase their knowledge regarding COVID-19 disease. By having enough knowledge, necessary preventive measures can be taken once an emergency occurred.

A comparison of various machine learning models for accurate detection of fake sews was done (Poddar et al., 2019). This study compares Naïve Bayes, Support Vector Machine (SVM), Logistic regression, and Decision tree classifier. The results indicate that the most accurate algorithms for detecting fake news in large datasets are SVM and Logic regression compared to other algorithms. However, Naïve Bayes achieved high accuracy when using small datasets.

Another study used logistic regression to classify the fake news (Nada et al., 2019). Some of the feature extraction techniques that had been used are simple such as bag-of-word, n-grams, and TF-IDF. This paper also constructs a model to give a better understanding of the fake news detection and classification. The proposed model achieved 72% of accuracy by using the algorithm.

Big Data Analytics for Healthcare. https://doi.org/10.1016/B978-0-323-91907-4.00014-5

Furthermore, Multinomial Naïve Bayes (MNB) and SVM are used for the detection of Bangla Fake News (Hussain et al., 2020). Before using the algorithms, Count Vectorizer and TF-IDF Vectorizer had been used to extract the features. The SVM algorithm had achieved higher accuracy compared to MNB algorithm.

Finally, a study is conducted for the distinguishing True and Fake News using text mining and machine learning algorithm (Lee et al., 2020). The results indicate that decision tree algorithm obtains the highest accuracy compared to others algorithm. However, decision tree algorithm has it owns downside which takes longer time to compute. SVM algorithm obtains 99.53% of precision with slightly lower percentage compared to decision tree algorithm.

The existing studies are compared in Table 18.1 based on their model, algorithm, strength, and weakness.

There are various existing systems for the detection of the COVID-19 news. For instance, Snope which focuses on fake news detection, or Corona Tracker and Domo which include Coronavirus Tracker feature. Furthermore, Domo, Ncov2019, and the World Health Organization (WHO) perform Coronavirus Tracking and include Coronavirus information/dashboard. BigMed system includes all features of fake news detection, Corona Tracker, and Coronavirus information/dashboard. Finally, this system also focuses on providing useful information for the users such as the daily news cases worldwide, the symptoms for this disease, and so forth.

3. Development methodology

There are various System Development Life Cycle and development methodologies (Augustine & Keikhosrokiani, 2021; Keikhosrokiani, 2019; Ravichandran & Keikhosrokiani, 2021). The spiral development methodology is used for developing BigMed system due to its flexibility. The changes can be made in the middle of process once changes and new requirements have been identified. Furthermore, this model has low risk at release since the risk has been identified in the last phase. The risk analysis is done in every iteration before the final release.

The spiral model consists of four main phases which are (1) identification of the objectives, (2) analyze and design, (3) develop and test, and (4) perform review and risk analysis. In the first phase, problem statements and objectives are identified before developing the system. Hence, the requirement gathering for BigMed system is done by studying existing works and system to determine the functionality of the system. Afterward, the analyze and design phase is carried. In this phase, the system constructs all suitable UML diagrams based on the requirements that had been studied in the first phase. Therefore, a prototype for analysis and design is done before starting the BigMed system. The third phase is developing and testing phase. This phase focuses on the process of writing codes for the system. All main functionalities are completed in this phase such as fake news detection and displaying information of COVID-19. Once the system coding is finished, multiple tests are carried out to ensure the functions can be run accordingly. The last phase is performing review and risk analysis. In this phase, the developed system is reviewed to ensure BigMed system satisfies all the requirements. The iteration will be done until the system is developed completely.

A general overview of BigMed system is illustrated in Fig. 18.1. BigMed focuses on two main artificial intelligence features which are fake news detection using machine learning and analytical dashboard using Power BI integrated to the web-based system. There are two main parties involved in BigMed system: (1) data analyst and (2) system user (public, healthcare professionals, ministries, etc.).

4. System design and implementation

4.1 System architecture and module design

System architecture for BigMed system is illustrated in Fig. 18.2 which shows user interaction with the system for inserting the news. Then BigMed system processes the data using machine learning to detect whether the news is fake or real. Then the result will be displayed to the user. In the back end, the model detection is carried out based on the model that had been trained before using machine learning. Once news detection is done, the system will then display the output whether the news is fake or not. For the dashboard part, the data is displayed based on the data stored in database. Multiple diagrams displayed in the real-time dashboard are shown in user interface section.

Two main modules are included in BigMed system which are (1) antimedical fake news modules and (2) dashboard module (Fig. 18.3). In the first module, data which is news related to COVID-19 will be inserted from social media to the system. The system will use machine learning techniques such as passive-aggressive classifier to classify the news into fake and real. Then, the results will be displayed to distinguish the fake and real news. The next module is the real-time analytical dashboard which concerns to display up-to-date, reliable, and authorized information about COVID-19 for preventive purposes.

TABLE 18.1 Comparison of existing studies.

No.	Title	Author and year	Summary	Model	Algorithm	Strength	Weakness
1.	Comparison of Various Machine Learning Models for Accurate Detection of Fake News	(Poddar et al., 2019)	Using multiple of algorithm to detect fake news	Computational model of probabilistic and geometric machine learning model	1. SVM 2. Logistic regression 3. Naïve Bayes 4. Decision tree	1. Better accuracy for large datasets (SVM and logistic regression) 2. Better accuracy for small datasets (Naïve Bayes)	1. Decision tree accuracy not achieved
2.	Fake News Detection Using Logistic Regression	(Nada et al., 2019)	Used Logistic regression language processing technique to classify fake news	Computational model	Logistic regression	1. The accuracy of the classifier is 72%	–
3.	Detection of Bangla Fake News using MNB and SVM Classifier	(Hussain et al., 2020)	Conduct experimental analysis on the detection of fake news based on multinomial Naïve Bayes (MNB) and Support Vector machine (SVM) algorithm	Computational model of probabilistic and geometric machine learning model	1. SVM 2. Multinomial Naïve Bayes (MNB)	1. Both algorithms achieved high accuracy with SVM 96.64% while MNB 93.32%	1. MNB accuracy little bit lower
4.	Distinguishing True and Fake News by Using Text Mining and Machine Learning Algorithm	(Lee et al., 2020)	Multiple of algorithm has been used in order to detect fake news	Computational model of probabilistic and geometric machine learning model	1. SVM 2. Decision tree 3. Naive Bayes 4. Logistic regression	1. The decision tree obtains the highest accuracy which is 99.57% while SVM 99.53% compared to logistic regression and Naïve Bayes 94%.	1. The decision tree takes longer time to compute.

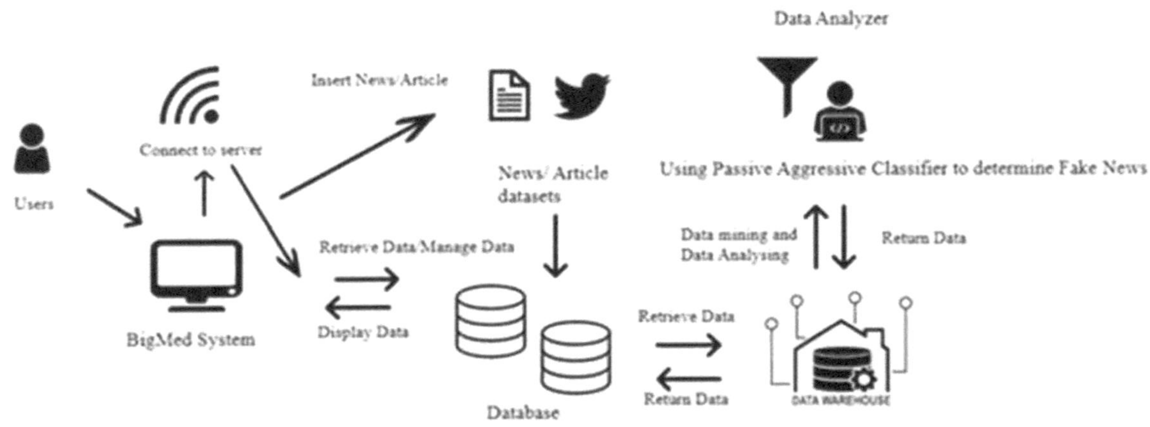

FIGURE 18.1 General overview of BigMed system.

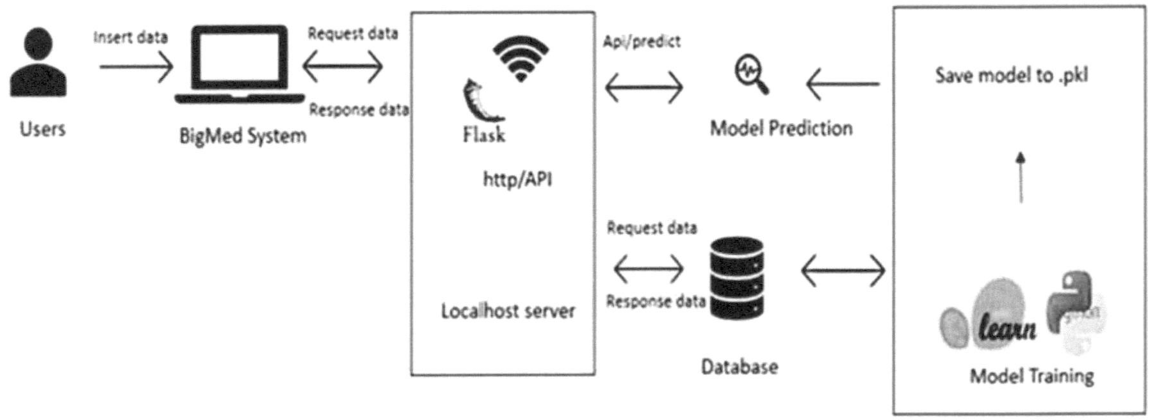

FIGURE 18.2 Architecture design for BigMed system.

4.2 Use case diagram

Use case diagram for BigMed is very simple with only one actor as shown in Fig. 18.4. Data analyst and admin are working in the back end. The actor or system user can enter news related to COVID-19 to the system. Then BigMed system will classify the result and display to the user whether the news is fake or real. In addition, the user can view the analytical dashboard for accessing the authorized information related to COVID-19 general information, daily cases, and information related to the prevention of this disease.

4.3 System interface design

BigMed is a web-based system consists of three main pages which are the Homepage, Fake News Detection/Classification, and the analytical dashboard (Fig. 18.5). The interface is user friendly and simple to enable every user to use the system without having problem. In homepage, the users are able to read validated and verified information related to coronavirus such as overview, prevention information to avoid coronavirus, vaccine information, and symptom details. The data is taken from the WHO website and store in the database. Furthermore, the users can click on the fake news page and insert any news to validate the status of the news. Finally, the analytical dashboard page of BigMed system displays multiple verified information such as the daily cases of coronavirus worldwide. In addition, users can observe the patterns of the coronavirus cases, deaths, and recovery cases.

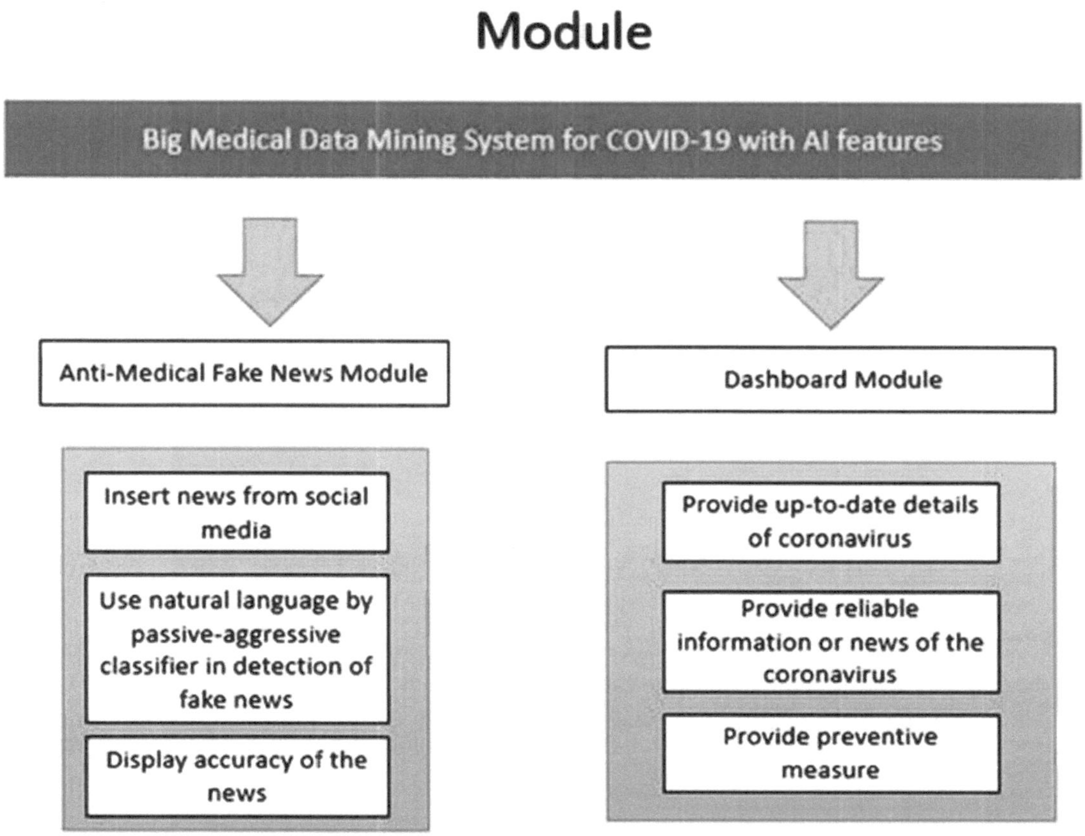

FIGURE 18.3 Overall module diagram for BigMed system.

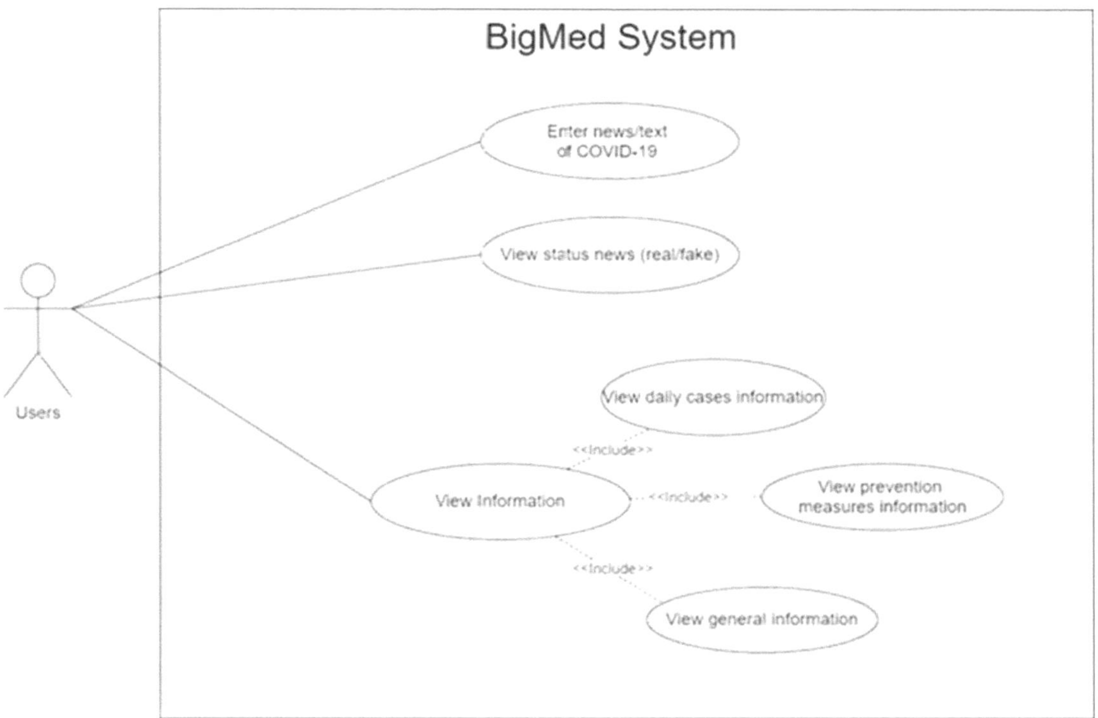

FIGURE 18.4 Use case diagram for BigMed.

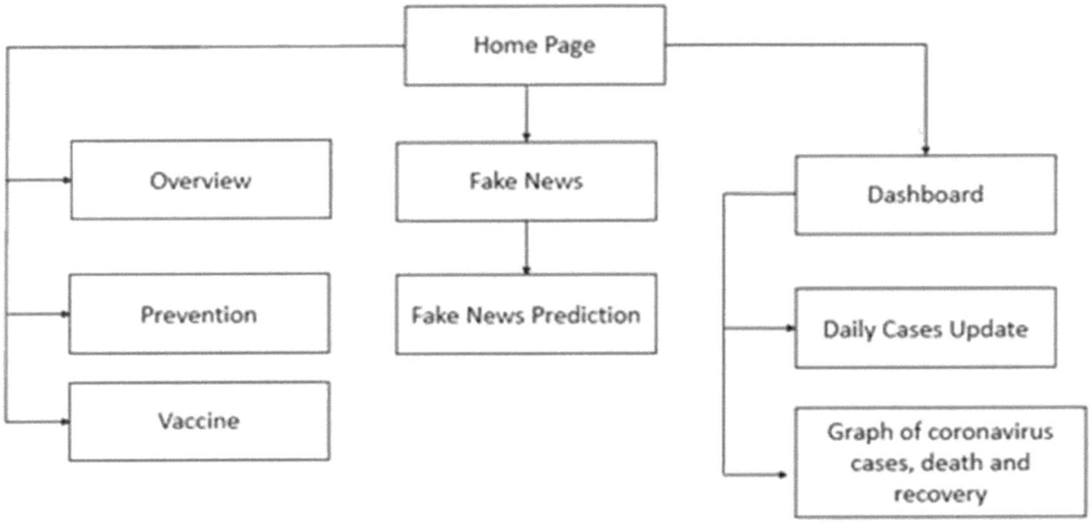

FIGURE 18.5 System interface design for BigMed.

4.4 Implementation strategy

To complete the BigMed System, top-down approach is used as the implementation strategy (Fig. 18.6). The problem is broken down into smaller pieces and been resolved phase by phase to make the process less complex. The implementation process begins with completing the fake news detection and classification module as these are the main and vital modules of BigMed system.

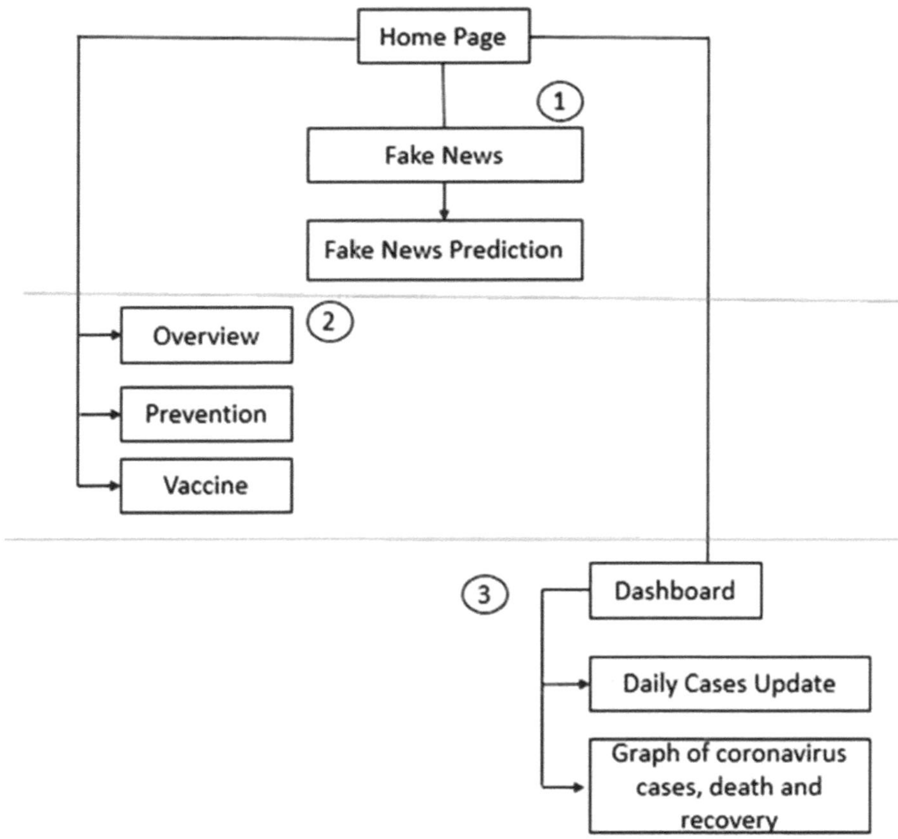

FIGURE 18.6 Implementation and completion flow of BigMed system.

The next phase of implementation process is focused on the home pages. The homepage consists of overview, prevention, and vaccine module. The data is collected from the WHO websites as one of the reliable sources of medical data.

Finally, the analytical dashboard of BigMed system is built. The analytical dashboard consists of the updates for daily coronavirus cases from different countries and data visualization. The data is collected in a spreadsheet from John Hopkins University which is updating daily. Furthermore, the dashboard consists of bar chart which shows the trends of daily cases, death cases, recovery cases, and provides prediction in the future.

5. Data analytics and user interface

5.1 Dataset and data preprocessing

The first step in building fake news detection and classification module is obtaining dataset which consists of over 1000 news. The data was not organized properly and includes some blank rows and columns. The data also consists of unnecessary attributes that are not used for BigMed system. Therefore, all unnecessary attributes, rows, and columns are removed from the dataset. The necessary attributes for the fake news detection and classification module are title, text, and label. The text is labeled into two classes of fake and real. This falls into supervised machine learning category since the data is labeled. As the data was imbalanced, resampling was done to include 500 real news and 500 of fake news in the dataset. The real news data has been taken from multiple reliable sources such as Healthline, ScienceDaily, medicalnewstoday, and WebMD websites, while most the fake news data has been taken from different sites. Some other data preprocessing steps such as tokenization, removing stop words, and feature extraction like Term Frequency-Inverse Document Frequency for natural language processing are done.

5.2 News detection and classification

Fake news detection or news classification is done using passive-aggressive classifier which is one of the machine learning algorithms. Multiple libraries such as panda, scikit-learn, and NumPy are used in python. Before going further, the preprocessing steps like tokenization, removing stop word, and feature extraction like Term Frequency-Inverse Document Frequency are done to find the important words and the most appeared words in the news. In this study, the combination of features extraction techniques and natural processing techniques is used with a passive-aggressive classification algorithm. The stop words had been removed before using the classifier and training the model. Then, the data has been split into two datasets which are the train dataset and test dataset. And finally, the passive-aggressive classifier has been used.

The classifier works by responding aggressively to incorrect prediction and remains passive when there is a correct prediction. The achieved max_df value is 0.7 which means to ignore the terms that appear in more than 70% of the documents. Based on the calculation, the system achieved 94.75% accuracy for the passive-aggressive classifier. Hence, it proves passive-aggressive classifier is one of the effective algorithms to detect fake news related to COVID-19 in the BigMed System.

Some examples of the news classifiers in BigMed system are shown in this section. For instance, if we extract the news from a reliable website (Fig. 18.7), paste the news in BigMed module and run it, it will consider the news as the "Real" news (Fig. 18.8).

Another example is shown in this section for testing fake news in BigMed system. For instance, if the news from Gossipblend.com (Fig. 18.9) is extracted and added in BigMed news classifier, the system will consider it as "Fake" news (Fig. 18.10).

5.3 Analytical dashboard

The analytical dashboard module is implemented using Power BI tool and integrated to the web-based system. It consists of four parts which are summary of cases, trend and forecasting, province and state breakdown, and lastly the fake news analysis. The source of data is obtained from John Hopkins University.

The trend and forecasting part is predicted by taking 10 points from the data and trying to predict the next day cases by using the previous 10 points data with 95% confidence interval. Then the dashboard displays forecasting for the daily new coronavirus cases, death, and recovery data. For the fake news analysis, the data had been taken from the datasets used for news classification. Some examples of BigMed analytical dashboard are shown in Figs. 18.11 and 18.12.

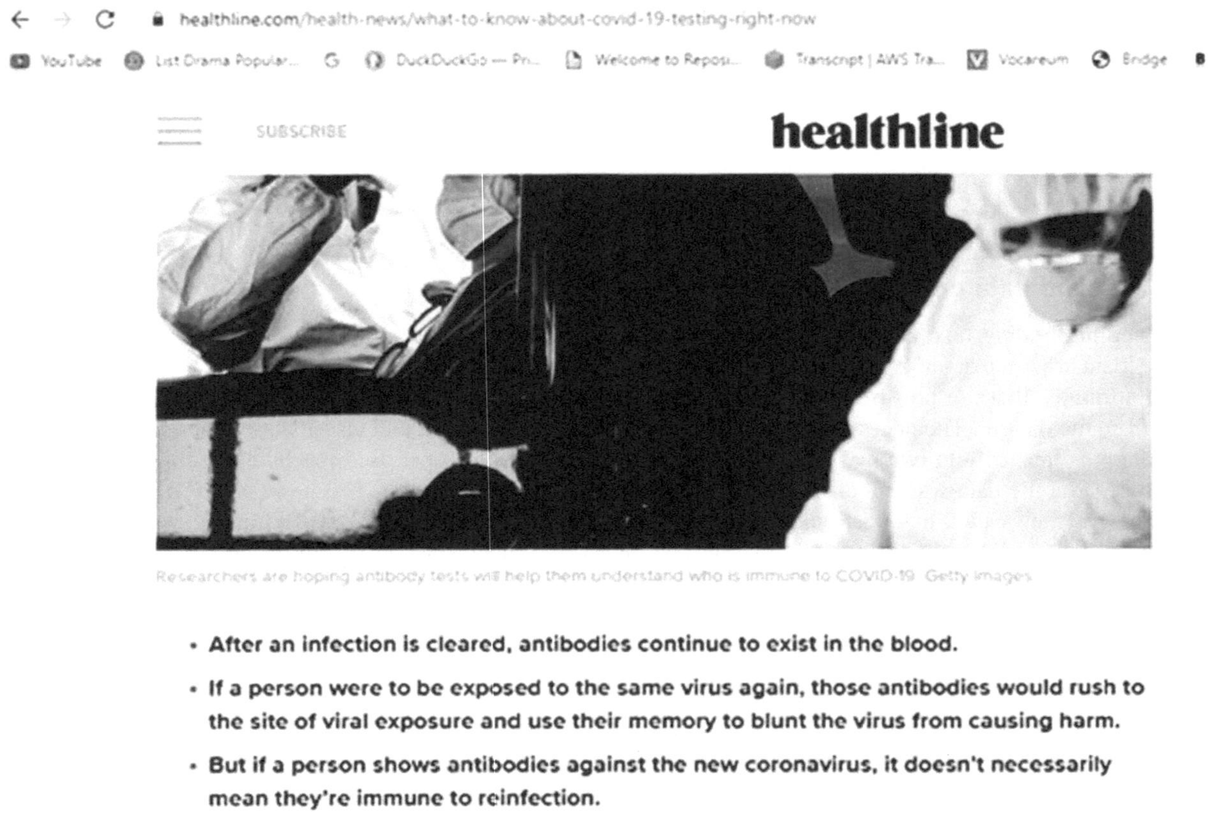

FIGURE 18.7 Healthline website related to coronavirus (real news).

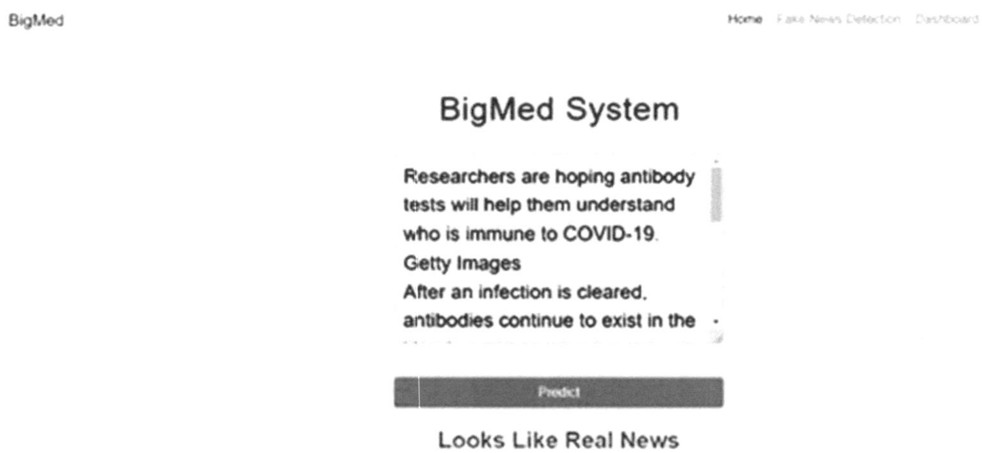

FIGURE 18.8 User interface for testing real news in BigMed system.

6. System testing and evaluation

6.1 Testing strategy

Testing is one of the vital parts to ensure the BigMed system can meet the objectives that had been proposed in the project and able to run successfully in every condition. Testing strategy describes how the software process is completed to ensure the quality and reliability of the system. BigMed system testing strategy consists of four main steps which are unit testing, integration testing, and system testing, and user acceptance testing.

FIGURE 18.9 News from Gossipblend.com (fake news).

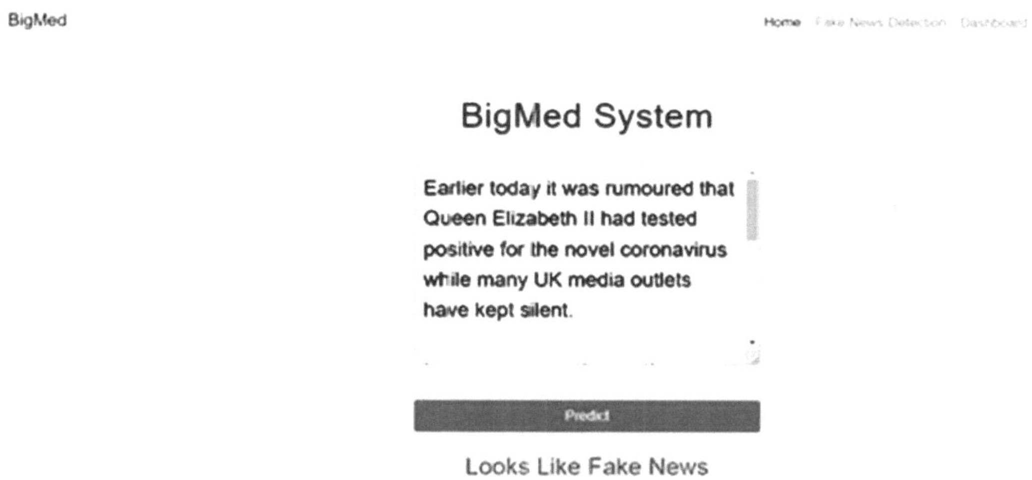

FIGURE 18.10 User interface for testing fake news in BigMed system.

6.1.1 Unit testing

The unit testing is performed by testing each function individually. The unit testing for BigMed system consists of two modules which are the fake news prediction module and the dashboard module. In both modules, it has multiple functionalities and features to be tested before integrating them into one system. Each function has been worked perfectly for unit testing.

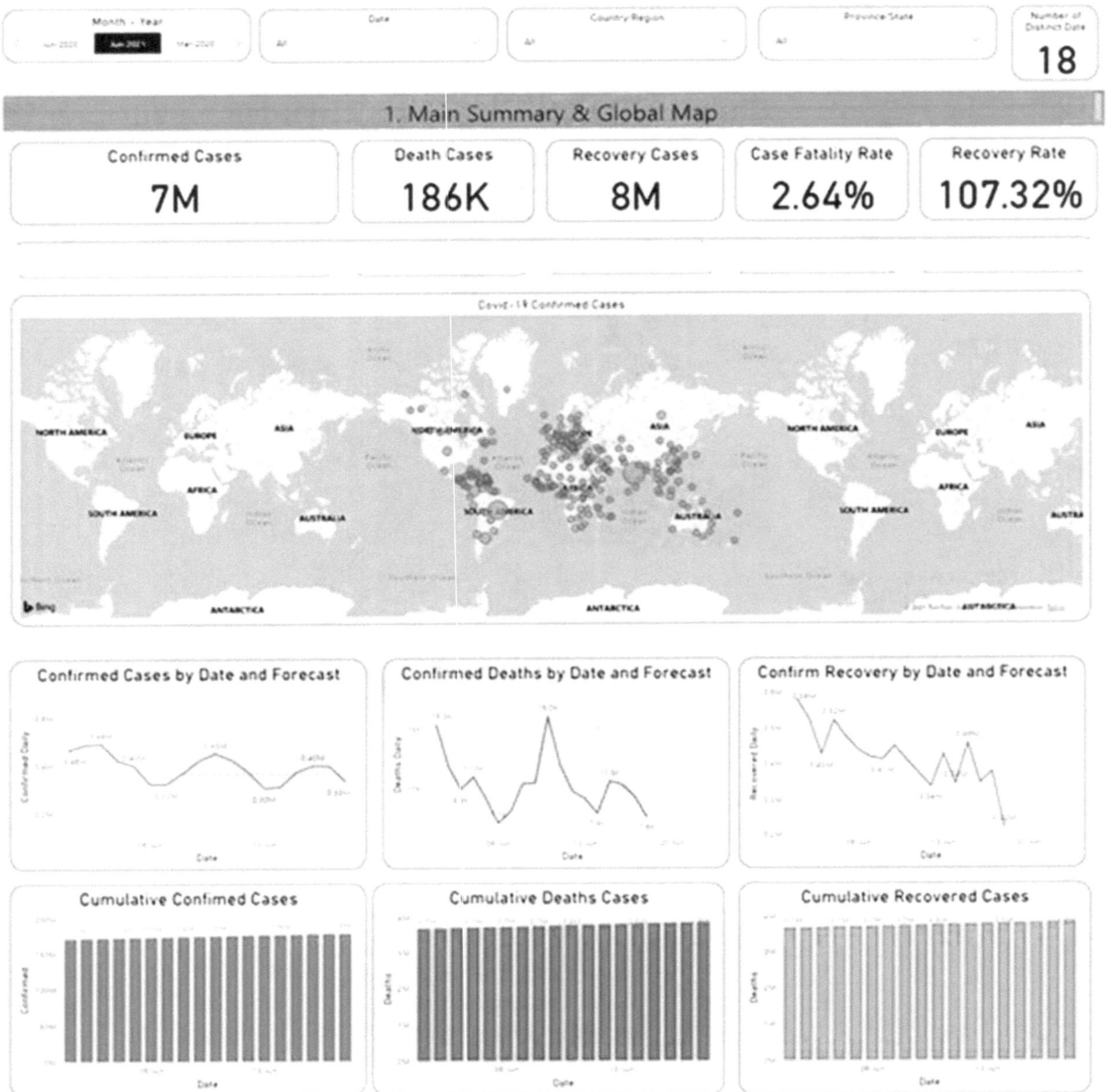

FIGURE 18.11 BigMed system analytical dashboard: trends and analysis.

6.1.2 Integration testing

After the completion of unit testing, the integration testing is carried out. In this step, both modules of BigMed system are combined into a system and ensure that the system can run perfectly. Multiple errors were occurred during the integration testing. Therefore, before fixing the errors, we must ensure each function works perfectly when both modules have been integrated.

6.1.3 System testing

System testing is performed before the completion of the development process. The testing has been done for the entire system which covered the fake news detection and dashboard module. In each of the modules, we ensured that all functions work accordingly. Finally, multiple test cases are done to ensure the output of the system is as expected and the objectives of the system are achieved.

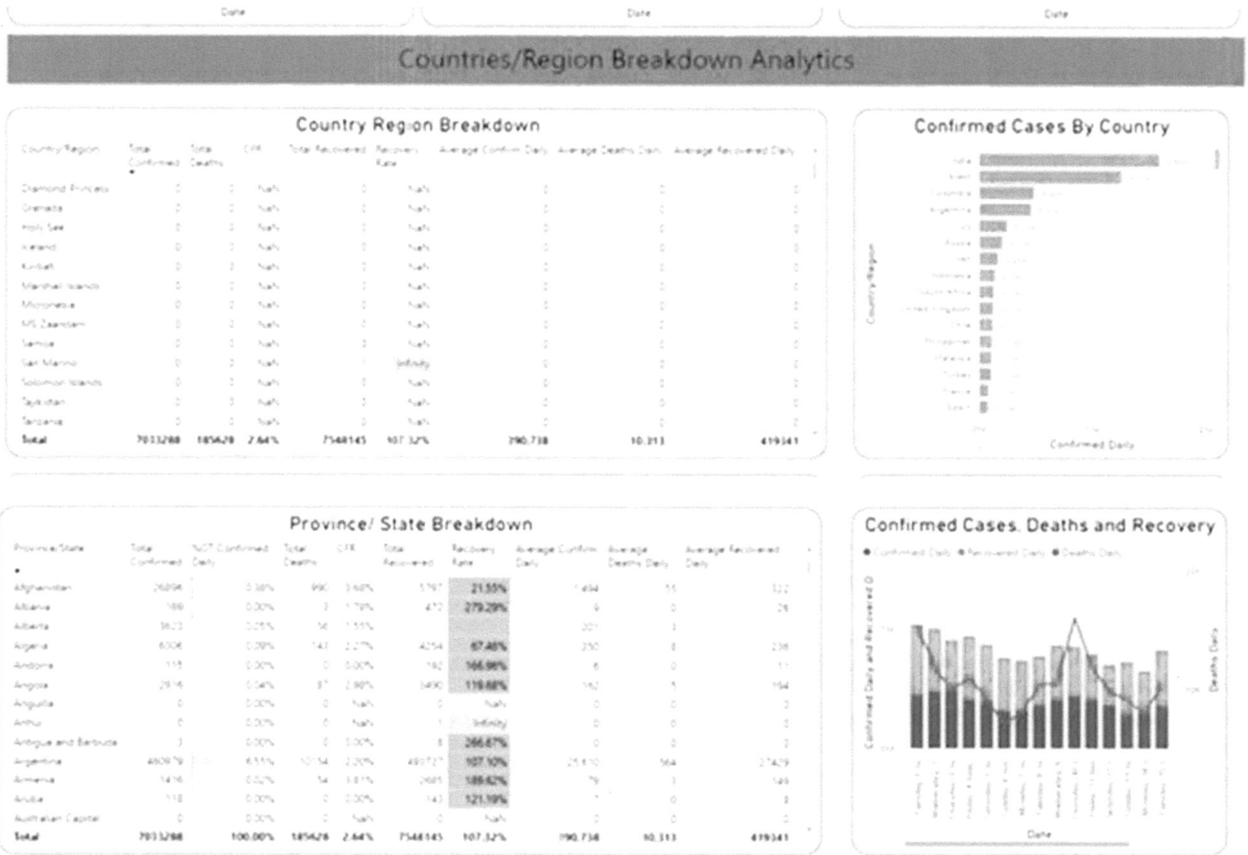

FIGURE 18.12 BigMed system analytical dashboard: country/region breakdown.

6.1.4 User acceptance test

User acceptance test is done by collecting data from the users after using BigMed. The total number of 16 users have tested the system and responded to the questionnaire. The questions were related to the system features, usability, and how the system can be improved from time to time. Majority of the respondents satisfy with the system features and believe that the system is useable and user friendly. Several features of BigMed System attracted the users such as the visualization trends, forecasting in the analytical dashboard, fake news detection engine, and the clear results of BigMed system. Finally, the users believe that the system can be improved by adding some features such as adding other languages for the fake news detection engine, adding more classifications for the fake news, detecting the fake news by using pictures or URL, and improving the user interface.

7. Conclusion

BigMed System is proposed to distinguish real and fake news and to provide awareness to people about the infectious coronavirus. The main goal of this system it to ensure all users receive credible source of news and avoid any kind of misinformation. After system implementation and testing, the requirements for the proposed system are met and the objectives are achieved successfully. BigMed provides an engine to recognize fake news related to coronavirus. User can insert the news in the engine to check whether it is fake or real Furthermore, an analytical dashboard is designed to provide proper and authorized information to educate the users about coronavirus. The main module of BigMed system, which is fake news detection, used machine learning algorithm such as passive-aggressive classifier and deploys it by using Flask. The dataset used for training the fake news detection engine consists of 1000 data, out of which 500 data are related to real news and the other 500 are related to fake news after resampling. Power BI analytical dashboard was designed and integrated to the web-based BigMed system to show the updated information related to coronavirus. BigMed system can assist the public, healthcare provider, ministries, etc., to combat fake news during COVID-19 pandemic, and it can provide awareness about coronavirus.

The system can be improved in the future by enhancing the fake news module to include more classifications of misinformation. In addition, the fake news module can be multilingual. Apart from that, in addition to passive-aggressive classifier, more algorithms can be tried to provide better accuracy for the fake news detection module. Finally, more data visualization and real-time information related to coronavirus can be provided by the system.

Acknowledgments

The authors are thankful to School of Computer Sciences, and Division of Research and Innovation, USM for providing financial support from Short Term Grant (304/PKOMP/6315435).

References

Alahdal, H., Basingab, F., & Alotaibi, R. (2020). An analytical study on the awareness, attitude and practice during the COVID-19 pandemic in Riyadh, Saudi Arabia [Article]. *Journal of Infection and Public Health, 13*(10), 1446–1452. https://doi.org/10.1016/j.jiph.2020.06.015

Augustine, C. A., & Keikhosrokiani, P. (2021). A habit-change support web-based system with big data analytical features for hospitals (doctive). In F. Saeed, F. Mohammed, & A. Al-Nahari (Eds.), *Innovative systems for intelligent health informatics* (pp. 91–101). Springer International Publishing. https://doi.org/10.1007/978-3-030-70713-2_10

Hussain, M. G., Hasan, M. R., Rahman, M., Protim, J., & Hasan, S. (2020). *Detection of Bangla fake news using MNB and SVM classifier.*

Islam, M. S., Ferdous, M. Z., & Potenza, M. N. (2020). Panic and generalized anxiety during the COVID-19 pandemic among Bangladeshi people: An online pilot survey early in the outbreak. *Journal of Affective Disorders, 276*, 30–37.

Keikhosrokiani, P. (2019). *Perspectives in the development of mobile medical information systems: Life Cycle, management, methodological approach and application* (1st ed.). Academic press. https://doi.org/10.1016/C2018-0-02485-8

Lee, H., Choe, I. P., In, J., & Kim, H. S. (2020). Distinguishing true and fake news by using text mining and machine learning algorithm. *American Journal of Data Mining and Knowledge Discovery, 5*(2), 20–26.

Nada, F., Khan, B. F., Maryam, A., Nooruz-Zuha, & Ahmad, Z. (2019). Fake News Detection Using Logistic Regression. *International Research Journal of Engineering and Technology, 06*(05).

Poddar, K., Amali, G., & S, U. (2019). *Comparison of various machine learning models for accurate detection of fake news.* https://doi.org/10.1109/i-PACT44901.2019.8960044

Ravichandran, B. D., & Keikhosrokiani, P. (2021). An emotional-persuasive habit-change support mobile application for heart disease patients (BeHabit). In F. Saeed, F. Mohammed, & A. Al-Nahari (Eds.), *Innovative systems for intelligent health informatics* (pp. 252–262). Springer International Publishing. https://doi.org/10.1007/978-3-030-70713-2_25

Scerri, M., & Grech, V. (2020). COVID-19, its novel vaccination and fake news — what a brew. *Early Human Development*, 105256. https://doi.org/10.1016/j.earlhumdev.2020.105256

Sood, S. (2020). Psychological effects of the coronavirus disease-2019 pandemic. *Research & Humanities in Medical Education, 7*(0), 23–26. https://www.rhime.in/ojs/index.php/rhime/article/view/264.

Wong, C. L., Chen, J., Chow, K. M., Law, B. M. H., Chan, D. N. S., So, W. K. W., Leung, A. W. Y., & Chan, C. W. H. (2020). Knowledge, attitudes and practices towards COVID-19 amongst ethnic minorities in Hong Kong [Article]. *International Journal of Environmental Research and Public Health, 17*(21), 1–13. https://doi.org/10.3390/ijerph17217878. Article 7878.

Section VI

Challenges and future of big data in healthcare

Chapter 19

Privacy security risks of big data processing in healthcare

Zhihan Lv[1] and Liang Qiao[2]

[1]*Faculty of Arts, Uppsala University, Uppsala, Sweden;* [2]*College of Computer Science & Technology, Qingdao University, Qingdao, Shandong, China*

1. Introduction

As Internet technology develops so fast, the analysis of big data has gradually penetrated the medical industry, and since the medical information is digitalized, so many electronic medical records, hospital information system, medical imaging, and other data emerged. Experts in related fields predict that the data in the medical field will exceed 35 ZB by 2020, which is 44 times more than that in 2009 (Stankovic, 2017). At present, big data has gradually changed the field of public healthcare including clinical operation, drug research and development, and personalized treatment. In 2016, the state council of China issued The Guidance on Promoting and Standardizing the Application and Development of Big Data in Healthcare. It reflects that China has incorporated the data generated in the healthcare sector into the strategic planning of big data development. Therefore, promoting data application in the field of healthcare, constructing a mutually integrated information platform, expanding data application in the field of healthcare, enriching services in the field of Internet and healthcare, and improving and strengthening the construction of related systems can effectively promote and serve the health of the public (Rizwan et al., 2018). While the development of big data in the field of healthcare has brought huge economic and social benefits to the society, the privacy and security of data has become increasingly prominent. The DarkOverlord stole 180,000 patient records through trespass; nearly half a million patient records are compromised after a hack of DataBreaches.net; a phishing attack on Washington medical staff result in more than 80,000 medical records released. The privacy breach of healthcare data has had a nasty impact, while in the context of big data, the way of privacy disclosure is more secretive. Therefore, correct identification of privacy security risks can reduce the probability of occurrence of privacy security of medical data (Emara, 2017; Mahmoud et al., 2018).

Based on this, an innovative analysis is made based on the existing data of China's healthcare field. In addition, questionnaires are issued under big data to collect and summarize the risk factors of healthcare data privacy and security assessed by doctors, nurses, managers, and technicians. The results are intended to lay the foundation for the follow-up research of healthcare big data (HBD).

2. Related work

2.1 HBD mining

At present, big data technology has been widely applied in healthcare, manufacturing, energy, transportation, environment, and many other fields (Cena, Gena, Houben, & Strohmaier, 2017). For example, Enayet, Razzaque, Hassan, Alamri and Fortino (2018) indicated that real-time access, sharing, storage, processing, and analysis of big data need to be realized. Villeneuve, Harwin, Holderbaum, Janko and Sherratt (2017) showed that detecting vital data of patients with chronic diseases facilitated doctors to make clear decisions. Chen, Hao, Hwang, Wang and Wang (2017) showed that accurate analysis of medical data contributes to early disease detection, patient care, community services, and other work, in addition to predicting disease outbreaks. Juddoo, George, Duquenoy and Windridge (2018) showed that in the health industry, the hierarchical framework was used to organize the dimension of data quality; the high-ranked dimension

Big Data Analytics for Healthcare. https://doi.org/10.1016/B978-0-323-91907-4.00020-0

categories in HBD can be determined to achieve data management and control. Caicedo, Prieto, Pezoa, Sobarzo and Ghani (2019) proposed a novel framework for Software Defined Network Teaching and Research. This teaching method can be applied to help medical practitioners engage in HBD research. At present, HBD analysis can help doctors make correct decisions and predict the occurrence of diseases.

2.2 Privacy issues of HBD

But as healthcare data develop, the frequency of data privacy and security issues is increasing. Kraemer, Braten, Tamkittikhun and Palma (2017) showed that with the development of current healthcare devices, more and more privacy issues and reliability hindered the complete transfer of healthcare monitoring data to the cloud service platform. Iyengar, Kundu and Pallis (2018) showed that the Internet could bring opportunities for popularizing and intelligently developing healthcare, but the privacy issues of patients, doctors, nurses, and healthcare providers were more concerned. Daniels, Rose and Farkas (2018) investigated the unclassified medical data and domain ontology, and inferred that confidential data were prone to privacy invasion, and found that the current problem of data leakage was relatively serious. He, Cai, Sun, Li, and Cheng (2017) showed that the release of user data might also seriously threaten user privacy, and third-party users could use data mining (DM) technology to infer sensitive information contained in the released data. To sum up, there are many privacy and security problems in current HBD, so it is of great significance to find risk indicators that can be quickly identified to improve the privacy protection of healthcare patients.

2.3 Solution of the privacy problem of HBD

At present, more experts and scholars have explored technologies or methods to solve the privacy security of big data. Bhuiyan et al. (2018) proposed a system solution based on blockchain technology, including providers, hospitals and clinics, insurance companies, and patients, and proposed to adopt a private blockchain solution to protect the privacy and security of data. Galletta et al. (2017) indicated that cloud technology could solve the problem of storage and analysis of tremendous MRI images in the medical field. However, the reliability, availability, and privacy of data are the main issues faced with currently. Al-Turjman and Alturjman (2018) indicated that with the advent of 5G technology, it had become a general trend to apply the Internet of things to the healthcare system; however, user verification was required before each interaction, which might damage and degrade the performance of the overall healthcare system. Fritchman et al. (2019) indicated that the healthcare industry needed to establish strict compliance and data management policies for data sharing, and encryption protocols could realize the security of healthcare data transmission. Angeletti, Chatzigiannakis and Vitaletti (2017) expressed the importance of privacy protection in the initial recruitment phase of clinical trials, which could be solved by not uploading data to public databases and ensuring the authenticity of data. But no study has yet fully assessed the potential risk of privacy leakage over the "life cycle" of medical data.

To sum up, HBD analysis can greatly benefit the development of the medical industry, but currently there is a lack of effective analysis tools and technologies, and there are still problems of medical data privacy and security. At present, there are many studies on the privacy and security of medical data, but there is no analysis of the privacy and security risks that may occur in each phase of the life cycle of healthcare data. Therefore, the development status of China's healthcare field is analyzed, and the possible privacy security risk factors in the four stages of data collection, data application, data storage, and data destruction in the life cycle of healthcare data are explored.

3. Methodology

3.1 Big data analysis in China's healthcare sector

Based on the health-related data released by the national bureau of statistics of China in recent years and the 2018 China Health Statistics Yearbook, the current work analyzes the development status of China's medical and healthcare field in recent years, including the number of medical and health institutions and medical personnel, and the crude mortality rate of major diseases in urban and rural areas; it also explores the medical and healthcare costs of major diseases, including the per capita medical expenses of outpatient and inpatient departments of public hospitals, medical and health expenses, the number of medical insurance participants, fund income and expenditure, and the average inpatient medical expenses of the top 10.

3.2 Key technologies of HBD mining

The key links of DM system implementation mainly include data migration, data storage, data query, DM, and data display. SAP Hana is a memory computing platform that supports enterprise-preset deployment and cloud deployment

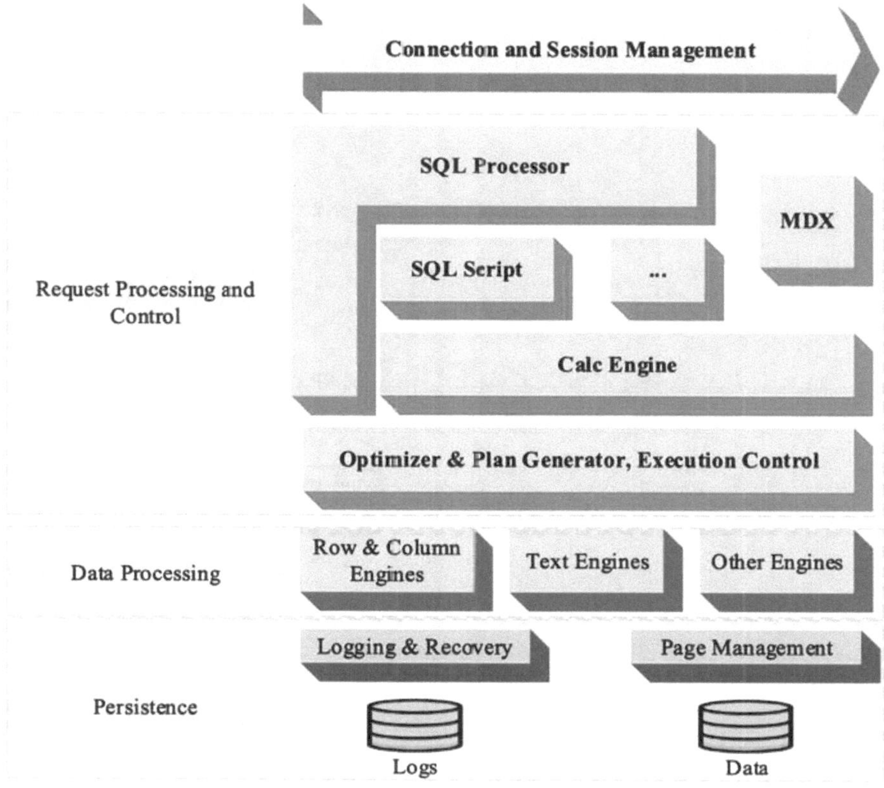

FIGURE 19.1 The architecture of Hana database system.

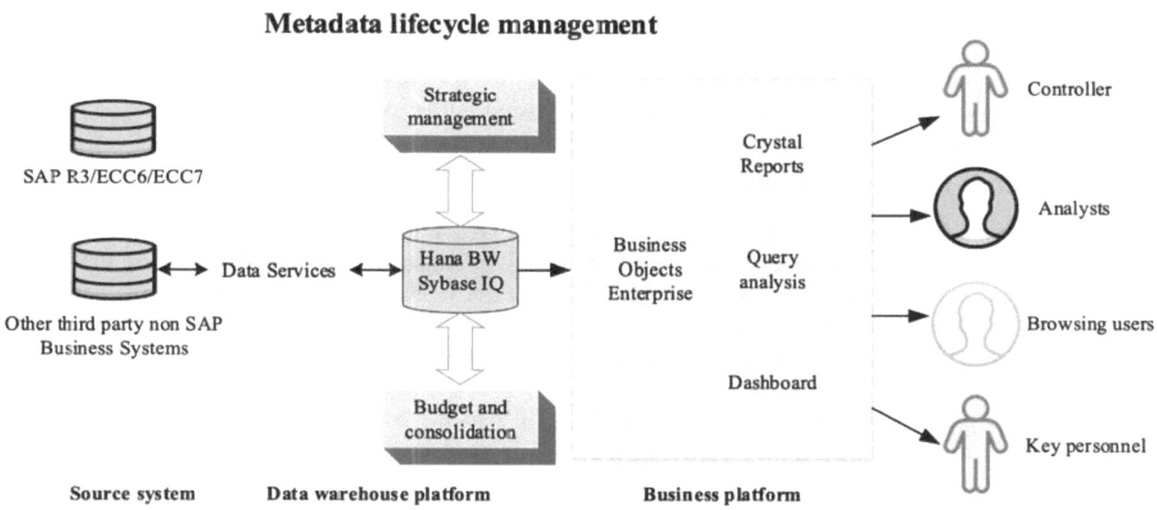

FIGURE 19.2 The basic architecture of BO.

mode and provides high-performance data query function. It is the first step to import the data from the csv file into the large database. The advantages of Hana database can help the system to complete large-scale data query and extraction. Fig. 19.1 presents the architecture of Hana database system.

BO (Business Object) is a component for data retrieval and processing, whose basic architecture is shown in Fig. 19.2. SAP BO is a simple real-world software abstraction. BOs are usually in the middle tier. SAP BO can automatically add a specific function in an application to obtain value-added effect and make knowledge reuse possible.

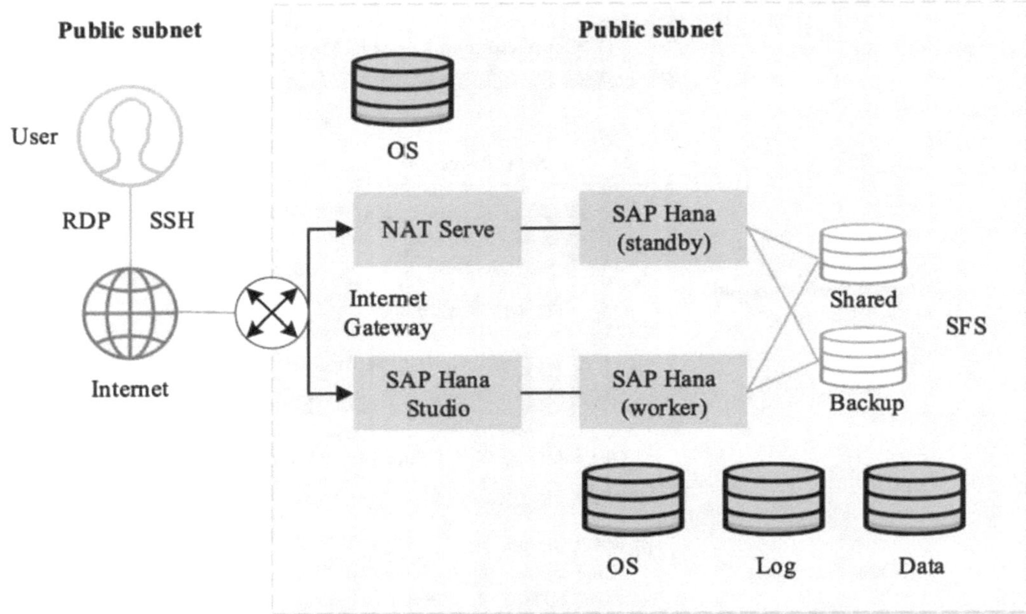

FIGURE 19.3 Typical deployment scheme of SAP Hana.

With the advantage of large memory, SAP Hana solution is to move all data-sensitive related computing logic into SAP Hana, thus eliminating the cost of data transmission. Compared with open source mining algorithm, Hana commercial mining algorithm can use the parallel computing ability of Hana platform to accelerate iterative computing by calling hardware acceleration capability. Fig. 19.3 indicates the typical deployment scenario.

The software and hardware facilities used in the system development environment are 1) database hardware environment: Dell PowerEdge R910 server, 256.0 GB memory; 2) Desktop software environment: Windows 10 operating system, Hana Studio 1.0.7; 3) Development language: SQLScript. The system framework is mainly composed of four parts (Fig. 19.4). Data source 1 and data source 2 represent the disease information table, respectively. Then, these two data sources are imported into the database through ETL tool, and specific views are generated by Hana modeling tool. Finally, the corresponding query and calculation are performed by the visualization tool provided by BO.

3.3 Establishment of indicator system for privacy and security risk assessment of HBD

Medical data collection is mainly divided into two kinds: one is passive collection, that is, in the process of patients' medical treatment, the doctor asks the patient information and records it in the electronic medical record; the other is active submission, that is, patients register information through the Internet or medical APP. In addition to the port burst attack, vulnerability attack is also a good means for attackers to attack the database. The common attack means include attacking the database without security patches, and using the common vulnerabilities of the website and a series of operations to attack. Fig. 19.5 shows the diagram of local database attack.

A total of 100 questionnaires are distributed to 25 doctors, 30 nurses, 15 administrators, and 30 technicians, and 92 questionnaires are collected, of which 89 are valid. Based on the questionnaire results, the privacy security risk factors of healthcare data are summarized. The main questions of the questionnaire are divided into four aspects: privacy security risks of data collection, storage, application, and destruction. The questionnaire specifically includes medical treatment process, private collection by medical institutions, malicious staff, external malicious attacks, infrastructure destruction, unclear relevant laws, incomplete identity authentication, incomplete disease diagnosis process, imperfect access system, inadequate protection measures, data encryption, weak personal privacy awareness, imperfect regulatory measures, data analysis, key loss, and data backup. In addition, Delphi method (Karamoozian, Wu, Chen, & Luo, 2019) is used to construct the indicator system for privacy and security risk assessment of healthcare data. Fig. 19.6 shows the specific construction method.

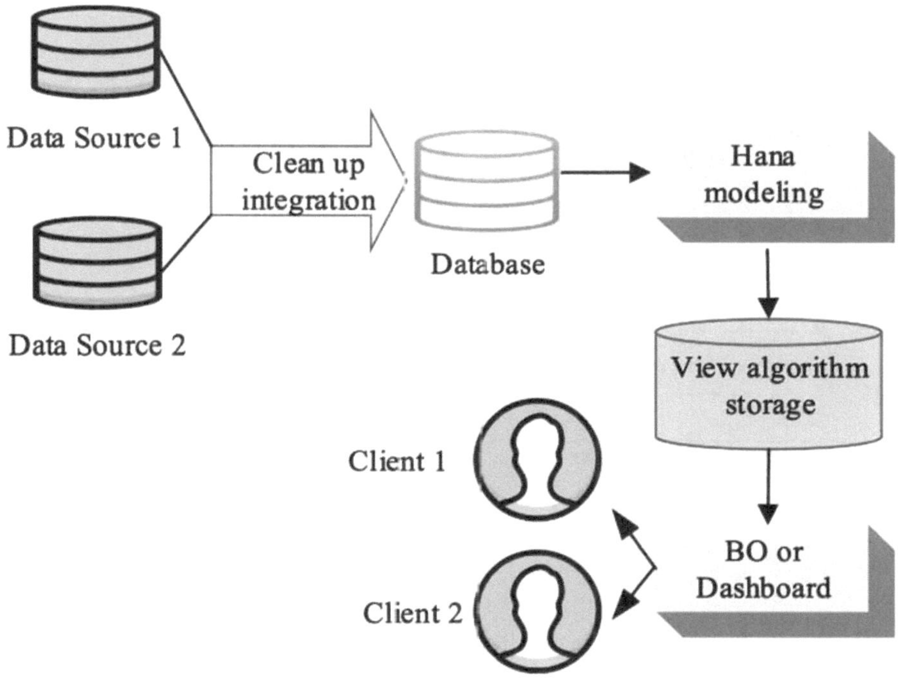

FIGURE 19.4 System composition framework.

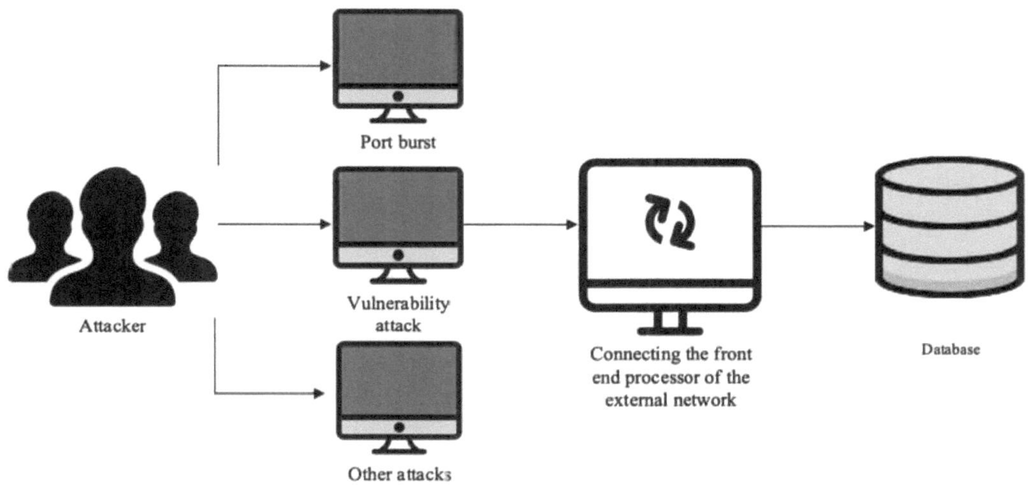

FIGURE 19.5 Diagram of local database attack.

3.4 Assessment model for privacy security risk

According to the information security risk, the risk assessment of information HBD privacy security is conducted from four aspects: threat frequency (T), asset importance (Z), utilization vulnerability (V), and vulnerability severity (E). Then, the risk size R of HBD is calculated as Eq. (1).

$$R = f(H, C) = f(H(T, V), C(Z, E)) \tag{19.1}$$

H is the uncertainty degree of risk occurrence; C represents losses caused by risks; T is the frequency of risk factors; V is the severity of exploitation vulnerability; Z is the importance of assets; E is the impact degree of vulnerability.

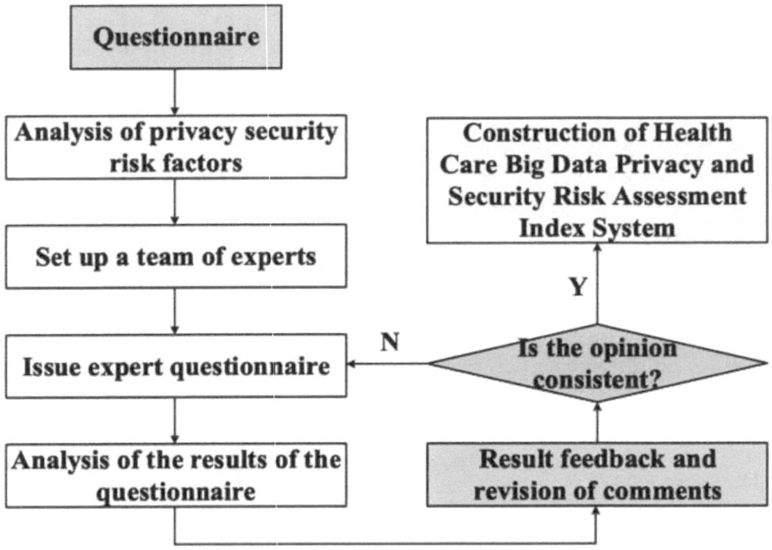

FIGURE 19.6 The construction process of the index system of privacy and security risk assessment for healthcare data.

Table 19.3 indicates that each risk factor is evaluated and scored, and each risk factor is defined as α, and the risk factors are, respectively, $\alpha_1, \alpha_2, ..., \alpha_6$. Assuming that the risk factors are scored p (δ_i, α_{ji}) at δ, then the conditional weight coefficient of each risk factor is expressed as Eq. (19.2).

$$p(\beta_j, \delta_i, \alpha_{ji}) = \frac{p(\delta_i, \alpha_{ji})}{\sum_{i=1}^{n} p(\delta_i, \alpha_{ji}, \beta_j)} \tag{19.2}$$

In Eq. (19.2), α_{ji} represents the ith risk factors in stage j; β_j is the jth risk stage.

Since information entropy can calculate the uncertainty of information, the entropy is used to determine the weight. In the cloud environment, the uncertainty degree of the above four aspects in the healthcare data is calculated as Eq. (19.3).

$$\begin{cases} H(\beta_j, \delta_i) = -\frac{1}{\ln n} \cdot \sum_{j}^{n} p(\beta_j, \delta_i, \alpha_{ji}) lnp(\beta_j, \delta_i, \alpha_{ji}) \\ H(\beta_j) = k_1 \cdot H(T_j) + k_2 \cdot H(V_j) \end{cases} \tag{19.3}$$

In Eq. (19.3), $H(\beta_j)$ is the uncertainty degree of stage j risk; T_j is the threat frequency of different risk factors in the jth risk stage; V_j is the severity of vulnerability to exploitation of different risk factors in the jth risk stage.

In addition to the uncertainty of risk factors, it is also necessary to calculate the losses caused by the occurrence of various risk factors. Then, the loss influence of different risk factors at different risk stages is calculated as Eq. (19.4).

$$\begin{cases} C(\beta_j, \delta_i) = \sum_{j}^{n} p(\beta_j, \delta_i, \alpha_{ji}) C(\beta_j, \delta_i, \alpha_{ji}) \\ C(\beta_j) = k_1 \cdot C(Z_j) + k_2 \cdot C(E_j) \end{cases} \tag{19.4}$$

In Eq. (19.4), C (β_j, δ_i) is the loss of the risk in stage j in δ_i; $C(\beta_j)$ is the loss in stage j; Z_j is the importance of assets of different risk factors in the jth risk stage; and E_j is the vulnerability influence degree of different risk factors in risk stage j.

Then, the risk size in each stage is calculated as Eq. (19.5).

$$R(\beta_j) = H(\beta_j) C(\beta_j) \tag{19.5}$$

In Eq. (19.5), the higher the value of $R(\beta_j)$ is, the greater the impact of healthcare data privacy and security risk in stage j is.

Since the degree of uncertainty of risk is related to the frequency of threat and the degree of vulnerability to exploitation, and the loss caused by the occurrence of risk is related to the importance of assets and the severity of vulnerability, the uncertainty of risk factors and the impact of loss, and the privacy security risk at each stage of HBD are calculated as Eq. (19.6).

$$\begin{cases} RH(\beta_j) = k_1 RT(\beta_j) + k_2 RV(\beta_j) \\ RC(\beta_j) = k_1 RZ(\beta_j) + k_2 RE(\beta_j) \\ R(\beta_j) = k_1 RH(\beta_j) + k_2 RC(\beta_j) \end{cases} \tag{19.6}$$

In Eq. (19.6), the risk status of privacy security needs to be determined based on R. When $0.8 \leq R \leq 1$, it belongs to extreme high risk; when $0.6 \leq R < 0.8$, it is considered as high risk; when $0.4 \leq R < 0.6$, it is considered as medium risk; when $0.2 \leq R < 0.4$, it is considered as low risk; and when $0 \leq R < 0.2$, the risk is extremely low.

The privacy disclosure behavior is a process, which is tested one by one through the module factors of the whole behavior process. In this process, all the instances obtained by the privacy instance generation operation are recorded as $inst_1, inst_2, ..., inst_m$. When all the calls in the process are checked, the mobile paths of all privacy instances form a set, which becomes the behavior path set, and can be expressed as the set of the final values of the *proc* attributes of all privacy instances, as Eq. (19.7).

$$BPS = \{inst_1.proc, inst_2.proc, ..., inst_m.proc\} \tag{19.7}$$

The privacy disclosure path is calculated by the attribute values of the instances moving along the path. Suppose $path_1 = p_1 t_1 p_2 t_2 ... p_{n-1} t_{n-1} p_n$ is a privacy leak path, and there is $n - 1$ transitions between its source location and decision location. Their Boolean expression is *ei*. If a privacy instance $inst_1$ moves on $path_1$, then all transitions should be triggered. In other words, the path PL can be calculated as Eq. (19.8).

$$PLpat\,h_1 = (ins\,t_1.Ctg, ins\,t_1.Cont, ins\,t_1.Proc, ins\,t_1.Dest) \tag{19.8}$$

There are j leak paths in the module m_1. The related expression of each path is e_j, and the module PLm_1 is calculated as Eq. (19.9).

$$PL\,m_1 = P\,L_{path_1} \vee P\,L_{path_2} \vee ... \vee P\,L_{path_m} \tag{19.9}$$

$\vee$ represents the union of attributes in an element.

The global privacy Petri net (PPN) contains at least one leak path in the unauthorized data access module and one leak path in the secret data transmission module, as Eq. (19.10).

$$P\,L_{global} = (P\,L_{da_1} \vee P\,L_{da_2} \vee .. \vee P\,L_{da_N}) \wedge (P\,L_{ct_1} \vee P\,L_{ct_2} \vee ... \vee P\,L_{ct_M}) \tag{19.10}$$

Suppose $path_1$ is a behavior path in the path set, which contains n_1 transitions and n_{1+1} locations. The weight of these transitions is ω_{t_i}, and the leakage possibility of the path is expressed as Eqs. (19.11) and (19.12).

$$p(\sigma_{path_1}) = \frac{1}{n_1} \sum_{i=1}^{n_1} \omega_{t_1} \tag{19.11}$$

$$\sigma_{path_1} = ins\,t_1.proc = p_1 t_1 p_2 ... p_{n-1} t_{n-1} p_n \tag{19.12}$$

If there are N behavior paths in the whole path set, the average probability of all paths is the privacy leakage probability of the behavior path set, calculated as Eq. (19.13).

$$p = \frac{1}{N} \sum_{i=1}^{N} p(\sigma_{path_1}) \tag{19.13}$$

Next, calculate the severity index of each behavior path. If the path passes through m PPN modules, the path severity is calculated as Eq. (19.14).

$$s(\sigma_{path_1}) = \frac{1}{m} \sum_{i=1}^{m} \omega_{\sigma_i} \tag{19.14}$$

Based on this, questionnaires are sent to relevant personnel in the hospital to score the privacy and security risks of information HBD from four aspects: threat frequency, asset importance, utilization vulnerability, and vulnerability severity. Likert scale 5 is used for evaluation, and Table 19.1 presents the specific evaluation methods.

TABLE 19.1 Assessment scale.

Categories	1	2	3	4	5
Threat frequency	Little probability to happen	Happening in few cases	Happening in some cases	Happening in most cases	Inevitable
Importance of assets	Little impact	A little impact	Normal impact	Big impact	Serious impact
Vulnerability of being used	Almost impossible to be used	Low chances of being used	Easy to be used	High probability of being used	Very high probability of being used
Fragility severity	Little impact on assets	A little impact on assets	Causing loss of assets	Big impact on assets	Serious impact on assets
Class	Extremely low	Low	Medium	High	Extremely high

4. Results

4.1 Analysis on the development status of China's medical and healthcare field

The current work compares the number and year-on-year growth rate of medical and health institutions in China from 2007 to 2017. Fig. 19.7A suggests that the number of medical and health institutions in China has remained almost unchanged since 2014, totally about 98,000. It also compares the changes in the number of hospitals, primary medical and health institutions, and professional public health institutions in China from 2007 to 2017. Fig. 19.7B concludes that from 2007 to 2017, the number of hospitals in China shows a slow and gradually rising trend, reaching 31,056 in 2017. However, the number of primary medical and health institutions in China is the largest, showing a gradual increase from 2008 to 2017, reaching 933,024 in 2017.

The current work compares the changes in the number of medical and health personnel, health technicians, practicing physicians, registered nurses, pharmacists and rural doctors, and health workers in China from 2009 to 2018. Fig. 19.8 indicates that the number of health personnel and health technical personnel in China shows a gradually increasing trend from 2009 to 2018, and reaches 12.30.03 million and 9.5292 million, respectively in 2018. The number of practicing physicians and registered nurses also shows a gradual increase, reaching 3,010,400 and 4,098,600, respectively in 2018.

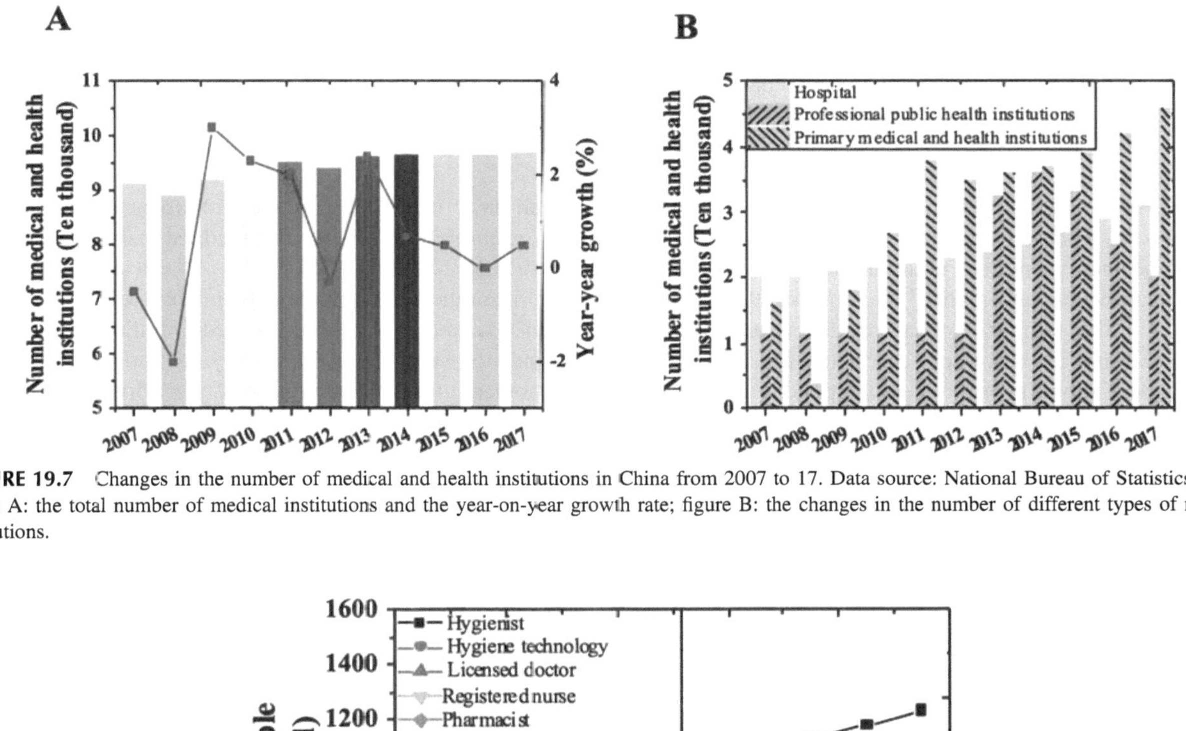

FIGURE 19.7 Changes in the number of medical and health institutions in China from 2007 to 17. Data source: National Bureau of Statistics. Note: figure A: the total number of medical institutions and the year-on-year growth rate; figure B: the changes in the number of different types of medical institutions.

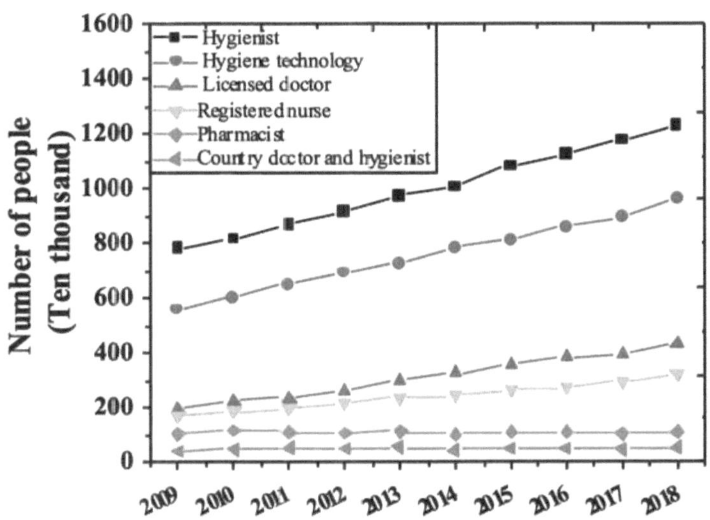

FIGURE 19.8 Changes in the number of medical and health personnel in China from 2009 to 18. Data source: National Bureau of Statistics.

TABLE 19.2 Per capita medical expenses from 2010 to 2017 of outpatient department and inpatient department of Chinese public hospitals.

Names of indexes	2010	2013	2014	2015	2016	2017
Outpatient department per capita medical expenses (yuan)	167.3	207.9	221.6	235.2	246.5	257.1
Inpatient department per capital medical expenses (yuan)	6415.9	7858.9	8290.5	8833.0	9229.7	9563.2

There are a small number of pharmacists, rural doctors, and health workers, while the number of rural doctors and health workers shows a decreasing trend, and only 907,100 people in 2018.

The public hospitals are taken as an example to compare the per capita medical expenses of outpatient department and inpatient department of Chinese hospitals from 2010 to 2017 (Table 19.2). Recently, the per capita medical expenses of outpatient departments and inpatient departments have also increased, but not greatly increase.

4.2 Analysis of medical and healthcare costs of major diseases in China

The work compares the differences between the total medical and health expenditure, government health expenditure, social expenditure, per capita health expenditure, urban per capita health expenditure and rural per capita expenditure in China from 2007 to 2017. Fig. 19.9 reflects that, in recent years, expenditures of different medical and healthcare expenses have shown gradual increase. Among them, the expenditure on social health is higher than the government's expenditure on health. In 2017, the total expenditure on health in China reached 5.2598.28 trillion yuan, while the per capita health expenditure in urban areas is higher than that in rural areas.

The work compares the differences among the number of urban basic medical insurance participants, the number of urban residents participating in medical insurance, the income and expenditure of urban basic medical insurance fund, and the income and expenditure of urban medical insurance fund from 2011 to 2017 (Fig. 19.10). All of them show a gradually rising trend. By the end of 2017, the number of basic urban medical insurance participants in China had reached 1176.814 million, and the number of urban residents participating in medical insurance had reached 873.587 million. The revenue and expenditure of the basic medical insurance fund for urban residents were 1793.16 billion yuan and 1442.17 billion yuan, respectively. The revenue and expenditure of the medical insurance fund for urban residents were 565.33 and 495.48 billion yuan, respectively.

The crude mortality from major diseases in urban and rural China in 2017 (1 in 100,000) is compared. Fig. 19.11 shows that the malignant tumors have the highest crude mortality rate. However, the crude death rate of heart disease, cerebrovascular disease, and respiratory diseases in rural areas is higher than that of urban residents, which shows that the crude

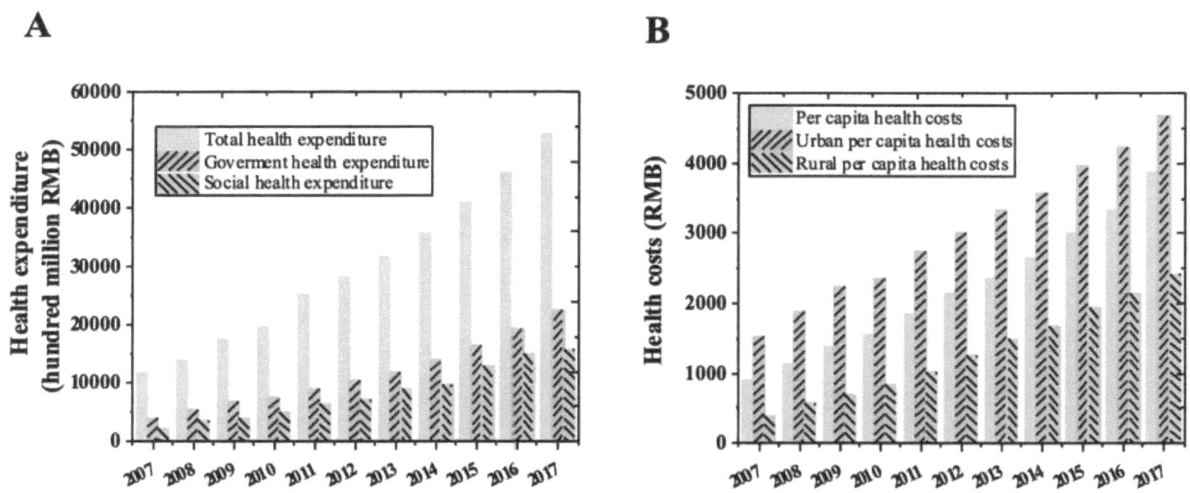

FIGURE 19.9 Changes in health care expenses in China. Data source: National Bureau of Statistics. Note: figure A: the health expenditure; figure B: the health costs.

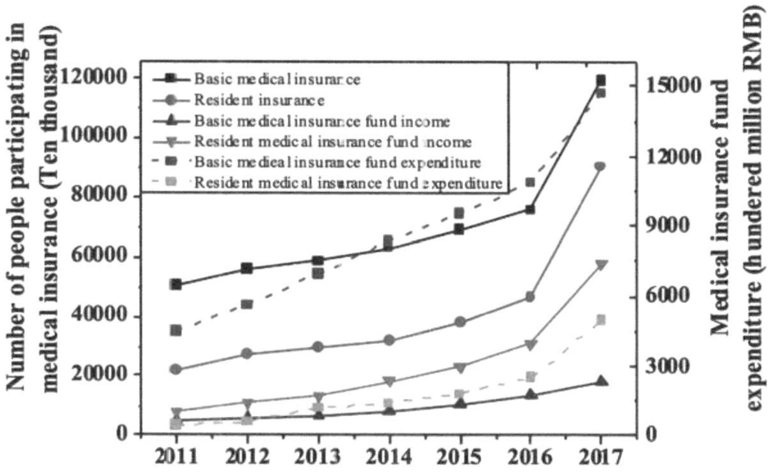

FIGURE 19.10 Changes in the number of Chinese medical insurance participants, fund income, and expenditure from 2007 to 17. Data source: National Bureau of Statistics.

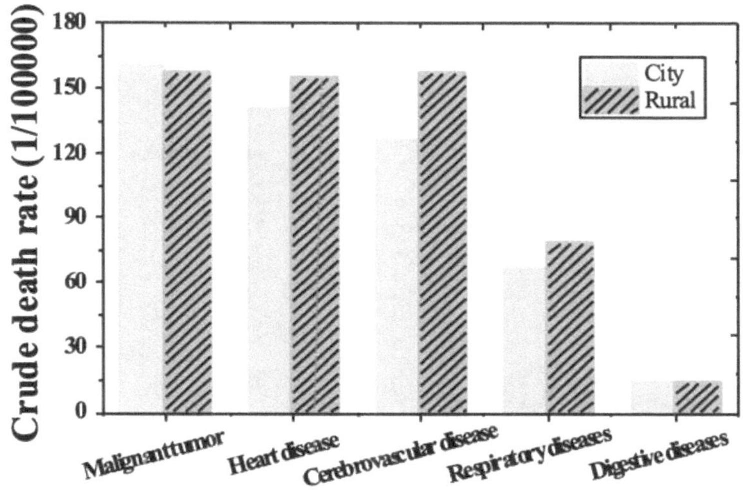

FIGURE 19.11 Comparison of crude mortality rates of major urban and rural diseases in China in 2017. Data source: National Bureau of Statistics.

mortality rate of Chinese rural residents is higher than that of urban residents. This may be due to the low income of rural residents in China and the high medical cost of treating heart and cerebrovascular diseases, which leads them to look down on diseases, or the poor facilities of primary medical care institutions.

The work compares the average hospitalization medical expenses of the top 10 diseases discharged from hospital in China in 2017. Table 19.3 demonstrates that the top 10 discharged patients are cerebral infarction, cesarean section, childhood bronchopneumonia, acute appendicitis, intracranial injury, senile cataract, inguinal hernia, bacterial pneumonia, cerebral hemorrhage, and lumbar disc herniation. Among these diseases, cerebral hemorrhage has the highest per capita medical expenses, followed by intracranial injury, and the highest average length of hospitalization is also cerebral hemorrhage, followed by intracranial injury. The results show that average hospitalization days are positively correlated with per capita medical expenses.

4.3 Testing of privacy and security risk assessment model for HBD in cloud environment

According to the literature, the coefficient of variation (CV) of the survey results is calculated. When the mean score of the expert is greater than 3 and the CV value is less than 0.3, the risk factor could be retained. The expert scores and CV calculation results are shown in Table 19.4. The mean values of the 16 risk factors are all greater than 3 and CV value is less than 0.3.

TABLE 19.3 The average hospital expenses of diseases ranking top 10 in the number of discharged patients in China in 2017.

Name of diseases	Number of discharged patients (105)	Average stay (d)	Per capita medical expense (RMB)
Cerebral infarction	31.22	10.7	9607.0
Caesarean birth	23.16	6.1	7794.7
Childhood bronchopneumonia	19.67	6.6	3195.7
Acute appendicitis	7.494	6.6	8403.4
Intracranial injury	7.01	12.0	12,361.6
Senile cataract	6.70	3.9	6952.2
Inguinal hernia	5.66	6.4	8226.3
Bacterial pneumonia	5.39	8.7	7314.0
Cerebral hemorrhage	5.23	14.5	18,254.6
Lumbar intervertebral disc protrusion	5.13	10.2	9412.5

TABLE 19.4 Risk factor score and coefficient of variation calculation result.

No	Risk factors	Average value	CV
1	Diagnosis process	3.5	0.172
2	Medical institutions collecting without permission	3.3	0.232
3	Malicious staff	3.2	0.262
4	External malicious attack	4.1	0.187
5	Infrastructure destroyed	4.2	0.198
6	Vague relevant law	3.2	0.252
7	Incomplete Id	3.7	0.201
8	Disease diagnosis process	3.7	0.162
9	Not perfect access system	3.1	0.220
10	Lack of protection	3.2	0.253
11	Data encryption	3.4	0.243
12	Weak personal privacy awareness	3.4	0.251
13	Not perfect regulatory measures	3.3	0.249
14	Data analysis	3.8	0.210
15	Lost key	3.9	0.276
16	Data backup	3.2	0.218

1, 2, 3, 4, 5, 6, 7, and 9 are summarized as risk factors of data collection in stage (β1), 4, 5, 7, 9, 10, and 11 are summarized as risk factors for the data storage stage (β2), 4, 6, 7, 8, 9, 10, 12, 14, and 15 are summarized as risk factors in data application stage (β3), and 3, 5, and 16 are summarized as risk factors of data destruction stage (β4). The risk uncertainty and risk size of each stage are compared (Fig. 19.12). The loss of risk is related to the importance of assets and the severity of vulnerability. The R value is calculated and it suggests that the R value of each stage is within the range of 0.2–0.4, which indicates that there are certain risks in all stages of HBD and they are all low risks.

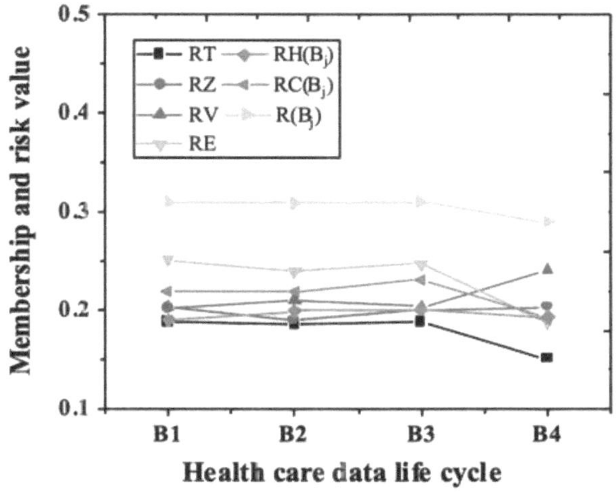

FIGURE 19.12 The risk membership degree and risk value of each stage.

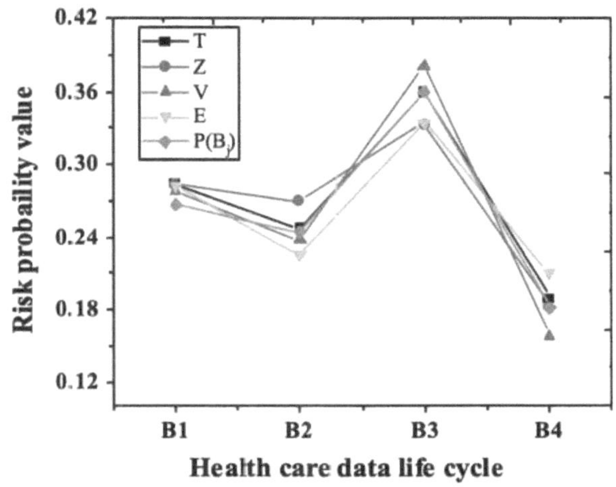

FIGURE 19.13 The risk probability value of each stage.

The risk probability values of different stages are calculated and shown in Fig. 19.13. Among the privacy risks in the four stages of the life cycle of HBD, the probability of privacy security risks is the highest in the data application (β3), while the probability of privacy data risks is the lowest in the data destruction (β4).

Fig. 19.12 and Fig. 19.13 reveal that 16 risk factors in the process of healthcare data collection, storage, application, and destruction have a low probability of privacy security. Then, the probability of 16 underlying risk factors listed in Table 19.4 is calculated and shown in Fig. 19.14. The probability of data analysis, medical treatment process, lack of protective measures, disease diagnosis process, imperfect access system, and incomplete identity authentication are greater than 0.6. The probability of security risk caused by malicious staff and data backup is low, only 0.15 and 0.14.

To sum up, the privacy and security protection of healthcare data is realized based on both technology and management (Fig. 19.15). When individuals conduct real-time tracking and operation of healthcare data, the privacy and security protection of HBD can be divided into the following aspects. I. The technology level. When big data is stored in the cloud, the direct access mode needs to be replaced by the storage threshold of increasing encryption keys. Dynamic encryption technology is used to encrypt data in the data transmission. In the DM, real-time security monitoring or anonymity technology should be used to protect patients' privacy. In addition, data traceability, identity authentication, access control, dynamic security monitoring, anonymity, DM, and destruction based on technology can also be used to protect the privacy of medical data. II. The management level. It can also improve the relevant laws on privacy protection of HBD based on management, establish an assessment mechanism for privacy disclosure and protection, set up privacy security standards, organize standardized management, implement supervision and management, and other technologies to realize the supervision of HBD.

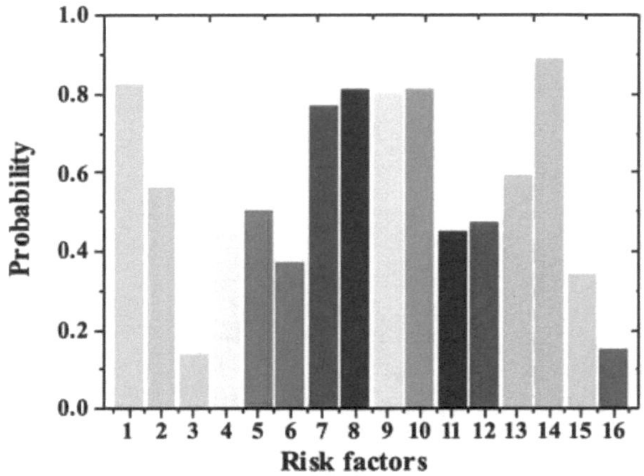

FIGURE 19.14 The probability of the occurrence of each risk factor.

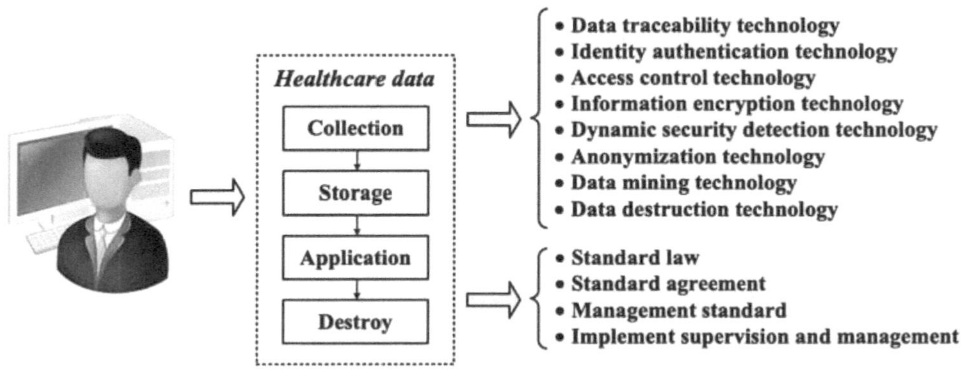

FIGURE 19.15 Privacy security protection measures based on healthcare big data.

4.4 Application of parallel random forest algorithm in hospital intelligent guidance

Parallel random forest (PRF) algorithm is based on Apache spark. The PRF algorithm is optimized from data parallelism and task parallelism. Regarding data parallelism, vertical data partition and data reuse are proposed to reduce the cost of data communication between distributed computing nodes. For task parallelism, a two-level parallel training method is proposed, which is trained in the decision tree level and the node level of each tree, respectively. The accuracy and performance of patients' treatment time prediction (PTTP) model and hospital queueing recommendation (HQR) model are analyzed to evaluate the application effect of the proposed PRF algorithm in hospital intelligent guidance system. The experimental data set is collected from the information management system of a cooperative hospital, covering 3 years (2017–19) of historical medical data. The hospital departments involved in the data set include emergency department (ED), laboratory, CT scan, MR scan, B-mode ultrasound, color Doppler ultrasound, nuclear medicine, and pharmacy. CT scanning task is taken as an example to analyze the prediction results of PTTP model from the treatment time. First, the distribution of the number of patients in CT scanning task is analyzed (Fig. 19.16A). In a week cycle, the number of patients in CT scanning task every day has two peaks. Some results of the CT scan task time-consuming model are shown in Fig. 19.16B.

The study compares and analyzes the average waiting time of patients with and without HQR system. 130 patients and 1800 medical records are used in each group (Fig. 19.17). Assisted with HQR system, the average queueing time of patients is significantly reduced. Moreover, the more tasks patients have, the more obvious the advantage is. The data sets of three groups of patients' recommendation requests are selected and executed on Spark clusters of different sizes to evaluate the performance of the HQR system. In the experiment, the data volume of patients' recommendation request is 500, 800, 1000, and 2000, respectively. Moreover, in each case, the computing node size of Spark cluster increases from 5 to 50, and Fig. 19.18 reflects the experimental results of performance comparison.

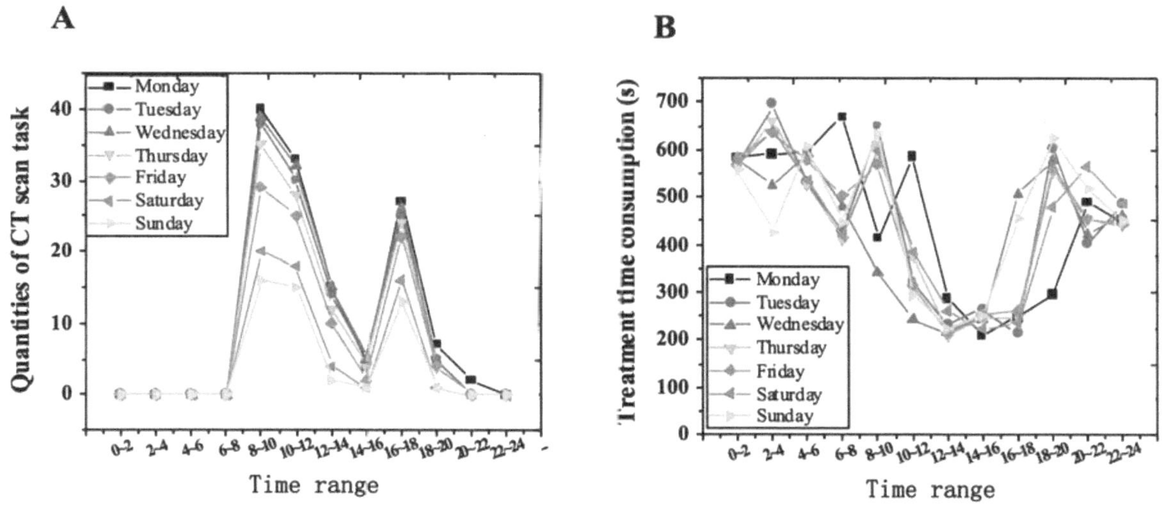

FIGURE 19.16 Time-consuming model of CT scanning task considering time factor. Note: Figure A: the number of CT scanning tasks per week; Figure B: the time-consuming model of CT scanning task.

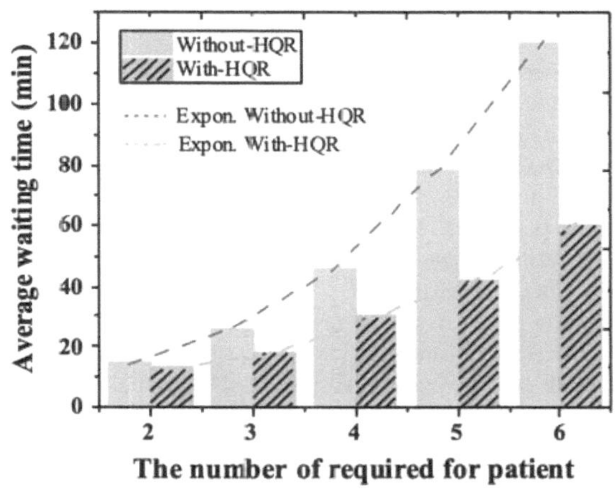

FIGURE 19.17 Analysis of the average queueing time of patients.

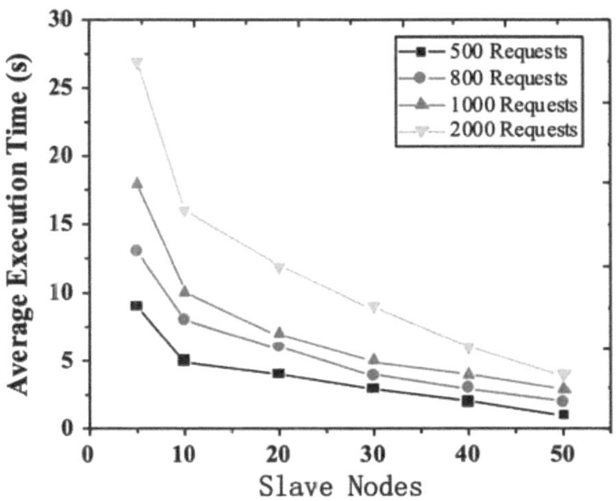

FIGURE 19.18 Performance evaluation of HQR system.

5. Conclusion

The work is designed to analyze the privacy security risks in the big data processing in China's healthcare sector when facing the cloud environment. Based on the case data analysis, the development status of China's health care field is analyzed under big data, and the privacy security risk factors existing in each stage of the life cycle of healthcare data are explored. The number of medical institutions, medical personnel, and insured persons in China's medical and healthcare field increases year by year, but the hospitalization costs also increase in recent years. In the life cycle of healthcare data, the data collection, storage, application, and destruction stage all have low privacy security risk, and the risk probability of data application stage is the highest, among which the probability of privacy security risk is the highest during data analysis. It indicates that it needs to strengthen the control of health care data to reduce the probability of privacy security risks. However, there are still some limitations. The work is conducted only based on big data, and a risk prediction system for HBD needs to be built in the future to strengthen the security control. The deep mining of healthcare data is of great significance for improving relevant policies, and the results can lay a foundation for the subsequent studies of healthcare data.

Acknowledgment

This work was supported in part by the National Natural Science Foundation of China (NSFC) under Grant Nos. 61902203, Key Research and Development Plan - Major Scientific and Technological Innovation Projects of ShanDong Province (2019JZZY020101).

References

Al-Turjman, F., & Alturjman, S. (2018). Context-sensitive access in industrial Internet of things (IIoT) healthcare applications. *IEEE Transactions on Industrial Informatics, 14*(6), 2736–2744. https://doi.org/10.1109/TII.2018.2808190

Angeletti, F., Chatzigiannakis, I., & Vitaletti, A. (2017). Privacy preserving data management in recruiting participants for digital clinical trials. In *HumanSys 2017 - Proceedings of the 1st international Workshop on human-centered sensing, networking, and systems, part of SenSys 2017* (pp. 7–12). Association for Computing Machinery, Inc. https://doi.org/10.1145/3144730.3144733

Bhuiyan, M. Z. A., Zaman, A., Wang, T., Wang, G., Tao, H., & Hassan, M. M. (2018). Blockchain and big data to transform the healthcare. In *Proceedings of the international conference on data processing and applications* (pp. 62–68).

Caicedo, C. V., Prieto, Y., Pezoa, J. E., Sobarzo, S. K., & Ghani, N. (2019). A novel framework for SDN teaching and research: A Chilean university case study. *IEEE Communications Magazine, 57*(11), 67–73. https://doi.org/10.1109/MCOM.001.1900261

Cena, F., Gena, C., Houben, G. J., & Strohmaier, M. (2017). Introduction to the special issue on big personal data in interactive intelligent systems. *ACM Transactions on Interactive Intelligent Systems, 7*(2), 1–5. https://doi.org/10.1145/3101102

Chen, M., Hao, Y., Hwang, K., Wang, L., & Wang, L. (2017). Disease prediction by machine learning over big data from healthcare Communities. *IEEE Access, 5*, 8869–8879. https://doi.org/10.1109/ACCESS.2017.2694446

Daniels, M., Rose, J., & Farkas, C. (2018). Protecting patients' data: An efficient method for health data privacy. In *Proceedings of the 13th international conference on availability, reliability and security* (pp. 1–10). https://doi.org/10.1145/3230833.3230865

Emara, K. (2017). Safety-aware location privacy in VANET: Evaluation and comparison. *IEEE Transactions on Vehicular Technology, 66*(12), 10718–10731. https://doi.org/10.1109/TVT.2017.2736885

Enayet, A., Razzaque, M. A., Hassan, M. M., Alamri, A., & Fortino, G. (2018). A mobility-aware optimal Resource allocation architecture for big data task execution on mobile cloud in smart Cities. *IEEE Communications Magazine, 56*(2), 110–117. https://doi.org/10.1109/MCOM.2018.1700293

Fritchman, K., Saminathan, K., Dowsley, R., Hughes, T., De Cock, M., Nascimento, A., & Teredesai, A. (2019). Privacy-preserving scoring of tree Ensembles: A novel framework for AI in healthcare. In *Proceedings - 2018 IEEE international conference on big data, big data 2018* (pp. 2413–2422). Institute of Electrical and Electronics Engineers Inc. https://doi.org/10.1109/BigData.2018.8622627

Galletta, A., Celesti, A., Tusa, F., Fazio, M., Bramanti, P., & Villari, M. (2017). Big MRI data dissemination and retrieval in a multi-cloud hospital storage system. In *ACM international conference proceeding series* (Vol. 128634, pp. 162–166). Association for Computing Machinery. https://doi.org/10.1145/3079452.3079507

He, Z., Cai, Z., Sun, Y., Li, Y., & Cheng, X. (2017). Customized privacy preserving for inherent data and latent data. *Personal and Ubiquitous Computing, 21*(1), 43–54. https://doi.org/10.1007/s00779-016-0972-2

Iyengar, A., Kundu, A., & Pallis, G. (2018). Healthcare informatics and privacy. *IEEE Internet Computing, 22*(2), 29–31. https://doi.org/10.1109/MIC.2018.022021660

Juddoo, S., George, C., Duquenoy, P., & Windridge, D. (2018). Data governance in the health industry: Investigating data quality dimensions within a big data context. *Applied System Innovation, 1*(4), 1–16. https://doi.org/10.3390/asi1040043

Karamoozian, A., Wu, D., Chen, C. L. P., & Luo, C. (2019). An approach for risk prioritization in construction Projects using analytic Network process and decision making trial and evaluation laboratory. *IEEE Access, 7*, 159842–159854. https://doi.org/10.1109/ACCESS.2019.2939067

Kraemer, F. A., Braten, A. E., Tamkittikhun, N., & Palma, D. (2017). Fog computing in healthcare-A Review and discussion. *IEEE Access, 5*, 9206–9222. https://doi.org/10.1109/ACCESS.2017.2704100

Mahmoud, M. M. E., Rodrigues, J. J. P. C., Ahmed, S. H., Shah, S. C., Al-Muhtadi, J. F., Korotaev, V. V., & De Albuquerque, V. H. C. (2018). Enabling technologies on cloud of things for smart healthcare. *IEEE Access, 6*, 31950–31967. https://doi.org/10.1109/ACCESS.2018.2845399

Rizwan, A., Zoha, A., Zhang, R., Ahmad, W., Arshad, K., Abu Ali, N., Alomainy, A., Imran, M. A., & Abbasi, Q. H. (2018). A Review on the Role of nano-communication in future healthcare systems: A big data Analytics perspective. *IEEE Access, 6*, 41903–41920. https://doi.org/10.1109/ACCESS.2018.2859340

Stankovic, J. A. (2017). Research directions for cyber physical systems in wireless and mobile healthcare. *ACM Transactions on Cyber-Physical Systems, 1*(1), 1–12. https://doi.org/10.1145/2899006

Villeneuve, E., Harwin, W., Holderbaum, W., Janko, B., & Sherratt, R. S. (2017). Reconstruction of angular kinematics from wrist-worn inertial sensor data for smart home healthcare. *IEEE Access, 5*, 2351–2363. https://doi.org/10.1109/ACCESS.2016.2640559

Chapter 20

Opportunities and challenges in healthcare with the management of big biomedical data

Gopi Battineni
University of Camerino, School of Medicinal and Health Products Sciences, Camerino, Italy

1. Introduction

Large innovations are quickly producing a lot of different omics information (Abdelhafez, 2014). However, this offers an incredible opportunity; in parallel, having extraordinary difficulties like data analysis turns out to be more unpredictable. The appearance of "data science" explains the commendable knowledge related to considering (usually large) data collections and explaining, cleaning, sorting out, putting away, and breaking them down for the motivations behind extricating information (Waller & Fawcett, 2013). It consolidates the controls of measurements, software engineering, and computational designing.

The term data science is a term represents the dealing of incoming data—all the science relies on last upon information, and a considerable lot of the exercises recorded above are treated as engineering (which is tied in with taking care of issues) and not science (which is about the disclosure of new information). On the off chance that However, data science is not the science of data in the particular industry (Provost & Fawcett, 2013), because the term data science in biomedicine "ranges a scope of organic and clinical examination challenges that are information escalated and explored in the formation of novel systems to progress biomedical science revelation. Fig. 20.1 explains the different stages to structure and store the healthcare data.

At the same time, biomedical analysts (scholars, doctor researchers, clinical trialists, and others) see a chance to change how they take care of their job utilizing the information streams that are currently accessible. A significant number of these researchers additionally did not consider the partnered informatics disciplines, considering them pertinent to a couple of spaces of request. Large informational collections, or information streams, are currently a major issue for these researchers, and they discover the expression "data science" valuable in catching the pressing factors on their exploration and conveyance missions (Dash et al., 2019).

Biomedical data can be accepted if patients consented to enter a particular report, or unconsented something else: the utilization of unconsented information has extra limits and security issues. Some of them are as follows:

Patient personal data including sex, age, date of birth, date of entry, or exit.
Common medical data such as weight, height, respiratory rate, blood pressure, cholesterol levels, and used medications.
Specialized lab acquired data: lipids, proteins, glycans, metabolites, and imaging.
Genetic data such as sequencing and genotype.
Epigenetic information and gene expressions.

Science and medication are not by any means the only exercises that have been troubled by the accessibility of information in volumes and speeds that were not seen earlier (Ristevski & Chen, 2018). Numerous efforts in fields such as transportation, money, media, amusement, land, etc., have seen an expanded capacity to catch, digitize, and store information and an accompanying expansion in business knowledge to improve measures, conveyance, and productivity. Regularly, web-based knowledge is the key data source in terms of online media, accounts, search engines, advertising,

Big Data Analytics for Healthcare. https://doi.org/10.1016/B978-0-323-91907-4.00017-0

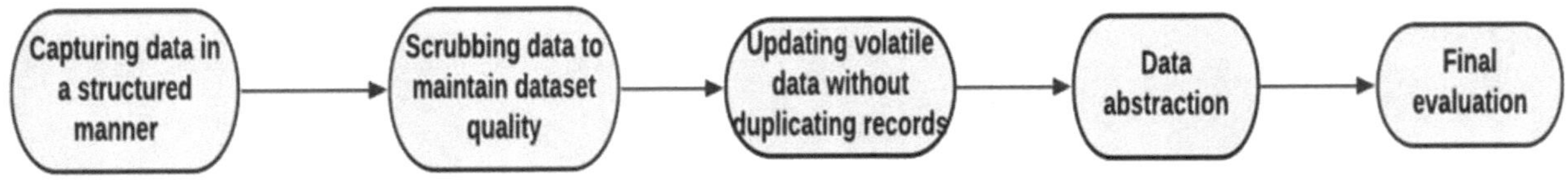

FIGURE 20.1 Healthcare data collection and processing steps.

and others (Masmoudi et al., 2017). It has created an intense need for specialists in software engineering, insights, and designing. These businesses do not have a solid custom of a particular subdiscipline of informatics, and they embraced the expression "data science" since it catches the types of challenges that they have and the kinds of experts they look for.

Despite the fact most components of data science have consistently been available in the informatics disciplines, there is by all accounts a specific range of abilities that is significant in current applications (Song & Zhu, 2016). The present difficulties incorporate huge informational collections that must be overseen cautiously because, for instance, they do not fit in the functioning memory of regular desktop computers. Likewise, there is a requirement for enormous scope comment and metadata that clarify how the information was created and what are noise sources. Nowadays incorporation of machine learning (ML) programs are getting big attention in dealing of larger datasets (L'Heureux et al., 2017).

The high-profile accomplishment of neural network algorithms in deep learning (DL) frameworks has made a functioning business sector for people with the data needed to assemble and convey these frameworks (Jan et al., 2019). Along these lines, there is by all accounts a particular range of abilities for data science that is a subset of the entirety of the informatics and that tends to the enfolding needs of those who require large data science (Jan et al., 2019; Zhang et al., 2018). Surprisingly, this workforce need has prompted the formation of area autonomous data science formulating programs in which learners get familiar with the vital abilities for which there right now is a solid market. They become specialists at overseeing information, yet might not have particular information in the space of the application, reliant on partners to give domain data to guarantee that the inquiries they pose and answer are significant and all well shaped.

It appears to be certain that biomedical information science has great challenges related to the data complexity and the difficulty of the science questions. But the data scientist with no organic or clinical information can most likely make commitments; they would require cautious management or coordinated effort because the idea of the information, the wellsprings of commotion, and the series of expectations that are sensible to make require a degree of complexity that is nontrivial (Ngiam & Khor, 2019). Hence, we accept that the best data science work is probably going to come from data scientists who have set aside the effort to plunge all the more profoundly into the domain and make a good judgment on a moment to minute premise about how the information may be distributed and be analyzed.

In this work, the author tries to explore the potential challenges that occurred with biomedical data and to distinguish the major problems that computer science analysts face in an analysis of large datasets.

2. Biomedical data types and role of machine learning

In this section, the author presents the types of biomedical data and their importance in clinical decisions. Besides, advantages of adding ML technologies for disease diagnosis and prediction of future outcomes are also discussed.

2.1 Electronic health records

An Electronic Health Record (EHR) is an advanced form of a patient's paper outline (Yanamadala et al., 2016). EHRs are ongoing, patient-focused records that make data accessible quickly and safely to approved clients. While an EHR includes the clinical and treatment accounts of patients, an EHR framework is worked to go past standard clinical information gathered in a provider's office and can be comprehensive of a more extensive perspective on a patient's consideration. EHRs are playing a major role in information technology (IT) and can

Contain a patient's clinical history, analyze, prescriptions, treatment plans, immunization dates, sensitivities, radiology pictures, and research center and test outcomes,

Permit admittance to evidence-based tools that healthcare providers can use to settle on choices about a patient's consideration,

Stabilize and computerize provider work progress.

One of the critical highlights of an EHR is that health data can be made and overseen by approved providers in a computerized design equipped for being imparted to different providers across more than one medical care association

(Lobach & Detmer, 2007). EHRs are worked to impart data to other medical service suppliers and associations— like labs, trained professionals, clinical imaging offices, drug stores, crisis offices, and school and work environment facilities—so they contain data from all clinicians engaged with a patient's consideration.

Present world reality has been fundamentally changed by computerized knowledge—mobile phones, smart tablets, and web-empowered gadgets have changed our daily routine and how we communicate.

A more noteworthy and more consistent progression of data inside an advanced medical care foundation, made by EHRs, incorporates and uses computerized advance and can change how care is conveyed and redressed. With EHRs, data is accessible at whatever point and any place it is required. Because of this, it is possible

- To improve patient care,
- Increase patient participation,
- Improve care coordination,
- Improve diagnostics and patient outcomes,
- Practice efficiencies and cost savings.

2.1.1 Advantages

EHRs and the capacity to trade biomedical data electronically can assist us with giving better potential and more secure consideration for patients while making substantial upgrades for user cooperation (Menachemi & Collum, 2011). EHRs assist health providers with better consideration for patients and give better medical services by

- Giving exact, state-of-the-art, and complete data about patients at the place of care,
- Empowering fast admittance to patient records for more planned, productive consideration,
- Safely imparting electronic data to patients and different clinicians,
- Aiding suppliers all the more adequately to analyze patients, diminish clinical mistakes, and give more secure consideration,
- Improving patient and provider collaboration and communication, just as medical care comfort,
- Empowering more secure, more dependable recommending,
- Assisting to provide more legible, total documentation, and precise billing and streamlined coding,
- Upgrading protection and security of patient information,
- Assisting providers with improving profitability and balance between work-life activities,
- Empowering suppliers to improve effectiveness and meet their business objectives,
- Reducing expenses through less paperwork, improved security, decreased duplication of testing, and improved wellbeing.

2.1.2 Other benefits

2.1.2.1 Reformed health care

EHRs are the initial step to changed medical services. The other advantages of EHRs include the following:

- Better medical services by improving all parts of patient consideration, including health, viability, patient-centeredness, correspondence, instruction, idealness, productivity, and equity.
- Better health by empowering customized ways of life in the whole population, including expanded actual work, optimal nutrition, avoidance of social pressure, and more extensive utilization of personalized care.
- Improved efficiencies and lower medical care costs by advancing preventive medication and improved coordination of medical care administrations, just as by diminishing waste and repetitive tests.
- Better clinical dynamic by coordinating patient data from various sources.

2.1.2.2 Significant use

Perhaps the most ideal approach to guarantee patients exploit the EHRs advantages is to accomplish significant use.

2.2 Medical scan images

Images are the biggest data source in medical services and, simultaneously, and the most difficult to analyze. Medical image data is obtained for various purposes, like situation analysis, diagnosis, intraoperative route, postemployable checking, and biomedical research (Willemink et al., 2020). Doctors today should depend to a great extent on clinical image examination performed by exhausted radiologists and sometimes investigate scans themselves. As pioneers in medical technologies apply artificial intelligence (AI) to do image analysis, this is a circumstance set to change.

Computer vision programming dependent on the most recent DL programs is now empowering computerized investigation to give precise outcomes that are conveyed inexplicably quicker than a manual cycle can accomplish (Mittal, Verma, et al., 2019). As these mechanized frameworks become unavoidable in the medical services industry, they may achieve revolutionary changes in the way radiologists, clinicians, and even patients use imaging innovation to screen therapy and improve results.

The most ideal approach to outline how computerized clinical image research can help patients, radiologists, and different clinicians is to show some examples. This section explores the developments in medical image analysis.

2.2.1 Computerized medical image analysis in CT scanning

The utilization of DL-based convolutional neural networks to investigate computerized tomography (CT) scans has seen a lot of improvement and development over the most recent few years however has mainly elaborate 2D slices from a patient's chest, midsection, or cerebrum (Polsinelli et al., 2020). However, leap forwards is in transit, as trendsetters have improved the presentation of DL frameworks that break down the whole 3D image series from a CT filter.

One organization represents considerable authority in DL technologies for medical settings, called Aidoc, as of late dispatched the principal full-body answer for CT scanning, which will bear the cost of radiologists a work process coordinated application, empowering them to examine outputs of the chest, c-spine, mid-region, and head, without the need to switch between discrete picture examination applications.

2.2.2 Boosting the speed, power, and comfort of magnetic resonance imaging

Similar to CT scanning, MRI is a nonintrusive strategy for looking at the inner functions of the body. Unlike CT scanning, MRI presents less danger to patients, since it does not originate radiation to catch pictures (Battineni et al., 2020). Its fundamental disadvantage, however, is the long assessment time. For example, a heart MRI can take over an hour to perform. By applying to this issue image investigation with the help of an ML algorithm, researchers have built up an answer that not just lessens time required for cardiovascular MRI assessments yet, in addition, expands the amount and nature of the information provided.

ViosWorks upgrades images from MRI scanners, conveying a 3D perspective on the heart with the expansion of envisioned and evaluated blood-stream information. As per Imaging Technology News, ViosWorks empowers the catch of 20 gigabytes of information in a small portion of the time needed for ordinary MRI innovation to obtain only 200 megabytes (Recent Advances in MRI Technology, Imaging Technology News, n.d.). This empowers a patient to inhale openly all through the assessment, in contrast to regular outputs, during which a patient may need to spend periods of holding breath. For example, during a heart MRI evaluation, a patient will be approached to remain still, without breathing, upward of multiple times during the assessment.

2.2.3 PET scans

In addition to the above scanning methods, another possibility called positron emission tomography (PET) is also widely using in clinical imaging procedures and are getting progressively helpful in assessing patients' reaction to therapy, particularly for cancer (Del Vecchio et al., 2010). Early and regular reaction assessment is fundamental, such as when utilizing chemo and radiation treatment to treat cellular breakdown in the lungs. At the point when doctors can diagnose patient response in the principal little while of treatment, they can adjust measurements, either by decreasing them to reduce poison in noninfected tissue or by increasing dose for patients whose tumors are not reacting emphatically.

Studies highlight that ML and DL can improve the viability of PET clinical image analysis (Wang et al., 2020). Algorithms can be created and prepared to overcome image noise, improve quality, and accumulate image data in larger portions and at a quicker rate than standard PET apparatus can. Subsequently, the amounts of radioactive tracer expected to catch solid images might be decreased, which is uplifting news for patients who should go through PET scans.

The decrease of harmfulness is not only an advantage to cancer patients. ML techniques can be trained to tumor classification among PET images, such as either being responsive or nonreceptive to treatment. This lightens the responsibility for radiologists and expands profitability, so more patients can profit by quick decisions, choices, and proper treatment conventions. Combining ML techniques with PET scanning and medical image assessment offers the accompanying benefits over traditional technologies and some of them are explained below.

Improved quality of image composures the requirement for follow-up checks, in this manner, decreasing patients' general exposure to the tracer medication.
Immediate high-quality images permit doctors to make quick decisions during the scanning, thus accelerating and improving the treatment accuracy.
Tumors can be observed much of the time and nonobtrusively to coordinate chemo and radiotherapy portions to therapy reaction, in this way, to improve the expectation and survivability of cancer cells in the lungs.

2.2.4 X-rays

The X-ray images are capturing in high number daily and they present a greater problem for doctors across the globe. For instance, it is reported that more than 22 million X-ray images are captured per year in National Health Services (NHS) of the United Kingdom, yet with insufficient radiologists to assess a huge amount, above 200,000 patients needed to hold for a month or more for their X-ray results (High-Resolution Detectors to Create Safer X-ray Diagnosis, Imaging Technology News, n.d.). By making it conceivable to automate the underlying screening of X-rays, medical image assessment software's can help radiologists stay aware of their responsibility. By screening each imaging through trained algorithms, machines can classify the X-ray content and raise alarms for those requiring insight analysis by an expert physician.

By considering the example of autonomous screening, which is a framework being utilized in developing nations to identify indications of tuberculosis identification among in chest X-rays. The solution was developed with the help of ML techniques to recognize irregularities with more precision than human screening staff, even though it has not yet demonstrated as exact as doctors who have practical experience in TB finding and treatment (Mittal, Kumar, et al., 2020).

Given the deficiencies of radiologists in low-income countries, however, an autonomous solution with a better-than-normal level of precision will definitely help a large number of patients who are getting premature diagnosis and treatment, and consequently, declining death rates.

On other hand, artificial neural networks are excluding subjectivity from the evaluation of skeletal tumor trouble on prostate malignant growth patients (Toney & Vesselle, 2014). As this type of malignant growth can spread from the prostate into a patient's bones, doctors utilize X-rays to distinguish when this occurs and assess the amount of the skeletal design that is influenced. A novel ML algorithm that has been built up that can peruse and decipher X-rays, and by estimating bone density, equitably measures the degree of tumor growth.

Not many clinicians, particularly radiologists, would prevent the worth from getting computerized help with the identification of clinical eccentricities from CT, MRI, X-ray, and PET images. Solutions for arranging and image classification from every particular imaging mode will certainly help doctors treat more patients, with the highest precision, and in a more ideal way than they can oversee utilizing manual techniques alone.

3. Current big data challenges in healthcare

Many companies are conducting data analysis to distinguish waste, increment in profits, and service delivery speed. While medical services associations can receive these equivalent operational rewards, devices like AI, ML, data mining, cloud storage, and data visualization additionally can support emergency clinics and different health providers to improve care results and save lives. Data challenges in medical care settings can cost large amounts of money (Buch et al., 2018). The big data components in healthcare include smartphones, EHR management, wearable devices like hand watches, patient portals, public records, research works, government bodies, and others (refer Fig. 20.2).

3.1 Big data and healthcare

Big data can help medical services change from a responsive, treatment-based approach to deal with a more incorporated, preventive model. Smart data utilization can speed the advancement of customized approaches for comprehensive patient engagement to prompt better personal care (Kaur et al., 2018). Data can reveal insight into health drivers for various percentages of the population. Data analysis assists providers with developing better practices dependent on strong evidence. Proper use of medical services data can counter any gender, racial, or cultural biases. The approaches mentioned in the next sections can be especially useful in medical care settings to resolve big data issues (refer Fig. 20.3).

3.1.1 Cloud computing

Cloud computing is defined as the storage of off-site data and computer resources—fundamental in attention to information challenges in medical services (Mittal, Battineni, et al., 2020). Besides allowing solutions of scalable storage, cloud

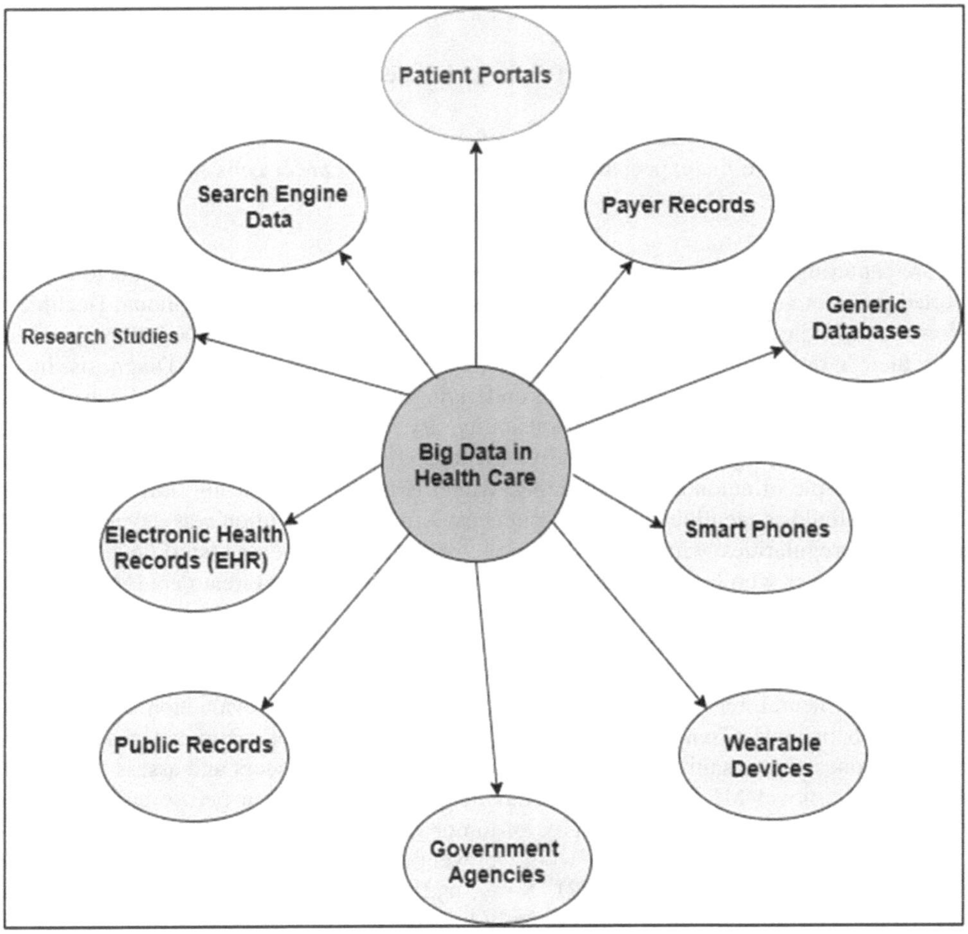

FIGURE 20.2 Big data in healthcare and its components.

computing brings costs through widespread access down to data across organizations and geographies. Further, distributed storage considers adaptable security and adapted information sharing. In medical care settings, secondary data can save lives, cloud computing guarantees uniform, on-request data links regardless of whether got to from an imaging center, specialist's center, ICU care units, or the accident location.

3.1.2 Artificial intelligence

AI discovers reiterations or irregularities in big data as it looks to imitate mankind intelligence without inclination or assumptions. AI can index aftereffects of specific medicines, endurance rates, and healing times in large quantities of patients in various locations. Additionally, it can reveal an associated medical issue that might be missed by occupied clinicians. This sort of machine knowledge permits decision-making based on data to people, since they essentially cannot separate that much information. AI examples used in medical services range from addressing heart arrhythmias appeared on electrocardiograms with more accuracy than prepared specialists in distinguishing tiny malignancy cells with a better than 95% of success rate.

3.1.3 Data mining

Data mining, which referred to as knowledge extraction from data, is the way toward identifying patterns and irregularities among big data (Mittal, Goyal, et al., 2019). Since portions of big data frequently are created in medical service frameworks, data mining is mandatory for discover necessary data and present it in an available configuration. After doing it properly, data mining enables users to engage data from many data sets and collection systems can be analyzed, examined, and used to design more powerful healthcare sources.

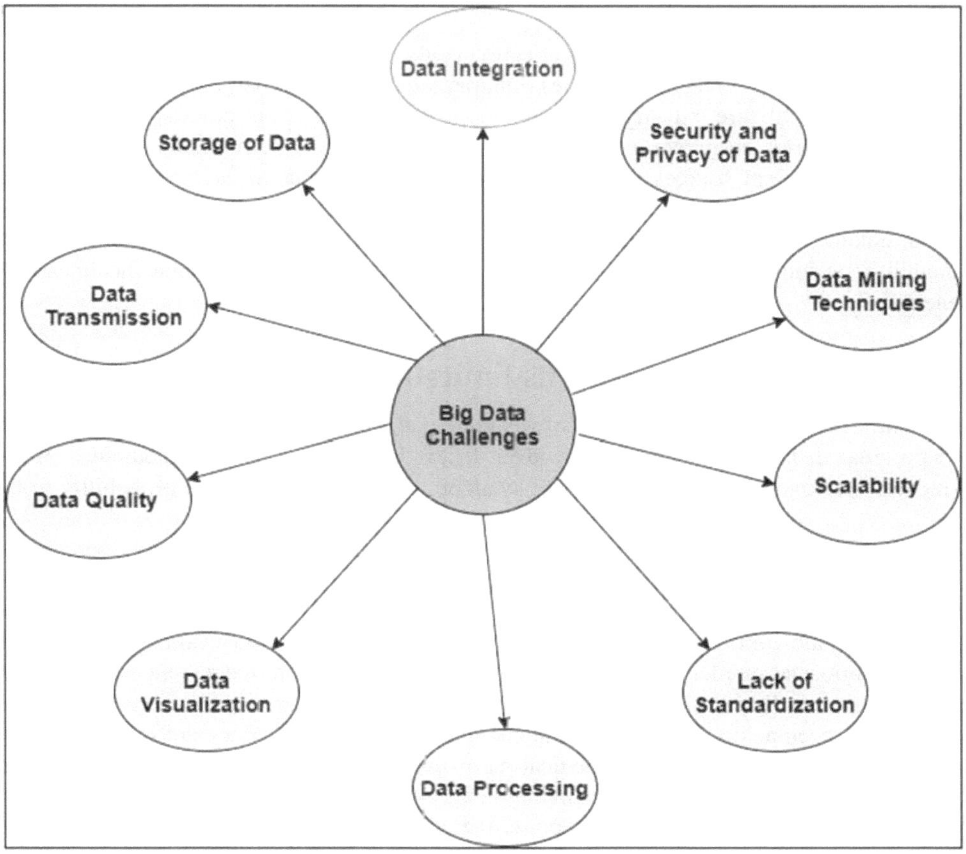

FIGURE 20.3 Big data and corresponding challenges.

3.1.4 *COVID-19 and data analytics*

Big data analytics is a framework as global medical and scientific researchers use data mining, AI, and other tools because of COVID-19 (Chintalapudi et al., 2021). Researchers, supported by technology, are examining data realms to comprehend the virus effects with an end goal to predict what will happen. AI projects with data mining to look for potential medicines by contrasting infection subtleties and those of existing medications. Similar efforts are in progress to assess various medicines and their viability and analyze the achievement of different barriers of social distancing carried out in good places.

3.2 Big data challenges in healthcare

3.2.1 *Lack of research*

In medical service centers, plenty of data challenges are occurring in daily routine. Research groups cannot generally get data on medical outcomes (Dhupia & Usha Rani, 2019). For instance, data security issues forced by government law control the access of medical data. Data fragmentation and the absence of uniform digitization slab effectiveness, with some information neglected on the grounds that it's stuck in storehouses. Some medical services frameworks might need to improve their utilization of big data software, yet need workers with the fundamental data training.

Another data challenge in medical care identifies with the decentralized idea of the major USA-based business frameworks could be digitalized; until now, many companies and fewer providers are using paper-based records. Inventions like AI can just work utilizing computerized data. This discontinuity of datasets makes it hard to build up a total image of medical services situations.

Other potential data challenges in medical care are adjusted by the dramatically better medical care results by meeting those difficulties. In case of patients not providing consent to utilize their personal data for security issues, it will lead to leakage of user information to third parties. Moreover, if data collection is not straightforward, people are not likely to share the type of data that is essential for preventing society from future pandemics.

3.2.2 Lack of expert skills in handling

To address the limitations of big data issues in medical care, healthcare centres and hospitals need data experts who have good knowledge in using IT systems to tackle the issues (Dhupia & Usha Rani, 2019; Jin et al., 2015). These data scientists require knowledge of the medical care industry and its methods, and experts from other sectors, these data analysts also require solid scientific, specialized, basic reasoning, and assessment abilities. Efficient data analysts should have the ability to reveal information from different sources and data sets, assessment of relative factors, and use it to showcase skills. Relational abilities also are significant, since data analysis is useless if it is not introduced clearly and adequately to the decision-makers and stakeholders. To overcome such issues, universities should need to introduce some courses on healthcare data analytics by introducing tools to conquer large medical datasets and help healthcare suppliers receive possibly large benefits.

4. Healthcare data management and its limitations

By integrating a patient's EHR with data from clinical wearable gadgets and customer level testing, an all-encompassing patient image can be created, providing specialists with a decent launch for ceaseless medicines. Besides, digitalizing patients' clinical records improves data accessibility and availability while improving the probability of information being reported.

Likewise, as the quantity of precise patient profiles develops, specialists can equally apply perceptive examination to preventive care and adopt a significantly more proactive strategy in distinguishing, expecting, diagnosing, and treating illnesses (Ginsburg & Phillips, 2018). Such data similarly fills in as invaluable contributions for clinical and drug research, speeding the cycle of groundbreaking thoughts and eventually improving public health. From the operational point, checking and controlling information identified by patient visits can possibly improve patient encounters with medical care suppliers by pinpointing and settling limitations in registering, testing, imaging, and data accessing.

While medical data has been achieving fundamental changes in healthcare, it does not come without difficulties. The convergence of EHRs puts a gigantic strain on medical care suppliers to oversee information in a manner that should guarantee integrity, interoperability, and security while agreeing with relating approaches and guidelines.

Big data can help medical care change from receptive, therapy-based methods to deal with a more coordinated, preventive model. Explicit data usage additionally can speed the improvement of customized approaches for more prominent patient commitment, which could prompt better consistency. However, maintaining such enormous data volumes of images, EHRs, telemedicine, and data from other sources would certainly create challenges in healthcare industries. This section explores the limitations that hospitals and others need to conquer and meet with the support of experts or data scientists. Some of them are listed below.

4.1 Data interoperability

With the goal for information to be generally helpful to any industry, it needs to produce steady significance and should be shared and moved among individuals, associations, and frameworks—this is called interoperability (What the Interoperability Rule Will Mean for Payers in 2021, n.d.). Interoperability has a huge significance in medical services as it unites patients' information from a scope of electronic medical systems, empowers patients to have an unlimited misunderstanding over what records can be imparted to whom, and simultaneously working with examination and advancement. However, as one of the persistent difficulties of the medical services industry, data interoperability is not just a specialized issue, for example, data consistency among various contexts and associations additionally requires an incorporated design of series, just as meetings' enthusiasm to share data.

4.2 Data quality

Data is treated as the fuel that controls the activities of any data framework; hence, guaranteeing data integrity additionally implies promising the framework's usefulness and adequacy (Arts et al., 2002). This cannot be more precise in the medical care industry where the accessibility of quality data directs the nature of therapy that the patients get. Unstructured data portrayed by the inadequacy, deficiency, incorrectness, duplication, nonnormalization, and insignificancy can prompt clinical errors that openly affect patients' health and safety, spoiling medical care suppliers' standing and prompting expensive claims.

Moreover, lower data quality can have huge effects on everyday activities, including inefficient inner and outer communications, incorrect payments, and postponed treatments. Incorrect data additionally has the capability of delaying clinical examination and improvement exercises by giving misinformation, bringing about wrong revelations—a genuine "trash in—trash out" condition.

4.3 Data insecurity

In the era where private data is digitized and gotten across the limits of associations, frameworks, and even lines, the medical care industry is looked up with the central issue of information security and patient protection. As per Verizon's 2018 Data Breach Investigations Report, security penetrates from the medical services area takes up generally 28% of every affirmed break, with most of the penetrates coming about because of human mistakes (Data Breach Investigations Report, n.d.). Furthermore, the business likewise needs to manage piles of terrible behaviour. In 2018, Australia's regular check-up framework – Health Engine had disclosed data validation of around 200 patients each month between March and August 2017 to cooperating law offices that we are searching for customers in close to home wounds claims.

In the age where private information is digitized and moved across the boundaries of organizations, systems, and even borders, the healthcare industry is faced with the big question of data security and patient privacy. According to Verizon's 2018 Data Breach Investigations Report, security breaches from the healthcare sector take up roughly 28% of all confirmed breaches, with the majority of the breaches resulting from human errors (Data Breach Investigations Report, n.d.). Additionally, the industry also needs to deal with heaps of bad conduct. In 2018, it was reported that Australia's doctor appointment system — health engine had intentionally disclosed personally identifiable information of around 200 patients per month between March and August 2017 to partnering law firms that were looking for clients with personal injury claims.

4.4 Policy settings

Understanding the security issues identified with patient data in the modern age, many nations on the planet have outfitted themselves with severe enactment to control the utilization of clinical information. Nonetheless, it is this prohibitive and complex administrative environment that has been keeping countries from understanding the true abilities of big data in medical care. For instance, in Australia, while existing guidelines are set up to ensure patients' health and secure their data (Health, n.d.), they viably limit the data linkage, prompting the unavailability and underutilization of public health datasets of country, especially for research purposes.

Since technological developments are occurring at a striking speed, medical care suppliers will without a doubt embrace the best innovation use cases in their tasks to improve proficiency and offer better types of assistance to patients. Under such situations, the public authority's limitation on information utilization will probably cause significant consistency issues and hamper the actual interaction of improving medical care. Policymakers, hence, need to discover the balance between the need for getting information and making information available and exploitable to make an obliging strategy setting that both works with developments and information sharing and guarantees information protection.

5. Conclusion

In this chapter, the author explored the advantages and limitations of biomedical data during the handling of big datasets. The data generation in medical fields is exponentially growing and data management in medical care requires an essential methodology whereby the three parts of data quality, security, and interoperability should be correctly addressed. In the event that users have a question about data strategy, they should need to contact the data management experts to help design and review the most upgraded structure. Therefore, the need for big data analysts and professionals is increasing and there is great demand for those who can handle large datasets to deliver better outcomes. It is additionally basic to comprehend the part of governments' help through an empowering yet extensive representation framework, which empowers business to use and oversee information in a manner that will yield the most qualities to patients.

References

Abdelhafez, H. A. (2014). Big data technologies and analytics: a review of emerging solutions. *International Journal of Business Analytics, 1*(2), 1–17. https://doi.org/10.4018/ijban.2014040101

Arts, D. G. T., De Keizer, N. F., & Scheffer, G. J. (2002). Defining and improving data quality in medical registries: a literature review, case study, and generic framework. *Journal of the American Medical Informatics Association, 9*(6), 600–611. https://doi.org/10.1197/jamia.M1087

Battineni, G., Chintalapudi, N., Amenta, F., & Traini, E. (2020). A comprehensive machine-learning model applied to magnetic resonance imaging (MRI) to predict Alzheimer's disease (AD) in older subjects. *Journal of Clinical Medicine, 9*(7), 2146. https://doi.org/10.3390/jcm9072146

Buch, V. H., Ahmed, I., & Maruthappu, M. (2018). Artificial intelligence in medicine: Current trends and future possibilities. *British Journal of General Practice, 68*(668), 143–144. https://doi.org/10.3399/bjgp18X695213

Chintalapudi, N., Battineni, G., & Amenta, F. (2021). Sentimental analysis of COVID-19 tweets using deep learning models. *Infectious Disease Reports, 13*(2), 329–339. https://doi.org/10.3390/idr13020032

Dash, S., Shakyawar, S. K., Sharma, M., & Kaushik, S. (2019). Big data in healthcare: management, analysis and future prospects. *Journal of Big Data, 6*(1), 1–25. https://doi.org/10.1186/s40537-019-0217-0

Data Breach Investigations Report. (n.d.). Retrieved from https://enterprise.verizon.com/en-sg/resources/reports/dbir/2018/. May 11, 2021.

Del Vecchio, S., Zannetti, A., Fonti, R., Iommelli, F., Pizzuti, L. M., Lettieri, A., & Salvatore, M. (2010). PET/CT in cancer research: from preclinical to clinical applications. *Contrast Media and Molecular Imaging, 5*(4), 190. https://doi.org/10.1002/cmmi.368

Dhupia, B., & Usha Rani, M. (2019). Research challenges in big data solutions in different applications. In *Springerbriefs in applied sciences and technology* (pp. 105–116). Springer Verlag. https://doi.org/10.1007/978-981-13-1456-8_9

Ginsburg, G. S., & Phillips, K. A. (2018). Precision medicine: from science to value. *Health Affairs, 37*(5), 694–701. https://doi.org/10.1377/hlthaff.2017.1624

Health. (n.d.). *National health act 1953-privacy guidelines for the medicare benefits and pharmaceutical benefits programs (06/03/2008).*

High resolution detectors to create safer X-ray diagnosis, Imaging technology news. (n.d.). Retrieved from https://www.itnonline.com/content/high-resolution-detectors-create-safer-x-ray-diagnosis. May 7, 2021.

Jan, B., Farman, H., Khan, M., Imran, M., Islam, I. U., Ahmad, A., Ali, S., & Jeon, G. (2019). Deep learning in big data analytics: a comparative study. *Computers & Electrical Engineering, 75*, 275–287. https://doi.org/10.1016/j.compeleceng.2017.12.009

Jin, X., Wah, B. W., Cheng, X., & Wang, Y. (2015). Significance and challenges of big data research. *Big Data Research, 2*(2), 59–64. https://doi.org/10.1016/j.bdr.2015.01.006

Kaur, P., Sharma, M., & Mittal, M. (2018). Big data and machine learning based secure healthcare framework. *Procedia Computer Science*. https://doi.org/10.1016/j.procs.2018.05.020

L'Heureux, A., Grolinger, K., Elyamany, H. F., & Capretz, M. A. M. (2017). Machine learning with big data: challenges and approaches. *IEEE Access, 5*, 7776–7797. https://doi.org/10.1109/ACCESS.2017.2696365

Lobach, D. F., & Detmer, D. E. (2007). Research challenges for electronic health records. *American Journal of Preventive Medicine, 32*(5 Suppl). https://doi.org/10.1016/j.amepre.2007.01.018

Masmoudi, A., Mezghani, E., Bellaaj, H., Drira, K., & Jmaiel, M. (2017). A web-based knowledge management system for scientific research team. In *Proceedings-2017 IEEE 26th international conference on enabling technologies: infrastructure for collaborative enterprises, WETICE 2017* (pp. 296–301). https://doi.org/10.1109/WETICE.2017.35

Menachemi, N., & Collum, T. H. (2011). Benefits and drawbacks of electronic health record systems. *Risk Management and Healthcare Policy, 4*, 47–55. https://doi.org/10.2147/RMHP.S12985

Mittal, M., Battineni, G., Goyal, L. M., Chhetri, B., Oberoi, S. V., Chintalapudi, N., & Amenta, F. (2020). Cloud-based framework to mitigate the impact of COVID-19 on seafarers' mental health. In *International maritime health*. https://doi.org/10.5603/IMH.2020.0038

Mittal, M., Goyal, L. M., Hemanth, D. J., & Sethi, J. K. (2019). Clustering approaches for high-dimensional databases: a review. *Wiley Interdisciplinary Reviews: Data Mining and Knowledge Discovery, 9*(3), e1300. https://doi.org/10.1002/widm.1300

Mittal, A., Kumar, D., Mittal, M., Saba, T., Abunadi, I., Rehman, A., & Roy, S. (2020). Detecting pneumonia using convolutions and dynamic capsule routing for chest X-ray images. *Sensors*. https://doi.org/10.3390/s20041068

Mittal, M., Verma, A., Kaur, I., Kaur, B., Sharma, M., Goyal, L. M., Roy, S., & Kim, T. H. (2019). An efficient edge detection approach to provide better edge connectivity for image analysis. *IEEE Access*. https://doi.org/10.1109/ACCESS.2019.2902579

Ngiam, K. Y., & Khor, I. W. (2019). Big data and machine learning algorithms for health-care delivery. *The Lancet Oncology, 20*(5), e262–e273. https://doi.org/10.1016/S1470-2045(19)30149-4

Polsinelli, M., Cinque, L., & Placidi, G. (2020). A light CNN for detecting COVID-19 from CT scans of the chest. *Pattern Recognition Letters, 140*, 95–100. https://doi.org/10.1016/j.patrec.2020.10.001

Provost, F., & Fawcett, T. (2013). Data science and its relationship to big data and data-driven decision making. *Big Data, 1*(1), 51–59. https://doi.org/10.1089/big.2013.1508

Recent Advances in MRI Technology, Imaging Technology News. (n.d.). Retrieved from https://www.itnonline.com/article/recent-advances-mri-technology. May 7, 2021.

Ristevski, B., & Chen, M. (2018). Big data analytics in medicine and healthcare. *Journal of Integrative Bioinformatics, 15*(3). https://doi.org/10.1515/jib-2017-0030

Song, I. Y., & Zhu, Y. (2016). Big data and data science: what should we teach? *Expert Systems, 33*(4), 364–373. https://doi.org/10.1111/exsy.12130

Toney, L. K., & Vesselle, H. J. (2014). Neural networks for nodal staging of non-small cell lung cancer with FDG PET and CT: importance of combining uptake values and sizes of nodes and primary tumor. *Radiology, 270*(1), 91–98. https://doi.org/10.1148/radiol.13122427

Waller, M. A., & Fawcett, S. E. (2013). Data science, predictive analytics, and big data: a revolution that will transform supply chain design and management. *Journal of Business Logistics, 34*(2), 77–84. https://doi.org/10.1111/jbl.12010

Wang, T., Lei, Y., Fu, Y., Curran, W. J., Liu, T., Nye, J. A., & Yang, X. (2020). Machine learning in quantitative PET: a review of attenuation correction and low-count image reconstruction methods. *Physica Medica, 76*, 294–306. https://doi.org/10.1016/j.ejmp.2020.07.028. Associazione Italiana di Fisica Medica.

What the Interoperability Rule Will Mean for Payers in 2021. (n.d.). Retrieved from https://healthpayerintelligence.com/news/what-the-interoperability-rule-will-mean-for-payers-in-2021. May 10, 2021.

Willemink, M. J., Koszek, W. A., Hardell, C., Wu, J., Fleischmann, D., Harvey, H., Folio, L. R., Summers, R. M., Rubin, D. L., & Lungren, M. P. (2020). Preparing medical imaging data for machine learning. *Radiology, 295*(1), 4–15. https://doi.org/10.1148/radiol.2020192224

Yanamadala, S., Morrison, D., Curtin, C., McDonald, K., & Hernandez-Boussard, T. (2016). Electronic health records and quality of care an observational study modeling impact on mortality, readmissions, and complications. *Medicine (United States), 95*(19). https://doi.org/10.1097/MD.0000000000003332

Zhang, Q., Yang, L. T., Chen, Z., & Li, P. (2018). A survey on deep learning for big data. *Information Fusion, 42*, 146–157. https://doi.org/10.1016/j.inffus.2017.10.006

Chapter 21

Future direction for healthcare based on big data analytics

Maria José Sousa[1], Paul Barach[2,3] and António Pesqueira[4]

[1]*Instituto Universitário de Lisboa, Business Research Unit, Lisboa, Portugal;* [2]*Interdisciplinary Research Institute for Health Law and Science, Sigmund Freud University Vienna, Vienna, Austria;* [3]*Jefferson College of Population Health, Philadelphia, PA, United States;* [4]*Bavarian Nordic A/S, Zürich, Switzerland*

1. Introduction

Disruptive technologies are displacing established technologies and shaking up the health sector industry through companies that are equipped with state-of-the-art technologies (Chui, Löffler, and Roberts, 2010). These technologies enable 3D printing, prototyping, and innovative applications of new product materials. Cloud technology, big data, artificial intelligence, and internet of things are triggering new ways of healthcare management and practice.

The health sector is moving to become more dynamic while it is being forced to adapt to new constraints that are emerging during the COVID-19 pandemic situation. Solutions are needed to new problems resulting from emergent needs around limited vital equipment, lack of key medications and protective equipment, revenue gaps, limited access to physicians and nurses, and increasing regulatory and media scrutiny.

New, cost-effective, approaches and treatments are needed to address the current public health and economical joint crises. More than ever, the need to support the codesign of healthcare services with patients and family careers is an essential part in the diagnostic process, as the health systems do not have the power and the resources to support all citizens. The recent years have provided several examples of how past business models in complex economies are being replaced mainly because they are obsolete, but also because of massive cost increases, and an unsustainable trajectory of health care spending to support new technologies. Several governments have passed transparency laws to address pervasive conflict of interests, requiring the reporting of the deep relationships between life sciences companies, healthcare delivery systems, and health care professionals. Researchers, doctors, patients, regulators, and investors—have a right to know if the research is biased, and the measures taken to minimize the possibility of bias.

Regulators and governmental authorities encourage a consistent approach to data disclosure in Europe and help guide further reporting actions at national levels. The European Medical Device Regulations directive requires detailed data reporting requirements, and several countries are also establishing new agency programs to evaluate the economic impact and performance of new drugs and technologies. These efforts are meant to gain better control of the run-away spending and assist in measuring the lasting impacts of new pharmaceutical products and devices. The new evaluation models use a customer-centric approach to assess cost-effective policy and service interventions to help improve the design (especially choice of primary end point) and interpretation of evaluative studies of new drugs and devices (Lilford et al., 2010). The new emerging evaluation models are more suited to deal with big data, namely, the flows of new trends of real-world patient data (Daniel, 2019). Companies are changing the traditional paradigms moving from face-to-face interactions to remote patient triage and monitoring using new advances in digital technology. As a main product of this research, a new model will be proposed for the adoption and implementation of technologies by the health sector.

2. Theoretical framework

2.1 Leadership conceptual framework

The study of the expression and the impacts of leadership are recurring themes in academic and professional environments. Leadership is effectively a widely studied phenomenon (Bass, 1990), in which the authors review 7500 studies on the

Big Data Analytics for Healthcare. https://doi.org/10.1016/B978-0-323-91907-4.00022-4

subject, suggesting better focus is needed on how best to implement these concepts. The management literature considers leadership a success factor in organizations and that specific leadership styles can lead to better financial and organizational performance. According to Levin, there are three major leadership styles (Lewin et al., 1939): (a) *Autocratic leaders* make decisions without consulting their team members. This can be appropriate when decisions need to be made quickly, when there is no need for team input, and when team agreement is not necessary for an outcome. However, this style can lead to high levels of absenteeism and staff turnover; (b) *Democratic leaders* make the final decision, but they include team members in the decision-making process. They encourage creativity and employees are often highly engaged in projects and decisions. As a result, team members tend to have high job satisfaction and high productivity; and (c) *Laissez-faire leaders* give their team members a lot of freedom to do their work, and to set their deadlines. They provide support with resources and advice if needed, but otherwise they do not get involved. This autonomy can lead to high job satisfaction, but it can be challenging if team members do not have the knowledge, skills, or self-motivation to do their work effectively.

The contingency school (Fiedler, 1996) suggests that what makes an effective leader is highly context dependent. The behavioral school also assumed that effective leaders adopt certain styles (Hersey & Blanchard, 1988, 1996), especially the ones studied in theory X and theory Y as (a) *Theory X* managers believe that the average employee has an inherent dislike of work and will avoid it if possible, they avoid responsibilities, and have relatively little ambition and (b) *Theory Y* managers believe that the expenditure of physical and mental effort in work is something natural, and the average employee, under proper conditions, will learn not only to accept but to seek responsibility.

Three major theoretical paradigms of leadership are used: the first, very focused on the profile and leading conditions; second, concerned with an indication of leadership behaviors which are more effective; and third, an aggregator, which explores the contingent variables that determine the success of leadership, either as background or even as consequential.

Burns (1978) proposes, based on a study of political leaders, that the leader types are in a continuum of behaviors ranging from transactional to transformational, arguing that transformational leadership is revealed when the leader can stimulate the followers to develop certain types of behaviors. This manifests beyond their personal interests and motivations and is focused only on the best interests of those they serve—the group and the organization. The model estimates that this type of leadership develops and stimulates ethical behaviors among the followers. This line of thought was taken up by Bass (1985, p. 258) and questions the differences, as some leaders combine both traits, even if there is a clear distinction between transactional and transformational leadership styles. Digital context is changing organizations, work relations, jobs, and the organizational culture—meaning e-leadership assumes more importance.

E-leadership is defined as a social influence process where changes in attitudes feelings, thoughts, behaviors, and organizations are brought about through the help of advanced IT (Avolio & Kahai, 2003; Mackenzie, 2010; Savolainen, 2014). Leaders need to deal with a new reality of managing employees at a distance which has created new challenges to motivate and engage remote workers. Effective interactions using remote IT tools between leaders and followers are one of the key challenges for the leaders because of the infrequent physical colocation which mostly misses the impact of nonverbal communication (Savolainen, 2014). Leaders need to make an extra effort to build close relationships with followers by sharing even more relevant information with them. Frequent quality meetings, both technologically aided and face to face, may facilitate openness in the relationship between leaders and followers, promoting trust-building and truth telling in a digitalized working-place (Savolainen, 2014). The use of digital services like WhatsApp and the development of an internal social network may also help leaders to share information with followers at a fast and effective pace. Employees welcome these asynchronous platforms to share their opinions even more freely and frequently. Few practices are as relevant as empowerment to facilitate social trust and foster personal responsibility and deep engagement among people (Brownell, 2010).

A new concept of digital leadership is emerging and includes many dimensions as shown in the following (Table 21.1):

2.2 Big data analytics and AI in the health sector

Globally, the health sector is changing. Artificial intelligence (AI) and significant data capabilities to process large set of data are enabling doctors to better diagnose type of diseases in their patients supported by extensive knowledge on the global patterns and trends (Al-Rahmi et al., 2019). AI has numerous applications for the healthcare industry. Machine learning, natural language processing, and robotics can predict an individual's risk of contracting HIV, assess a patient's risk of inpatient violence, and assist in surgeries. The quality of data determines the reliability of outputted information (Bresciani et al., 2021). Flawed or bias underlying data can result in faulty learning and generate erroneous outputs. Minority populations are often underrepresented in data, making them particularly vulnerable to over- or underdiagnosis when AI strategies are used to inform decision-making (Adrian et al., 2018; Awan et al., 2021).

TABLE 21.1 Health digital leadership competencies.

Domains	Examples of leadership competencies
Leadership and strategic vision	Inspire the health workers, create a shared vision, and successfully manage change, in order to achieve the strategic vision of the organization. A commitment to lifelong learning and improvement of all the health workers to achieve high levels of quality and performance.
Internal and external communications	Communicate clearly and concisely with internal and external stakeholders. Facilitate the interactions with all the health sector actors, based on big data analytics.
Ethics and social responsibility	Align individual and organizational conduct with ethical and professional standards, including the responsibility to the patients and the community.
Health context	Apply business principles to the health context, understanding the healthcare system, and deciding based on big data analytics.

Source: Systematization of Health Studies from 2019 to 2020.

Homogeneous data forms the basis of many AI tools, which means that their outputs do not apply to a diverse population. For example, if a deep learning tool predicts an individual's risk of contracting HIV learned from a dataset that only included males, the tool would not have the same power to reliably and accurately predict the risk in female patients. Using the tool as-is would result in ultimately harmful or unnecessary interventions. The purpose of AI is to help the provider make the best decision that ultimately benefits the patient—all patients. Often, how the data predicts the outcomes (which variables are more influential) and how the information is combined are unclear to the end-user, making clinical decisions difficult. This "black box" problem means the provider cannot assess the accuracy of the methods that lead the system to its output which can lead to lose of confidence in the technology undermining the utility of AI tools (Table 21.2).

On a global scale, physicians are becoming more digital, spending more time online. Not only to search for information or educational purposes, but also recommending specific websites to their patients to educate and empower them to search for specific useful information or search for new therapies or treatments (Subbe & Barach, 2020).

Moreover, the combination of social media networks, cloud computing solutions, digital, big data analytics (Ashaari et al., 2020, ch. 27), and mobile skills are influencing new health policies (Table 21.3).

Health organizations are using more digital technologies including CRM, Master data management, Business Intelligence, Digital Asset Management (DAM), Call Centers Software Systems, Business Intelligence and Information Management, Business Process Improvement systems, Decision support systems, and Digital Systems Management. On the other hand, researchers, investors, regulators, providers, patients, and HCPs are looking for new innovative services and products like telemedicine services. Telemedicine has blossomed during COVID with many health systems leveraging their telehealth technology to allow clinicians to see patients who are at home, including in remote areas and regions in

TABLE 21.2 Big data analytics and AI.

Continuing medical education (CME)
Medical Guidelines
Scientific articles
Clinical studies
News about the industry and related topics
Literature citation database
Congresses calendar, agendas, and proceedings
Medical education videos
Clinical trial data
Peer-to-peer portals and information sharing libraries
Product specifications

Source: Systematization of Health Studies from 2019 to 2020.

TABLE 21.3 Health technologies applications.

Mobile solutions	Mobile apps to support the patients through disease diagnoses, facilitating participation in clinical trials, and monitor various biometrics. Also, mobile-friendly websites services enable to deliver content, images, and videos to a growing number of users, that it is also possible to include the Health Care Providers (HCPs) and Patients;
Scientific and medical product portals for doctors and pharmacies	Facilitate the search for information and as knowledge portals
Medical resource portals	Knowledge portals
Web conferences	Share information among health professionals, researchers, and policymakers
Web Document databases and online repositories for articles sharing	Increase health knowledge.
Social networking	Veeva chatter, Yammer, and Lync, with medical teams and specialized commercial services for medical, inquiries, product education, and side effects reporting
Integrated telemedicine	Presence for more efficient end-to-end care management
Impact of technology in health policy	More efficient, but also more inclusive and social policies

Source: Systematization of Health Studies from 2019 to 2020.

developing countries. Electronic intensive care unit (e-ICU) monitoring programs, which allow nurses and physicians to remotely monitor the status of 60−100 patients in ICUs in multiple hospitals, are ideal for monitoring sicker patients. Technological and staffing complexities make it impossible to create such a program on short notice, but rapid deployment can reduce health care workers' contact with infected patients in the ICU.

Community telemedicine or mobile integrated health care programs allow patients to be treated in their homes, with higher-level medical support provided virtually. For sicker patients at home, such programs can facilitate evaluation before hospital transfer, potentially allowing them to bypass the ED and be placed directly in a hospital bed, reducing exposure for health care workers and other patients.

Much medical decision making is cognitive, and telemedicine can provide rapid access to subspecialists who are not immediately available in person. New ways and methods of engagement between physicians and patients are possible including scheduling appointments via internet; self-medication programs for specific nonrisk patients with medical control through mobile apps and telemedicine control; 3D printing for custom-making drugs for individual patients for correct dosage instead of "one-size-fits-all dosage," facilitating access globally to health.

Disasters and pandemics pose unique challenges to health care delivery. Though telehealth will not solve them all, it's well suited for scenarios in which infrastructure remains intact and clinicians are available to see patients. Payment and regulatory structures, state licensing, credentialing across hospitals, and program implementation all take time to work through. Health authorities, regulatory agencies, and payers are requesting more digital services and using more digital products through online and mobile usage to address traditional and new requirements. Mobile apps and web-services along with digital tools will allow positive solutions to patients (Table 21.4).

3. Empirical methodological approach

A survey that contained questions concerning leadership actions and big data analysis and transfer was designed (Annex 1). The theoretical framework was used to build the survey, which is based on demographic questions (i.e., country and job position) and a scale of validated 25 statements (about Applications Trends of Technologies in Health Sector, Big Data Analysis and Transfer, and Leadership themes).

The survey used a 5-point Likert scale ("strongly disagree" to "strongly agree") categorical response format. An email invitation to complete an electronic form of the survey (http://www.googleforms.com) was sent to a convenience sample of experts on May 20, 2020.

Data was analyzed using Statistical Package for the Social Science, version 26.0. First was made a descriptive analysis of the demographic characteristics of the respondents and then it was assessed the reliability of the survey by measuring the alpha coefficients of each of the five scales that were computed to measure the scales' internal reliability.

TABLE 21.4 Application trends in the health sector.

Telemedicine
Predictive and remote patient monitoring and maintenance
Digital products and digital processes
Customers and partners digital relationships
New related ecosystems based on digital platforms without industry boundaries
New opportunities for people to develop their skills
Digital work in the form of intelligent alerts and intelligent robots
Collaboration between people and machines
Remote work
New types of jobs

Source: Systematization of Health Studies from 2019 to 2020.

3.1 Results

3.1.1 Profile of the experts

The profiles of the respondents regarding their positions, academic degree, type of organizations, and countries of origin are presented below (Table 21.5). Table 21.5 demonstrates the professional positions of the respondents including experts, researchers, institutional representatives, or policymakers. The positions of the respondents are rank ordered as follows: Researchers (n = 4), Institutional Representatives (n = 5), Experts (n = 24), and Policymakers (n = 1).

The respondents represent several countries (Table 21.6). There were 34 expert respondents primarily from Brazil (n = 17) and South Africa (n = 7), that consented to participate in the e-HealthCare research.

TABLE 21.5 Descriptive statistics – job position of the experts.

Job Position	N	%
Expert	24	70.6
Institutional representative	5	14.7
Policymaker	1	2.9
Researcher	4	11.8
Total	34	100

TABLE 21.6 Country of the experts.

Country	N	%
Brazil	17	50.0
China	3	8.8
India	4	11.8
Russia	3	8.8
South Africa	7	20.6
Total	34	100

3.1.2 Analysis of the reliability

A Cronbach's alpha coefficient analysis was conducted to estimate the internal consistency and reliability of the items of the questionnaire. The small sample size, 34 respondents, posed limitations on the external generalizability of our findings. The Cronbach alpha coefficient of reliability ranges from 0 to 1 and provides an overall assessment of a measure's reliability (Cronbach, 1951). The Cronbach alpha was calculated by correlating the score for each scale item with the total score for each observation, and then comparing that to the variance for all individual item scores as follows:

$$\alpha = (\mathrm{kk}-1)\left(1-\sum \mathrm{ki} = 1\sigma 2\mathrm{yi}\sigma 2\mathrm{x}\right)\alpha = (\mathrm{kk}-1)\left(1-\sum \mathrm{i}= 1\mathrm{k}\sigma \mathrm{yi}2\sigma \mathrm{x}2\right)$$

where

kk refers to the number of scale items

σ2yiσyi2 refers to the variance associated with the item i

σ2xσx2 refers to the variance associated with the observed total scores.

Table 21.7 presents the means of factor scores and the reliability coefficients (Cronbach's alpha) for the three scales corresponding to the three domains. The global Cronbach alpha was 0.986. An alpha >0.9 represents a very high reliability of the data, and can be used in further statistical analysis, as follows.

3.1.3 Data analysis

After verifying the reliability of the scale items, the Means and Standard Deviation of the responses was calculated. The mean calculation is based on the following formula to measure the average of the numbers:

$$\mathrm{X} = \sum \mathrm{xN}$$

where

$\sum$ represents the summation.

X represents scores.

N represents a number of scores.

The standard deviation calculation is based on the following formula to measures the spread of the data around the mean value:

where

σ = standard deviation.

Xi = each value of dataset.

μ = the arithmetic mean of the data.

N = the total number of data points.

$\sum$ (Xi − x)2 = The sum of (Xi − x)2 for all data points.

Table 21.8 demonstrates the different subdimensions broken into technology, leadership, and sustainability trends, as the model proposed for the Health Sector.

4. Discussion

It was observed significant differences between respondents in all the dimensions regarding the applications trends of technologies in health sector. The standard deviation values were very high. This can be explained based on the differences of maturity of the countries in regard to the dimensions of our model: Applications Trends of Technologies in Health Sector, Big Data Analytics, and Leadership.

TABLE 21.7 Reliability coefficients.

Dimensions	Mean	Cronbach alpha
Applications trends of technologies in health sector	4.121	0.968
Big data analytics	4.045	0.977
Leadership	4.129	0.955

TABLE 21.8 Descriptive statistics of the proposed dimensions and sub-dimensions.

Applications trends of technologies in health sector	Mean	S.D.
Telemedicine	4.18	0.191
Predictive and remote patient monitoring and maintenance	4.09	0.191
Digital products and digital processes	4.09	0.195
Customers and partners digital relationships	4.12	0.178
New related ecosystems based on digital platforms without industry boundaries	4.12	0.188
New opportunities for people to develop their skills	4.29	0.177
Digital work in the form of intelligent alerts and intelligent robots	3.82	0.166
Collaboration between people and machines	4.12	0.178
Remote work	4.12	0.183
New types of jobs	4.26	0.181
Big data analytics		
CME – continuing medical education	4.15	0.194
Medical guidelines	4.12	0.183
Scientific articles	4.26	0.181
Clinical studies	4.12	0.173
News about the industry and related topics	3.79	0.183
Literature citation database	4.03	0.171
Congresses calendar, agendas, and proceedings	3.97	0.161
Medical education videos	3.85	0.207
Clinical trial data	4.09	0.176
Peer-to-peer portals and information sharing libraries	4.15	0.189
Product specifications	3.97	0.196
Leadership		
Leadership and strategic vision	4.15	0.185
Internal and external communications	3.88	0.173
Ethics and social responsibility	4.15	0.164
Health context	4.29	0.166

The data presented in this study supports the reliability and face validity of the survey developed to assess the perceptions of the experts, institutional representatives, policymakers, and researchers.

The first dimension analyzed, *Applications Trends of Technologies in Health Sector*, suggests that the focus should be on people development with the highest mean values 4.29 and 4.26, respectively, underscoring the items New Opportunities for People to Develop Their Skills and New types of Jobs. The second dimension *Big Data Analytics* suggests that the focus should be on data analytics for being used in science and education with the highest mean values 4.26, 4.15, and 4.15, respectively. This points to the importance of scientific articles, peer-to-peer portals and information sharing libraries, and continuing medical education. The third dimension, *Leadership*, suggests that the focus should be on leadership, strategic vision, and context with the highest mean values 4.29, 4.15, and 4.15, respectively. This highlights the importance of health context, leadership and strategic vision, and ethics and social responsibility.

The study findings suggest that the leadership, technologies, and big data analytics dimensions need to be increased to support the health sector sustainability. Technology is a powerful trigger to improve the efficiency and efficacy of the sector, promoting digital transformation. The big data analytics will lead the health professionals to respond to the new challenges in a more efficient way, and the leadership will need to have the strength to create a compelling strategic vision for the sector.

There are several limitations to the study. Focusing perceptions is reliant on self-reports of current and retrospective perceptions, which may be a source of richness but also bias. Second, it is not possible to tell if there are significant differences between the responders and the nonresponders to the survey. Because of the anonymity of the subjects, nonrespondents could not be contacted. Third, the overall response rate to our questionnaire was low, perhaps in part because of the use of an e-mail survey.

5. Implications and future research

5.1 Theoretical implications of the study findings

The study results provide theoretical contributions with a material impact on a variety of adjacent fields. It elaborates on a literature review on key emerging leadership and technologies as big data analytics and AI themes and that also can influence the economic and political leadership levels. It proposes the need to forge stronger links between technology and leadership, underpinned by the principles of organizational sustainability and transparency. It also presented an innovative theoretical perspective on the leadership concept that is associated with enhancing the potential of innovation and development for the health sector.

5.2 Policy implications

The study contributes to the political discussion of public policies that are urgently needed in and also can contribute to the creation of a transparent culture of sustainability in the health sector. This effort can be done through the identification of the most relevant dimensions regarding technology, big data analytics and leadership. Moreover, new policies can promote the investment in technologies as opportunities to stimulate bold economic growth. Another critical role of policy is to define new regulations that are agile and competitive while strongly adhering to principals of transparent ethical business practices. This will help stimulate a framework for digital innovation to address and respond to societal challenges.

5.3 Future research avenues

With the exponential growth of technology (e.g., big data analytics, AI, data mining, and others) in the health sector, it is important to reassess the future status of technology innovations and the way leadership is responding to these changes. With the recent pandemic crisis, their resolution will be enhanced by embracing new digital technology. New leadership styles are needed to support and fund new ways of working and exchanging ideas and data. It is also important to better understand the impact of these new regulations and frameworks on the way doctors and health care professionals are adapting. New studies are needed to broaden the research and focus more attention on these issues. There is an urgent need to develop appropriate strategies to assure that healthcare technologies have the right capacity and are governed by ethical leadership to effectively select and support the right technologies that can improve the welfare of patients, institutions, and healthcare professionals.

6. Conclusions

This chapter identifies the leading emerging disruptive technologies in the health sector. It makes an exploration of the importance of big data analytics and the importance in times of crisis of humble and forward-thinking leadership that will impact the strategic vision and capabilities of the healthcare sector. Technologies create opportunities for community engagement, and innovation that can lead to many lasting changes. For example, telemedicine can cause innovation in the leadership models. On the other hand, technologies have given rise to new ways for health professionals to share their knowledge and learn from others. The health sector needs to develop new skills by enhancing their competitive capacity (Hartman & Whooley, 2016) through the adoption of health technologies, supported by agile regulations, improved working conditions, and grounded in ethical and transparent principles. This research suggests that the health sector will most benefit from a deeper understanding and support of three key dimensions: *technologies*; strong *leadership*; and the ability to play an active part in promoting measures based on big data analytics and favoring *sustainable* development.

Annex 1

Questionnaire

Age: ____________________________

1. Gender: M: F:
2. Leadership role: _________________________________
3. Please select your job position (Table 21.9):

TABLE 21.9 Respondents job position.

Job Position
Expert
Researcher
Institutional representative
Policymaker

4. Please select your country (Table 21.10):

TABLE 21.10 Respondents country.

Country
Brazil
China
India
Russia

5. Trends of Health Technologies, Leadership, and Big Data Analytics for Sustainability

Please rate the next items regarding the importance of the dimensions of Application Trends of Technologies in the health sector, big data analytics, and leadership. Select the level of perceived importance using the scale ranging from Not important (1) to Very Important (5) (Table 21.11):

TABLE 21.11 List of applications trends of technologies in health sector.

Applications trends of technologies in Health sector
Telemedicine
Predictive and remote patient monitoring and maintenance
Digital products and digital processes
Customers and partners digital relationships
New related ecosystems based on digital platforms without industry boundaries
New opportunities for people to develop their skills
Digital work in the form of intelligent alerts and intelligent robots
Collaboration between people and machines

Continued

TABLE 21.11 List of applications trends of technologies in health sector.—cont'd

Applications trends of technologies in Health sector
Remote work
New types of jobs
Big data analytics
CME – Continuing medical education
Medical Guidelines
Scientific articles
Clinical studies
News about the industry and related topics
Literature citation database
Congresses calendar, agendas, and proceedings
Medical education videos
Clinical trial data
Peer-to-peer portals and information sharing libraries
Product specifications
Leadership
Leadership and strategic vision
Internal and external communications
Ethics and social responsibility
Health context

References

Adrian, C., Abdullah, R., Atan, R., & Jusoh, Y. Y. (2018). Conceptual model development of big data analytics implementation assessment effect on decision-making. *The International Journal of Interactive Multimedia and Artificial Intelligence, 5*(1), 101–106.

Al-Rahmi, W. M., Yahaya, N., Aldraiweesh, A. A., Alturki, U., Alamri, M. M., Sukri, M., Kamin, Y., Aljeraiwi, A., & Alhamed, O. A. (2019). Big data adoption and knowledge management sharing: An empirical investigation on their adoption and sustainability as a purpose of education. *IEEE Access, 7*, 47245–47258.

Ashaari, M. A., Amran, A., Ahmad, N. H., Bakri, H., & Nazri, S. (2020). Big data analytics technology capability and data-driven decision making in Malaysian higher education institutions: A conceptual framework. *IOP Conference Series: Materials Science and Engineering, 874*(1), 012021.

Avolio, B. J., & Kahai, S. S. (2003). Adding the "E" to E-leadership: How it may impact your leadership. *Organizational Dynamics, 31*(4), 325–338.

Awan, U., Shamim, S., Khan, Z., Zia, N. U., Shariq, S. M., & Khan, M. N. (2021). Big data analytics capability and decision-making: The role of data-driven insight on circular economy performance. *Technological Forecasting and Social Change, 168*.

Bass, B. M. (1985). *Leadership and performance beyond expectations*. Hardcover.

Bass, B. M. (1990). *Handbook of leadership: Theory, research, and managerial application*. New York: Free Press, Collier Macmillan.

Bresciani, S., Ciampi, F., Meli, F., & Ferraris, A. (2021). Using big data for co-innovation processes: Mapping the field of data-driven innovation, proposing theoretical developments and providing a research agenda. *International Journal of Information Management*, 102347.

Brownell, J. (2010). Leadership in the service of hospitality. *Cornell Hospitality Quarterly, 51*(3), 363–378.

Burns, J. M. (1978). *Leadership*. New York: Harper & Row.

Chui, M., Loffler, M., & Roberts, R. (2010). The internet of things. *McKinsey Quarterly, 2*(2), 1–9.

Cronbach, L. (1951). Coefficient alpha and the internal structure of tests. *Psycho, 16*, 297–334.

Daniel, B. K. (2019). Big data and data science: A critical review of issues for educational research. *British Journal of Educational Technology, 50*(1), 101–113.

Fiedler, F. (1996). Research on leadership selection and training: One view of the future. *Administrative Science Quarterly, 41*(2), 241–250.

Hartman, S. W., & Whooley, P. (2016). Are China and the United States in a competitive zero-sum economic game? *The International Trade Journal, 30*(5), 434–448.

Hersey, P., & Blanchard, K. (1988). *Management of organizational behaviour: Utilizing human resources* (5th ed.). Englewood Cliffs, New Jersey: Prentice-Hall.

Hersey, P., & Blanchard, K. (1996). *Management of organizational behaviour: Utilizing human resources* (7th ed.). Englewood Cliffs, New Jersey: Prentice-Hall.

Lewin, K., Lippit, R., & White, R. K. (1939). Patterns of aggressive behavior in experimentally created "social climates.". *The Journal of Social Psychology, 10*, 271–279.

Lilford, R., Chilton, P. J., Hemming, K., Brown, C., Girling, A., & Barach, P. (2010). Evaluating policy and service interventions: Framework to guide selection and interpretation of study end points. *British Medical Journal, 341*, c4413.

Mackenzie, M. L. (2010). Manager communication and workplace trust: Understanding manager and employee perceptions in the E-world. *International Journal of Information Management, 30*, 529–541.

Savolainen, R. (2014). Emotions as motivators for information seeking: A conceptual analysis. *Library & Information Science Research, 36*(1), 59–65.

Subbe, C., & Barach, P. (2020). Safety 3.0 and the end of the superstar clinician. In E. Vanderheiden, & C. H. Mayer (Eds.), *Navigating mistakes, errors and failures—their hidden potential in cultural context* (pp. 515–535). Springer Nature Switzerland AG 515.

Section VII

Case studies of big data in healthcare arena

Chapter 22

Big data in orthopedics: between hypes and hopes

Carlo Biz[1] and Nicola Luigi Bragazzi[2]

[1]*University of Padova, Orthopedics and Orthopedic Oncology, Department of Surgery, Oncology and Gastroenterology DISCOG, Padova, Italy;* [2]*Laboratory for Industrial and Applied Mathematics (LIAM), Department of Mathematics and Statistics, York University, Toronto, ON, Canada*

1. Introduction

The global burden of disease (GBD) is the societal and clinical burden imposed by a given disorder, in terms of economic–financial and humanistic costs generated by ineffective treatment and inadequate management. Quantitatively, monitoring and tracking these costs can help all relevant stakeholders (public health policy- and decision-makers, as well as practitioners) verify the progress and the effectiveness of the adopted interventions, relying on an array of reliable indicators and validated measures (Schwend, 2020). These include, for instance, the years of life lost (YLLs), the years lived with disability (YLDs), and the disability-adjusted life years (DALYs), which enable to assess life lost due to death (like casualty or premature death) or disabilities, respectively, which hinder to live life at 100% health. GBD-related metrics is of paramount importance in allocating funding and distributing logistic-organizational and human resources, especially in developing countries and territories, where there is, often, a lack of infrastructures and facilities (Schwend, 2020). Compared to medical and public/global health specializations, surgical specialties have been generally overlooked when it comes to financing. On the other hand, musculoskeletal diseases, since infanthood, contribute to a significant portion of the GBD (Schwend, 2020; Sebbag et al., 2019).

According to a recent systematic analysis of the World Health Organization (WHO) Burden of Diseases Database, worldwide, in 183 countries, the total count of DALYs generated by musculoskeletal diseases has been computed to increase from about 80 million to approximately 108 million in the period 2000–2015. Similarly, YLDs have increased from around 77 millions to circa 104 millions, with musculoskeletal diseases ranking second as cause generating YLDs globally. A comparable trend was reported for YLLs, which have increased from about three millions to slightly more than four millions. The burden of musculoskeletal diseases is particularly dramatically relevant in European countries and territories, being remarkable as well in developing countries. To counteract and mitigate, at least partially, such a burden, recently, the WHO has promoted the delivery of essential surgical services and provisions through its Emergency and Essential Surgical Care Project and Global Initiative (Schwend, 2020).

Thanks to its latest scientific advancements and technological achievements, medicine, including orthopedics, is entering a new, unprecedented era, characterized by the production and release of an incredible amount of data, termed as big data. They are characterized by several key dimensions, including velocity (big data can be generated, processed, and analyzed in real time), volume (referring to the wealth of data, the magnitude of which challenges classical storage, processing, and analytical capacities and infrastructures), variety (referring to the diversity of data sources, administrative, patient reported, healthcare generated, etc.), veracity (credibility, reliability, and accuracy of data), and value (raw data that, once processed, become smart, applicable, and actionable).

Different channels and sources can produce big data: from large-scale surveys, databases, repositories, and registries (epidemiological/clinical big data) to wet-lab and next-generation sequencing and high-throughput technologies (molecular

Big Data Analytics for Healthcare. https://doi.org/10.1016/B978-0-323-91907-4.00010-8

big data), smartphones and other mobile devices, sensors, wearable technologies, imaging techniques (computational big data), and nonconventional data streams such as social networks, and web queries (infodemiological or digital big data).

This chapter will provide a brief overview on the potential uses of big data in the field of orthopedics (Koziara et al., 2021), broken down according to source/channel (Table 22.1), showing practical examples and applications of big data (summarized in Table 22.2), as well as their shortcomings and limitations (Table 22.3).

TABLE 22.1 Types of big data and their sources/channels in the field of orthopedics.

Type of big data	Sources/channels
Epidemiological big data	Epidemiological survey
	Claims-based database (administrative database)
	Electronic health records (EHRs)/electronic medical records (EMRs)
Molecular big data	Microarray chips
Big data generated by information and communication technologies	Smartphones
	Sensors and wearable technologies
	Imaging techniques (i.e., radiography)
Computational/digital big data	"Nonconventional data streams"
	Web searches
	Website page consultation (i.e., Wikipedia)

TABLE 22.2 Types of big data and examples of potential uses/applications in the field of orthopedics.

Type of big data	Examples of potential uses/applications
Epidemiological big data	Epidemiological assessment (incidence, prevalence, comorbidities, and mortality rates)
	Epidemiological nowcasting/forecasting for funding and resources allocation optimization
	Economic assessment (costs evaluation)
	Evaluation and comparison of different orthopedic treatment and management options
	Identification of diagnostic and prognostic markers
	Evaluation and assessment of mid- and long-term clinical outcomes
Molecular big data	Patient profiling and stratification
	Personalized/individualized orthopedics
	Characterization of the effects and actions of drugs at the cellular and molecular levels
	Identification of potential druggable targets
Big data generated by information and communication technologies	Collection of patient-reported outcomes
	Customization and personalized of healthcare provision delivery
Computational/digital big data	Patient health-related literacy assessment
	Patient education and empowerment

TABLE 22.3 Shortcomings and limitations of big data in current orthopedics research.

Type of big data	Limitation/issue
Epidemiological big data	Discrepancies between registry-based studies and individual (single- or multicenter) investigations
	Discrepancies among database-based studies
	Privacy and bioethical issues
Molecular big data	Conflicting results among studies (depending on the type of tissue studied, the type of molecular technique used, etc.)
	"False discovery" of markers
Big data generated by information and communication technologies	Privacy and bioethical issues due to the pervasive and ubiquitous nature of the devices
Computational/digital big data	Lack of transparency concerning the algorithm

2. Roles and applications of epidemiological big data in current orthopedics research

Epidemiological big data can come from large-scale, often nation-wide surveys. These data can inform public health policies as well as evidence-based medicine and, more specifically, orthopedics. A recent bibliometric study conducted by Romanini et al. (2021) has found a significantly increasing rate of studies relying on registries-based research in the recent years.

While randomized controlled trials represent the gold standard for building a body of rigorous and clinically relevant evidence, they may not always reflect real-life patient populations, as such limiting the generalizability and external validity of their findings. Real-life or real-world evidence, collected during daily clinical practice, provides a complementary perspective to tightly controlled trials (McIsaac, 2020). In this respect, big data–based studies can add to well-designed "small data"–based investigations and randomized controlled trials.

There exist very large databases, such as the UK National Joint Registry (Koziara et al., 2021; Muir, 2017), The National Hip Fracture Database, the Swedish Hip Arthroplasty Registry, or the Trauma Audit and Research Network (Koziara et al., 2021). More specifically, big data can be used to quantify the socioeconomic burden of a given orthopedic disorder, estimate, and project its epidemiological trends to optimize the allocation of funding and resources, better informing nation-wide international strategies. For instance, Ha et al. (2016) assessed the epidemiological trends of hip fractures in South Korea in terms of incidence and mortality in the period from 2008 to 2012, forecasting the volume of hip fractures until 2025 utilizing a nation-wide claims-based database. Authors found an increase in the incidence of hip fractures, higher among women and in the older age group. Opposite trends could be reported for overall standardized mortality ratios, which were higher among men and higher than those in the general population regardless of the age group, even if they were decreasing.

Similar studies have been conducted, for example, for distal radius (Kwon et al., 2016), spinal (Kim, Jang, Park, & Lee et al., 2016), hip (Lin et al., 2018) and osteoporotic fractures (Kim, Jang, Park, & Kim et al., 2016), complications of spinal surgery (Ratliff et al., 2016), and other orthopedic traumas and injuries (Yang et al., 2016), among others.

Besides quantifying and forecasting epidemiological trends, big data can be exploited to investigate the determinants of comorbidities and identify prognostic markers. For example, Lu et al. (2020) mined two large orthopedic databases, a prospective surgical outcomes one, and a claims-based private insurance one, to discover the determinants of an increased risk for revision surgery among patients undergoing primary total shoulder arthroplasties in the period from 2007 to 2016. Some specific comorbidities (high body mass index, metabolic impairments such as diabetes, congestive heart failure, and dyspnea) as well as age could be identified as major factors increasing the likelihood of revision.

Furthermore, big data can be utilized to explore the mid-term and long-term clinical outcomes of a given surgical procedure and its superiority over another one (the competitor). For example, Spaans et al. (2018) investigated the effects of combining bone impaction grafting with a dual-mobility cup to reduce the risk of dislocation rate after performing revision hip arthroplasty and preserve the integrity of the acetabulum, avoiding its destruction, potentially induced by the aseptic loosening of the prosthesis. Authors found the combination of the two procedures resulted in satisfactory clinical outcomes and a good midterm survival of the cup.

Big data is particularly helpful when the studied orthopedic disease is rare, such as medial clavicle injuries. For example, Bakir et al. (Bakir et al., 2019, 2020) in Germany performed a nation-wide, registry-based survey to epidemiologically characterize medial clavicle fractures and sternoclavicular joint dislocations in a sample of 114,003 patients, from 2012 to 2014. Authors found that such injuries were often accompanied by thoracic, cranio-cerebral, and upper extremity (shoulder/upper arm) injuries. Authors also assessed the outcomes of different surgical options, ranging from plate osteosynthesis to surgery with K-wires, absorbable materials, or tension flange.

Big data can help uncover relationships between diseases and comorbidities, in that they tend to cocluster. Diseasome is the "human disease network": a big data–based study of the diseasome can contribute to a better understanding of the so-called "system or network medicine" (Barabási, 2007; Zanzoni et al., 2009). Xie et al. (2017) performed a big data–based, cross-sectional study, dissecting the relationship between metabolic syndrome (and its components, high body mass index, dyslipidemia, and hypertension) and knee osteoarthritis in a sample of 5764 participants. Authors were able to confirm such a correlation and found that the accumulation of the various components of the metabolic syndrome resulted in a higher prevalence rate of radiographic knee osteoarthritis, also after adjusting for confounding factors.

Finally, big data can be used to verify the implementation of recommendations and decision-making processes. For example, Jacquet et al. (Jacquet et al., 2019) exploited big data to monitor and track the compliance with guidelines in terms of rates of conservative treatment options for the management of meniscal lesions, including meniscus degeneration. Authors compared these options versus surgical approaches, like meniscus repair and meniscectomy: for this purpose, they mined the French agency for information on hospital care (ATIH) database from 2005 to 2017. The meniscectomy rate was found to gradually decrease during the study period, especially in private hospitals, while an opposite trend could be detected for meniscus repair interventions. However, disparity in surgical practices in terms of significant regional and age group variations could be found, warranting ad hoc interventions from stakeholders.

On the other hand, as previously mentioned, there are still open issues that need to be addressed and solved. Big data–based studies can offer a different point of view, but some conflicting findings with regard to randomized controlled studies and small, well-conducted investigations can be found. Sochacki et al. (2018) have found statistically significant discrepancies between the two types of study designs/methods. Authors pooled together 207 studies, of which 201 were original research publications, totaling 15,780 individuals, with 54% of the total sample being female. The remaining 6 studies were based on databases, totaling 20,825 participants, 60% of which were female. Differences could be detected in terms of age, body mass index, female percentage, and length of follow-up. Further, a higher major complication rate (femoral neck fracture, hip dislocation, reoperation and revision surgery, and conversion to arthroplasty) characterized the database-based studies.

Such discrepancies could be due to the unique nature of the database used in the study: each orthopedic database significantly varies in the methods deployed to collect and capture data and the population(s) it specifically represents (Bedard et al., 2018). Bedard et al. (2018) systematically compared different major databases containing data about orthopedic patients undergoing primary total hip arthroplasty (namely, the National Surgical Quality Improvement Programs or NSQIP, the Nationwide Inpatient Sample or NIS, the Medicare Standard Analytic Files or MED, and the Humana administrative claims database or HAC). The databases differed in terms of the number of patients (ranging from 22,644 to 371,715), whereas discrepancies in terms of age and gender distribution were clinically negligible. However, differences in terms of comorbidities prevalence and postoperative complications rate were clinically meaningful.

Summarizing, big data repositories, registries, and databases are increasingly common in orthopedics research: there are, however, significant considerable variations in socio-demographic characteristics, comorbidities and major complication rates between individual (single- or multicenter) and database-based studies, and even among registry studies themselves (for example, clinical vs. administrative database). This should be accounted for when critically appraising orthopedics research and in risk adjustment modeling (Patel et al., 2016; Slobogean et al., 2015).

In particular, administrative databases (Patel et al., 2016) can provide researchers and scholars, as well as practitioners and policy- and decision-makers with a lot of information concerning disease epidemiology, comorbidities, disparities, and inequalities in access to healthcare and clinical outcomes. Furthermore, they can inform in a data-driven fashion the decision-making processes underlying orthopedic surgical procedures, in terms of preoperative risk stratification parameters, in order to significantly curb/minimize peri-operative morbidity and mortality rates. On the other hand, administrative databases (Patel et al., 2016; Slobogean et al., 2015) may suffer from clerical inaccuracies, recording bias (due to the very nature of the database and secondary to economic–financial incentives underlying the collection, and maintenance of the dataset), temporal changes in nosology and nomenclature systems as well as in billing codes, and, finally, a dearth of several clinically relevant parameters, including orthopedics-specific variables and outcomes.

Conversely, clinical studies, especially those relying on "Small Data," even though well designed and well conducted, are generally statistically underpowered and are plagued by several biases, including participants sampling and selection bias, which hinders to generalize the findings, with samples being not representative of the entire population. It is also difficult to stratify according to treatment/orthopedic surgical procedure, if the sample is particularly heterogenous and the sample size does not allow to make sufficiently statistically robust and reliable calculations. Confidence and certainty can increase with "big data," paralleling, however, the growth of complexity, and associated computational costs (Slobogean et al., 2015). Also big data–based databases can be affected by biases, as previously mentioned, such as recording or association biases and other statistical artifacts, like "reverse epidemiology" or "reverse causality" (Imam & Coleman, 2019).

3. Roles and applications of molecular big data in current orthopedics research

Wet-lab and high-throughput technologies, including microarray chips, next-generation sequencing, and whole-exome sequencing, can generate a wealth of molecular big data, paving the way for a personalized/individualized rather than "one-size-fits-it-all" orthopedics.

Molecular big data can elucidate the mechanisms underlying the etiopathogenesis of a given orthopedic disease and identify new potential druggable targets for the development of ad hoc pharmacological therapies. Personalized orthopedics can benefit from genome-wide association and postgenomics studies (Bragazzi et al., 2020; Moreau, 2017).

According to a recent bibliometric study carried out by Mani et al. (2021), two major hotspots of orthopedics research are osteoarthritis (24%), and orthopedic basic science (22%), emphasizing the importance of translational orthopedics in the contemporary research (Mediouni et al., 2020). Recently, in 2019, Mediouni (2019) has devised a T-model, aimed at bridging and filling in the gap between basic and clinical sciences in orthopedics, enhancing the skills and competences of the orthopedic surgeons, on the one hand, and giving value to the role of the cellular and molecular biologist/bioengineers, on the other hand.

The unique and unprecedented convergence between different disciplines, such as nano-(bio-) engineering, 3D computational simulation, mathematical modeling, and advanced and sophisticated biostatistical techniques and artificial intelligence (Data Mining, Machine, and Deep Learning), are shaping new paths and opportunities in the field of orthopedics research, enriching it, making it more multi- and interdisciplinary and complex, and more able to address the biomedical challenges. Similarly, Dr. Elias Zerhouni (2003), who has served as Director of the National Institutes of Health (NIH) from 2002 to 2008, has indicated such a unique convergence as the future roadmap in the field of scholarly research.

Osteoarthritis is a chronic-degenerative disorder that affects joints and is clinically and epidemiologically common globally. The etiopathogenesis is complex, multifactorial, even if it has to be fully elucidated yet. However, the major cellular event underlying osteoarthritis is cartilage degradation. Genomics/postgenomics assays can help dissect the basis of this disease and identify the genes in terms of cascades and networks that may play a key role driving the pathogenesis of osteoarthritis. In the existing scholarly literature, several molecular profiling studies have been conducted at the level of different tissues (namely, cartilage, subchondral bone, and synovium), contributing to the identification of pathways involved in matrix metabolism, bone turnover, and inflammation. However, some conflicting findings have been obtained, which requires a better integration among studies, in terms of replicability and reproducibility (Liu et al., 2020).

Moreover, molecular big data can capture the landscape of several orthopedic diseases and events, like osteosarcoma (Behjati et al., 2017), arthrofibrosis (Morrey et al., 2017), orthopedic contractures and injuries (Huang et al., 2019), idiopathic osteonecrosis of the femoral head (Sakamoto et al., 2017), scoliosis (Lin et al., 2020; Zhao et al., 2021), either idiopathic or congenital, and other congenital skeletal disorders (Bonafe et al., 2015), among others.

4. Roles and applications of big data generated by imaging techniques and wearable technologies/smart sensors in current orthopedics research

Latest technological achievements in the field of mobile health (mHealth) with smartphones, smart devices, and wearable sensors (Lightsey et al., 2021; Ramkumar et al., 2017) are revolutionizing orthopedics surgery and, for instance, arthroplasty, also enabling remote patient monitoring. For example, Pellegrini et al. (2021) have developed a mHealth-based intervention (NEAT!2), that should be effective in reducing sedentary time in a sample of 92 adults undergoing a knee replacement at 3 and 6 months after surgery. NEAT!2 is a smartphone application that, using data collected from the mobile device's internal accelerometer, interrupts prolonged bouts of sitting by calling the participant and/or vibrating. A similar approach had been devised and implemented for people suffering from diabetes (Pellegrini et al., 2015).

Radiomics is an "emerging translational field of research" aimed at mining, merging, processing, analyzing, and extracting clinically meaningful patterns and interpretations from large-scale, high-dimensional datasets generated by clinical imaging techniques and tools (Rizzo et al., 2018). In the field of orthopedics research, radiomics can be utilized for the characterization and profiling of osteosarcoma patients (Wu et al., 2018) and prediction of lung metastasis (Pereira et al., 2021). However, also given its recency, still too much has to be explored in this field. On the other hand, it can be anticipated that radiomics and other big data generated by wearable/smart devices and sensors will profoundly impact both orthopedics practice and research.

5. Roles and applications of infodemiological big data in current orthopedics research

Infodemiology (from "information" and "epidemiology") and infoveillance (from "information" and "surveillance") represent an emerging discipline, at the intersection of computer, data, and behavioral science, aimed at dissecting the determinants of computational/digital activities (such as web queries, use of social networks, and consumption of online material) (Eysenbach, 2002, 2006).

For instance, Ciaffi et al. (2021) explored the digital interest for back pain in Italy, using Google Trends, an open-source tool that enables to investigate the volume of web searches related to a given search term. Authors consulted as well related Wikipedia page view statistics. Web queries and Wikipedia, as well as social networks, represent "nonconventional or novel data streams" (Bragazzi et al., 2016; Gianfredi et al., 2018). Digital queries were processed and analyzed, to uncover secular trends and seasonal patterns. Authors found an increase in the interest for back pain, with searches concentrating in cold (winter) months and decreasing during hot (spring/summer) months.

Moreover, Yamaguchi et al. (2020) carried out a Google search for commonly searched keywords related to pain, in Japan and in the United States. For this purpose, authors exploited Google Trends and found that accurate and reliable medical information did not appear among the top 100 results.

The quality of orthopedics-related website and, more in general, online material is highly heterogenous and variable both in terms of content and information provided. For instance, Winship et al. (2014) assessed the quality of sites concerning 10 commonly diagnosed pediatric orthopedics disorders retrieved from two popular search engines. Authors found that quality was high for nonprofit and academic webpages, whereas the content displayed on commercial websites and also on sites run by physicians was characterized by very low quality. Quality varied also depending on the type of orthopedic disease, being higher for "osteochondroma" and "developmental dysplasia of the hip" and lower for "polydactyly" and "brachial plexus birth palsy." Diagnostic criteria and markers were well explained, differently from prognosis, which resulted to be more difficult to understand and follow.

This holds true also for websites concerning adult orthopedic diseases and related surgical procedures, such as knee osteotomy (Broderick et al., 2020, 2021), spinal surgery (Guo et al., 2019), or hip arthroscopy (Bryant et al., 2018), among others.

Orthopedic patients use the internet as a low-cost and easily available resource to learn about their condition/disorder, as well as about potential treatment options and orthopedic surgeons (Hautala et al., 2021). According to a recent survey, conducted in an orthopedic clinic at a Level I trauma center in the United States of America, sampling 138 trauma patients aged 47.1 years, 51.1% of which were female, 55.8% of them surfed the web for retrieving injury-related information. However, about two-thirds of them consulted at least one unreliable source. Online material uptake and consumption were associated to age, gender, employment status, and health-related literacy.

Practitioners and residents in the field of orthopedics should be aware of these findings in that the web is often consulted by patients with musculoskeletal diseases. Moreover, the web can be used to deliver high-quality material and empower the patient. According to a recently published systematic review of the literature, synthesizing 10 clinical trials from 14 studies totaling 4172 orthopedic patients (Ellsworth et al., 2016), providing patients with web-based education resulted in a significantly improved health-related literacy (9 out of 10 trials), and increased satisfaction (7 out 10 trials). However, there is a dearth of data and inconsistent evidence concerning the impact of web-based patient education and empowerment in terms of clinical outcomes, and health-related behaviors and attitudes.

6. "Participatory orthopedics": integrating basic and translational orthopedics and citizen science

Big data can also contribute to an emerging superspecialization within orthopedics: the so-called participatory orthopedics, in such a way promoting public participation in the field of orthopedics research, creating "global collaborative social networks," and integrating basic and translational orthopedics and citizen science (Anoushiravani et al., 2016; Dekkers et al., 2018).

Participatory orthopedics gives a new value and importance to the patient, who is the "real teacher," quoting a famous statement of the Canadian physician Sir William Osler (1849–1919) enunciated in 1903 (Radu et al., 2021). The latest scientific and technological advancements and current trends in clinical practice and research have gradually shifted the practitioners' attention and interest toward patient's "subjective" outcomes (satisfaction, pain, quality of life, etc.), besides "objective" clinical outcomes (healthcare resources uptake and consumption, healthcare processes and provisions delivery, morbidity and mortality rates).

However, for most orthopedic surgeons, the world of patient-reported outcomes represents a still "unchartered health care environment" (Fiddes et al., 2013), the navigation of which, by incorporating "mission, values, and culture" (Shaha et al., 2016), can really advance orthopedics practice and research.

7. Conclusions and future prospects

Big data is increasingly having a more and more relevant role, being highly ubiquitous and pervasive in contemporary society, permeating it and paving the way for new, unprecedented perspectives in biomedicine, including orthopedics. Big data can be a real paradigm shift that revolutionizes orthopedics and musculoskeletal clinical research (Helfet et al., 2014). However, there are some methodological issues that should be properly addressed and some ethical issues that should be considered. Therefore, further research in the field is warranted.

References

Anoushiravani, A. A., Patton, J., Sayeed, Z., El-Othmani, M. M., & Saleh, K. J. (2016). Big data, big research: Implementing population health-based research models and integrating care to reduce cost and improve outcomes. *Orthopedic Clinics of North America, 47*(4), 717–724. https://doi.org/10.1016/j.ocl.2016.05.008. Epub 2016 August 8. PMID: 27637658.

Bakir, M. S., Unterkofler, J., Haralambiev, L., Kim, S., Carbon, R., Ekkernkamp, A., & Schulz-Drost, S. (2020). Medial injuries of the clavicle: More prevalent than expected? A big data analysis of incidence, age, and gender distribution based on nationwide routine data. *European Journal of Trauma and Emergency Surgery*. https://doi.org/10.1007/s00068-019-01293-0. Epub ahead of print. PMID: 31960070.

Bakir, M. S., Unterkofler, J., Hönning, A., Haralambiev, L., Kim, S., Ekkernkamp, A., & Schulz-Drost, S. (2019). Shoulder girdle injuries involving the medial clavicle differ from lateral clavicle injuries with a focus on concomitant injuries and management strategies: A retrospective study based on nationwide routine data. *PLoS One, 14*(10), e0224370. https://doi.org/10.1371/journal.pone.0224370. PMID: 31652299; PMCID: PMC6814233.

Barabási, A. L. (2007). Network medicine—from obesity to the "diseasome". *New England Journal of Medicine, 357*(4), 404–407. https://doi.org/10.1056/NEJMe078114. Epub 2007 July 25. PMID: 17652657.

Bedard, N. A., Pugely, A. J., McHugh, M. A., Lux, N. R., Bozic, K. J., & Callaghan, J. J. (2018). Big data and total hip arthroplasty: How do large databases compare? *The Journal of Arthroplasty, 33*(1), 41–45.e3. https://doi.org/10.1016/j.arth.2017.09.003. Epub 2017 September 13. PMID: 29017802.

Behjati, S., Tarpey, P. S., Haase, K., Ye, H., Young, M. D., Alexandrov, L. B., Farndon, S. J., Collord, G., Wedge, D. C., Martincorena, I., Cooke, S. L., Davies, H., Mifsud, W., Lidgren, M., Martin, S., Latimer, C., Maddison, M., Butler, A. P., Teague, J. W., … Campbell, P. J. (2017). Recurrent mutation of IGF signalling genes and distinct patterns of genomic rearrangement in osteosarcoma. *Nature Communications, 8*, 15936. https://doi.org/10.1038/ncomms15936. PMID: 28643781; PMCID: PMC5490007.

Bonafe, L., Cormier-Daire, V., Hall, C., Lachman, R., Mortier, G., Mundlos, S., Nishimura, G., Sangiorgi, L., Savarirayan, R., Sillence, D., Spranger, J., Superti-Furga, A., Warman, M., & Unger, S. (2015). Nosology and classification of genetic skeletal disorders: 2015 revision. *American Journal of Medical Genetics, Part A, 167A*(12), 2869–2892. https://doi.org/10.1002/ajmg.a.37365. Epub 2015 September 23. PMID: 26394607.

Bragazzi, N. L., Dini, G., Toletone, A., Brigo, F., & Durando, P. (2016). Leveraging big data for exploring occupational diseases-related interest at the level of scientific community, media coverage and novel data streams: The example of silicosis as a pilot study. *PLoS One, 11*(11), e0166051. https://doi.org/10.1371/journal.pone.0166051. PMID: 27806115; PMCID: PMC5091866.

Bragazzi, N. L., Khoramipour, K., Chaouachi, A., & Chamari, K. (2020). Toward sportomics: Shifting from sport genomics to sport postgenomics and metabolomics specialties. Promises, challenges, and future perspectives. *International Journal of Sports Physiology and Performance*. https://doi.org/10.1123/ijspp.2020-0648. Epub ahead of print. PMID: 32963119.

Broderick, J. M., McCarthy, A., & Hogan, N. (2020). Knee osteotomy: Quality tools and readability data of information on the internet. *Data Brief, 34*, 106624. https://doi.org/10.1016/j.dib.2020.106624. PMID: 33354604; PMCID: PMC7744941.

Broderick, J. M., McCarthy, A., & Hogan, N. (2021). Osteotomy around the knee: Assessment of quality, content and readability of online information. *The Knee, 28*, 139–150. https://doi.org/10.1016/j.knee.2020.11.010. Epub 2020 December 23. PMID: 33360380.

Bryant, J., Mohan, R., Koottappillil, B., Wong, K., & Yi, P. H. (2018). Minimally invasive spine surgery: Analyzing internet-based education material. *Clinical Spine Surgery, 31*(3), E166–E170. https://doi.org/10.1097/BSD.0000000000000602. PMID: 29315116.

Ciaffi, J., Meliconi, R., Landini, M. P., Mancarella, L., Brusi, V., Faldini, C., & Ursini, F. (2021). Seasonality of back pain in Italy: An infodemiology study. *International Journal of Environmental Research and Public Health, 18*(3), 1325. https://doi.org/10.3390/ijerph18031325. PMID: 33535709; PMCID: PMC7908346.

Dekkers, T., Melles, M., Groeneveld, B. S., & de Ridder, H. (2018). Web-based patient education in orthopedics: Systematic review. *Journal of Medical Internet Research, 20*(4), e143. https://doi.org/10.2196/jmir.9013. PMID: 29685869; PMCID: PMC5938597.

Ellsworth, B., Patel, H., & Kamath, A. F. (2016). Assessment of quality and content of online information about hip arthroscopy. *Arthroscopy, 32*(10), 2082–2089. https://doi.org/10.1016/j.arthro.2016.03.019. Epub 2016 May 24. PMID: 27234649.

Eysenbach, G. (2002). Infodemiology: The epidemiology of (mis)information. *Americas Journal of Medicine, 113*(9), 763–765. https://doi.org/10.1016/s0002-9343(02)01473-0. PMID: 12517369.

Eysenbach, G. (2006). Infodemiology: Tracking flu-related searches on the web for syndromic surveillance. *AMIA Annual Symposium proceedings, 2006*, 244–248. PMID: 17238340; PMCID: PMC1839505.

Fiddes, P. J., Brooks, P. M., & Komesaroff, P. (2013). The patient is the teacher: Ambulatory patient-centred student-based interprofessional education where the patient is the teacher who improves patient care outcomes. *Internal Medicine Journal, 43*(7), 747–750. https://doi.org/10.1111/imj.12197. PMID: 23841759.

Gianfredi, V., Bragazzi, N. L., Nucci, D., Martini, M., Rosselli, R., Minelli, L., & Moretti, M. (2018). Harnessing big data for communicable tropical and sub-tropical disorders: Implications from a systematic review of the literature. *Front Public Health, 6*, 90. https://doi.org/10.3389/fpubh.2018.00090. PMID: 29619364; PMCID: PMC5871696.

Guo, W. J., Wang, W. K., Xu, D., Qiao, Z., Shi, Y. L., & Luo, P. (2019). Evaluating the quality, content, and readability of online resources for failed back spinal surgery. *Spine, 44*(7), 494–502. https://doi.org/10.1097/BRS.0000000000002870. PMID: 30234809.

Ha, Y. C., Kim, T. Y., Lee, A., Lee, Y. K., Kim, H. Y., Kim, J. H., Park, C. M., & Jang, S. (2016). Current trends and future projections of hip fracture in South Korea using nationwide claims data. *Osteoporosis International, 27*(8), 2603–2609. https://doi.org/10.1007/s00198-016-3576-9. Epub 2016 April 25. PMID: 27112763.

Hautala, G. S., Comadoll, S. M., Raffetto, M. L., Ducas, G. W., Jacobs, C. A., Aneja, A., & Matuszewski, P. E. (2021). Most orthopaedic trauma patients are using the internet, but do you know where they're going? *Injury*. https://doi.org/10.1016/j.injury.2021.02.029. S0020-1383(21)00132-7. Epub ahead of print. PMID: 33653619.

Helfet, D. L., Hanson, B. P., & De Faoite, D. (2014). Big data: The paradigm shift needed to revolutionize musculoskeletal clinical research. *American Journal of Orthopedics, 43*(9), 399–400. PMID: 25251523.

Huang, P., Gu, J., Wu, J., Geng, L., Hong, Y., Wang, S., & Wang, M. (2019). Microarray analysis of the molecular mechanisms associated with age and body mass index in human meniscal injury. *Molecular Medicine Reports, 19*(1), 93–102. https://doi.org/10.3892/mmr.2018.9685. Epub 2018 November 21. Erratum in: Mol. Med. Rep. 2019 October, 20(4), 3968. PMID: 30483788; PMCID: PMC6297773.

Imam, T. H., & Coleman, K. J. (2019). Obesity and mortality in end-stage renal disease. Is it time to reverse the "reverse epidemiology"—at least in peritoneal dialysis? *Journal of Renal Nutrition, 29*(4), 269–275. https://doi.org/10.1053/j.jrn.2018.09.005. Epub 2018 November 15. PMID: 30448394.

Jacquet, C., Pujol, N., Pauly, V., Beaufils, P., & Ollivier, M. (2019). Analysis of the trends in arthroscopic meniscectomy and meniscus repair procedures in France from 2005 to 2017. *Orthopaedics & Traumatology: Surgery & Research, 105*(4), 677–682. https://doi.org/10.1016/j.otsr.2019.01.024. Epub 2019 April 23. PMID: 31027979.

Kim, H. Y., Jang, E. J., Park, B., Kim, T. Y., Shin, S. A., Ha, Y. C., & Jang, S. (2016). Development of a Korean fracture risk score (KFRS) for predicting osteoporotic fracture risk: Analysis of data from the Korean national health insurance service. *PLoS One, 11*(7), e0158918. https://doi.org/10.1371/journal.pone.0158918. PMID: 27399597; PMCID: PMC4939957.

Kim, T. Y., Jang, S., Park, C. M., Lee, A., Lee, Y. K., Kim, H. Y., Cho, E. H., & Ha, Y. C. (2016). Trends of incidence, mortality, and future projection of spinal fractures in Korea using nationwide claims data. *Journal of Korean Medical Science, 31*(5), 801–805. https://doi.org/10.3346/jkms.2016.31.5.801. Epub 2016 March 25. PMID: 27134505; PMCID: PMC4835609.

Koziara, M., Gaukroger, A., Hing, C., & Eardley, W. (2021). Introduction to big data in trauma and orthopaedics. *Orthopaedics and Trauma, 35*(2), 84–89.

Kwon, G. D., Jang, S., Lee, A., Park, C. M., Lee, Y. K., Kim, T. Y., Kim, H. Y., Park, E. J., & Ha, Y. C. (2016). Incidence and mortality after distal radius fractures in adults aged 50 Years and older in Korea. *Journal of Korean Medical Science, 31*(4), 630–634. https://doi.org/10.3346/jkms.2016.31.4.630. Epub 2016 February 22. PMID: 27051250; PMCID: PMC4810349.

Lightsey, H. M., 4th, Yeung, C. M., Samartzis, D., & Makhni, M. C. (2021). The past, present, and future of remote patient monitoring in spine care: An overview. *European Spine Journal*. https://doi.org/10.1007/s00586-021-06921-1. Epub ahead of print. PMID: 34241698.

Lin, K. B., Yang, N. P., Lee, Y. H., Chan, C. L., Wu, C. H., Chen, H. C., & Chang, N. T. (2018). The incidence and factors of hip fractures and subsequent morbidity in Taiwan: An 11-year population-based cohort study. *PLoS One, 13*(2), e0192388. https://doi.org/10.1371/journal.pone.0192388. PMID: 29447190; PMCID: PMC5813923.

Lin, M., Zhao, S., Liu, G., Huang, Y., Yu, C., Zhao, Y., Wang, L., Zhang, Y., Yan, Z., Wang, S., Liu, S., Liu, J., Ye, Y., Chen, Y., Yang, X., Tong, B., Wang, Z., Yang, X., Niu, Y., … Qiu, G. (2020). Deciphering Disorders Involving Scoliosis and COmorbidities (DISCO) study. Identification of novel FBN1 variations implicated in congenital scoliosis. *Journal of Human Genetics, 65*(3), 221–230. https://doi.org/10.1038/s10038-019-0698-x. Epub 2019 December 11. PMID: 31827250; PMCID: PMC6983459.

Liu, W., Jiao, Y., Tian, C., Hasty, K., Song, L., Kelly, D. M., Li, J., Chen, H., Gu, W., & Liu, S. (2020). Gene expression profiling studies using microarray in osteoarthritis: Genes in common and different conditions. *Archivum Immunologiae et Therapiae Experimentalis, 68*(5), 28. https://doi.org/10.1007/s00005-020-00592-4. PMID: 32914280.

Lu, Y., Khazi, Z. M., Patel, B. H., Agarwalla, A., Cancienne, J., Werner, B. C., & Forsythe, B. (2020). Big data in total shoulder arthroplasty: An in-depth comparison of national outcomes databases. *Journal of the American Academy of Orthopaedic Surgeons, 28*(14), e626–e632. https://doi.org/10.5435/JAAOS-D-19-00173. PMID: 32692100.

Mani, O., Nucci, A. M., Scaglione, M., Bonicoli, E., Parchi, P. D., & Piolanti, N. (2021). Bibliometric trend analysis in a decade of European Orthopaedic literature. *Acta BioMedica, 92*(3), e2021280. https://doi.org/10.23750/abm.v92i3.9512. PMID: 34212934.

McIsaac, D. I. (2020). Real-world evaluation of enhanced recovery after surgery: Big data under the microscope. *British Journal of Anaesthesia, 124*(5), 510–512. https://doi.org/10.1016/j.bja.2020.01.012. Epub 2020 February 27. PMID: 32115185.

Mediouni, M. (2019). A new generation of orthopaedic surgeons "Tmodel". *Current Orthopaedic Practice, 30*, 444–445.

Mediouni, M., Madiouni, R., Gardner, M., & Vaughan, N. (2020). Translational medicine: Challenges and new orthopaedic vision (Mediouni-Model). *Current Orthopaedic Practice, 31*(2), 196–200. https://doi.org/10.1097/BCO.0000000000000846

Moreau, A. (2017). The next personalized medicine evolution in orthopedics: How diagnosing and treating scoliosis are about to change. *Personalized Medicine, 14*(2), 89–92. https://doi.org/10.2217/pme-2016-0094. Epub 2017 January 19. PMID: 28757885; PMCID: PMC5480784.

Morrey, M. E., Abdel, M. P., Riester, S. M., Dudakovic, A., van Wijnen, A. J., Morrey, B. F., & Sanchez-Sotelo, J. (2017). Molecular landscape of arthrofibrosis: Microarray and bioinformatic analysis of the temporal expression of 380 genes during contracture genesis. *Gene, 610*, 15–23. https://doi.org/10.1016/j.gene.2017.01.025. Epub 2017 February 3. PMID: 28167142.

Muir, D. (2017). Is there anything to learn from a national joint registry? *Foot and Ankle Clinics, 22*(2), 465–475. https://doi.org/10.1016/j.fcl.2017.01.004. Epub 2017 March 30. PMID: 28502358.

Patel, A. A., Singh, K., Nunley, R. M., & Minhas, S. V. (2016). Administrative databases in orthopaedic research: Pearls and pitfalls of big data. *Journal of the American Academy of Orthopaedic Surgeons, 24*(3), 172–179. https://doi.org/10.5435/JAAOS-D-13-00009. PMID: 26836377.

Pellegrini, C. A., Hoffman, S. A., Daly, E. R., Murillo, M., Iakovlev, G., & Spring, B. (2015). Acceptability of smartphone technology to interrupt sedentary time in adults with diabetes. *Translational Behavioral Medicine, 5*(3), 307–314. https://doi.org/10.1007/s13142-015-0314-3. PMID: 26327936; PMCID: PMC4537463.

Pellegrini, C. A., Lee, J., DeVivo, K. E., Harpine, C. E., Del Gaizo, D. J., & Wilcox, S. (2021). Reducing sedentary time using an innovative mHealth intervention among patients with total knee replacement: Rationale and study protocol. *Contemporary Clinical Trials Communications, 22*, 100810. https://doi.org/10.1016/j.conctc.2021.100810. PMID: 34195473; PMCID: PMC8239442.

Pereira, H. M., Leite Duarte, M. E., Ribeiro Damasceno, I., de Oliveira Moura Santos, L. A., & Nogueira-Barbosa, M. H. (2021). Machine learning-based CT radiomics features for the prediction of pulmonary metastasis in osteosarcoma. *British Journal of Radiology*, 20201391. https://doi.org/10.1259/bjr.20201391. Epub ahead of print. PMID: 34111978.

Radu, R., Hernández-Ortega, S., Borrega, O., Palmeri, A., Athanasiou, D., Brooke, N., Chapí, I., Le Corvec, A., Guglieri, M., Perera-Lluna, A., Garrido-Aguirre, J., Ryll, B., & Nafria Escalera, B. (2021). Global collaborative social network (Share4Rare) to promote citizen science in rare disease research: Platform development study. *JMIR Form Res, 5*(3), e22695. https://doi.org/10.2196/22695. PMID: 33779572; PMCID: PMC8088870.

Ramkumar, P. N., Muschler, G. F., Spindler, K. P., Harris, J. D., McCulloch, P. C., & Mont, M. A. (2017). Open mHealth architecture: A primer for tomorrow's orthopedic surgeon and introduction to its use in lower extremity arthroplasty. *The Journal of Arthroplasty, 32*(4), 1058–1062. https://doi.org/10.1016/j.arth.2016.11.019. Epub 2016 November 17. PMID: 27956125.

Ratliff, J. K., Balise, R., Veeravagu, A., Cole, T. S., Cheng, I., Olshen, R. A., & Tian, L. (2016). Predicting occurrence of spine surgery complications using "big data" modeling of an administrative claims database. *Journal of Bone and Joint Surgery, 98*(10), 824–834. https://doi.org/10.2106/JBJS.15.00301. PMID: 27194492.

Rizzo, S., Botta, F., Raimondi, S., Origgi, D., Fanciullo, C., Morganti, A. G., & Bellomi, M. (2018). Radiomics: The facts and the challenges of image analysis. *European Radiology Experimental, 2*(1), 36. https://doi.org/10.1186/s41747-018-0068-z. PMID: 30426318; PMCID: PMC6234198.

Romanini, E., Schettini, I., Torre, M., Venosa, M., Tarantino, A., Calvisi, V., & Zanoli, G. (2021). The rise of registry-based research: A bibliometric analysis. *Acta Orthopaedica*, 1–5. https://doi.org/10.1080/17453674.2021.1937459. Epub ahead of print. PMID: 34139929.

Sakamoto, Y., Yamamoto, T., Sugano, N., Takahashi, D., Watanabe, T., Atsumi, T., Nakamura, J., Hasegawa, Y., Akashi, K., Narita, I., Miyamoto, T., Takeuchi, T., Ikari, K., Amano, K., Fujie, A , Kubo, T., Tada, Y., Kaneuji, A., Nakamura, H., … Ikegawa, S. (2017). Genome-wide association study of idiopathic osteonecrosis of the femoral head. *Scientific Reports, 7*(1), 15035. https://doi.org/10.1038/s41598-017-14778-y. PMID: 29118346; PMCID: PMC5678103.

Schwend, R. M. (2020). The burden of pediatric musculoskeletal diseases worldwide. *Orthopedic Clinics of North America, 51*(2), 207–217. https://doi.org/10.1016/j.ocl.2019.11.005. Epub 2020 January 31. PMID: 32138858.

Sebbag, E., Felten, R., Sagez, F., Sibilia, J., Devilliers, H., & Arnaud, L. (2019). The world-wide burden of musculoskeletal diseases: A systematic analysis of the world health organization burden of diseases database. *Annals of the Rheumatic Diseases, 78*(6), 844–848. https://doi.org/10.1136/annrheumdis-2019-215142. Epub 2019 April 15. PMID: 30987966.

Shaha, S. H., Sayeed, Z., Anoushiravani, A. A., El-Othmani, M. M., & Saleh, K. J. (2016). Big data, big problems: Incorporating mission, values, and culture in provider affiliations. *Orthopedic Clinics of North America, 47*(4), 725–732. https://doi.org/10.1016/j.ocl.2016.05.009. Epub 2016 August 8. PMID: 27637659.

Slobogean, G. P., Giannoudis, P. V., Frihagen, F., Forte, M. L., Morshed, S., & Bhandari, M. (2015). Bigger data, bigger problems. *Journal of Orthopaedic Trauma, 29*(Suppl. 12), S43–S46. https://doi.org/10.1097/BOT.0000000000000463. PMID: 26584266.

Sochacki, K. R., Jack, R. A., 2nd, Safran, M. R., Nho, S. J., & Harris, J. D. (2018). There is a significant discrepancy between "big data" database and original research publications on hip arthroscopy outcomes: A systematic review. *Arthroscopy, 34*(6), 1998–2004. https://doi.org/10.1016/j.arthro.2018.01.018. Epub 2018 February 21. PMID: 29477605.

Spaans, E. A., Koenraadt, K. L. M., Wagenmakers, R., van den Hout, J. A. A. M., Te Stroet, M. A. J., & Bolder, S. B. T. (2018). Midterm survival analysis of a cemented dual-mobility cup combined with bone impaction grafting in 102 revision hip arthroplasties. *Hip International, 28*(2), 161–167. https://doi.org/10.5301/hipint.5000548. Epub 2017 November 9. PMID: 28967056.

Winship, B., Grisell, M., Yang, C. B., Chen, R. X., & Bauer, A. S. (2014). The quality of pediatric orthopaedic information on the internet. *Journal of Pediatric Orthopaedics, 34*(4), 474–477. https://doi.org/10.1097/BPO.0000000000000125. PMID: 24276228; PMCID: PMC5016082.

Wu, Y., Xu, L., Yang, P., Lin, N., Huang, X., Pan, W., Li, H., Lin, P., Li, B., Bunpetch, V., Luo, C., Jiang, Y., Yang, D., Huang, M., Niu, T., & Ye, Z. (2018). Survival prediction in high-grade osteosarcoma using radiomics of diagnostic computed tomography. *EBioMedicine, 34*, 27–34. https://doi.org/10.1016/j.ebiom.2018.07.006. Epub 2018 July 17. PMID: 30026116; PMCID: PMC6116348.

Xie, D. X., Wei, J., Zeng, C., Yang, T., Li, H., Wang, Y. L., Long, H. Z., Wu, Z. Y., Qian, Y. X., Li, K. H., & Lei, G. H. (2017). Association between metabolic syndrome and knee osteoarthritis: A cross-sectional study. *BMC Musculoskeletal Disorders, 18*(1), 533. https://doi.org/10.1186/s12891-017-1890-9. PMID: 29246142; PMCID: PMC5732466.

Yamaguchi, Y., Lee, D., Nagai, T., Funamoto, T., Tajima, T., & Chosa, E. (2020). Googling musculoskeletal-related pain and ranking of medical associations' patient information pages: Google ads keyword planner analysis. *Journal of Medical Internet Research, 22*(8), e18684. https://doi.org/10.2196/18684. PMID: 32795991; PMCID: PMC7455867.

Yang, N. P., Phan, D. V., Lee, Y. H., Hsu, J. C., Pan, R. H., Chan, C. L., Chang, N. T., & Chu, D. (2016). Retrospective one-million-subject fixed-cohort survey of utilization of emergency departments due to traumatic causes in Taiwan, 2001-2010. *World Journal of Emergency Surgery, 11*(1), 41. https://doi.org/10.1186/s13017-016-0098-x. PMID: 27579054; PMCID: PMC5004311.

Zanzoni, A., Soler-López, M., & Aloy, P. (2009). A network medicine approach to human disease. *FEBS Letters, 583*(11), 1759–1765. https://doi.org/10.1016/j.febslet.2009.03.001. Epub 2009 March 6. PMID: 19269289.

Zerhouni, E. (2003). The NIH roadmap. *Science, 302*, 63–72.

Zhao, S., Zhang, Y., Chen, W., Li, W., Wang, S., Wang, L., Zhao, Y., Lin, M., Ye, Y., Lin, J., Zheng, Y., Liu, J., Zhao, H., Yan, Z., Yang, Y., Huang, Y., Lin, G., Chen, Z., Zhang, Z., … Wu, N. (2021). Deciphering Disorders Involving Scoliosis and COmorbidities (DISCO) study. Diagnostic yield and clinical impact of exome sequencing in early-onset scoliosis (EOS). *Journal of Medical Genetics, 58*(1), 41–47. https://doi.org/10.1136/jmedgenet-2019-106823. Epub 2020 May 7. PMID: 32381727; PMCID: PMC7802082.

Chapter 23

Predicting onset (type-2) of diabetes from medical records using binary class classification

Md Habib Al Mamun and Pantea Keikhosrokiani
School of Computer Sciences, Universiti Sains Malaysia, Minden, Penang, Malaysia

1. Introduction

1.1 Background of the study

Currently, the world has been struggling from a serious health problem of diabetes. Almost 3.2 million deaths are recorded annually caused to diabetes (Tabish, 2007). A lot of complications are followed from diabetes such as cardiovascular disease, blindness and visual disability, kidney failure, etc. An updated study demonstrated that 415 million people are affected and it is estimated to increase to 642 million by the year 2040 (Al-Lawati, 2017). The number is predicted to rise by 25% in 2030 and 51% in 2045 (Saeedi et al., 2019). Additionally, around 193 million people left uninvestigated because of asymptomatic nature of diabetes, particularly in type-2 diabetes. Cost is another factor for the case remaining diagnostics. Health care expenses for diabetes are projected to be 500 billion dollars for 2030 and this is around 12% of total health care spending globally (Marinov et al., 2011).Thus, diabetes has become one of the main priorities in health sector and a vast amount of medical data has been generating from heath service provider. Therefore, data mining can play a vital role by extracting and analyzing the vast amount of data and connects the discovered data insight to the human knowledge which can address the problem in the health sector.

1.2 Problem statement, objectives, and scope of the study

Many people are remained uninvestigated for diabetes as (a) diabetes is often asymptomatic, (b) investigations are costly, and (c) the process of doctor and diagnostic center appointment is sluggish. Data mining techniques can provide a solution which addresses the mentioned problems and lessens the workload of health service providers. This study aims to build a data mining model for predicting onset diabetes from a medical dataset with high level of accuracy in a fastest way. Scope of this study is to build a data mining model based on dataset regarding the pregnant women who are suffering from diabetes. In this project, eight classification algorithms—including REPTree, J48, Naive Bayes, Logistic, Sequential Minimal Optimization (SMO), ZeroR, PART, and IBk—are performed on the Pima Indians Diabetes Database (PIDD) dataset for building the classification model. Furthermore, the authors test the model by a new unseen dataset to ensure the prediction capability of the model.

2. Paper review

2.1 Defining the field

2.1.1 Onset/type-2 diabetes

Onset diabetic issue is a lifelong illness and it occurs if the body does not create enough insulin, or if the cells of the body are unable to consume the insulin appropriately. The condition is heavily influenced by lifestyle activities, e.g., such as

Big Data Analytics for Healthcare. https://doi.org/10.1016/B978-0-323-91907-4.00012-1

drinking, workout, dietary and habits. In addition, this leads to other problems like high blood pressure, weight problems, and dyslipidemia which affect people's life expectancy (Wexler et al., 2006). Cardiovascular and kidney failure are other crucial problems which occur with the onset of diabetes. Therefore, early detection and prevention techniques of onset diabetes are very crucial things to avoid life-threatening impediments.

2.1.2 Data mining

Data mining is a nonconventional process which is done on certain large data sets to find out valid, novel, useful, and clear patterns of data. Fayyad et al. represented a five-step data mining process that takes data as input and delivers knowledge as output. The first three steps—selection, preprocessing, transformation—are the data preparation. Then the data mining process takes place in the fourth step, which uses an algorithm to find the pattern of data. Finally, knowledge comes from the fifth step of interpretation and evaluation. "Data mining is an iterative process" (Weiss & Davison, 2010). If the result after the data mining process is not acceptable or requires further improvements, an adjustment may be required at any step. Therefore, the process is repeated after some adjustments are made.

2.1.3 Data mining task

Data mining task is divided into mainly two categories: prediction and description. In general, predictive data mining is based on supervised data and descriptive work on unsupervised data. In predictive mining, the purpose is to predict unknown or future values based on another existing dataset by applying the appropriate algorithm which will derive a model from the dataset. On the other hand, the descriptive method finds the data, describes the pattern, and brings up some new, meaningful, and remarkable information from the dataset. For the convenience of discussion, the main points of the data mining task and required algorithms are presented in Fig. 23.1.

2.1.4 Data mining-classifications and regression

For example, a bank manager wants to examine which loan applicant is unsafe or safe for the bank. In order to know the situation, predictive mining is a must. The most important prediction task is classification and regression (Teoh Yi Zhe & Keikhosrokiani, 2021). This procedure binds an object to either a predetermined class or a numerical value. Then the algorithm generates a prediction model and it is generated from a training dataset. By applying the model on new data, the process comes up with a prediction. The important attributes of this prediction model are that the algorithm itself does all the prediction tasks by using classification or regression or both.

2.1.5 Data mining-clustering

Clustering is an unsupervised and descriptive mining task. The main purpose is uncovering secret patterns and features of learning from data. No labels are given to the algorithm. However, clustering automatically splits the data into a distinct meaningful cluster based on characteristics. The main goal of clustering is to build a model in a very simple way. Another reason is that clustering allows data compression or dimensionality reduction. For example, a human can identify a "dog" even if it has a different size and color. The clustering algorithm automates this process.

FIGURE 23.1 Data mining task and algorithms.

2.1.6 Data mining-association rules

Association rules analysis is a descriptive task to discover how items are associated with each other. The discovered association is called the association rules. For example, you are a sales manager. A customer purchased a mobile and camera from your shop. What would you recommend him/her next? In this scenario, association analysis can provide the best solution. Sequential Pattern Mining is a very vital technique used in association analysis which aims for a pattern among items in a sequence, rather than in a set of items.

2.1.7 Data mining-text, link, content

Let us say the manager wants to analyze the millions of reviews on our e-commerce site to know the customer's feedback about our product. In this case, text mining can identify the actual feeling of the users, whether it is positive, negative, or neutral (Ying et al., 2021). The main challenge is data structure. Therefore, specialized algorithms—classifications, clustering, and association rules—are needed to analyze the text. For text classification, the Naïve Bayes algorithm is very popular, and a support vector machine (SVM) is unparalleled when requiring higher accuracy. For text or document clustering, K-means is a widely used algorithm. Therefore, for text mining, it can be divided by a description or a prediction model as it would use both at the same time (Malik et al., 2021).

2.2 Related works

Perveen et al. (2016) discussed in their study "Performance Analysis of Data Mining Classification Techniques to Predict Diabetes" that Adaboost, Bagging ensemble machine learning approaches, and J48 Tree algorithm have a role in predicting whether an individual has diabetes or not based upon the risk factors. The result accomplished after the experiment suggested that the Adaboost method performed better than the Bagging and the J48 decision tree algorithm (Perveen et al., 2016).

A data mining method of genetic programming for predicting diabetes is introduced in existing studies. The result depicted that the genetic programming method achieved optimal accuracy compared to other implemented methods. This optimal accuracy can be improved by employing the classifier algorithm (Pradhan & Bamnote, 2014).

In a study entitled "Early Predictive System for Diabetes Mellitus Disease," Orabi et al. (2016) introduced a layout of a system for predicting diabetes of an individual at a certain age. The decision tree classification algorithm is used to build the system. The result has illustrated that the system performed very well and provided the result with higher accuracy (Orabi et al., 2016).

For predicting the risk factors of diabetes, Nai-Arun et al. used some data mining classification algorithms, e.g., decisiont tree (DT), artificial neural network (ANN), logistic regression (LR), and Naive Bayes (NB) for designing a model in the study "Comparison of Classifiers for the Risk of Diabetes Prediction." In order to enhance the performance, the Bagging and the Boosting methods have been used in building this model. The best outcomes are achieved by the random forest classification method among all the experimented algorithms (Nai-Arun & Moungmai, 2015).

A diabetes prediction model using ANN and DT classification methods has been designed by Rashid et al. (2016) in their study "An Intelligent Approach for Diabetes Classification, Prediction and Description." The result showed that this model can identify the symptoms of diabetes from patient data with maximum accuracy (Rashid et al., 2016).

Joshi and Chawan (2018) conducted a study entitled "Diabetes Prediction Using Machine Learning Techniques" for designing a system which will predict the early stage diabetes with a maximum accuracy level. They combined different classification algorithms—SVM, LR, and ANN. The result showed that the model can predict diabetes at an earlier stage with an optimum accuracy (Joshi & Chawan, 2018).

The paper "Prediction of Diabetes Diagnosis Using Classification Based Data Mining Techniques" by Selvakumar et al. (2017) has compared some classification algorithm such LR, multilayer perception, and KNN for predicting the diabetes. The result showed that binary LR achieved the best output for the diabetes prediction (Selvakumar et al., 2017).

Cahn et al. (2018) has designed a diabetes prediction model using LR classification algorithm in their study "Use of a Machine Learning Algorithm Improves Prediction of Progression to Diabetes." The study concluded that the model can deliver a clinical intervention with best accuracy (Cahn et al., 2018).

A study was done to design and identify a model that classifies cardiovascular disease and predicts the presence or absence of the disease in patients using machine learning methods with accurate predictions. The results indicate that SVM and LR methods are the most efficient for diagnosing cardiovascular disease (Jinjri et al., 2021).

The obese patient's level of possibility to lose weight was classified to high (Good health), medium (Normal), and low (Poor health) based on the patient's diet and exercise data. Machine learning techniques such as k-nearest neighbor (KNN) and decision tree are used in this study to classify the diet and exercise data and find out the level of possibility to reduce weight. Analysis of this study shows that the decision tree provides the best accuracy for diet and exercise data where it is recorded as 71.54% and 63.63%, respectively (Pinto et al., 2021).

3. Proposed methodology

3.1 Model diagram

Fig. 23.2 illustrates the procedure for building the proposed classification model for diabetes prediction. The model is divided into two phases of (1) Training Phase and (2) Prediction Phase. The study followed four steps in the training phase which are (a) loading PIMA Indian dataset, (b) data analysis and data preprocess for creating different version of dataset, (c) create model by using eight types of classification algorithm, (d) model assessment, and finally, (e) selecting appropriate model based on the performance analysis. In prediction phase, a new unseen data has been tested for testing the model in predicting onset diabetes.

3.2 Brief description of algorithms used

This study used eight popular algorithms as the classifier for building prediction model based on their accuracy. The algorithms are briefly described in this section.

3.2.1 Decision tree algorithm (REPTree, J48)

Decision tree is a machine learning algorithm which is used for supervised learning. Decision tree generally simulates human thinking in tree structure for making a decision easily. Firstly, decision tree picks an attribute to be root node. Secondly, it creates a branch for each possible attribute value and separates the instance into multiple subsets. Thirdly, every subset links to a branch of the root node. Finally, the algorithm repeats the process iteratively on each branch (Kohavi, 1996). The typical algorithms of decision tree are REPTree, J48, and so on.

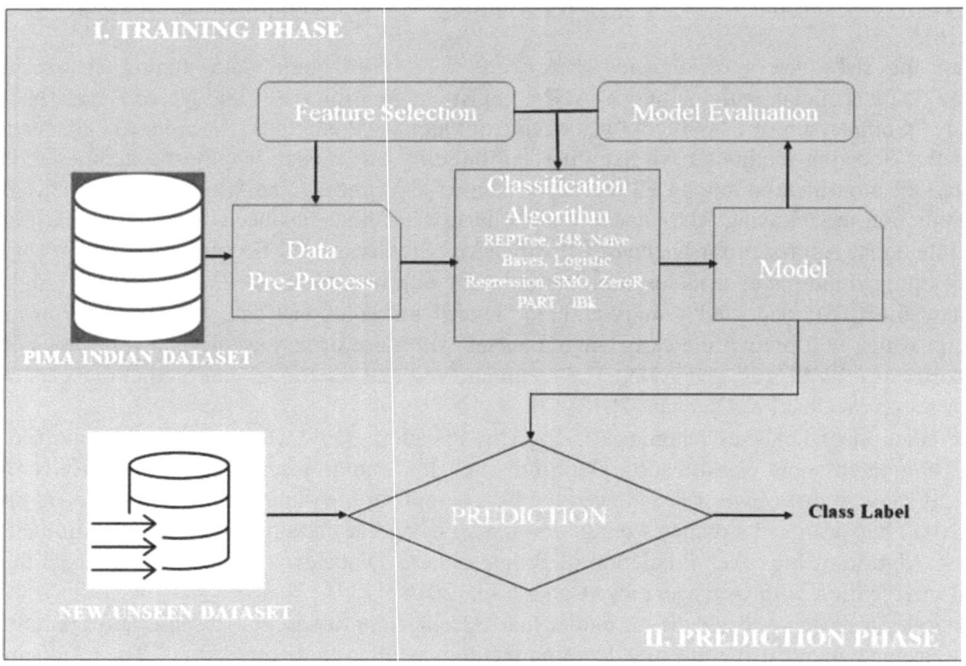

FIGURE 23.2 Proposed model diagram.

3.2.2 Naive Bayesian (Naive Bayes)

Naive Bayes is a probabilistic classifier founded on Bayes theorem which offers a method of calculating the probability of a hypothesis developed our prior knowledge. Naïve Bayes is a machine learning algorithm that is used for huge volume of data and is a classification technique that classifies all features as autonomous and separate from each other (Sneha & Gangil, 2019). Prediction of membership probability is created for every class. For instance, the probability of data points is linked to a specific class and the class is evaluated as highly appropriate class while it is acquired highest probability.

3.2.3 Functions (Logistic, SMO)

Logistic Regression (LR) is the most commonly used machine learning algorithm in healthcare. LR approach is applied to predict the result of dependent variable with constant-independent variables which facilitate to diagnose and predict disease in a different way (Kemppainen et al., 2018). LR is a linear combination of independent variables and it limits the cost function value between 0 and 1. Sequential minimal optimization algorithm (SMO) is a machine learning algorithm which is broadly used for training SVMs. SMO is used as one of the methods to resolve the SVM training problem that is more effective than standard quadratic programming solvers (Rifkin & Poggio, 2002).

3.2.4 Rule based (ZeroR, PART)

ZeroR is the simplest rule-based classification technique which focuses on the target and ignores all predictors. ZeroR does not have predictability power and it just estimates the class. ZeroR is very effective for deciding a baseline performance. On the other hand, PART is a partial decision tree algorithm. It is basically an upgraded version of C4.5 and RIPPER algorithms. Unlike C4.5 and RIPPER, to create appropriate rules, PART does not need to execute global optimization (Frank & Witten, 1998).

3.2.5 LAZY (IBk)

IBk is a machine learning algorithm which follows LAZY method. It is an instance-based learning approach similar to KNN techniques. The fundamental function of this algorithm is that every unseen instance is always contrasted with current ones using a Euclidean distance metrics and the nearest existing instance is employed to assign the class for the test sample (Witten et al., 2016).

3.3 Data mining tools

In this project, WEKA data mining software is utilized for doing the experiment. The software platform is developed by the University of Waikato in New Zealand. The software integrates a lot of data mining algorithm for classification, clustering, rules base analysis, and so on. The software supports a wide range of dataset format and can be converted from another format to its own "arrf" data format. Graphical user interface and its simplicity are the main beauty of the software. The main goal of this project is to build a binary classification model to predict onset diabetes using the WEKA tools.

3.4 Dataset

The recommended technique is assessed on Pima Indian Diabetes Dataset which is originally from the National Institute of Diabetes and Digestive and Kidney Diseases. The dataset is taken from Kaggle, a Google company for data scientist. The dataset recorded some clinical details of female individuals. There are 768 instances logged under eight attributes as input variable and one class attribute as output variable. All attributes have different numerical values. The class "0" suggests negative for diabetes and "1" treated as positive for diabetes. Table 23.1 presents the detail of the dataset used in this study.

3.5 Evaluation measures

To measure the performance of the chosen algorithms. the study applied mainly four evaluation criteria such as F-measure, Precision, Recall, and Accuracy. Table 23.2 presented definition of the evaluation measure and its formula. Prior to doing

TABLE 23.1 Dataset description.

Att. No.	Attribute	Specification	Abbreviation	Variables	Instance
1	Pregnancies	Number of times pregnant	Preg	Input	768
2	Glucose	Plasma glucose concentration 2 h in an oral glucose tolerance test	Plas	Input	
3	BloodPressure	Diastolic blood pressure (mm Hg)	Pres	Input	
4	SkinThickness	Triceps skin fold thickness (mm)	Skin	Input	
5	Insulin	2-Hour serum insulin (mu U/ml)	Insu	Input	
6	BMI	Body mass index (weight in kg/(height in m)2)	Mass	Input	
7	DiabetesPedigreeFunction	Diabetes pedigree function	Pedi	Input	
8	Age	Age (years)	Age	Input	
9	Outcome	Class variable (0 or 1) 268 of 768 are 1, the others are 0	Class	Output	

TABLE 23.2 Definition of evaluation measures.

Sl	Measure	Definition	Formula	Elements of formula
1	F-measure (F)	The F-measure is computed as the mean of precision and recall by providing each the same weighting. F-measure balances precision and recall.	F = 2* (P * R)/(P + R)	TP = True positive TN = True negative FP = false positive FN = false negative P = precision R = recall
2	Precision (P)	Precision is the ratio of correctly predicted positive observations to the total predicted positive observations. It measures model's accuracy in classifying a sample as positive.	P = TP/(TP + FP)	
3	Recall (R)	Recall quantifies the number of correct positive predictions. It determines how accurately a prediction model is able to identify the relevant data.	R = TP/(TP + FN)	
4	Accuracy (A)	Accuracy is a way to measure how often the algorithm classifies a data point correctly. Accuracy can predict the positive and negative cases correctly.	A = (TP + TN)/(TP + FP + FN + TN)	

this, the study applied a technique called Confusion Matrix to summarize the performance of classification algorithms because an unequal observation or more than two classes in dataset may mislead the result. The confusion metrics calculate a model's accuracy by evaluating predicted values with actual values. It also can identify when a classification algorithm mislabels one another (Mailund, 2017). Additionally, this study measures classifier's performance on the basis of classified instances.

4. Result and discussion

4.1 Classifier's performance based on of classified instance

Correctly classified instances mean the sum of true positive (TP) and true negative (TN). On the other hand, incorrectly classified instances mean the sum of false positive (FP) and false negative (FN). Table 23.3 shows that there are 768

TABLE 23.3 Classifier's performance based on of classified instance.

Total number of instance	Classification algorithms	Correctly classified instances	Incorrectly classified instances
768	Logistic regression	593 (77.21%)	175 (22.79%)
	SMO	594 (77.34%)	174 (22.64%)
	REPTree	578 (75.26%)	190 (24.74%)
	J48	567 (73.83%)	201 (26.17%)
	Naive Bayes	586 (76.30%)	182 (23.70%)
	ZeroR	500 (65.10%)	268 (34.90%)
	PART	578 (75.26%)	190 (24.74%)
	IBk	539 (70.18%)	229 (29.82%)

instances in the dataset. SMO algorithm is showing the maximum correctly classified instance which is 77.34%. Logistics is showing in second highest, scoring almost the same as SMO which is 77.21%. Therefore, SMO and Logistic can predict the chance of being type-2 diabetes more accurately than other classification algorithm.

4.2 Confusion matrix

The confusion matrix shows how good a classification model is by defining what it gets right and what it gets wrong. The confusion matrix for this study is shown in numbers in Table 23.4 with A and B representing the class labels. The PIDD has 768 instances, and the target variable was either "functional" or "nonfunctional." The right side of the matrix tells that column "a" is functional, and "b" is nonfunctional. The columns tell how the model classified the samples.

For example, in the matrix related to Logistic Regression model, the first column contains all the samples which the model thinks are "a," total 555. The second column contains all the samples which the model thinks are "b," total 213. The rows, on the other hand, represent reality. The first row contains all the samples which really are "a," total 500 of them. The second row contains all the samples which really are "b," total 268 of them. Knowing the columns and rows, the study gets the following details:

The top-left and bottom-right of the matrix are showing things the model classifies correctly. That means, $440 + 153 = 593$ is correctly classified.

Furthremore, the bottom left and top right of the matrix are showing where the model is confused. That means, $115 + 60 = 175$ is confused.

As a result, all correct classifications are on the top left to bottom right diagonal. Everything off that diagonal is an incorrect classification of some sort. The result of the confusion matrix shows that SMO and LR model has lowest number of confusion which is 174 and 175, respectively.

4.3 F-measure

The f-score (or f-measure) is calculated based on the precision and recall. Fig. 23.3 presents a comparison among the algorithms for the f-score. The figure shows that logistic has the highest f-score which is 84%, while SMO scored 83%. Therefore, Logistic model can predict the chance of being affected by type-2 diabetes more accurately than other classification algorithm.

4.4 Precision

Fig. 23.4 shows the comparison for precision that calculates positive predictive value. Here J48 and Naive Bayes perform better than other algorithms with 80%, followed by Logistic model which has slightly lower with 79%. Therefore, in terms of precision, J48, Bayes, and Logistic model can predict more accurately than others.

TABLE 23.4 Confusion matrix for classifiers.

1	**Logistic Regression**	**A**	**B**	**Total instance**
	A-tested negative	440	60	500
	B-tested positive	115	153	268
	Total instance	555	213	768
2	**SMO**	**A**	**B**	**Total instance**
	A-tested negative	449	51	500
	B-tested positive	123	145	268
	Total instance	572	196	768
3	**REPTree**	**A**	**B**	**Total instance**
	A-tested negative	423	77	500
	B-tested positive	113	155	268
	Total instance	536	232	768
4	**J48**	**A**	**B**	**Total instance**
	A-tested negative	407	93	500
	B-tested positive	108	160	268
	Total instance	515	253	768
5	**Naive Bayes**	**A**	**B**	**Total instance**
	A-tested negative	422	78	500
	B-tested positive	104	164	268
	Total instance	526	242	768
6	**ZeroR**	**A**	**B**	**Total instance**
	A-tested negative	500	0	500
	B-tested positive	268	0	268
	Total instance	768	0	768
7	**PART**	**A**	**B**	**Total instance**
	A-tested negative	422	78	500
	B-tested positive	112	156	268
	Total instance	534	234	768
8	**IBk**	**A**	**B**	**Total instance**
	A-tested negative	397	103	500
	B-tested positive	126	142	268
	Total instance	523	245	768

4.5 Recall

Recall is the ability of a model to find all the relevant cases within a data set. Fig. 23.5 shows a comparison for a recall measure among the eight algorithms used in this study. The result shows that ZeroR scored the highest followed by SMO and Logistic with 100%, 89%, and 88% respectively. Therefore, in the context of recall, ZeroR SMO and Logistic model have more accuracy than other models.

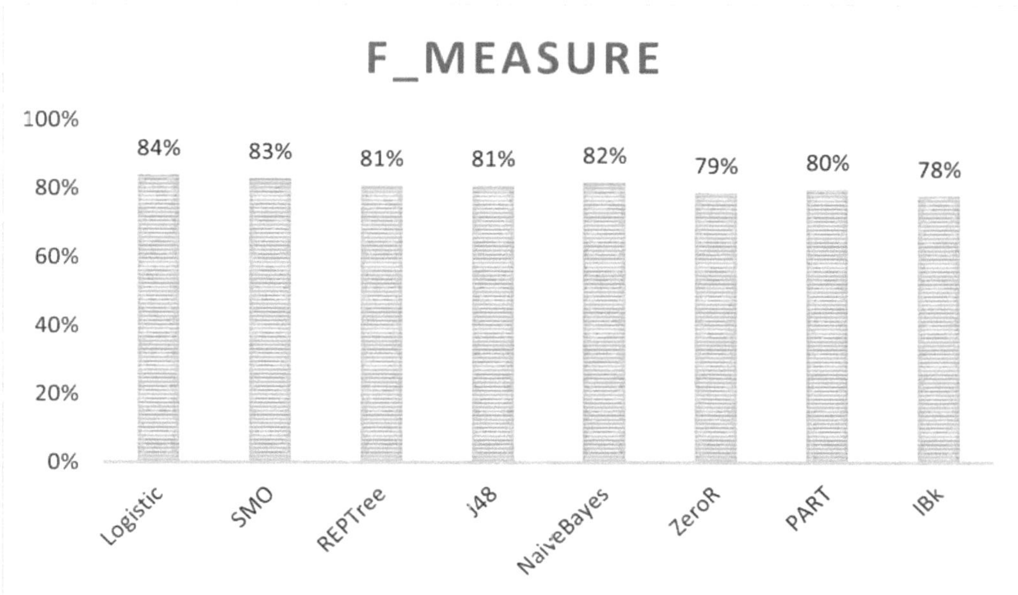

FIGURE 23.3 Comparison of F-measure.

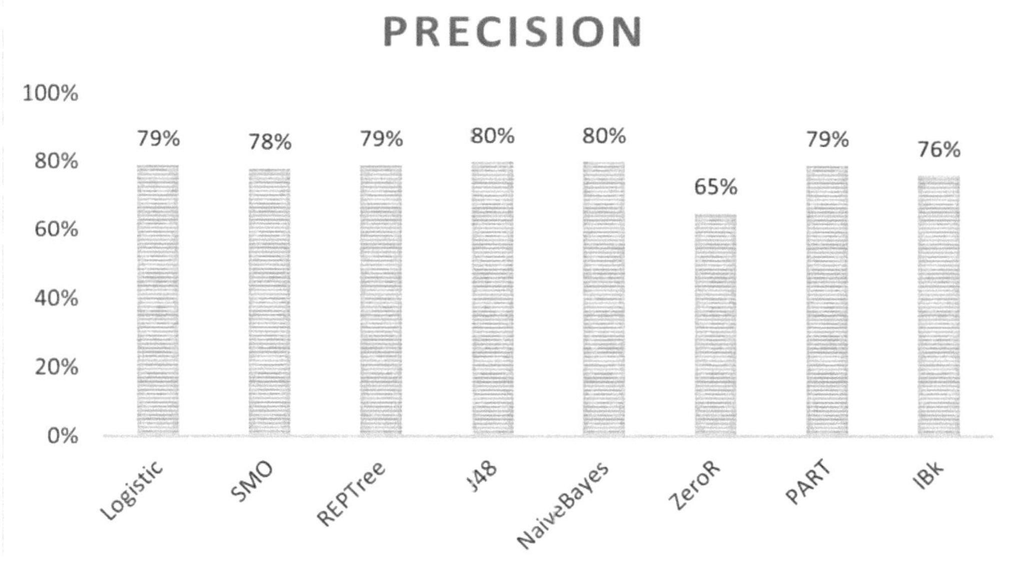

FIGURE 23.4 Comparison of precision.

4.6 Accuracy

Accuracy is defined as the percentage of correct predictions for the test data. The comparison of performance accuracy for the algorithms is shown in Fig. 23.6. It is observed that Logistic achieved the highest accuracy of 77.47% over the other algorithms. SMO scored 76.80%.

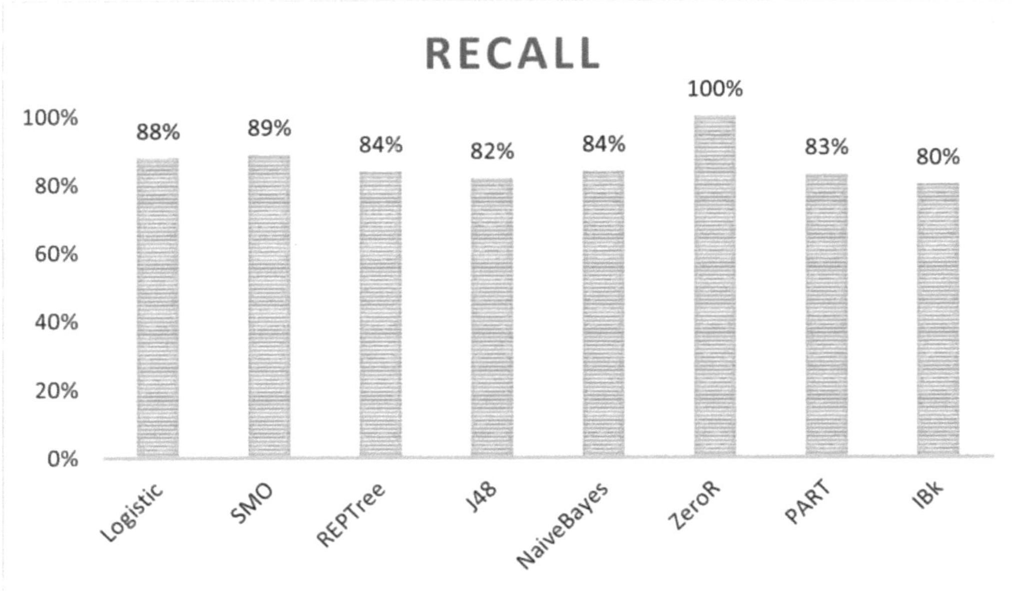

FIGURE 23.5 Comparison of recall.

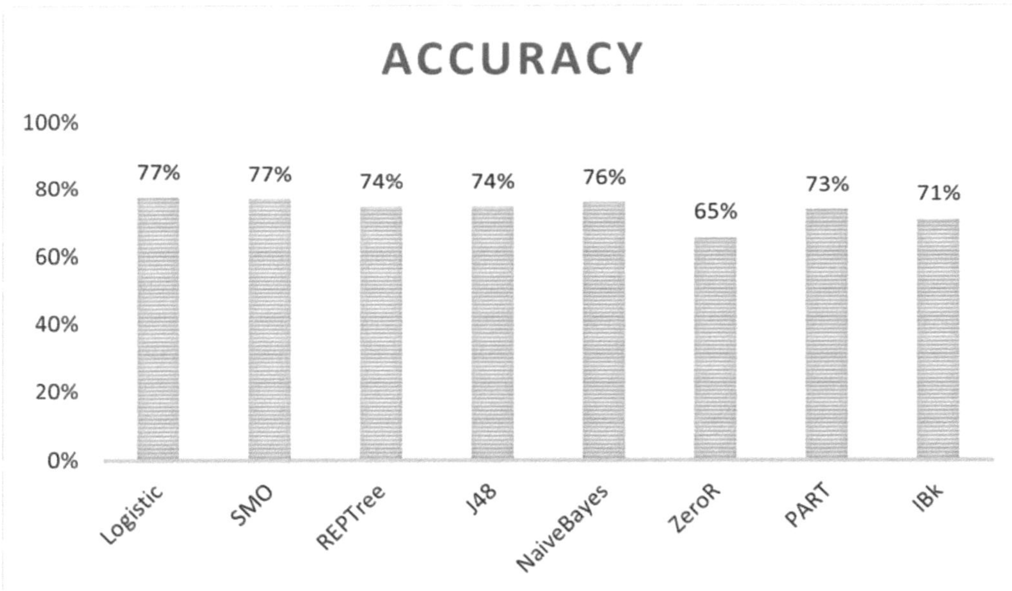

FIGURE 23.6 Comparison of accuracy.

4.7 Comparative analysis summary

Table 23.5 presented the analysis summary that has been evaluated by F-measure, Precision, Recall, and Accuracy. Among four measures, LR model achieved higher f-score, precision, and accuracy. Additionally, Logistic model performed well in identifying correctly classified instance and finding the confusion of instances in the dataset. Therefore, Logistic model appeared best fit to predict onset (type-2) of diabetes from medical records.

TABLE 23.5 Comparative analysis summary.

Classification algorithms	F-score	Precision	Recall	Accuracy
Logistic	0.84	0.79	0.88	77.47%
SMO	0.83	0.78	0.89	76.80%
REPTree	0.81	0.79	0.84	74.46%
J48	0.81	0.80	0.82	74.49%
Naive Bayes	0.82	0.80	0.84	75.75%
ZeroR	0.79	0.65	1.00	65.11%
PART	0.80	0.79	0.83	73.45%
IBk	0.78	0.76	0.80	70.62%

5. Conclusion

Diabetes prediction at early stage can address one of the critical issues in the public health sector. In this study, a methodical step was followed for developing a prediction model to forecast illnesses such as diabetes with maximum level of accuracy. Throughout this project, eight classification algorithms are executed on PIDD dataset by using the WEKA machine learning tool. After measuring the confusion matrix, f-score, precision, recall, and accuracy level, the LR model has achieved the highest performance with accuracy of 77.47%. Thus, this binary-class "Logistic regression" model has been chosen for predicting the onset diabetes from medical records. This study can be expanded in the future for large-scale implementations in healthcare sectors.

References

Al-Lawati, J. A. (2017). Diabetes mellitus: A local and global public health emergency! *Oman Medical Journal, 32*(3), 177–179. https://doi.org/10.5001/omj.2017.34

Cahn, A., Shoshan, A., Sagiv, T., Yesharim, R., Raz, I., & Goshen, R. (2018). Use of a machine learning algorithm improves prediction of progression to diabetes. *Diabetes, 67*(Suppl. 1), 1286-P. https://doi.org/10.2337/db18-1286-p

Frank, E., & Witten, I. (1998). Generating accurate rule sets without global optimization. In *Machine learning: Proceedings of the fifteenth international conference* (pp. 144–151).

Jinjri, W. M., Keikhosrokiani, P., & Abdullah, N. L. (2021). Machine learning algorithms for the classification of cardiovascular disease-a comparative study. In *2021 international conference on information technology, ICIT 2021-proceedings* (pp. 132–138). Institute of Electrical and Electronics Engineers Inc. https://doi.org/10.1109/ICIT52682.2021.9491677

Joshi, T. N., & Chawan, P. P. M. (2018). Diabetes prediction using machine learning techniques. *International Journal of Engineering Research and Applications (IJERA), 8*, 9–13. https://doi.org/10.9790/9622-0801020913

Kemppainen, L. M., Kemppainen, T. T., Reippainen, J. A., Salmenniemi, S. T., & Vuolanto, P. H. (2018). Use of complementary and alternative medicine in Europe: Health-related and sociodemographic determinants. *Scandinavian Journal of Public Health, 46*(4), 448–455. https://doi.org/10.1177/1403494817733869

Kohavi, R. (1996). Scaling up the accuracy of Naïve Bayes classifiers: A decision-tree hybrid. In *KDD'96: Proceedings of the second international conference on knowledge discovery and data mining* (pp. 202–207).

Mailund, T. (2017). Introduction to R programming. In *Beginning data science in R* (pp. 1–28). Springer Nature. https://doi.org/10.1007/978-1-4842-2671-1_1

Malik, E. F., Keikhosrokiani, P., & Asl, M. P. (2021). Text Mining Life Cycle for a Spatial Reading of Viet Thanh Nguyen's The Refugees (2017). In *2021 International Congress of Advanced Technology and Engineering (ICOTEN)* (pp. 1–9). https://doi.org/10.1109/ICOTEN52080.2021.9493520

Marinov, M., Mosa, A. S. M., Yoo, I., & Boren, S. A. (2011). Data-mining technologies for diabetes: A systematic review. *Journal of Diabetes Science and Technology, 5*(6), 1549–1556. https://doi.org/10.1177/193229681100500631

Nai-Arun, N., & Moungmai, R. (2015). Comparison of classifiers for the risk of diabetes prediction. In *Procedia computer science* (Vol. 69, pp. 132–142). Elsevier B.V. https://doi.org/10.1016/j.procs.2015.10.014

Orabi, K. M., Kamal, Y. M., & Rabah, T. M. (2016). Early predictive system for diabetes mellitus disease. In *Lecture notes in computer science (including subseries lecture notes in artificial intelligence and lecture notes in bioinformatics)* (Vol. 9728, pp. 420–427). Springer Verlag. https://doi.org/10.1007/978-3-319-41561-1_31

Perveen, S., Shahbaz, M., Guergachi, A., & Keshavjee, K. (2016). Performance analysis of data mining classification techniques to predict diabetes. In *Procedia computer science* (Vol. 82, pp. 115–121). Elsevier B.V. https://doi.org/10.1016/j.procs.2016.04.016

Pinto, K. A., Abdullah, N. L., & Keikhosrokiani, P. (2021). Diet & exercise classification using machine learning to predict obese patient's weight loss. *International Congress of Advanced Technology and Engineering*, 4–5.

Pradhan, M., & Bamnote, G. R. (2014). Design of classifier for detection of diabetes mellitus using genetic programming. In *Advances in intelligent systems and computing* (Vol. 327, pp. 763–770). Springer Verlag. https://doi.org/10.1007/978-3-319-11933-5_86

Rashid, T. A., Abdullah, S. M., & Abdullah, R. M. (2016). An intelligent approach for diabetes classification, prediction and description. In *Advances in intelligent systems and computing* (Vol. 424, pp. 323–335). Springer Verlag. https://doi.org/10.1007/978-3-319-28031-8_28

Rifkin, R. M., & Poggio, T. (2002). *Everything old is new again: A fresh look at historical approaches in machine learning* (Ph.D. dissertation). Cambridge, MA: Massachusetts Institute of Technology.

Saeedi, P., Petersohn, I., Salpea, P., Malanda, B., Karuranga, S., Unwin, N., Colagiuri, S., Guariguata, L., Motala, A. A., Ogurtsova, K., Shaw, J. E., Bright, D., & Williams, R. (2019). Global and regional diabetes prevalence estimates for 2019 and projections for 2030 and 2045: Results from the International Diabetes Federation diabetes atlas, 9th edition. *Diabetes Research and Clinical Practice, 157*. https://doi.org/10.1016/j.diabres.2019.107843

Selvakumar, S., Kannan, K. S., & Gothainachiyar, S. (2017). Prediction of diabetes diagnosis using classification based data mining techniques. *International Journal of Statistics and Systems, 12*(2), 183–188.

Sneha, N., & Gangil, T. (2019). Analysis of diabetes mellitus for early prediction using optimal features selection. *Journal of Big Data, 6*(1). https://doi.org/10.1186/s40537-019-0175-6

Tabish, S. A. (2007). Is diabetes becoming the biggest epidemic of the twenty-first century? *International Journal of Health Sciences, 1*(2), V–VIII. http://www.ncbi.nlm.nih.gov/pubmed/21475425.

Teoh Yi Zhe, I., & Keikhosrokiani, P. (2021). Knowledge workers mental workload prediction using optimised ELANFIS. *Applied Intelligence, 51*(4), 2406–2430. https://doi.org/10.1007/s10489-020-01928-5

Weiss, G. M., & Davison, B. D. (2010). Data mining. In H. Bidgoli (Ed.), *Handbook of technology management: Vol. II*. John Wiley and Sons.

Wexler, D. J., Grant, R. W., Wittenberg, E., Bosch, J. L., Cagliero, E., Delahanty, L., Blais, M. A., & Meigs, J. B. (2006). Correlates of health-related quality of life in type 2 diabetes. *Diabetologia, 49*(7), 1489–1497. https://doi.org/10.1007/s00125-006-0249-9

Witten, I. H., Frank, E., Hall, M. A., & Pal, C. J. (2016). Data mining: Practical machine learning tools and techniques. In *Data mining: Practical machine learning tools and techniques* (pp. 1–621). Elsevier Inc. http://www.sciencedirect.com/science/book/9780128042915.

Ying, S. Y., Keikhosrokiani, P., & Asl, M. P. (2021). Comparison of data analytic techniques for a spatial opinion mining in literary works: A review paper. In *Lecture notes on data engineering and communications technologies* (Vol. 72, pp. 523–535). Springer Science and Business Media Deutschland GmbH. https://doi.org/10.1007/978-3-030-70713-2_49

Chapter 24

Screening programs incorporating big data analytics

Kevin Sheng-Kai Ma[1,2]

[1]*Center for Global Health, Perelman School of Medicine, University of Pennsylvania, Philadelphia, PA, United States;* [2]*Graduate Institute of Biomedical Electronics and Bioinformatics, College of Electrical Engineering and Computer Science, National Taiwan University, Taipei, Taiwan*

1. Introduction: disease screening and screening programs

Prevention is better than cure. That is, accurate and timely screening allows for effective prevention, through providing a stratified profile of disease. To achieve so, screening tests are designed and done to identify possible anomalies or lesions that are early signs of diseases in symptom-free populations. As such, although a screening test is not considered diagnostic, it can be used to effectively and efficiently determine a subset of the general population from which individuals are recommended to undergo additional medical or clinical examinations, so as to confirm the presence or absence of certain diseases. In this chapter, we will first go through the goals, measures, and utility of screening programs; then introduce how clinicians and epidemiologists determine whether a specific screening program is valid; next give examples of state-of-the-art screening programs that incorporate big data analytics; and finally discuss challenges that investigators working on big data—facilitated screening are faced with.

1.1 Goals and measures for screening programs

Screening refers to the routine procedure that investigates whether clinically healthy populations are under the risk of unsuspected conditions that require treatment. Major components of screening involve the following: (1) whether tools used to detect potentially abnormal signs are accurate and (2) whether the proposed treatment can justify the considerations for disease screening. Specifically, the considerations for disease screening are based on three recognized benefits (Box 24.1).

There are several subgroups among the general population, also known as vulnerable individuals or groups at risk, who we should consider screening. Implementation of these screening programs in many countries has success in preventive medicine at national and global levels. For instance, screening programs provided for pregnant women have turned out as an effective strategy to control and to prevent the spread of hepatitis B virus (HBV) infection. In this case, screening is considered as being justified since such implementation in an evidence-based sense can prevent infants from becoming HBV carriers. Likewise, disease screening for immigrants or refugees from certain areas of endemicity is adopted to determine susceptible family contacts for which vaccination (Ma, Lee et al., 2021) is recommended. As such, liabilities and benefits of screening include consequent improved disease prognosis, prevention of postoperation complications (Wu

BOX 24.1 Rationales and benefits of disease screening.

The capability to determine individuals with certain traits that need to be treated.

The prevention of transmission or infections following disease development.

Used as a measure of preexisting conditions before prevention, such as vaccination and/or surgery, is implemented.

Big Data Analytics for Healthcare. https://doi.org/10.1016/B978-0-323-91907-4.00023-6

et al., 2020), reduced medical costs, and optimized allocation of medical resources (Ma & Tsai, 2020). In particular, screening as an access to early detection can allow timely implementation of available treatment of suspected abnormalities at an early stage, thus reducing the odds of diseases developing into a severe form, or transmission to others, and can also help identify at risk individuals close to the screened subject.

However, there are several limitations to conventional screening programs. First, errors in screening can lead to adverse economic, ethical, and legal outcomes, since a false-positive or false-negative screening can result in unnecessary medical investigations, biased diagnoses, and even adverse psychological impact. Also, false-positive test results can lead to job loss and cause economic burden. That is, medicolegal liabilities should be carefully managed per the implementation of screening programs and the interpretation of screening test results required. Second, although the screening of blood samples and blood-derived products has been widely adopted in many national screening programs for the control of HBV and hepatitis C virus (HCV), the practicability of universal screening for all at risk groups, such as health care workers, and susceptible subgroups in the general population is limited due to the labor-intensive nature of the procedure and data interpretation of screening.

As such, novel programs that seek to incorporate technologies of high efficiency, such as big data analytics, have been designed and carried out. With the application of big data analytics, screening programs are allowed to measure variables from the micro- and molecular level, to the macro- and social level, all at the same visit; such merit exempts screening programs from being limited to the capacity of involving only one or a few variables per visit. Accordingly, with big data—facilitated screening, profiles of temporal changes throughout the entire body can be provided in multiple follow-ups, which creates a personalized database that contains the detailed genotype and phenotype of each subject (Torkamani et al., 2017). As a feedback, through training the predictive algorithms with those large datasets, the performance and accuracy for disease screening can be further improved (Khera et al., 2018; Perkins et al., 2018; Schüssler-Fiorenza Rose et al., 2019).

1.2 Measures and utility of a screening program

Acceptable screening tests constitute satisfying results in terms of several epidemiological measures, including the sensitivity, specificity, and positive predictive value (PPV). In a nutshell, sensitivity and specificity refer to the concordance of a screening test with respect to a given referent, while PPV and negative predictive value (NPV), respectively, represent the likelihood that a screening test can identify whether the screened individuals do or do not have a target condition, based on the screening results (Table 24.1). Since screening tests provide an overview of stratified profiles, instead of precise diagnoses that are generated in later steps of the clinical decision-making process, the goals are to minimize false negatives and false positives through designing tests that may clearly separate populations with and without a given disease of interest. In big data analytics, especially in an era where techniques such as machine learning are widely employed, elements in the confusion matrix are therefore given clinical interpretations. For instance, the recall term in the confusion matrix represents sensitivity or total positive rate in an epidemiological sense; in the same way, precision equals PPV (Wiemken & Kelley, 2019) (Table 24.1).

1.3 Databases and training sets of screening programs

To promote public health, trends of providing nationwide screening programs for chronic or infectious diseases are more and more common in countries with social welfare systems. Common screening programs include cancer screening such as colorectal cancer, breast cancer, prostate cancer, cervical cancer, and oral cancer (Ma, Tan et al., 2021), screening of infectious diseases, such as human immunodeficiency virus/acquired immune deficiency syndrome, HBV, HCV, methicillin-resistant *Staphylococcus aureus* (Kuo et al., 2020), tuberculosis (Chiang et al., 2021), and the coronavirus disease 2019, screening of chronic diseases, such as diabetes, cardiovascular diseases (Ma, Chiang et al., 2021b; Ma, Liou et al., 2021), and autoimmune diseases, such as human leukocyte antigen (HLA) screening for ankylosing spondylitis, and screening of drug allergy, such as HLA screening for a species of fatal adverse drug reactions (ADRs) (Ma et al., 2020) and Stevens—Johnson syndrome (Ma, Chung et al., 2021; Ma, Saeed et al., 2021).

1.4 Nationwide screening programs

The practice of disease screening is an important component of public health and social warfare. In particular, due to the large healthcare burden of chronic diseases such as cancer, diabetes, and cardiovascular diseases (Chiang et al., 2022), and infectious diseases, nationwide screening programs of easy access have been implemented in many countries. Examples of

TABLE 24.1 **The two-by-two (2 × 2) table and confusion matrix used to summarize and present epidemiological data.**

		Conditions, as determined by golden standards			
	Total population	**Condition positive**	**Condition negative**	**Prevalence** $= \frac{\text{Condition positive}}{\text{Total population}}$	
Test outcomes	Test positive	True positive	False positive, type I error	Positive predictive value (PPV), Precision $= \frac{\text{True positive}}{\text{Test positive}}$	False discovery rate $= \frac{\text{False positive}}{\text{Test positive}}$
	Test negative	False negative, type II error	True negative	False omission rate $= \frac{\text{False negative}}{\text{Test negative}}$	Negative predictive value $= \frac{\text{True negative}}{\text{Test negative}}$
	Accuracy $= \frac{\text{True positive + True negative}}{\text{Total population}}$	Total positive rate, Sensitivity, Recall $= \frac{\text{True positive}}{\text{Condition positive}}$	False positive rate, Fall − out $= \frac{\text{False positive}}{\text{Condition negative}}$	Positive likelihood ratio $= \frac{\text{Total positive rate}}{\text{False positive rate}}$	Diagnostic odds ratio $= \frac{\text{Positive likelihood ratio}}{\text{Negative likelihood ratio}}$
		False negative rate, Miss rate $= \frac{\text{False negative}}{\text{Condition positive}}$	True negative rate, Specificity $= \frac{\text{True negative}}{\text{Condition negative}}$	Negative likelihood ratio $= \frac{\text{True negative rate}}{\text{False negative rate}}$	

Note that the positive predictive value, a frequently presented outcome in screening program, equals to precision, a common derivative in big data analytics; in the same way, sensitivity of a screening program, defined as total positive rate, equals to the recall computed through machine learning–based algorithm.

some of these screening programs are given in the next couple of sections in this chapter. As such, results and findings in these screening programs naturally provide a database with abundant clinically relevant information (Price et al., 2017), including demographic characteristics, social behaviors and history, including contact and traveling history for infectious disease (Ma, 2021), medical history and diagnostic records, lab tests, including genetic tests, image findings, including radiographs, and, most importantly, the status of whether or not they eventually developed a disease or not, including the severity and staging of such diseases. Studies realized with these databases have also resulted in evidence and insights in clinical epidemiology (Ma, Hasturk et al., 2021; Ma, Illescas Ralda et al., 2021; Ma, Lai et al., 2021; Ma, Chiang et al., 2021). To ensure the validity of these databases, in most screening programs from which the data are subjected to further machine learning—facilitated analytics, only physicians with specific qualifications (such as subspecialty board certification) and extensive experience (for instance, at least having performed hundreds of certain surgeries within the past one or two years) were certified to participate in these screening programs. In those screening programs, as we want to collect substantial data to optimize next generation screening programs with big data analytics, completeness of involved procedures and findings during the procedures had to be photo-documented. Moreover, a selection of the documentation of these procedures should be assessed by an external committee of experts.

Thus, in the era of big data analytics, the implementation of these policies guarantees the quality of data. With these validated, large-scaled datasets, we are allowed to establish automatic, or at least semiautomatic, screening programs that incorporate models trained with such real-world clinically relevant data. To verify whether these model-facilitated screening programs are more accurate and efficient, evidence of the highest level in the pyramid of evidence-based medicine (EBM) is warranted to support any claim of such utility.

2. Evidence-based medicine for big data analytics—facilitated screening programs

To study screening programs that incorporate big data analytics, such as machine learning-facilitated interpretation of multiomics, electronic health records (EHRs), and clinical images including radiographs, one should always keep in mind how to critically appraise the clinical efficacy and utility of such novel programs. As such, concepts in EBM, which serve as the gold standards to determine efficacy, efficiency, and utility of interventions in clinical trials, may be applied.

2.1 Principles of evidence-based medicine

EBM concerns the judicious, reasonable, and explicit use of best and up-to-date evidence in making clinical decisions for patients, through integrating clinical expertise of physicians and patient preference with the best available options provided by the latest research. It is a framework aiming to incorporate conclusions from clinical research of high quality in clinical decision-making. Hence, practice of EBM requires efficient literature-searching skills, and formal rules to critically appraise scientific evidence to determine whether certain clinical literature may be applied clinically or not. Successful application of EBM involves appropriately relating clinical manifestations of individual patients and clinical experience of individual practitioners, with the most applicable scientific evidence provided and suggested by past clinical studies. In such a context, the scientific evidence of the highest level is randomized controlled trials (Fig. 24.1) conducted on rigorously selected participants that can prove the efficacy and potential adverse effect of interventions, such as new drugs, medical devices, screening programs, or health promotion campaigns, in comparison with existing options of golden standard, with the lowest risk of bias (Sackett et al., 1996). Overall, the practice of EBM is a process of problem-based and lifelong self-directed learning in which patient care creates the need for clinically relevant information of diagnosis, prognosis, therapeutic modalities, as well as other aspects in healthcare.

The EBM process entails thorough review of previously published data in past studies that are related to specific clinical scenarios, during which the first step, identifying and defining clinical questions, and the second step, systematically searching in research databases, provide a productive way of keeping up with up-do-date literature (Table 24.2). As such, EBM is well known for translating the practice of systematically reading and critically appraising peer-review studies into a pragmatic process that expands practitioners' domain knowledge and accordingly benefits individual patients. Keeping this in mind, we should then understand that instead of being a "cookbook" with recipes, EBM is a framework of how knowledge evolves and is updated in a way toward a paradigm shift, particularly since EBM is more of a bottom up approach that integrates the most suitable external evidence with individual physicians' clinical expertise and patients' values, and ultimately, such process of improvement brings cost-effectiveness and better health care (Evidence-Based Medicine Working Group, 1992). That said, although external clinical evidence can influence, it can never replace, individual physicians' clinical expertise, it is physicians with expertise who decide whether the external evidence can apply to the individual patient and how conclusions from these evidences should be integrated into the process of clinical

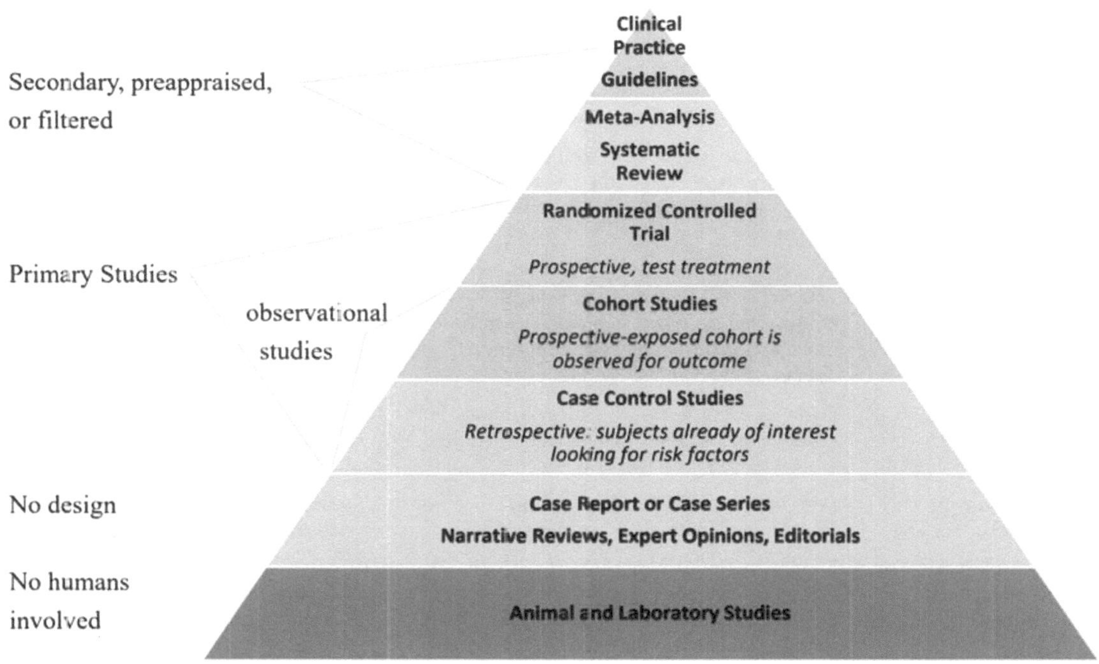

FIGURE 24.1 The hierarchy and levels of evidence. The hierarchy of evidence supports the use of results from large-scale epidemiological studies, such as randomized controlled trials, or even better, metaanalysis of these studies, to formulate clinical guidelines. Examples of systematic reviews and metaanalyses of randomized controlled trials include those published by the Cochrane Collaboration.

decision-making. That is, external evidence, including guidelines published by any committee of experts, practically is to be joined with individual clinical expertise when it comes to deciding whether and how this evidence matches an individual patient's clinical conditions, predicament, and preferences, and finally, whether this external evidence should be applied. Similar to applying machine learning—based techniques for clinical decision support systems, EBM serves as a workflow toward best practice; moreover, either EBM workflow or machine learning—based programs are designed to support, instead of totally replace, clinical expertise of individual physicians.

Furthermore, with methodologies of systematic reviews and metaanalyses, researchers are allowed to identify a series of studies on a clinical question, determine the most applicable ones, and then, critically appraise and analyze them to generate forest plots that indicate a summary of the best available and applicable evidence. With these methodologies, EBM-oriented clinicians and researchers are enabled and obliged to (1) use summarized evidence in clinical practice; (2) involve in developing and updating selected evidence-based guidelines or systematic reviews in their area of expertise; and (3) enroll patients in clinical trials on diagnosis, prognosis, and treatment, on which their clinical expertise is based. Moreover, since EBM has turned out as a powerful mechanism of recommendation that supports clinical decisions with well-documented evidence from considerable previous clinical studies (Table 24.2), which is surprisingly similar to the nature of big data medicine, that real-world evidence serves as a guidance for future practice, it can be inferred that the spirit of big data medicine share a lot in common with the concept of EBM, and that the development of big data medicine may facilitate and nourish that of EBM. But before we can officially claim the clinical impact and utility of big data medicine, still we have to first learn what constitutes the principles of EBM, which may be applied to judge whether big data—facilitated medical technology has passed that examination.

2.2 Gap between clinical research and best practices

Applying the principles of EBM facilitates the decision-making process when there are novel and appealing options, which fills in the gap between the latest clinical studies and best practices through bringing qualified available clinical evidence to current modalities. Such a gap has always existed and will be there when new modalities, including big data—supported algorithms, are proposed. As for one example of such gap, despite strong evidence suggested by studies in the 1970s that thrombolytic therapy and the use of aspirin can effectively manage and treat acute myocardial infarction, it took another 10 years to have these treatments accepted and adopted as routine protocols for patients with acute myocardial infarction.

TABLE 24.2 Levels of evidence and grading system in evidence-based medicine.

Strength of recommendation and quality of evidence	Methodological quality of supporting evidence and its examples	Clarity of balance between desirable and undesirable effect
IA strong recommendation, high-quality evidence	Consistent evidence from well-performed randomized controlled trials or exceptionally strong evidence from unbiased observational studies	Desirable effects clearly outweigh undesirable effects or vice versa
IB strong recommendation, moderate-quality evidence	Evidence from randomized controlled trials with important limitations (inconsistent results, methodological flaws, indirect, or imprecise) or exceptionally strong evidence from unbiased observational studies	Desirable effects clearly outweigh undesirable effects or vice versa
IC strong recommendation, low-quality evidence	Evidence for at least one critical outcome from observational studies, randomized controlled trials with serious flaws or indirect evidence	Desirable effects clearly outweigh undesirable effects or vice versa
ID strong recommendation, very low-quality evidence	Evidence for at least one critical outcome from unsystematic clinical observations or very indirect evidence	Desirable effects clearly outweigh undesirable effects or vice versa
IIA Weak recommendation, high-quality evidence	Consistent evidence from well-performed randomized controlled trials or exceptionally strong evidence from unbiased observational studies	Desirable effects closely balanced with undesirable effects
IIB Weak recommendation, moderate-quality evidence	Evidence from randomized controlled trials with important limitations (inconsistent results, methodological flaws, indirect, or imprecise) or exceptionally strong evidence from unbiased observational studies	Desirable effects closely balanced with undesirable effects
IIC Weak recommendation, low-quality evidence	Evidence for at least one critical outcome from observational studies, from randomized controlled trials with serious flaws or indirect evidence	Uncertainty in the estimates of desirable effects, harms, and burden; desirable effects, harms, and burden may be closely balanced
IID Weak recommendation, very low-quality evidence	Evidence for at least one critical outcome from unsystematic clinical observations or very indirect evidence	Major uncertainty in the estimates of desirable effects, harms, and burden; Desirable effects may or may not be balanced with undesirable effects which may be closely balanced

With this framework, clinicians and researchers systematically develop clinical practice recommendations through grading the quality of evidence, for the specific clinical question they are interested in. Ideally, systematic reviews based on randomized controlled trials provide the best quality of evidence. Several versions of this framework are proposed, and the subsequent guidelines, including the Grading of Recommendations Assessment, Development and Evaluation (GRADE) approach, can be followed.

Likewise, such gaps may exist in a way where, although scientific evidence is available, its practical application is complex. On the one hand, there is a lack of consolidated frameworks that help researchers and clinicians synthesize and come up with systematic results based on published scientific research; on the other hand, such a gap manifests as the inability to translate available evidence obtained in research to clinically relevant options which will benefit both healthcare professionals and the general populations. Both forms of such gap reflect a lack of appropriate frames and strategies that can effectively bring about improvement in professional conduct. Thus, even if we already witness high performance of many examples in disease screening and detecting suspected anomalies, there are still many practical barriers to breakthroughs before implementing and integrating these big data–based tools into daily clinical practice. To assess whether these tools are qualified for clinical use, evidence of the top hierarchy (Fig. 24.1) discussed in the next section is needed.

2.3 Hierarchy and levels of clinical evidence and information

EBM is characterized by the categorization of several levels of clinical evidence, which are ranked according to the robustness of their study designs that exempt them from various risks of biases in medical research (Fig. 24.1 and Table 24.2).

The principles of EBM stress that any medical decisions with regard to the optimal diagnostic or therapy procedure should be based on scientific evidence from clinical research, and that although clinical experience and expert opinion are of great help, they are not the major foundation in clinical decision-making. To accordingly make such clinical decisions about interventions, be it instructions, screening, medications, or surgery, for each individual patient, we have to acknowledge that it is always a complicated process in which physicians and patients communicate with each other to select the best available options for each individual patient. When it comes to launching a screen program that is to be implemented on a national scale, the communication process becomes even more complicated, for which much more robust evidence that can convince multidisciplinary representatives is needed.

As EBM involves the use of the highest level of clinical research evidence, it was actually impossible before the 1990s, when electronic databases were not yet applicable for medical reference management. After the 2000s, with the popularization of electronic records, the Internet, a rising number of new clinical options that well-trained clinicians did not hear of or learn about while they are still in school, and an increase in healthcare cost and expense, the medical field has been more and more placing emphasis on applying EBM in every clinical scenario; such increasingly available resources and motivations are in line with that of the development of big data analytics in healthcare.

Overall, EBM has become the paradigm and guidance useful in providing clues to unsolved clinical questions on which our intuitive clinical observations can actually result in more harm than good. Moreover, in most countries, physicians apply EBM to treatment planning for a single patient with the support of governmental authorities and the pharmaceutical industry. Applying such a consolidated framework allows for the development of practical guidelines for disease prevention and management, a filtered database with the best clinical and scientific evidence from domain knowledge, that is edited and continuously updated by experts with the latest peer-reviewed data and objective information. Thus, the integration of evidence and data in clinical research allows for the development of EBM, and at the same time, whether or not big data analytics may effectively reshape the landscape of clinical medicine, should be viewed with the concepts of EBM (Fig. 24.1).

3. Screening programs incorporating big data analytics

As we have discussed earlier in this chapter, common disease screening supported on a nationwide scale includes those for diseases that are potentially fatal or diseases with severe complications and sequelae that may result in a low quality of life. Here, examples of big data–facilitated cancer screening, big data–facilitated screening for complications of diabetes, and big data-based alerts for potential ADRs are given.

3.1 Cancer screening programs in the era of big data analytics

In an era without the help of predictive analytics, cancer risk stratification suffers from the lack of domain knowledge on prognostic factors, the lack of systematically collected prognostic data, labor-intensive data input (Morita et al., 1999), and, sometimes, overreliance on individual clinicians' opinion when it comes to prognosis estimation (Christakis & Lamont, 2000). Despite the existing prognostic aids for certain cancers (Alexander et al., 2017), those difficulties that oncologists are faced with may result in biased treatment plans for end-of-life care and acute care use (Sborov et al., 2019), due mainly to the lack of a risk stratification system that can indicate individual prognosis such as 1-year survival rate (Lakin et al., 2016).

After the paradigm shift toward patient-centered care (Burwell, 2015), clinicians aimed at tailoring care based on an individual patient's risk for outcomes, which requires population data on course of care and clinical findings that can be provided by comprehensive datasets including that of Medicare (Kline et al., 2015). On the other hand, with data integrating EHRs, radiographs, results of genetic tests (Struewing et al., 1997), and data on utilization of medical resources, predictive analytics allows for decision aids that promote value-based clinical decision-making (Conn, 2014). That is, predictive analytics and consequent risk stratification strategies in oncology result from the need for predictions of genomic and molecular risk, acute care use, adverse effects (Ma, Tan, et al., 2021), and life expectancy. Of all, evidence-based applications of predictive analytics toward cancer risk stratification include risk management for patients with cancer, radiomics, and pathology interpretation (Box 24.2).

3.1.1 Risk management for patients with cancer

Risk management in oncology involves interventions provided timely to patients at high risks of poor prognosis, which can be achieved with predictive algorithms (Brooks et al , 2015; Elfiky et al., 2018). Such prediction may be applied to

BOX 24.2 Fields of evidence-based big data–driven cancer risk stratification.

Risk prediction for mortality, length of hospital stay, readmissions, and discharge diagnoses during the treatment course.

Computer-aided detection of lesions through radiomics for the detection, classification, and monitoring of tumors.

Precise pathological staging based on clinical and laboratory evidence such as images of biopsies and genomic data.

optimize multiple steps during the treatment course, including chemotherapy (Brooks et al., 2015), surgery (Yeo et al., 2016), or before discharge (Manning et al., 2018). To achieve so, programs that can efficiently extract data from electronic medical records (EMRs) or EHRs are developed. For example, the deep learning–supported framework used by Google has been reported to accurately predict in-hospital mortality (Bertsimas et al., 2018), prolonged length of hospital stay, readmissions (Fieber et al., 2018), and discharge diagnoses.

3.1.2 Radiomics

Radiomics involves texture analysis based on radiographic findings to reveal the status of tumors and their progression, which may provide characteristics beneficial for the detection, classification, and monitoring of solid tumors (Bi et al., 2019). Computer-aided detection has been applied to facilitate the detection of malignant lung nodules in computed tomography (CT) and prostate lesions through magnetic resonance imaging and can also provide clues to cancer staging (Chan et al., 2008). When incorporating big data analytics, machine learning–based programs have been shown to predict the risk of metastasis based on CTs (Aerts et al., 2014; Coroller et al., 2015). Applications of radiomics also include the detection and prediction of response to treatment, such as the ability to inform an estimated tumor size after chemotherapy and radiotherapy (Sorace et al., 2018).

3.1.3 Pathology interpretation

Predictive analytics has the potential to minimize the heterogeneity of interpathologist findings and interpretations of examples including bronchoscopic biopsies for non–small cell lung cancer (Yu et al., 2016). This is important as pathological findings, providing the pathological staging which is more accurate than that obtained from other clinical findings, serve as the final judgment that leads to the diagnosis and consequent treatment strategies based on such an assessment. Through incorporating images of biopsies, genomic data, and big data analytics, machine learning–based programs are allowed to automatically detect metastatic breast malignancies from images of sentinel lymph node biopsies and predict their prognoses, with a satisfying area under the receiving operator characteristic curve (AUROC) for malignancy detection that is comparable to pathologists' performance, thus accelerating the clinical workflow and lessening the burden of pathologists (Bejnordi et al., 2017).

Overall, predictive algorithms merging clinical-, genetic-, and molecular-level information with applications in the estimation of the use of medical resources and medical costs, clinician decision support, and genomic risk stratification (Ma & Velarde Lopez, 2021) are of the potential to shape and improve cancer patients care, which turns out as a useful tool toward precision oncology.

3.2 Diabetes screening programs in the era of big data analytics

Diabetes is a global epidemic with a continuously increasing prevalence (Wild et al., 2004). Despite the gold standard of using glycated hemoglobin tests (HbA1c) to determine whether an individual is having clinically evident diabetes or not, screening programs focusing on peripheral complications, including diabetic foot ulcers, diabetic ketoacidosis, diabetic nephropathy, diabetic retinopathy (DR), and diabetes-associated periodontitis, have been proposed as candidates to realize early detection and screening of diabetes. Among these complications of diabetes, DR is the number one cause of blindness and vision loss in developed countries (Yau et al., 2012). There is abundant evidence showing that early diagnosis and intervention can prevent visual loss from DR, and many developed countries have established DR screening programs aimed at early screening, diagnosis, and treatment of DR (Huemer et al., 2020). Such programs could rely on the analysis of fundus photographs by trained personnel, which are of relatively high cost and accuracies varying among clinicians; on the contrary, deep learning continues the long trend of automatic and assisted analysis of retinal images (Esteva et al., 2017) and has been shown to lower the cost, improve diagnostic accuracy, and increase patient's accessibility to DR screening tools (Abràmoff et al., 2013).

One well-known example of DR screening algorithms is the IDx-DR system. The IDx-DR system incorporates data on biomarkers from multiple detectors, among which some utilize convolutional neural networks. IDx-DR improved on the Iowa Detection Program (IDP) by including separate algorithms to quantify the quality of images and the detection of suspected diabetic lesions (Abràmoff et al., 2013). With the use of deep learning, IDx-DR algorithms improved on those of IDP, with the verification of the same dataset, Messidor-2. The verification results against Messidor-2 suggested that the specificity of IDx-DR was significantly higher than that of IDP, while both IDx-DR and IDP manifest high sensitivity (Abràmoff et al., 2016). Moreover, IDx-DR is also verified through real-world evidence in a diabetic care program (van der Heijden et al., 2018). Despite cross-trial discrepancies in performance on detecting more than mild cases of DR, IDx-DR turned out to be the first fully autonomous AI-based diagnostic system that is approved by the food and drug administration (FDA). According to the FDA approval, the IDx-DR system is designed to work in connection with a nonpupil dilating fundus camera, using a macula- and a disc-centered image for analysis, and requires all four pictures from both eyes to yield a result.

To sum up, state-of-the-art systems, such as the above-discussed IDx-DR, RetmarkerDR, EyeArt, Google, Singapore SERI-NUS, Bosch DR algorithm, and Retinalyze, have turned out as potential approaches or options that support existing screening initiatives, which has the flexibility to be incorporated in a variety of application programming interfaces. Some of these big data–facilitated screening for multilevel complications of diabetes are even FDA approved and are commercially available.

3.3 Drug allergy screening in the era of big data analytics

Allergies are immune-mediated hypersensitivity reactions with symptoms ranging from minor skin rashes to severe anaphylaxis (Blumenthal et al., 2017). Patients receiving medical care are at particular risk of developing an allergic reaction due to many exposures with potential adverse effects (Bates et al., 1995). Because some allergic reactions may cause irreversible damage to patients and may result in liability for malpractice (Jeffres et al., 2018), close monitoring and surveillance for allergic reactions are crucial for patient safety and improved quality of health care (Benn et al., 2009; Crandall et al., 2018).

For such purpose, patient safety monitoring systems in hospitals which receive voluntary safety event reports from first-line personnel are integrated to detect patient safety signals in health care facilities (Okafor et al., 2015). The bases for such systems are safety reports that contain a large volume of data, and ideal outcomes of these systems are alerts that return in-time feedback to health care personnel or actions to prevent similar events in the future (Mahajan, 2010).

However, the rarity of allergic reactions makes ADRs unlikely to be classified as a standalone safety event category that can be easily monitored and identified (Ma et al., 2020). Obstacles that healthcare professionals are faced with include the fact that manual screening of keyword-filtered safety reports is time- and labor intensive; excessively sensitive parameters are associated with false-positive cases, and an excessively restricted keyword library is associated with missed cases. It has been pointed out in a study that among 101 keywords related to allergic symptoms, causative reagents, and treatments, which were used to retrieve 128000 hospital safety reports over a 10-year period, only 4.7% of the reports turned out as true allergic reactions. Given such limitations, machine learning–supported programs are employed to more accurately identify true drug allergies through safety reports (Young et al., 2019) and medical records (Bates et al., 1995; Budnitz et al., 2005).

As for the use of computational models and ADRs, studies have identified ADRs with the adverse event reporting system database of the FDA. From which over 1.6 million case reports collected from 2004 to 2009 were used as the training dataset for Bayesian networks, and accordingly, 10 species of Cinryze-associated thrombotic events were detected in patients with angioedema (Gandhi et al., 2012). Using the same database, the susceptibility to hypersensitivity reactions to antineoplastic medications can be inferred using parameters derived from Bayesian neural networks; specifically, signals of docetaxel- and paclitaxel-induced mild, severe, and fatal hypersensitivity are suggested (Kadoyama et al., 2011). On the other hand, such an approach may also estimate the different risks of hypersensitivity resulting from the use of several drugs; for instance, it was predicted that oxaliplatin and carboplatin can cause severe and fatal hypersensitivity reactions and that the use of dexamethasone-mediated oxaliplatin was associated with mild but not severe or fatal hypersensitivity reactions (Sakaeda et al., 2011). Likewise, studies have suggested the utility of Bayesian networks as a diagnostic tool for the evaluation of ADRs, with which differential diagnoses on drug-induced cutaneous reactions could be made (Lanctôt & Naranjo, 1995; Naranjo et al., 1994). These findings suggest the potential of soft computational models to accurately interpret data in ADR reports.

4. Challenges of big data–acilitated screening programs

Despite privacy concerns due to technical obstacles highlighted in the General Data Protection Regulation of the European Union on data protection, limitations and challenges of big data analytics-facilitated screening programs include: data acquisition, overdiagnoses of diseases, external validation with prospective studies, and subsequent risk of bias (Box 24.3).

4.1 Acquisition of high-quality clinical data

As of 2020, through published studies that tested machine learning–facilitated healthcare programs, full access to all datasets and codes was reported to be severely limited, to an extent that these resources are unavailable in 93%–95% of published studies. Compared to big data analytics in other fields, data sources are scarce in the field of clinical medicine. Likewise, big data–facilitated screening programs that incorporate risk-based stratification models are subjected to the lack of quality data in multiple aspects of patient data. For instance, in claims-based datasets, emergency department visits and inpatient lab data are often not registered and aggregated into an accessible registry timely and efficiently. In particular, the acquisition of an accurate date of death of an individual registered in claims-based datasets often requires linking to multiple external data sources in which the date is registered, thus hindering the ability of mortality prediction. Additionally, in most health registries, precise data on patients' lifestyle variables and behaviors in daily life and at home are hard to collect, which in fact constitutes the vast majority of their lifetime.

To solve this issue of data acquisition, novel approaches to collecting real-time data, through measures such as wearable medical devices, may help prevent unnecessary hospitalizations via acquiring patterns that turn out as early signs of diseases. In a similar sense, real-world data sources that integrate health records from every health-seeking behavior may empower real-time collection of EHRs-based data. Predictive algorithms for disease screening that are based on real-world data are more applicable and are immediately actionable than algorithms based on randomized clinical trials, since the latter often exclude potentially relevant segments of the general population. Examples of those real-world datasets include well-established oncology databases from the American Society of Clinical Oncology CancerLinQ and Flatiron Health which could serve this purpose, although limitations per their dependence on manual curation, or per the structural variability of the user interface, have been reported.

4.2 Overdiagnoses in big data–facilitated screening programs

Overdiagnosis as a common concern in disease screening programs can generate waste and harm. Overdiagnosis takes place when asymptomatic abnormalities that in fact are not clinically relevant are detected and reported. These abnormalities are not clinically relevant as they disappear spontaneously or do not progress (Brodersen et al., 2018). Overdiagnoses in big data–facilitated screening programs can be attributed to the purpose and nature of screening programs: providing an overall profile stratified by risks, instead of jumping to precise diagnoses. Specifically, since in big data screening multiple features of the body are monitored over time, highly sensitive technologies are bound to detect numerous abnormalities without being able to tell which features will be clinically manifest; in such case, only some automatically detected abnormalities will become symptomatic, while the rest represent overdiagnoses. As a result, a high percentage of screened individuals may be labeled with multiple clinically harmless conditions (Perkins et al., 2018; Torkamani et al., 2017).

On the other hand, unlike false-positive findings that are measured by specificity, overdiagnoses are increased by the sensitivity of screening tests. Novel screening technologies, including fine-grained molecular tests, or in the case of big data–facilitated programs with data collected through wearable devices, compared with conventional methods, often

BOX 24.3 Challenges in the development of clinically acceptable big data–facilitated screening programs

Lack of high-quality clinical data that are collected on a real-time basis in common databases such as health registry or claims-based datasets.

Overdiagnoses resulting from the detection of clinically irrelevant and harmless abnormalities that will never be symptomatic.

Lack of prospective assessment and external validation through clinical trials or observational studies designed in a real-world clinical setting.

Lack of representativeness and generalizability due to intrinsic biases as a result of factors such as the composition of the training datasets.

identify more and milder abnormalities. For instance, mild but clinically irrelevant cases of atrial fibrillation are more likely to be detected by a smartwatch than by insertable cardiac monitoring. Consequences of such overdiagnoses include the chance of medical professionals to treat these newly detected cases of mild but irrelevant features, exactly like how they treat patients with well-documented severe conditions that are evidence of high-risk ending in the disease spectrum, also known as spectrum bias.

In the same way, although algorithms incorporating multiple variables can be more predictive, for instance, compared with conventional genetic tests, the use of polygenic risk scores can identify a significantly larger at risk population, over a threefold risk for five screened diseases. However, when applying polygenic risk scores to conduct five isolated diagnoses, only 20% of the tested population was at high risk for at least one of the screened diseases (Khera et al., 2018). Thus, if such analytical tools are used to make a series of diagnoses in an ultralarge population, it can be inferred that almost everyone will be labeled as having a high risk of something. That said, such risk scores, when used properly, can also help redefine low risk-representing traits as harmless features, which can then reduce the chance of overdiagnosis. Statistically, this is due to the bias—variance tradeoff, in which when we are building predictive algorithms, we are actually tempted to include more predictor variables to optimally enhance the accuracy and the capability of the model to reflect real-world complexity. However, since it is difficult to reliably assess all multiple variables at once, the great accuracy thus may be outweighed by an increase in the variance or noise, which represents loss of precision.

Another pragmatic approach to minimize the risk of overdiagnosis in big data—facilitated screening is to follow conventional screening principles, such as guidelines developed by the World Health Organization. In such a case, targeting only serious and potentially severe conditions that require treatment, in turn, can limit the number of overdiagnosed abnormalities that are clinically irrelevant.

4.3 External validation with prospective studies

Successful predictive algorithms are usually defined by improvement in statistical endpoints, such as PPV and AUROC, while few studies have suggested the impact of predictive algorithms on clinically relevant endpoints, including overall survival or time to diagnosis, particularly for fatal diseases such as cancer and severe ADRs (Topol, 2019). Specifically, as of 2020, a metaanalysis pointed out that only 10 records were found for randomized clinical trials that tested the clinical efficacy of deep learning—based interventions using medical images. Of 81 nonrandomized clinical studies included in the metaanalysis, only 10% of which were prospective studies and merely 7.4% were validated in a real-world clinical setting. In these studies that compared the performance of machine learning—facilitated approaches versus well-trained clinicians, the median number of human graders/experts in the comparator group was merely four. As mentioned earlier in this chapter, interclinician accuracy varies, most studies are subjected to risk of bias, and thus, it remains unclear clinically, how powerful big data analytics—facilitated healthcare programs are, which includes screening programs. Subsequently, the risk of bias was high in 58 of the 81 studies investigated in the metaanalysis (Nagendran et al., 2020).

In response to such challenge, the FDA's Digital Health Innovation Action Plan has launched a precertification program that serves as a pipeline for streamlined prospective assessment of analytic tools for clinical use, which may be a venue for software medical devices that incorporate predictive algorithms to obtain regulatory approval. Likewise, further standardization tools for the validation of predictive screening algorithms have been formulated for prospective evaluation and regulatory approval (Parikh et al., 2019; Wolff et al., 2019).

4.4 Ensuring representativeness and mitigating bias

Another risk of training predictive analytic models with retrospective data is that the intrinsic biases of these big data—supported programs may be reinforced in clinical care. Predictive algorithms trained with subjective clinical data could systematically bias against patients of different subgroups in the general population (Mullainathan & Obermeyer, 2017). For instance, for a predictive algorithm trained with genomic data designed to screen a particular disease, the training datasets, if contain only low numbers of individuals from certain minor ethnic groups, may be prone to inaccurate classification of genetic variants for these ethnic groups (Manrai et al., 2016); that is, such lack of data can compromise the generalizability of the predictive screening algorithm. Thus, when developing predictive algorithms for clinical risk stratification, (1) representativeness of all target populations in the training set and (2) audit mechanisms with which systematic biases on minor ethnic groups can be prevented, should be taken into consideration (Parikh et al., 2019).

5. Conclusions: toward next generation big data analytics—facilitated disease screening

In this chapter, goals, rationales, and measures of screening programs are illustrated, including useful tools that are applied to determine whether a screening program is of high validity. These tools comprise common outcome measures that have also been adopted in the era of big data analytics, during which such analytics have been applied to optimize the efficacy and efficiency of disease screening in various clinical specialties. Overall, preventive precision medicine based on big data analytics promises to realize disease prevention through entailing novel approaches to disease screening, which are highlighted in medical education (Ma, Chang et al., 2021). In such trends, big data provides us with access to domain knowledge of disease development. However, the use of big data analytics does not generically guarantee real-world efficacy of state-of-the-art big data—facilitated screening programs. In fact, to fill in the gap between clinical information and best practices, it requires patience, tolerance, and wisdom for clinical and research professionals, ethical committees, funding agencies, and policymakers to solve existing issues with inadequate data, overdiagnosis, lack of prospective studies of high-level evidence in EBM, and subsequent risk of bias, to ultimately create useful tools that facilitate precision medicine.

Specifically, although big data—supported preventive and precision medicine may offer an opportunity to eliminate uncertainty, its benefits can be overshadowed by medical waste and socioeconomic burden resulting from overdiagnoses; meanwhile, new measures of risk management may alleviate our intolerance of risk and disease, which to an extent has increased the risk of overdiagnoses (Pathirana et al., 2017). Before we can solve these potential problems of big data—facilitated screening programs, we have to first recognize and define an acceptable range of risk, morbidity, and mortality that exist in society, so as not to regard and highlight all that are registered as abnormal, as clinically relevant features. Multicenter or multinational prospective and prognostic studies, with a long follow-up period, may improve our understanding of the natural course of abnormal findings and quantify overdiagnosis, and thus optimize clinical utility of big data—facilitated disease screening. In summary, with effort made to acquire a clearer understanding of multiple markers and the value of repeated measurement of markers, we are all set to establish screening programs allowing for optimized clinically relevant disease risk stratification, in the context of preventive precision medicine.

References

Abràmoff, M. D., Folk, J. C., Han, D. P., Walker, J. D., Williams, D. F., Russell, S. R., Massin, P., Cochener, B., Gain, P., Tang, L., Lamard, M., Moga, D. C., Quellec, G., & Niemeijer, M. (2013). Automated analysis of retinal images for detection of referable diabetic retinopathy. *JAMA Ophthalmology, 131*(3), 351—357. https://doi.org/10.1001/jamaophthalmol.2013.1743

Abràmoff, M. D., Lou, Y., Erginay, A., Clarida, W., Amelon, R., Folk, J. C., & Niemeijer, M. (2016). Improved automated detection of diabetic retinopathy on a publicly available dataset through integration of deep learning. *Investigative Ophthalmology and Visual Science, 57*(13), 5200—5206. https://doi.org/10.1167/iovs.16-19964

Aerts, H. J. W. L., Velazquez, E. R., Leijenaar, R. T. H., Parmar, C., Grossmann, P., Carvalho, S., Bussink, J., Monshouwer, R., Haibe-Kains, B., Rietveld, D., Hoebers, F., Rietbergen, M. M., Leemans, C. R., Dekker, A., Quackenbush, J., Gillies, R. J., & Lambin, P. (2014). Decoding tumour phenotype by noninvasive imaging using a quantitative radiomics approach. *Nature Communications, 5*. https://doi.org/10.1038/ncomms5006

Alexander, M., Wolfe, R., Ball, D., Conron, M., Stirling, R. G., Solomon, B., MacManus, M., Officer, A., Karnam, S., Burbury, K., & Evans, S. M. (2017). Lung cancer prognostic index: A risk score to predict overall survival after the diagnosis of non-small-cell lung cancer. *British Journal of Cancer, 117*(5), 744—751. https://doi.org/10.1038/bjc.2017.232

Bates, D. W., Cullen, D. J., Laird, N., Petersen, L. A., Small, S. D., Servi, D., Laffel, G., Sweitzer, B. J., Shea, B. F., Hallisey, R., Vander Vliet, M., Nemeskal, R., & Leape, L. L. (1995). Incidence of adverse drug events and potential adverse drug events: Implications for prevention. *Journal of the American Medical Association: The Journal of the American Medical Association, 274*(1), 29—34. https://doi.org/10.1001/jama.1995.03530010043033

Benn, J., Koutantji, M., Wallace, L., Spurgeon, P., Rejman, M., Healey, A., & Vincent, C. (2009). Feedback from incident reporting: Information and action to improve patient safety. *Quality and Safety in Health Care, 18*(1), 11—21. https://doi.org/10.1136/qshc.2007.024166

Bertsimas, D., Dunn, J., Pawlowski, C., Silberholz, J., Weinstein, A., Zhuo, Y. D., Chen, E., & Elfiky, A. A. (2018). Applied informatics decision support tool for mortality predictions in patients with cancer. *JCO Clinical Cancer Informatics, 2018*(2), 1—11. https://doi.org/10.1200/CCI.18.00003

Bejnordi, B. E., Veta, M., Van Diest, P. J., Van Ginneken, B., Karssemeijer, N., Litjens, G., Van Der Laak, J. A. W. M., Hermsen, M., Manson, Q. F., Balkenhol, M., Geessink, O., Stathonikos, N., Van Dijk, M. C. R. F., Bult, P., Beca, F., Beck, A. H., Wang, D., Khosla, A., … Gargeya, R. (2017). Diagnostic assessment of deep learning algorithms for detection of lymph node metastases in women with breast cancer. *JAMA — Journal of the American Medical Association, 318*(22), 2199—2210. https://doi.org/10.1001/jama.2017.14585

Bi, W. L., Hosny, A., Schabath, M. B., Giger, M. L., Birkbak, N. J., Mehrtash, A., Allison, T., Arnaout, O., Abbosh, C., Dunn, I. F., Mak, R. H., Tamimi, R. M., Tempany, C. M., Swanton, C., Hoffmann, U., Schwartz, L. H., Gillies, R. J., Huang, R. Y., & Aerts, H. J. W. L. (2019). Artificial intelligence in cancer imaging: Clinical challenges and applications. *CA Cancer Journal for Clinicians, 69*(2), 127–157. https://doi.org/10.3322/caac.21552

Blumenthal, K. G., Lai, K. H., Huang, M., Wallace, Z. S., Wickner, P. G., & Zhou, L. (2017). Adverse and hypersensitivity reactions to prescription nonsteroidal anti-inflammatory agents in a large health care system. *Journal of Allergy and Clinical Immunology: In Practice, 5*(3), 737–743.e3. https://doi.org/10.1016/j.jaip.2016.12.006

Brodersen, J., Schwartz, L. M., Heneghan, C., O'Sullivan, J. W., Aronson, J. K., & Woloshin, S. (2018). Overdiagnosis: What it is and what it isn't. *BMJ Evidence-Based Medicine, 23*(1), 1–3. https://doi.org/10.1136/ebmed-2017-110886

Brooks, G. A., Kansagra, A. J., Rao, S. R., Weitzman, J. I., Linden, E. A., & Jacobson, J. O. (2015). A clinical prediction model to assess risk for chemotherapy-related hospitalization in patients initiating palliative chemotherapy. *JAMA Oncology, 1*(4), 441–447. https://doi.org/10.1001/jamaoncol.2015.0828

Budnitz, D. S., Pollock, D. A., Mendelsohn, A. B., Weidenbach, K. N., McDonald, A. K., & Annest, J. L. (2005). Emergency department visits for outpatient adverse drug events: Demonstration for a national surveillance system. *Annals of Emergency Medicine, 45*(2), 197–206. https://doi.org/10.1016/j.annemergmed.2004.09.020

Burwell, S. M. (2015). Setting value-based payment goals - HHS efforts to improve U.S. health care. *New England Journal of Medicine, 372*(10), 897–899. https://doi.org/10.1056/NEJMp1500445

Chan, H. P., Hadjiiski, L., Zhou, C., & Sahiner, B. (2008). Computer-aided diagnosis of lung cancer and pulmonary embolism in computed tomography-a review. *Academic Radiology, 15*(5), 535–555. https://doi.org/10.1016/j.acra.2008.01.014

Chiang, C., Chiang, C., Pickering, J. W., et al. (2022). Performance of the European Society of Cardiology 0/1-Hour, 0/2-Hour, and 0/3-Hour Algorithms for Rapid Triage of Acute Myocardial Infarction : An International Collaborative Meta-analysis. *Annals of Internal Medicine, 175*(1), 101–113. https://doi.org/10.7326/M21-1499

Chiang, C. H., Tang, P. U., Lee, G. H., Chiang, T. H., Chiang, C. H., Ma, K. S. K., & Fang, C. T. (2021). Prevalence of nontuberculous mycobacterium infections versus tuberculosis among autopsied HIV patients in sub-saharan Africa: A systematic review and meta-analysis. *American Journal of Tropical Medicine and Hygiene, 104*(2), 628–633. https://doi.org/10.4269/ajtmh.20-0973

Crandall, K. M., Almuhanna, A., Cady, R., Fahey, L., Floyd, T. T., Freiburg, D., Hilliard, M. A., Kalburgi, S., Khan, N. I., Patrick, D., Pavuluri, P., Potter, K., Scafidi, L., Sigman, L., & Shah, R. K. (2018). 10,000 good catches: Increasing safety event reporting in a pediatric health care system. *Pediatric Quality & Safety, 3*(2), e072. https://doi.org/10.1097/pq9.0000000000000072

Christakis, N. A., & Lamont, E. B. (2000). Extent and determinants of error in doctors' prognoses in terminally ill patients: Prospective cohort study. *British Medical Journal, 320*(7233), 469–472.

Conn, J. (2014). Predictive analytics tools help hospitals reduce preventable readmissions. *Modern Healthcare, 44*(31), 16–17.

Coroller, T. P., Grossmann, P., Hou, Y., Rios Velazquez, E., Leijenaar, R. T. H., Hermann, G., Lambin, P., Haibe-Kains, B., Mak, R. H., & Aerts, H. J. W. L. (2015). CT-based radiomic signature predicts distant metastasis in lung adenocarcinoma. *Radiotherapy and Oncology, 114*(3), 345–350. https://doi.org/10.1016/j.radonc.2015.02.015

Elfiky, A. A., Pany, M. J., Parikh, R. B., & Obermeyer, Z. (2018). Development and application of a machine learning approach to assess short-term mortality risk among patients with cancer starting chemotherapy. *JAMA Network Open, 1*(3), e180926. https://doi.org/10.1001/jamanetworkopen.2018.0926

Esteva, A., Kuprel, B., Novoa, R. A., Ko, J., Swetter, S. M., Blau, H. M., & Thrun, S. (2017). Dermatologist-level classification of skin cancer with deep neural networks. *Nature, 542*(7639), 115–118. https://doi.org/10.1038/nature21056

Evidence-Based Medicine Working Group. (1992). Evidence-based medicine: A new approach to teaching the practice of medicine. *The Journal of the American Medical Association, 268*(17), 2420–2425. https://doi.org/10.1001/jama.1992.03490170092032

Fieber, J. H., Sharoky, C. E., Collier, K. T., Hoffman, R. L., Wirtalla, C., Kelz, R. R., & Paulson, E. C. (2018). A preoperative prediction model for risk of multiple admissions after colon cancer surgery. *Journal of Surgical Research, 231*, 380–386. https://doi.org/10.1016/j.jss.2018.05.079

Gandhi, P. K., Gentry, W. M., & Bottorff, M. B. (2012). Thrombotic events associated with C1 esterase inhibitor products in patients with hereditary angioedema: Investigation from the United States food and drug administration adverse event reporting system database. *Pharmacotherapy, 32*(10), 902–909. https://doi.org/10.1002/j.1875-9114.2012.01126

van der Heijden, A. A., Abramoff, M. D., Verbraak, F., van Hecke, M. V., Liem, A., & Nijpels, G. (2018). Validation of automated screening for referable diabetic retinopathy with the IDx-DR device in the Hoorn Diabetes Care System. *Acta Ophthalmologica, 96*(1), 63–68. https://doi.org/10.1111/aos.13613

Huemer, J., Wagner, S. K., & Sim, D. A. (2020). The evolution of diabetic retinopathy screening programmes: A chronology of retinal photography from 35 mm slides to artificial intelligence. *Clinical Ophthalmology, 14*, 2021–2035. https://doi.org/10.2147/OPTH.S261629

Jeffres, M. N., Hall-Lipsy, E. A., King, S. T., & Cleary, J. D. (2018). Systematic review of professional liability when prescribing β-lactams for patients with a known penicillin allergy. *Annals of Allergy, Asthma and Immunology, 121*(5), 530–536. https://doi.org/10.1016/j.anai.2018.03.010

Kadoyama, K., Kuwahara, A., Yamamori, M., Brown, J. B., Sakaeda, T., & Okuno, Y. (2011). Hypersensitivity reactions to anticancer agents: Data mining of the public version of the FDA adverse event reporting system, AERS. *Journal of Experimental and Clinical Cancer Research, 30*(1). https://doi.org/10.1186/1756-9966-30-93

Khera, A. V., Chaffin, M., Aragam, K. G., Haas, M. E., Roselli, C., Choi, S. H., Natarajan, P., Lander, E. S., Lubitz, S. A., Ellinor, P. T., & Kathiresan, S. (2018). Genome-wide polygenic scores for common diseases identify individuals with risk equivalent to monogenic mutations. *Nature Genetics, 50*(9), 1219–1224. https://doi.org/10.1038/s41588-018-0183-z

Kline, R. M., Bazell, C., Smith, E., Schumacher, H., Rajkumar, R., & Conway, P. H. (2015). Centers for Medicare and Medicaid Services: Using an episode-based payment model to improve oncology care. *Journal of Oncology Practice, 11*(2), 114–116. https://doi.org/10.1200/JOP.2014.002337

Kuo, C. F., Lio, C. F., Chen, H. T., Wang, Y. T. T., Ma, K. S. K., Chou, Y. T., Chang, F. C., & Tsai, S. Y. (2020). Discordance of vancomycin minimum inhibitory concentration for methicillin-resistant *Staphylococcus aureus* at 2 μg/mL between Vitek II, E-test, and Broth Microdilution. *PeerJ, 2020*(3). https://doi.org/10.7717/peerj.8963

Lakin, J. R., Robinson, M. G., Bernacki, R. E., Powers, B. W., Block, S. D., Cunningham, R., & Obermeyer, Z. (2016). Estimating 1-year mortality for high-risk primary care patients using the "surprise" question. *JAMA Internal Medicine, 176*(12), 1863–1865. https://doi.org/10.1001/jamainternmed.2016.5928

Lanctôt, K. L., & Naranjo, C. A. (1995). Comparison of the Bayesian approach and a simple algorithm for assessment of adverse drug events. *Clinical Pharmacology and Therapeutics, 58*(6), 692–698. https://doi.org/10.1016/0009-9236(95)90026-8

Ma, K. S. K., Saeed, H. N., Chodosh, J., Wang, C. W., Chung, Y. C., Wei, L. C., Kuo, M. T., Liang, C. M., Chang, J. W. C., Chung, W. H., Chen, C. B., & Ma, D. H. K. (2021). Ocular manifestations of anti-neoplastic immune checkpoint inhibitor-associated Stevens-Johnson syndrome/toxic epidermal necrolysis in cancer patients. *Ocular Surface, 22*, 47–50. https://doi.org/10.1016/j.jtos.2021.06.010, 34216790.

Ma, K. S. K. (2021). Integrating travel history via big data analytics under universal healthcare framework for disease control and prevention in the COVID-19 pandemic. *Journal of Clinical Epidemiology, 130*, 147–148. https://doi.org/10.1016/j.jclinepi.2020.08.016

Ma, K. S., Chang, H. C., & Krupat, E. (2021). Teaching evidence-based medicine with electronic databases for preclinical education. *Advances in Physiology Education, 45*(4), 849–855. https://doi.org/10.1152/advan.00057.2021

Ma, K. S.-K., Chiang, C.-H., Lopez, A. A. V., & Wang, L.-T. (2021). Cohort study of periodontitis-associated signaling pathways in myocardial infarction following Atherosclerotic cardiovascular diseases. *Metabolism, 116*, 154478. https://doi.org/10.1016/j.metabol.2020.154478

Ma, K.S.K., Chung, W.H., Hsueh, Y.J., Chen, S.Y., Tokunaga, K., Kinoshita, S., Ma, D.H.K., & Ueta, M. (2021). Human leucocyte antigen association of patients with Stevens-Johnson syndrome/toxic epidermal necrolysis with severe ocular complications in Han Chinese. British Journal of Ophthalmology. https://doi.org/10.1136/bjophthalmol-2020-317105. 33441319

Ma, K. S., Hasturk, H., Carreras, I., et al. (2021). Dementia and the Risk of Periodontitis: A Population-Based Cohort Study. *Journal of Dental Research*. https://doi.org/10.1177/00220345211037220

Ma, K. S., Illescas Ralda, M. M., Veeravalli, J. J., et al. (2021). Patients with juvenile idiopathic arthritis are at increased risk for obstructive sleep apnoea: a population-based cohort study. *European Journal of Orthodontics*. https://doi.org/10.1093/ejo/cjab050

Ma, K. S., Lai, J., Chiu, L., Chiu, L., Van Dyke, T. E., & Wei, J. C. (2021). Fibromyalgia and periodontitis: Bidirectional associations in population-based 15-year retrospective cohorts. *Journal of Periodontology*. https://doi.org/10.1002/JPER.21-0256

Ma, K. S., Lee, C., Liu, K., Wei, J. C., Lee, Y. T., & Wang, L. T. (2021). Safety and Seroconversion of Immunotherapies against SARS-CoV-2 Infection: A Systematic Review and Meta-Analysis of Clinical Trials. *Pathogens, 10*(12). https://doi.org/10.3390/pathogens10121537

Ma, K. S.-K., Liou, Y.-J., Huang, P.-H., Lin, P.-S., Chen, Y.-W., & Chang, R.-F. (2021). Identifying medically-compromised patients with periodontitis-associated cardiovascular diseases using convolutional neural network-facilitated multilabel classification of panoramic radiographs. In *2021 international conference on applied artificial intelligence (ICAPAI)*. https://doi.org/10.1109/ICAPAI49758.2021.9462069

Ma, K. S.-K., Tan, J., & Velarde Lopez, A. A. (2021). Sociodemographics, lifestyle determinants, and viral infections in patients with head and neck cancer undergoing radiotherapy in Taiwan: A prospective cohort study. *Journal of Clinical Oncology, 39*(15_Suppl. 1), 10553. https://doi.org/10.1200/jco.2021.39.15_suppl.10553

Ma, K. S. K., & Tsai, S. Y. (2020). Big data-driven personal protective equipment stockpiling framework under universal healthcare for disease control and prevention in the COVID-19 era. *International Journal of Surgery, 79*, 290–291. https://doi.org/10.1016/j.ijsu.2020.05.091

Ma, K. S.-K., & Velarde Lopez, A. A. (2021). Prognostic biomarkers for primary Sjögren's syndrome-associated non-Hodgkin's lymphoma. *Journal of Clinical Oncology, 39*(15_Suppl. 1), e19563. https://doi.org/10.1200/jco.2021.39.15_suppl.e19563

Ma, K. S. K., Wei, J. C. C., & Chung, W. H. (2020). Correspondence to "hypersensitivity reactions with allopurinol and febuxostat: A study using the Medicare claims data". *Annals of the Rheumatic Diseases*. https://doi.org/10.1136/annrheumdis-2020-218090

Mahajan, R. P. (2010). Critical incident reporting and learning. *British Journal of Anaesthesia, 105*(1), 69–75. https://doi.org/10.1093/bja/aeq133

Manning, A. M., Casper, K. A., Peter, K. S., Wilson, K. M., Mark, J. R., & Collar, R. M. (2018). Can predictive modeling identify head and neck oncology patients at risk for readmission? *Otolaryngology – Head and Neck Surgery, 159*(4), 669–674. https://doi.org/10.1177/0194599818775938

Manrai, A. K., Funke, B. H., Rehm, H. L., Olesen, M. S., Maron, B. A., Szolovits, P., Margulies, D. M., Loscalzo, J., & Kohane, I. S. (2016). Genetic misdiagnoses and the potential for health disparities. *New England Journal of Medicine, 375*(7), 655–665. https://doi.org/10.1056/NEJMsa1507092

Morita, T., Tsunoda, J., Inoue, S., & Chihara, S. (1999). The palliative prognostic index: A scoring system for survival prediction of terminally ill cancer patients. *Supportive Care in Cancer, 7*(3), 128–133. https://doi.org/10.1007/s005200050242

Mullainathan, S., & Obermeyer, Z. (2017). Does machine learning automate moral hazard and error? *American Economic Review, 107*(5), 476–480. https://doi.org/10.1257/aer.p20171084

Nagendran, M., Chen, Y., Lovejoy, C. A., Gordon, A. C., Komorowski, M., Harvey, H., Topol, E. J., Ioannidis, J. P. A., Collins, G. S., & Maruthappu, M. (2020). Artificial intelligence versus clinicians: Systematic review of design, reporting standards, and claims of deep learning studies. *BMJ, 368*, m689. https://doi.org/10.1136/bmj.m689

Naranjo, C. A., Kwok, M. C. O., Lanctôt, K. L., Zhao, H., Spielberg, S. P., & Shear, N. H. (1994). Enhanced differential diagnosis of anticonvulsant hypersensitivity reactions by an integrated Bayesian and biochemical approach. *Clinical Pharmacology & Therapeutics, 56*(5), 564–575. https://doi.org/10.1038/clpt.1994.178

Okafor, N. G., Doshi, P. B., Miller, S. K., McCarthy, J. J., Hoot, N. R., Darger, B. F., Benitez, R. C., & Chathampally, Y. G. (2015). Voluntary medical incident reporting tool to improve physician reporting of medical errors in an emergency department. *Western Journal of Emergency Medicine, 16*(7), 1073–1078. https://doi.org/10.5811/westjem.2015.8.27390

Parikh, R. B., Obermeyer, Z., & Navathe, A. S. (2019). Regulation of predictive analytics in medicine. *Science, 363*(6429), 810–812. https://doi.org/10.1126/science.aaw0029

Pathirana, T., Clark, J., & Moynihan, R. (2017). Mapping the drivers of overdiagnosis to potential solutions. *BMJ, 358*, j3879. https://doi.org/10.1136/bmj.j3879

Perkins, B. A., Caskey, C. T., Brar, P., Dec, E., Karow, D. S., Kahn, A. M., Hou, Y. C. C., Shah, N., Boeldt, D., Coughlin, E., Hands, G., Lavrenko, V., Yu, J., Procko, A., Appis, J., Dale, A. M., Guo, L., Jönsson, T. J., Wittmann, B. M., … Venter, J. C. (2018). Precision medicine screening using whole-genome sequencing and advanced imaging to identify disease risk in adults. *Proceedings of the National Academy of Sciences of the United States of America, 115*(14), 3686–3691. https://doi.org/10.1073/pnas.1706096114

Price, N. D., Magis, A. T., Earls, J. C., Glusman, G., Levy, R., Lausted, C., McDonald, D. T., Kusebauch, U., Moss, C. L., Zhou, Y., Qin, S., Moritz, R. L., Brogaard, K., Omenn, G. S., Lovejoy, J. C., & Hood, L. (2017). A wellness study of 108 individuals using personal, dense, dynamic data clouds. *Nature Biotechnology, 35*(8), 747–756. https://doi.org/10.1038/nbt.3870

Sackett, D. L., Rosenberg, W. M. C., Gray, J. A. M., Haynes, R. B., & Richardson, W. S. (1996). Evidence based medicine: What it is and what it isn't. *BMJ, 312*(7023), 71–72. https://doi.org/10.1136/bmj.312.7023.71

Sakaeda, T., Kadoyama, K., Yabuuchi, H., Niijima, S., Seki, K., Shiraishi, Y., & Okuno, Y. (2011). Platinum agent-induced hypersensitivity reactions: Data mining of the public version of the FDA adverse event reporting system, AERS. *International Journal of Medical Sciences, 8*(4), 332–338. https://doi.org/10.7150/ijms.8.332

Sborov, K., Giaretta, S., Koong, A., Aggarwal, S., Aslakson, R., Gensheimer, M. F., Chang, D. T., & Pollom, E. L. (2019). Impact of accuracy of survival predictions on quality of end-of-life care among patients with metastatic cancer who receive radiation therapy. *Journal of Oncology Practice, 15*(3), E262–E270. https://doi.org/10.1200/JOP.18.00516

Schüssler-Fiorenza Rose, S. M., Contrepois, K., Moneghetti, K. J., Zhou, W., Mishra, T., Mataraso, S., Dagan-Rosenfeld, O., Ganz, A. B., Dunn, J., Hornburg, D., Rego, S., Perelman, D., Ahadi, S., Sailani, M. R., Zhou, Y., Leopold, S. R., Chen, J., Ashland, M., Christle, J. W., … Snyder, M. P. (2019). A longitudinal big data approach for precision health. *Nature Medicine, 25*(5), 792–804. https://doi.org/10.1038/s41591-019-0414-6

Sorace, A. G., Wu, C., Barnes, S. L., Jarrett, A. M., Avery, S., Patt, D., Goodgame, B., Luci, J. J., Kang, H., Abramson, R. G., Yankeelov, T. E., & Virostko, J. (2018). Repeatability, reproducibility, and accuracy of quantitative mri of the breast in the community radiology setting. *Journal of Magnetic Resonance Imaging, 48*(3), 695–707. https://doi.org/10.1002/jmri.26011

Struewing, J. P., Hartge, P., Wacholder, S., Baker, S. M., Berlin, M., McAdams, M., Timmerman, M. M., Brody, L. C., & Tucker, M. A. (1997). The risk of cancer associated with specific mutations of BRCA1 and BRCA2 among Ashkenazi Jews. *New England Journal of Medicine, 336*(20), 1401–1408. https://doi.org/10.1056/NEJM199705153362001

Topol, E. J. (2019). High-performance medicine: The convergence of human and artificial intelligence. *Nature Medicine, 25*(1), 44–56. https://doi.org/10.1038/s41591-018-0300-7

Torkamani, A., Andersen, K. G., Steinhubl, S. R., & Topol, E. J. (2017). High-definition medicine. *Cell, 170*(5), 828–843. https://doi.org/10.1016/j.cell.2017.08.007

Wiemken, T. L., & Kelley, R. R. (2019). Machine learning in epidemiology and health outcomes research. *Annual Review of Public Health, 41*, 21–36. https://doi.org/10.1146/annurev-publhealth-040119-094437

Wild, S., Roglic, G., Green, A., Sicree, R., & King, H. (2004). Global prevalence of diabetes: Estimates for the year 2000 and projections for 2030. *Diabetes Care, 27*(5), 1047–1053. https://doi.org/10.2337/diacare.27.5.1047

Wolff, R. F., Moons, K. G. M., Riley, R. D., Whiting, P. F., Westwood, M., Collins, G. S., Reitsma, J. B., Kleijnen, J., & Mallett, S. (2019). PROBAST: A tool to assess the risk of bias and applicability of prediction model studies. *Annals of Internal Medicine, 170*(1), 51–58. https://doi.org/10.7326/M18-1376

Wu, M. C., Ma, K. S. K., Wang, Y. H., & Wei, J. C. C. (2020). Impact of tonsillectomy on irritable bowel syndrome: A nationwide population-based cohort study. *PLoS One, 15*(9). https://doi.org/10.1371/journal pone.0238242

Yau, J. W. Y., Rogers, S. L., Kawasaki, R., Lamoureux, E. L., Kowalski, J. W., Bek, T., Chen, S. J., Dekker, J. M., Fletcher, A., Grauslund, J., Haffner, S., Hamman, R. F., Ikram, M. K., Kayama, T., Klein, B. E. K., Klein, R., Krishnaiah, S., Mayurasakorn, K., O'Hare, J. P., … Wong, T. Y. (2012). Global prevalence and major risk factors of diabetic retinopathy. *Diabetes Care, 35*(3), 556–564. https://doi.org/10.2337/dc11-1909

Yeo, H., Mao, J., Abelson, J. S., Lachs, M., Finlayson, E., Milsom, J., & Sedrakyan, A. (2016). Development of a nonparametric predictive model for readmission risk in elderly adults after colon and rectal cancer surgery. *Journal of the American Geriatrics Society, 64*(11), e125–e130. https://doi.org/10.1111/jgs.14448

Young, I. J. B., Luz, S., & Lone, N. (2019). A systematic review of natural language processing for classification tasks in the field of incident reporting and adverse event analysis. *International Journal of Medical Informatics, 132*. https://doi.org/10.1016/j.ijmedinf.2019.103971

Yu, K. H., Zhang, C., Berry, G. J., Altman, R. B., Ré, C., Rubin, D. L., & Snyder, M. (2016). Predicting non-small cell lung cancer prognosis by fully automated microscopic pathology image features. *Nature Communications, 7*. https://doi.org/10.1038/ncomms12474

Index

Note: 'Page numbers followed by "f" indicate figures and "t" indicate tables.'

C

D

I

K

L

M

N

O

P

Made in United States
Troutdale, OR
06/27/2024

20836776R00197